Family Maps
of
Hale County, Alabama
Deluxe Edition

With Homesteads, Roads, Waterways, Towns, Cemeteries, Railroads, and More

Family Maps
of
Hale County, Alabama
Deluxe Edition

With Homesteads, Roads, Waterways, Towns, Cemeteries, Railroads, and More

by Gregory A. Boyd, J.D.

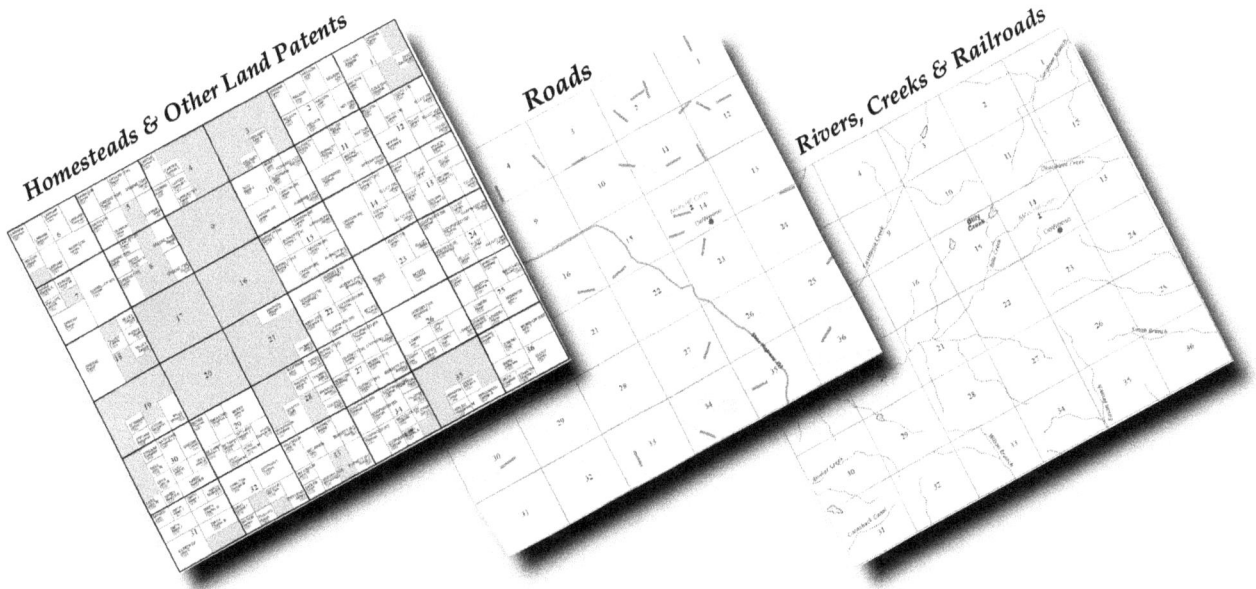

Homesteads & Other Land Patents

Roads

Rivers, Creeks & Railroads

Featuring 3 *Maps Per Township…*

Arphax Publishing Co.
www.arphax.com

Family Maps of Hale County, Alabama, Deluxe Edition: With Homesteads, Roads, Waterways, Towns, Cemeteries, Railroads, and More.
by Gregory A. Boyd, J.D.

ISBN 1-4203-1377-0

Copyright © 2007, 2010 by Boyd IT, Inc., All rights reserved.
Printed in the United States of America

Published by Arphax Publishing Co., 2210 Research Park Blvd., Norman, Oklahoma, USA 73069
www.arphax.com

First Edition

ATTENTION HISTORICAL & GENEALOGICAL SOCIETIES, UNIVERSITIES, COLLEGES, CORPORATIONS, FAMILY REUNION COORDINATORS, AND PROFESSIONAL ORGANIZATIONS: Quantity discounts are available on bulk purchases of this book. For information, please contact Arphax Publishing Co., at the address listed above, or at (405) 366-6181, or visit our web-site at www.arphax.com and contact us through the "Bulk Sales" link.

—LEGAL—

The contents of this book rely on data published by the United States Government and its various agencies and departments, including but not limited to the General Land Office–Bureau of Land Management, the Department of the Interior, and the U.S. Census Bureau. The author has relied on said government agencies or re-sellers of its data, but makes no guarantee of the data's accuracy or of its representation herein, neither in its text nor maps. Said maps have been proportioned and scaled in a manner reflecting the author's primary goal—to make patentee names readable. This book will assist in the discovery of possible relationships between people, places, locales, rivers, streams, cemeteries, etc., but "proving" those relationships or exact geographic locations of any of the elements contained in the maps will require the use of other source material, which could include, but not be limited to: land patents, surveys, the patentees' applications, professionally drawn road-maps, etc.

Neither the author nor publisher makes any claim that the contents herein represent a complete or accurate record of the data it presents and disclaims any liability for reader's use of the book's contents. Many circumstances exist where human, computer, or data delivery errors could cause records to have been missed or to be inaccurately represented herein. Neither the author nor publisher shall assume any liability whatsoever for errors, inaccuracies, omissions or other inconsistencies herein.

No part of this book may be reproduced, stored, or transmitted by any means (electronic, mechanical, photocopying, recording, or otherwise, as applicable) without the prior written permission of the publisher.

This book is dedicated to my wonderful family:

Vicki, Jordan, & Amy Boyd

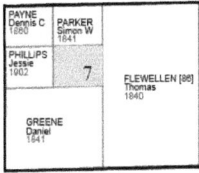

Contents

- Part I -

The Big Picture

- Part II -

Township Map Groups

(each Map Group contains a Patent Index, Patent Map, Road Map, & Historical Map)

Appendices

Preface

The quest for the discovery of my ancestors' origins, migrations, beliefs, and life-ways has brought me rewards that I could never have imagined. The *Family Maps* series of books is my first effort to share with historical and genealogical researchers, some of the tools that I have developed to achieve my research goals. I firmly believe that this effort will allow many people to reap the same sorts of treasures that I have.

Our Federal government's General Land Office of the Bureau of Land Management (the "GLO") has given genealogists and historians an incredible gift by virtue of its enormous database housed on its web-site at glorecords.blm.gov. Here, you can search for and find millions of parcels of land purchased by our ancestors in about thirty states.

This GLO web-site is one of the best FREE on-line tools available to family researchers. But, it is not for the faint of heart, nor is it for those unwilling or unable to to sift through and analyze the thousands of records that exist for most counties.

My immediate goal with this series is to spare you the hundreds of hours of work that it would take you to map the Land Patents for this county. Every Hale County homestead or land patent that I have gleaned from public GLO databases is mapped here. Consequently, I can usually show you in an instant, where your ancestor's land is located, as well as the names of nearby land-owners.

Originally, that was my primary goal. But after speaking to other genealogists, it became clear that there was much more that they wanted. Taking their advice set me back almost a full year, but I think you will agree it was worth the wait. Because now, you can learn so much more.

Now, this book answers these sorts of questions:

- Are there any variant spellings for surnames that I have missed in searching GLO records?
- Where is my family's traditional home-place?
- What cemeteries are near Grandma's house?
- My Granddad used to swim in such-and-such-Creek—where is that?
- How close is this little community to that one?
- Are there any other people with the same surname who bought land in the county?
- How about cousins and in-laws—did they buy land in the area?

And these are just for starters!

The rules for using the *Family Maps* books are simple, but the strategies for success are many. Some techniques are apparent on first use, but many are gained with time and experience. Please take the time to notice the roads, cemeteries, creek-names, family names, and unique first-names throughout the whole county. You cannot imagine what YOU might be the first to discover.

I hope to learn that many of you have answered age-old research questions within these pages or that you have discovered relationships previously not even considered. When these sorts of things happen to you, will you please let me hear about it? I would like nothing better. My contact information can always be found at www.arphax.com.

One more thing: please read the "How To Use This Book" chapter; it starts on the next page. This will give you the very best chance to find the treasures that lie within these pages.

My family and I wish you the very best of luck, both in life, and in your research.   Greg Boyd

How to Use This Book - A Graphical Summary

Part I
"The Big Picture"

Map A ▸ *Counties in the State*
Map B ▸ *Surrounding Counties*
Map C ▸ *Congressional Townships (Map Groups) in the County*
Map D ▸ *Cities & Towns in the County*
Map E ▸ *Cemeteries in the County*
Surnames in the County ▸ *Number of Land-Parcels for Each Surname*
Surname/Township Index ▸ *Directs you to Township Map Groups in Part II*

The <u>*Surname/Township Index*</u> *can direct you to any number of* **Township Map Groups**

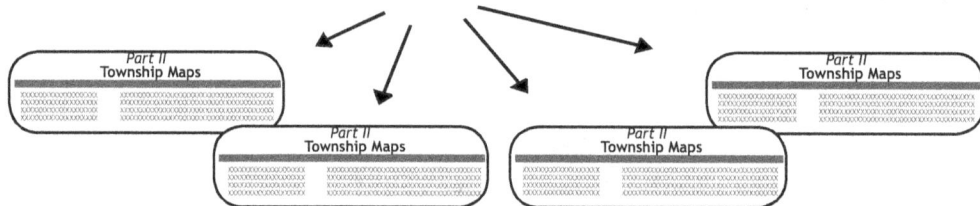

Part II
Township Maps

Part II
Township Maps

Part II
Township Maps

Part II
Township Maps

Part II
Township Map Groups
(1 for each Township in the County)

Each Township Map Group contains all four of of the following tools . . .

Land Patent Index ▸ *Every-name Index of Patents Mapped in this Township*
Land Patent Map ▸ *Map of Patents as listed in above Index*
Road Map ▸ *Map of Roads, City-centers, and Cemeteries in the Township*
Historical Map ▸ *Map of Railroads, Lakes, Rivers, Creeks, City-Centers, and Cemeteries*

Appendices

Appendix A ▸ *Congressional Authority enabling Patents within our Maps*
Appendix B ▸ *Section-Parts / Aliquot Parts (a comprehensive list)*
Appendix C ▸ *Multi-patentee Groups (Individuals within Buying Groups)*

How to Use This Book

The two "Parts" of this *Family Maps* volume seek to answer two different types of questions. Part I deals with broad questions like: what counties surround Hale County, are there any ASHCRAFTs in Hale County, and if so, in which Townships or Maps can I find them? Ultimately, though, Part I should point you to a particular Township Map Group in Part II.

Part II concerns itself with details like: where exactly is this family's land, who else bought land in the area, and what roads and streams run through the land, or are located nearby. The Chart on the opposite page, and the remainder of this chapter attempt to convey to you the particulars of these two "parts", as well as how best to use them to achieve your research goals.

Part I
"The Big Picture"

Within Part I, you will find five "Big Picture" maps and two county-wide surname tools.

These include:

- Map A - Where Hale County lies within the state
- Map B - Counties that surround Hale County
- Map C - Congressional Townships of Hale County (+ Map Group Numbers)
- Map D - Cities & Towns of Hale County (with Index)
- Map E - Cemeteries of Hale County (with Index)
- Surnames in Hale County Patents (with Parcel-counts for each surname)
- Surname/Township Index (with Parcel-counts for each surname by Township)

The five "Big-Picture" Maps are fairly self-explanatory, yet should not be overlooked. This is particularly true of Maps "C", "D", and "E", all of which show Hale County and its Congressional Townships (and their assigned Map Group Numbers).

Let me briefly explain this concept of Map Group Numbers. These are a device completely of our own invention. They were created to help you quickly locate maps without having to remember the full legal name of the various Congressional Townships. It is simply easier to remember "Map Group 1" than a legal name like: "Township 9-North Range 6-West, 5th Principal Meridian." But the fact is that the TRUE legal name for these Townships IS terribly important. These are the designations that others will be familiar with and you will need to accurately record them in your notes. This is why both Map Group numbers AND legal descriptions of Townships are almost always displayed together.

Map "C" will be your first introduction to "Map Group Numbers", and that is all it contains: legal Township descriptions and their assigned Map Group Numbers. Once you get further into your research, and more immersed in the details, you will likely want to refer back to Map "C" from time to time, in order to regain your bearings on just where in the county you are researching.

Remember, township boundaries are a completely artificial device, created to standardize land descriptions. But do not let them become a boundary in your mind when choosing which townships to research. Your relative's in-laws, children, cousins, siblings, and mamas and papas, might just as easily have lived in the township next to the one your grandfather lived in—rather than in the one where he actually lived. So Map "C" can be your guide to which other Townships/Map Groups you likewise ought to analyze.

Of course, the same holds true for County lines; this is the purpose behind Map "B". It shows you surrounding counties that you may want to consider for further reserarch.

Map "D", the Cities and Towns map, is the first map with an index. Map "E" is the second (Cemeteries). Both, Maps "D" and "E" give you broad views of City (or Cemetery) locations in the County. But they go much further by pointing you toward pertinent Township Map Groups so you can locate the patents, roads, and waterways located near a particular city or cemetery.

Once you are familiar with these *Family Maps* volumes and the county you are researching, the "Surnames In Hale County" chapter (or its sister chapter in other volumes) is where you'll likely start your future research sessions. Here, you can quickly scan its few pages and see if anyone in the county possesses the surnames you are researching. The "Surnames in Hale County" list shows only two things: surnames and the number of parcels of land we have located for that surname in Hale County. But whether or not you immediately locate the surnames you are researching, please do not go any further without taking a few moments to scan ALL the surnames in these very few pages.

You cannot imagine how many lost ancestors are waiting to be found by someone willing to take just a little longer to scan the "Surnames In Hale County" list. Misspellings and typographical errors abound in most any index of this sort. Don't miss out on finding your Kinard that was written Rynard or Cox that was written Lox. If it looks funny or wrong, it very often is. And one of those little errors may well be your relative.

Now, armed with a surname and the knowledge that it has one or more entries in this book, you are ready for the "Surname/Township Index." Unlike the "Surnames In Hale County", which has only one line per Surname, the "Surname/Township Index" contains one line-item for each Township Map Group in which each surname is found. In other words, each line represents a different Township Map Group that you will need to review.

Specifically, each line of the Surname/Township

Index contains the following four columns of information:

1. Surname
2. Township Map Group Number (these Map Groups are found in Part II)
3. Parcels of Land (number of them with the given Surname within the Township)
4. Meridian/Township/Range (the legal description for this Township Map Group)

The key column here is that of the Township Map Group Number. While you should definitely record the Meridian, Township, and Range, you can do that later. Right now, you need to dig a little deeper. That Map Group Number tells you where in Part II that you need to start digging.

But before you leave the "Surname/Township Index", do the same thing that you did with the "Surnames in Hale County" list: take a moment to scan the pages of the Index and see if there are similarly spelled or misspelled surnames that deserve your attention. Here again, is an easy opportunity to discover grossly misspelled family names with very little effort. Now you are ready to turn to . . .

Part II
"Township Map Groups"

You will normally arrive here in Part II after being directed to do so by one or more "Map Group Numbers" in the Surname/Township Index of Part I.

Each Map Group represents a set of four tools dedicated to a single Congressional Township that is either wholly or partially within the county. If you are trying to learn all that you can about a particular family or their land, then these tools should usually be viewed in the order they are presented.

These four tools include:

1. a Land Patent Index
2. a Land Patent Map
3. a Road Map, and
4. an Historical Map

As I mentioned earlier, each grouping of this sort is assigned a Map Group Number. So, let's now move on to a discussion of the four tools that make up one of these Township Map Groups.

Land Patent Index

Each Township Map Group's Index begins with a title, something along these lines:

MAP GROUP 1: Index to Land Patents
Township 16-North Range 5-West (2ⁿᵈ PM)

The Index contains seven (7) columns. They are:

1. ID (a unique ID number for this Individual and a corresponding Parcel of land in this Township)
2. Individual in Patent (name)
3. Sec. (Section), and
4. Sec. Part (Section Part, or Aliquot Part)
5. Date Issued (Patent)
6. Other Counties (often means multiple counties were mentioned in GLO records, or the section lies within multiple counties).
7. For More Info . . . (points to other places within this index or elsewhere in the book where you can find more information)

While most of the seven columns are self-explanatory, I will take a few moments to explain the "Sec. Part." and "For More Info" columns.

The "Sec. Part" column refers to what surveryors and other land professionals refer to as an Aliquot Part. The origins and use of such a term mean little to a non-surveyor, and I have chosen to simply call these sub-sections of land what they are: a "Section Part". No matter what we call them, what we are referring to are things like a quarter-section or half-section or quarter-quarter-section. See Appendix "B" for most of the "Section Parts" you will come across (and many you will not) and what size land-parcel they represent.

The "For More Info" column of the Index may seem like a small appendage to each line, but please

recognize quickly that this is not so. And to understand the various items you might find here, you need to become familiar with the Legend that appears at the top of each Land Patent Index.

Here is a sample of the Legend . . .

LEGEND

"For More Info . . . " column

A = Authority (Legislative Act, See Appendix "A")
B = Block or Lot (location in Section unknown)
C = Cancelled Patent
F = Fractional Section
G = Group (Multi-Patentee Patent, see Appendix "C")
V = Overlaps another Parcel
R = Re-Issued (Parcel patented more than once)

Most parcels of land will have only one or two of these items in their "For More Info" columns, but when that is not the case, there is often some valuable information to be gained from further investigation. Below, I will explain what each of these items means to you you as a researcher.

A = Authority
(Legislative Act, See Appendix "A")
All Federal Land Patents were issued because some branch of our government (usually the U.S. Congress) passed a law making such a transfer of title possible. And therefore every patent within these pages will have an "A" item next to it in the index. The number after the "A" indicates which item in Appendix "A" holds the citation to the particular law which authorized the transfer of land to the public. As it stands, most of the Public Land data compiled and released by our government, and which serves as the basis for the patents mapped here, concerns itself with "Cash Sale" homesteads. So in some Counties, the law which authorized cash sales will be the primary, if not the only, entry in the Appendix.

B = Block or Lot (location in Section unknown)
A "B" designation in the Index is a tip-off that the EXACT location of the patent within the map is not apparent from the legal description. This Patent will nonetheless be noted within the proper

Section along with any other Lots purchased in the Section. Given the scope of this project (many states and many Counties are being mapped), trying to locate all relevant plats for Lots (if they even exist) and accurately mapping them would have taken one person several lifetimes. But since our primary goal from the onset has been to establish relationships between neighbors and families, very little is lost to this goal since we can still observe who all lived in which Section.

C = Cancelled Patent

A Cancelled Patent is just that: cancelled. Whether the original Patentee forfeited his or her patent due to fraud, a technicality, non-payment, or whatever, the fact remains that it is significant to know who received patents for what parcels and when. A cancellation may be evidence that the Patentee never physically re-located to the land, but does not in itself prove that point. Further evidence would be required to prove that. *See also*, Re-issued Patents, *below*.

F = Fractional Section

A Fractional Section is one that contains less than 640 acres, almost always because of a body of water. The exact size and shape of land-parcels contained in such sections may not be ascertainable, but we map them nonetheless. Just keep in mind that we are not mapping an actual parcel to scale in such instances. Another point to consider is that we have located some fractional sections that are not so designated by the Bureau of Land Management in their data. This means that not all fractional sections have been so identified in our indexes.

G = Group
(Multi-Patentee Patent, see Appendix "C")

A "G" designation means that the Patent was issued to a GROUP of people (Multi-patentees). The "G" will always be followed by a number. Some such groups were quite large and it was impractical if not impossible to display each individual in our maps without unduly affecting readability. EACH person in the group is named in the Index, but they won't all be found on the Map. You will find the name of the first person in such a Group

on the map with the Group number next to it, enclosed in [square brackets].

To find all the members of the Group you can either scan the Index for all people with the same Group Number or you can simply refer to Appendix "C" where all members of the Group are listed next to their number.

O = Overlaps another Parcel

An Overlap is one where PART of a parcel of land gets issued on more than one patent. For genealogical purposes, both transfers of title are important and both Patentees are mapped. If the ENTIRE parcel of land is re-issued, that is what we call it, a Re-Issued Patent (*see below*). The number after the "O" indicates the ID for the overlapping Patent(s) contained within the same Index. Like Re-Issued and Cancelled Patents, Overlaps may cause a map-reader to be confused at first, but for genealogical purposes, all of these parties' relationships to the underlying land is important, and therefore, we map them.

R = Re-Issued (Parcel patented more than once)

The label, "Re-issued Patent" describes Patents which were issued more than once for land with the EXACT SAME LEGAL DESCRIPTION. Whether the original patent was cancelled or not, there were a good many parcels which were patented more than once. The number after the "R" indicates the ID for the other Patent contained within the same Index that was for the same land. A quick glance at the map itself within the relevant Section will be the quickest way to find the other Patentee to whom the Parcel was transferred. They should both be mapped in the same general area.

I have gone to some length describing all sorts of anomalies either in the underlying data or in their representation on the maps and indexes in this book. Most of this will bore the most ardent reseracher, but I do this with all due respect to those researchers who will inevitably (and rightfully) ask: *"Why isn't so-and-so's name on the exact spot that the index says it should be?"*

In most cases it will be due to the existence of a Multi-Patentee Patent, a Re-issued Patent, a Cancelled Patent, or Overlapping Parcels named in separate Patents. I don't pretend that this discussion will answer every question along these lines, but I hope it will at least convince you of the complexity of the subject.

Not to despair, this book's companion web-site will offer a way to further explain "odd-ball" or errant data. Each book (County) will have its own web-page or pages to discuss such situations. You can go to www.arphax.com to find the relevant web-page for Hale County.

Land Patent Map

On the first two-page spread following each Township's Index to Land Patents, you'll find the corresponding Land Patent Map. And here lies the real heart of our work. For the first time anywhere, researchers will be able to observe and analyze, on a grand scale, most of the original land-owners for an area AND see them mapped in proximity to each one another.

We encourage you to make vigorous use of the accompanying Index described above, but then later, to abandon it, and just stare at these maps for a while. This is a great way to catch misspellings or to find collateral kin you'd not known were in the area.

Each Land Patent Map represents one Congressional Township containing approximately 36-square miles. Each of these square miles is labeled by an accompanying Section Number (1 through 36, in most cases). Keep in mind, that this book concerns itself solely with Hale County's patents. Townships which creep into one or more other counties will not be shown in their entirety in any one book. You will need to consult other books, as they become available, in order to view other countys' patents, cities, cemeteries, etc.

But getting back to Hale County: each Land Patent Map contains a Statistical Chart that looks like the following:

Township Statistics

Parcels Mapped	:	173
Number of Patents	:	163
Number of Individuals	:	152
Patentees Identified	:	151
Number of Surnames	:	137
Multi-Patentee Parcels	:	4
Oldest Patent Date	:	11/27/1820
Most Recent Patent	:	9/28/1917
Block/Lot Parcels	:	0
Parcels Re-Issued	:	3
Parcels that Overlap	:	8
Cities and Towns	:	6
Cemeteries	:	6

This information may be of more use to a social statistician or historian than a genealogist, but I think all three will find it interesting.

Most of the statistics are self-explanatory, and what is not, was described in the above discussion of the Index's Legend, but I do want to mention a few of them that may affect your understanding of the Land Patent Maps.

First of all, Patents often contain more than one Parcel of land, so it is common for there to be more Parcels than Patents. Also, the Number of Individuals will more often than not, not match the number of Patentees. A Patentee is literally the person or PERSONS named in a patent. So, a Patent may have a multi-person Patentee or a single-person patentee. Nonetheless, we account for all these individuals in our indexes.

On the lower-righthand side of the Patent Map is a Legend which describes various features in the map, including Section Boundaries, Patent (land) Boundaries, Lots (numbered), and Multi-Patentee Group Numbers. You'll also find a "Helpful Hints" Box that will assist you.

One important note: though the vast majority of Patents mapped in this series will prove to be reasonably accurate representations of their actual locations, we cannot claim this for patents lying along state and county lines, or waterways, or that have been platted (lots).

Shifting boundaries and sparse legal descriptions in the GLO data make this a reality that we have nonetheless tried to overcome by estimating these patents' locations the best that we can.

Road Map

On the two-page spread following each Patent Map you will find a Road Map covering the exact same area (the same Congressional Township).

For me, fully exploring the past means that every once in a while I must leave the library and travel to the actual locations where my ancestors once walked and worked the land. Our Township Road Maps are a great place to begin such a quest.

Keep in mind that the scaling and proportion of these maps was chosen in order to squeeze hundreds of people-names, road-names, and place-names into tinier spaces than you would traditionally see. These are not professional road-maps, and like any secondary genealogical source, should be looked upon as an entry-way to original sources—in this case, original patents and applications, professionally produced maps and surveys, etc.

Both our Road Maps and Historical Maps contain cemeteries and city-centers, along with a listing of these on the left-hand side of the map. I should note that I am showing you city center-points, rather than city-limit boundaries, because in many instances, this will represent a place where settlement began. This may be a good time to mention that many cemeteries are located on private property, Always check with a local historical or genealogical society to see if a particular cemetery is publicly accessible (if it is not obviously so). As a final point, look for your surnames among the road-names. You will often be surprised by what you find.

Historical Map

The third and final map in each Map Group is our attempt to display what each Township might have looked like before the advent of modern roads. In frontier times, people were usually more determined to settle near rivers and creeks than they were near roads, which were often few and far between. As was the case with the Road Map, we've included the same cemeteries and city-centers. We've also included railroads, many of which came along before most roads.

While some may claim "Historical Map" to be a bit of a misnomer for this tool, we settled for this label simply because it was almost as accurate as saying "Railroads, Lakes, Rivers, Cities, and Cemeteries," and it is much easier to remember.

In Closing . . .

By way of example, here is *A Really Good Way to Use a Township Map Group.* First, find the person you are researching in the Township's Index to Land Patents, which will direct you to the proper Section and parcel on the Patent Map. But before leaving the Index, scan all the patents within it, looking for other names of interest. Now, turn to the Patent Map and locate your parcels of land. Pay special attention to the names of patent-holders who own land surrounding your person of interest. Next, turn the page and look at the same Section(s) on the Road Map. Note which roads are closest to your parcels and also the names of nearby towns and cemeteries. Using other resources, you may be able to learn of kin who have been buried here, plus, you may choose to visit these cemeteries the next time you are in the area.

Finally, turn to the Historical Map. Look once more at the same Sections where you found your research subject's land. Note the nearby streams, creeks, and other geographical features. You may be surprised to find family names were used to name them, or you may see a name you haven't heard mentioned in years and years—and a new research possibility is born.

Many more techniques for using these *Family Maps* volumes will no doubt be discovered. If from time to time, you will navigate to Hale County's web-page at www.arphax.com (use the "Research" link), you can learn new tricks as they become known (or you can share ones you have employed). But for now, you are ready to get started. So, go, and good luck.

– Part I –

The Big Picture

Map A - Where Hale County, Alabama Lies Within the State

Lauderdale	Limestone	Madison	Jackson
Colbert			
Franklin	Lawrence	Morgan	Dekalb
		Marshall	
Marion	Winston	Cullman	Cherokee
		Blount	Etowah
	Walker	Saint Clair	Calhoun
Lamar	Fayette		Cleburne
		Jefferson	Talladega
Pickens	Tuscaloosa	Shelby	Clay	Randolph
		Bibb	Coosa	Tallapoosa	Chambers
Greene	Hale	Chilton		
	Perry	Autauga	Elmore	Lee
Sumter			Macon	Russell
	Marengo	Dallas	Montgomery	
		Lowndes	Bullock	
Choctaw	Wilcox	Butler	Pike	Barbour
		Crenshaw		
Clarke	Monroe	Conecuh		Dale	Henry
Washington			Coffee	
		Covington	Geneva	Houston
Mobile	Escambia			
Baldwin				

Legend

— State Boundary

— County Boundaries

▢ Hale County, Alabama

Helpful Hints

1 We start with Map "A" which simply shows us where within the State this county lies.

2 Map "B" zooms in further to help us more easily identify surrounding Counties.

3 Map "C" zooms in even further to reveal the Congressional Townships that either lie within or intersect Hale County.

Map B - Hale County, Alabama and Surrounding Counties

Lowndes

Pickens

Jefferson

Mississippi

Tuscaloosa

Shelby

Noxubee

Greene

Bibb

Alabama

Kemper

Hale

Chilton

Perry

Sumter

Lauderdale

Dallas

Marengo

Choctaw

Clarke

Wilcox

Copyright © 2007 Boyd IT, Inc. All Rights Reserved

——— Legend ———

━━━ State Boundaries (when applicable)

——— County Boundary

———— Helpful Hints ————
1 Many Patent-holders and their
   families settled across county
   lines. It is always a good idea to
   check nearby counties for your
   families.

2 Refer to Map "A" to see a
   broader view of where this
   County lies within the State,
   and Map "C" to see which
   Congressional Townships lie
   within Hale County.

Map C - Congressional Townships of Hale County, Alabama

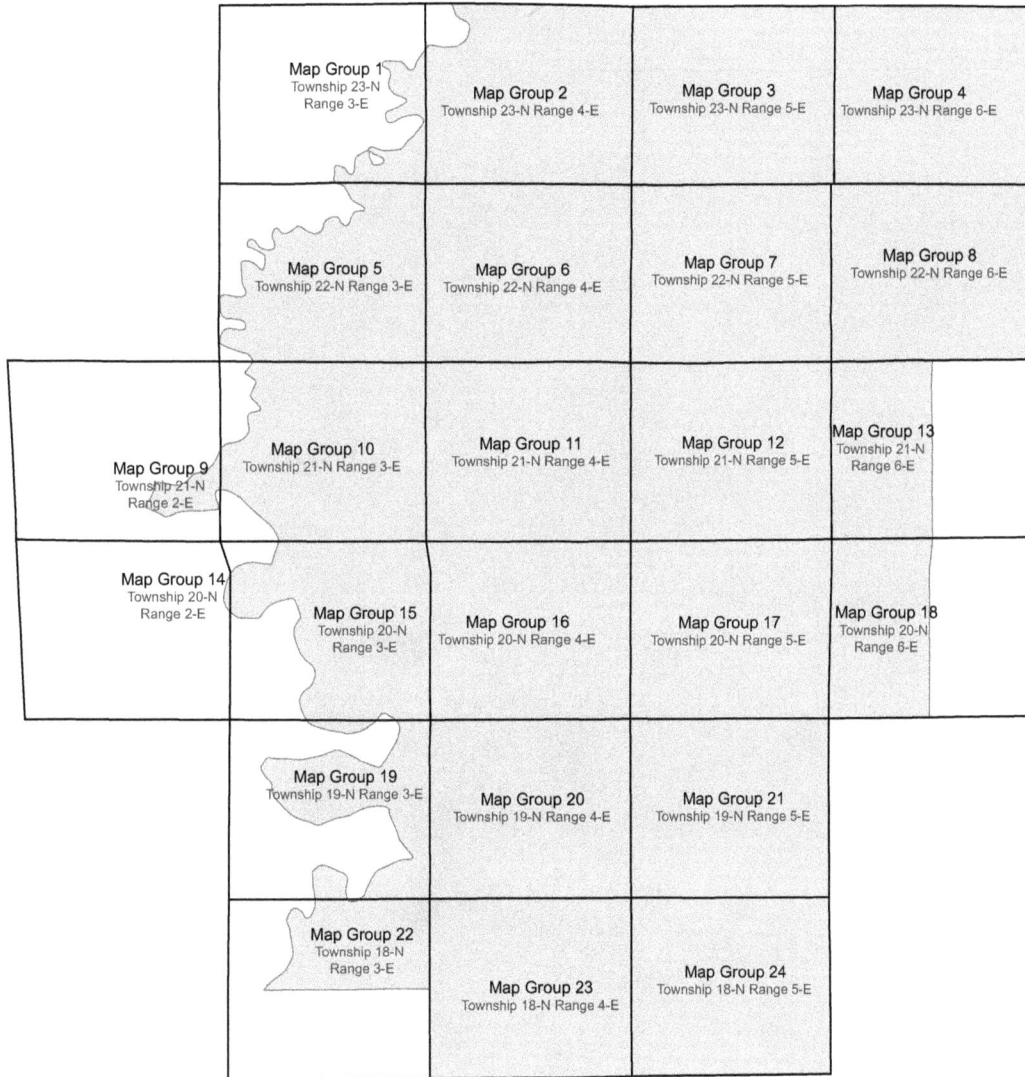

Map Group 1 Township 23-N Range 3-E	Map Group 2 Township 23-N Range 4-E	Map Group 3 Township 23-N Range 5-E	Map Group 4 Township 23-N Range 6-E
Map Group 5 Township 22-N Range 3-E	Map Group 6 Township 22-N Range 4-E	Map Group 7 Township 22-N Range 5-E	Map Group 8 Township 22-N Range 6-E
Map Group 9 Township 21-N Range 2-E	Map Group 10 Township 21-N Range 3-E	Map Group 11 Township 21-N Range 4-E	Map Group 12 Township 21-N Range 5-E	Map Group 13 Township 21-N Range 6-E
Map Group 14 Township 20-N Range 2-E	Map Group 15 Township 20-N Range 3-E	Map Group 16 Township 20-N Range 4-E	Map Group 17 Township 20-N Range 5-E	Map Group 18 Township 20-N Range 6-E
	Map Group 19 Township 19-N Range 3-E	Map Group 20 Township 19-N Range 4-E	Map Group 21 Township 19-N Range 5-E
	Map Group 22 Township 18-N Range 3-E	Map Group 23 Township 18-N Range 4-E	Map Group 24 Township 18-N Range 5-E

——— Legend ———

Hale County, Alabama

Congressional Townships

——— Helpful Hints ———

1 Many Patent-holders and their families settled across county lines. It is always a good idea to check nearby counties for your families (See Map "B").

2 Refer to Map "A" to see a broader view of where this county lies within the State, and Map "B" for a view of the counties surrounding Hale County.

Map D Index: Cities & Towns of Hale County, Alabama

The following represents the Cities and Towns of Hale County, along with the corresponding Map Group in which each is found. Cities and Towns are displayed in both the Road and Historical maps in the Group.

City/Town	Map Group No.
Akron	5
Allenville	23
Arcola	22
Casemore	20
Cedarville	20
Cypress	2
Darrah	5
Dominick	12
East Port Landing	10
Evansville	5
Gallion	23
Gilmore Quarters	19
Greensboro	17
Harper Hill	7
Havana	7
Hogglesville	8
Ingram	7
Lake Bend Landing	19
Laneville	24
Lock Five	19
Melton	16
Millwood	15
Moundville	2
New Prospect	5
Newbern	21
Oak Grove	23
Oak Village	5
Phipps	4
Port Royal	19
Powers	2
Prairieville	23
Rosemary	21
Sawyerville	11
Stewart	6
Sunshine	24
Wateroak	8
Wedgeworth	10
Whitsitt	21

Map D - Cities & Towns of Hale County, Alabama

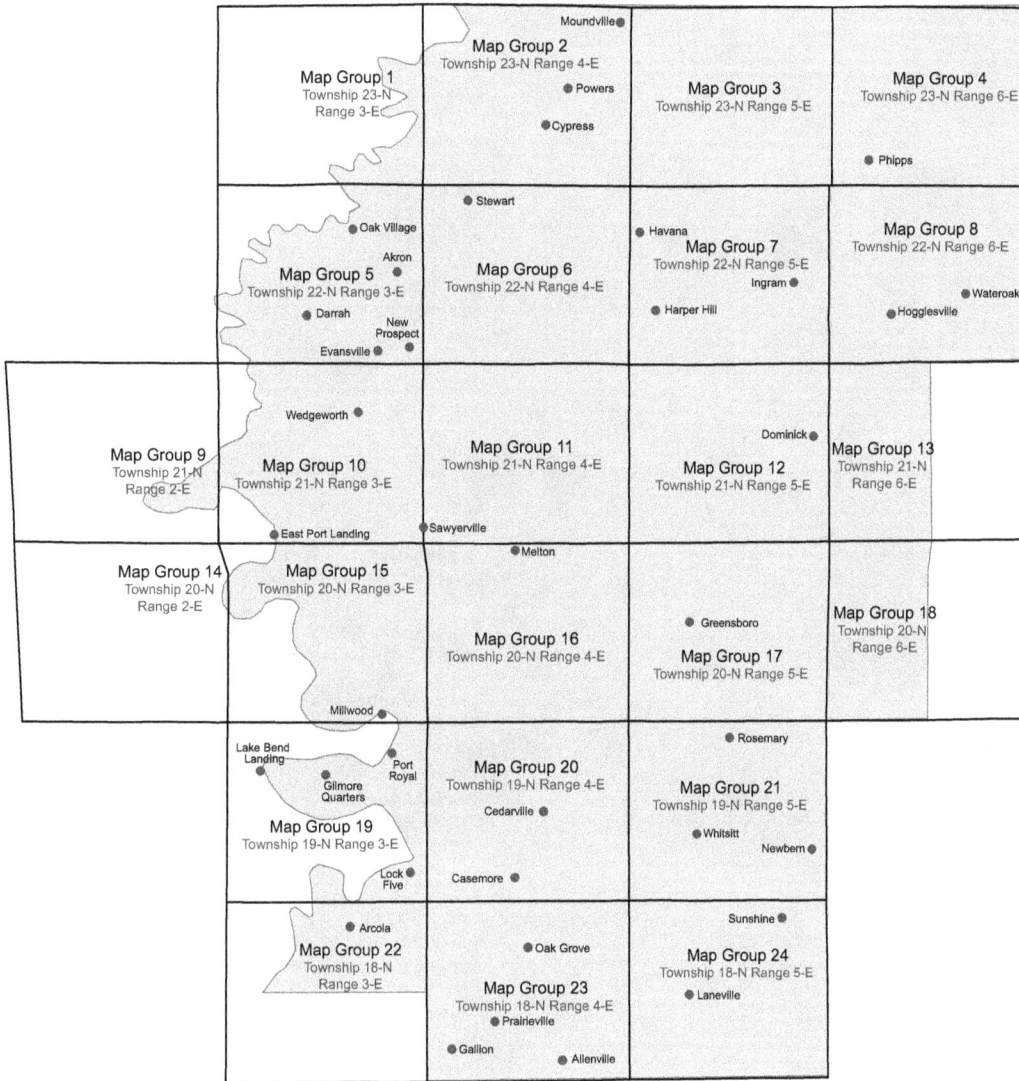

Map Group 1
Township 23-N
Range 3-E

Map Group 2
Township 23-N Range 4-E

Moundville●

● Powers

● Cypress

Map Group 3
Township 23-N Range 5-E

Map Group 4
Township 23-N Range 6-E

● Phipps

● Stewart

● Oak Village
Akron
Map Group 5 ●
Township 22-N Range 3-E
● Darrah
New
Prospect
Evansville ● ●

Map Group 6
Township 22-N Range 4-E

● Havana
Map Group 7
Township 22-N Range 5-E
Ingram ●
● Harper Hill

Map Group 8
Township 22-N Range 6-E
● Wateroak
● Hogglesville

Map Group 9
Township 21-N
Range 2-E

Wedgeworth ●

Map Group 10
Township 21-N Range 3-E

● East Port Landing

Map Group 11
Township 21-N Range 4-E

●Sawyerville

Dominick ●

Map Group 12
Township 21-N Range 5-E

Map Group 13
Township 21-N
Range 6-E

Map Group 14
Township 20-N
Range 2-E

Map Group 15
Township 20-N Range 3-E

● Melton

Map Group 16
Township 20-N Range 4-E

Millwood ●

● Greensboro

Map Group 17
Township 20-N Range 5-E

Map Group 18
Township 20-N
Range 6-E

Lake Bend
Landing ●
● Gilmore
Quarters
Map Group 19
Township 19-N Range 3-E
Lock ●
Five

Port
Royal
Map Group 20
Township 19-N Range 4-E
Cedarville ●

Casemore ●

● Rosemary

Map Group 21
Township 19-N Range 5-E
● Whitsitt
Newbern ●

● Arcola
Map Group 22
Township 18-N
Range 3-E

● Oak Grove

Map Group 23
Township 18-N Range 4-E
● Prairieville
● Gallion
● Allenville

Sunshine ●
Map Group 24
Township 18-N Range 5-E
● Laneville

──── Helpful Hints ────

1 Cities and towns are marked only at their center-points as published by the USGS and/or NationalAtlas.gov. This often enables us to more closely approximate where these might have existed when first settled.

2 To see more specifically where these Cities & Towns are located within the county, refer to both the Road and Historical maps in the Map-Group referred to above. See also, the Map "D" Index on the opposite page.

Map E Index: Cemeteries of Hale County, Alabama

The following represents many of the Cemeteries of Hale County, along with the corresponding Township Map Group in which each is found. Cemeteries are displayed in both the Road and Historical maps in the Map Groups referred to below.

Cemetery	Map Group No.	Cemetery	Map Group No.
Akron New Cem.	5	Mount Hebron Cem.	6
Alexander Cem.	24	Mount Herman Cem.	13
Allenville Cem.	23	Mount Moriah Cem.	16
Antioch Cem.	12	Mount Olive Cem.	23
Bethlehem Cem.	10	Mount Zion Cem.	5
Bethlehem Cem.	10	Mount Zion Cem.	16
Boston Cem.	16	New Haven Cem.	12
Burk Cem.	16	New Hope Cem.	8
Burrough Cem.	12	New Shiloh Cem.	8
Burroughs Cem.	12	Newbern Cem.	21
Burton Cem.	17	Oak Grove Cem.	23
Carthage Cem.	3	Oak Hill Cem.	3
Casemore Cem.	20	Oakwood Cem.	17
Chambers Cem.	8	Old Shiloh Cem.	8
China Grove Cem.	4	Pickens Cem.	16
Concord Cem.	6	Pickens Cem.	19
Cottrell Cem.	24	Pine Flat Cem.	8
Crooks Cem.	16	Pine Grove Cem.	17
Curry Cem.	16	Pine Grove Cem.	20
Curry Grove Cem.	24	Pisgah Cem.	8
Eaton Cem.	20	Pleasant Grove Cem.	17
Erie Cem.	15	Pleasant Hill Cem.	3
Evans Cem.	15	Pleasant Valley Cem.	8
Evening Star Cem.	22	Pruitt Springs Cem.	7
Five Mile Cem.	6	Ramey Cem.	16
Fowler Cem.	24	Ramey Chapel Cem.	12
Greenleaf Cem.	3	Redick Cem.	17
Greenleaf Cem.	17	Rhodes Chapel Cem.	12
Greensboro Cem.	17	Rhone Cem.	11
Greer Cem.	24	Robertson Cem.	11
Grimes Cem.	4	Saint Andrews Cem.	23
Harris Cem.	6	Saint Johns Cem.	12
Harris Cem.	7	Saint Marys Cem.	17
Hatche Cem.	16	Saint Pauls Cem.	20
Havana Cem.	6	Sample Cem.	5
Hill Place Cem.	17	Shelton Cem.	12
Holley Cem.	8	Springhill Cem.	6
Hunter Chapel Cem.	24	Star of Bethlehem Cem.	7
Jackson Chapel Cem.	10	Stokes Cem.	17
Jenkins Place Cem.	17	Taylor Cem.	16
Jerusalem Cem.	17	Terrell Cem.	21
Jerusalem Cem.	22	Tunstall Cem.	24
Jones Cem.	24	Union Grove Cem.	17
Langham Cem.	11	Washington Cem.	19
Lewis Cem.	3	Washington Cem.	21
Liberty Cem.	7	Weaver Cem.	17
Limestone Cem.	15	Whitsitt-Perry Cem.	7
Long Cem.	6	Williams Cem.	6
Long Cem.	16	Willis-Scott Cem.	23
Macedonia Cem.	7	Wilson Cem.	11
Martian Cem.	11	Woods Cem.	3
Martin Mission Cem.	6		
May Cem.	17		
Mays Cem.	10		
McCoy Cem.	17		
McCreary Cem.	21		
Micken Cem.	20		
Mileous Chapel Cem.	6		
Morning Star Cem.	12		

Map E - Cemeteries of Hale County, Alabama

Map Group 1 Township 23-N Range 3-E	Map Group 2 Township 23-N Range 4-E	⚑Carthage ⚑Oak Hill ⚑Lewis ⚑Woods Pleasant Hill Map Group 3 Township 23-N Range 5-E Greenleaf ⚑	⚑Grimes Map Group 4 Township 23-N Range 6-E ⚑China Grove

(map graphic with cemetery locations)

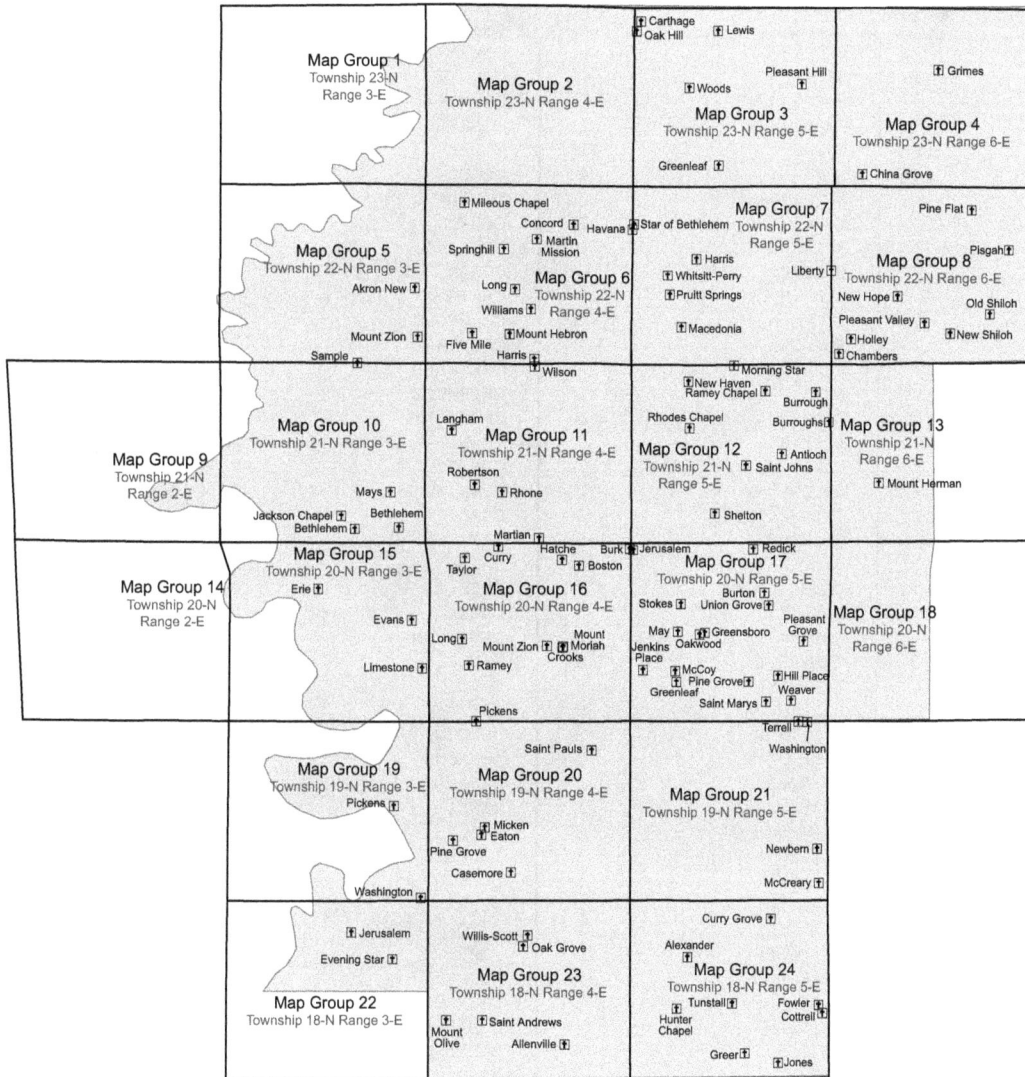

--- Legend ---

☐ Hale County, Alabama

☐ Congressional Townships

Copyright © 2007 Boyd IT, Inc. All Rights Reserved

--- Helpful Hints ---

1 Cemeteries are marked at locations as published by the USGS and/or NationalAtlas.gov.

2 To see more specifically where these Cemeteries are located, refer to the Road & Historical maps in the Map-Group referred to above. See also, the Map "E" Index on the opposite page to make sure you don't miss any of the Cemeteries located within this Congressional township.

Surnames in Hale County, Alabama Patents

The following list represents the surnames that we have located in Hale County, Alabama Patents and the number of parcels that we have mapped for each one. Here is a quick way to determine the existence (or not) of Patents to be found in the subsequent indexes and maps of this volume.

Surname	# of Land Parcels	Surname	# of Land Parcels	Surname	# of Land Parcels	Surname	# of Land Parcels
ABBOTT	2	BREWER	2	COMPANY	34	ELLIOT	2
ABERNATHY	3	BRILEY	2	CONNER	1	ELLIOTT	43
ADAM	1	BRITTON	5	CONNOR	4	ELLIS	8
ADAMS	5	BRODNAX	1	COOK	21	EVANS	2
ADCOCK	2	BROWN	12	COOPE	1	EVRIET	5
ALLEN	12	BRYAN	1	COOPER	4	FAIRCLOTH	1
ALLISON	8	BUCHANNAN	3	COPELAND	2	FARISH	1
ALSOBROOKE	1	BUCK	2	COUNTS	3	FERRIS	2
ALSTON	2	BUCKHALTER	1	COUSINS	5	FIELD	1
ANDERS	4	BUFORD	3	COWAN	2	FIELDS	1
ANDERSON	45	BURDIN	3	CRAIG	5	FILES	2
ANDREWS	1	BURKE	9	CRAWFORD	5	FINLEY	1
ARINGTON	1	BURRELL	1	CRENSHAW	3	FINNEY	3
ARNOLD	9	BURROUGHS	12	CRESWELL	3	FISHER	12
ARRINGTON	8	BURY	1	CRISWELL	2	FITZ	1
ASH	2	BUSHARD	1	CROOM	12	FLEMING	8
AVERA	4	BUZZARD	1	CROW	1	FLEMMING	4
AVERITT	2	CABANISS	1	CUMMINGS	9	FOLLEY	1
AVERY	10	CADE	2	CUNNINGHAM	2	FORD	1
BAGGETT	1	CALDWELL	3	CURRY	5	FORNIER	1
BALDWIN	1	CALHOUN	5	DABNEY	2	FORSTER	1
BANNON	2	CALLOWAY	1	DAILEY	2	FOSTER	12
BARBER	3	CALWELL	2	DALE	2	FOURNIER	1
BARNES	5	CAMACK	5	DANCE	1	FOWLER	13
BARRETT	1	CAMAK	20	DAVIDSON	5	FRAZIER	5
BARRON	3	CAMPBELL	4	DAVIS	24	FREEMAN	4
BARTEE	7	CARAWAY	6	DAVITT	1	FRIEDMAN	35
BARTON	1	CARDER	2	DAY	5	FRIERSON	11
BATES	7	CARLISLE	2	DERDEN	8	FULLER	4
BATTLE	34	CARR	1	DESMOND	3	FULTOM	1
BAUMGARTHER	1	CARROLL	1	DEVANE	1	FULTON	10
BAXTER	1	CARROWAY	1	DEW	3	GABEL	3
BEALE	7	CARSON	6	DIAL	14	GADDIE	2
BEARD	2	CARTER	5	DICKENS	6	GADEIL	1
BECK	1	CARVER	1	DICKINS	9	GAGE	5
BELL	9	CHAMBERS	15	DILLARD	1	GAINSLEY	1
BENNETT	6	CHAMPION	2	DIXON	1	GAREY	5
BERRY	2	CHANDLER	10	DOBBINS	6	GARRETSON	1
BESTOR	2	CHANDRON	8	DOCKERY	3	GARRETT	2
BIRMINGHAM	3	CHAPMAN	6	DOCKREY	1	GAY	1
BISHOP	12	CHATHAM	1	DONALDSON	1	GEDDIE	24
BLACKBURN	2	CHILDS	4	DONELSON	2	GEDIE	2
BLACKWOOD	1	CHILES	7	DONOR	1	GEORGE	5
BLAND	5	CHRISTOPHER	3	DONUGH	2	GEWIN	1
BLOCKER	1	CLAREY	1	DORDON	5	GIBBS	1
BLOUNT	5	CLARKE	1	DOROUGH	2	GIDDIE	1
BOATNER	1	CLARY	7	DOWDLE	2	GIFFORD	1
BOGGS	4	CLEMENT	8	DRUMMOND	5	GILHAM	1
BOHANNAN	1	CLEMENTS	25	DUKE	8	GILL	2
BOLTON	4	CLEVELAND	2	DUNKIN	2	GILMORE	5
BORDEN	36	CO	1	DUNLAP	2	GLADNEY	1
BOUNDS	2	COATES	3	DUNN	1	GLENN	10
BOYD	6	COATS	10	EARBEE	4	GLOVER	36
BRADFORD	3	COCHRAN	1	EASLEY	1	GODDEN	3
BRANCH	1	COCKE	1	EDDINS	10	GOODDIN	1
BRANDON	1	COLBURN	2	EDMINSTON	2	GOODEN	1
BRANTLEY	4	COLBY	1	EDMISTON	1	GOODWIN	8
BRANTLY	1	COLE	3	EDMONDSTON	2	GOOLE	1
BRASFIELD	2	COLEMAN	1	EDMUNDSTON	1	GRANT	2
BRASSFIELD	1	COLEY	1	EDWARDS	1	GRANTHAM	11
BREADY	1	COLINS	2	EGNER	4	GRAVES	2
BREAZEALE	1	COLLINS	17	ELAM	1	GRAY	27

Surname	# of Land Parcels	Surname	# of Land Parcels	Surname	# of Land Parcels	Surname	# of Land Parcels
GREATHOUSE	2	HOLTAM	1	LIDDELL	4	MCKEAN	2
GREEN	12	HOOKS	2	LILES	7	MCKEE	1
GREENE	13	HOPKINS	4	LINCOLN	1	MCKENNIE	1
GREER	18	HOPPER	1	LINGALEY	2	MCKERNIE	1
GRIFFIN	22	HOPSON	5	LIPSCOMB	14	MCLANE	1
GRIGGS	2	HORN	4	LITCHFIELD	2	MCLAUREN	2
GRONTHAM	1	HORNE	1	LITTLE	1	MCLAURIN	1
GUIN	1	HORTON	3	LIVINGSTON	3	MCLEAN	1
GULLEY	1	HOUPT	2	LLOYD	2	MCMASTER	10
GUNN	17	HOUSE	3	LOFTES	3	MCMASTERS	5
GUY	12	HOWARD	3	LOFTIS	5	MCMILLAN	8
GWIN	1	HOWELL	1	LOGAN	20	MCMILLEN	1
HADEN	2	HUBBARD	1	LOMAX	2	MCMILLIAN	12
HAGOOD	3	HUCKABEE	14	LONG	6	MCNALLY	1
HALBERT	2	HUDDLESTON	1	LOVEMAN	35	MCPHAIL	1
HALL	3	HUDSON	2	LOW	2	MCRAE	4
HALLBROOKS	1	HURLY	2	LOWREY	1	MCRARY	2
HALLY	1	HUTCHINS	25	LOWRY	1	MCRORY	1
HAMER	1	HUTT	1	LUCKEY	4	MEADE	3
HAMILTON	1	IDOM	2	LUCKY	5	MEADER	1
HAMLETT	1	INGE	2	LUDLOW	2	MEADOR	12
HAMMONDS	1	INGRAM	9	LUMMAS	1	MEARS	1
HANCOCK	1	INGREM	2	LUMMUS	3	MEEK	1
HANIS	4	JACK	5	LUMPKIN	1	MEEKS	1
HANNA	12	JACKSON	10	LYON	3	MEIGS	1
HANNAN	1	JAMES	2	LYONS	1	MELTON	6
HANY	1	JAMISON	1	MABRY	2	MERIWEATHER	17
HARBIN	2	JANNWAY	7	MADISON	12	MERIWETHER	1
HARDIN	5	JEFFRIES	1	MALONE	1	MERRIWEATHER	4
HARDING	4	JEMISON	60	MANESS	2	MERRYWEATHER	3
HARDWICK	15	JENKINS	16	MANNING	2	MIDDLEBROOKS	10
HARDY	2	JENNINGS	4	MANSKER	2	MILES	1
HARGROVE	2	JIMISON	6	MARR	2	MILLEN	1
HARMAN	1	JOHNSON	50	MARRAST	2	MILLER	1
HARPER	16	JOHNSTON	23	MARS	1	MINTER	10
HARRELL	1	JONES	43	MARTIN	59	MITCHELL	5
HARRIS	24	KAMBER	1	MARTINIER	1	MON	1
HARRISON	5	KEATON	21	MARTINIERE	3	MONETT	2
HARRISS	1	KEETON	1	MASON	3	MONTGOMERY	1
HARRY	7	KEITH	1	MASSINGALE	1	MOODY	5
HART	2	KELLY	1	MAXWELL	1	MOORE	6
HARVEY	2	KEMP	1	MAY	48	MORGAN	5
HATTER	7	KENNARD	1	MAYES	1	MORRIS	3
HATTOX	1	KENNEDY	20	MAYFIELD	2	MORRISON	24
HAYES	1	KENNON	6	MCALPIN	19	MORRISSETT	6
HAYS	2	KEY	3	MCCAIN	1	MORRISSON	1
HEAD	1	KINARD	5	MCCARTER	8	MOSS	10
HEDLESTON	11	KING	6	MCCLURE	1	MUNNERLYN	6
HEMPHILL	1	KIRKSEY	1	MCCONNEL	1	MURFF	12
HENDERSON	4	KNIGHT	5	MCCONNELL	4	MURPHREY	7
HENDON	2	KNOBLOCK	2	MCCOWN	3	MURPHRY	2
HENLEY	11	KNOWLES	1	MCCOY	2	MURPHY	22
HENNON	1	KNOX	2	MCCRAE	1	MUSSINA	5
HENRY	5	KORNEGAY	1	MCCRARY	5	MYERS	4
HERNDON	12	LAKE	1	MCCRAY	1	NASH	2
HESTER	9	LANDRUM	2	MCCRORY	7	NEAL	1
HILL	16	LANDRY	4	MCDANIEL	1	NEIGHBOURS	5
HILLHOUSE	2	LANE	19	MCDONALD	16	NELSON	24
HINES	21	LANGFORD	8	MCDOWALL	1	NERTZ	1
HINTON	13	LASETER	2	MCDOWELL	1	NEVIN	11
HOBSON	5	LASTER	1	MCFARLAND	6	NEWNUM	1
HODGES	1	LATNER	2	MCGAW	2	NEWTON	2
HOGGLE	18	LAVENDER	16	MCGEE	5	NICHOLSON	1
HOLBROOK	8	LAWLESS	12	MCGEHEE	27	NORDIN	2
HOLLEY	9	LAWRENCE	4	MCGIFFERT	2	NORRIS	1
HOLLINGSWORTH	1	LAWSON	6	MCGIFFORD	10	NORWOOD	3
HOLLIS	6	LEAVELL	3	MCGRIFFORD	1	OBANNON	3
HOLLY	3	LEAVENS	1	MCGRUDER	1	OLIVER	2
HOLMAN	1	LEE	8	MCINTIRE	2	ORMON	2
HOLSTON	8	LEWIS	33	MCKANE	4	ORMOND	4

Surname	# of Land Parcels	Surname	# of Land Parcels	Surname	# of Land Parcels	Surname	# of Land Parcels
OSBORN	12	RHODES	18	STEELE	4	WATSON	9
OVERTON	1	RICARD	3	STEINWINDER	2	WATT	5
OWENS	21	RICE	3	STEPHENS	16	WATTS	1
PAGE	1	RICHARDS	12	STEPHENSON	6	WEAGWORTH	1
PARISH	3	RICHARDSON	7	STEVENS	7	WEATHERRED	1
PARK	1	RIDDLE	1	STEWARD	7	WEATHERSPOON	2
PARKER	7	RIDGEWAY	1	STEWART	11	WEAVER	6
PARR	3	RIDGILL	1	STICKNEY	11	WEBB	18
PATTERSON	1	ROAN	6	STOKES	7	WEBSTER	3
PATTISON	1	ROANE	1	STONE	4	WEDGEWORTH	21
PATTON	3	ROBERTS	2	STOREY	1	WEDGWORTH	5
PAUL	1	ROBERTSON	14	STRADWICK	1	WEEKS	3
PAYNE	10	ROBINSON	1	STRICKLAND	1	WELBORN	3
PEACOCK	1	RODEN	1	STRINGFELLON	2	WELLS	2
PEARSON	1	ROE	1	STRINGFELLOW	11	WELSH	1
PECK	8	ROGERS	7	SUMMERS	2	WEST	1
PEIRCE	1	ROSS	1	SUMMEY	9	WESTBROOK	3
PERKINS	1	ROSSER	1	SUMMY	5	WHEELING	2
PERMENTER	3	ROSSON	1	SUMNERS	3	WHITE	16
PERRIN	7	ROUDET	1	SURGINER	1	WHITEHEAD	11
PERRITT	1	ROYALL	1	SUTTON	1	WHITFIELD	1
PERRY	12	RUFF	3	SWANN	1	WHITSETT	7
PETEET	1	RUFFIN	1	SWIFT	3	WHITSITT	1
PETERSON	8	RUSSEL	1	TALBOT	3	WHITWORTH	4
PETETE	1	RUSSELL	14	TALIAFERRO	6	WIER	1
PHARES	15	RYAN	23	TALLIAFERRO	1	WILBORN	1
PHARIS	4	SAMPLE	14	TANKERSLEY	1	WILBURNE	1
PHARRES	5	SAMUEL	1	TANNER	1	WILLIAMS	63
PHILLIPS	10	SANDERS	6	TAPPAN	1	WILLIAMSON	2
PHIPPS	3	SANDERSON	1	TARRANT	2	WILLINGHAM	8
PICKENS	23	SATTERWHITE	1	TAYLOE	1	WILLSON	1
PIERCE	2	SAUNDERS	3	TAYLOR	14	WILSON	56
PILKERTON	1	SCARLETT	2	TERRY	9	WIN	1
POOL	3	SCISM	1	TEW	1	WINDHAM	7
POPE	12	SCOTT	55	THIGPEN	14	WINGATE	1
POUNDS	1	SEABROOK	1	THOMAS	6	WINN	2
POWERS	7	SEAL	3	THOMASON	1	WISDOM	1
PRATHER	2	SEALE	34	THOMPSON	7	WITHERS	22
PRESTWOOD	1	SEALES	1	THORNTON	1	WITHERSPOON	16
PRICE	1	SEXTON	1	THRASH	1	WOLSTENHOLME	1
PRICKET	1	SHACKELFORD	1	THURMOND	1	WOOD	2
PRICKETT	2	SHACKLEFORD	9	TIDMORE	32	WOODALL	3
PRISOC	8	SHAFFER	5	TINGLE	11	WOODARD	2
PRISOCK	4	SHAMBLIN	1	TOLAND	6	WOODWARD	1
PRITCHARD	1	SHAW	1	TOLER	6	WOOLLEY	1
PRUITT	3	SHELDON	6	TOOSING	3	WOOTEN	3
PUCKETT	4	SHEPHERD	1	TORBERT	2	WOOTON	1
PURDOM	1	SHIVERS	1	TORBUT	2	WRIGHT	15
PURNELL	8	SHULTZ	1	TOWNSEND	3	WYATT	3
PURSELL	1	SIKES	1	TRAVIS	12	WYNNE	8
PURTEL	1	SIMMONS	3	TRUE	2	YARBOROUGH	14
PURTTE	2	SIMMS	2	TUBB	7	YOUNG	3
RABORN	1	SIMPSON	1	TUBBS	1		
RACKLEY	4	SIMS	94	TUCKER	3		
RAGLAND	1	SKINNER	1	TURNER	7		
RAINNER	1	SLAUGHTER	3	VARNELL	1		
RAMIE	1	SMALL	2	VAUGHAN	2		
RANDOLPH	2	SMELLEY	5	VEST	1		
RANEY	2	SMITH	32	VIARS	1		
RASSER	2	SNEDECOR	27	WADE	1		
RATLIFF	7	SORRELL	2	WADKINS	1		
RAVESIES	9	SPARKS	10	WALKER	9		
RAVISIES	1	SPEED	14	WALLACE	8		
RAY	2	SPENCE	4	WALLER	6		
READ	1	SPENCER	1	WALTERS	1		
REDDING	4	SPIVEY	1	WALTHALL	3		
REED	6	STALLINGS	1	WALTON	3		
REEVES	1	STANFILL	2	WARD	2		
REID	1	STARKE	1	WARREN	9		
REYNOLDS	1	STEEDMAN	4	WATKINS	6		

Surname/Township Index

This Index allows you to determine which *Township Map Group(s)* contain individuals with the following surnames. Each *Map Group* has a corresponding full-name index of all individuals who obtained patents for land within its Congressional township's borders. After each index you will find the Patent Map to which it refers, and just thereafter, you can view the township's Road Map and Historical Map, with the latter map displaying streams, railroads, and more.

So, once you find your Surname here, proceed to the Index at the beginning of the **Map Group** indicated below.

Surname	Map Group	Parcels of Land	Meridian/Township/Range		
ABBOTT	**21**	1	St Stephens	19-N	5-E
" "	**13**	1	St Stephens	21-N	6-E
ABERNATHY	**7**	3	St Stephens	22-N	5-E
ADAM	**12**	1	St Stephens	21-N	5-E
ADAMS	**7**	4	St Stephens	22-N	5-E
" "	**24**	1	St Stephens	18-N	5-E
ADCOCK	**10**	2	St Stephens	21-N	3-E
ALLEN	**8**	7	St Stephens	22-N	6-E
" "	**18**	4	St Stephens	20-N	6-E
" "	**7**	1	St Stephens	22-N	5-E
ALLISON	**11**	4	St Stephens	21-N	4-E
" "	**12**	4	St Stephens	21-N	5-E
ALSOBROOKE	**12**	1	St Stephens	21-N	5-E
ALSTON	**24**	2	St Stephens	18-N	5-E
ANDERS	**6**	2	St Stephens	22-N	4-E
" "	**11**	1	St Stephens	21-N	4-E
" "	**5**	1	St Stephens	22-N	3-E
ANDERSON	**5**	16	St Stephens	22-N	3-E
" "	**11**	12	St Stephens	21-N	4-E
" "	**6**	12	St Stephens	22-N	4-E
" "	**12**	5	St Stephens	21-N	5-E
ANDREWS	**16**	1	St Stephens	20-N	4-E
ARINGTON	**21**	1	St Stephens	19-N	5-E
ARNOLD	**8**	8	St Stephens	22-N	6-E
" "	**11**	1	St Stephens	21-N	4-E
ARRINGTON	**19**	7	St Stephens	19-N	3-E
" "	**10**	1	St Stephens	21-N	3-E
ASH	**18**	1	St Stephens	20-N	6-E
" "	**13**	1	St Stephens	21-N	6-E
AVERA	**24**	3	St Stephens	18-N	5-E
" "	**8**	1	St Stephens	22-N	6-E
AVERITT	**8**	2	St Stephens	22-N	6-E
AVERY	**18**	7	St Stephens	20-N	6-E
" "	**11**	1	St Stephens	21-N	4-E
" "	**13**	1	St Stephens	21-N	6-E
" "	**6**	1	St Stephens	22-N	4-E
BAGGETT	**24**	1	St Stephens	18-N	5-E
BALDWIN	**1**	1	St Stephens	23-N	3-E
BANNON	**24**	2	St Stephens	18-N	5-E
BARBER	**6**	3	St Stephens	22-N	4-E
BARNES	**20**	5	St Stephens	19-N	4-E
BARRETT	**23**	1	St Stephens	18-N	4-E
BARRON	**7**	2	St Stephens	22-N	5-E
" "	**24**	1	St Stephens	18-N	5-E

Surname	Map Group	Parcels of Land	Meridian/Township/Range		
BARTEE	**5**	7	St Stephens	22-N	3-E
BARTON	**7**	1	St Stephens	22-N	5-E
BATES	**12**	3	St Stephens	21-N	5-E
" "	**10**	2	St Stephens	21-N	3-E
" "	**11**	1	St Stephens	21-N	4-E
" "	**6**	1	St Stephens	22-N	4-E
BATTLE	**2**	31	St Stephens	23-N	4-E
" "	**1**	2	St Stephens	23-N	3-E
" "	**3**	1	St Stephens	23-N	5-E
BAUMGARTHER	**23**	1	St Stephens	18-N	4-E
BAXTER	**11**	1	St Stephens	21-N	4-E
BEALE	**2**	7	St Stephens	23-N	4-E
BEARD	**20**	2	St Stephens	19-N	4-E
BECK	**11**	1	St Stephens	21-N	4-E
BELL	**17**	3	St Stephens	20-N	5-E
" "	**21**	2	St Stephens	19-N	5-E
" "	**18**	2	St Stephens	20-N	6-E
" "	**24**	1	St Stephens	18-N	5-E
" "	**9**	1	St Stephens	21-N	2-E
BENNETT	**24**	2	St Stephens	18-N	5-E
" "	**17**	2	St Stephens	20-N	5-E
" "	**8**	2	St Stephens	22-N	6-E
BERRY	**10**	2	St Stephens	21-N	3-E
BESTOR	**3**	2	St Stephens	23-N	5-E
BIRMINGHAM	**6**	3	St Stephens	22-N	4-E
BISHOP	**3**	8	St Stephens	23-N	5-E
" "	**2**	3	St Stephens	23-N	4-E
" "	**6**	1	St Stephens	22-N	4-E
BLACKBURN	**21**	1	St Stephens	19-N	5-E
" "	**18**	1	St Stephens	20-N	6-E
BLACKWOOD	**8**	1	St Stephens	22-N	6-E
BLAND	**8**	5	St Stephens	22-N	6-E
BLOCKER	**4**	1	St Stephens	23-N	6-E
BLOUNT	**2**	4	St Stephens	23-N	4-E
" "	**12**	1	St Stephens	21-N	5-E
BOATNER	**4**	1	St Stephens	23-N	6-E
BOGGS	**8**	4	St Stephens	22-N	6-E
BOHANNAN	**18**	1	St Stephens	20-N	6-E
BOLTON	**6**	2	St Stephens	22-N	4-E
" "	**7**	2	St Stephens	22-N	5-E
BORDEN	**24**	20	St Stephens	18-N	5-E
" "	**21**	15	St Stephens	19-N	5-E
" "	**16**	1	St Stephens	20-N	4-E
BOUNDS	**21**	1	St Stephens	19-N	5-E
" "	**13**	1	St Stephens	21-N	6-E
BOYD	**21**	3	St Stephens	19-N	5-E
" "	**8**	3	St Stephens	22-N	6-E
BRADFORD	**13**	3	St Stephens	21-N	6-E
BRANCH	**23**	1	St Stephens	18-N	4-E
BRANDON	**3**	1	St Stephens	23-N	5-E
BRANTLEY	**17**	3	St Stephens	20-N	5-E
" "	**12**	1	St Stephens	21-N	5-E
BRANTLY	**17**	1	St Stephens	20-N	5-E
BRASFIELD	**1**	2	St Stephens	23-N	3-E
BRASSFIELD	**1**	1	St Stephens	23-N	3-E
BREADY	**22**	1	St Stephens	18-N	3-E
BREAZEALE	**11**	1	St Stephens	21-N	4-E
BREWER	**11**	1	St Stephens	21-N	4-E
" "	**7**	1	St Stephens	22-N	5-E
BRILEY	**18**	1	St Stephens	20-N	6-E

Surname	Map Group	Parcels of Land	Meridian/Township/Range		
BRILEY (Cont'd)	**12**	1	St Stephens	21-N	5-E
BRITTON	**11**	5	St Stephens	21-N	4-E
BRODNAX	**5**	1	St Stephens	22-N	3-E
BROWN	**10**	3	St Stephens	21-N	3-E
" "	**5**	3	St Stephens	22-N	3-E
" "	**24**	2	St Stephens	18-N	5-E
" "	**23**	1	St Stephens	18-N	4-E
" "	**11**	1	St Stephens	21-N	4-E
" "	**8**	1	St Stephens	22-N	6-E
" "	**2**	1	St Stephens	23-N	4-E
BRYAN	**23**	1	St Stephens	18-N	4-E
BUCHANNAN	**20**	3	St Stephens	19-N	4-E
BUCK	**3**	2	St Stephens	23-N	5-E
BUCKHALTER	**21**	1	St Stephens	19-N	5-E
BUFORD	**6**	2	St Stephens	22-N	4-E
" "	**10**	1	St Stephens	21-N	3-E
BURDIN	**3**	3	St Stephens	23-N	5-E
BURKE	**24**	9	St Stephens	18-N	5-E
BURRELL	**5**	1	St Stephens	22-N	3-E
BURROUGHS	**2**	12	St Stephens	23-N	4-E
BURY	**10**	1	St Stephens	21-N	3-E
BUSHARD	**8**	1	St Stephens	22-N	6-E
BUZZARD	**8**	1	St Stephens	22-N	6-E
CABANISS	**24**	1	St Stephens	18-N	5-E
CADE	**21**	1	St Stephens	19-N	5-E
" "	**18**	1	St Stephens	20-N	6-E
CALDWELL	**8**	2	St Stephens	22-N	6-E
" "	**10**	1	St Stephens	21-N	3-E
CALHOUN	**3**	3	St Stephens	23-N	5-E
" "	**7**	2	St Stephens	22-N	5-E
CALLOWAY	**21**	1	St Stephens	19-N	5-E
CALWELL	**10**	1	St Stephens	21-N	3-E
" "	**6**	1	St Stephens	22-N	4-E
CAMACK	**7**	5	St Stephens	22-N	5-E
CAMAK	**7**	20	St Stephens	22-N	5-E
CAMPBELL	**10**	2	St Stephens	21-N	3-E
" "	**7**	2	St Stephens	22-N	5-E
CARAWAY	**2**	6	St Stephens	23-N	4-E
CARDER	**5**	2	St Stephens	22-N	3-E
CARLISLE	**8**	2	St Stephens	22-N	6-E
CARR	**12**	1	St Stephens	21-N	5-E
CARROLL	**11**	1	St Stephens	21-N	4-E
CARROWAY	**2**	1	St Stephens	23-N	4-E
CARSON	**10**	6	St Stephens	21-N	3-E
CARTER	**17**	2	St Stephens	20-N	5-E
" "	**20**	1	St Stephens	19-N	4-E
" "	**21**	1	St Stephens	19-N	5-E
" "	**11**	1	St Stephens	21-N	4-E
CARVER	**5**	1	St Stephens	22-N	3-E
CHAMBERS	**24**	8	St Stephens	18-N	5-E
" "	**17**	2	St Stephens	20-N	5-E
" "	**18**	2	St Stephens	20-N	6-E
" "	**11**	2	St Stephens	21-N	4-E
" "	**14**	1	St Stephens	20-N	2-E
CHAMPION	**3**	2	St Stephens	23-N	5-E
CHANDLER	**7**	5	St Stephens	22-N	5-E
" "	**20**	2	St Stephens	19-N	4-E
" "	**12**	2	St Stephens	21-N	5-E
" "	**13**	1	St Stephens	21-N	6-E
CHANDRON	**16**	5	St Stephens	20-N	4-E

Surname	Map Group	Parcels of Land	Meridian/Township/Range		
CHANDRON (Cont'd)	**20**	3	St Stephens	19-N	4-E
CHAPMAN	**12**	3	St Stephens	21-N	5-E
" "	**7**	3	St Stephens	22-N	5-E
CHATHAM	**18**	1	St Stephens	20-N	6-E
CHILDS	**21**	2	St Stephens	19-N	5-E
" "	**17**	2	St Stephens	20-N	5-E
CHILES	**5**	7	St Stephens	22-N	3-E
CHRISTOPHER	**18**	2	St Stephens	20-N	6-E
" "	**21**	1	St Stephens	19-N	5-E
CLAREY	**8**	1	St Stephens	22-N	6-E
CLARKE	**11**	1	St Stephens	21-N	4-E
CLARY	**7**	5	St Stephens	22-N	5-E
" "	**8**	2	St Stephens	22-N	6-E
CLEMENT	**8**	5	St Stephens	22-N	6-E
" "	**13**	3	St Stephens	21-N	6-E
CLEMENTS	**6**	12	St Stephens	22-N	4-E
" "	**11**	4	St Stephens	21-N	4-E
" "	**4**	4	St Stephens	23-N	6-E
" "	**10**	3	St Stephens	21-N	3-E
" "	**5**	2	St Stephens	22-N	3-E
CLEVELAND	**1**	2	St Stephens	23-N	3-E
CO	**9**	1	St Stephens	21-N	2-E
COATES	**21**	3	St Stephens	19-N	5-E
COATS	**24**	6	St Stephens	18-N	5-E
" "	**21**	4	St Stephens	19-N	5-E
COCHRAN	**11**	1	St Stephens	21-N	4-E
COCKE	**23**	1	St Stephens	18-N	4-E
COLBURN	**8**	2	St Stephens	22-N	6-E
COLBY	**4**	1	St Stephens	23-N	6-E
COLE	**24**	3	St Stephens	18-N	5-E
COLEMAN	**13**	1	St Stephens	21-N	6-E
COLEY	**4**	1	St Stephens	23-N	6-E
COLINS	**5**	2	St Stephens	22-N	3-E
COLLINS	**11**	6	St Stephens	21-N	4-E
" "	**5**	6	St Stephens	22-N	3-E
" "	**6**	2	St Stephens	22-N	4-E
" "	**3**	2	St Stephens	23-N	5-E
" "	**4**	1	St Stephens	23-N	6-E
COMPANY	**11**	17	St Stephens	21-N	4-E
" "	**5**	6	St Stephens	22-N	3-E
" "	**9**	4	St Stephens	21-N	2-E
" "	**10**	4	St Stephens	21-N	3-E
" "	**6**	3	St Stephens	22-N	4-E
CONNER	**22**	1	St Stephens	18-N	3-E
CONNOR	**22**	4	St Stephens	18-N	3-E
COOK	**8**	14	St Stephens	22-N	6-E
" "	**12**	3	St Stephens	21-N	5-E
" "	**7**	3	St Stephens	22-N	5-E
" "	**16**	1	St Stephens	20-N	4-E
COOPE	**5**	1	St Stephens	22-N	3-E
COOPER	**5**	2	St Stephens	22-N	3-E
" "	**7**	2	St Stephens	22-N	5-E
COPELAND	**20**	1	St Stephens	19-N	4-E
" "	**18**	1	St Stephens	20-N	6-E
COUNTS	**8**	3	St Stephens	22-N	6-E
COUSINS	**12**	4	St Stephens	21-N	5-E
" "	**18**	1	St Stephens	20-N	6-E
COWAN	**20**	2	St Stephens	19-N	4-E
CRAIG	**18**	3	St Stephens	20-N	6-E
" "	**23**	2	St Stephens	18-N	4-E

Surname	Map Group	Parcels of Land	Meridian/Township/Range
CRAWFORD	**21**	2	St Stephens 19-N 5-E
" "	**13**	2	St Stephens 21-N 6-E
" "	**12**	1	St Stephens 21-N 5-E
CRENSHAW	**21**	2	St Stephens 19-N 5-E
" "	**24**	1	St Stephens 18-N 5-E
CRESWELL	**9**	3	St Stephens 21-N 2-E
CRISWELL	**9**	1	St Stephens 21-N 2-E
" "	**10**	1	St Stephens 21-N 3-E
CROOM	**24**	11	St Stephens 18-N 5-E
" "	**21**	1	St Stephens 19-N 5-E
CROW	**3**	1	St Stephens 23-N 5-E
CUMMINGS	**5**	7	St Stephens 22-N 3-E
" "	**20**	2	St Stephens 19-N 4-E
CUNNINGHAM	**11**	1	St Stephens 21-N 4-E
" "	**2**	1	St Stephens 23-N 4-E
CURRY	**18**	4	St Stephens 20-N 6-E
" "	**21**	1	St Stephens 19-N 5-E
DABNEY	**19**	2	St Stephens 19-N 3-E
DAILEY	**12**	2	St Stephens 21-N 5-E
DALE	**12**	2	St Stephens 21-N 5-E
DANCE	**12**	1	St Stephens 21-N 5-E
DAVIDSON	**10**	4	St Stephens 21-N 3-E
" "	**12**	1	St Stephens 21-N 5-E
DAVIS	**8**	7	St Stephens 22-N 6-E
" "	**12**	5	St Stephens 21-N 5-E
" "	**7**	5	St Stephens 22-N 5-E
" "	**3**	2	St Stephens 23-N 5-E
" "	**21**	1	St Stephens 19-N 5-E
" "	**15**	1	St Stephens 20-N 3-E
" "	**18**	1	St Stephens 20-N 6-E
" "	**11**	1	St Stephens 21-N 4-E
" "	**5**	1	St Stephens 22-N 3-E
DAVITT	**12**	1	St Stephens 21-N 5-E
DAY	**11**	2	St Stephens 21-N 4-E
" "	**7**	2	St Stephens 22-N 5-E
" "	**12**	1	St Stephens 21-N 5-E
DERDEN	**10**	5	St Stephens 21-N 3-E
" "	**11**	3	St Stephens 21-N 4-E
DESMOND	**2**	3	St Stephens 23-N 4-E
DEVANE	**3**	1	St Stephens 23-N 5-E
DEW	**5**	2	St Stephens 22-N 3-E
" "	**21**	1	St Stephens 19-N 5-E
DIAL	**6**	12	St Stephens 22-N 4-E
" "	**5**	1	St Stephens 22-N 3-E
" "	**3**	1	St Stephens 23-N 5-E
DICKENS	**17**	4	St Stephens 20-N 5-E
" "	**24**	2	St Stephens 18-N 5-E
DICKINS	**24**	9	St Stephens 18-N 5-E
DILLARD	**12**	1	St Stephens 21-N 5-E
DIXON	**20**	1	St Stephens 19-N 4-E
DOBBINS	**6**	6	St Stephens 22-N 4-E
DOCKERY	**4**	3	St Stephens 23-N 6-E
DOCKREY	**4**	1	St Stephens 23-N 6-E
DONALDSON	**4**	1	St Stephens 23-N 6-E
DONELSON	**19**	2	St Stephens 19-N 3-E
DONOR	**4**	1	St Stephens 23-N 6-E
DONUGH	**10**	2	St Stephens 21-N 3-E
DORDON	**10**	3	St Stephens 21-N 3-E
" "	**11**	2	St Stephens 21-N 4-E
DOROUGH	**10**	2	St Stephens 21-N 3-E

Surname	Map Group	Parcels of Land	Meridian/Township/Range		
DOWDLE	**7**	2	St Stephens	22-N	5-E
DRUMMOND	**20**	4	St Stephens	19-N	4-E
" "	**19**	1	St Stephens	19-N	3-E
DUKE	**10**	4	St Stephens	21-N	3-E
" "	**13**	2	St Stephens	21-N	6-E
" "	**8**	2	St Stephens	22-N	6-E
DUNKIN	**8**	2	St Stephens	22-N	6-E
DUNLAP	**1**	2	St Stephens	23-N	3-E
DUNN	**2**	1	St Stephens	23-N	4-E
EARBEE	**19**	4	St Stephens	19-N	3-E
EASLEY	**21**	1	St Stephens	19-N	5-E
EDDINS	**2**	4	St Stephens	23-N	4-E
" "	**12**	3	St Stephens	21-N	5-E
" "	**17**	2	St Stephens	20-N	5-E
" "	**6**	1	St Stephens	22-N	4-E
EDMINSTON	**5**	2	St Stephens	22-N	3-E
EDMISTON	**5**	1	St Stephens	22-N	3-E
EDMONDSTON	**5**	2	St Stephens	22-N	3-E
EDMUNDSTON	**5**	1	St Stephens	22-N	3-E
EDWARDS	**20**	1	St Stephens	19-N	4-E
EGNER	**4**	4	St Stephens	23-N	6-E
ELAM	**4**	1	St Stephens	23-N	6-E
ELLIOT	**6**	1	St Stephens	22-N	4-E
" "	**7**	1	St Stephens	22-N	5-E
ELLIOTT	**7**	18	St Stephens	22-N	5-E
" "	**3**	12	St Stephens	23-N	5-E
" "	**6**	7	St Stephens	22-N	4-E
" "	**24**	2	St Stephens	18-N	5-E
" "	**2**	2	St Stephens	23-N	4-E
" "	**21**	1	St Stephens	19-N	5-E
" "	**13**	1	St Stephens	21-N	6-E
ELLIS	**1**	5	St Stephens	23-N	3-E
" "	**8**	2	St Stephens	22-N	6-E
" "	**11**	1	St Stephens	21-N	4-E
EVANS	**11**	1	St Stephens	21-N	4-E
" "	**8**	1	St Stephens	22-N	6-E
EVRIET	**8**	5	St Stephens	22-N	6-E
FAIRCLOTH	**12**	1	St Stephens	21-N	5-E
FARISH	**21**	1	St Stephens	19-N	5-E
FERRIS	**10**	2	St Stephens	21-N	3-E
FIELD	**21**	1	St Stephens	19-N	5-E
FIELDS	**12**	1	St Stephens	21-N	5-E
FILES	**19**	2	St Stephens	19-N	3-E
FINLEY	**12**	1	St Stephens	21-N	5-E
FINNEY	**24**	2	St Stephens	18-N	5-E
" "	**10**	1	St Stephens	21-N	3-E
FISHER	**8**	12	St Stephens	22-N	6-E
FITZ	**19**	1	St Stephens	19-N	3-E
FLEMING	**3**	5	St Stephens	23-N	5-E
" "	**6**	2	St Stephens	22-N	4-E
" "	**4**	1	St Stephens	23-N	6-E
FLEMMING	**6**	4	St Stephens	22-N	4-E
FOLLEY	**18**	1	St Stephens	20-N	6-E
FORD	**13**	1	St Stephens	21-N	6-E
FORNIER	**22**	1	St Stephens	18-N	3-E
FORSTER	**10**	1	St Stephens	21-N	3-E
FOSTER	**2**	5	St Stephens	23-N	4-E
" "	**12**	4	St Stephens	21-N	5-E
" "	**4**	2	St Stephens	23-N	6-E
" "	**10**	1	St Stephens	21-N	3-E

Surname	Map Group	Parcels of Land	Meridian/Township/Range		
FOURNIER	**16**	1	St Stephens	20-N	4-E
FOWLER	**15**	7	St Stephens	20-N	3-E
" "	**4**	5	St Stephens	23-N	6-E
" "	**10**	1	St Stephens	21-N	3-E
FRAZIER	**18**	5	St Stephens	20-N	6-E
FREEMAN	**12**	3	St Stephens	21-N	5-E
" "	**24**	1	St Stephens	18-N	5-E
FRIEDMAN	**4**	35	St Stephens	23-N	6-E
FRIERSON	**6**	7	St Stephens	22-N	4-E
" "	**24**	2	St Stephens	18-N	5-E
" "	**3**	2	St Stephens	23-N	5-E
FULLER	**3**	4	St Stephens	23-N	5-E
FULTOM	**7**	1	St Stephens	22-N	5-E
FULTON	**6**	10	St Stephens	22-N	4-E
GABEL	**3**	2	St Stephens	23-N	5-E
" "	**24**	1	St Stephens	18-N	5-E
GADDIE	**4**	2	St Stephens	23-N	6-E
GADEIL	**4**	1	St Stephens	23-N	6-E
GAGE	**18**	4	St Stephens	20-N	6-E
" "	**23**	1	St Stephens	18-N	4-E
GAINSLEY	**23**	1	St Stephens	18-N	4-E
GAREY	**24**	2	St Stephens	18-N	5-E
" "	**11**	2	St Stephens	21-N	4-E
" "	**8**	1	St Stephens	22-N	6-E
GARRETSON	**24**	1	St Stephens	18-N	5-E
GARRETT	**20**	1	St Stephens	19-N	4-E
" "	**21**	1	St Stephens	19-N	5-E
GAY	**8**	1	St Stephens	22-N	6-E
GEDDIE	**3**	9	St Stephens	23-N	5-E
" "	**4**	8	St Stephens	23-N	6-E
" "	**8**	4	St Stephens	22-N	6-E
" "	**7**	3	St Stephens	22-N	5-E
GEDIE	**8**	2	St Stephens	22-N	6-E
GEORGE	**8**	5	St Stephens	22-N	6-E
GEWIN	**12**	1	St Stephens	21-N	5-E
GIBBS	**5**	1	St Stephens	22-N	3-E
GIDDIE	**4**	1	St Stephens	23-N	6-E
GIFFORD	**1**	1	St Stephens	23-N	3-E
GILHAM	**6**	1	St Stephens	22-N	4-E
GILL	**24**	1	St Stephens	18-N	5-E
" "	**6**	1	St Stephens	22-N	4-E
GILMORE	**10**	3	St Stephens	21-N	3-E
" "	**24**	2	St Stephens	18-N	5-E
GLADNEY	**3**	1	St Stephens	23-N	5-E
GLENN	**2**	9	St Stephens	23-N	4-E
" "	**8**	1	St Stephens	22-N	6-E
GLOVER	**23**	14	St Stephens	18-N	4-E
" "	**22**	8	St Stephens	18-N	3-E
" "	**20**	7	St Stephens	19-N	4-E
" "	**6**	2	St Stephens	22-N	4-E
" "	**19**	1	St Stephens	19-N	3-E
" "	**21**	1	St Stephens	19-N	5-E
" "	**16**	1	St Stephens	20-N	4-E
" "	**7**	1	St Stephens	22-N	5-E
" "	**3**	1	St Stephens	23-N	5-E
GODDEN	**5**	3	St Stephens	22-N	3-E
GOODDIN	**8**	1	St Stephens	22-N	6-E
GOODEN	**8**	1	St Stephens	22-N	6-E
GOODWIN	**8**	6	St Stephens	22-N	6-E
" "	**13**	1	St Stephens	21-N	6-E

Surname	Map Group	Parcels of Land	Meridian/Township/Range
GOODWIN (Cont'd)	**4**	1	St Stephens 23-N 6-E
GOOLE	**20**	1	St Stephens 19-N 4-E
GRANT	**15**	1	St Stephens 20-N 3-E
" "	**10**	1	St Stephens 21-N 3-E
GRANTHAM	**13**	9	St Stephens 21-N 6-E
" "	**24**	1	St Stephens 18-N 5-E
" "	**12**	1	St Stephens 21-N 5-E
GRAVES	**10**	2	St Stephens 21-N 3-E
GRAY	**2**	22	St Stephens 23-N 4-E
" "	**10**	2	St Stephens 21-N 3-E
" "	**23**	1	St Stephens 18-N 4-E
" "	**6**	1	St Stephens 22-N 4-E
" "	**3**	1	St Stephens 23-N 5-E
GREATHOUSE	**4**	2	St Stephens 23-N 6-E
GREEN	**11**	4	St Stephens 21-N 4-E
" "	**6**	4	St Stephens 22-N 4-E
" "	**10**	2	St Stephens 21-N 3-E
" "	**24**	1	St Stephens 18-N 5-E
" "	**3**	1	St Stephens 23-N 5-E
GREENE	**2**	11	St Stephens 23-N 4-E
" "	**16**	1	St Stephens 20-N 4-E
" "	**1**	1	St Stephens 23-N 3-E
GREER	**24**	13	St Stephens 18-N 5-E
" "	**6**	3	St Stephens 22-N 4-E
" "	**23**	1	St Stephens 18-N 4-E
" "	**7**	1	St Stephens 22-N 5-E
GRIFFIN	**4**	11	St Stephens 23-N 6-E
" "	**3**	4	St Stephens 23-N 5-E
" "	**18**	2	St Stephens 20-N 6-E
" "	**24**	1	St Stephens 18-N 5-E
" "	**19**	1	St Stephens 19-N 3-E
" "	**16**	1	St Stephens 20-N 4-E
" "	**7**	1	St Stephens 22-N 5-E
" "	**8**	1	St Stephens 22-N 6-E
GRIGGS	**17**	2	St Stephens 20-N 5-E
GRONTHAM	**13**	1	St Stephens 21-N 6-E
GUIN	**11**	1	St Stephens 21-N 4-E
GULLEY	**12**	1	St Stephens 21-N 5-E
GUNN	**3**	17	St Stephens 23-N 5-E
GUY	**8**	6	St Stephens 22-N 6-E
" "	**7**	5	St Stephens 22-N 5-E
" "	**3**	1	St Stephens 23-N 5-E
GWIN	**7**	1	St Stephens 22-N 5-E
HADEN	**2**	2	St Stephens 23-N 4-E
HAGOOD	**5**	3	St Stephens 22-N 3-E
HALBERT	**20**	1	St Stephens 19-N 4-E
" "	**21**	1	St Stephens 19-N 5-E
HALL	**16**	1	St Stephens 20-N 4-E
" "	**12**	1	St Stephens 21-N 5-E
" "	**3**	1	St Stephens 23-N 5-E
HALLBROOKS	**6**	1	St Stephens 22-N 4-E
HALLY	**6**	1	St Stephens 22-N 4-E
HAMER	**21**	1	St Stephens 19-N 5-E
HAMILTON	**4**	1	St Stephens 23-N 6-E
HAMLETT	**11**	1	St Stephens 21-N 4-E
HAMMONDS	**23**	1	St Stephens 18-N 4-E
HANCOCK	**16**	1	St Stephens 20-N 4-E
HANIS	**6**	3	St Stephens 22-N 4-E
" "	**11**	1	St Stephens 21-N 4-E
HANNA	**5**	7	St Stephens 22-N 3-E

Surname	Map Group	Parcels of Land	Meridian/Township/Range		
HANNA (Cont'd)	21	4	St Stephens	19-N	5-E
" "	6	1	St Stephens	22-N	4-E
HANNAN	24	1	St Stephens	18-N	5-E
HANY	6	1	St Stephens	22-N	4-E
HARBIN	21	2	St Stephens	19-N	5-E
HARDIN	21	4	St Stephens	19-N	5-E
" "	12	1	St Stephens	21-N	5-E
HARDING	24	4	St Stephens	18-N	5-E
HARDWICK	2	14	St Stephens	23-N	4-E
" "	3	1	St Stephens	23-N	5-E
HARDY	23	2	St Stephens	18-N	4-E
HARGROVE	4	2	St Stephens	23-N	6-E
HARMAN	24	1	St Stephens	18-N	5-E
HARPER	18	9	St Stephens	20-N	6-E
" "	3	4	St Stephens	23-N	5-E
" "	24	3	St Stephens	18-N	5-E
HARRELL	20	1	St Stephens	19-N	4-E
HARRIS	6	12	St Stephens	22-N	4-E
" "	11	11	St Stephens	21-N	4-E
" "	20	1	St Stephens	19-N	4-E
HARRISON	12	4	St Stephens	21-N	5-E
" "	20	1	St Stephens	19-N	4-E
HARRISS	12	1	St Stephens	21-N	5-E
HARRY	11	4	St Stephens	21-N	4-E
" "	6	2	St Stephens	22-N	4-E
" "	12	1	St Stephens	21-N	5-E
HART	6	2	St Stephens	22-N	4-E
HARVEY	11	1	St Stephens	21-N	4-E
" "	7	1	St Stephens	22-N	5-E
HATTER	5	7	St Stephens	22-N	3-E
HATTOX	6	1	St Stephens	22-N	4-E
HAYES	24	1	St Stephens	18-N	5-E
HAYS	9	2	St Stephens	21-N	2-E
HEAD	21	1	St Stephens	19-N	5-E
HEDLESTON	2	9	St Stephens	23-N	4-E
" "	6	2	St Stephens	22-N	4-E
HEMPHILL	24	1	St Stephens	18-N	5-E
HENDERSON	12	4	St Stephens	21-N	5-E
HENDON	21	2	St Stephens	19-N	5-E
HENLEY	16	5	St Stephens	20-N	4-E
" "	20	3	St Stephens	19-N	4-E
" "	10	3	St Stephens	21-N	3-E
HENNON	6	1	St Stephens	22-N	4-E
HENRY	11	5	St Stephens	21-N	4-E
HERNDON	15	6	St Stephens	20-N	3-E
" "	10	5	St Stephens	21-N	3-E
" "	11	1	St Stephens	21-N	4-E
HESTER	3	4	St Stephens	23-N	5-E
" "	4	4	St Stephens	23-N	6-E
" "	11	1	St Stephens	21-N	4-E
HILL	6	8	St Stephens	22-N	4-E
" "	10	5	St Stephens	21-N	3-E
" "	23	2	St Stephens	18-N	4-E
" "	8	1	St Stephens	22-N	6-E
HILLHOUSE	7	1	St Stephens	22-N	5-E
" "	3	1	St Stephens	23-N	5-E
HINES	15	18	St Stephens	20-N	3-E
" "	19	3	St Stephens	19-N	3-E
HINTON	10	13	St Stephens	21-N	3-E
HOBSON	6	3	St Stephens	22-N	4-E

Surname	Map Group	Parcels of Land	Meridian/Township/Range
HOBSON (Cont'd)	**11**	2	St Stephens 21-N 4-E
HODGES	**21**	1	St Stephens 19-N 5-E
HOGGLE	**8**	17	St Stephens 22-N 6-E
" "	**7**	1	St Stephens 22-N 5-E
HOLBROOK	**6**	8	St Stephens 22-N 4-E
HOLLEY	**6**	6	St Stephens 22-N 4-E
" "	**5**	3	St Stephens 22-N 3-E
HOLLINGSWORTH	**18**	1	St Stephens 20-N 6-E
HOLLIS	**7**	6	St Stephens 22-N 5-E
HOLLY	**2**	2	St Stephens 23-N 4-E
" "	**6**	1	St Stephens 22-N 4-E
HOLMAN	**8**	1	St Stephens 22-N 6-E
HOLSTON	**7**	8	St Stephens 22-N 5-E
HOLTAM	**22**	1	St Stephens 18-N 3-E
HOOKS	**24**	2	St Stephens 18-N 5-E
HOPKINS	**10**	4	St Stephens 21-N 3-E
HOPPER	**21**	1	St Stephens 19-N 5-E
HOPSON	**18**	5	St Stephens 20-N 6-E
HORN	**8**	3	St Stephens 22-N 6-E
" "	**3**	1	St Stephens 23-N 5-E
HORNE	**8**	1	St Stephens 22-N 6-E
HORTON	**21**	3	St Stephens 19-N 5-E
HOUPT	**15**	1	St Stephens 20-N 3-E
" "	**9**	1	St Stephens 21-N 2-E
HOUSE	**21**	3	St Stephens 19-N 5-E
HOWARD	**13**	3	St Stephens 21-N 6-E
HOWELL	**23**	1	St Stephens 18-N 4-E
HUBBARD	**5**	1	St Stephens 22-N 3-E
HUCKABEE	**24**	13	St Stephens 18-N 5-E
" "	**21**	1	St Stephens 19-N 5-E
HUDDLESTON	**6**	1	St Stephens 22-N 4-E
HUDSON	**23**	1	St Stephens 18-N 4-E
" "	**24**	1	St Stephens 18-N 5-E
HURLY	**7**	2	St Stephens 22-N 5-E
HUTCHINS	**17**	22	St Stephens 20-N 5-E
" "	**12**	3	St Stephens 21-N 5-E
HUTT	**7**	1	St Stephens 22-N 5-E
IDOM	**12**	2	St Stephens 21-N 5-E
INGE	**6**	1	St Stephens 22-N 4-E
" "	**3**	1	St Stephens 23-N 5-E
INGRAM	**7**	7	St Stephens 22-N 5-E
" "	**20**	2	St Stephens 19-N 4-E
INGREM	**24**	1	St Stephens 18-N 5-E
" "	**12**	1	St Stephens 21-N 5-E
JACK	**2**	4	St Stephens 23-N 4-E
" "	**6**	1	St Stephens 22-N 4-E
JACKSON	**10**	6	St Stephens 21-N 3-E
" "	**7**	3	St Stephens 22-N 5-E
" "	**5**	1	St Stephens 22-N 3-E
JAMES	**22**	2	St Stephens 18-N 3-E
JAMISON	**18**	1	St Stephens 20-N 6-E
JANNWAY	**3**	5	St Stephens 23-N 5-E
" "	**6**	1	St Stephens 22-N 4-E
" "	**7**	1	St Stephens 22-N 5-E
JEFFRIES	**5**	1	St Stephens 22-N 3-E
JEMISON	**4**	35	St Stephens 23-N 6-E
" "	**2**	17	St Stephens 23-N 4-E
" "	**1**	5	St Stephens 23-N 3-E
" "	**24**	2	St Stephens 18-N 5-E
" "	**10**	1	St Stephens 21-N 3-E

Surname	Map Group	Parcels of Land	Meridian/Township/Range		
JENKINS	**13**	7	St Stephens	21-N	6-E
" "	**8**	3	St Stephens	22-N	6-E
" "	**21**	2	St Stephens	19-N	5-E
" "	**12**	2	St Stephens	21-N	5-E
" "	**3**	2	St Stephens	23-N	5-E
JENNINGS	**10**	4	St Stephens	21-N	3-E
JIMISON	**5**	4	St Stephens	22-N	3-E
" "	**10**	1	St Stephens	21-N	3-E
" "	**6**	1	St Stephens	22-N	4-E
JOHNSON	**4**	16	St Stephens	23-N	6-E
" "	**8**	8	St Stephens	22-N	6-E
" "	**12**	6	St Stephens	21-N	5-E
" "	**13**	6	St Stephens	21-N	6-E
" "	**24**	4	St Stephens	18-N	5-E
" "	**11**	3	St Stephens	21-N	4-E
" "	**23**	2	St Stephens	18-N	4-E
" "	**17**	2	St Stephens	20-N	5-E
" "	**18**	2	St Stephens	20-N	6-E
" "	**7**	1	St Stephens	22-N	5-E
JOHNSTON	**4**	11	St Stephens	23-N	6-E
" "	**8**	8	St Stephens	22-N	6-E
" "	**3**	3	St Stephens	23-N	5-E
" "	**11**	1	St Stephens	21-N	4-E
JONES	**6**	18	St Stephens	22-N	4-E
" "	**5**	13	St Stephens	22-N	3-E
" "	**7**	5	St Stephens	22-N	5-E
" "	**2**	4	St Stephens	23-N	4-E
" "	**13**	3	St Stephens	21-N	6-E
KAMBER	**22**	1	St Stephens	18-N	3-E
KEATON	**2**	20	St Stephens	23-N	4-E
" "	**3**	1	St Stephens	23-N	5-E
KEETON	**2**	1	St Stephens	23-N	4-E
KEITH	**18**	1	St Stephens	20-N	6-E
KELLY	**3**	1	St Stephens	23-N	5-E
KEMP	**3**	1	St Stephens	23-N	5-E
KENNARD	**18**	1	St Stephens	20-N	6-E
KENNEDY	**10**	20	St Stephens	21-N	3-E
KENNON	**2**	4	St Stephens	23-N	4-E
" "	**15**	1	St Stephens	20-N	3-E
" "	**6**	1	St Stephens	22-N	4-E
KEY	**3**	2	St Stephens	23-N	5-E
" "	**4**	1	St Stephens	23-N	6-E
KINARD	**8**	3	St Stephens	22-N	6-E
" "	**12**	2	St Stephens	21-N	5-E
KING	**11**	3	St Stephens	21-N	4-E
" "	**21**	1	St Stephens	19-N	5-E
" "	**6**	1	St Stephens	22-N	4-E
" "	**3**	1	St Stephens	23-N	5-E
KIRKSEY	**12**	1	St Stephens	21-N	5-E
KNIGHT	**7**	5	St Stephens	22-N	5-E
KNOBLOCK	**4**	2	St Stephens	23-N	6-E
KNOWLES	**3**	1	St Stephens	23-N	5-E
KNOX	**24**	1	St Stephens	18-N	5-E
" "	**2**	1	St Stephens	23-N	4-E
KORNEGAY	**2**	1	St Stephens	23-N	4-E
LAKE	**17**	1	St Stephens	20-N	5-E
LANDRUM	**22**	1	St Stephens	18-N	3-E
" "	**16**	1	St Stephens	20-N	4-E
LANDRY	**11**	4	St Stephens	21-N	4-E
LANE	**6**	8	St Stephens	22-N	4-E

Surname	Map Group	Parcels of Land	Meridian/Township/Range		
LANE (Cont'd)	**10**	6	St Stephens	21-N	3-E
" "	**11**	3	St Stephens	21-N	4-E
" "	**16**	1	St Stephens	20-N	4-E
" "	**3**	1	St Stephens	23-N	5-E
LANGFORD	**8**	8	St Stephens	22-N	6-E
LASETER	**5**	2	St Stephens	22-N	3-E
LASTER	**5**	1	St Stephens	22-N	3-E
LATNER	**8**	1	St Stephens	22-N	6-E
" "	**4**	1	St Stephens	23-N	6-E
LAVENDER	**7**	16	St Stephens	22-N	5-E
LAWLESS	**8**	11	St Stephens	22-N	6-E
" "	**11**	1	St Stephens	21-N	4-E
LAWRENCE	**24**	4	St Stephens	18-N	5-E
LAWSON	**8**	3	St Stephens	22-N	6-E
" "	**24**	2	St Stephens	18-N	5-E
" "	**15**	1	St Stephens	20-N	3-E
LEAVELL	**2**	3	St Stephens	23-N	4-E
LEAVENS	**1**	1	St Stephens	23-N	3-E
LEE	**12**	3	St Stephens	21-N	5-E
" "	**7**	3	St Stephens	22-N	5-E
" "	**10**	1	St Stephens	21-N	3-E
" "	**8**	1	St Stephens	22-N	6-E
LEWIS	**3**	19	St Stephens	23-N	5-E
" "	**5**	7	St Stephens	22-N	3-E
" "	**1**	3	St Stephens	23-N	3-E
" "	**9**	2	St Stephens	21-N	2-E
" "	**20**	1	St Stephens	19-N	4-E
" "	**4**	1	St Stephens	23-N	6-E
LIDDELL	**6**	4	St Stephens	22-N	4-E
LILES	**7**	6	St Stephens	22-N	5-E
" "	**12**	1	St Stephens	21-N	5-E
LINCOLN	**24**	1	St Stephens	18-N	5-E
LINGALEY	**12**	2	St Stephens	21-N	5-E
LIPSCOMB	**10**	11	St Stephens	21-N	3-E
" "	**21**	3	St Stephens	19-N	5-E
LITCHFIELD	**24**	1	St Stephens	18-N	5-E
" "	**21**	1	St Stephens	19-N	5-E
LITTLE	**19**	1	St Stephens	19-N	3-E
LIVINGSTON	**15**	1	St Stephens	20-N	3-E
" "	**11**	1	St Stephens	21-N	4-E
" "	**12**	1	St Stephens	21-N	5-E
LLOYD	**5**	2	St Stephens	22-N	3-E
LOFTES	**24**	2	St Stephens	18-N	5-E
" "	**3**	1	St Stephens	23-N	5-E
LOFTIS	**7**	5	St Stephens	22-N	5-E
LOGAN	**5**	20	St Stephens	22-N	3-E
LOMAX	**23**	2	St Stephens	18-N	4-E
LONG	**6**	6	St Stephens	22-N	4-E
LOVEMAN	**4**	35	St Stephens	23-N	6-E
LOW	**15**	1	St Stephens	20-N	3-E
" "	**18**	1	St Stephens	20-N	6-E
LOWREY	**20**	1	St Stephens	19-N	4-E
LOWRY	**19**	1	St Stephens	19-N	3-E
LUCKEY	**3**	4	St Stephens	23-N	5-E
LUCKY	**3**	5	St Stephens	23-N	5-E
LUDLOW	**21**	2	St Stephens	19-N	5-E
LUMMAS	**5**	1	St Stephens	22-N	3-E
LUMMUS	**5**	3	St Stephens	22-N	3-E
LUMPKIN	**24**	1	St Stephens	18-N	5-E
LYON	**2**	2	St Stephens	23-N	4-E

Surname	Map Group	Parcels of Land	Meridian/Township/Range		
LYON (Cont'd)	**23**	1	St Stephens	18-N	4-E
LYONS	**7**	1	St Stephens	22-N	5-E
MABRY	**21**	2	St Stephens	19-N	5-E
MADISON	**12**	11	St Stephens	21-N	5-E
" "	**15**	1	St Stephens	20-N	3-E
MALONE	**23**	1	St Stephens	18-N	4-E
MANESS	**23**	1	St Stephens	18-N	4-E
" "	**20**	1	St Stephens	19-N	4-E
MANNING	**23**	2	St Stephens	18-N	4-E
MANSKER	**6**	1	St Stephens	22-N	4-E
" "	**7**	1	St Stephens	22-N	5-E
MARR	**2**	2	St Stephens	23-N	4-E
MARRAST	**17**	1	St Stephens	20-N	5-E
" "	**18**	1	St Stephens	20-N	6-E
MARS	**18**	1	St Stephens	20-N	6-E
MARTIN	**19**	30	St Stephens	19-N	3-E
" "	**24**	7	St Stephens	18-N	5-E
" "	**3**	7	St Stephens	23-N	5-E
" "	**7**	5	St Stephens	22-N	5-E
" "	**20**	4	St Stephens	19-N	4-E
" "	**17**	2	St Stephens	20-N	5-E
" "	**11**	2	St Stephens	21-N	4-E
" "	**23**	1	St Stephens	18-N	4-E
" "	**6**	1	St Stephens	22-N	4-E
MARTINIER	**23**	1	St Stephens	18-N	4-E
MARTINIERE	**16**	2	St Stephens	20-N	4-E
" "	**23**	1	St Stephens	18-N	4-E
MASON	**9**	2	St Stephens	21-N	2-E
" "	**19**	1	St Stephens	19-N	3-E
MASSINGALE	**3**	1	St Stephens	23-N	5-E
MAXWELL	**4**	1	St Stephens	23-N	6-E
MAY	**10**	26	St Stephens	21-N	3-E
" "	**11**	6	St Stephens	21-N	4-E
" "	**1**	6	St Stephens	23-N	3-E
" "	**19**	5	St Stephens	19-N	3-E
" "	**17**	2	St Stephens	20-N	5-E
" "	**5**	2	St Stephens	22-N	3-E
" "	**20**	1	St Stephens	19-N	4-E
MAYES	**2**	1	St Stephens	23-N	4-E
MAYFIELD	**17**	1	St Stephens	20-N	5-E
" "	**18**	1	St Stephens	20-N	6-E
MCALPIN	**11**	10	St Stephens	21-N	4-E
" "	**14**	8	St Stephens	20-N	2-E
" "	**15**	1	St Stephens	20-N	3-E
MCCAIN	**3**	1	St Stephens	23-N	5-E
MCCARTER	**17**	4	St Stephens	20-N	5-E
" "	**11**	3	St Stephens	21-N	4-E
" "	**12**	1	St Stephens	21-N	5-E
MCCLURE	**20**	1	St Stephens	19-N	4-E
MCCONNEL	**24**	1	St Stephens	18-N	5-E
MCCONNELL	**24**	2	St Stephens	18-N	5-E
" "	**13**	1	St Stephens	21-N	6-E
" "	**8**	1	St Stephens	22-N	6-E
MCCOWN	**3**	2	St Stephens	23-N	5-E
" "	**2**	1	St Stephens	23-N	4-E
MCCOY	**19**	1	St Stephens	19-N	3-E
" "	**12**	1	St Stephens	21-N	5-E
MCCRAE	**3**	1	St Stephens	23-N	5-E
MCCRARY	**6**	5	St Stephens	22-N	4-E
MCCRAY	**6**	1	St Stephens	22-N	4-E

Surname	Map Group	Parcels of Land	Meridian/Township/Range
MCCRORY	**7**	7	St Stephens 22-N 5-E
MCDANIEL	**19**	1	St Stephens 19-N 3-E
MCDONALD	**24**	5	St Stephens 18-N 5-E
" "	**21**	5	St Stephens 19-N 5-E
" "	**12**	3	St Stephens 21-N 5-E
" "	**4**	2	St Stephens 23-N 6-E
" "	**3**	1	St Stephens 23-N 5-E
MCDOWALL	**4**	1	St Stephens 23-N 6-E
MCDOWELL	**9**	1	St Stephens 21-N 2-E
MCFARLAND	**8**	5	St Stephens 22-N 6-E
" "	**16**	1	St Stephens 20-N 4-E
MCGAW	**20**	2	St Stephens 19-N 4-E
MCGEE	**24**	5	St Stephens 18-N 5-E
MCGEHEE	**5**	9	St Stephens 22-N 3-E
" "	**6**	9	St Stephens 22-N 4-E
" "	**11**	8	St Stephens 21-N 4-E
" "	**10**	1	St Stephens 21-N 3-E
MCGIFFERT	**1**	2	St Stephens 23-N 3-E
MCGIFFORD	**1**	9	St Stephens 23-N 3-E
" "	**2**	1	St Stephens 23-N 4-E
MCGRIFFORD	**1**	1	St Stephens 23-N 3-E
MCGRUDER	**5**	1	St Stephens 22-N 3-E
MCINTIRE	**19**	2	St Stephens 19-N 3-E
MCKANE	**12**	3	St Stephens 21-N 5-E
" "	**7**	1	St Stephens 22-N 5-E
MCKEAN	**7**	2	St Stephens 22-N 5-E
MCKEE	**18**	1	St Stephens 20-N 6-E
MCKENNIE	**2**	1	St Stephens 23-N 4-E
MCKERNIE	**7**	1	St Stephens 22-N 5-E
MCLANE	**11**	1	St Stephens 21-N 4-E
MCLAUREN	**15**	1	St Stephens 20-N 3-E
" "	**10**	1	St Stephens 21-N 3-E
MCLAURIN	**9**	1	St Stephens 21-N 2-E
MCLEAN	**22**	1	St Stephens 18-N 3-E
MCMASTER	**12**	5	St Stephens 21-N 5-E
" "	**6**	5	St Stephens 22-N 4-E
MCMASTERS	**12**	2	St Stephens 21-N 5-E
" "	**6**	2	St Stephens 22-N 4-E
" "	**7**	1	St Stephens 22-N 5-E
MCMILLAN	**2**	5	St Stephens 23-N 4-E
" "	**3**	2	St Stephens 23-N 5-E
" "	**11**	1	St Stephens 21-N 4-E
MCMILLEN	**3**	1	St Stephens 23-N 5-E
MCMILLIAN	**2**	7	St Stephens 23-N 4-E
" "	**3**	4	St Stephens 23-N 5-E
" "	**4**	1	St Stephens 23-N 6-E
MCNALLY	**20**	1	St Stephens 19-N 4-E
MCPHAIL	**4**	1	St Stephens 23-N 6-E
MCRAE	**23**	2	St Stephens 18-N 4-E
" "	**3**	2	St Stephens 23-N 5-E
MCRARY	**6**	2	St Stephens 22-N 4-E
MCRORY	**4**	1	St Stephens 23-N 6-E
MEADE	**19**	3	St Stephens 19-N 3-E
MEADER	**11**	1	St Stephens 21-N 4-E
MEADOR	**10**	7	St Stephens 21-N 3-E
" "	**11**	5	St Stephens 21-N 4-E
MEARS	**3**	1	St Stephens 23-N 5-E
MEEK	**13**	1	St Stephens 21-N 6-E
MEEKS	**12**	1	St Stephens 21-N 5-E
MEIGS	**13**	1	St Stephens 21-N 6-E

Surname	Map Group	Parcels of Land	Meridian/Township/Range		
MELTON	11	4	St Stephens	21-N	4-E
" "	10	2	St Stephens	21-N	3-E
MERIWEATHER	5	17	St Stephens	22-N	3-E
MERIWETHER	5	1	St Stephens	22-N	3-E
MERRIWEATHER	5	4	St Stephens	22-N	3-E
MERRYWEATHER	5	3	St Stephens	22-N	3-E
MIDDLEBROOKS	21	8	St Stephens	19-N	5-E
" "	24	2	St Stephens	18-N	5-E
MILES	21	1	St Stephens	19-N	5-E
MILLEN	11	1	St Stephens	21-N	4-E
MILLER	20	1	St Stephens	19-N	4-E
MINTER	2	6	St Stephens	23-N	4-E
" "	1	4	St Stephens	23-N	3-E
MITCHELL	5	2	St Stephens	22-N	3-E
" "	4	2	St Stephens	23-N	6-E
" "	12	1	St Stephens	21-N	5-E
MON	11	1	St Stephens	21-N	4-E
MONETT	10	1	St Stephens	21-N	3-E
" "	11	1	St Stephens	21-N	4-E
MONTGOMERY	16	1	St Stephens	20-N	4-E
MOODY	18	5	St Stephens	20-N	6-E
MOORE	24	3	St Stephens	18-N	5-E
" "	23	1	St Stephens	18-N	4-E
" "	16	1	St Stephens	20-N	4-E
" "	10	1	St Stephens	21-N	3-E
MORGAN	8	4	St Stephens	22-N	6-E
" "	23	1	St Stephens	18-N	4-E
MORRIS	8	2	St Stephens	22-N	6-E
" "	3	1	St Stephens	23-N	5-E
MORRISON	8	17	St Stephens	22-N	6-E
" "	4	6	St Stephens	23-N	6-E
" "	11	1	St Stephens	21-N	4-E
MORRISSETT	24	6	St Stephens	18-N	5-E
MORRISSON	11	1	St Stephens	21-N	4-E
MOSS	2	9	St Stephens	23-N	4-E
" "	23	1	St Stephens	18-N	4-E
MUNNERLYN	11	5	St Stephens	21-N	4-E
" "	12	1	St Stephens	21-N	5-E
MURFF	18	9	St Stephens	20-N	6-E
" "	17	2	St Stephens	20-N	5-E
" "	13	1	St Stephens	21-N	6-E
MURPHREY	10	7	St Stephens	21-N	3-E
MURPHRY	10	2	St Stephens	21-N	3-E
MURPHY	10	13	St Stephens	21-N	3-E
" "	9	6	St Stephens	21-N	2-E
" "	15	3	St Stephens	20-N	3-E
MUSSINA	10	3	St Stephens	21-N	3-E
" "	19	2	St Stephens	19-N	3-E
MYERS	19	4	St Stephens	19-N	3-E
NASH	24	2	St Stephens	18-N	5-E
NEAL	3	1	St Stephens	23-N	5-E
NEIGHBOURS	12	4	St Stephens	21-N	5-E
" "	7	1	St Stephens	22-N	5-E
NELSON	24	12	St Stephens	18-N	5-E
" "	21	10	St Stephens	19-N	5-E
" "	7	2	St Stephens	22-N	5-E
NERTZ	18	1	St Stephens	20-N	6-E
NEVIN	3	11	St Stephens	23-N	5-E
NEWNUM	13	1	St Stephens	21-N	6-E
NEWTON	10	2	St Stephens	21-N	3-E

Surname	Map Group	Parcels of Land	Meridian/Township/Range		
NICHOLSON	**17**	1	St Stephens	20-N	5-E
NORDIN	**11**	2	St Stephens	21-N	4-E
NORRIS	**11**	1	St Stephens	21-N	4-E
NORWOOD	**9**	3	St Stephens	21-N	2-E
OBANNON	**24**	3	St Stephens	18-N	5-E
OLIVER	**12**	2	St Stephens	21-N	5-E
ORMON	**4**	2	St Stephens	23-N	6-E
ORMOND	**24**	4	St Stephens	18-N	5-E
OSBORN	**8**	10	St Stephens	22-N	6-E
" "	**22**	1	St Stephens	18-N	3-E
" "	**19**	1	St Stephens	19-N	3-E
OVERTON	**20**	1	St Stephens	19-N	4-E
OWENS	**8**	9	St Stephens	22-N	6-E
" "	**7**	8	St Stephens	22-N	5-E
" "	**4**	3	St Stephens	23-N	6-E
" "	**3**	1	St Stephens	23-N	5-E
PAGE	**18**	1	St Stephens	20-N	6-E
PARISH	**2**	3	St Stephens	23-N	4-E
PARK	**1**	1	St Stephens	23-N	3-E
PARKER	**2**	4	St Stephens	23-N	4-E
" "	**12**	1	St Stephens	21-N	5-E
" "	**6**	1	St Stephens	22-N	4-E
" "	**3**	1	St Stephens	23-N	5-E
PARR	**11**	3	St Stephens	21-N	4-E
PATTERSON	**5**	1	St Stephens	22-N	3-E
PATTISON	**5**	1	St Stephens	22-N	3-E
PATTON	**12**	1	St Stephens	21-N	5-E
" "	**13**	1	St Stephens	21-N	6-E
" "	**7**	1	St Stephens	22-N	5-E
PAUL	**1**	1	St Stephens	23-N	3-E
PAYNE	**8**	10	St Stephens	22-N	6-E
PEACOCK	**20**	1	St Stephens	19-N	4-E
PEARSON	**20**	1	St Stephens	19-N	4-E
PECK	**11**	5	St Stephens	21-N	4-E
" "	**17**	1	St Stephens	20-N	5-E
" "	**18**	1	St Stephens	20-N	6-E
" "	**7**	1	St Stephens	22-N	5-E
PEIRCE	**4**	1	St Stephens	23-N	6-E
PERKINS	**21**	1	St Stephens	19-N	5-E
PERMENTER	**7**	3	St Stephens	22-N	5-E
PERRIN	**1**	7	St Stephens	23-N	3-E
PERRITT	**20**	1	St Stephens	19-N	4-E
PERRY	**12**	6	St Stephens	21-N	5-E
" "	**7**	4	St Stephens	22-N	5-E
" "	**24**	1	St Stephens	18-N	5-E
" "	**4**	1	St Stephens	23-N	6-E
PETEET	**21**	1	St Stephens	19-N	5-E
PETERSON	**12**	6	St Stephens	21-N	5-E
" "	**13**	2	St Stephens	21-N	6-E
PETETE	**21**	1	St Stephens	19-N	5-E
PHARES	**4**	7	St Stephens	23-N	6-E
" "	**8**	5	St Stephens	22-N	6-E
" "	**7**	2	St Stephens	22-N	5-E
" "	**19**	1	St Stephens	19-N	3-E
PHARIS	**11**	4	St Stephens	21-N	4-E
PHARRES	**4**	5	St Stephens	23-N	6-E
PHILLIPS	**8**	5	St Stephens	22-N	6-E
" "	**22**	1	St Stephens	18-N	3-E
" "	**20**	1	St Stephens	19-N	4-E
" "	**21**	1	St Stephens	19-N	5-E

Surname	Map Group	Parcels of Land	Meridian/Township/Range
PHILLIPS (Cont'd)	**13**	1	St Stephens 21-N 6-E
" "	**3**	1	St Stephens 23-N 5-E
PHIPPS	**4**	3	St Stephens 23-N 6-E
PICKENS	**24**	16	St Stephens 18-N 5-E
" "	**11**	4	St Stephens 21-N 4-E
" "	**17**	2	St Stephens 20-N 5-E
" "	**21**	1	St Stephens 19-N 5-E
PIERCE	**4**	2	St Stephens 23-N 6-E
PILKERTON	**7**	1	St Stephens 22-N 5-E
POOL	**12**	1	St Stephens 21-N 5-E
" "	**13**	1	St Stephens 21-N 6-E
" "	**8**	1	St Stephens 22-N 6-E
POPE	**2**	6	St Stephens 23-N 4-E
" "	**6**	4	St Stephens 22-N 4-E
" "	**7**	2	St Stephens 22-N 5-E
POUNDS	**11**	1	St Stephens 21-N 4-E
POWERS	**12**	4	St Stephens 21-N 5-E
" "	**18**	3	St Stephens 20-N 6-E
PRATHER	**12**	2	St Stephens 21-N 5-E
PRESTWOOD	**21**	1	St Stephens 19-N 5-E
PRICE	**3**	1	St Stephens 23-N 5-E
PRICKET	**5**	1	St Stephens 22-N 3-E
PRICKETT	**5**	2	St Stephens 22-N 3-E
PRISOC	**12**	7	St Stephens 21-N 5-E
" "	**7**	1	St Stephens 22-N 5-E
PRISOCK	**12**	3	St Stephens 21-N 5-E
" "	**11**	1	St Stephens 21-N 4-E
PRITCHARD	**14**	1	St Stephens 20-N 2-E
PRUITT	**24**	3	St Stephens 18-N 5-E
PUCKETT	**5**	3	St Stephens 22-N 3-E
" "	**10**	1	St Stephens 21-N 3-E
PURDOM	**17**	1	St Stephens 20-N 5-E
PURNELL	**16**	5	St Stephens 20-N 4-E
" "	**5**	2	St Stephens 22-N 3-E
" "	**11**	1	St Stephens 21-N 4-E
PURSELL	**12**	1	St Stephens 21-N 5-E
PURTEL	**12**	1	St Stephens 21-N 5-E
PURTTE	**12**	2	St Stephens 21-N 5-E
RABORN	**20**	1	St Stephens 19-N 4-E
RACKLEY	**20**	2	St Stephens 19-N 4-E
" "	**17**	2	St Stephens 20-N 5-E
RAGLAND	**8**	1	St Stephens 22-N 6-E
RAINNER	**4**	1	St Stephens 23-N 6-E
RAMIE	**3**	1	St Stephens 23-N 5-E
RANDOLPH	**17**	2	St Stephens 20-N 5-E
RANEY	**10**	1	St Stephens 21-N 3-E
" "	**11**	1	St Stephens 21-N 4-E
RASSER	**4**	2	St Stephens 23-N 6-E
RATLIFF	**4**	6	St Stephens 23-N 6-E
" "	**3**	1	St Stephens 23-N 5-E
RAVESIES	**19**	8	St Stephens 19-N 3-E
" "	**22**	1	St Stephens 18-N 3-E
RAVISIES	**19**	1	St Stephens 19-N 3-E
RAY	**19**	1	St Stephens 19-N 3-E
" "	**12**	1	St Stephens 21-N 5-E
READ	**11**	1	St Stephens 21-N 4-E
REDDING	**11**	4	St Stephens 21-N 4-E
REED	**18**	3	St Stephens 20-N 6-E
" "	**7**	3	St Stephens 22-N 5-E
REEVES	**24**	1	St Stephens 18-N 5-E

Surname	Map Group	Parcels of Land	Meridian/Township/Range
REID	**20**	1	St Stephens 19-N 4-E
REYNOLDS	**18**	1	St Stephens 20-N 6-E
RHODES	**12**	11	St Stephens 21-N 5-E
" "	**13**	2	St Stephens 21-N 6-E
" "	**24**	1	St Stephens 18-N 5-E
" "	**17**	1	St Stephens 20-N 5-E
" "	**18**	1	St Stephens 20-N 6-E
" "	**6**	1	St Stephens 22-N 4-E
" "	**3**	1	St Stephens 23-N 5-E
RICARD	**8**	3	St Stephens 22-N 6-E
RICE	**21**	3	St Stephens 19-N 5-E
RICHARDS	**2**	12	St Stephens 23-N 4-E
RICHARDSON	**8**	5	St Stephens 22-N 6-E
" "	**6**	1	St Stephens 22-N 4-E
" "	**7**	1	St Stephens 22-N 5-E
RIDDLE	**9**	1	St Stephens 21-N 2-E
RIDGEWAY	**10**	1	St Stephens 21-N 3-E
RIDGILL	**23**	1	St Stephens 18-N 4-E
ROAN	**24**	3	St Stephens 18-N 5-E
" "	**21**	3	St Stephens 19-N 5-E
ROANE	**21**	1	St Stephens 19-N 5-E
ROBERTS	**11**	2	St Stephens 21-N 4-E
ROBERTSON	**19**	9	St Stephens 19-N 3-E
" "	**11**	3	St Stephens 21-N 4-E
" "	**23**	1	St Stephens 18-N 4-E
" "	**20**	1	St Stephens 19-N 4-E
ROBINSON	**14**	1	St Stephens 20-N 2-E
RODEN	**9**	1	St Stephens 21-N 2-E
ROE	**5**	1	St Stephens 22-N 3-E
ROGERS	**3**	3	St Stephens 23-N 5-E
" "	**24**	2	St Stephens 18-N 5-E
" "	**23**	1	St Stephens 18-N 4-E
" "	**2**	1	St Stephens 23-N 4-E
ROSS	**6**	1	St Stephens 22-N 4-E
ROSSER	**4**	1	St Stephens 23-N 6-E
ROSSON	**3**	1	St Stephens 23-N 5-E
ROUDET	**16**	1	St Stephens 20-N 4-E
ROYALL	**20**	1	St Stephens 19-N 4-E
RUFF	**11**	3	St Stephens 21-N 4-E
RUFFIN	**23**	1	St Stephens 18-N 4-E
RUSSEL	**8**	1	St Stephens 22-N 6-E
RUSSELL	**8**	12	St Stephens 22-N 6-E
" "	**13**	2	St Stephens 21-N 6-E
RYAN	**8**	14	St Stephens 22-N 6-E
" "	**7**	4	St Stephens 22-N 5-E
" "	**12**	3	St Stephens 21-N 5-E
" "	**24**	2	St Stephens 18-N 5-E
SAMPLE	**5**	11	St Stephens 22-N 3-E
" "	**10**	3	St Stephens 21-N 3-E
SAMUEL	**3**	1	St Stephens 23-N 5-E
SANDERS	**17**	4	St Stephens 20-N 5-E
" "	**18**	2	St Stephens 20-N 6-E
SANDERSON	**23**	1	St Stephens 18-N 4-E
SATTERWHITE	**4**	1	St Stephens 23-N 6-E
SAUNDERS	**17**	3	St Stephens 20-N 5-E
SCARLETT	**6**	2	St Stephens 22-N 4-E
SCISM	**22**	1	St Stephens 18-N 3-E
SCOTT	**11**	18	St Stephens 21-N 4-E
" "	**10**	12	St Stephens 21-N 3-E
" "	**1**	11	St Stephens 23-N 3-E

Surname	Map Group	Parcels of Land	Meridian/Township/Range
SCOTT (Cont'd)	5	7	St Stephens 22-N 3-E
" "	9	4	St Stephens 21-N 2-E
" "	6	2	St Stephens 22-N 4-E
" "	16	1	St Stephens 20-N 4-E
SEABROOK	21	1	St Stephens 19-N 5-E
SEAL	21	3	St Stephens 19-N 5-E
SEALE	12	19	St Stephens 21-N 5-E
" "	21	9	St Stephens 19-N 5-E
" "	3	2	St Stephens 23-N 5-E
" "	16	1	St Stephens 20-N 4-E
" "	17	1	St Stephens 20-N 5-E
" "	6	1	St Stephens 22-N 4-E
" "	7	1	St Stephens 22-N 5-E
SEALES	21	1	St Stephens 19-N 5-E
SEXTON	20	1	St Stephens 19-N 4-E
SHACKELFORD	13	1	St Stephens 21-N 6-E
SHACKLEFORD	13	7	St Stephens 21-N 6-E
" "	18	2	St Stephens 20-N 6-E
SHAFFER	8	2	St Stephens 22-N 6-E
" "	24	1	St Stephens 18-N 5-E
" "	19	1	St Stephens 19-N 3-E
" "	13	1	St Stephens 21-N 6-E
SHAMBLIN	4	1	St Stephens 23-N 6-E
SHAW	5	1	St Stephens 22-N 3-E
SHELDON	24	6	St Stephens 18-N 5-E
SHEPHERD	15	1	St Stephens 20-N 3-E
SHIVERS	17	1	St Stephens 20-N 5-E
SHULTZ	23	1	St Stephens 18-N 4-E
SIKES	10	1	St Stephens 21-N 3-E
SIMMONS	7	2	St Stephens 22-N 5-E
" "	4	1	St Stephens 23-N 6-E
SIMMS	7	2	St Stephens 22-N 5-E
SIMPSON	11	1	St Stephens 21-N 4-E
SIMS	1	21	St Stephens 23-N 3-E
" "	2	14	St Stephens 23-N 4-E
" "	6	13	St Stephens 22-N 4-E
" "	10	10	St Stephens 21-N 3-E
" "	11	9	St Stephens 21-N 4-E
" "	19	6	St Stephens 19-N 3-E
" "	5	4	St Stephens 22-N 3-E
" "	17	3	St Stephens 20-N 5-E
" "	13	3	St Stephens 21-N 6-E
" "	7	3	St Stephens 22-N 5-E
" "	8	3	St Stephens 22-N 6-E
" "	14	2	St Stephens 20-N 2-E
" "	9	2	St Stephens 21-N 2-E
" "	18	1	St Stephens 20-N 6-E
SKINNER	20	1	St Stephens 19-N 4-E
SLAUGHTER	13	3	St Stephens 21-N 6-E
SMALL	11	2	St Stephens 21-N 4-E
SMELLEY	8	5	St Stephens 22-N 6-E
SMITH	8	14	St Stephens 22-N 6-E
" "	13	7	St Stephens 21-N 6-E
" "	3	4	St Stephens 23-N 5-E
" "	24	3	St Stephens 18-N 5-E
" "	7	3	St Stephens 22-N 5-E
" "	11	1	St Stephens 21-N 4-E
SNEDECOR	15	12	St Stephens 20-N 3-E
" "	19	8	St Stephens 19-N 3-E
" "	10	4	St Stephens 21-N 3-E

Surname	Map Group	Parcels of Land	Meridian/Township/Range		
SNEDECOR (Cont'd)	**14**	3	St Stephens	20-N	2-E
SORRELL	**24**	2	St Stephens	18-N	5-E
SPARKS	**2**	5	St Stephens	23-N	4-E
" "	**13**	4	St Stephens	21-N	6-E
" "	**3**	1	St Stephens	23-N	5-E
SPEED	**11**	12	St Stephens	21-N	4-E
" "	**17**	1	St Stephens	20-N	5-E
" "	**18**	1	St Stephens	20-N	6-E
SPENCE	**2**	2	St Stephens	23-N	4-E
" "	**8**	1	St Stephens	22-N	6-E
" "	**3**	1	St Stephens	23-N	5-E
SPENCER	**4**	1	St Stephens	23-N	6-E
SPIVEY	**11**	1	St Stephens	21-N	4-E
STALLINGS	**11**	1	St Stephens	21-N	4-E
STANFILL	**21**	2	St Stephens	19-N	5-E
STARKE	**21**	1	St Stephens	19-N	5-E
STEEDMAN	**8**	4	St Stephens	22-N	6-E
STEELE	**1**	4	St Stephens	23-N	3-E
STEINWINDER	**6**	1	St Stephens	22-N	4-E
" "	**7**	1	St Stephens	22-N	5-E
STEPHENS	**8**	6	St Stephens	22-N	6-E
" "	**17**	3	St Stephens	20-N	5-E
" "	**21**	2	St Stephens	19-N	5-E
" "	**12**	2	St Stephens	21-N	5-E
" "	**5**	2	St Stephens	22-N	3-E
" "	**19**	1	St Stephens	19-N	3-E
STEPHENSON	**11**	6	St Stephens	21-N	4-E
STEVENS	**12**	3	St Stephens	21-N	5-E
" "	**7**	3	St Stephens	22-N	5-E
" "	**8**	1	St Stephens	22-N	6-E
STEWARD	**8**	7	St Stephens	22-N	6-E
STEWART	**12**	6	St Stephens	21-N	5-E
" "	**19**	2	St Stephens	19-N	3-E
" "	**20**	2	St Stephens	19-N	4-E
" "	**8**	1	St Stephens	22-N	6-E
STICKNEY	**7**	5	St Stephens	22-N	5-E
" "	**19**	4	St Stephens	19-N	3-E
" "	**11**	2	St Stephens	21-N	4-E
STOKES	**17**	4	St Stephens	20-N	5-E
" "	**18**	2	St Stephens	20-N	6-E
" "	**13**	1	St Stephens	21-N	6-E
STONE	**17**	2	St Stephens	20-N	5-E
" "	**12**	2	St Stephens	21-N	5-E
STOREY	**5**	1	St Stephens	22-N	3-E
STRADWICK	**18**	1	St Stephens	20-N	6-E
STRICKLAND	**16**	1	St Stephens	20-N	4-E
STRINGFELLON	**11**	1	St Stephens	21-N	4-E
" "	**6**	1	St Stephens	22-N	4-E
STRINGFELLOW	**11**	10	St Stephens	21-N	4-E
" "	**6**	1	St Stephens	22-N	4-E
SUMMERS	**5**	1	St Stephens	22-N	3-E
" "	**4**	1	St Stephens	23-N	6-E
SUMMEY	**12**	3	St Stephens	21-N	5-E
" "	**7**	3	St Stephens	22-N	5-E
" "	**18**	1	St Stephens	20-N	6-E
" "	**11**	1	St Stephens	21-N	4-E
" "	**13**	1	St Stephens	21-N	6-E
SUMMY	**18**	1	St Stephens	20-N	6-E
" "	**11**	1	St Stephens	21-N	4-E
" "	**12**	1	St Stephens	21-N	5-E

Surname	Map Group	Parcels of Land	Meridian/Township/Range		
SUMMY (Cont'd)	6	1	St Stephens	22-N	4-E
" "	7	1	St Stephens	22-N	5-E
SUMNERS	4	3	St Stephens	23-N	6-E
SURGINER	23	1	St Stephens	18-N	4-E
SUTTON	2	1	St Stephens	23-N	4-E
SWANN	23	1	St Stephens	18-N	4-E
SWIFT	24	3	St Stephens	18-N	5-E
TALBOT	9	3	St Stephens	21-N	2-E
TALIAFERRO	20	4	St Stephens	19-N	4-E
" "	23	1	St Stephens	18-N	4-E
" "	19	1	St Stephens	19-N	3-E
TALLIAFERRO	23	1	St Stephens	18-N	4-E
TANKERSLEY	5	1	St Stephens	22-N	3-E
TANNER	6	1	St Stephens	22-N	4-E
TAPPAN	5	1	St Stephens	22-N	3-E
TARRANT	8	2	St Stephens	22-N	6-E
TAYLOE	12	1	St Stephens	21-N	5-E
TAYLOR	8	9	St Stephens	22-N	6-E
" "	10	3	St Stephens	21-N	3-E
" "	7	2	St Stephens	22-N	5-E
TERRY	7	5	St Stephens	22-N	5-E
" "	4	3	St Stephens	23-N	6-E
" "	8	1	St Stephens	22-N	6-E
TEW	24	1	St Stephens	18-N	5-E
THIGPEN	8	7	St Stephens	22-N	6-E
" "	18	4	St Stephens	20-N	6-E
" "	7	3	St Stephens	22-N	5-E
THOMAS	21	2	St Stephens	19-N	5-E
" "	13	2	St Stephens	21-N	6-E
" "	11	1	St Stephens	21-N	4-E
" "	12	1	St Stephens	21-N	5-E
THOMASON	11	1	St Stephens	21-N	4-E
THOMPSON	10	3	St Stephens	21-N	3-E
" "	4	2	St Stephens	23-N	6-E
" "	5	1	St Stephens	22-N	3-E
" "	6	1	St Stephens	22-N	4-E
THORNTON	20	1	St Stephens	19-N	4-E
THRASH	20	1	St Stephens	19-N	4-E
THURMOND	17	1	St Stephens	20-N	5-E
TIDMORE	3	15	St Stephens	23-N	5-E
" "	7	12	St Stephens	22-N	5-E
" "	4	2	St Stephens	23-N	6-E
" "	21	1	St Stephens	19-N	5-E
" "	17	1	St Stephens	20-N	5-E
" "	13	1	St Stephens	21-N	6-E
TINGLE	3	7	St Stephens	23-N	5-E
" "	8	3	St Stephens	22-N	6-E
" "	4	1	St Stephens	23-N	6-E
TOLAND	11	6	St Stephens	21-N	4-E
TOLER	3	6	St Stephens	23-N	5-E
TOOSING	2	3	St Stephens	23-N	4-E
TORBERT	15	1	St Stephens	20-N	3-E
" "	10	1	St Stephens	21-N	3-E
TORBUT	10	2	St Stephens	21-N	3-E
TOWNSEND	11	2	St Stephens	21-N	4-E
" "	15	1	St Stephens	20-N	3-E
TRAVIS	6	9	St Stephens	22-N	4-E
" "	24	3	St Stephens	18-N	5-E
TRUE	10	1	St Stephens	21-N	3-E
" "	5	1	St Stephens	22-N	3-E

Surname	Map Group	Parcels of Land	Meridian/Township/Range		
TUBB	**3**	4	St Stephens	23-N	5-E
" "	**4**	2	St Stephens	23-N	6-E
" "	**8**	1	St Stephens	22-N	6-E
TUBBS	**3**	1	St Stephens	23-N	5-E
TUCKER	**23**	1	St Stephens	18-N	4-E
" "	**20**	1	St Stephens	19-N	4-E
" "	**16**	1	St Stephens	20-N	4-E
TURNER	**17**	3	St Stephens	20-N	5-E
" "	**11**	1	St Stephens	21-N	4-E
" "	**5**	1	St Stephens	22-N	3-E
" "	**6**	1	St Stephens	22-N	4-E
" "	**3**	1	St Stephens	23-N	5-E
VARNELL	**24**	1	St Stephens	18-N	5-E
VAUGHAN	**24**	2	St Stephens	18-N	5-E
VEST	**20**	1	St Stephens	19-N	4-E
VIARS	**6**	1	St Stephens	22-N	4-E
WADE	**23**	1	St Stephens	18-N	4-E
WADKINS	**6**	1	St Stephens	22-N	4-E
WALKER	**12**	5	St Stephens	21-N	5-E
" "	**21**	4	St Stephens	19-N	5-E
WALLACE	**24**	7	St Stephens	18-N	5-E
" "	**12**	1	St Stephens	21-N	5-E
WALLER	**19**	3	St Stephens	19-N	3-E
" "	**22**	1	St Stephens	18-N	3-E
" "	**20**	1	St Stephens	19-N	4-E
" "	**16**	1	St Stephens	20-N	4-E
WALTERS	**21**	1	St Stephens	19-N	5-E
WALTHALL	**18**	3	St Stephens	20-N	6-E
WALTON	**21**	2	St Stephens	19-N	5-E
" "	**15**	1	St Stephens	20-N	3-E
WARD	**19**	1	St Stephens	19-N	3-E
" "	**20**	1	St Stephens	19-N	4-E
WARREN	**21**	5	St Stephens	19-N	5-E
" "	**12**	3	St Stephens	21-N	5-E
" "	**7**	1	St Stephens	22-N	5-E
WATKINS	**19**	3	St Stephens	19-N	3-E
" "	**5**	2	St Stephens	22-N	3-E
" "	**6**	1	St Stephens	22-N	4-E
WATSON	**14**	2	St Stephens	20-N	2-E
" "	**11**	2	St Stephens	21-N	4-E
" "	**12**	2	St Stephens	21-N	5-E
" "	**24**	1	St Stephens	18-N	5-E
" "	**10**	1	St Stephens	21-N	3-E
" "	**7**	1	St Stephens	22-N	5-E
WATT	**5**	5	St Stephens	22-N	3-E
WATTS	**5**	1	St Stephens	22-N	3-E
WEAGWORTH	**5**	1	St Stephens	22-N	3-E
WEATHERRED	**2**	1	St Stephens	23-N	4-E
WEATHERSPOON	**2**	2	St Stephens	23-N	4-E
WEAVER	**24**	6	St Stephens	18-N	5-E
WEBB	**13**	8	St Stephens	21-N	6-E
" "	**12**	4	St Stephens	21-N	5-E
" "	**2**	3	St Stephens	23-N	4-E
" "	**3**	3	St Stephens	23-N	5-E
WEBSTER	**4**	3	St Stephens	23-N	6-E
WEDGEWORTH	**24**	5	St Stephens	18-N	5-E
" "	**10**	5	St Stephens	21-N	3-E
" "	**11**	5	St Stephens	21-N	4-E
" "	**5**	5	St Stephens	22-N	3-E
" "	**6**	1	St Stephens	22-N	4-E

Surname	Map Group	Parcels of Land	Meridian/Township/Range		
WEDGWORTH	**10**	3	St Stephens	21-N	3-E
" "	**5**	1	St Stephens	22-N	3-E
" "	**4**	1	St Stephens	23-N	6-E
WEEKS	**12**	2	St Stephens	21-N	5-E
" "	**8**	1	St Stephens	22-N	6-E
WELBORN	**3**	3	St Stephens	23-N	5-E
WELLS	**24**	2	St Stephens	18-N	5-E
WELSH	**5**	1	St Stephens	22-N	3-E
WEST	**4**	1	St Stephens	23-N	6-E
WESTBROOK	**21**	3	St Stephens	19-N	5-E
WHEELING	**7**	2	St Stephens	22-N	5-E
WHITE	**11**	7	St Stephens	21-N	4-E
" "	**22**	3	St Stephens	18-N	3-E
" "	**20**	2	St Stephens	19-N	4-E
" "	**16**	2	St Stephens	20-N	4-E
" "	**12**	1	St Stephens	21-N	5-E
" "	**1**	1	St Stephens	23-N	3-E
WHITEHEAD	**5**	11	St Stephens	22-N	3-E
WHITFIELD	**3**	1	St Stephens	23-N	5-E
WHITSETT	**7**	4	St Stephens	22-N	5-E
" "	**21**	3	St Stephens	19-N	5-E
WHITSITT	**19**	1	St Stephens	19-N	3-E
WHITWORTH	**5**	2	St Stephens	22-N	3-E
" "	**20**	1	St Stephens	19-N	4-E
" "	**10**	1	St Stephens	21-N	3-E
WIER	**5**	1	St Stephens	22-N	3-E
WILBORN	**7**	1	St Stephens	22-N	5-E
WILBURNE	**3**	1	St Stephens	23-N	5-E
WILLIAMS	**11**	21	St Stephens	21-N	4-E
" "	**6**	21	St Stephens	22-N	4-E
" "	**10**	7	St Stephens	21-N	3-E
" "	**12**	4	St Stephens	21-N	5-E
" "	**13**	3	St Stephens	21-N	6-E
" "	**24**	2	St Stephens	18-N	5-E
" "	**21**	1	St Stephens	19-N	5-E
" "	**15**	1	St Stephens	20-N	3-E
" "	**8**	1	St Stephens	22-N	6-E
" "	**2**	1	St Stephens	23-N	4-E
" "	**3**	1	St Stephens	23-N	5-E
WILLIAMSON	**7**	2	St Stephens	22-N	5-E
WILLINGHAM	**10**	7	St Stephens	21-N	3-E
" "	**11**	1	St Stephens	21-N	4-E
WILLSON	**2**	1	St Stephens	23-N	4-E
WILSON	**11**	16	St Stephens	21-N	4-E
" "	**2**	13	St Stephens	23-N	4-E
" "	**5**	5	St Stephens	22-N	3-E
" "	**7**	5	St Stephens	22-N	5-E
" "	**13**	4	St Stephens	21-N	6-E
" "	**6**	4	St Stephens	22-N	4-E
" "	**4**	4	St Stephens	23-N	6-E
" "	**8**	2	St Stephens	22-N	6-E
" "	**23**	1	St Stephens	18-N	4-E
" "	**20**	1	St Stephens	19-N	4-E
" "	**12**	1	St Stephens	21-N	5-E
WIN	**10**	1	St Stephens	21-N	3-E
WINDHAM	**10**	4	St Stephens	21-N	3-E
" "	**5**	2	St Stephens	22-N	3-E
" "	**11**	1	St Stephens	21-N	4-E
WINGATE	**12**	1	St Stephens	21-N	5-E
WINN	**13**	2	St Stephens	21-N	6-E

Surname	Map Group	Parcels of Land	Meridian/Township/Range		
WISDOM	**17**	1	St Stephens	20-N	5-E
WITHERS	**15**	18	St Stephens	20-N	3-E
`"` `"`	**16**	4	St Stephens	20-N	4-E
WITHERSPOON	**6**	7	St Stephens	22-N	4-E
`"` `"`	**12**	3	St Stephens	21-N	5-E
`"` `"`	**2**	3	St Stephens	23-N	4-E
`"` `"`	**23**	1	St Stephens	18-N	4-E
`"` `"`	**17**	1	St Stephens	20-N	5-E
`"` `"`	**1**	1	St Stephens	23-N	3-E
WOLSTENHOLME	**5**	1	St Stephens	22-N	3-E
WOOD	**21**	2	St Stephens	19-N	5-E
WOODALL	**12**	3	St Stephens	21-N	5-E
WOODARD	**20**	2	St Stephens	19-N	4-E
WOODWARD	**20**	1	St Stephens	19-N	4-E
WOOLLEY	**1**	1	St Stephens	23-N	3-E
WOOTEN	**7**	3	St Stephens	22-N	5-E
WOOTON	**7**	1	St Stephens	22-N	5-E
WRIGHT	**10**	8	St Stephens	21-N	3-E
`"` `"`	**4**	4	St Stephens	23-N	6-E
`"` `"`	**19**	2	St Stephens	19-N	3-E
`"` `"`	**15**	1	St Stephens	20-N	3-E
WYATT	**4**	2	St Stephens	23-N	6-E
`"` `"`	**8**	1	St Stephens	22-N	6-E
WYNNE	**15**	7	St Stephens	20-N	3-E
`"` `"`	**10**	1	St Stephens	21-N	3-E
YARBOROUGH	**11**	10	St Stephens	21-N	4-E
`"` `"`	**10**	4	St Stephens	21-N	3-E
YOUNG	**1**	2	St Stephens	23-N	3-E
`"` `"`	**4**	1	St Stephens	23-N	6-E

– Part II –

Township Map Groups

Map Group 1: Index to Land Patents

Township 23-North Range 3-East (St Stephens)

After you locate an individual in this Index, take note of the Section and Section Part then proceed to the Land Patent map on the pages immediately following. You should have no difficulty locating the corresponding parcel of land.

The "For More Info" Column will lead you to more information about the underlying Patents. See the *Legend* at right, and the "How to Use this Book" chapter, for more information.

```
                        LEGEND
              "For More Info . . . " column
A = Authority (Legislative Act, See Appendix "A")
B = Block or Lot (location in Section unknown)
C = Cancelled Patent
F = Fractional Section
G = Group  (Multi-Patentee Patent, see Appendix "C")
V = Overlaps another Parcel
R = Re-Issued (Parcel patented more than once)

(A & G items require you to look in the Appendixes referred
to above. All other Letter-designations followed by a number
require you to locate line-items in this index that possess
the ID number found after the letter).
```

ID	Individual in Patent	Sec.	Sec. Part	Date Issued	Other Counties	For More Info . . .
8	BALDWIN, Archibald P	35	NW	1830-11-01	Greene	A1 F R11
4	BATTLE, Alfred	12	SE	1830-11-01	Greene	A1 G19 F R41
5	" "	13	NE	1830-11-01	Greene	A1 G19 F R43
48	BRASFIELD, John C	11	NESW	1837-11-07	Greene	A1
49	" "	11	SENW	1837-11-07	Greene	A1
6	BRASSFIELD, Alfred	11	NENW	1839-09-20	Greene	A1
50	CLEVELAND, John G	11	SWNW	1839-09-20	Greene	A1
51	" "	11	W½SW	1839-09-20	Greene	A1
69	DUNLAP, William	13	A	1830-11-01	Greene	A1 G78
70	"	13	SW	1830-11-01	Greene	A1 G78 F R72
61	ELLIS, Stephen	26	SE	1830-11-01	Greene	A1 G81 F R54
59	" "	34	A	1830-11-01	Greene	A1 G80
60	" "	34	B	1830-11-01	Greene	A1 G80
57	" "	34	NW	1830-11-01	Greene	A1
58	" "	35	W½	1830-11-01	Greene	A1 F
35	GIFFORD, James	12	SENE	1837-03-30	Greene	A1
9	GREENE, Daniel	24	SE	1830-11-01	Greene	A1 F
4	JEMISON, Robert	12	SE	1830-11-01	Greene	A1 G19 F R41
5	" "	13	NE	1830-11-01	Greene	A1 G19 F R43
53	" "	24	SW	1830-11-01	Greene	A1 F
54	" "	26	SE	1830-11-01	Greene	A1 G154 F R61
55	" "	34	SE	1830-11-01	Greene	A1 G154
52	LEAVENS, Joshua B	12	SW	1830-11-01	Greene	A1 F R12
33	LEWIS, Felix G	11	NWNW	1839-03-15	Greene	A1
75	LEWIS, William M	23	SW	1838-08-28	Greene	A1
76	" "	26	W½NW	1838-08-28	Greene	A1
69	MAY, William	13	A	1830-11-01	Greene	A1 G78
70	" "	13	SW	1830-11-01	Greene	A1 G78 F R72
77	" "	14	NE	1830-11-01	Greene	A1 F R1
79	" "	23	SE	1830-11-01	Greene	A1 F R21
80	" "	23	SENE	1834-10-21	Greene	A1
78	" "	14	SE	1838-08-28	Greene	A1 F
36	MCGIFFERT, James	12	NENE	1839-09-20	Greene	A1
37	" "	12	W½NE	1839-09-20	Greene	A1
10	MCGIFFORD, David	11	SESW	1839-09-20	Greene	A1
41	MCGIFFORD, James	12	SE	1830-11-01	Greene	A1 F R4
43	" "	13	NE	1830-11-01	Greene	A1 F R5
45	" "	13	NW	1830-11-01	Greene	A1 G197 F
40	" "	12	E½NW	1834-10-21	Greene	A1
42	" "	12	W½NW	1837-03-30	Greene	A1
38	" "	11	SE	1837-04-01	Greene	A1 F
44	" "	24	A	1837-04-01	Greene	A1 F
39	" "	11	W½NE	1839-03-15	Greene	A1
46	MCGRIFFORD, James	11	E½NE	1839-03-15	Greene	A1
71	MINTER, William J	13	S½SE	1837-04-01	Greene	A1
74	" "	24	E½NE	1837-04-01	Greene	A1

ID	Individual in Patent	Sec.	Sec. Part	Date Issued	Other Counties	For More Info . . .
72	MINTER, William J (Cont'd)	13	SW	1839-09-20	Greene	A1 F R70
73	" "	23	N½NE	1839-09-20	Greene	A1
7	PARK, Andrew	14	W½NW	1839-09-20	Greene	A1
45	PAUL, James	13	NW	1830-11-01	Greene	A1 G197 F
34	PERRIN, Freeman	36	W½NE	1839-09-20		A1
63	PERRIN, Truman	35	S½	1834-11-04	Greene	A1 F
64	" "	36	E½NW	1834-11-04		A1 V65, 66
65	" "	36	NENW	1834-11-04		A1 V64
67	" "	36	SW	1834-11-04		A1
68	" "	36	W½SE	1834-11-04		A1
66	" "	36	SENW	1837-04-01		A1 V64
12	SCOTT, David	12	SW	1830-11-01	Greene	A1 G222 R52
13	" "	23	NW	1830-11-01	Greene	A1 G222
14	" "	25	B	1830-11-01	Greene	A1 G222 F
15	" "	25	NE	1830-11-01	Greene	A1 G222 F
16	" "	26	E½NE	1830-11-01	Greene	A1 G222
17	" "	26	SW	1830-11-01	Greene	A1 G222 F
59	" "	34	A	1830-11-01	Greene	A1 G80
60	" "	34	B	1830-11-01	Greene	A1 G80
18	" "	34	SW	1830-11-01	Greene	A1 G222
19	" "	35	NE	1830-11-01	Greene	A1 G222 F
11	" "	35	NW	1830-11-01	Greene	A1 F R8
12	SIMS, Edward	12	SW	1830-11-01	Greene	A1 G222 R52
13	" "	23	NW	1830-11-01	Greene	A1 G222
21	" "	23	SE	1830-11-01	Greene	A1 F R79
23	" "	24	S½	1830-11-01	Greene	A1 F
24	" "	25	A	1830-11-01	Greene	A1 F
14	" "	25	B	1830-11-01	Greene	A1 G222 F
15	" "	25	NE	1830-11-01	Greene	A1 G222 F
26	" "	25	SW	1830-11-01	Greene	A1 F
27	" "	25	W½NW	1830-11-01	Greene	A1
16	" "	26	E½NE	1830-11-01	Greene	A1 G222
54	" "	26	SE	1830-11-01	Greene	A1 G154 F R61
61	" "	26	SE	1830-11-01	Greene	A1 G81 F R54
17	" "	26	SW	1830-11-01	Greene	A1 G222 F
55	" "	34	SE	1830-11-01	Greene	A1 G154
18	" "	34	SW	1830-11-01	Greene	A1 G222
30	" "	35	N½	1830-11-01	Greene	A1 F
19	" "	35	NE	1830-11-01	Greene	A1 G222 F
20	" "	14	SESW	1834-10-21	Greene	A1
22	" "	23	SWNE	1834-10-21	Greene	A1
25	" "	25	E½SE	1839-09-20	Greene	A1
28	" "	26	E½NW	1839-09-20	Greene	A1
29	" "	26	W½NE	1839-09-20	Greene	A1
1	STEELE, Aaron	14	NE	1837-04-01	Greene	A1 F R77
2	" "	14	NESW	1839-09-20	Greene	A1
3	" "	14	W½SW	1839-09-20	Greene	A1
47	STEELE, James N	14	NENW	1840-11-10	Greene	A1
62	WHITE, Thomas	24	NW	1830-11-01	Greene	A1 F
56	WITHERSPOON, Samuel M	36	E½NE	1837-04-01		A1
81	WOOLLEY, Zachariah	25	SENE	1853-08-01	Greene	A1
31	YOUNG, Ezekiel W	11		1839-09-20	Greene	A1 F
32	" "	14	SENW	1839-09-20	Greene	A1

Patent Map

T23-N R3-E
St Stephens Meridian

Map Group 1

Township Statistics

Parcels Mapped	:	81
Number of Patents	:	79
Number of Individuals	:	31
Patentees Identified	:	35
Number of Surnames	:	27
Multi-Patentee Parcels	:	18
Oldest Patent Date	:	11/1/1830
Most Recent Patent	:	8/1/1853
Block/Lot Parcels	:	6
Parcels Re - Issued	:	8
Parcels that Overlap	:	3
Cities and Towns	:	0
Cemeteries	:	0

Note: the area contained in this map amounts to far less than a full Township. Therefore, its contents are completely on this single page (instead of a "normal" 2-page spread).

Legend

———— Patent Boundary

——— Section Boundary

░░░ No Patents Found (or Outside County)

1., 2., 3., ... Lot Numbers (when beside a name)

[ ] Group Number (see Appendix "C")

Scale: Section = 1 mile X 1 mile (generally, with some exceptions)

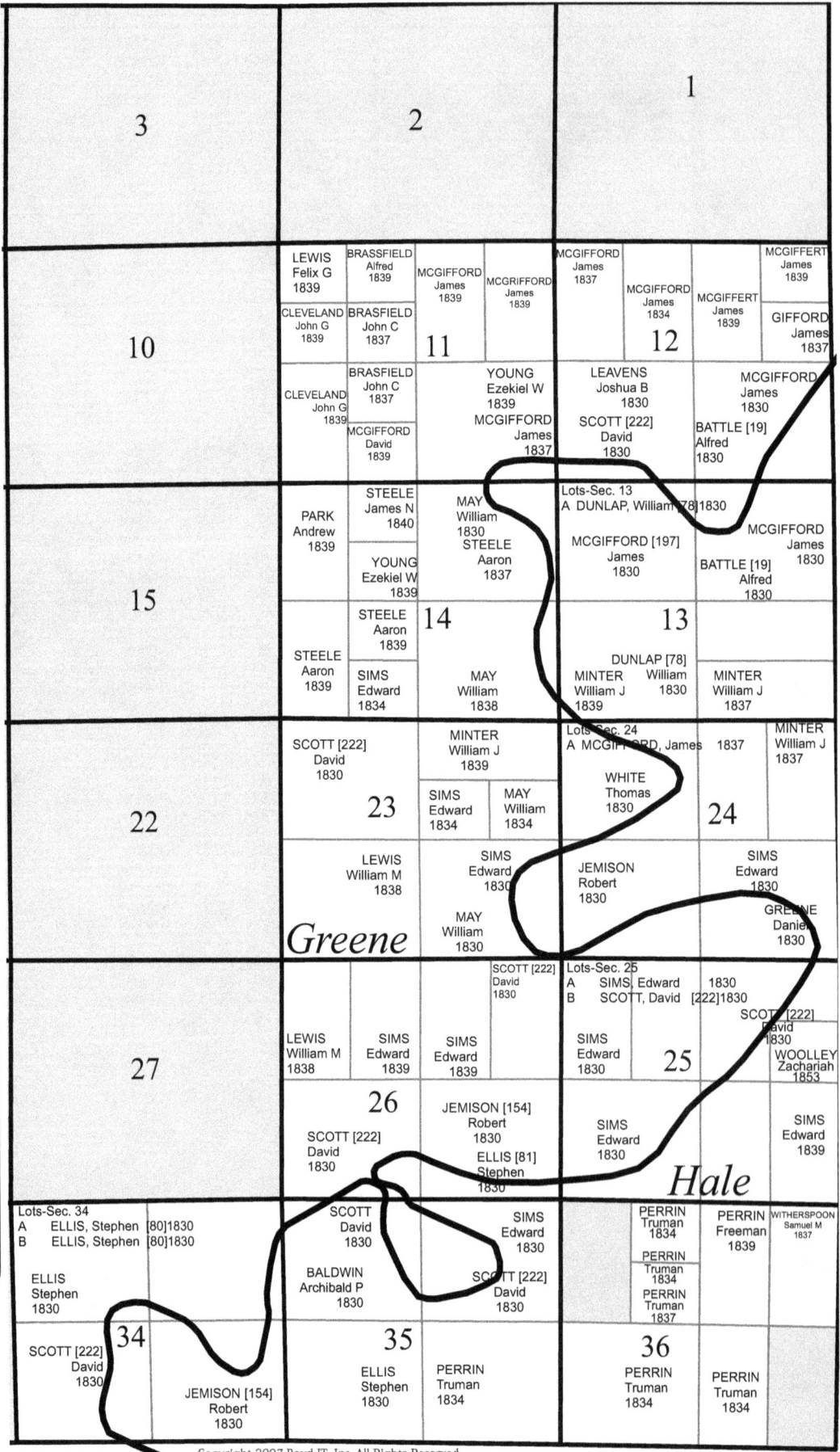

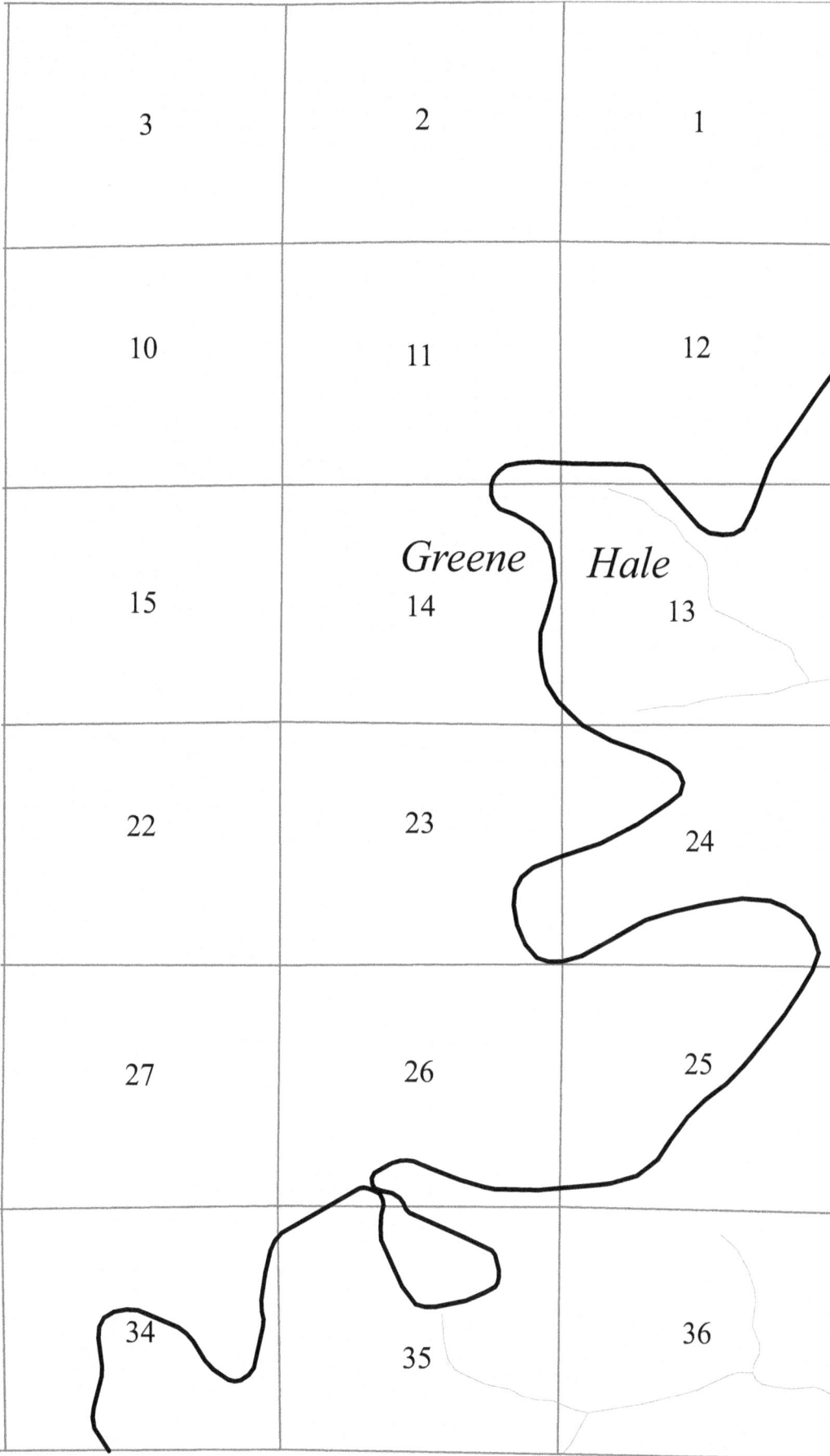

Road Map
T23-N R3-E
St Stephens Meridian

Map Group 1

Note: the area contained in this map amounts to far less than a full Township. Therefore, its contents are completely on this single page (instead of a "normal" 2-page spread).

Cities & Towns
None

Cemeteries
None

3	2	1
10	11	12
15	14 *Greene*	13 *Hale*
22	23	24
27	26	25
34	35	36

Legend
— Section Lines
═ Interstates
▬ Highways
— Other Roads
● Cities/Towns
✝ Cemeteries

Scale: Section = 1 mile X 1 mile
(generally, with some exceptions)

Historical Map

T23-N R3-E
St Stephens Meridian

Map Group 1

Note: the area contained in this map amounts to far less than a full Township. Therefore, its contents are completely on this single page (instead of a "normal" 2-page spread).

Cities & Towns
None

Cemeteries
None

Legend

——————— Section Lines

+++++++ Railroads

�(shaded) Large Rivers & Bodies of Water

- - - - - - - Streams/Creeks & Small Rivers

● Cities/Towns

‡ Cemeteries

Scale: Section = 1 mile X 1 mile
(there are some exceptions)

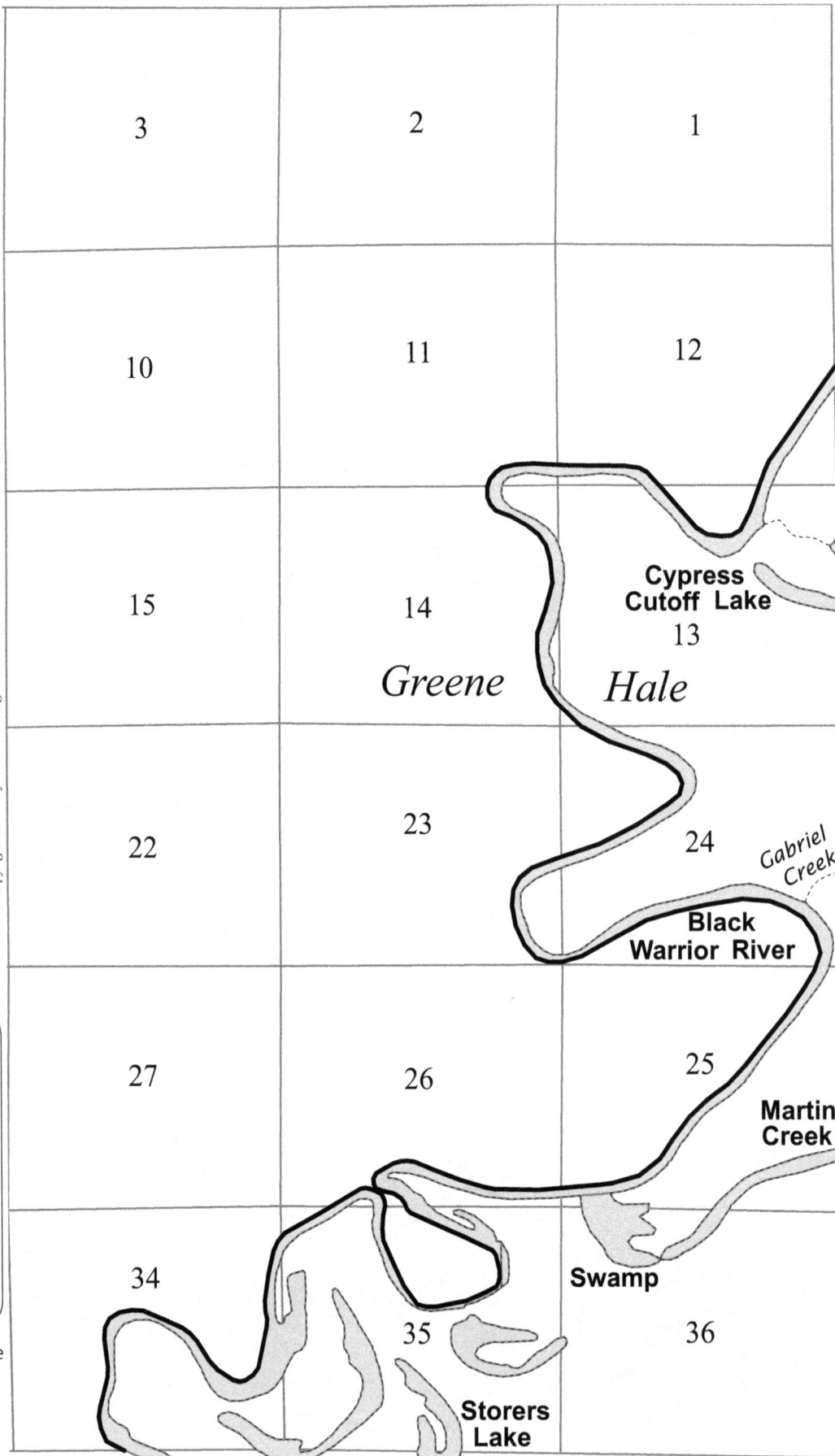

3

2

1

10

11

12

15

14

Cypress Cutoff Lake

13

Greene

Hale

22

23

24

Gabriel Creek

Black Warrior River

27

26

25

Martin Creek

34

35

Swamp

36

Storers Lake

Map Group 2: Index to Land Patents

Township 23-North Range 4-East (St Stephens)

After you locate an individual in this Index, take note of the Section and Section Part then proceed to the Land Patent map on the pages immediately following. You should have no difficulty locating the corresponding parcel of land.

The "For More Info" Column will lead you to more information about the underlying Patents. See the *Legend* at right, and the "How to Use this Book" chapter, for more information.

ID	Individual in Patent	Sec.	Sec. Part	Date Issued	Other Counties	For More Info . . .
102	BATTLE, Alfred	13	E½SE	1830-11-01		A1 G17
109	" "	13	E½SW	1830-11-01		A1 G19
91	" "	13	W½SE	1830-11-01		A1
110	" "	13	W½SW	1830-11-01		A1 G19
111	" "	14	E½SW	1830-11-01		A1 G19
112	" "	14	W½SE	1830-11-01		A1 G19
113	" "	14	W½SW	1830-11-01		A1 G19
114	" "	15	E½SE	1830-11-01		A1 G19
92	" "	15	W½SE	1830-11-01		A1
98	" "	22	E½NE	1830-11-01		A1
105	" "	23	E½NE	1830-11-01		A1 G21
106	" "	23	E½NW	1830-11-01		A1 G21
107	" "	23	W½NE	1830-11-01		A1 G21
108	" "	23	W½NW	1830-11-01		A1 G21
103	" "	7	SE	1830-11-01	Greene	A1 G16 F
104	" "	7	SW	1830-11-01	Greene	A1 G16
116	" "	8	E½SE	1830-11-01	Greene	A1 G20
117	" "	8	E½SW	1830-11-01	Greene	A1 G20
115	" "	8	W½SW	1830-11-01	Greene	A1 G19
89	" "	13	E½NW	1832-01-10		A1
90	" "	13	W½NW	1832-01-10		A1
93	" "	17	NENE	1837-04-01		A1
94	" "	17	SENW	1837-04-01		A1
95	" "	17	W½NE	1837-04-01		A1
96	" "	19	E½SW	1837-04-01		A1
97	" "	19	W½SE	1837-04-01		A1
101	" "	9	W½SW	1837-04-01		A1
88	" "	10	W½SW	1839-09-20		A1
99	" "	8	E½NE	1839-09-20	Greene	A1
87	" "	10	NESW	1852-01-01		A1
100	" "	8	W½NE	1852-01-01	Greene	A1 F
236	BEALE, John	4	W½NW	1830-11-01		A1 G25
237	" "	5	E½SE	1830-11-01	Greene	A1 G25
238	" "	5	W½SE	1830-11-01	Greene	A1 G25
272	BEALE, John S	5	N½NW	1830-11-01	Greene	A1 G23
273	" "	5	SW	1830-11-01	Greene	A1 G23 F R128
274	" "	6	NE	1830-11-01	Greene	A1 G23 F R122
275	" "	8	NW	1830-11-01	Greene	A1 G24 F R127
118	BISHOP, Archibald	36	NWNE	1834-10-01		A1
328	BISHOP, William A	17	E½SE	1852-01-01		A1
329	" "	17	SENE	1852-01-01		A1
272	BLOUNT, James G	5	N½NW	1830-11-01	Greene	A1 G23
273	" "	5	SW	1830-11-01	Greene	A1 G23 F R128
274	" "	6	NE	1830-11-01	Greene	A1 G23 F R122
275	" "	8	NW	1830-11-01	Greene	A1 G24 F R127
172	BROWN, Harry	10	SESW	1904-09-28		A2

ID	Individual in Patent	Sec.	Sec. Part	Date Issued	Other Counties	For More Info . . .
272	BURROUGHS, Benjamin	5	N½NW	1830-11-01	Greene	A1 G23
128	" "	5	SW	1830-11-01	Greene	A1 G37 F R273
273	" "	5	SW	1830-11-01	Greene	A1 G23 F R128
120	" "	6	E½SE	1830-11-01	Greene	A1
122	" "	6	NE	1830-11-01	Greene	A1 F R274
274	" "	6	NE	1830-11-01	Greene	A1 G23 F R122
129	" "	7	NE	1830-11-01	Greene	A1 G37 F
127	" "	8	NW	1830-11-01	Greene	A1 F R275
126	" "	7	NW	1830-11-05	Greene	A1 F
123	" "	6	W½NW	1837-04-01	Greene	A1
124	" "	6	W½SE	1837-04-01	Greene	A1
125	" "	6	W½SW	1837-04-01	Greene	A1
119	" "	6	E½NW	1839-09-20	Greene	A1
121	" "	6	E½SW	1839-09-20	Greene	A1
178	CARAWAY, James	20	NE	1839-09-20		A1
179	" "	21	SENW	1839-09-20		A1
180	" "	21	W½NW	1839-09-20		A1
181	" "	24	E½NE	1839-09-20		A1
182	" "	24	NENW	1839-09-20		A1
183	" "	24	NWNE	1839-09-20		A1
184	CARROWAY, James	24	SESW	1837-03-30		A1
289	CUNNINGHAM, Joseph P	33	W½SW	1830-11-01		A1
233	DESMOND, John B	28	NW	1858-06-01		A1
235	" "	29	NE	1858-06-01		A1
234	" "	28	W½NE	1860-12-01		A1
173	DUNN, Henry C	30	N½SW	1897-08-30		A2
315	EDDINS, Simeon J	4	NESE	1853-08-01		A1
316	" "	4	SENW	1853-08-01		A1
318	" "	4	SWNE	1853-08-01		A1
317	" "	4	SESE	1853-11-15		A1
278	ELLIOTT, Johnson	32	NWSE	1835-10-01		A1
279	" "	32	SWNE	1835-10-01		A1
103	FOSTER, James	7	SE	1830-11-01	Greene	A1 G16 F
104	" "	7	SW	1830-11-01	Greene	A1 G16
239	FOSTER, John D	3	S½NW	1853-08-01		A1
270	FOSTER, John L	10	E½NE	1858-06-01		A1
271	" "	11	W½NW	1858-06-01		A1
311	GLENN, Simeon	26	E½NW	1830-11-01		A1 G93
310	" "	26	W½SW	1830-11-01		A1
312	" "	27	E½SE	1830-11-01		A1 G93
313	" "	27	W½SE	1830-11-01		A1 G93
314	" "	34	E½NW	1830-11-01		A1 G93
307	" "	23	W½SW	1837-03-30		A1
308	" "	26	W½NW	1837-03-30		A1
309	" "	26	W½SE	1837-03-30		A1
319	GLENN, Simion	34	SWNW	1835-10-01		A1
175	GRAY, Hezekiah	4	E½NE	1850-04-01		A1 G119
176	" "	4	NENW	1850-04-01		A1 G119
202	GRAY, James	35	W½NE	1830-11-01		A1
196	" "	26	E½SW	1831-07-01		A1
204	" "	25	W½SW	1834-10-01		A1 G120
191	" "	22	E½SW	1837-03-20		A1
192	" "	22	SENW	1837-03-20		A1
193	" "	22	W½NE	1837-03-20		A1
194	" "	22	W½SE	1837-03-20		A1
197	" "	27	E½NE	1837-03-20		A1
198	" "	27	E½NW	1837-03-20		A1
199	" "	27	E½SW	1837-03-20		A1
190	" "	22	E½SE	1837-03-30		A1
195	" "	22	W½SW	1837-03-30		A1
200	" "	27	NWNE	1837-03-30		A1
188	" "	20	SE	1837-04-01		A1
201	" "	27	SWNE	1837-04-01		A1
203	" "	22	NENW	1839-09-20		A1 G121
189	" "	21	SESE	1844-07-10		A1
246	GRAY, John	35	E½SE	1830-11-01		A1
247	" "	35	W½SE	1830-11-01		A1 G122
324	GRAY, Thomas	34	E½SE	1830-11-01		A1 G123
175	GRAY, William	4	E½NE	1850-04-01		A1 G119
176	" "	4	NENW	1850-04-01		A1 G119
102	GREENE, Daniel	13	E½SE	1830-11-01		A1 G17
135	" "	14	W½NW	1830-11-01		A1
136	" "	15	E½NE	1830-11-01		A1

ID	Individual in Patent	Sec.	Sec. Part	Date Issued	Other Counties	For More Info . . .
137	GREENE, Daniel (Cont'd)	19	W½SW	1830-11-01		A1
138	" "	25	E½SE	1830-11-01		A1
143	" "	26	E½NE	1830-11-01		A1 G128
139	" "	27	W½SW	1830-11-01		A1
140	" "	30	W½NW	1830-11-01		A1
141	" "	36	E½NW	1830-11-01		A1 G127
142	" "	36	W½NW	1830-11-01		A1 G127
144	" "	36	W½SW	1830-11-01		A1 G126
175	HADEN, Anselm L	4	E½NE	1850-04-01		A1 G119
176	" "	4	NENW	1850-04-01		A1 G119
130	HARDWICK, Benjamin F	11	NWNE	1858-06-01		A1
131	" "	2	SWSE	1858-06-01		A1
160	HARDWICK, Garland	1	E½SE	1830-11-01		A1
161	" "	1	W½SE	1830-11-01		A1
162	" "	12	E½NE	1830-11-01		A1
167	" "	12	E½SE	1830-11-01		A1 G137
164	" "	12	W½NE	1830-11-01		A1
166	" "	12	W½SW	1835-10-01		A1
165	" "	12	W½SE	1837-04-01		A1
163	" "	12	SESW	1839-09-20		A1
168	HARDWICK, Garlanda	11	SWNE	1835-10-01		A1
170	HARDWICK, George M	3	NENW	1837-03-20		A1
171	" "	4	NWNE	1837-04-01		A1
169	" "	10	E½SE	1840-11-10		A1
205	HEDLESTON, James	30	W½SE	1830-11-01		A1
212	" "	31	W½NE	1830-11-01		A1
210	" "	31	NWSE	1834-10-16		A1
213	" "	32	SWSE	1834-10-16		A1
208	" "	31	E½SE	1834-10-21		A1
211	" "	31	SWSE	1834-10-21		A1
206	" "	31	E½NE	1837-04-01		A1
209	" "	31	E½SW	1837-04-01		A1
207	" "	31	E½NW	1839-09-20		A1
174	HOLLY, Henry	32	NESE	1834-10-16		A1
214	HOLLY, James	32	SENW	1834-10-21		A1
215	JACK, James	32	N½SW	1837-04-01		A1
216	" "	32	NWNE	1837-04-01		A1
217	" "	32	SESE	1837-04-01		A1
218	" "	32	W½NW	1837-04-01		A1
303	JEMISON, Robert	11	E½NE	1830-11-01		A1 G155
297	" "	11	E½SE	1830-11-01		A1
167	" "	12	E½SE	1830-11-01		A1 G137
109	" "	13	E½SW	1830-11-01		A1 G19
110	" "	13	W½SW	1830-11-01		A1 G19
111	" "	14	E½SW	1830-11-01		A1 G19
112	" "	14	W½SE	1830-11-01		A1 G19
113	" "	14	W½SW	1830-11-01		A1 G19
114	" "	15	E½SE	1830-11-01		A1 G19
298	" "	24	E½SE	1830-11-01		A1
299	" "	24	W½SE	1830-11-01		A1
300	" "	3	E½NE	1830-11-01		A1
301	" "	3	W½NE	1830-11-01		A1
302	" "	5	NE	1830-11-01	Greene	A1
128	" "	5	SW	1830-11-01	Greene	A1 G37 F R273
129	" "	7	NE	1830-11-01	Greene	A1 G37 F
115	" "	8	W½SW	1830-11-01	Greene	A1 G19
248	JONES, John	25	W½NW	1830-11-01		A1
330	JONES, William D	25	E½NE	1830-11-01		A1
331	" "	25	E½NW	1830-11-01		A1
332	" "	25	W½NE	1830-11-01		A1
267	KEATON, John	15	E½NW	1830-11-01		A1 G163
268	" "	15	W½NW	1830-11-01		A1 G163
253	" "	19	E½SE	1831-06-01		A1
254	" "	20	SW	1831-06-01		A1
265	" "	9	W½NE	1831-06-01		A1 R230
250	" "	14	E½NE	1832-01-10		A1
255	" "	21	W½SW	1832-01-10		A1
252	" "	15	SWNE	1834-10-01		A1
260	" "	9	E½NW	1834-10-01		A1
262	" "	9	E½SW	1834-10-21		A1
249	" "	10	W½NW	1837-04-01		A1
251	" "	15	E½SW	1837-04-01		A1
256	" "	22	W½NW	1837-04-01		A1

ID	Individual in Patent	Sec.	Sec. Part	Date Issued	Other Counties	For More Info . . .
257	KEATON, John (Cont'd)	4	E½SW	1837-04-01		A1
258	" "	4	W½SE	1837-04-01		A1
259	" "	9	E½NE	1837-04-01		A1
263	" "	9	NWNW	1837-04-01		A1
264	" "	9	SWNW	1837-04-01		A1
266	" "	9	W½SE	1837-04-01		A1
261	" "	9	E½SE	1839-03-15		A1
269	KEETON, John	15	NWNE	1837-04-01		A1
342	KENNON, William	27	W½NW	1830-11-01		A1
343	" "	28	E½NE	1830-11-01		A1
144	" "	36	W½SW	1830-11-01		A1 G126
204	" "	25	W½SW	1834-10-01		A1 G120
219	KNOX, James	13	E½NE	1830-11-01		A1
203	KORNEGAY, Thomas W	22	NENW	1839-09-20		A1 G121
185	LEAVELL, James G	29	W½NW	1861-08-01		A1
186	" "	30	E½NW	1861-08-01		A1
187	" "	30	NE	1861-08-01		A1
295	LYON, Peter	12	NESW	1835-10-01		A1
296	" "	3	NWNW	1837-04-01		A1
116	MARR, William M	8	E½SE	1830-11-01	Greene	A1 G20
117	" "	8	E½SW	1830-11-01	Greene	A1 G20
325	MAYES, Thomas	14	E½NW	1831-01-04		A1
82	MCCOWN, Alexander	3	W½SE	1839-09-20		A1
220	MCGIFFORD, James	18	W½	1830-11-01		A1 F R339
304	MCKENNIE, Robert	17	NENW	1837-03-30		A1
141	MCMILLAN, Alexander	36	E½NW	1830-11-01		A1 G127
142	" "	36	W½NW	1830-11-01		A1 G127
84	" "	36	W½SE	1830-11-01		A1
83	" "	36	W½SW	1839-09-20		A1
221	MCMILLAN, James	3	E½SE	1840-11-10		A1
85	MCMILLIAN, Alexander	36	E½SE	1839-09-20		A1
86	" "	36	S½NE	1839-09-20		A1
222	MCMILLIAN, James	11	NWSW	1839-09-20		A1
229	MCMILLIAN, James W	13	NWNE	1838-08-28		A1
227	" "	10	E½NW	1839-09-20		A1
228	" "	11	SWSW	1839-09-20		A1
230	" "	9	W½NE	1839-09-20		A1 R265
336	MINTER, William J	17	W½NW	1837-04-01		A1
337	" "	17	W½SW	1837-04-01		A1
338	" "	18	E½	1837-04-01		A1 F
339	" "	18	W½	1837-04-01		A1 F R220
340	" "	19	N½	1837-04-01		A1
341	" "	20	NW	1837-04-01		A1
286	MOSS, Johnson	1	E½NE	1830-11-01		A1 G204
280	" "	1	W½NE	1830-11-01		A1
284	" "	2	SENE	1834-10-14		A1
285	" "	2	W½NE	1834-10-21		A1
281	" "	2	E½SE	1835-10-01		A1
282	" "	2	NENE	1835-10-01		A1
283	" "	2	NW	1837-03-20		A1
287	MOSS, Johnston	1	E½NW	1830-11-01		A1
288	" "	1	W½NW	1830-11-01		A1
333	PARISH, William G	14	E½SE	1830-11-01		A1
334	" "	24	W½NW	1830-11-01		A1
335	" "	8	W½SE	1830-11-01	Greene	A1
105	PARKER, James	23	E½NE	1830-11-01		A1 G21
106	" "	23	E½NW	1830-11-01		A1 G21
107	" "	23	W½NE	1830-11-01		A1 G21
108	" "	23	W½NW	1830-11-01		A1 G21
344	POPE, Willis	28	E½SE	1837-04-01		A1
345	" "	28	NESW	1837-04-01		A1
346	" "	28	NWSE	1837-04-01		A1
347	" "	28	SESW	1837-04-01		A1
348	" "	28	SWSE	1837-04-01		A1
349	" "	28	W½SW	1837-04-01		A1
286	RICHARDS, John D	1	E½NE	1830-11-01		A1 G204
240	" "	1	E½SW	1830-11-01		A1
241	" "	11	E½SW	1830-11-01		A1
244	" "	11	W½SE	1830-11-01		A1 G218
242	" "	12	E½NW	1830-11-01		A1
267	" "	15	E½NW	1830-11-01		A1 G163
268	" "	15	W½NW	1830-11-01		A1 G163
236	" "	4	W½NW	1830-11-01		A1 G25

ID	Individual in Patent	Sec.	Sec. Part	Date Issued	Other Counties	For More Info . . .
243	RICHARDS, John D (Cont'd)	4	W½SW	1830-11-01		A1
237	" "	5	E½SE	1830-11-01	Greene	A1 G25
238	" "	5	W½SE	1830-11-01	Greene	A1 G25
275	" "	8	NW	1830-11-01	Greene	A1 G24 F R127
306	ROGERS, Simeon G	21	NESE	1840-11-10		A1
244	SIMS, Edward	11	W½SE	1830-11-01		A1 G218
154	" "	23	E½SE	1830-11-01		A1
155	" "	23	W½SE	1830-11-01		A1
156	" "	24	W½SW	1830-11-01		A1
157	" "	25	W½SE	1830-11-01		A1
143	" "	26	E½NE	1830-11-01		A1 G128
311	" "	26	E½NW	1830-11-01		A1 G93
158	" "	26	E½SE	1830-11-01		A1
159	" "	26	W½NE	1830-11-01		A1
312	" "	27	E½SE	1830-11-01		A1 G93
313	" "	27	W½SE	1830-11-01		A1 G93
314	" "	34	E½NW	1830-11-01		A1 G93
324	" "	34	E½SE	1830-11-01		A1 G123
247	" "	35	W½SE	1830-11-01		A1 G122
231	SPARKS, Jesse	23	NESW	1837-03-20		A1
232	" "	23	SESW	1837-03-30		A1
290	SPARKS, Joseph R	24	SENW	1837-11-07		A1
291	" "	24	SWNE	1837-11-07		A1
320	SPARKS, Stephen	24	NESW	1837-03-30		A1
145	SPENCE, David	25	SESW	1835-10-01		A1
177	SPENCE, Isaac B	25	NESW	1834-11-04		A1
276	SUTTON, John	14	W½NE	1831-01-04		A1
292	TOOSING, Joseph	1	W½SW	1830-11-01		A1
303	" "	11	E½NE	1830-11-01		A1 G155
293	" "	12	W½NW	1830-11-01		A1
294	WEATHERRED, Marquis L	32	NENW	1837-04-01		A1
326	WEATHERSPOON, Thomas	3	E½SW	1831-01-04		A1
327	" "	3	W½SW	1831-01-04		A1
132	WEBB, Berry	11	E½NW	1835-10-01		A1
133	" "	2	E½SW	1837-03-20		A1
134	" "	2	W½SW	1839-03-15		A1
277	WILLIAMS, John	36	NENE	1839-09-20		A1
146	WILLSON, David	29	E½SW	1835-10-01		A1
147	WILSON, David	29	W½SW	1830-11-01		A1
151	" "	33	E½SW	1830-11-01		A1
152	" "	33	NE	1830-11-01		A1
148	" "	30	E½SE	1834-10-16		A1
149	" "	32	SENE	1834-10-16		A1
153	" "	33	SWNW	1834-10-16		A1
150	" "	33	E½NW	1837-04-01		A1
225	WILSON, James S	29	E½SE	1834-10-16		A1
226	" "	30	SESW	1834-10-21		A1
245	WILSON, John D	34	NWNW	1909-10-07		A1
322	WILSON, Thomas E	32	NENE	1835-10-01		A1
323	" "	33	NWNW	1835-10-01		A1
321	" "	29	W½SE	1837-04-01		A1
223	WITHERSPOON, James P	32	SESW	1837-04-01		A1
224	" "	32	SWSW	1837-04-01		A1
305	WITHERSPOON, Samuel M	30	SWSW	1837-04-01		A1

Patent Map

T23-N R4-E
St Stephens Meridian

Map Group 2

Township Statistics

Parcels Mapped	:	268
Number of Patents	:	256
Number of Individuals	:	82
Patentees Identified	:	94
Number of Surnames	:	57
Multi-Patentee Parcels	:	45
Oldest Patent Date	:	11/1/1830
Most Recent Patent	:	10/7/1909
Block/Lot Parcels	:	0
Parcels Re - Issued	:	5
Parcels that Overlap	:	0
Cities and Towns	:	3
Cemeteries	:	0

Greene

Hale

Section 6:
BURROUGHS Benjamin 1837
BURROUGHS Benjamin 1839
BURROUGHS Benjamin 1830
BEALE [23] John S 1830

Section 5:
BEALE [23] John S 1830
JEMISON Robert 1830

Section 4:
GRAY [119] Hezekiah 1850
HARDWICK George M 1837
GRAY [119] Hezekiah 1850
BEALE [25] John 1830
EDDINS Simeon J 1853
EDDINS Simeon J 1853
RICHARDS John D 1830
KEATON John 1837
KEATON John 1837
EDDINS Simeon J 1853
EDDINS Simeon J 1853
BEALE [23] John S 1830
BEALE [25] John 1830
BEALE [25] John 1830

Section 7:
BURROUGHS Benjamin 1837
BURROUGHS Benjamin 1839
BURROUGHS Benjamin 1837
BURROUGHS Benjamin 1830
BURROUGHS [37] Benjamin 1830
BURROUGHS Benjamin 1830
BURROUGHS [37] Benjamin 1830

Section 8:
BEALE [24] John S 1830
BURROUGHS Benjamin 1830
BATTLE Alfred 1852
BATTLE Alfred 1839

Section 9:
KEATON John 1837
KEATON John 1837
KEATON John 1834
MCMILLIAN James W 1839
KEATON John 1837
KEATON John 1831

Section 16, 17, 18, 19, 20, 21:
MINTER William J 1837
MCGIFFORD James 1830
MINTER William J 1837
MINTER William J 1837
MCKENNIE Robert 1837
BATTLE Alfred 1837
BATTLE Alfred 1837
BATTLE Alfred 1837
BISHOP William A 1852
BISHOP William A 1852

BATTLE [16] Alfred 1830
BATTLE [16] Alfred 1830
BATTLE [19] Alfred 1830
BATTLE [20] Alfred 1830
BATTLE [20] Alfred 1830
PARISH William G 1830
BATTLE Alfred 1837
KEATON John 1834
KEATON John 1837
KEATON John 1839

MINTER William J 1837
GREENE Daniel 1830
BATTLE Alfred 1837
BATTLE Alfred 1837
KEATON John 1831
MINTER William J 1837
KEATON John 1831
GRAY James 1837
CARAWAY James 1839
CARAWAY James 1839
CARAWAY James 1839
KEATON John 1832
ROGERS Simeon G 1840
GRAY James 1844

Section 28, 29, 30, 31, 32, 33:
GREENE Daniel 1830
LEAVELL James G 1861
LEAVELL James G 1861
LEAVELL James G 1861
DESMOND John B 1858
DESMOND John B 1858
DESMOND John B 1860
KENNON William 1830

DUNN Henry C 1897
WITHERSPOON Samuel M 1837
HEDLESTON James 1830
WILSON David 1834
WILSON James S 1834
WILLSON David 1835
WILSON Thomas E 1837
WILSON James S 1834
POPE Willis 1837
POPE Willis 1837
POPE Willis 1837
POPE Willis 1837
POPE Willis 1837
POPE Willis 1837

HEDLESTON James 1839
HEDLESTON James 1830
HEDLESTON James 1837
JACK James 1837
WEATHERRED Marquis L 1837
JACK James 1837
HOLLY James 1834
ELLIOTT Johnson 1835
WILSON David 1834
WILSON Thomas E 1835
WILSON Thomas E 1835
WILSON David 1837
WILSON David 1834
WILSON David 1830

HEDLESTON James 1837
HEDLESTON James 1834
HEDLESTON James 1834
HEDLESTON James 1834
WITHERSPOON James P 1837
WITHERSPOON James P 1837
JACK James 1837
HOLLY Henry 1834
ELLIOTT Johnson 1835
HEDLESTON James 1834
HOLLY Henry 1834
JACK James 1837
CUNNINGHAM Joseph P 1830
WILSON David 1830

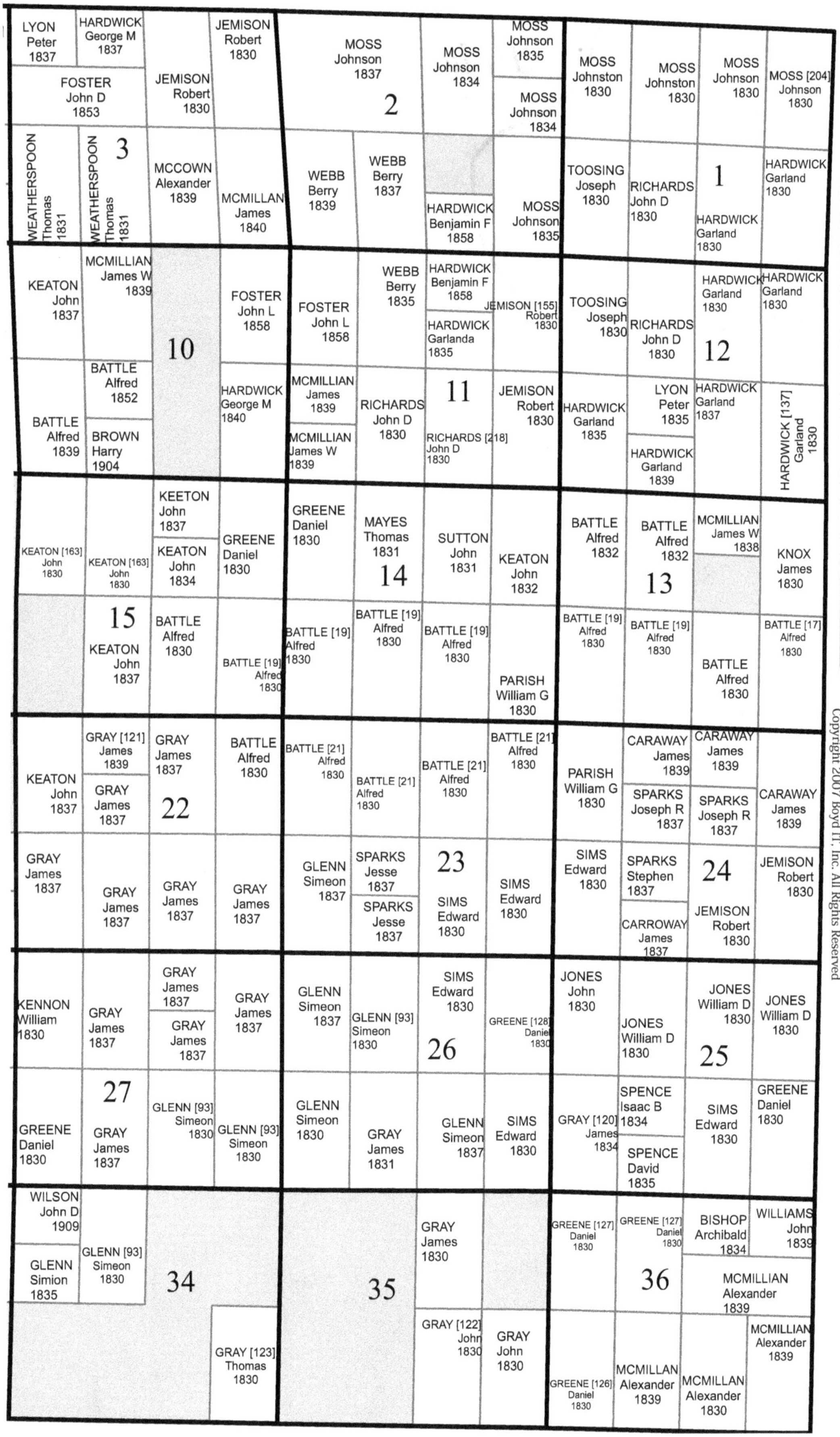

Section 2 (top-left area):

LYON Peter 1837 | HARDWICK George M 1837 | JEMISON Robert 1830

FOSTER John D 1853 | JEMISON Robert 1830

WEATHERSPOON Thomas 1831 | WEATHERSPOON Thomas 1831 | 3 | MCCOWN Alexander 1839 | MCMILLAN James 1840

MOSS Johnson 1837 | 2 | MOSS Johnson 1834 | MOSS Johnson 1835 | MOSS Johnson 1834

WEBB Berry 1839 | WEBB Berry 1837 | HARDWICK Benjamin F 1858 | MOSS Johnson 1835

MOSS Johnston 1830 | MOSS Johnston 1830 | MOSS Johnson 1830 | MOSS [204] Johnson 1830

TOOSING Joseph 1830 | RICHARDS John D 1830 | 1 | HARDWICK Garland 1830 | HARDWICK Garland 1830

Section 10-12:

KEATON John 1837 | MCMILLIAN James W 1839 | 10 | FOSTER John L 1858 | FOSTER John L 1858 | WEBB Berry 1835 | HARDWICK Benjamin F 1858

BATTLE Alfred 1852 | HARDWICK George M 1840 | MCMILLIAN James 1839 | HARDWICK Garlanda 1835 | JEMISON [155] Robert 1830

BATTLE Alfred 1839 | BROWN Harry 1904 | MCMILLIAN James W 1839 | RICHARDS John D 1830 | 11 | RICHARDS [218] John D 1830 | JEMISON Robert 1830 | HARDWICK Garland 1835

TOOSING Joseph 1830 | RICHARDS John D 1830 | 12 | HARDWICK Garland 1830 | HARDWICK Garland 1830 | LYON Peter 1835 | HARDWICK Garland 1837 | HARDWICK [137] Garland 1830 | HARDWICK Garland 1839

Section 15-13:

KEATON [163] John 1830 | KEATON [163] John 1830 | 15 | KEATON John 1837 | KEETON John 1837 | KEATON John 1834 | GREENE Daniel 1830 | GREENE Daniel 1830 | BATTLE Alfred 1830 | MAYES Thomas 1831 | 14 | SUTTON John 1831 | KEATON John 1832 | BATTLE Alfred 1832 | BATTLE Alfred 1832 | MCMILLIAN James W 1838 | 13 | KNOX James 1830

BATTLE Alfred 1830 | BATTLE [19] Alfred 1830 | BATTLE [19] Alfred 1830 | BATTLE [19] Alfred 1830 | BATTLE [19] Alfred 1830 | PARISH William G 1830 | BATTLE [19] Alfred 1830 | BATTLE [19] Alfred 1830 | BATTLE Alfred 1830 | BATTLE [17] Alfred 1830

Section 22-24:

KEATON John 1837 | GRAY [121] James 1839 | GRAY James 1837 | GRAY James 1837 | 22 | BATTLE Alfred 1830 | BATTLE [21] Alfred 1830 | BATTLE [21] Alfred 1830 | BATTLE [21] Alfred 1830 | BATTLE [21] Alfred 1830 | CARAWAY James 1839 | CARAWAY James 1839 | SPARKS Joseph R 1837 | SPARKS Joseph R 1837 | CARAWAY James 1839

GRAY James 1837 | GRAY James 1837 | GRAY James 1837 | GRAY James 1837 | GLENN Simeon 1837 | SPARKS Jesse 1837 | 23 | SPARKS Jesse 1837 | SIMS Edward 1830 | SIMS Edward 1830 | SIMS Edward 1830 | SPARKS Stephen 1837 | CARROWAY James 1837 | 24 | JEMISON Robert 1830 | JEMISON Robert 1830

Section 27-25:

KENNON William 1830 | GRAY James 1837 | 27 | GLENN [93] Simeon 1830 | GRAY James 1837 | GRAY James 1837 | GRAY James 1837 | GRAY James 1837 | GLENN [93] Simeon 1830 | GLENN Simeon 1837 | GLENN [93] Simeon 1830 | GLENN Simeon 1830 | 26 | GRAY James 1831 | SIMS Edward 1830 | GREENE [128] Daniel 1830 | GLENN Simeon 1837 | SIMS Edward 1830 | JONES John 1830 | JONES William D 1830 | SPENCE Isaac B 1834 | SPENCE David 1835 | GRAY [120] James 1834 | JONES William D 1830 | 25 | JONES William D 1830 | SIMS Edward 1830 | GREENE Daniel 1830

GREENE Daniel 1830

Section 34-36:

WILSON John D 1909 | GLENN Simion 1835 | GLENN [93] Simeon 1830 | 34 | 35 | GRAY [123] Thomas 1830 | GRAY James 1830 | GRAY [122] John 1830 | GRAY John 1830 | GREENE [127] Daniel 1830 | GREENE [127] Daniel 1830 | BISHOP Archibald 1834 | WILLIAMS John 1839 | 36 | MCMILLIAN Alexander 1839 | MCMILLIAN Alexander 1839 | GREENE [126] Daniel 1830 | MCMILLAN Alexander 1839 | MCMILLAN Alexander 1830

Helpful Hints

1. This Map's INDEX can be found on the preceding pages.
2. Refer to Map "C" to see where this Township lies within Hale County, Alabama.
3. Numbers within square brackets [ ] denote a multi-patentee land parcel (multi-owner). Refer to Appendix "C" for a full list of members in this group.
4. Areas that look to be crowded with Patentees usually indicate multiple sales of the same parcel (Re-issues) or Overlapping parcels. See this Township's Index for an explanation of these and other circumstances that might explain "odd" groupings of Patentees on this map.

Legend

—— Patent Boundary
▬▬ Section Boundary
▓ No Patents Found (or Outside County)
1., 2., 3., ... Lot Numbers (when beside a name)
[ ] Group Number (see Appendix "C")

Scale: Section = 1 mile X 1 mile (generally, with some exceptions)

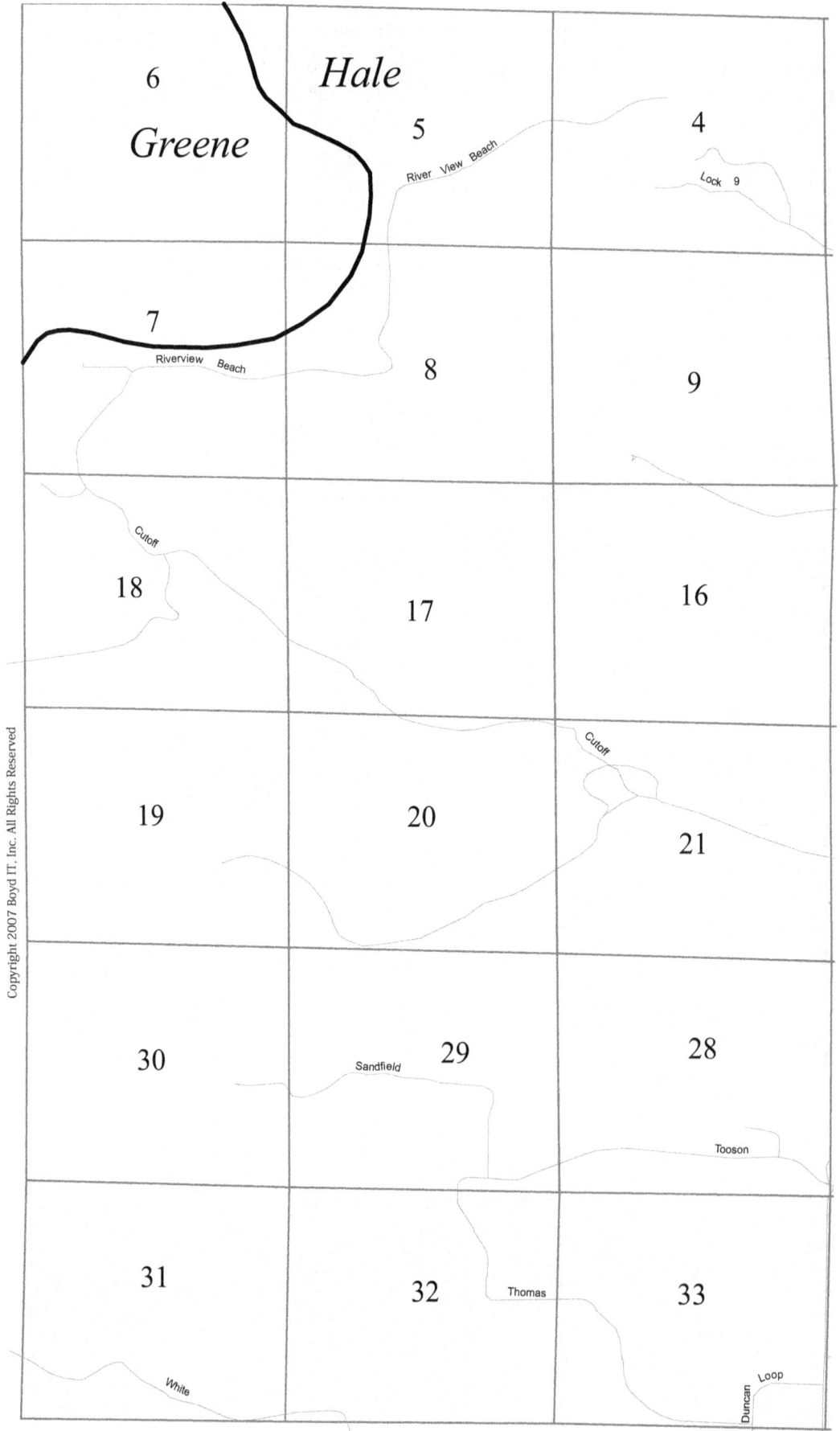

Road Map

T23-N R4-E
St Stephens Meridian

Map Group 2

Cities & Towns
Cypress
Moundville
Powers

Cemeteries
None

6	*Hale*	4
Greene	5	
7	8	9
18	17	16
19	20	21
30	29	28
31	32	33

River View Beach

Lock 9

Riverview Beach

Cutoff

Cutoff

Sandfield

Tooson

Thomas

White

Duncan Loop

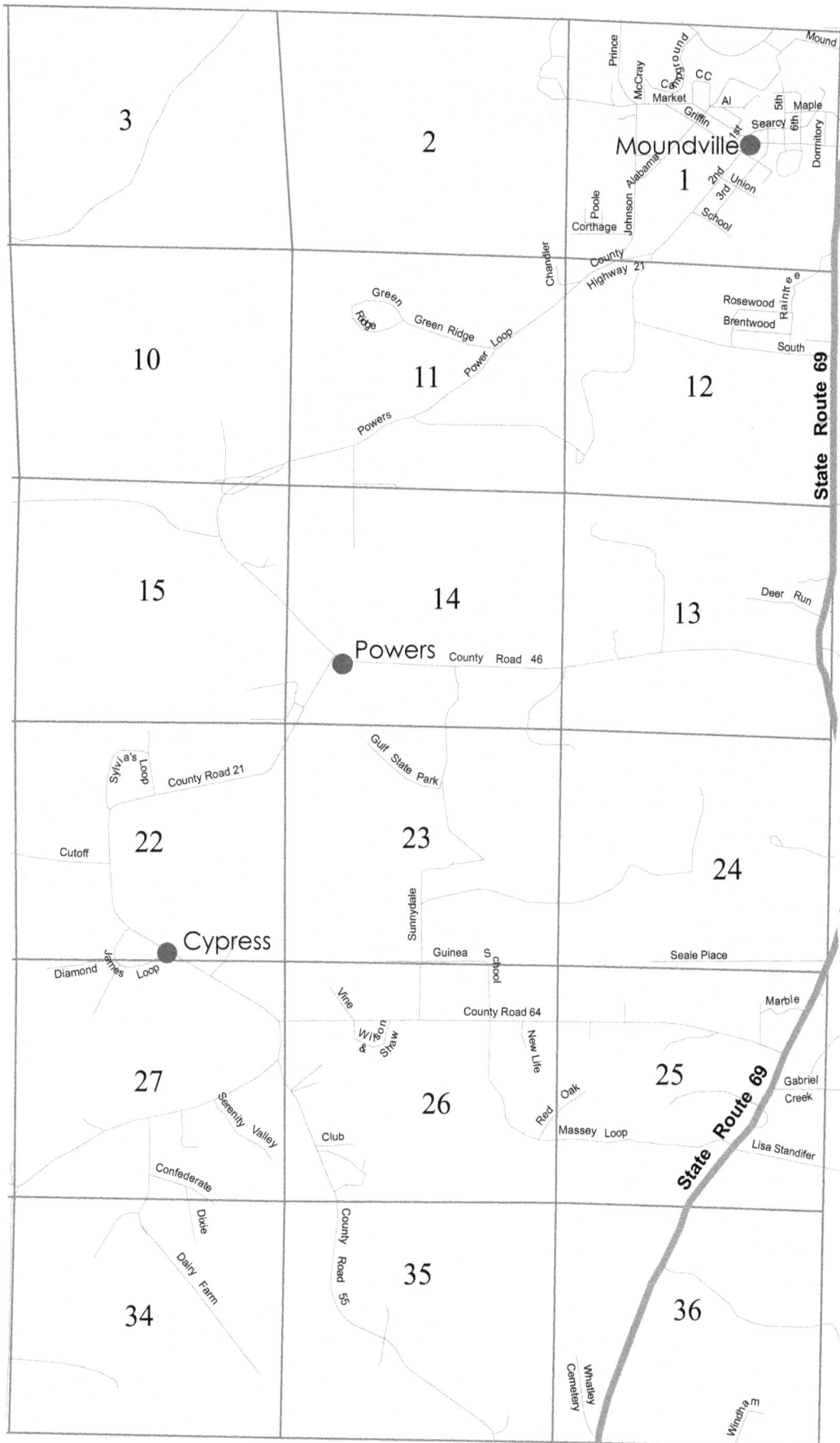

Helpful Hints

1. This road map has a number of uses, but primarily it is to help you: a) find the present location of land owned by your ancestors (at least the general area), b) find cemeteries and city-centers, and c) estimate the route/roads used by Census-takers & tax-assessors.

2. If you plan to travel to Hale County to locate cemeteries or land parcels, please pick up a modern travel map for the area before you do. Mapping old land parcels on modern maps is not as exact a science as you might think. Just the slightest variations in public land survey coordinates, estimates of parcel boundaries, or road-map deviations can greatly alter a map's representation of how a road either does or doesn't cross a particular parcel of land.

Legend

- Section Lines
- Interstates
- Highways
- Other Roads
- Cities/Towns
- Cemeteries

Scale: Section = 1 mile X 1 mile (generally, with some exceptions)

Historical Map

T23-N R4-E
St Stephens Meridian

Map Group 2

Cities & Towns
Cypress
Moundville
Powers

Cemeteries
None

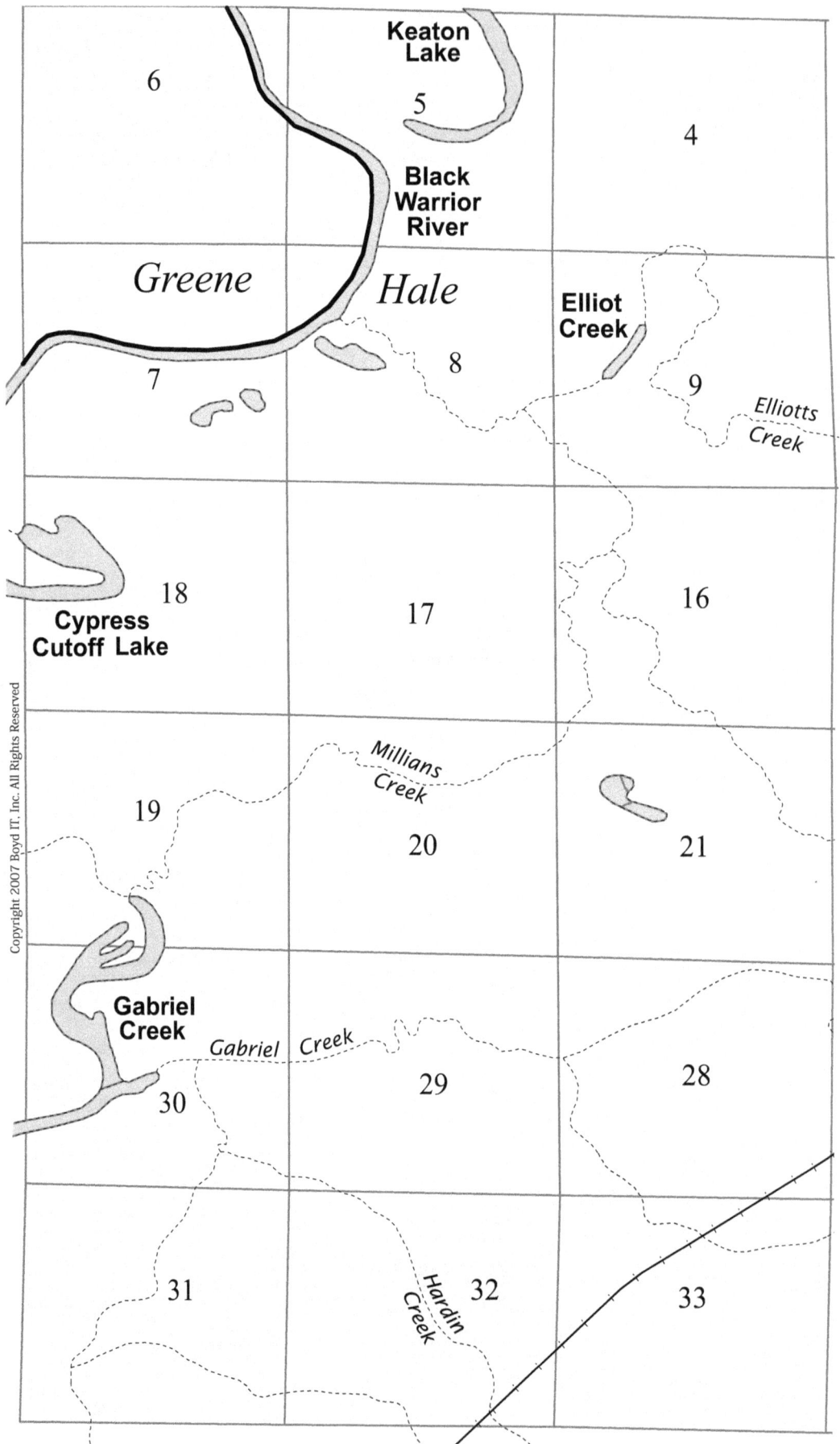

6

Keaton Lake

5

4

Black Warrior River

Greene

Hale

Elliot Creek

7

8

9

Elliotts Creek

18

17

16

Cypress Cutoff Lake

19

Millians Creek

20

21

Gabriel Creek

Gabriel Creek

30

29

28

31

Hardin Creek

32

33

Touson
Lake

Wiggins
Lake

3

2

1

Moundville ●

10

11

Elliotts Creek

12

15

14

13

● Powers

22

Millians Creek

23

24

Cypress ●

26

25

27

Gabriel Creek

34

35

Gile Creek

36

Helpful Hints

1. This Map takes a different look at the same Congressional Township displayed in the preceding two maps. It presents features that can help you better envision the historical development of the area: a) Water-bodies (lakes & ponds), b) Water-courses (rivers, streams, etc.), c) Railroads, d) City/town center-points (where they were oftentimes located when first settled), and e) Cemeteries.

2. Using this "Historical" map in tandem with this Township's Patent Map and Road Map, may lead you to some interesting discoveries. You will often find roads, towns, cemeteries, and waterways are named after nearby landowners: sometimes those names will be the ones you are researching. See how many of these research gems you can find here in Hale County.

Legend

————————	Section Lines
—+—+—+—+—	Railroads
▭	Large Rivers & Bodies of Water
··········	Streams/Creeks & Small Rivers
●	Cities/Towns
♰	Cemeteries

Scale: Section = 1 mile X 1 mile
(there are some exceptions)

65

Map Group 3: Index to Land Patents

Township 23-North Range 5-East (St Stephens)

After you locate an individual in this Index, take note of the Section and Section Part then proceed to the Land Patent map on the pages immediately following. You should have no difficulty locating the corresponding parcel of land.

The "For More Info" Column will lead you to more information about the underlying Patents. See the *Legend* at right, and the "How to Use this Book" chapter, for more information.

```
                        LEGEND
            "For More Info . . . " column
A = Authority (Legislative Act, See Appendix "A")
B = Block or Lot (location in Section unknown)
C = Cancelled Patent
F = Fractional Section
G = Group  (Multi-Patentee Patent, see Appendix "C")
V = Overlaps another Parcel
R = Re-Issued (Parcel patented more than once)

(A & G items require you to look in the Appendixes referred
to above. All other Letter-designations followed by a number
require you to locate line-items in this index that possess
the ID number found after the letter).
```

ID	Individual in Patent	Sec.	Sec. Part	Date Issued	Other Counties	For More Info . . .
351	BATTLE, Alfred	19	E½SW	1832-01-10		A1 G18
372	BESTOR, Daniel	32	E½NW	1895-01-31		A2
549	BESTOR, Samuel	32	W½SW	1895-01-31		A2
555	BISHOP, William A	22	NESE	1853-11-15		A1
556	" "	26	NWSW	1858-06-01		A1
557	" "	26	SWNW	1858-06-01		A1
558	" "	27	NESE	1858-06-01		A1
559	" "	27	NWSE	1858-06-01		A1
560	" "	27	SENE	1858-06-01		A1
561	" "	34	SWNW	1858-06-01		A1
562	" "	35	SWNW	1858-06-01		A1
565	BRANDON, William	20	NWSE	1858-06-01		A1
521	BUCK, Morgan E	22	NWSW	1880-02-20		A2
522	" "	22	SWNW	1880-02-20		A2
474	BURDIN, John	28	SENW	1839-09-20		A1
475	" "	28	W½NW	1839-09-20		A1
476	" "	34	NWNW	1839-09-20		A1
397	CALHOUN, Elias	32	SESE	1858-06-01		A1
398	" "	33	SESW	1858-06-01		A1
399	" "	33	SWSE	1858-06-01		A1
442	CHAMPION, James	14	NESW	1883-03-10		A1
443	" "	14	NWSE	1883-03-10		A1
477	COLLINS, John	23	NWSE	1850-04-01		A1
554	COLLINS, Washington	23	SESE	1850-09-02		A1
478	CROW, John	1	W½SW	1827-07-02		A1
405	DAVIS, George	18	W½NE	1825-06-20		A1 G74
404	" "	4	W½NE	1825-06-20		A1 G73
404	DEVANE, Irelon C	4	W½NE	1825-06-20		A1 G73
388	DIAL, David M	32	E½NE	1824-01-19		A1
384	ELLIOTT, David	29	SE	1831-08-01		A1 G79
375	" "	20	S½SW	1839-09-20		A1
378	" "	29	SWNE	1839-09-20		A1
379	" "	29	W½NW	1839-09-20		A1
380	" "	30	E½NE	1839-09-20		A1
382	" "	32	W½NE	1839-09-20		A1
383	" "	33	W½NW	1839-09-20		A1
376	" "	20	SWSE	1858-06-01		A1
377	" "	29	NWNE	1858-06-01		A1
381	" "	32	NESE	1858-06-01		A1
498	ELLIOTT, Johnson	22	E½NW	1839-09-20		A1
499	" "	22	W½NE	1839-09-20		A1
410	FLEMING, George W	12	NWNE	1839-09-20		A1
411	" "	12	SWNE	1839-09-20		A1
573	FLEMING, William M	12	NWSE	1858-06-01		A1
574	" "	12	SENE	1858-06-01		A1
575	" "	12	SWSE	1858-06-01		A1

ID	Individual in Patent	Sec.	Sec. Part	Date Issued	Other Counties	For More Info . . .
551	FRIERSON, Theodore	26	NESE	1892-01-18		A2
552	" "	26	SENE	1892-01-18		A2
396	FULLER, Edward H	21	NENW	1839-09-20		A1
506	FULLER, Littleton S	20	SWNE	1837-03-30		A1
505	" "	20	E½NE	1839-09-20		A1
507	FULLER, Littleton T	21	NWNW	1839-09-20		A1
440	GABEL, Israel	13	NWSW	1839-09-20		A1
441	" "	13	SENW	1839-09-20		A1
406	GEDDIE, George	26	NESW	1895-01-31		A2
407	" "	26	NWSE	1895-01-31		A2
408	" "	26	SENW	1895-01-31		A2
409	" "	26	SWNE	1895-01-31		A2
435	GEDDIE, Hiram	36	NWSW	1858-06-01		A1
439	GEDDIE, Isaac D	14	S½SE	1895-02-23		A2
444	GEDDIE, James D	14	NENE	1858-06-01		A1
445	" "	14	NESE	1858-06-01		A1
446	" "	14	SENE	1858-06-01		A1
374	GLADNEY, David B	2	NWNW	1858-06-01		A1
544	GLOVER, Richmond V	2	NWSE	1917-11-12		A2
447	GRAY, James	35	E½NE	1837-04-01		A1 V417
534	GREEN, Phillip H	28	N½SE	1898-07-25		A1
422	GRIFFIN, Hardy M	24	NWSW	1858-06-01		A1
423	" "	24	SESW	1858-06-01		A1
424	" "	26	NWNE	1858-06-01		A1
421	" "	24	NESE	1861-07-01		A1 R430
351	GUNN, Peter	19	E½SW	1832-01-10		A1 G18
533	GUNN, Peter R	20	W½NW	1825-08-05		A1
531	" "	19	NESE	1834-10-01		A1
532	" "	19	W½SE	1834-10-01		A1
405	GUNN, Radford	18	W½NE	1825-06-20		A1 G74
536	" "	19	E½NE	1825-06-20		A1
538	" "	19	W½NE	1825-06-20		A1 G131
535	" "	17	E½SE	1839-09-20		A1
537	" "	20	NWNE	1839-09-20		A1
539	GUNN, Radford M	20	NESW	1837-03-30		A1
540	" "	20	NWSW	1837-03-30		A1
545	GUNN, Robert B	17	E½NE	1839-09-20		A1
546	" "	9	S½SE	1839-09-20		A1
547	" "	9	SESW	1839-09-20		A1
550	GUNN, Samuel	19	W½NW	1824-10-20		A1
564	GUNN, William B	18	E½NE	1825-06-20		A1
563	" "	15	SWSW	1839-09-20		A1
483	GUY, John J	36	NWSE	1891-06-29		A2
437	HALL, Horace	10	SESW	1895-02-23		A2
403	HARDWICK, Garland	29	E½NW	1825-09-01		A1
479	HARPER, John	3	E½SW	1824-01-19		A1
481	" "	4	E½SW	1824-01-19		A1
482	" "	10	W½SW	1825-06-20		A1 G138
480	" "	3	W½NW	1825-06-20		A1
385	HESTER, David	4	W½NW	1831-01-04		A1
386	" "	8	NENW	1837-03-30		A1
387	" "	8	SENW	1837-04-01		A1
518	HESTER, Mcduff C	12	NENE	1905-03-30		A2
569	HILLHOUSE, William	34	N½SE	1839-09-20		A1
412	HORN, George W	33	SWSW	1839-09-20		A1
541	INGE, Richard	28	W½SW	1825-06-20		A1
578	JANNWAY, William W	21	SWNW	1858-06-01		A1
579	" "	22	NESW	1858-06-01		A1
580	" "	22	S½SW	1861-08-01		A1
581	" "	22	SWSE	1861-08-01		A1
582	" "	27	N½NW	1861-08-01		A1
502	JENKINS, Leonce A	14	E½NW	1894-10-22		A2
517	JENKINS, Matthew T	14	W½NE	1890-03-19		A2
438	JOHNSTON, Howell H	12	SW	1899-03-24		A2
457	JOHNSTON, James M	24	SESE	1919-10-04		A2
458	" "	24	W½SE	1919-10-04		A2
484	KEATON, John	31	NW	1839-09-20		A1
509	KELLY, Mamie L	14	NWSW	1906-02-16		A2 G164
355	KEMP, Barney	1	E½NE	1849-09-01		A1
503	KEY, Lewis C	36	NENE	1860-10-01		A1
504	" "	36	W½NE	1860-10-01		A1
365	KING, Charles	14	SESW	1920-04-16		A2
570	KNOWLES, William	2	NENW	1839-09-20		A1

ID	Individual in Patent	Sec.	Sec. Part	Date Issued	Other Counties	For More Info . . .
495	LANE, John W	8	W½NW	1830-11-01		A1 G170
353	LEWIS, Andrew J	10	NESW	1839-09-20		A1
363	LEWIS, Charles A	12	W½NW	1837-04-01		A1
362	" "	12	E½NW	1839-09-20		A1
364	" "	2	SWSE	1839-09-20		A1
359	" "	1	NENW	1858-06-01		A1
360	" "	11	E½NW	1858-06-01		A1
361	" "	11	NWNW	1858-06-01		A1
402	LEWIS, Frederick	2	NWNE	1896-06-15		A2
425	LEWIS, Henry C	4	E½NE	1892-06-10		A2
449	LEWIS, James	10	W½NE	1825-06-20		A1
455	" "	9	NE	1825-06-20		A1
456	" "	9	W½NW	1825-09-10		A1
453	" "	4	W½SW	1837-04-01		A1 V572
448	" "	10	E½NE	1839-03-15		A1
452	" "	3	E½SE	1839-03-15		A1
450	" "	10	W½SE	1839-09-20		A1
451	" "	14	W½NW	1839-09-20		A1
454	" "	9	N½SE	1839-09-20		A1
520	LEWIS, Monroe	10	SESE	1896-02-26		A2
357	LOFTES, Berryman H	32	E½SW	1839-09-20		A1
400	LUCKEY, Francis V	26	NENE	1858-06-01		A1
413	LUCKEY, George W	26	SESW	1858-06-01		A1
414	" "	26	SWSW	1858-06-01		A1
415	" "	35	NWNW	1858-06-01		A1
401	LUCKY, Francis V	25	N½NW	1858-06-01		A1
416	LUCKY, George W	35	NESE	1854-07-15		A1
417	" "	35	SENE	1854-07-15		A1 V447
572	LUCKY, William	4	SWSW	1848-04-15		A1 V453
571	" "	36	SENE	1852-01-01		A1
459	MARTIN, James	32	W½SE	1824-01-19		A1
466	MARTIN, James T	27	SESW	1840-11-10		A1
465	" "	22	NWSE	1850-04-01		A1
524	MARTIN, Moses	34	E½NW	1839-03-15		A1
525	" "	34	NE	1839-03-15		A1
523	" "	27	S½SE	1839-09-20		A1
576	MARTIN, William S	33	NWSW	1839-09-20		A1
352	MASSINGALE, Alfred	7	SE	1825-06-20		A1
486	MCCAIN, John	2	E½SE	1825-06-20		A1
548	MCCOWN, Sampson	5	E½SW	1826-12-01		A1 G189
495	" "	8	W½NW	1830-11-01		A1 G170
373	MCCRAE, Daniel	30	E½NW	1825-06-20		A1 G190
460	MCDONALD, James	10	NESE	1839-09-20		A1
350	MCMILLAN, Alexander	31	SW	1839-09-20		A1
461	MCMILLAN, James	31	E½NE	1839-09-20		A1
373	MCMILLEN, James	30	E½NW	1825-06-20		A1 G190
462	MCMILLIAN, James	17	W½NE	1825-09-01		A1
464	" "	9	W½SW	1825-09-01		A1
463	" "	32	W½NW	1832-01-10		A1
467	MCMILLIAN, James W	30	SWNE	1839-09-20		A1
495	MCRAE, Malcolm	8	W½NW	1830-11-01		A1 G170
548	MCRAE, Malcom	5	E½SW	1826-12-01		A1 G189
351	MEARS, John	19	E½SW	1832-01-10		A1 G18
538	MORRIS, John	19	W½NE	1825-06-20		A1 G131
501	NEAL, Leonard B	24	NWNE	1858-06-01		A1
392	NEVIN, Dixon H	28	NENE	1903-12-17		A2
393	" "	28	NENW	1909-07-22		A2
394	" "	28	NWNE	1909-07-22		A2
431	NEVIN, Henry	24	SENE	1852-01-01		A1
426	" "	13	E½SE	1858-06-01		A1
427	" "	13	SWSE	1858-06-01		A1
428	" "	24	NENE	1858-06-01		A1
429	" "	24	NENW	1858-06-01		A1
430	" "	24	NESE	1891-11-23		A2 R421
432	NEVIN, Henry P	24	S½NW	1914-01-17		A2
433	" "	24	SWNE	1914-01-17		A2
500	OWENS, Lacy	26	S½SE	1860-10-01		A1
395	PARKER, Edmond	1	NWNW	1899-12-07		A1
354	PHILLIPS, Andrew	4	E½NW	1824-01-19		A1
583	PRICE, Wilson	11	SWSE	1839-09-20		A1
351	RAMIE, Robert	19	E½SW	1832-01-10		A1 G18
508	RATLIFF, Lorenzo M	2	NENE	1858-06-01		A1
487	RHODES, John P	35	SWNE	1852-01-01		A1

ID	Individual in Patent	Sec.	Sec. Part	Date Issued	Other Counties	For More Info . . .
529	ROGERS, Newbern E	2	S½NE	1897-08-30		A2
530	"	2	S½NW	1897-08-30		A2
568	ROGERS, William H	3	E½NE	1858-06-01		A1
436	ROSSON, Hiram	9	E½NW	1825-09-01		A1
358	SAMUEL, Bill	34	NESW	1894-12-07		A2
384	SEALE, William	29	SE	1831-08-01		A1 G79
577	"	28	S½NE	1839-09-20		A1
526	SMITH, Moses	19	E½NW	1825-08-05		A1
527	"	19	SESE	1839-09-20		A1
528	"	30	NWNE	1839-09-20		A1
351	SMITH, Moss	19	E½SW	1832-01-10		A1 G18
473	SPARKS, Jesse	29	SW	1824-01-19		A1
485	SPENCE, John M	22	NWNW	1910-10-10		A2
390	TIDMORE, David	33	NESW	1837-04-01		A1
391	"	33	NWSE	1837-04-01		A1
389	"	33	E½NE	1839-09-20		A1
471	TIDMORE, Jeremiah	36	S½SE	1839-09-20		A1
469	"	35	E½NW	1858-06-01		A1
470	"	35	NWSE	1858-06-01		A1
488	TIDMORE, John	35	NWNE	1854-07-15		A1
510	TIDMORE, Mark	35	S½SE	1858-06-01		A1
512	"	36	S½SW	1858-06-01		A1
511	"	36	NESW	1860-10-01		A1
513	"	36	SENW	1860-10-01		A1
514	"	36	W½NW	1860-10-01		A1
515	TIDMORE, Mary	33	SENW	1839-09-20		A1
516	"	33	SWNE	1839-09-20		A1
519	TIDMORE, Miree	34	S½SE	1891-09-15		A2
366	TINGLE, Cyrus	14	SWSW	1858-06-01		A1
369	"	23	NESW	1858-06-01		A1
370	"	23	NWNW	1858-06-01		A1
371	"	23	SWSW	1858-06-01		A1
367	"	22	E½NE	1891-06-30		A2
368	"	22	SESE	1891-06-30		A2
472	TINGLE, Jesse S	12	SESE	1858-06-01		A1
434	TOLER, Henry W	28	E½SW	1885-06-30		A2
489	TOLER, John	20	NESE	1858-06-01		A1
490	"	21	N½SW	1858-06-01		A1
491	"	21	NWSE	1858-06-01		A1
492	"	21	SENW	1858-06-01		A1
493	"	21	SWNE	1858-06-01		A1
542	TUBB, Richard P	1	SENW	1858-06-01		A1
543	"	1	W½NE	1858-06-01		A1
566	TUBB, William E	23	NENW	1852-01-01		A1
567	"	23	NWSW	1852-01-01		A1
509	TUBBS, Mamie L	14	NWSW	1906-02-16		A2 G164
494	TURNER, John	26	NENW	1858-06-01		A1
356	WEBB, Berry	2	E½SW	1826-05-15		A1
482	WEBB, James	10	W½SW	1825-06-20		A1 G138
468	"	2	W½SW	1825-06-20		A1
419	WELBORN, George W	34	NWSW	1858-06-01		A1
418	"	33	SESE	1860-04-02		A1
420	"	34	S½SW	1860-04-02		A1
496	WHITFIELD, John W	28	S½SE	1893-05-26		A2
553	WILBURNE, Thomas	31	SE	1825-06-20		A1
497	WILLIAMS, John	30	W½NW	1825-06-20		A1

Patent Map

T23-N R5-E
St Stephens Meridian

Map Group 3

Township Statistics

Parcels Mapped	:	234
Number of Patents	:	187
Number of Individuals	:	131
Patentees Identified	:	125
Number of Surnames	:	86
Multi-Patentee Parcels	:	10
Oldest Patent Date	:	1/19/1824
Most Recent Patent	:	4/16/1920
Block/Lot Parcels	:	0
Parcels Re - Issued	:	1
Parcels that Overlap	:	4
Cities and Towns	:	0
Cemeteries	:	6

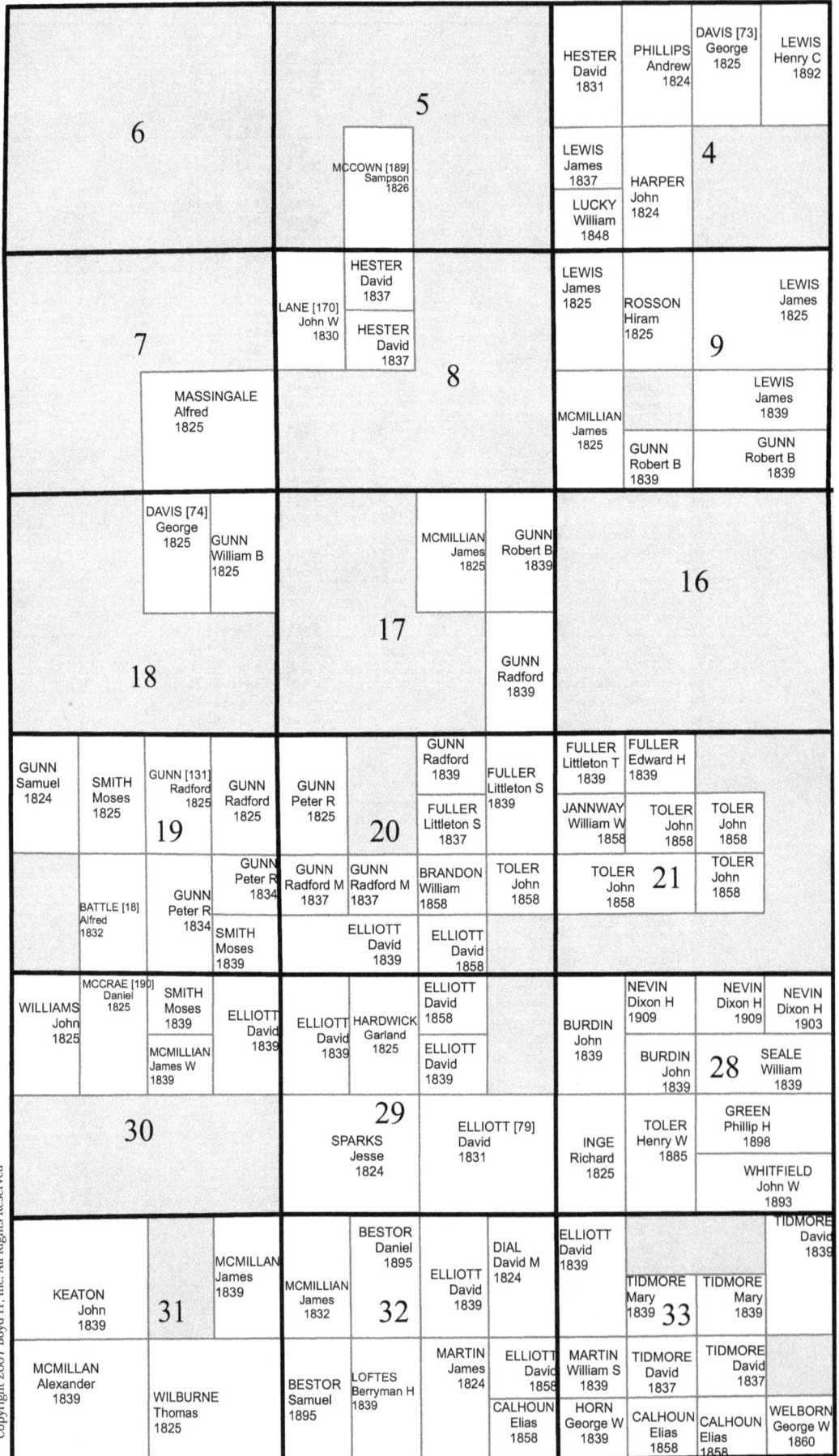

Copyright 2007 Boyd IT, Inc. All Rights Reserved

Section 3
HARPER John 1825

ROGERS William H 1858

HARPER John 1824

LEWIS James 1839

Section 2
GLADNEY David B 1858

KNOWLES William 1839

LEWIS Frederick 1896

RATLIFF Lorenzo M 1858

ROGERS Newbern E 1897

ROGERS Newbern E 1897

WEBB James 1825

WEBB Berry 1826

GLOVER Richmond V 1917

MCCAIN John 1825

LEWIS Charles A 1839

Section 1
PARKER Edmond 1899

LEWIS Charles A 1858

TUBB Richard P 1858

KEMP Barney 1849

TUBB Richard P 1858

CROW John 1827

Section 10
LEWIS James 1825

LEWIS James 1839

HARPER [138] John 1825

LEWIS Andrew J 1839

MCDONALD James 1839

HALL Horace 1895

LEWIS James 1839

LEWIS Monroe 1896

Section 11
LEWIS Charles A 1858

LEWIS Charles A 1858

PRICE Wilson 1839

Section 12
LEWIS Charles A 1837

LEWIS Charles A 1839

FLEMING George W 1839

FLEMING George W 1839

HESTER Mcduff C 1905

FLEMING William M 1858

JOHNSTON Howell H 1899

FLEMING William M 1858

FLEMING William M 1858

TINGLE Jesse S 1858

Section 15
GUNN William B 1839

Section 14
LEWIS James 1839

JENKINS Leonce A 1894

JENKINS Matthew T 1890

GEDDIE James D 1858

GEDDIE James D 1858

KELLY [164] Mamie L 1906

CHAMPION James 1883

CHAMPION James 1883

GEDDIE James D 1858

TINGLE Cyrus 1858

KING Charles 1920

GEDDIE Isaac D 1895

Section 13
GABEL Israel 1839

GABEL Israel 1839

NEVIN Henry 1858

NEVIN Henry 1858

NEVIN Henry 1858

Section 22
SPENCE John M 1910

ELLIOTT Johnson 1839

ELLIOTT Johnson 1839

TINGLE Cyrus 1891

BUCK Morgan E 1880

BUCK Morgan E 1880

JANNWAY William W 1858

MARTIN James T 1850

BISHOP William A 1853

JANNWAY William W 1861

JANNWAY William W 1861

TINGLE Cyrus 1891

Section 23
TINGLE Cyrus 1858

TUBB William E 1852

TUBB William E 1852

TINGLE Cyrus 1858

COLLINS John 1850

TINGLE Cyrus 1858

COLLINS Washington 1850

Section 24
NEVIN Henry 1858

NEAL Leonard B 1858

NEVIN Henry 1858

NEVIN Henry P 1914

NEVIN Henry P 1914

NEVIN Henry 1852

GRIFFIN Hardy M 1858

JOHNSTON James M 1919

GRIFFIN Hardy M 1861 NEVIN Henry 1891

GRIFFIN Hardy M 1858

JOHNSTON James M 1919

Section 27
JANNWAY William W 1861

MARTIN James T 1840

MARTIN Moses 1839

Section 26
TURNER John 1858

BISHOP William A 1858

BISHOP William A 1858

GEDDIE George 1895

GRIFFIN Hardy M 1858

GEDDIE George 1895

LUCKEY Francis V 1858

FRIERSON Theodore 1892

BISHOP William A 1858

BISHOP William A 1858

GEDDIE George 1895

GEDDIE George 1895

FRIERSON Theodore 1892

LUCKEY George W 1858

LUCKEY George W 1858

OWENS Lacy 1860

Section 25
LUCKY Francis V 1858

Section 34
BURDIN John 1839

MARTIN Moses 1839

MARTIN Moses 1839

BISHOP William A 1858

WELBORN George W 1858

SAMUEL Bill 1894

HILLHOUSE William 1839

WELBORN George W 1860

TIDMORE Miree 1891

Section 35
LUCKEY George W 1858

TIDMORE Jeremiah 1858

TIDMORE John 1854

GRAY James 1837

BISHOP William A 1858

RHODES John P 1852

LUCKY George W 1854

TIDMORE Jeremiah 1858

LUCKY George W 1854

TIDMORE Mark 1858

Section 36
TIDMORE Mark 1860

KEY Lewis C 1860

KEY Lewis C 1860

TIDMORE Mark 1860

LUCKY William 1852

GEDDIE Hiram 1858

TIDMORE Mark 1860

GUY John J 1891

TIDMORE Mark 1858

TIDMORE Jeremiah 1839

Helpful Hints

1. This Map's INDEX can be found on the preceding pages.

2. Refer to Map "C" to see where this Township lies within Hale County, Alabama.

3. Numbers within square brackets [ ] denote a multi-patentee land parcel (multi-owner). Refer to Appendix "C" for a full list of members in this group.

4. Areas that look to be crowded with Patentees usually indicate multiple sales of the same parcel (Re-issues) or Overlapping parcels. See this Township's Index for an explanation of these and other circumstances that might explain "odd" groupings of Patentees on this map.

Legend

———— Patent Boundary

▬▬▬▬ Section Boundary

No Patents Found (or Outside County)

1., 2., 3., ... Lot Numbers (when beside a name)

[ ] Group Number (see Appendix "C")

Scale: Section = 1 mile X 1 mile (generally, with some exceptions)

Road Map

T23-N R5-E
St Stephens Meridian

Map Group 3

Copyright 2007 Boyd IT, Inc. All Rights Reserved

Mound

Burke

Park

Park Manor

Owens

Beck

Sunset

Sunrise

Taskaloosa

Okamulgee

Choctaw

Desoto

Coyote

Slide

Mink

4

Terry Acres

Heather

Sandy Fork

Carthage Cem.

6

Skelton

5

Lewis
Cem.

Bamboo

Oak Hill
Cem.

Ivy

County Road 67

Pine Ridge

Whispering
Pine

Cities & Towns
None

Industrial

Hampton Hills

7

McNeil

Valley View Garden

Valley

8

9

County

Road 52

18

17

Wyatt   Hill

16

Woods
Cem.

Rattlesnake

Lynda

Hickory

White Oak

Cedar

County Road   44

Jack
McClain

Cherry

Broadleaf

Crabapple

19

20

21

State Route 69

State Route 69

Cemeteries
Carthage Cemetery
Greenleaf Cemetery
Lewis Cemetery
Oak Hill Cemetery
Pleasant Hill Cemetery
Woods Cemetery

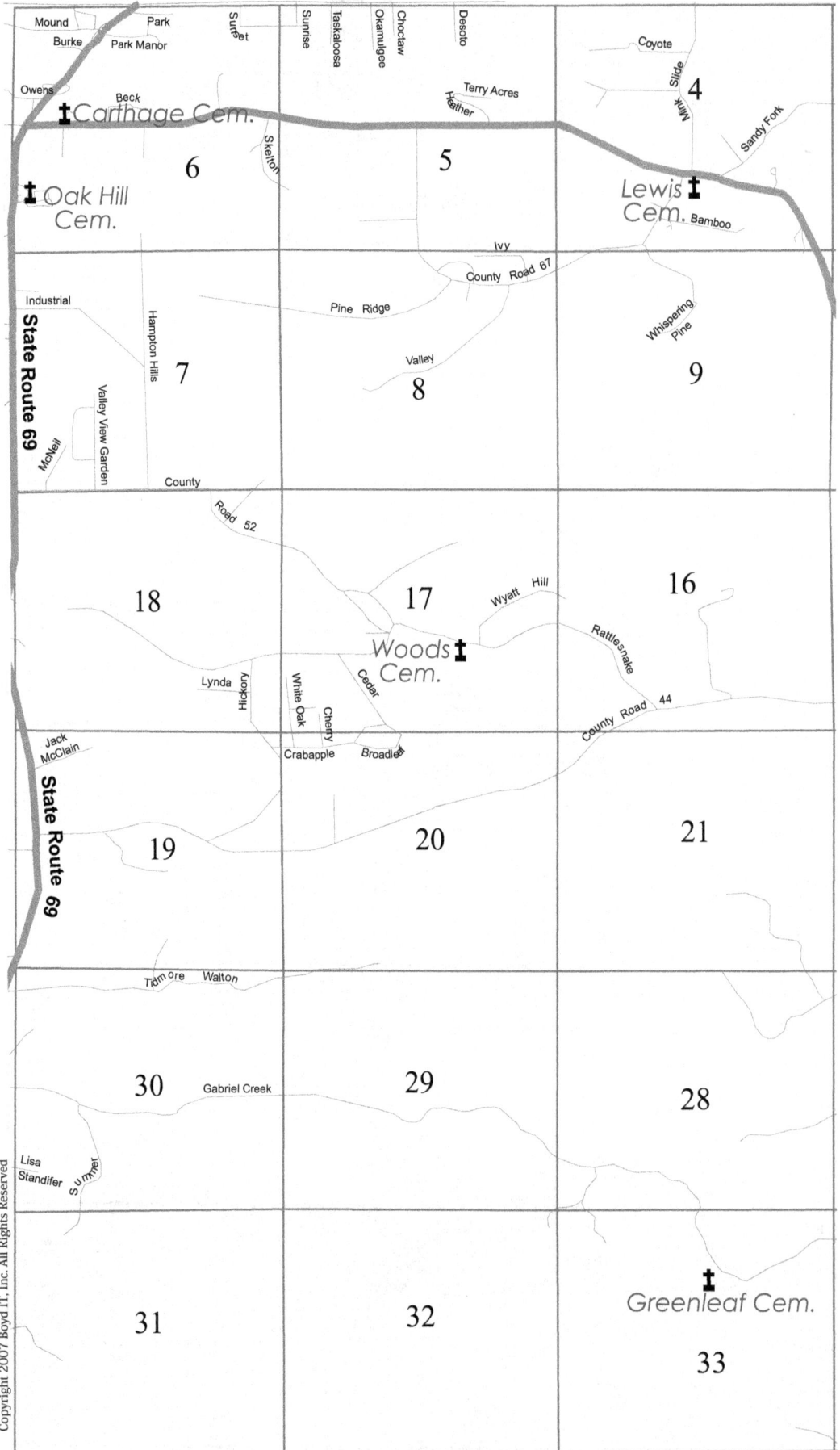

Tidmore

Walton

30

Gabriel Creek

29

28

Lisa
Standifer

Summer

31

32

Greenleaf Cem.

33

3

Wildwood

R.P Davis

Sandy Fork

2

1

10

County Road 50

11

12

15

County Road 44

14

‡ *Pleasant Hill Cem.*

13

22

Beckom Bottom

23

24

27

Gabriel Creek

26

25

Beckom Bottom

China Grove

34

35

36

Greenleaf

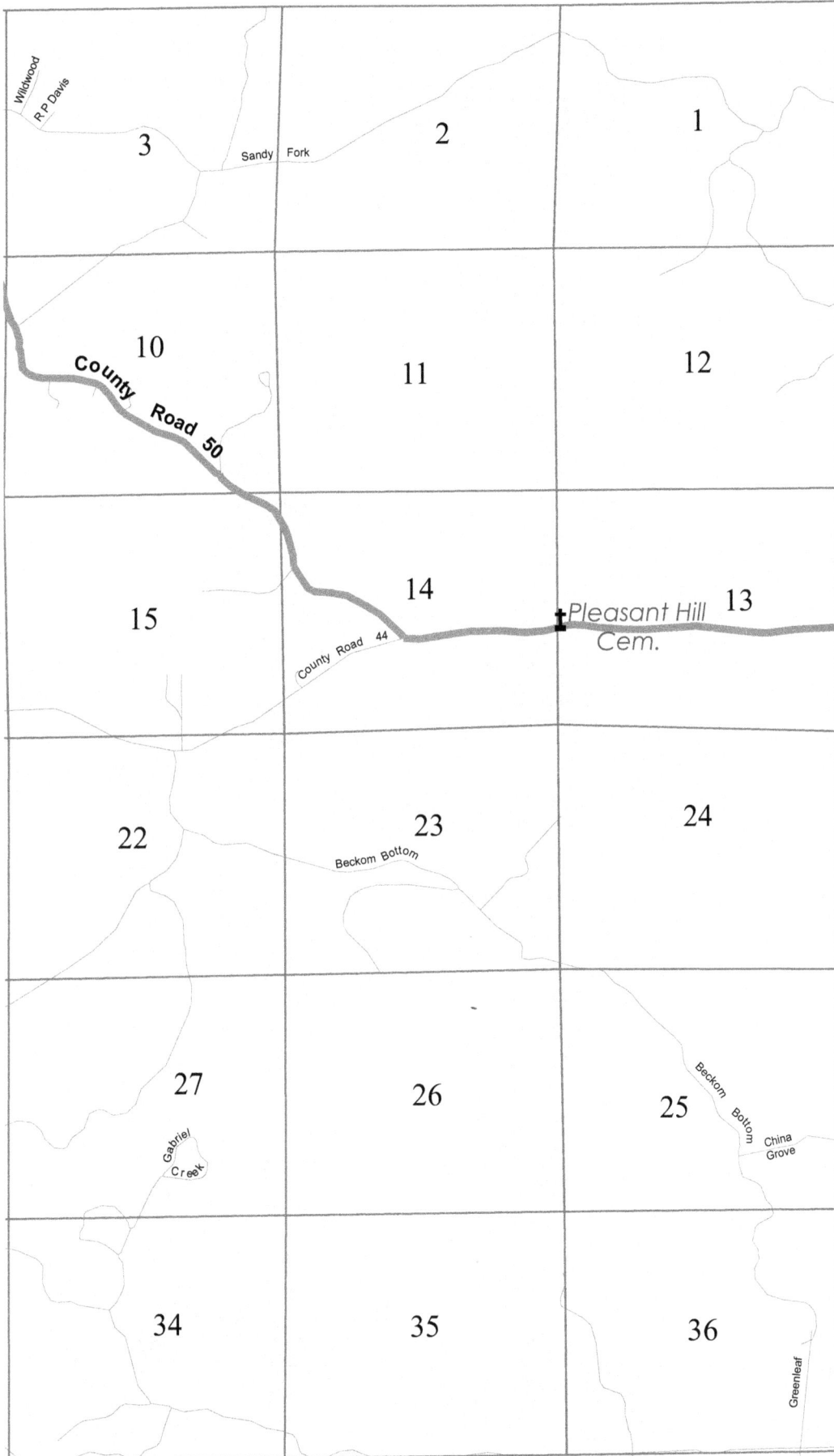

Helpful Hints

1. This road map has a number of uses, but primarily it is to help you: a) find the present location of land owned by your ancestors (at least the general area), b) find cemeteries and city-centers, and c) estimate the route/roads used by Census-takers & tax-assessors.

2. If you plan to travel to Hale County to locate cemeteries or land parcels, please pick up a modern travel map for the area before you do. Mapping old land parcels on modern maps is not as exact a science as you might think. Just the slightest variations in public land survey coordinates, estimates of parcel boundaries, or road-map deviations can greatly alter a map's representation of how a road either does or doesn't cross a particular parcel of land.

Legend

——————	Section Lines
════════	Interstates
▬▬▬▬▬	Highways
——————	Other Roads
●	Cities/Towns
‡	Cemeteries

Scale: Section = 1 mile X 1 mile
(generally, with some exceptions)

73

Historical Map

T23-N R5-E
St Stephens Meridian

Map Group 3

Cities & Towns
None

Cemeteries
Carthage Cemetery
Greenleaf Cemetery
Lewis Cemetery
Oak Hill Cemetery
Pleasant Hill Cemetery
Woods Cemetery

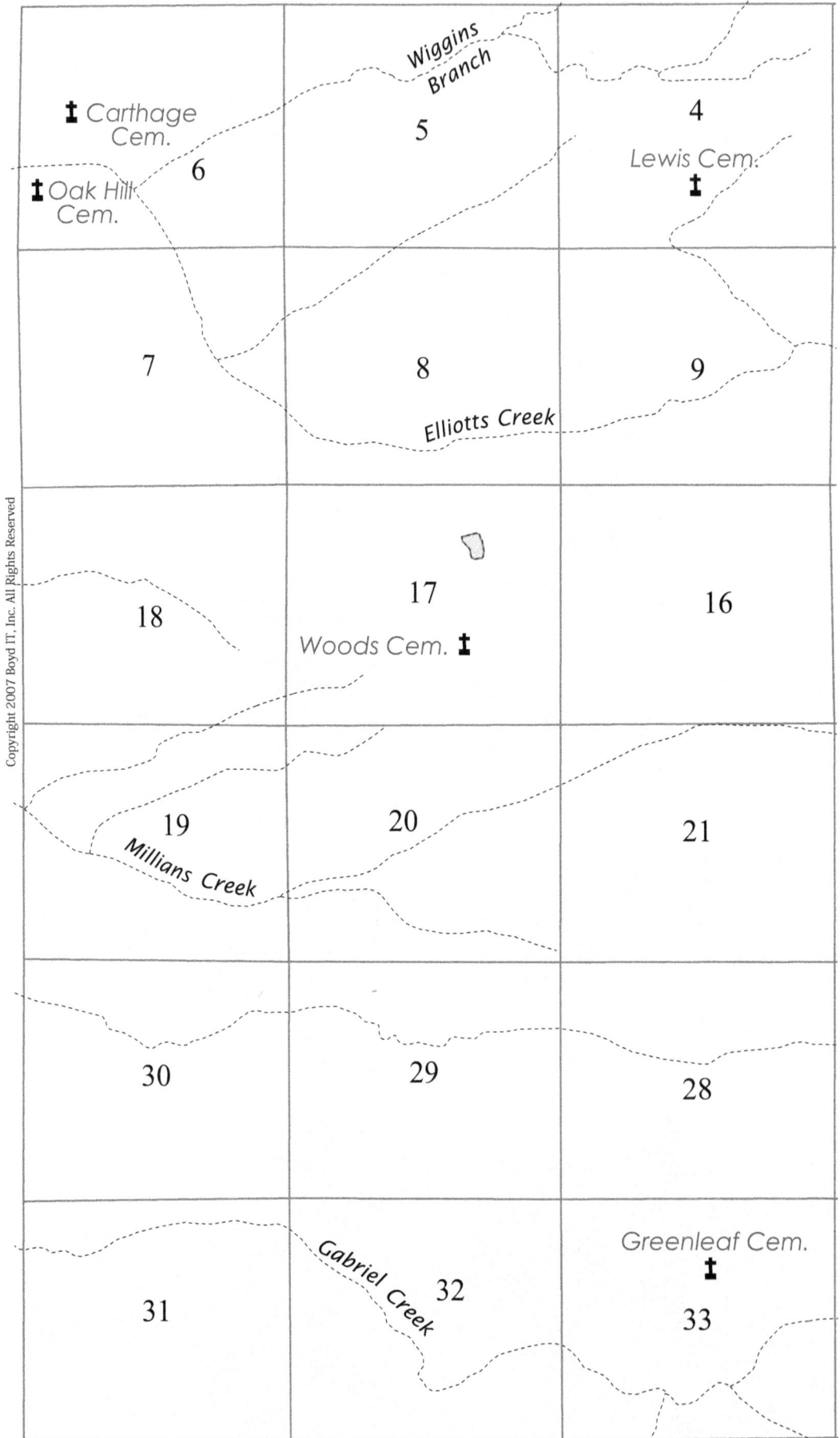

Carthage Cem.

Oak Hill Cem.

Wiggins Branch

5

4

Lewis Cem.

7

8

9

Elliotts Creek

18

17

Woods Cem.

16

19

20

21

Millians Creek

30

29

28

31

Gabriel Creek

32

Greenleaf Cem.

33

6

3

2

1

Elliotts Creek   12

11

10

13

15   14   ✝ *Pleasant Hill Cem.*

22   23   24

Millians Creek

27   26   25

34   35   36

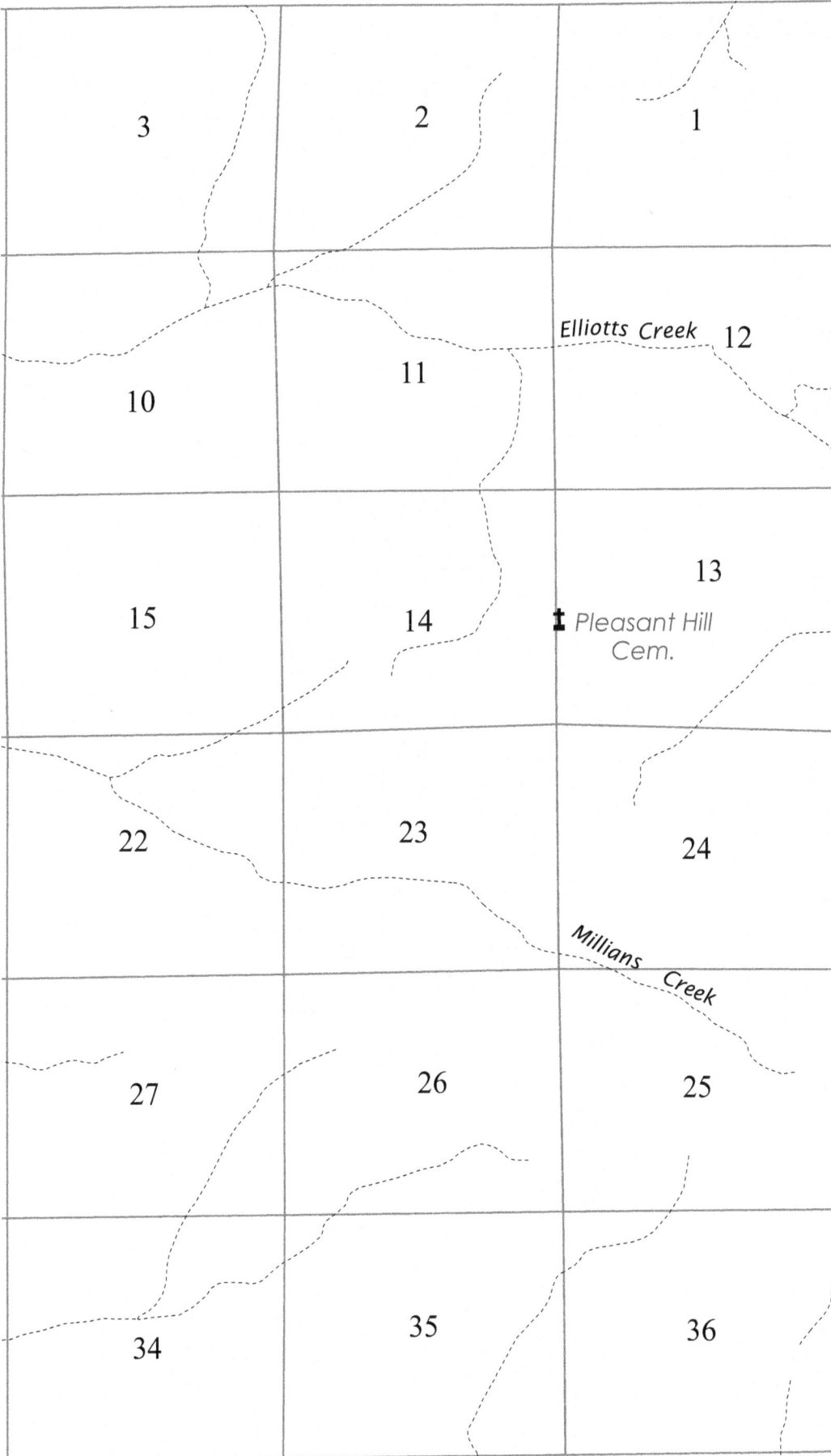

Helpful Hints

1. This Map takes a different look at the same Congressional Township displayed in the preceding two maps. It presents features that can help you better envision the historical development of the area: a) Water-bodies (lakes & ponds), b) Water-courses (rivers, streams, etc.), c) Railroads, d) City/town center-points (where they were oftentimes located when first settled), and e) Cemeteries.

2. Using this "Historical" map in tandem with this Township's Patent Map and Road Map, may lead you to some interesting discoveries. You will often find roads, towns, cemeteries, and waterways are named after nearby landowners: sometimes those names will be the ones you are researching. See how many of these research gems you can find here in Hale County.

L e g e n d

——————— Section Lines

+—+—+—+—+ Railroads

▭ Large Rivers & Bodies of Water

- - - - - - - Streams/Creeks & Small Rivers

● Cities/Towns

✝ Cemeteries

Scale: Section = 1 mile X 1 mile
(there are some exceptions)

Map Group 4: Index to Land Patents

Township 23-North Range 6-East (St Stephens)

After you locate an individual in this Index, take note of the Section and Section Part then proceed to the Land Patent map on the pages immediately following. You should have no difficulty locating the corresponding parcel of land.

The "For More Info" Column will lead you to more information about the underlying Patents. See the *Legend* at right, and the "How to Use this Book" chapter, for more information.

```
                    LEGEND
        "For More Info . . . " column
A = Authority (Legislative Act, See Appendix "A")
B = Block or Lot (location in Section unknown)
C = Cancelled Patent
F = Fractional Section
G = Group  (Multi-Patentee Patent, see Appendix "C")
V = Overlaps another Parcel
R = Re-Issued (Parcel patented more than once)

(A & G items require you to look in the Appendixes referred
to above. All other Letter-designations followed by a number
require you to locate line-items in this index that possess
the ID number found after the letter).
```

ID	Individual in Patent	Sec.	Sec. Part	Date Issued	Other Counties	For More Info . . .
743	BLOCKER, Michael P	11	NWNW	1858-06-01		A1
685	BOATNER, Isham	1	SWNE	1837-11-07		A1
588	CLEMENTS, Amanda R	36	NESW	1910-12-01		A1
693	CLEMENTS, James R	2	S½SE	1893-05-26		A2
694	" "	2	S½SW	1893-05-26		A2
716	CLEMENTS, Joseph B	2	NESE	1915-05-07		A2
633	COLBY, Charles W	26	NWNW	1910-06-23		A2
768	COLEY, Thomas J	14	SW	1903-11-24		A2
723	COLLINS, Levin	2	SWNW	1849-05-01		A1
699	DOCKERY, John	5	NESE	1834-10-16		A1
700	" "	5	NWNE	1854-07-15		A1
701	" "	5	NWNW	1854-07-15		A1
651	DOCKREY, Francis M	4	NW	1860-12-01		A1
652	DONALDSON, Francis M	30	SESE	1903-05-19		A2
741	DONOR, Mary E	6	N½NE	1892-01-18		A2
638	EGNER, David	2	NWSE	1835-10-01		A1
639	" "	2	NWSW	1839-09-20		A1
662	EGNER, George H	1	NWNW	1839-03-15		A1
663	" "	2	NESW	1839-09-20		A1
702	ELAM, John	2	NENW	1849-09-01		A1
664	FLEMING, George W	7	W½NW	1839-09-20		A1
745	FOSTER, Moses	7	SWSW	1834-10-16		A1
744	" "	18	NWNW	1839-09-20		A1
778	FOWLER, William H	18	NENE	1861-01-01		A1
779	" "	18	W½NE	1861-01-01		A1
780	" "	6	S½SE	1861-01-01		A1
781	" "	8	E½NW	1861-01-01		A1
782	" "	8	NWNW	1861-01-01		A1
619	FRIEDMAN, Bernard	28	N½SW	1888-06-09		A1 G86
620	" "	28	W½NW	1888-06-09		A1 G86
597	" "	10	E½SE	1888-06-30		A1 G86
598	" "	10	S½NW	1888-06-30		A1 G86
599	" "	10	SESW	1888-06-30		A1 G86
600	" "	10	SWNE	1888-06-30		A1 G86
601	" "	10	SWSE	1888-06-30		A1 G86
602	" "	10	W½SW	1888-06-30		A1 G86
603	" "	12	N½SE	1888-06-30		A1 G86
604	" "	12	W½	1888-06-30		A1 G86
605	" "	14	E½NE	1888-06-30		A1 G86
606	" "	14	NW	1888-06-30		A1 G86
607	" "	14	SE	1888-06-30		A1 G86
608	" "	14	SWNE	1888-06-30		A1 G86
609	" "	18	SWNW	1888-06-30		A1 G86
610	" "	20	S½SE	1888-06-30		A1 G86
611	" "	22	SENE	1888-06-30		A1 G86
612	" "	22	SESE	1888-06-30		A1 G86

ID	Individual in Patent	Sec.	Sec. Part	Date Issued	Other Counties	For More Info . . .
613	FRIEDMAN, Bernard (Cont'd)	24	E½	1888-06-30		A1 G86
614	" "	24	E½NW	1888-06-30		A1 G86
615	" "	24	E½SW	1888-06-30		A1 G86
616	" "	24	NWNW	1888-06-30		A1 G86
617	" "	26	S½SE	1888-06-30		A1 G86
618	" "	26	S½SW	1888-06-30		A1 G86
621	" "	30	E½SW	1888-06-30		A1 G86
622	" "	34	E½SW	1888-06-30		A1 G86
623	" "	34	N½NE	1888-06-30		A1 G86
624	" "	34	NW	1888-06-30		A1 G86
625	" "	34	SWNE	1888-06-30		A1 G86
626	" "	36	E½SE	1888-06-30		A1 G86
627	" "	36	N½	1888-06-30		A1 G86
628	" "	36	NWSW	1888-06-30		A1 G86
631	" "	8	NENE	1888-06-30		A1 G86
629	" "	6	N½SE	1888-09-12		A1 G86
630	" "	6	S½NE	1888-09-12		A1 G86
653	GADDIE, Gabriel	28	SENE	1860-12-01		A1
654	" "	28	SENW	1860-12-01		A1
655	GADEIL, Gabriel	26	N½NE	1860-10-01		A1
584	GEDDIE, Alexander	34	E½SE	1891-01-15		A2
585	" "	34	NWSE	1891-01-15		A2
586	" "	34	SENE	1891-01-15		A2
648	GEDDIE, Delaney	6	S½SW	1897-01-28		A2
656	GEDDIE, Gabriel	21	SWSE	1858-06-01		A1
657	" "	27	NWSW	1858-06-01		A1
658	" "	28	NWSE	1858-06-01		A1
715	GEDDIE, John T	32	SESE	1901-12-17		A2
689	GIDDIE, James D	29	W½SW	1839-09-20		A1
753	GOODWIN, Peter	11	SWSE	1858-06-01		A1
775	GREATHOUSE, William C	26	N½SE	1896-04-23		A2
776	" "	26	S½NE	1896-04-23		A2
632	GRIFFIN, Berry K	1	NENE	1850-04-01		A1
659	GRIFFIN, George A	10	E½NE	1893-05-26		A2
660	" "	10	NENW	1893-05-26		A2
661	" "	10	NWNE	1893-05-26		A2
697	GRIFFIN, John A	30	NESE	1860-12-01		A1
698	" "	30	SWSE	1860-12-01		A1
724	GRIFFIN, Lindsey G	17	NWSW	1858-06-01		A1
725	" "	18	NESW	1858-06-01		A1
726	" "	19	NENE	1858-06-01		A1
727	" "	20	NENW	1858-06-01		A1
728	" "	20	NWNE	1858-06-01		A1
742	HAMILTON, Mary J	18	NESE	1884-03-20		A1
703	HARGROVE, John	2	W½NE	1839-09-20		A1
704	" "	21	E½SW	1841-01-09		A1
691	HESTER, James G	18	NWSW	1860-10-01		A1
754	HESTER, Richard N	30	NENW	1861-07-01		A1
755	" "	30	NWNE	1861-07-01		A1
756	" "	30	S½NW	1861-07-01		A1
619	JEMISON, Robert	28	N½SW	1888-06-09		A1 G86
620	" "	28	W½NW	1888-06-09		A1 G86
597	" "	10	E½SE	1888-06-30		A1 G86
598	" "	10	S½NW	1888-06-30		A1 G86
599	" "	10	SESW	1888-06-30		A1 G86
600	" "	10	SWNE	1888-06-30		A1 G86
601	" "	10	SWSE	1888-06-30		A1 G86
602	" "	10	W½SW	1888-06-30		A1 G86
603	" "	12	N½SE	1888-06-30		A1 G86
604	" "	12	W½	1888-06-30		A1 G86
605	" "	14	E½NE	1888-06-30		A1 G86
606	" "	14	NW	1888-06-30		A1 G86
607	" "	14	SE	1888-06-30		A1 G86
608	" "	14	SWNE	1888-06-30		A1 G86
609	" "	18	SWNW	1888-06-30		A1 G86
610	" "	20	S½SE	1888-06-30		A1 G86
611	" "	22	SENE	1888-06-30		A1 G86
612	" "	22	SESE	1888-06-30		A1 G86
613	" "	24	E½	1888-06-30		A1 G86
614	" "	24	E½NW	1888-06-30		A1 G86
615	" "	24	E½SW	1888-06-30		A1 G86
616	" "	24	NWNW	1888-06-30		A1 G86
617	" "	26	S½SE	1888-06-30		A1 G86

ID	Individual in Patent	Sec.	Sec. Part	Date Issued	Other Counties	For More Info . . .
618	JEMISON, Robert (Cont'd)	26	S½SW	1888-06-30		A1 G86
621	" "	30	E½SW	1888-06-30		A1 G86
622	" "	34	E½SW	1888-06-30		A1 G86
623	" "	34	N½NE	1888-06-30		A1 G86
624	" "	34	NW	1888-06-30		A1 G86
625	" "	34	SWNE	1888-06-30		A1 G86
626	" "	36	E½SE	1888-06-30		A1 G86
627	" "	36	N½	1888-06-30		A1 G86
628	" "	36	NWSW	1888-06-30		A1 G86
631	" "	8	NENE	1888-06-30		A1 G86
629	" "	6	N½SE	1888-09-12		A1 G86
630	" "	6	S½NE	1888-09-12		A1 G86
591	JOHNSON, Austin	26	NENW	1852-01-01		A1
634	JOHNSON, Daniel J	18	SWSW	1912-11-15		A2 G158
637	JOHNSON, Daniel R	26	NWSW	1913-03-03		A2
670	JOHNSON, Horace	19	NESE	1839-09-20		A1
671	" "	19	NWSE	1839-09-20		A1
672	" "	24	NWSW	1860-12-01		A1
673	" "	24	SWNW	1860-12-01		A1
686	JOHNSON, Jacob	18	W½SE	1839-09-20		A1
687	" "	29	SWNW	1841-01-09		A1
688	" "	30	NENE	1850-09-02		A1
634	JOHNSON, Shelottie	18	SWSW	1912-11-15		A2 G158
765	JOHNSON, Stephen	19	NWNE	1858-06-01		A1
771	JOHNSON, Thomas	20	SWSW	1858-06-01		A1
787	JOHNSON, William	8	NESE	1860-10-01		A1
788	" "	8	SW	1860-10-01		A1
789	" "	8	SWNW	1860-10-01		A1
790	" "	8	W½SE	1860-10-01		A1
645	JOHNSTON, David	3	NE	1843-05-01		A1
640	" "	1	NWSE	1849-05-01		A1
641	" "	1	SENW	1849-05-01		A1
642	" "	1	SESE	1849-05-01		A1
643	" "	12	NENE	1849-05-01		A1
644	" "	2	NWNW	1849-05-01		A1
675	JOHNSTON, Howell	21	SWNE	1837-11-07		A1
784	JOHNSTON, William H	30	NWSE	1858-06-01		A1
785	" "	30	SENE	1858-06-01		A1
786	" "	30	SWNE	1858-06-01		A1
783	" "	30	NWNW	1885-05-04		A1
692	KEY, James M	31	SWSW	1858-06-01		A1
720	KNOBLOCK, Julius J	6	E½NW	1897-09-22		A2
721	" "	6	N½SW	1897-09-22		A2
594	LATNER, Barton C	34	W½SW	1891-01-15		A2
665	LEWIS, George W	6	W½NW	1889-03-16		A2
619	LOVEMAN, Emanuel	28	N½SW	1888-06-09		A1 G86
620	" "	28	W½NW	1888-06-09		A1 G86
597	" "	10	E½SE	1888-06-30		A1 G86
598	" "	10	S½NW	1888-06-30		A1 G86
599	" "	10	SESW	1888-06-30		A1 G86
600	" "	10	SWNE	1888-06-30		A1 G86
601	" "	10	SWSE	1888-06-30		A1 G86
602	" "	10	W½SW	1888-06-30		A1 G86
603	" "	12	N½SE	1888-06-30		A1 G86
604	" "	12	W½	1888-06-30		A1 G86
605	" "	14	E½NE	1888-06-30		A1 G86
606	" "	14	NW	1888-06-30		A1 G86
607	" "	14	SE	1888-06-30		A1 G86
608	" "	14	SWNE	1888-06-30		A1 G86
609	" "	18	SWNW	1888-06-30		A1 G86
610	" "	20	S½SE	1888-06-30		A1 G86
611	" "	22	SENE	1888-06-30		A1 G86
612	" "	22	SESE	1888-06-30		A1 G86
613	" "	24	E½	1888-06-30		A1 G86
614	" "	24	E½NW	1888-06-30		A1 G86
615	" "	24	E½SW	1888-06-30		A1 G86
616	" "	24	NWNW	1888-06-30		A1 G86
617	" "	26	S½SE	1888-06-30		A1 G86
618	" "	26	S½SW	1888-06-30		A1 G86
621	" "	30	E½SW	1888-06-30		A1 G86
622	" "	34	E½SW	1888-06-30		A1 G86
623	" "	34	N½NE	1888-06-30		A1 G86
624	" "	34	NW	1888-06-30		A1 G86

ID	Individual in Patent	Sec.	Sec. Part	Date Issued	Other Counties	For More Info . . .
625	LOVEMAN, Emanuel (Cont'd)	34	SWNE	1888-06-30		A1 G86
626	" "	36	E½SE	1888-06-30		A1 G86
627	" "	36	N½	1888-06-30		A1 G86
628	" "	36	NWSW	1888-06-30		A1 G86
631	" "	8	NENE	1888-06-30		A1 G86
629	" "	6	N½SE	1888-09-12		A1 G86
630	" "	6	S½NE	1888-09-12		A1 G86
760	MAXWELL, Robert	19	SESE	1849-09-01		A1
636	MCDONALD, Daniel	18	SESE	1834-10-14		A1
635	" "	17	SWSW	1834-11-04		A1
590	MCDOWALL, Archibald G	2	SENE	1858-06-01		A1
750	MCMILLIAN, Neal	20	NWNW	1834-10-21		A1
649	MCPHAIL, Duncan	8	NWNE	1834-10-21		A1
650	MCRORY, Elizur	32	SWSE	1848-07-01		A1
592	MITCHELL, Axham	22	N½NE	1880-02-20		A2
593	" "	22	N½NW	1880-02-20		A2
730	MORRISON, Malcom R	22	NWSW	1896-06-15		A2
731	" "	22	SESW	1896-06-15		A2
732	" "	22	SWSE	1896-06-15		A2
733	" "	22	SWSW	1896-06-15		A2
751	MORRISON, Norman	36	S½SW	1899-02-06		A2
752	" "	36	W½SE	1899-02-06		A2
706	ORMON, John	12	W½NE	1860-12-01		A1
705	" "	12	SENE	1861-07-01		A1
696	OWENS, Jemison	34	SWSE	1860-10-01		A1
757	OWENS, Robert A	20	E½SW	1890-03-19		A2
758	" "	20	NWSE	1890-03-19		A2
667	PEIRCE, Gordon	9	E½NE	1832-01-10		A1
762	PERRY, Samuel C	32	W½NW	1860-10-01		A1
589	PHARES, Anderson C	28	NENE	1906-07-21		A1
676	PHARES, Isaac	20	NWSW	1860-10-01		A1
679	" "	26	SWNW	1860-10-01		A1
677	" "	26	NESW	1860-12-01		A1
678	" "	26	SENW	1860-12-01		A1
769	PHARES, Thomas J	28	S½SE	1891-06-30		A2
770	" "	28	S½SW	1891-06-30		A2
680	PHARRES, Isaac	19	E½NW	1858-06-01		A1
681	" "	19	NESW	1858-06-01		A1
682	" "	19	S½NE	1858-06-01		A1
683	" "	19	SWSE	1858-06-01		A1
684	" "	20	SWNW	1858-06-01		A1
791	PHIPPS, William	15	SWNE	1853-08-01		A1
793	" "	22	SENW	1858-06-01		A1
792	" "	22	NESW	1860-10-01		A1
668	PIERCE, Gordon	28	NENW	1837-11-07		A1
669	" "	28	W½NE	1837-11-07		A1
761	RAINNER, Ruffin	13	SWNE	1860-04-02		A1
595	RASSER, Benjamin	10	NWNW	1834-10-16		A1
596	" "	4	SESE	1834-10-16		A1
711	RATLIFF, John	8	SENE	1837-11-07		A1
710	" "	5	NWSE	1839-09-20		A1
707	" "	22	N½SE	1858-06-01		A1
708	" "	23	E½SW	1858-06-01		A1
709	" "	23	NWSW	1858-06-01		A1
729	RATLIFF, Lorenzo M	5	NENE	1854-07-15		A1
719	ROSSER, Josiah	9	SWNW	1839-09-20		A1
713	SATTERWHITE, John	2	NENE	1839-09-20		A1
714	SHAMBLIN, John	20	NENE	1839-09-20		A1
748	SIMMONS, Nancy	18	SESW	1860-12-01		A1
587	SPENCER, Alexander	8	SWNE	1839-09-20		A1
749	SUMMERS, Nancy	18	E½NW	1860-10-01		A1
690	SUMNERS, James D	4	SW	1891-06-30		A2
766	SUMNERS, Thomas B	10	NESW	1908-10-29		A2
767	" "	10	NWSE	1908-10-29		A2
695	TERRY, James W	32	N½NE	1891-06-30		A2
772	TERRY, Thomas S	32	E½NW	1890-03-19		A2
773	" "	32	S½NE	1890-03-19		A2
759	THOMPSON, Robert A	18	SENE	1884-03-20		A1
763	THOMPSON, Samuel O	4	NESE	1893-07-19		A2
646	TIDMORE, David	32	E½SW	1860-10-01		A1
647	" "	32	N½SE	1860-10-01		A1
712	TINGLE, John S	12	S½SE	1861-07-01		A1
764	TUBB, Samuel	3	W½SW	1839-09-20		A1

ID	Individual in Patent	Sec.	Sec. Part	Date Issued	Other Counties	For More Info . . .
777	TUBB, William E	8	SESE	1837-04-01		A1
747	WEBSTER, Moses	15	NWNW	1834-10-16		A1
746	WEBSTER, Moses S	22	SWNE	1839-03-15		A1
794	WEBSTER, William	21	SENW	1834-10-16		A1
722	WEDGWORTH, Larkin	28	NESE	1839-09-20		A1
717	WEST, Joseph D	5	SWNW	1839-09-20		A1
734	WILSON, Margaret S	20	NESE	1904-07-02		A2
735	" "	20	SENE	1904-07-02		A2
736	" "	20	SENW	1904-07-02		A2
737	" "	20	SWNE	1904-07-02		A2
674	WRIGHT, Horatia W	4	NWNE	1858-06-01		A1
738	WRIGHT, Margia	4	E½NE	1891-06-29		A2
739	" "	4	NWSE	1891-06-29		A2
740	" "	4	SWNE	1891-06-29		A2
666	WYATT, Giles H	32	W½SW	1860-10-01		A1
718	WYATT, Joseph T	30	W½SW	1891-01-15		A2
774	YOUNG, William B	1	NESE	1839-09-20		A1

Patent Map

T23-N R6-E
St Stephens Meridian

Map Group 4

Township Statistics

Parcels Mapped	:	211
Number of Patents	:	146
Number of Individuals	:	105
Patentees Identified	:	102
Number of Surnames	:	72
Multi-Patentee Parcels	:	36
Oldest Patent Date	:	1/10/1832
Most Recent Patent	:	5/7/1915
Block/Lot Parcels	:	0
Parcels Re - Issued	:	0
Parcels that Overlap	:	0
Cities and Towns	:	1
Cemeteries	:	2

Copyright 2007 Boyd IT, Inc. All Rights Reserved

Section 6
LEWIS George W 1889
KNOBLOCK Julius J 1897
DONOR Mary E 1892
FRIEDMAN [86] Bernard 1888
KNOBLOCK Julius J 1897
FRIEDMAN [86] Bernard 1888
GEDDIE Delaney 1897
FOWLER William H 1861

Section 5
DOCKERY John 1854
DOCKERY John 1854
RATLIFF Lorenzo M 1854
WEST Joseph D 1839
RATLIFF John 1839
DOCKERY John 1834

Section 4
DOCKREY Francis M 1860
WRIGHT Horatia W 1858
WRIGHT Margia 1891
WRIGHT Margia 1891
SUMNERS James D 1891
WRIGHT Margia 1891
THOMPSON Samuel O 1893
RASSER Benjamin 1834

Section 7
FLEMING George W 1839
FOSTER Moses 1834

Section 8
FOWLER William H 1861
JOHNSON William 1860
FOWLER William H 1861
MCPHAIL Duncan 1834
FRIEDMAN [86] Bernard 1888
SPENCER Alexander 1839
RATLIFF John 1837
JOHNSON William 1860
JOHNSON William 1860
JOHNSON William 1860
TUBB William E 1837

Section 9
ROSSER Josiah 1839
PEIRCE Gordon 1832

Section 18
FOSTER Moses 1839
SUMMERS Nancy 1860
FOWLER William H 1861
FRIEDMAN [86] Bernard 1888
FOWLER William H 1861
THOMPSON Robert A 1884
HESTER James G 1860
GRIFFIN Lindsey G 1858
JOHNSON Jacob 1839
HAMILTON Mary J 1884
GRIFFIN Lindsey G 1858
JOHNSON [158] Daniel J 1912
SIMMONS Nancy 1860
MCDONALD Daniel 1834

Section 17
GRIFFIN Lindsey G 1858
MCDONALD Daniel 1834

Section 16

Section 19
PHARRES Isaac 1858
JOHNSON Stephen 1858
GRIFFIN Lindsey G 1858
PHARRES Isaac 1858
PHARRES Isaac 1858
JOHNSON Horace 1839
JOHNSON Horace 1839
PHARRES Isaac 1858
MAXWELL Robert 1849

Section 20
MCMILLIAN Neal 1834
GRIFFIN Lindsey G 1858
GRIFFIN Lindsey G 1858
SHAMBLIN John 1839
PHARRES Isaac 1858
WILSON Margaret S 1904
WILSON Margaret S 1904
WILSON Margaret S 1904
PHARES Isaac 1860
OWENS Robert A 1890
WILSON Margaret S 1904
JOHNSON Thomas 1858
OWENS Robert A 1890
FRIEDMAN [86] Bernard 1888

Section 21
WEBSTER William 1834
JOHNSTON Howell 1837
HARGROVE John 1841
GEDDIE Gabriel 1858

Section 30
JOHNSTON William H 1885
HESTER Richard N 1861
HESTER Richard N 1861
JOHNSON Jacob 1850
HESTER Richard N 1861
JOHNSTON William H 1858
JOHNSTON William H 1858
WYATT Joseph T 1891
JOHNSTON William H 1858
GRIFFIN John A 1860
FRIEDMAN [86] Bernard 1888
GRIFFIN John A 1860
DONALDSON Francis M 1903

Section 29
JOHNSON Jacob 1841
GIDDIE James D 1839

Section 28
FRIEDMAN [86] Bernard 1888
PIERCE Gordon 1837
PIERCE Gordon 1837
PHARES Anderson C 1906
GADDIE Gabriel 1860
GADDIE Gabriel 1860
FRIEDMAN [86] Bernard 1888
GEDDIE Gabriel 1858
WEDGWORTH Larkin 1839
PHARES Thomas J 1891
PHARES Thomas J 1891

Section 31
KEY James M 1858

Section 32
PERRY Samuel C 1860
TERRY Thomas S 1890
TERRY James W 1891
TERRY Thomas S 1890
TIDMORE David 1860
WYATT Giles H 1860
TIDMORE David 1860
MCRORY Elizur 1848
GEDDIE John T 1901

Section 33

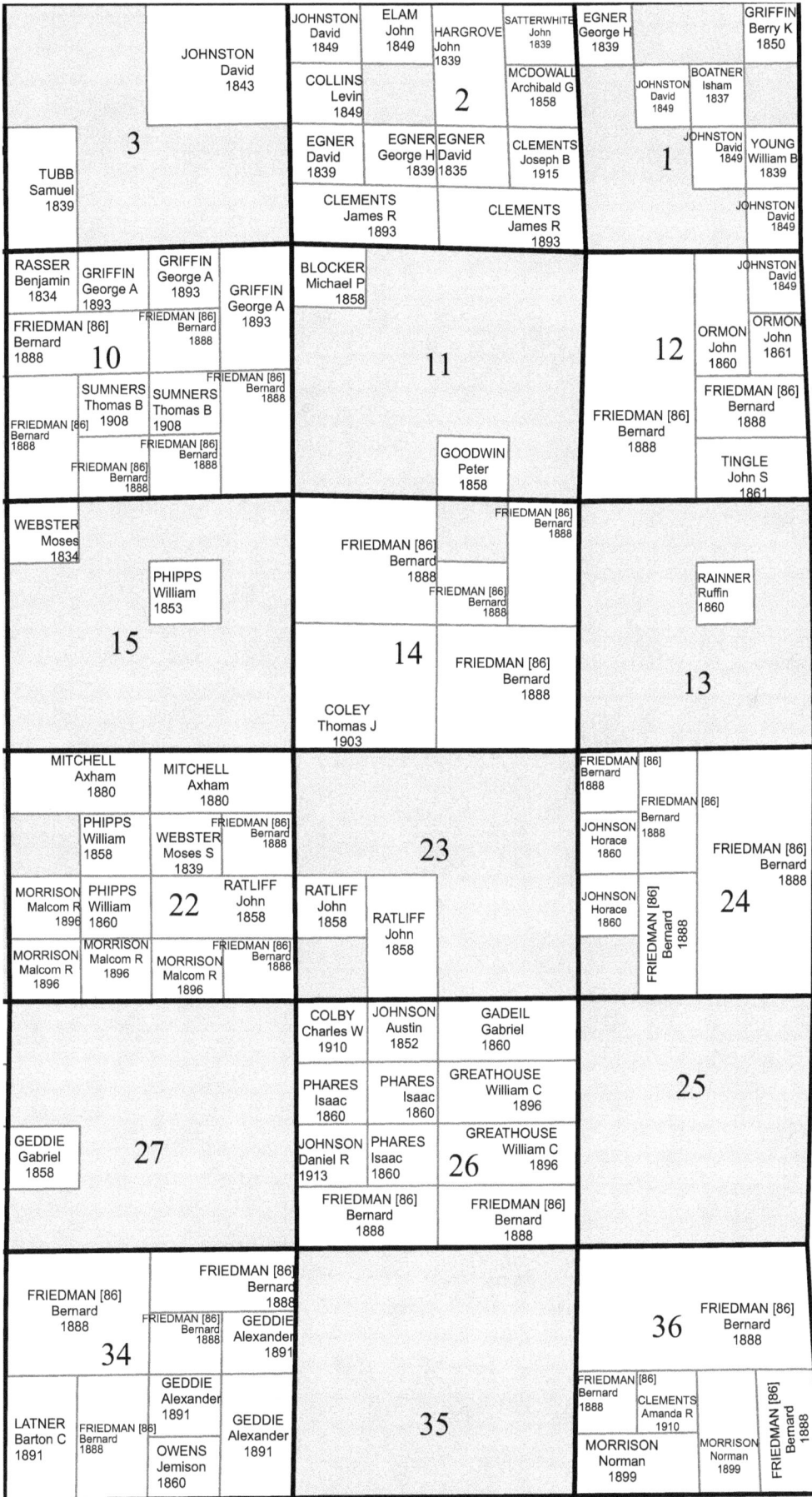

Helpful Hints

1. This Map's INDEX can be found on the preceding pages.

2. Refer to Map "C" to see where this Township lies within Hale County, Alabama.

3. Numbers within square brackets [ ] denote a multi-patentee land parcel (multi-owner). Refer to Appendix "C" for a full list of members in this group.

4. Areas that look to be crowded with Patentees usually indicate multiple sales of the same parcel (Re-issues) or Overlapping parcels. See this Township's Index for an explanation of these and other circumstances that might explain "odd" groupings of Patentees on this map.

Legend

Patent Boundary

Section Boundary

No Patents Found (or Outside County)

1., 2., 3., ... Lot Numbers (when beside a name)

[ ] Group Number (see Appendix "C")

Scale: Section = 1 mile X 1 mile (generally, with some exceptions)

83

Road Map

T23-N R6-E
St Stephens Meridian

Map Group 4

Cities & Towns
Phipps

Cemeteries
China Grove Cemetery
Grimes Cemetery

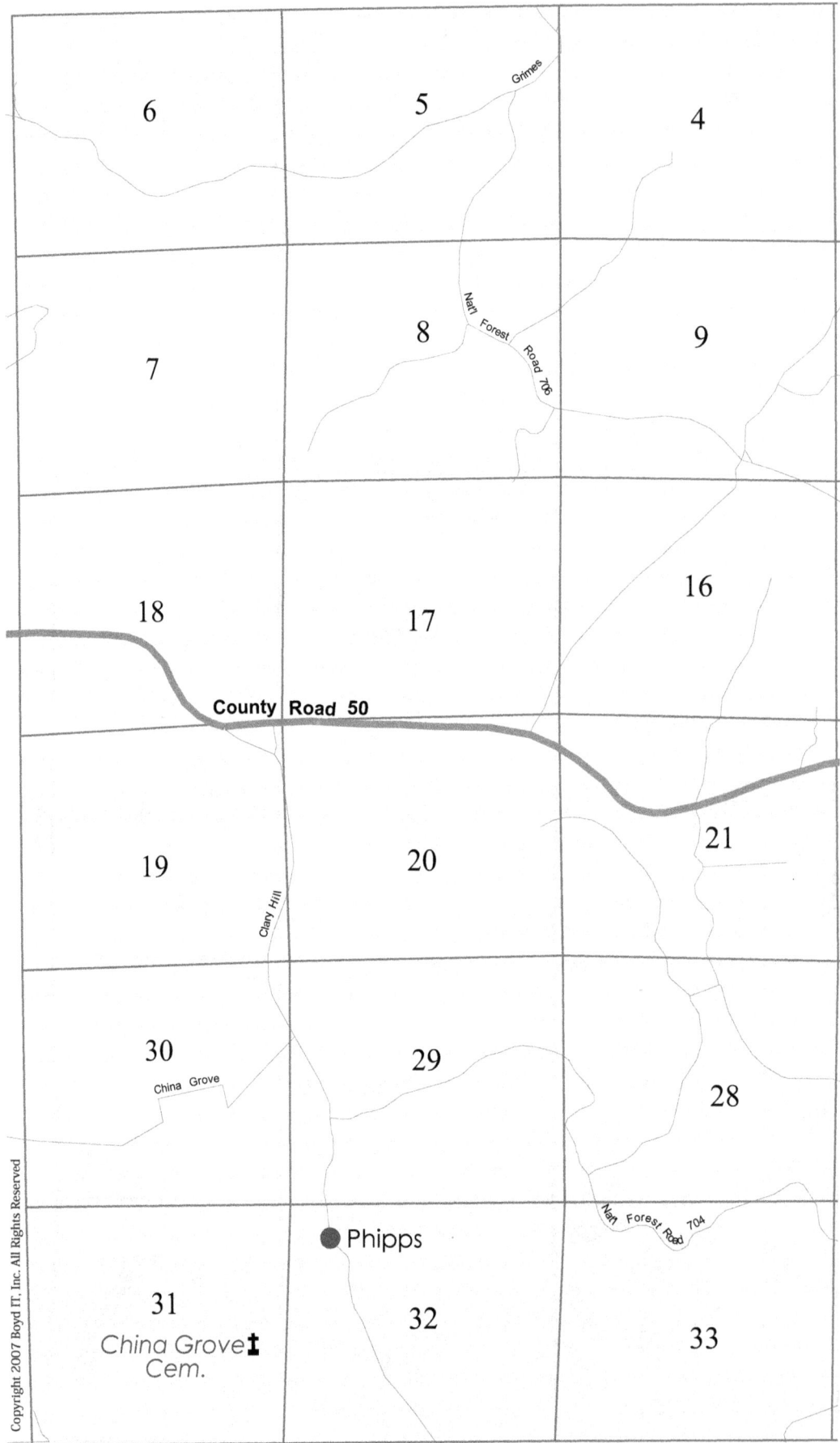

6

5

4

Grimes

7

8

Nat'l Forest Road 706

9

18

17

16

County Road 50

19

Clary Hill

20

21

30

China Grove

29

28

31

China Grove Cem.

● Phipps

32

Nat'l Forest Road 704

33

3

2

1

Nat'l Forest Road 705

10

11

12

Nat'l Forest Road 710

✝ *Grimes Cem.*

15

14

13

County Road 50

22

23

24

Nat'l Forest Road 718 A

26

Eagle

25

Nat'l Forest Road 704 B

Nat'l Forest Road 708

27

Nat'l Forest Road 718 B

34

35

County Road 49

36

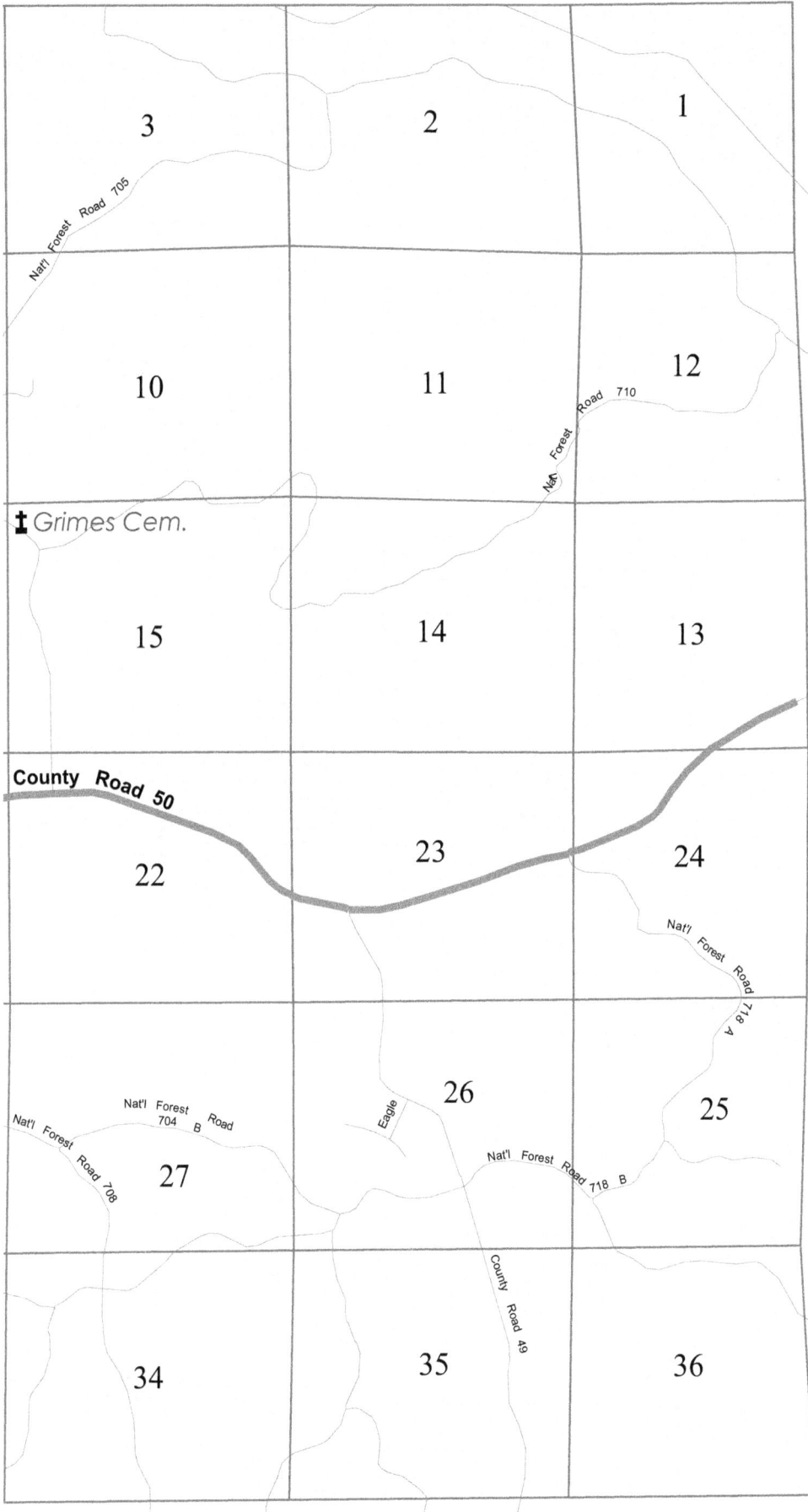

Helpful Hints

1. This road map has a number of uses, but primarily it is to help you: a) find the present location of land owned by your ancestors (at least the general area), b) find cemeteries and city-centers, and c) estimate the route/roads used by Census-takers & tax-assessors.

2. If you plan to travel to Hale County to locate cemeteries or land parcels, please pick up a modern travel map for the area before you do. Mapping old land parcels on modern maps is not as exact a science as you might think. Just the slightest variations in public land survey coordinates, estimates of parcel boundaries, or road-map deviations can greatly alter a map's representation of how a road either does or doesn't cross a particular parcel of land.

Legend

————	Section Lines
═══	Interstates
▬▬▬	Highways
————	Other Roads
●	Cities/Towns
✝	Cemeteries

Scale: Section = 1 mile X 1 mile
(generally, with some exceptions)

Historical Map

T23-N R6-E
St Stephens Meridian

Map Group 4

___Cities & Towns___
Phipps

___Cemeteries___
China Grove Cemetery
Grimes Cemetery

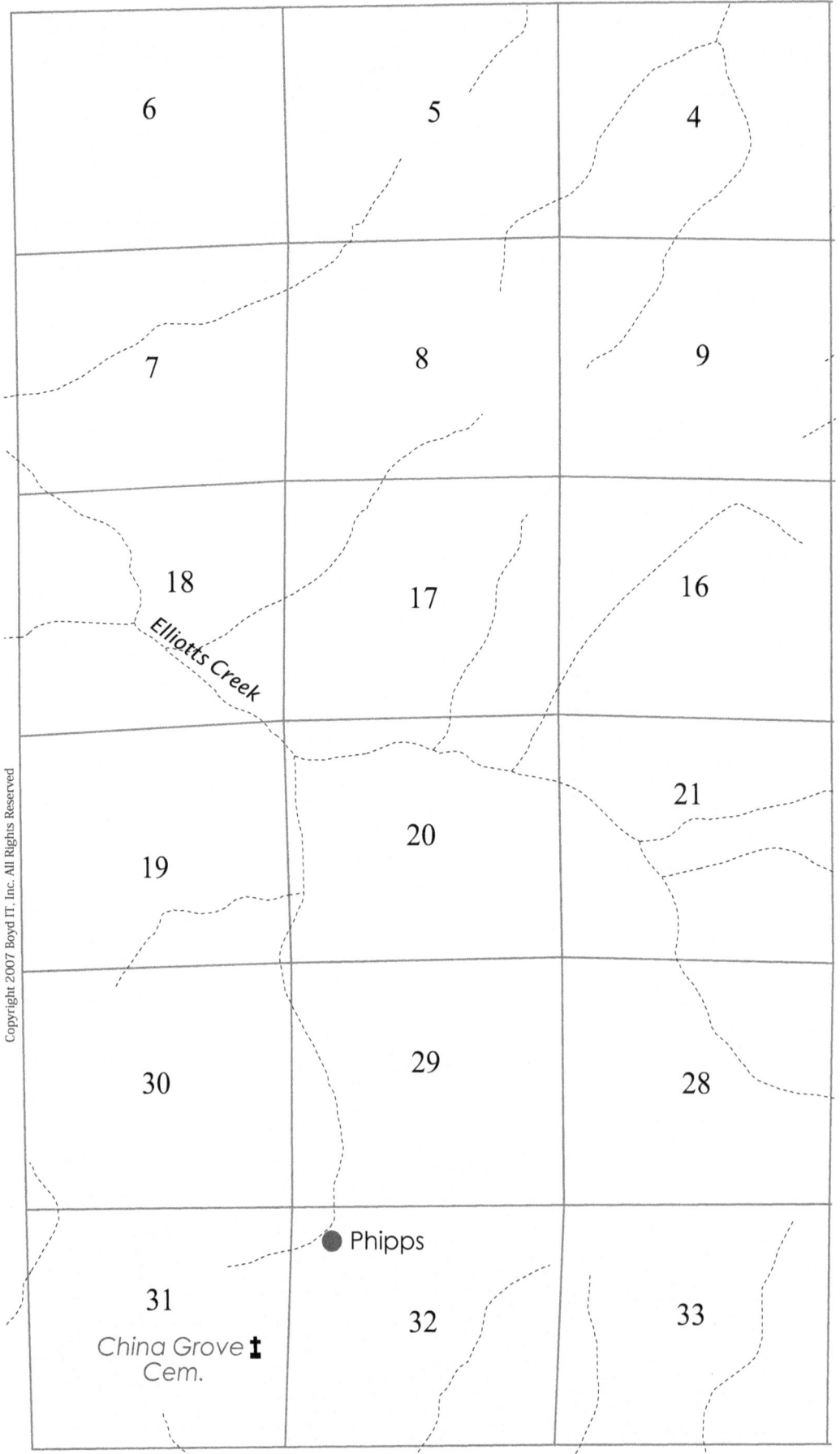

6

5

4

7

8

9

18

Elliotts Creek

17

16

19

20

21

30

29

28

● Phipps

31

32

33

China Grove
Cem.

3

2

1

South Sandy Creek

10

11

12

✝ Grimes Cem.

15

14

13

Elliotts Creek

22

23

24

27

26

25

34

35

36

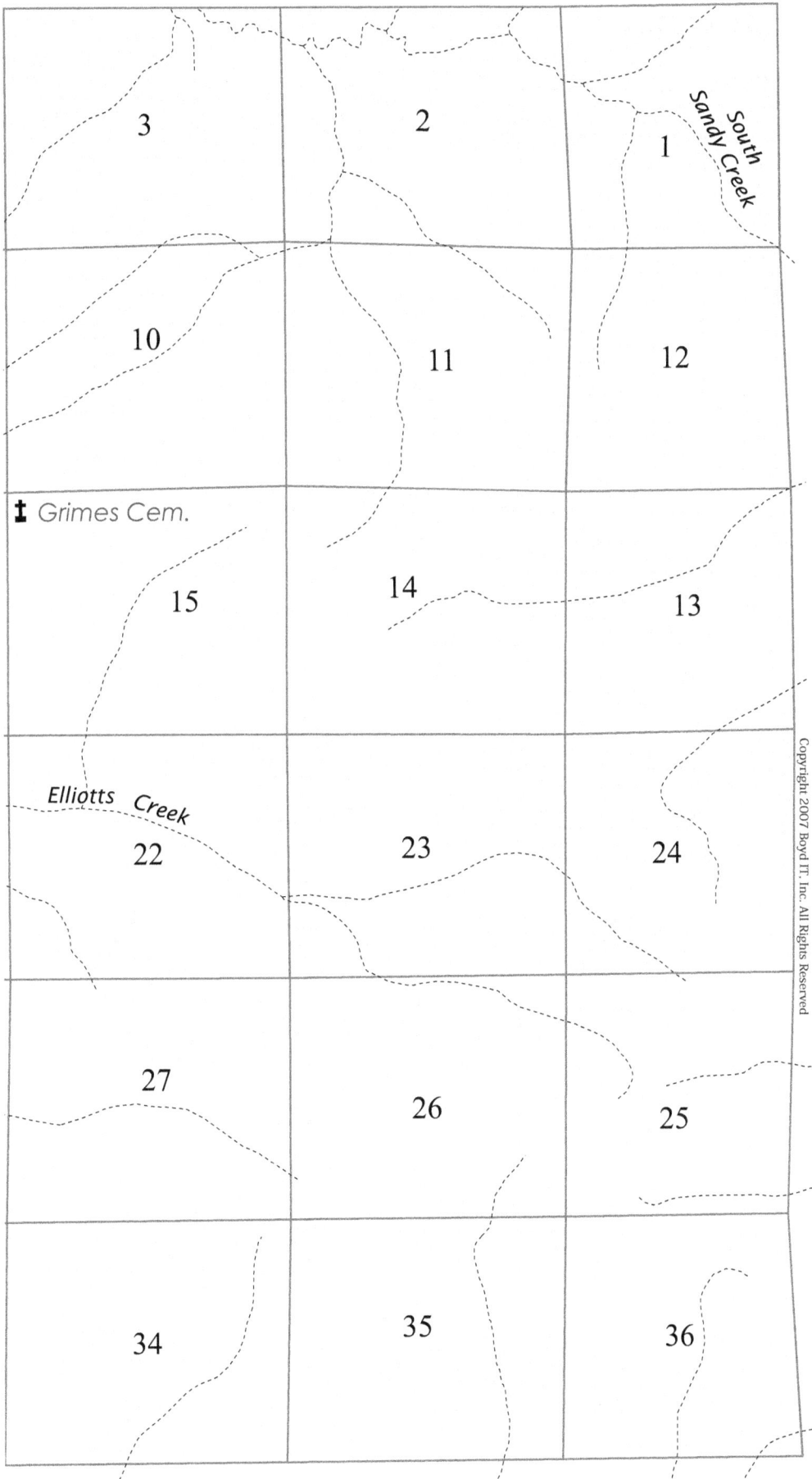

Helpful Hints

1. This Map takes a different look at the same Congressional Township displayed in the preceding two maps. It presents features that can help you better envision the historical development of the area: a) Water-bodies (lakes & ponds), b) Water-courses (rivers, streams, etc.), c) Railroads, d) City/town center-points (where they were oftentimes located when first settled), and e) Cemeteries.

2. Using this "Historical" map in tandem with this Township's Patent Map and Road Map, may lead you to some interesting discoveries. You will often find roads, towns, cemeteries, and waterways are named after nearby landowners: sometimes those names will be the ones you are researching. See how many of these research gems you can find here in Hale County.

Legend

———————	Section Lines
─┼─┼─┼─┼─┼─	Railroads
▭	Large Rivers & Bodies of Water
- - - - - - -	Streams/Creeks & Small Rivers
●	Cities/Towns
✝	Cemeteries

Scale: Section = 1 mile X 1 mile
(there are some exceptions)

Map Group 5: Index to Land Patents

Township 22-North Range 3-East (St Stephens)

After you locate an individual in this Index, take note of the Section and Section Part then proceed to the Land Patent map on the pages immediately following. You should have no difficulty locating the corresponding parcel of land.

The "For More Info" Column will lead you to more information about the underlying Patents. See the *Legend* at right, and the "How to Use this Book" chapter, for more information.

```
                    LEGEND
        "For More Info . . . " column
A = Authority (Legislative Act, See Appendix "A")
B = Block or Lot (location in Section unknown)
C = Cancelled Patent
F = Fractional Section
G = Group  (Multi-Patentee Patent, see Appendix "C")
V = Overlaps another Parcel
R = Re-Issued (Parcel patented more than once)

(A & G items require you to look in the Appendixes referred
to above. All other Letter-designations followed by a number
require you to locate line-items in this index that possess
the ID number found after the letter).
```

ID	Individual in Patent	Sec.	Sec. Part	Date Issued	Other Counties	For More Info . . .
881	ANDERS, James	13	W½SW	1829-03-06		A1
981	ANDERSON, Thomas J	13	W½SE	1824-10-20		A1
995	" "	24	E½NE	1824-10-20		A1 G7
996	" "	24	W½NE	1824-10-20		A1 G7
983	" "	25	E½NE	1824-10-20		A1
984	" "	25	E½NW	1824-10-20		A1
985	" "	25	E½SE	1824-10-20		A1
986	" "	25	W½NE	1824-10-20		A1
987	" "	25	W½SE	1824-10-20		A1
988	" "	25	W½SW	1824-10-20		A1
991	" "	26	W½NE	1824-10-20		A1
992	" "	26	W½SE	1824-10-20		A1
993	" "	34	E½NE	1825-04-25		A1
994	" "	34	W½NE	1825-04-25		A1
989	" "	26	E½NE	1825-05-25		A1
990	" "	26	E½SE	1825-05-25		A1
982	" "	24	E½SE	1825-09-15		A1
894	BARTEE, James H	20	NESW	1851-03-01		A1
895	" "	20	S½NE	1858-08-20		A1
896	" "	21	W½NW	1858-08-20		A1
927	BARTEE, John L	20	N½NE	1858-08-20		A1
928	" "	20	N½SE	1858-08-20		A1
997	BARTEE, Thomas W	21	S½NE	1897-05-20		A1
998	" "	22	SWNW	1897-05-20		A1
938	BRODNAX, John S B	20	SENW	1916-03-14		A1
796	BROWN, Alexander	28	SWSE	1837-03-30		A1
795	" "	28	SESW	1837-05-15		A1
952	BROWN, Kembron	29	SWSW	1839-05-01		A1
956	BURRELL, Lieuvirt	22	SESE	1914-05-13		A1
921	CARDER, John	26	E½NW	1825-09-15		A1
920	"	23	SE	1826-06-10		A1
964	CARVER, Pullum	7	W½SW	1826-02-01	Greene	A1
1004	CHILES, Thompson	8	S½NE	1825-09-15	Greene	A1 F
1002	" "	18	N½SW	1826-02-01	Greene	A1 F
1003	" "	19	NE	1835-09-28	Greene	A1 F
1000	" "	17	NW	1837-03-30	Greene	A1 F
1001	" "	17	NWSE	1837-08-01	Greene	A1
1007	CHILES, William	19	N½NW	1824-10-20	Greene	A1 F
1008	" "	19	S½NW	1825-09-15	Greene	A1 F
918	CLEMENTS, Jesse B	34	E½NW	1825-05-25		A1 G59
919	" "	34	W½NW	1825-05-25		A1 G59
935	COLINS, John R	28	NENW	1897-03-02		A1
936	" "	29	NENE	1897-03-02		A1
840	COLLINS, Daniel R	29	SWNE	1858-08-20		A1
937	COLLINS, John R	28	SWNW	1858-08-20		A1
939	COLLINS, John S	29	SESE	1835-09-28		A1

ID	Individual in Patent	Sec.	Sec. Part	Date Issued	Other Counties	For More Info . . .
950	COLLINS, Joshua C	28	NWNW	1837-11-02		A1
951	" "	33	NWNE	1837-11-02		A1
1027	COLLINS, Williamson	28	NWSW	1897-01-15		A1
1009	COMPANY, Sims Banks And	13	E½SE	1824-10-20		A1 G157
843	" "	24	E½NW	1824-10-20		A1 G221
844	" "	24	W½NW	1824-10-20		A1 G221
1010	" "	25	E½SW	1824-10-20		A1 G157
1011	" "	34	E½SE	1825-04-25		A1 G157
1012	" "	34	W½SE	1825-04-25		A1 G157
867	COOPE, George	36	W½NW	1825-05-25		A1 G67
869	COOPER, George	36	E½NW	1825-05-25		A1 G69
868	" "	36	W½NE	1825-05-25		A1 G68
891	CUMMINGS, James	23	W½NW	1835-09-25		A1
885	" "	14	NESW	1835-09-28		A1
890	" "	23	SENW	1835-09-28		A1
888	" "	22	S½NE	1837-05-15		A1
886	" "	22	N½SE	1858-08-20		A1
887	" "	22	NESW	1858-08-20		A1
889	" "	22	SENW	1858-08-20		A1
922	DAVIS, John	29	NWSE	1840-11-10		A1
849	DEW, Duncan	32	E½NE	1837-05-15		A1
850	" "	33	E½NW	1837-05-15		A1
841	DIAL, David M	35	E½NE	1825-05-25		A1 R826
923	EDMINSTON, John	13	W½NW	1831-08-25		A1
930	EDMINSTON, John M	23	NENW	1835-10-20		A1
924	EDMISTON, John	14	SESE	1835-09-28		A1 V858
931	EDMONDSTON, John M	14	SESW	1837-08-01		A1
932	" "	14	W½SW	1837-08-01		A1
893	EDMUNDSTON, James	15	NWSE	1837-08-01		A1
845	GIBBS, Dixon	21	NWSW	1840-11-10		A1
798	GODDEN, Amzi	29	E½SW	1840-11-10		A1
799	" "	32	E½SE	1840-11-10		A1
800	" "	32	W½SE	1840-11-10		A1
961	HAGOOD, Parten	15	NENE	1837-08-01		A1
962	HAGOOD, Partin	15	SENE	1840-11-10		A1
963	HAGOOD, Portin	14	NENE	1835-10-20		A1
802	HANNA, Andrew M	32	E½NW	1840-11-10		A1 G135
801	" "	32	N½SW	1840-11-10		A1
803	" "	32	S½SW	1840-11-10		A1 G135
804	" "	32	W½NE	1840-11-10		A1 G135
971	HANNA, Robert C	24	E½SW	1831-09-01		A1
972	" "	24	W½SE	1835-10-28		A1
970	" "	23	SW	1837-05-15		A1
802	" "	32	E½NW	1840-11-10		A1 G135
803	" "	32	S½SW	1840-11-10		A1 G135
804	" "	32	W½NE	1840-11-10		A1 G135
968	HATTER, Richard	34	E½SW	1825-04-25		A1
969	" "	34	W½SW	1825-04-25		A1
918	" "	34	E½NW	1825-05-25		A1 G59
919	" "	34	W½NW	1825-05-25		A1 G59
967	" "	33	W½SE	1826-02-01		A1
965	" "	33	NESE	1835-09-28		A1
966	" "	33	SWNE	1835-09-28		A1
897	HOLLEY, James	1	NW	1835-09-25		A1
899	" "	2	E½NE	1835-09-25		A1
898	" "	1	W½SE	1837-05-15		A1 R847
977	HUBBARD, Samuel	33	W½SW	1837-05-15		A1 G149
947	JACKSON, Joseph	36	E½SW	1825-05-25		A1 G152
900	JEFFRIES, James	20	W½NW	1858-08-20		A1
1009	JIMISON, William	13	E½SE	1824-10-20		A1 G157
1010	" "	25	E½SW	1824-10-20		A1 G157
1011	" "	34	E½SE	1825-04-25		A1 G157
1012	" "	34	W½SE	1825-04-25		A1 G157
810	JONES, Cadwallader	20	S½SE	1908-08-03		A1
811	" "	20	SESW	1908-08-03		A1
901	JONES, James	11	NE	1826-02-01		A1 G160
902	" "	11	NW	1826-02-01		A1 G160
903	" "	12	NW	1826-02-01		A1 G160
904	" "	2	SW	1826-02-01		A1 G160 F
905	" "	2	W½SE	1826-02-01		A1 G160 F
901	JONES, John	11	NE	1826-02-01		A1 G160
902	" "	11	NW	1826-02-01		A1 G160
903	" "	12	NW	1826-02-01		A1 G160

ID	Individual in Patent	Sec.	Sec. Part	Date Issued	Other Counties	For More Info . . .
904	JONES, John (Cont'd)	2	SW	1826-02-01		A1 G160 F
905	" "	2	W½SE	1826-02-01		A1 G160 F
901	JONES, Thomas	11	NE	1826-02-01		A1 G160
902	" "	11	NW	1826-02-01		A1 G160
903	" "	12	NW	1826-02-01		A1 G160
904	" "	2	SW	1826-02-01		A1 G160 F
905	" "	2	W½SE	1826-02-01		A1 G160 F
901	JONES, William	11	NE	1826-02-01		A1 G160
902	" "	11	NW	1826-02-01		A1 G160
903	" "	12	NW	1826-02-01		A1 G160
904	" "	2	SW	1826-02-01		A1 G160 F
905	" "	2	W½SE	1826-02-01		A1 G160 F
1015	" "	12	E½SE	1827-02-10		A1
1017	" "	2	W½NW	1827-02-10		A1
1014	" "	12	E½NE	1829-06-01		A1
1018	" "	3	E½	1830-12-01	Greene	A1 F
1016	" "	12	W½NE	1837-03-20		A1
1013	" "	1	E½SE	1837-03-30		A1
915	LASETER, Jeremiah	28	SWNE	1840-11-10		A1
916	" "	28	SWSW	1840-11-10		A1
917	LASTER, Jeremiah	32	W½NW	1840-11-10		A1
933	LEWIS, John M	25	W½NW	1826-02-01		A1
973	LEWIS, Robert C	15	E½SE	1837-03-30		A1
975	" "	22	NENE	1837-03-30		A1
976	" "	22	NWNE	1837-08-01		A1
974	" "	15	SWSE	1858-08-20		A1
977	LEWIS, Rufus G	33	W½SW	1837-05-15		A1 G149
1022	LEWIS, William M	31	E½	1837-03-30	Greene	A1 F
864	LLOYD, Elisha	33	NWNW	1837-05-15		A1
865	" "	33	SWNW	1837-05-15		A1
814	LOGAN, Clemens	14	W½NW	1837-03-30		A1
813	" "	10	S½SE	1840-11-10	Greene	A1
815	LOGAN, Clements	11	NESE	1835-09-28		A1
879	LOGAN, Isaac	28	E½NE	1825-05-25		A1
877	" "	27	NWNW	1835-10-28		A1
876	" "	27	NENW	1837-03-30		A1
878	" "	27	S½NW	1837-05-15		A1
875	" "	22	W½SW	1840-11-10		A1
882	LOGAN, James C	10	NE	1825-05-25	Greene	A1 F
883	" "	9	E½S½	1826-06-10	Greene	A1 F
884	" "	9	SW	1837-08-01	Greene	A1 R943
892	LOGAN, James D	22	NWNW	1852-01-01		A1
929	LOGAN, John L	10	SW	1835-10-01	Greene	A1 F
954	LOGAN, Leroy	15	E½NW	1843-02-01		A1
955	" "	15	NWNE	1843-02-01		A1
959	LOGAN, Matilda H	21	SESE	1837-11-02		A1
1006	LOGAN, William C	13	W½NE	1830-12-15		A1
1005	" "	13	NENW	1835-10-20		A1
1029	LOGAN, Willis	15	SWNE	1835-10-20		A1
1028	" "	14	NWNE	1837-03-30		A1
953	LUMMAS, Lavinia	20	NWSW	1837-11-02		A1
1019	LUMMUS, William	19	SE	1835-09-28	Greene	A1
1020	" "	20	SWSW	1835-09-28		A1
1021	" "	29	SWSE	1837-03-30		A1
945	MAY, Jonathan	35	E½SW	1825-05-25		A1
946	" "	35	W½SW	1825-05-25		A1
817	MCGEHEE, Dabney	10	NW	1825-04-25	Greene	A1 F
816	" "	10		1831-01-03	Greene	A1 F
818	" "	3	A	1837-03-30	Greene	A1 F
823	" "	9	N½NW	1837-03-30	Greene	A1
819	" "	3	SENW	1837-11-02	Greene	A1
820	" "	3	SESW	1837-11-02	Greene	A1
821	" "	3	W½NW	1837-11-02	Greene	A1
822	" "	3	W½SW	1837-11-02	Greene	A1
934	MCGEHEE, John M	1	E½NE	1858-08-20		A1
907	MCGRUDER, James	28	SENW	1902-02-03		A2
948	MERIWEATHER, Joseph	18	W½NW	1824-10-20	Greene	A1
1031	MERIWEATHER, Zachariah	17	E½NE	1837-11-02	Greene	A1
1032	" "	17	E½SE	1837-11-02	Greene	A1
1033	" "	17	SWSE	1837-11-02	Greene	A1
1035	MERIWEATHER, Zachry	17	N½	1824-10-20	Greene	A1 F
1036	" "	17	SW	1824-10-20	Greene	A1
1037	" "	18	E½NW	1824-10-20	Greene	A1 F

ID	Individual in Patent	Sec.	Sec. Part	Date Issued	Other Counties	For More Info . . .
1038	MERIWEATHER, Zachry (Cont'd)	18	N½	1824-10-20	Greene	A1 F
1039	" "	18	S½SW	1824-10-20	Greene	A1 F
1040	" "	7	S½	1824-10-20	Greene	A1 F
1043	" "	8	N½SW	1824-10-20	Greene	A1 F
1044	" "	8	S½	1824-10-20	Greene	A1 F
1045	" "	8	S½SW	1824-10-20	Greene	A1
1046	" "	8	SW	1824-10-20	Greene	A1 F
1041	" "	7	SE	1825-04-20	Greene	A1 F
1042	" "	7	W½NE	1825-04-20	Greene	A1 F
1047	" "	8	W½NW	1825-04-20	Greene	A1 F
926	MERIWETHER, John H	20	NENW	1837-11-02		A1
1030	MERRIWEATHER, Willis	19	S½	1826-08-20	Greene	A1 F
1034	MERRIWEATHER, Zachariah	7	E½SW	1837-03-30	Greene	A1
1048	MERRIWEATHER, Zachry	17	W½	1825-09-15	Greene	A1 F
1049	"	8	N½NE	1825-09-15	Greene	A1 F
1050	MERRYWEATHER, Zachry	18	E½	1825-04-25	Greene	A1 F
1051	" "	18	N½NE	1825-04-25	Greene	A1
1052	" "	18	S½NE	1825-04-25	Greene	A1 F
880	MITCHELL, Isaac W	33	E½SW	1826-12-20		A1
906	MITCHELL, James L	33	E½NE	1825-09-15		A1
925	PATTERSON, John G	28	NWSE	1837-03-15		A1
812	PATTISON, Claiborne	28	NESW	1837-05-15		A1
824	PRICKET, Dabney	35	E½SE	1825-05-25		A1 G213
826	PRICKETT, Dabney	35	E½NE	1825-05-25		A1 G214 R841
825	" "	35	E½NW	1825-05-25		A1
827	PUCKETT, Dabney	26	E½SW	1824-10-20		A1
828	" "	35	W½NE	1824-10-20		A1
829	" "	36	W½SW	1824-10-20		A1
805	PURNELL, Benjamin	29	NESE	1840-11-10		A1
806	" "	30	NENE	1897-02-17	Greene	A1
947	ROE, Churchwell	36	E½SW	1825-05-25		A1 G152
839	SAMPLE, Daniel B	35	W½NW	1825-09-15		A1
837	" "	27	SWSE	1835-10-20		A1
836	" "	27	SESE	1837-03-20		A1
834	" "	26	W½NW	1837-03-30		A1
835	" "	27	N½SE	1840-11-10		A1
833	" "	26	NWSW	1843-02-01		A1
832	" "	22	SESW	1858-08-20		A1
838	" "	28	NWNE	1862-04-01		A1
830	" "	21	NESE	1897-01-15		A1
831	" "	21	W½SE	1897-01-15		A1
1023	SAMPLE, William R	22	NENW	1852-01-01		A1
995	SCOTT, David	24	E½NE	1824-10-20		A1 G7
843	" "	24	E½NW	1824-10-20		A1 G221
996	" "	24	W½NE	1824-10-20		A1 G7
844	" "	24	W½NW	1824-10-20		A1 G221
826	" "	35	E½NE	1825-05-25		A1 G214 R841
824	" "	35	E½SE	1825-05-25		A1 G213
868	" "	36	W½NE	1825-05-25		A1 G68
797	SHAW, Alexander	30	W½	1824-10-20	Greene	A1 F
869	SIMS, Edward	36	E½NW	1825-05-25		A1 G69
867	" "	36	W½NW	1825-05-25		A1 G67
851	" "	30	SE	1826-06-10	Greene	A1 F
852	" "	31	W½	1826-06-10	Greene	A1 F R979
807	STEPHENS, Benjamin W	7	NWNW	1835-09-25	Greene	A1
908	STEPHENS, James	7	E½NW	1826-02-01	Greene	A1 F
909	STOREY, James	3	W½	1826-02-01	Greene	A1 F
866	SUMMERS, Francis	30	NWNE	1840-11-10	Greene	A1
870	TANKERSLEY, George	9	N½NE	1837-05-15	Greene	A1
977	TAPPAN, John	33	W½SW	1837-05-15		A1 G149
873	THOMPSON, Henry B	30	E½	1825-05-25	Greene	A1 F R874
874	" "	30	E½	1825-05-25	Greene	A1 F R873
957	TRUE, Martin	35	W½SE	1825-05-25		A1
980	TURNER, Samuel M	12	SW	1835-09-28		A1
808	WATKINS, Bryan	12	W½SE	1827-02-10		A1
809	" "	21	SENW	1840-11-10		A1
941	WATT, John	8	E½NW	1824-10-20	Greene	A1 F
943	" "	9	SW	1825-09-15	Greene	A1 F R884
940	" "	2	W½	1826-02-01		A1 F
942	" "	9	SE	1826-06-10	Greene	A1 F
1024	WATT, William T	3	NESW	1837-08-01	Greene	A1
944	WATTS, John	7	E½NE	1825-09-15	Greene	A1 F
960	WEAGWORTH, Matthew	24	W½SW	1833-05-30		A1

ID	Individual in Patent	Sec.	Sec. Part	Date Issued	Other Counties	For More Info . . .
913	WEDGEWORTH, James	36	W½SE	1826-08-20		A1
910	" "	27	SW	1840-11-10		A1
911	" "	28	E½SE	1840-11-10		A1
912	" "	33	SESE	1840-11-10		A1
949	WEDGEWORTH, Joseph	13	E½SW	1825-09-15		A1
914	WEDGWORTH, James	36	E½SE	1837-03-15		A1
958	WELSH, Martin	29	NW	1897-01-15		A1
853	WHITEHEAD, Edwin D	11	SESE	1837-05-15		A1
854	" "	11	SW	1837-05-15		A1
855	" "	11	W½SE	1837-05-15		A1
856	" "	13	SENW	1837-05-15		A1
857	" "	14	E½NW	1837-05-15		A1
858	" "	14	E½SE	1837-05-15		A1 V924
859	" "	14	SWNE	1837-05-15		A1
861	" "	23	E½NE	1837-05-15		A1
862	" "	23	W½NE	1837-05-15		A1
863	" "	27	NE	1840-11-10		A1
860	" "	14	W½SE	1843-02-01		A1
979	WHITWORTH, Samuel J	31	W½	1824-10-20	Greene	A1 F R852
978	" "	31	E½W½	1825-05-25	Greene	A1 F
842	WIER, David S	26	SWSW	1837-03-15		A1
846	WILSON, Drury A	1	SW	1858-08-20		A1
847	" "	1	W½SE	1858-08-20		A1 R898
848	" "	2	E½SE	1858-08-20		A1
1025	WILSON, William	2	E½NW	1858-08-20		A1
1026	" "	2	W½NE	1858-08-20		A1
872	WINDHAM, George	29	SENE	1837-03-15		A1
871	" "	29	NWSW	1837-11-02		A1
999	WOLSTENHOLME, Thomas	7	SWNW	1837-05-15	Greene	A1

Patent Map

T22-N R3-E
St Stephens Meridian

Map Group 5

Township Statistics

Parcels Mapped	:	258
Number of Patents	:	242
Number of Individuals	:	120
Patentees Identified	:	118
Number of Surnames	:	81
Multi-Patentee Parcels	:	25
Oldest Patent Date	:	10/20/1824
Most Recent Patent	:	3/14/1916
Block/Lot Parcels	:	1
Parcels Re - Issued	:	5
Parcels that Overlap	:	2
Cities and Towns	:	5
Cemeteries	:	3

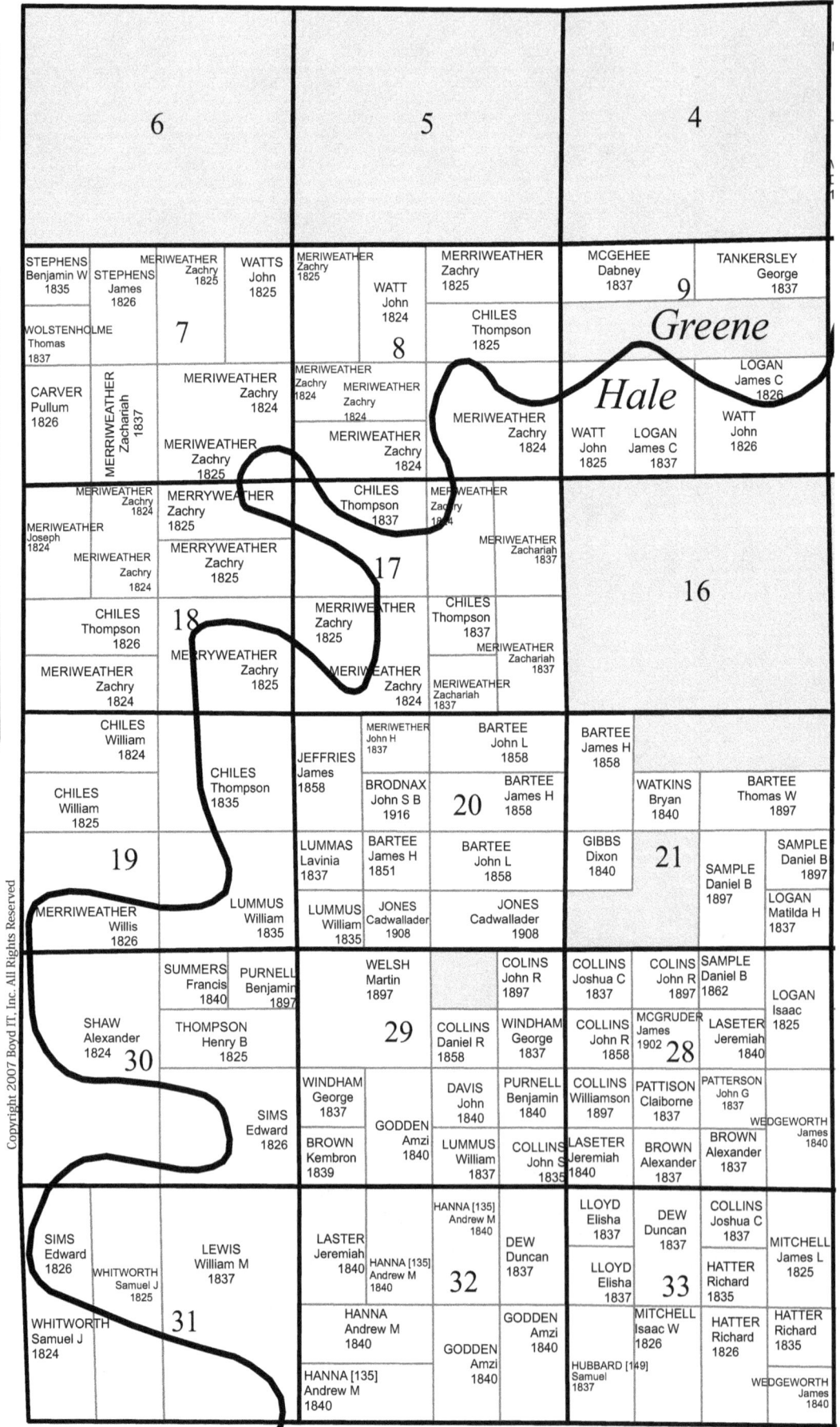

6

5

4

7

STEPHENS Benjamin W 1835

STEPHENS James 1826

MERIWEATHER Zachry 1825

WATTS John 1825

WOLSTENHOLME Thomas 1837

CARVER Pullum 1826

MERIWEATHER Zachariah 1837

MERIWEATHER Zachry 1824

MERIWEATHER Zachry 1825

8

MERIWEATHER Zachry 1825

WATT John 1824

MERIWEATHER Zachry 1824

MERIWEATHER Zachry 1824

MERIWEATHER Zachry 1824

MERIWEATHER Zachry 1824

MERRIWEATHER Zachry 1825

CHILES Thompson 1825

MERIWEATHER Zachry 1824

Greene

Hale

MCGEHEE Dabney 1837

9

TANKERSLEY George 1837

LOGAN James C 1826

WATT John 1825

LOGAN James C 1837

WATT John 1826

MERIWEATHER Zachry 1824

MERRYWEATHER Zachry 1825

MERIWEATHER Joseph 1824

MERIWEATHER Zachry 1824

18

CHILES Thompson 1826

MERIWEATHER Zachry 1824

MERRYWEATHER Zachry 1825

CHILES Thompson 1837

17

MERRIWEATHER Zachry 1825

MERIWEATHER Zachry 1825

CHILES Thompson 1837

MERIWEATHER Zachry 1824

MERIWEATHER Zachary 1837

MERIWEATHER Zachariah 1837

MERIWEATHER Zachariah 1837

16

CHILES William 1824

CHILES William 1825

19

CHILES Thompson 1835

MERRIWEATHER Willis 1826

LUMMAS Lavinia 1837

LUMMUS William 1835

JEFFRIES James 1858

MERIWETHER John H 1837

BRODNAX John S B 1916

20

BARTEE John L 1858

BARTEE James H 1858

BARTEE James H 1851

BARTEE John L 1858

LUMMUS William 1835

JONES Cadwallader 1908

JONES Cadwallader 1908

BARTEE James H 1858

WATKINS Bryan 1840

BARTEE Thomas W 1897

GIBBS Dixon 1840

21

SAMPLE Daniel B 1897

SAMPLE Daniel B 1897

LOGAN Matilda H 1837

30

SHAW Alexander 1824

SUMMERS Francis 1840

PURNELL Benjamin 1897

THOMPSON Henry B 1825

SIMS Edward 1826

WELSH Martin 1897

29

WINDHAM George 1837

BROWN Kembron 1839

GODDEN Amzi 1840

COLINS John R 1897

COLLINS Daniel R 1858

WINDHAM George 1837

DAVIS John 1840

LUMMUS William 1837

COLLINS Joshua C 1837

COLLINS John R 1858

PURNELL Benjamin 1840

COLLINS John S 1835

COLINS John R 1897

MCGRUDER James 1902

COLLINS Williamson 1897

LASETER Jeremiah 1840

SAMPLE Daniel B 1862

28

LASETER Jeremiah 1840

PATTISON Claiborne 1837

LOGAN Isaac 1825

PATTERSON John G 1837

BROWN Alexander 1837

WEDGEWORTH James 1840

31

SIMS Edward 1826

WHITWORTH Samuel J 1825

WHITWORTH Samuel J 1824

LEWIS William M 1837

LASTER Jeremiah 1840

HANNA [135] Andrew M 1840

HANNA Andrew M 1840

HANNA [135] Andrew M 1840

HANNA [135] Andrew M 1840

32

GODDEN Amzi 1840

DEW Duncan 1837

GODDEN Amzi 1840

LLOYD Elisha 1837

LLOYD Elisha 1837

HUBBARD [149] Samuel 1837

DEW Duncan 1837

33

MITCHELL Isaac W 1826

COLLINS Joshua C 1837

HATTER Richard 1835

HATTER Richard 1826

MITCHELL James L 1825

HATTER Richard 1835

WEDGEWORTH James 1840

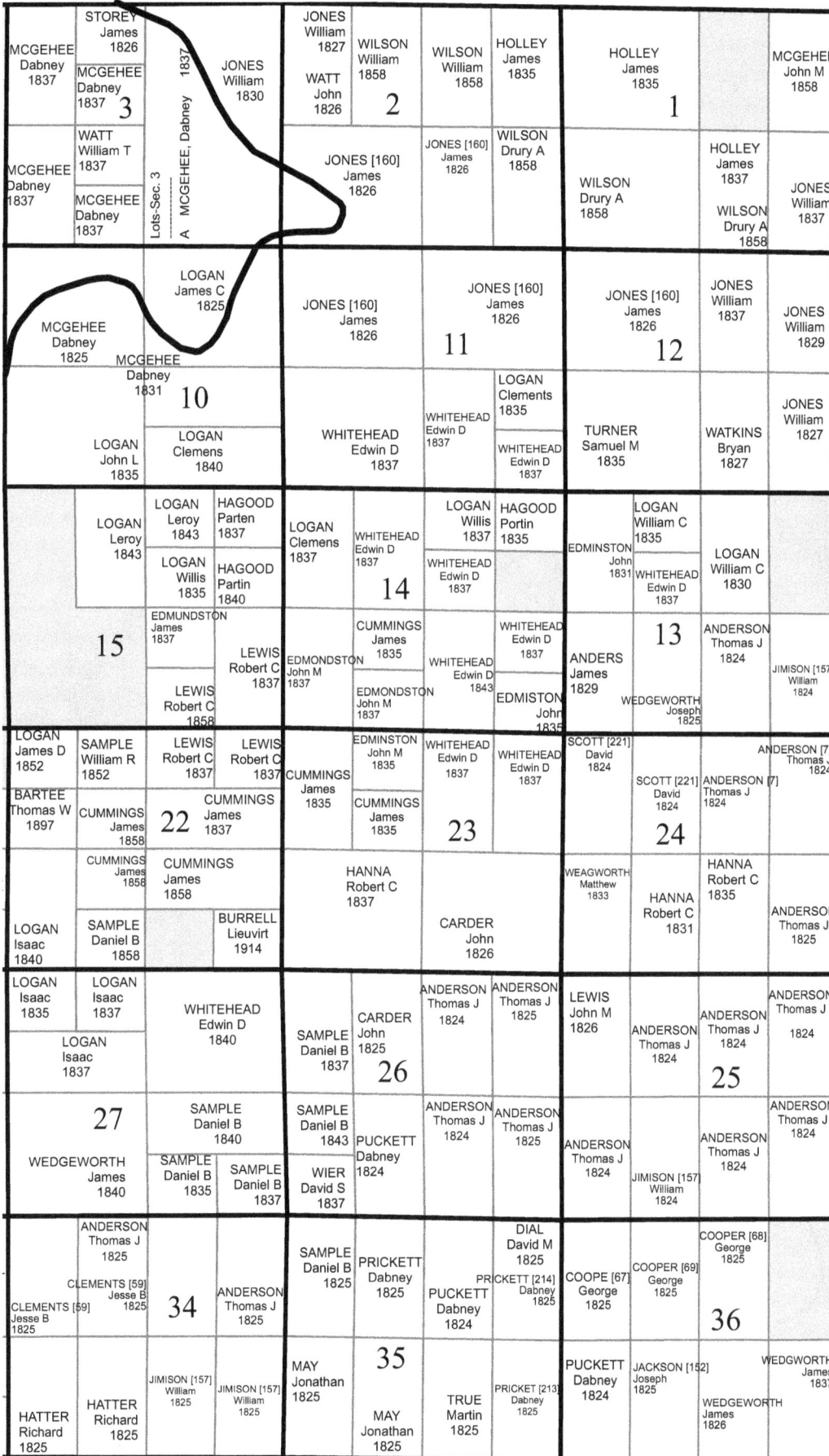

Section 3

STOREY James 1826

MCGEHEE Dabney 1837

MCGEHEE Dabney 1837

MCGEHEE Dabney 1837

MCGEHEE Dabney 1837

WATT William T 1837

MCGEHEE Dabney 1837

JONES William 1830

Lots-Sec. 3

A MCGEHEE, Dabney

Section 2

JONES William 1827

WATT John 1826

WILSON William 1858

WILSON William 1858

HOLLEY James 1835

JONES [160] James 1826

JONES [160] James 1826

WILSON Drury A 1858

Section 1

HOLLEY James 1835

WILSON Drury A 1858

HOLLEY James 1837

WILSON Drury A 1858

MCGEHEE John M 1858

JONES William 1837

Section 10

LOGAN James C 1825

MCGEHEE Dabney 1825

MCGEHEE Dabney 1831

LOGAN John L 1835

LOGAN Clemens 1840

Section 11

JONES [160] James 1826

JONES [160] James 1826

WHITEHEAD Edwin D 1837

Section 12

JONES [160] James 1826

JONES [160] William 1837

JONES William 1829

LOGAN Clements 1835

TURNER Samuel M 1835

WATKINS Bryan 1827

JONES William 1827

WHITEHEAD Edwin D 1837

WHITEHEAD Edwin D 1837

Section 15

LOGAN Leroy 1843

LOGAN Leroy 1843

LOGAN Willis 1835

HAGOOD Parten 1837

HAGOOD Partin 1840

EDMUNDSTON James 1837

LEWIS Robert C 1837

LEWIS Robert C 1858

Section 14

LOGAN Clemens 1837

WHITEHEAD Edwin D 1837

CUMMINGS James 1835

EDMONDSTON John M 1837

EDMONDSTON John M 1837

LOGAN Willis 1837

HAGOOD Portin 1835

WHITEHEAD Edwin D 1837

WHITEHEAD Edwin D 1837

EDMISTON John 1835

Section 13

LOGAN William C 1835

EDMINSTON John 1831

WHITEHEAD Edwin D 1837

LOGAN William C 1830

ANDERS James 1829

WEDGEWORTH Joseph 1825

ANDERSON Thomas J 1824

JIMISON [157] William 1824

Section 22

LOGAN James D 1852

SAMPLE William R 1852

BARTEE Thomas W 1897

CUMMINGS James 1858

CUMMINGS James 1858

LOGAN Isaac 1840

LEWIS Robert C 1837

LEWIS Robert C 1837

CUMMINGS James 1837

CUMMINGS James 1858

SAMPLE Daniel B 1858

BURRELL Lieuvirt 1914

Section 23

EDMINSTON John M 1835

CUMMINGS James 1835

CUMMINGS James 1835

HANNA Robert C 1837

CARDER John 1826

WHITEHEAD Edwin D 1837

WHITEHEAD Edwin D 1837

Section 24

SCOTT [221] David 1824

SCOTT [221] David 1824

ANDERSON [7] Thomas J 1824

WEAGWORTH Matthew 1833

HANNA Robert C 1831

ANDERSON [7] Thomas J 1824

ANDERSON [7] Thomas J 1824

HANNA Robert C 1835

ANDERSON Thomas J 1825

Section 27

LOGAN Isaac 1835

LOGAN Isaac 1837

LOGAN Isaac 1837

WEDGEWORTH James 1840

WHITEHEAD Edwin D 1840

SAMPLE Daniel B 1840

SAMPLE Daniel B 1835

SAMPLE Daniel B 1837

Section 26

SAMPLE Daniel B 1837

SAMPLE Daniel B 1843

CARDER John 1825

WIER David S 1837

ANDERSON Thomas J 1824

ANDERSON Thomas J 1825

ANDERSON Thomas J 1824

ANDERSON Thomas J 1825

Section 25

LEWIS John M 1826

ANDERSON Thomas J 1824

ANDERSON Thomas J 1824

ANDERSON Thomas J 1824

ANDERSON Thomas J 1824

ANDERSON Thomas J 1824

JIMISON [157] William 1824

ANDERSON Thomas J 1824

ANDERSON Thomas J 1824

Section 34

ANDERSON Thomas J 1825

CLEMENTS [59] Jesse B 1825

CLEMENTS [59] Jesse B 1825

ANDERSON Thomas J 1825

JIMISON [157] William 1825

HATTER Richard 1825

HATTER Richard 1825

JIMISON [157] William 1825

Section 35

SAMPLE Daniel B 1825

MAY Jonathan 1825

MAY Jonathan 1825

PRICKETT Dabney 1825

TRUE Martin 1825

PUCKETT Dabney 1824

PRICKETT [214] Dabney 1825

PRICKET [213] Dabney 1825

DIAL David M 1825

PUCKETT Dabney 1824

Section 36

COOPE [67] George 1825

COOPER [69] George 1825

COOPER [68] George 1825

PUCKETT Dabney 1824

JACKSON [152] Joseph 1825

WEDGEWORTH James 1826

WEDGWORTH James 1837

Helpful Hints

1. This Map's INDEX can be found on the preceding pages.

2. Refer to Map "C" to see where this Township lies within Hale County, Alabama.

3. Numbers within square brackets [ ] denote a multi-patentee land parcel (multi-owner). Refer to Appendix "C" for a full list of members in this group.

4. Areas that look to be crowded with Patentees usually indicate multiple sales of the same parcel (Re-issues) or Overlapping parcels. See this Township's Index for an explanation of these and other circumstances that might explain "odd" groupings of Patentees on this map.

Legend

Patent Boundary

Section Boundary

No Patents Found (or Outside County)

1., 2., 3., ... Lot Numbers (when beside a name)

[ ] Group Number (see Appendix "C")

Scale: Section = 1 mile X 1 mile (generally, with some exceptions)

Road Map

T22-N R3-E
St Stephens Meridian

Map Group 5

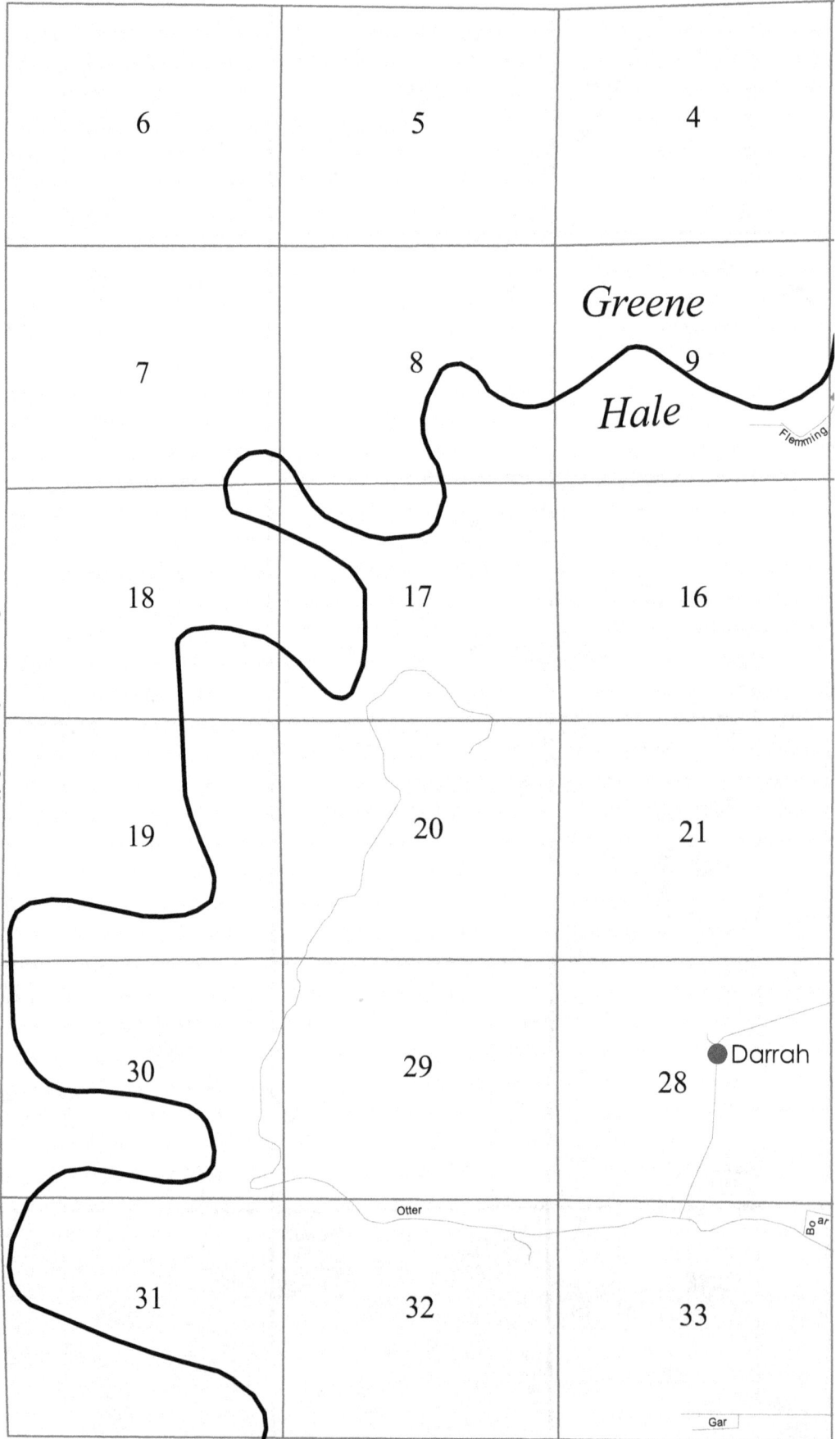

Cities & Towns
Akron
Darrah
Evansville
New Prospect
Oak Village

Cemeteries
Akron New Cemetery
Mount Zion Cemetery
Sample Cemetery

6	5	4
7	8	*Greene* 9 *Hale* Flemming
18	17	16
19	20	21
30	29	28 ●Darrah
31	32 Otter	33 Bo ar Gar

3

2

1

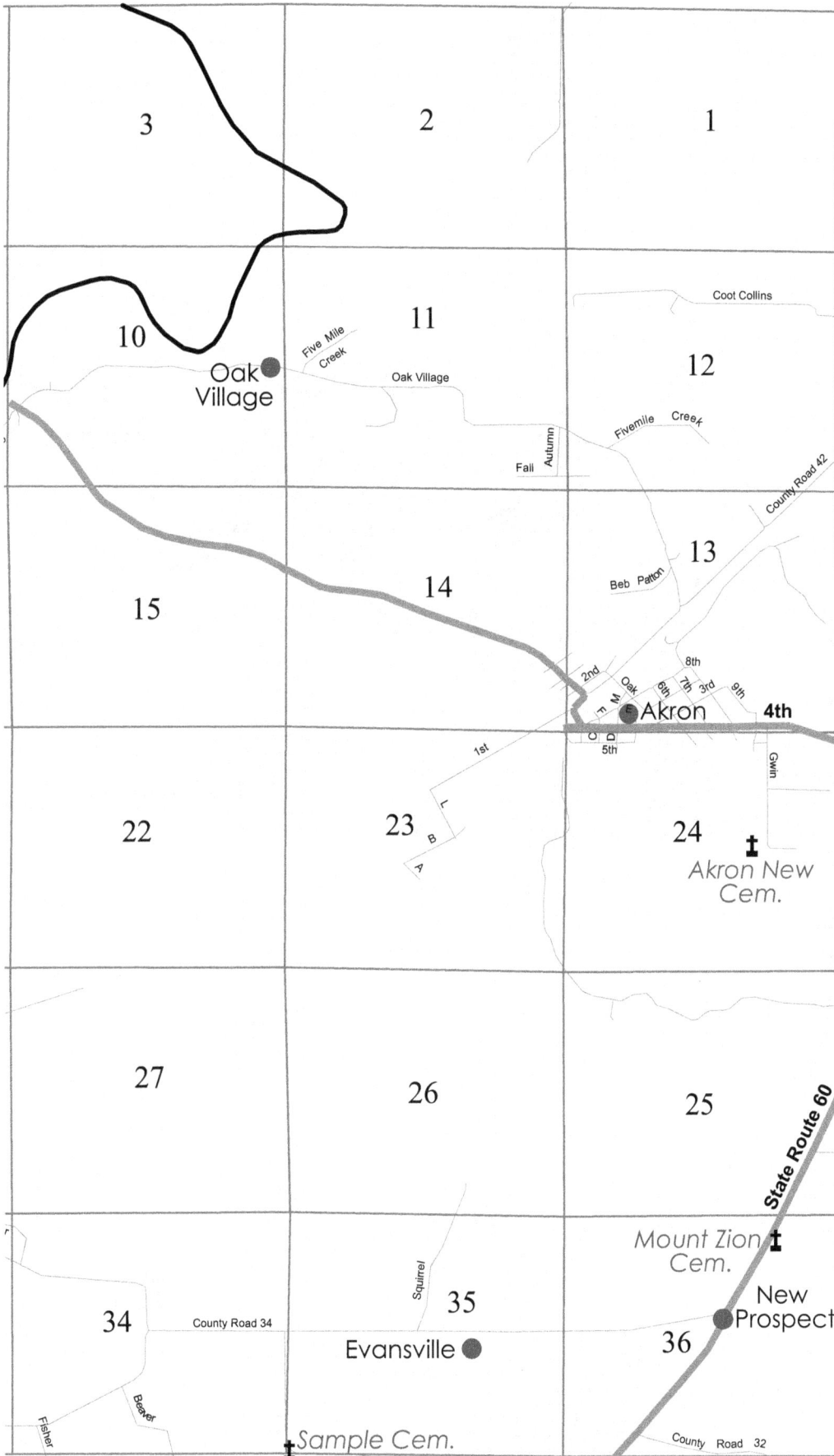

Coot Collins

11

10

12

Oak Village

Five Mile Creek

Oak Village

Fivemile Creek

Autumn

Fall

County Road 42

13

15

14

Beb Patton

8th

2nd

7th 3rd

9th

1st

6th

Oak

Akron

4th

5th

Gwin

22

23

24

A B L

Akron New Cem.

27

26

25

State Route 60

Mount Zion Cem.

Squirrel

35

New Prospect

County Road 34

34

Evansville

36

Fisher

Beaver

Sample Cem.

County Road 32

Scale: Section = 1 mile X 1 mile (generally, with some exceptions)

Historical Map

T22-N R3-E
St Stephens Meridian

Map Group 5

Cities & Towns
Akron
Darrah
Evansville
New Prospect
Oak Village

Cemeteries
Akron New Cemetery
Mount Zion Cemetery
Sample Cemetery

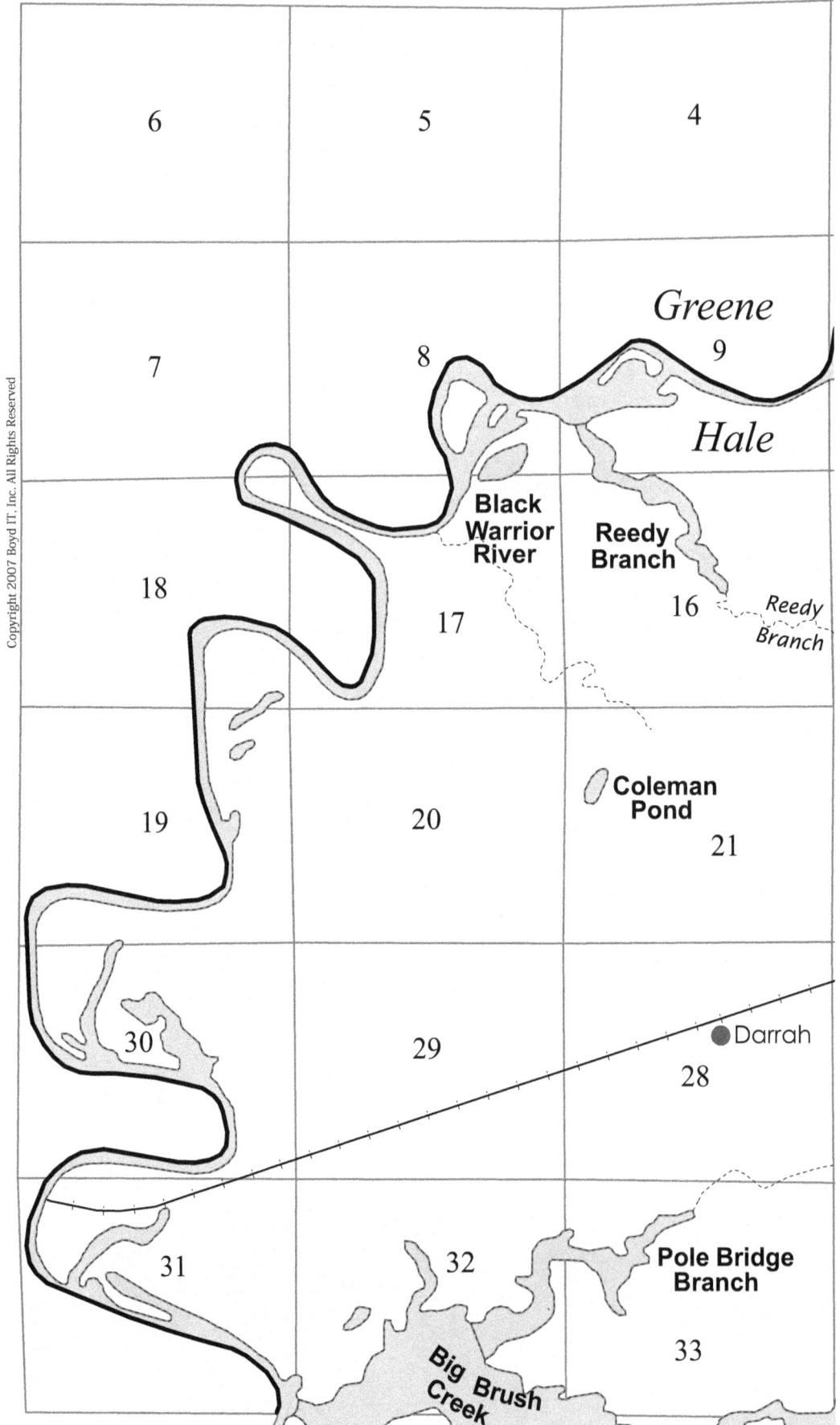

6

5

4

7

8

Greene

9

Hale

Black Warrior River

Reedy Branch

Reedy Branch

18

17

16

19

20

Coleman Pond

21

30

29

● Darrah

28

31

32

Pole Bridge Branch

Big Brush Creek

33

2 **Martin Slough**

1

3

Martin Slough

Fivemile Creek

Oak Village

Fivemile Creek

11

12

10

15

14

13

Akron

22

23

24

† *Akron New Cem.*

27

26

25

Pole Bridge Branch

Mount Zion † *Cem.*

35

New Prospect

34

Evansville

36

† *Sample Cem.*

Helpful Hints

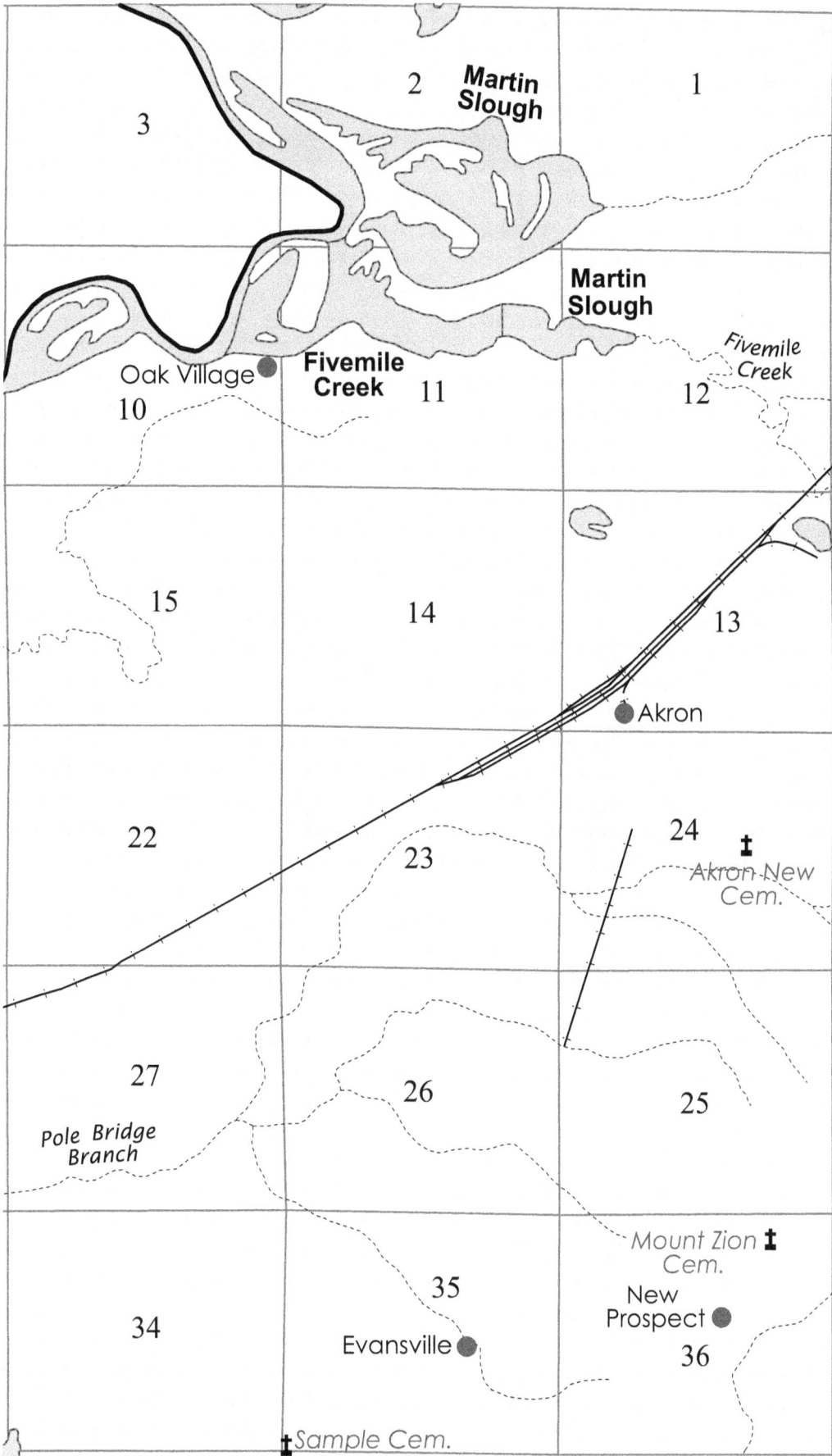

1. This Map takes a different look at the same Congressional Township displayed in the preceding two maps. It presents features that can help you better envision the historical development of the area: a) Water-bodies (lakes & ponds), b) Water-courses (rivers, streams, etc.), c) Railroads, d) City/town center-points (where they were oftentimes located when first settled), and e) Cemeteries.

2. Using this "Historical" map in tandem with this Township's Patent Map and Road Map, may lead you to some interesting discoveries. You will often find roads, towns, cemeteries, and waterways are named after nearby landowners: sometimes those names will be the ones you are researching. See how many of these research gems you can find here in Hale County.

L e g e n d

————————	Section Lines
+‒+‒+‒+‒+‒+	Railroads
▨	Large Rivers & Bodies of Water
------------	Streams/Creeks & Small Rivers
●	Cities/Towns
†	Cemeteries

Scale: Section = 1 mile X 1 mile
(there are some exceptions)

Map Group 6: Index to Land Patents

Township 22-North Range 4-East (St Stephens)

After you locate an individual in this Index, take note of the Section and Section Part then proceed to the Land Patent map on the pages immediately following. You should have no difficulty locating the corresponding parcel of land.

The "For More Info" Column will lead you to more information about the underlying Patents. See the *Legend* at right, and the "How to Use this Book" chapter, for more information.

ID	Individual in Patent	Sec.	Sec. Part	Date Issued	Other Counties	For More Info . . .
1163	ANDERS, James	31	E½SE	1826-08-20		A1
1164	" "	33	E½NE	1827-02-10		A1
1270	ANDERSON, Thomas J	19	E½NW	1824-10-20		A1
1274	" "	19	E½SE	1824-10-20		A1 G5
1275	" "	19	W½NW	1824-10-20		A1 G5
1276	" "	19	W½SE	1824-10-20		A1 G5
1273	" "	30	E½NE	1824-10-20		A1
1277	" "	30	E½NW	1824-10-20		A1 G5
1278	" "	30	W½NE	1824-10-20		A1 G5
1279	" "	30	W½NW	1824-10-20		A1 G5
1280	" "	30	W½SW	1824-10-20		A1 G6
1272	" "	19	W½NE	1825-05-25		A1
1271	" "	19	E½SW	1825-06-20		A1
1269	" "	18	W½SW	1826-08-20		A1
1101	AVERY, David	36	SWSE	1897-08-16		A1
1054	BARBER, Abraham	23	W½NE	1824-10-20		A1
1053	" "	14	W½SE	1825-04-20		A1
1055	" "	24	SWSE	1837-03-30		A1
1201	BATES, John M	31	E½SW	1825-05-25		A1 G14
1208	BIRMINGHAM, Joshua	35	E½NE	1826-02-01		A1
1209	" "	35	E½NW	1826-02-01		A1
1210	" "	35	W½SE	1833-05-30		A1
1149	BISHOP, Henry N	28	E½NW	1824-10-20		A1
1127	BOLTON, Elizabeth	36	NENE	1837-11-02		A1
1240	BOLTON, Robert	36	NESE	1837-03-30		A1
1143	BUFORD, Goodlow	8	E½NW	1824-10-20		A1 G36
1142	" "	8	W½NW	1824-10-20		A1
1214	CALWELL, Margaret	36	W½NE	1837-11-02		A1
1274	CLEMENTS, Benjamin	19	E½SE	1824-10-20		A1 G5
1275	" "	19	W½NW	1824-10-20		A1 G5
1276	" "	19	W½SE	1824-10-20		A1 G5
1081	" "	27	E½NE	1824-10-20		A1 G58
1085	" "	28	W½NE	1824-10-20		A1 G56
1277	" "	30	E½NW	1824-10-20		A1 G5
1082	" "	30	E½SE	1824-10-20		A1 G55
1278	" "	30	W½NE	1824-10-20		A1 G5
1279	" "	30	W½NW	1824-10-20		A1 G5
1083	" "	30	W½SE	1824-10-20		A1 G55
1084	" "	31	E½NW	1824-10-20		A1 G55
1188	CLEMENTS, Jesse B	21	W½SE	1824-10-20		A1 G60
1165	COLLINS, James	29	W½SE	1824-10-20		A1
1183	COLLINS, James W	29	E½SW	1824-10-20		A1 G63
1123	COMPANY, Sims Banks And	10	E½NW	1824-10-20		A1 G229
1124	" "	10	W½NE	1824-10-20		A1 G229
1125	" "	10	W½NW	1824-10-20		A1 G229
1102	DIAL, David M	29	W½SW	1824-10-20		A1

ID	Individual in Patent	Sec.	Sec. Part	Date Issued	Other Counties	For More Info . . .
1082	DIAL, David M (Cont'd)	30	E½SE	1824-10-20		A1 G55
1108	" "	30	E½SW	1824-10-20		A1 G76
1083	" "	30	W½SE	1824-10-20		A1 G55
1280	" "	30	W½SW	1824-10-20		A1 G6
1103	" "	31	E½NE	1824-10-20		A1
1084	" "	31	E½NW	1824-10-20		A1 G55
1105	" "	31	W½NW	1824-10-20		A1
1106	" "	31	W½SE	1824-10-20		A1
1201	" "	31	E½SW	1825-05-25		A1 G14
1107	" "	32	W½NW	1825-05-25		A1
1104	" "	31	W½NE	1825-09-15		A1
1066	DOBBINS, Alexander	13	E½NW	1824-10-20		A1
1067	" "	13	W½NW	1824-10-20		A1
1068	" "	15	E½SE	1824-10-20		A1
1069	" "	15	W½SE	1824-10-20		A1
1070	" "	15	W½SW	1824-10-20		A1
1071	" "	22	W½NE	1824-10-20		A1
1184	EDDINS, James W	26	W½SW	1826-10-02		A1
1193	ELLIOT, John	13	E½NE	1826-02-01		A1
1110	ELLIOTT, David R	24	NWSE	1858-08-20		A1
1111	" "	24	SWNE	1858-08-20		A1
1136	ELLIOTT, George	13	W½SE	1837-11-02		A1
1265	ELLIOTT, Thomas	24	E½NE	1824-10-20		A1
1267	" "	24	NENW	1837-03-15		A1
1268	" "	24	NWNE	1837-03-15		A1
1266	" "	24	E½SE	1837-03-30		A1
1236	FLEMING, Plinny R	32	E½SE	1824-10-20		A1 G84
1237	" "	32	W½SE	1824-10-20		A1 G84
1202	FLEMMING, John M	33	W½NW	1824-10-20		A1
1203	FLEMMING, John R	32	E½NE	1825-05-25		A1
1204	" "	32	W½NE	1825-05-25		A1
1238	FLEMMING, Plinny R	33	W½SW	1825-05-25		A1
1118	FRIERSON, Edward L	5	E½NW	1824-10-20		A1
1178	FRIERSON, James M	14	E½SW	1825-05-25		A1
1310	FRIERSON, William V	17	W½SW	1824-10-20		A1 R1299
1311	" "	23	E½SE	1824-10-20		A1
1312	" "	23	W½SE	1824-10-20		A1
1313	" "	24	W½NW	1824-10-20		A1
1314	" "	26	W½NW	1824-10-20		A1
1229	FULTON, Paul	20	E½NW	1824-10-20		A1
1230	" "	20	E½SW	1824-10-20		A1
1232	" "	20	W½SE	1824-10-20		A1
1235	" "	29	W½NW	1824-10-20		A1 G87 R1088
1234	" "	29	E½NW	1825-04-20		A1
1231	" "	20	W½NW	1825-05-25		A1
1233	" "	20	W½SW	1825-05-25		A1
1228	" "	19	E½NE	1825-09-15		A1
1296	FULTON, William F	31	NWSW	1835-09-25		A1
1297	" "	31	SWSW	1837-03-15		A1
1189	GILHAM, Jesse	24	W½SW	1827-03-01		A1
1157	GILL, Isaac	23	SENE	1839-05-01		A1
1072	GLOVER, Allen	13	E½SE	1837-11-02		A1
1073	" "	14	E½SE	1837-11-02		A1
1166	GRAY, James	12	SE	1837-05-15		A1
1099	GREEN, Daniel	10	E½SW	1824-10-20		A1 G124
1100	" "	10	W½SE	1824-10-20		A1 G124
1098	" "	15	W½NW	1824-10-20		A1 G125
1097	" "	14	NENE	1835-10-01		A1
1242	GREER, Robert	24	SENW	1840-11-10		A1
1243	" "	24	SESW	1840-11-10		A1
1244	" "	25	NWNW	1840-11-10		A1
1158	HALLBROOKS, Jacob	26	E½NW	1837-11-02		A1
1137	HALLY, George	7	NWNE	1835-10-28		A1
1130	HANIS, Evan	33	W½SE	1824-10-20		A1
1085	HANIS, Evin	28	W½NE	1824-10-20		A1 G56
1196	HANIS, John	34	W½SW	1824-10-20		A1 G134
1241	HANNA, Robert C	29	E½SE	1824-10-20		A1 G136
1215	HANY, Margaret	36	W½SW	1824-10-20		A1
1131	HARRIS, Evan	33	W½NE	1825-05-25		A1
1132	HARRIS, Evan R	33	SESW	1837-03-30		A1
1133	HARRIS, Evin	33	NESW	1835-09-25		A1
1197	HARRIS, John	33	E½SE	1825-10-01		A1 G139
1222	HARRIS, Noah	34	W½NW	1837-03-20		A1

ID	Individual in Patent	Sec.	Sec. Part	Date Issued	Other Counties	For More Info . . .
1223	HARRIS, Page	27	E½NW	1824-10-20		A1
1224	" "	27	NESE	1835-09-22		A1
1225	" "	27	NESW	1835-10-01		A1
1226	HARRIS, Page W	27	SESE	1837-03-30		A1
1227	" "	27	W½SE	1837-03-30		A1
1262	HARRIS, Sherrard	32	E½NW	1825-05-25		A1
1263	HARRIS, Sherrod W	28	E½SW	1831-08-25		A1
1198	HARRY, John J	34	E½SE	1824-10-20		A1 V1255
1199	" "	36	E½SW	1825-04-20		A1
1114	HART, Derrel	35	E½SW	1837-05-15		A1
1117	HART, Durrell	35	W½NE	1825-05-25		A1
1207	HATTOX, Jonathan	34	E½NE	1826-06-10		A1
1167	HEDLESTON, James	6	E½NW	1835-10-28		A1
1168	"	6	W½NE	1835-10-28		A1
1298	HENNON, William	2	E½SE	1825-05-25		A1 G144
1144	HILL, Green	10	E½SE	1824-10-20		A1
1099	" "	10	E½SW	1824-10-20		A1 G124
1100	" "	10	W½SE	1824-10-20		A1 G124
1145	" "	10	W½SW	1824-10-20		A1
1146	" "	12	W½SW	1824-10-20		A1
1217	HILL, Middleton M	11	E½NE	1825-09-15		A1 R1218
1218	" "	11	E½NE	1825-09-15		A1 R1217
1219	" "	11	E½SW	1825-09-15		A1
1220	" "	11	W½SE	1825-09-15		A1 R1221
1221	" "	11	W½SE	1825-09-15		A1 R1220
1080	HOBSON, Baker	3	E½NE	1824-10-20		A1 G145
1079	" "	3	W½NE	1824-10-20		A1
1078	" "	2	W½NW	1825-05-25		A1
1088	HOLBROOK, Bunell	29	W½NW	1825-09-15		A1 R1235
1089	HOLBROOK, Burrel	28	E½SE	1824-10-20		A1 G147
1090	"	28	W½SE	1824-10-20		A1 G147
1091	HOLBROOK, Burrell	17	E½SE	1826-02-01		A1
1092	"	17	W½SE	1826-02-01		A1
1161	HOLBROOK, Jacob	21	W½SW	1824-10-20		A1 G148
1159	"	28	W½NW	1824-10-20		A1
1160	"	29	E½NE	1824-10-20		A1
1138	HOLLEY, George	7	E½NE	1837-03-30		A1
1139	" "	7	E½NW	1837-03-30		A1
1140	" "	7	SWNE	1837-03-30		A1
1147	HOLLEY, Henry	5	NWSW	1835-09-22		A1
1148	"	6	NESE	1835-09-22		A1
1169	HOLLEY, James	5	E½SW	1829-03-06		A1
1141	HOLLY, George	5	SWSW	1835-10-28		A1
1170	HUDDLESTON, James	5	W½NW	1829-03-06		A1
1077	INGE, Anne R	11	W½NW	1824-10-20		A1
1171	JACK, James	6	NENE	1837-05-15		A1
1316	JANNWAY, William W	36	SENE	1860-10-01		A1
1108	JIMISON, William	30	E½SW	1824-10-20		A1 G76
1174	JONES, James	17	E½SW	1824-10-20		A1 G160
1176	" "	7	E½SE	1824-10-20		A1 G160
1175	" "	18	E½NW	1826-02-01		A1 G160
1177	" "	7	SW	1826-02-01		A1 G160
1172	" "	18	E½SW	1827-02-10		A1
1173	" "	18	W½NW	1827-02-10		A1
1174	JONES, John	17	E½SW	1824-10-20		A1 G160
1176	" "	7	E½SE	1824-10-20		A1 G160
1175	" "	18	E½NW	1826-02-01		A1 G160
1177	" "	7	SW	1826-02-01		A1 G160
1216	JONES, Mary H	7	SWNW	1835-09-25		A1 R1305
1174	JONES, Thomas	17	E½SW	1824-10-20		A1 G160
1176	" "	7	E½SE	1824-10-20		A1 G160
1175	" "	18	E½NW	1826-02-01		A1 G160
1177	" "	7	SW	1826-02-01		A1 G160
1281	" "	7	W½SE	1827-02-10		A1
1306	JONES, William	15	W½NE	1824-10-20		A1 G162
1174	" "	17	E½SW	1824-10-20		A1 G160
1299	" "	17	W½SW	1824-10-20		A1 R1310
1300	" "	20	E½NE	1824-10-20		A1
1302	" "	20	W½NE	1824-10-20		A1
1307	" "	3	E½SE	1824-10-20		A1 G161
1308	" "	3	E½SW	1824-10-20		A1 G161
1176	" "	7	E½SE	1824-10-20		A1 G160
1298	" "	2	E½SE	1825-05-25		A1 G144

ID	Individual in Patent	Sec.	Sec. Part	Date Issued	Other Counties	For More Info . . .
1301	JONES, William (Cont'd)	20	E½SE	1825-05-25		A1
1303	" "	21	W½NW	1825-05-25		A1
1175	" "	18	E½NW	1826-02-01		A1 G160
1177	" "	7	SW	1826-02-01		A1 G160
1304	" "	6	SWSW	1835-09-22		A1
1305	" "	7	SWNW	1835-10-20		A1 R1216
1309	KENNON, William	1	W½SW	1825-05-25		A1 G166
1200	KING, John	22	E½SW	1824-10-20		A1
1241	LANE, John W	29	E½SE	1824-10-20		A1 G136
1235	" "	29	W½NW	1824-10-20		A1 G87 R1088
1236	" "	32	E½SE	1824-10-20		A1 G84
1237	" "	32	W½SE	1824-10-20		A1 G84
1206	" "	33	E½NW	1824-10-20		A1 G173
1143	" "	8	E½NW	1824-10-20		A1 G36
1309	" "	1	W½SW	1825-05-25		A1 G166
1197	" "	33	E½SE	1825-10-01		A1 G139
1245	LIDDELL, Robert W	6	E½SW	1837-03-30		A1
1246	" "	6	NWSE	1837-03-30		A1
1247	" "	6	SESE	1837-03-30		A1
1248	" "	6	SWSE	1837-03-30		A1
1135	LONG, Gabriel	21	E½NE	1824-10-20		A1
1211	LONG, Lunerford	21	E½NW	1824-10-20		A1
1212	" "	21	E½SW	1824-10-20		A1
1213	" "	21	W½NE	1824-10-20		A1
1188	" "	21	W½SE	1824-10-20		A1 G60
1239	LONG, Reuben	36	NW	1825-04-20		A1
1109	MANSKER, David	13	W½NE	1825-09-15		A1
1179	MARTIN, James	12	E½NE	1824-10-20		A1
1282	MCCRARY, Thomas	25	E½SE	1897-02-17		A1
1283	" "	25	NENW	1897-02-17		A1
1284	" "	25	SENE	1897-02-17		A1
1285	" "	25	SWSE	1897-02-17		A1
1286	" "	25	W½NE	1897-02-17		A1
1287	MCCRAY, Thomas	25	NESW	1837-11-02		A1
1061	MCGEHEE, Abraham	10	E½NE	1824-10-20		A1
1062	" "	12	W½NE	1824-10-20		A1
1056	" "	1	E½SE	1825-05-25		A1 R1057
1057	" "	1	E½SE	1825-05-25		A1 R1056
1058	" "	1	E½SW	1825-05-25		A1
1059	" "	1	W½SE	1825-05-25		A1 R1060
1060	" "	1	W½SE	1825-05-25		A1 R1059
1298	" "	2	E½SE	1825-05-25		A1 G144
1064	" "	2	E½SW	1825-05-25		A1 G195
1063	" "	2	W½SE	1825-05-25		A1
1065	" "	2	W½SW	1825-05-25		A1 G195
1289	MCMASTER, Thomas	25	W½SW	1824-10-20		A1
1291	" "	26	E½SE	1824-10-20		A1
1292	" "	26	E½SW	1824-10-20		A1
1290	" "	26	E½NE	1825-05-25		A1
1288	" "	25	SESW	1835-10-28		A1
1180	MCMASTERS, James	24	NESW	1837-11-02		A1
1293	MCMASTERS, Thomas	25	S½NW	1837-11-02		A1
1294	MCRARY, Thomas	25	NWSE	1837-08-01		A1
1295	" "	36	NWSE	1837-08-01		A1
1181	PARKER, James	1	E½NE	1825-04-20		A1
1307	POPE, Willis	3	E½SE	1824-10-20		A1 G161
1308	" "	3	E½SW	1824-10-20		A1 G161
1317	" "	3	W½SE	1824-10-20		A1
1318	" "	3	W½SW	1824-10-20		A1
1264	RHODES, Solomon	26	W½NE	1824-10-20		A1
1156	RICHARDSON, Hiram	26	W½SE	1825-04-20		A1
1205	ROSS, John	13	E½SW	1837-03-30		A1
1253	SCARLETT, Samuel	13	W½SW	1837-05-15		A1
1254	" "	14	SENE	1837-05-15		A1
1161	SCOTT, David	21	W½SW	1824-10-20		A1 G148
1183	" "	29	E½SW	1824-10-20		A1 G63
1086	SEALE, Benton	25	NENE	1858-08-20		A1
1123	SIMS, Edward	10	E½NW	1824-10-20		A1 G229
1124	" "	10	W½NE	1824-10-20		A1 G229
1125	" "	10	W½NW	1824-10-20		A1 G229
1121	" "	22	W½SW	1824-10-20		A1 G232
1120	" "	28	E½NE	1824-10-20		A1 G231
1089	" "	28	E½SE	1824-10-20		A1 G147

ID	Individual in Patent	Sec.	Sec. Part	Date Issued	Other Counties	For More Info . . .
1090	SIMS, Edward (Cont'd)	28	W½SE	1824-10-20		A1 G147
1122	" "	28	W½SW	1824-10-20		A1 G233
1080	" "	3	E½NE	1824-10-20		A1 G145
1196	" "	34	W½SW	1824-10-20		A1 G134
1064	" "	2	E½SW	1825-05-25		A1 G195
1065	" "	2	W½SW	1825-05-25		A1 G195
1119	" "	27	W½NW	1825-05-25		A1 G231
1187	STEINWINDER, Jefferson	36	SESE	1837-08-01		A1
1129	STRINGFELLON, Enock	35	W½SW	1837-08-01		A1
1126	STRINGFELLOW, Eli	23	E½SE	1827-07-02		A1
1162	SUMMY, Jacob	1	W½NE	1824-10-20		A1
1112	TANNER, David	27	SESW	1837-08-01		A1
1128	THOMPSON, Elizabeth	35	SWNW	1837-03-15		A1
1074	TRAVIS, Amos	15	E½NE	1824-10-20		A1
1306	" "	15	W½NE	1824-10-20		A1 G162
1075	" "	22	E½NE	1837-03-30		A1
1076	" "	23	W½NW	1837-03-30		A1
1115	TRAVIS, Doctor W	15	E½NW	1824-10-20		A1 G239
1098	" "	15	W½NW	1824-10-20		A1 G125
1190	TRAVIS, Jesse	14	E½NW	1824-10-20		A1
1191	" "	14	W½NE	1824-10-20		A1
1115	" "	15	E½NW	1824-10-20		A1 G239
1192	" "	14	W½NW	1825-04-20		A1
1249	TURNER, Samuel M	23	NENE	1835-09-25		A1
1315	VIARS, William	35	NWNW	1840-11-10		A1
1134	WADKINS, G W	12	E½SW	1824-10-20		A1 G240
1134	WADKINS, John	12	E½SW	1824-10-20		A1 G240
1134	WADKINS, Lacy	12	E½SW	1824-10-20		A1 G240
1134	WADKINS, Lucy	12	E½SW	1824-10-20		A1 G240
1134	WADKINS, Mary	12	E½SW	1824-10-20		A1 G240
1134	WADKINS, Tabitha	12	E½SW	1824-10-20		A1 G240
1087	WATKINS, Bryan	19	W½SW	1830-12-15		A1
1185	WEDGEWORTH, James	32	W½SW	1824-10-20		A1
1081	WILLIAMS, Charles	27	E½NE	1824-10-20		A1 G58
1094	" "	27	W½NE	1824-10-20		A1
1093	" "	22	W½SE	1825-09-15		A1
1095	" "	34	E½NW	1837-03-30		A1
1096	" "	34	W½NE	1837-03-30		A1
1120	WILLIAMS, David	28	E½NE	1824-10-20		A1 G231
1119	" "	27	W½NW	1825-05-25		A1 G231
1113	" "	22	E½SE	1837-05-15		A1
1121	WILLIAMS, Henry	22	W½SW	1824-10-20		A1 G232
1152	" "	21	E½SE	1825-05-25		A1
1155	" "	22	W½NW	1835-10-20		A1
1151	" "	15	SESW	1837-03-15		A1
1153	" "	22	NENW	1837-03-15		A1
1150	" "	15	NESW	1837-05-15		A1
1154	" "	22	SENW	1837-05-15		A1
1182	WILLIAMS, James S	32	E½SW	1835-09-25		A1
1194	WILLIAMS, John G	23	NENW	1850-03-01		A1
1195	" "	23	SENW	1850-03-01		A1
1122	WILLIAMS, Samuel	28	W½SW	1824-10-20		A1 G233
1206	" "	33	E½NW	1824-10-20		A1 G173
1255	" "	34	SE	1837-08-01		A1 V1198
1116	WILSON, Drury	27	W½SW	1824-10-20		A1
1186	WILSON, Jane	34	E½SW	1824-10-20		A1
1250	WILSON, Samuel M	6	NWSW	1858-08-20		A1
1251	" "	6	W½SW	1858-08-20		A1
1256	WITHERSPOON, Samuel	23	W½SW	1824-10-20		A1
1257	" "	4	E½NW	1824-10-20		A1
1258	" "	4	W½NW	1824-10-20		A1
1260	" "	5	SWNE	1835-10-28		A1
1259	" "	5	N½NE	1837-05-15		A1
1261	" "	6	SENE	1837-05-15		A1
1252	WITHERSPOON, Samuel M	5	SENE	1835-10-01		A1

Patent Map

T22-N R4-E
St Stephens Meridian

Map Group 6

Township Statistics

Parcels Mapped	:	266
Number of Patents	:	261
Number of Individuals	:	136
Patentees Identified	:	144
Number of Surnames	:	87
Multi-Patentee Parcels	:	51
Oldest Patent Date	:	10/20/1824
Most Recent Patent	:	8/16/1897
Block/Lot Parcels	:	0
Parcels Re - Issued	:	7
Parcels that Overlap	:	2
Cities and Towns	:	1
Cemeteries	:	10

Section 3
HOBSON [145] Baker 1824
HOBSON Baker 1824
POPE Willis 1824
JONES [161] William 1824
POPE Willis 1824
JONES [161] William 1824

Section 2
HOBSON Baker 1825
MCGEHEE [195] Abraham 1825
MCGEHEE [195] Abraham 1825
MCGEHEE Abraham 1825
HENNON [144] William 1825

Section 1
SUMMY Jacob 1824
PARKER James 1825
KENNON [166] William 1825
MCGEHEE Abraham 1825
MCGEHEE Abraham 1825
MCGEHEE Abraham 1825

Section 10
SIMS [229] Edward 1824
SIMS [229] Edward 1824
SIMS [229] Edward 1824
MCGEHEE Abraham 1824
HILL Green 1824
GREEN [124] Daniel 1824
GREEN [124] Daniel 1824
HILL Green 1824

Section 11
INGE Anne R 1824
HILL Middleton M 1825
HILL Middleton M 1825
HILL Middleton M 1825

Section 12
HILL Middleton M 1825
MCGEHEE Abraham 1824
MARTIN James 1824
HILL Green 1824
WADKINS [240] G W 1824
GRAY James 1837

Section 15
GREEN [125] Daniel 1824
JONES [162] William 1824
TRAVIS [239] Doctor W 1824
TRAVIS Amos 1824
DOBBINS Alexander 1824
WILLIAMS Henry 1837
WILLIAMS Henry 1837

Section 14
TRAVIS Jesse 1825
TRAVIS Jesse 1824
TRAVIS Jesse 1824
DOBBINS Alexander 1824
FRIERSON James M 1825
BARBER Abraham 1825

Section 13
GREEN Daniel 1835
SCARLETT Samuel 1837
DOBBINS Alexander 1824
DOBBINS Alexander 1824
MANSKER David 1825
ELLIOT John 1826
SCARLETT Samuel 1837
ROSS John 1837
ELLIOTT George 1837
GLOVER Allen 1837
GLOVER Allen 1837

Section 22
WILLIAMS Henry 1835
WILLIAMS Henry 1837
WILLIAMS Henry 1837
DOBBINS Alexander 1824
TRAVIS Amos 1837
KING John 1824
SIMS [232] Edward 1824
WILLIAMS Charles 1825
WILLIAMS David 1837

Section 23
TRAVIS Amos 1837
WILLIAMS John G 1850
WILLIAMS John G 1850
BARBER Abraham 1824
GILL Isaac 1839
FRIERSON William V 1824
FRIERSON William V 1824
WITHERSPOON Samuel 1824
STRINGFELLOW Eli 1827
TURNER Samuel M 1835

Section 24
FRIERSON William V 1824
ELLIOTT Thomas 1837
ELLIOTT Thomas 1837
GREER Robert 1840
ELLIOTT David R 1858
ELLIOTT Thomas 1824
GILHAM Jesse 1827
MCMASTERS James 1837
GREER Robert 1840
ELLIOTT David R 1858
ELLIOTT Thomas 1837
BARBER Abraham 1837

Section 27
SIMS [231] Edward 1825
HARRIS Page 1824
CLEMENTS [58] Benjamin 1824
WILLIAMS Charles 1824
WILSON Drury 1824
HARRIS Page 1835
TANNER David 1837
HARRIS Page W 1837
HARRIS Page 1835
HARRIS Page W 1837

Section 26
FRIERSON William V 1824
HALLBROOKS Jacob 1837
RHODES Solomon 1824
MCMASTER Thomas 1825
EDDINS James W 1826
MCMASTER Thomas 1824
RICHARDSON Hiram 1825
MCMASTER Thomas 1824

Section 25
GREER Robert 1840
MCCRARY Thomas 1897
MCCRARY Thomas 1897
SEALE Benton 1858
MCMASTERS Thomas 1837
MCCRARY Thomas 1897
MCCRAY Thomas 1837
MCRARY Thomas 1837
MCMASTER Thomas 1824
MCCRARY Thomas 1897
MCMASTER Thomas 1835
MCCRARY Thomas 1897

Section 34
HARRIS Noah 1837
WILLIAMS Charles 1837
WILLIAMS Charles 1837
HATTOX Jonathan 1826
HANIS [134] John 1824
WILSON Jane 1824
WILLIAMS Samuel 1837
HARRY John J 1824

Section 35
VIARS William 1840
HART Durrell 1825
BIRMINGHAM Joshua 1826
THOMPSON Elizabeth 1837
BIRMINGHAM Joshua 1826
STRINGFELLON Enock 1837
HART Derrel 1837
BIRMINGHAM Joshua 1833

Section 36
LONG Reuben 1825
CALWELL Margaret 1837
BOLTON Elizabeth 1837
JANNWAY William W 1860
HANY Margaret 1824
HARRY John J 1825
MCRARY Thomas 1837
BOLTON Robert 1837
AVERY David 1897
STEINWINDER Jefferson 1837

Helpful Hints

1. This Map's INDEX can be found on the preceding pages.

2. Refer to Map "C" to see where this Township lies within Hale County, Alabama.

3. Numbers within square brackets [ ] denote a multi-patentee land parcel (multi-owner). Refer to Appendix "C" for a full list of members in this group.

4. Areas that look to be crowded with Patentees usually indicate multiple sales of the same parcel (Re-issues) or Overlapping parcels. See this Township's Index for an explanation of these and other circumstances that might explain "odd" groupings of Patentees on this map.

Legend

————— Patent Boundary

━━━━━ Section Boundary

No Patents Found (or Outside County)

1., 2., 3., ... Lot Numbers (when beside a name)

[ ] Group Number (see Appendix "C")

Scale: Section = 1 mile X 1 mile (generally, with some exceptions)

Road Map

T22-N R4-E
St Stephens Meridian

Map Group 6

Cities & Towns

Stewart

Cemeteries

Concord Cemetery
Five Mile Cemetery
Harris Cemetery
Havana Cemetery
Long Cemetery
Martin Mission Cemetery
Mileous Chapel Cemetery
Mount Hebron Cemetery
Springhill Cemetery
Williams Cemetery

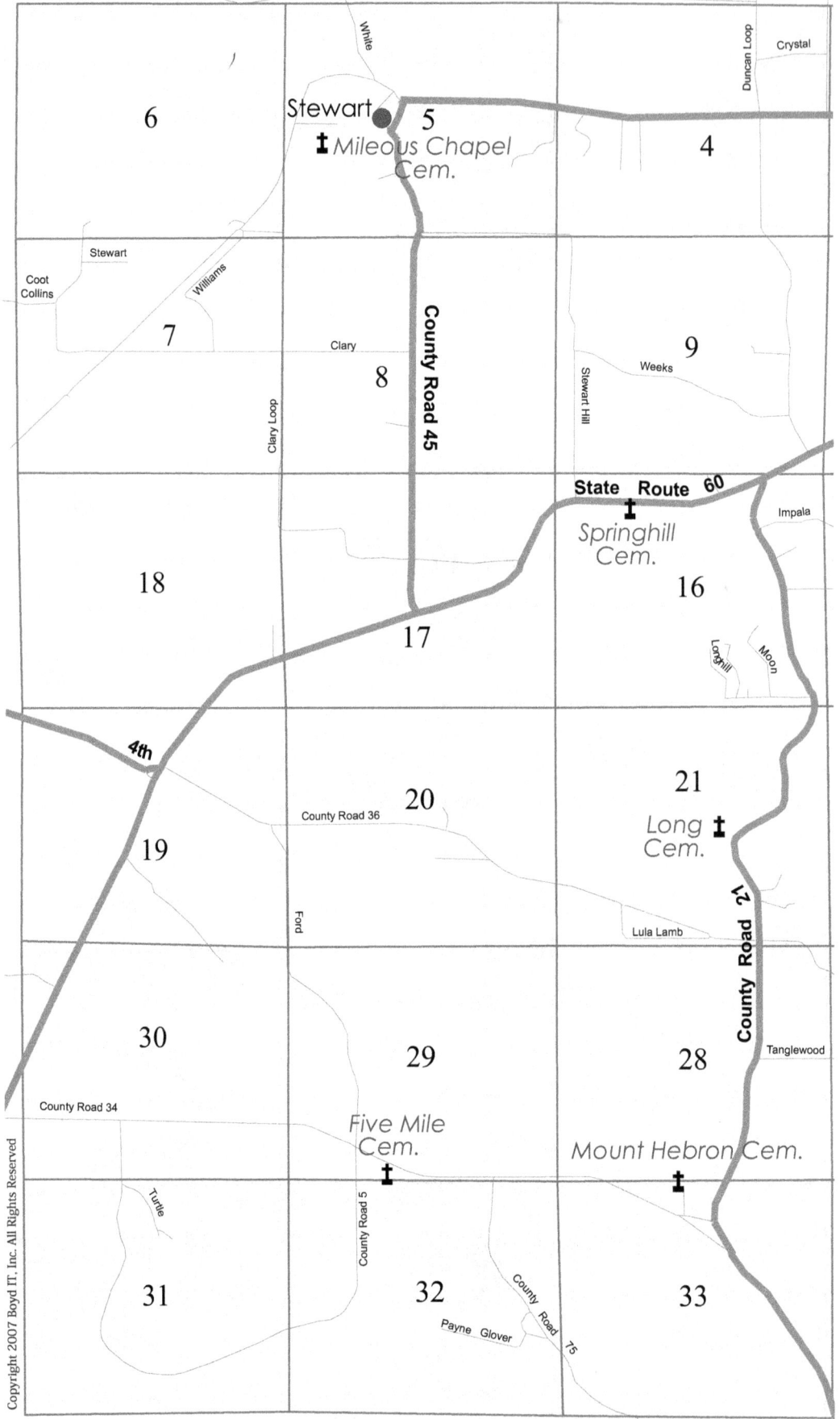

6

White

Duncan Loop

Crystal

Stewart

5

4

Mileous Chapel Cem.

Stewart

Coot Collins

Williams

7

Clary

8

County Road 45

Clary Loop

Stewart Hill

Weeks

9

State Route 60

Impala

Springhill Cem.

18

17

16

Longhill

Moon

4th

20

County Road 36

21

Long Cem.

19

Ford

Lula Lamb

County Road 2

30

County Road 34

29

Five Mile Cem.

28

Mount Hebron Cem.

Tanglewood

County Road 2

Turtle

County Road 5

31

32

Payne Glover

County Road 75

33

Copyright 2007 Boyd IT. Inc. All Rights Reserved

108

Cedarwood

County Road 55 Woodland Park

Windham

Gile Creek

County Road 42

3

2

Ashley

Al Hwy 69

1

Chancey

State Route 69

Star

10

✝ Concord Cem.

St Luke

✝ Havana Cem.

Black Walnut

11

12

Crimson

✝ Martin Mission Cem.

County Road 59

15

14

13

22

23

24

✝ Williams Cem.

Williams

27

26

25

Lonesome Dove

34

35

36

Parker

✝ Harris Cem.

Hubbard

Copyright 2007 Boyd IT, Inc. All Rights Reserved

Helpful Hints

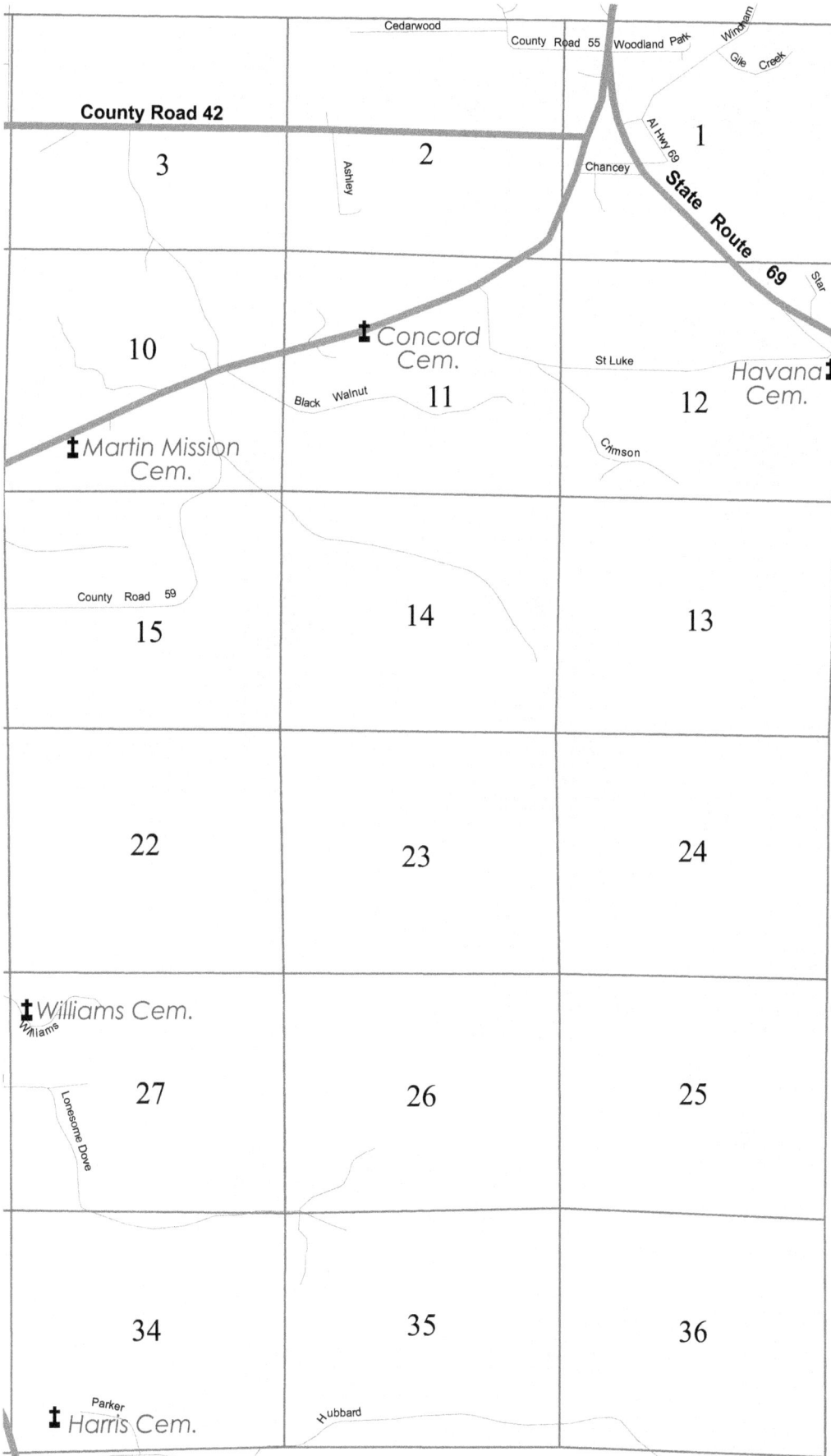

1. This road map has a number of uses, but primarily it is to help you: a) find the present location of land owned by your ancestors (at least the general area), b) find cemeteries and city-centers, and c) estimate the route/roads used by Census-takers & tax-assessors.

2. If you plan to travel to Hale County to locate cemeteries or land parcels, please pick up a modern travel map for the area before you do. Mapping old land parcels on modern maps is not as exact a science as you might think. Just the slightest variations in public land survey coordinates, estimates of parcel boundaries, or road-map deviations can greatly alter a map's representation of how a road either does or doesn't cross a particular parcel of land.

Legend

——————— Section Lines

══════════ Interstates

▬▬▬▬▬▬ Highways

——————— Other Roads

● Cities/Towns

✝ Cemeteries

Scale: Section = 1 mile X 1 mile
(generally, with some exceptions)

Historical Map

T22-N R4-E
St Stephens Meridian

Map Group 6

Cities & Towns
Stewart

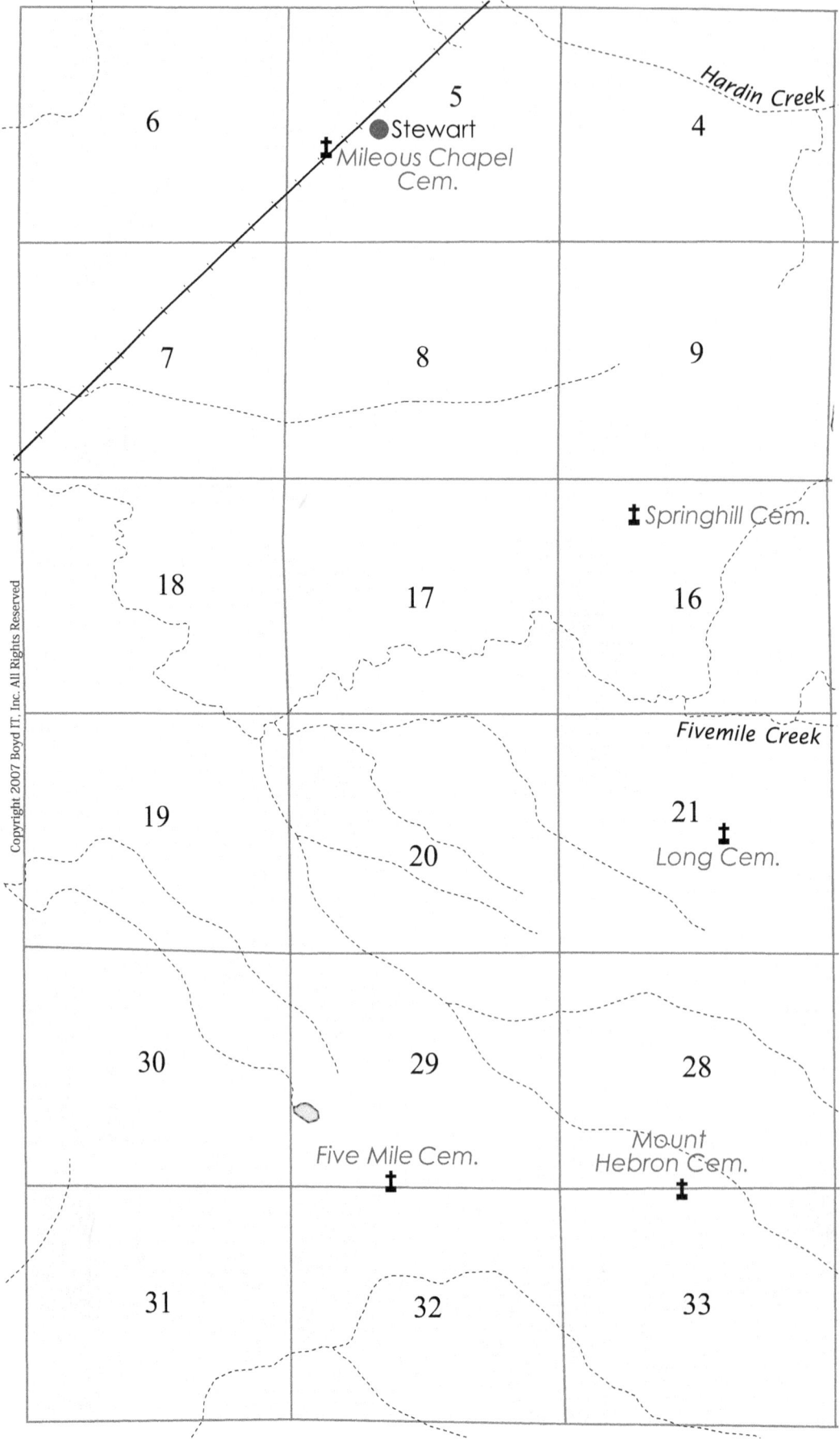

Cemeteries
Concord Cemetery
Five Mile Cemetery
Harris Cemetery
Havana Cemetery
Long Cemetery
Martin Mission Cemetery
Mileous Chapel Cemetery
Mount Hebron Cemetery
Springhill Cemetery
Williams Cemetery

Hardin Creek

6

5

● Stewart
✝ *Mileous Chapel Cem.*

4

7

8

9

18

✝ *Springhill Cem.*

17

16

Fivemile Creek

19

20

21
✝
Long Cem.

30

29

28

Five Mile Cem.
✝

Mount Hebron Cem.
✝

31

32

33

Copyright 2007 Boyd IT. Inc. All Rights Reserved

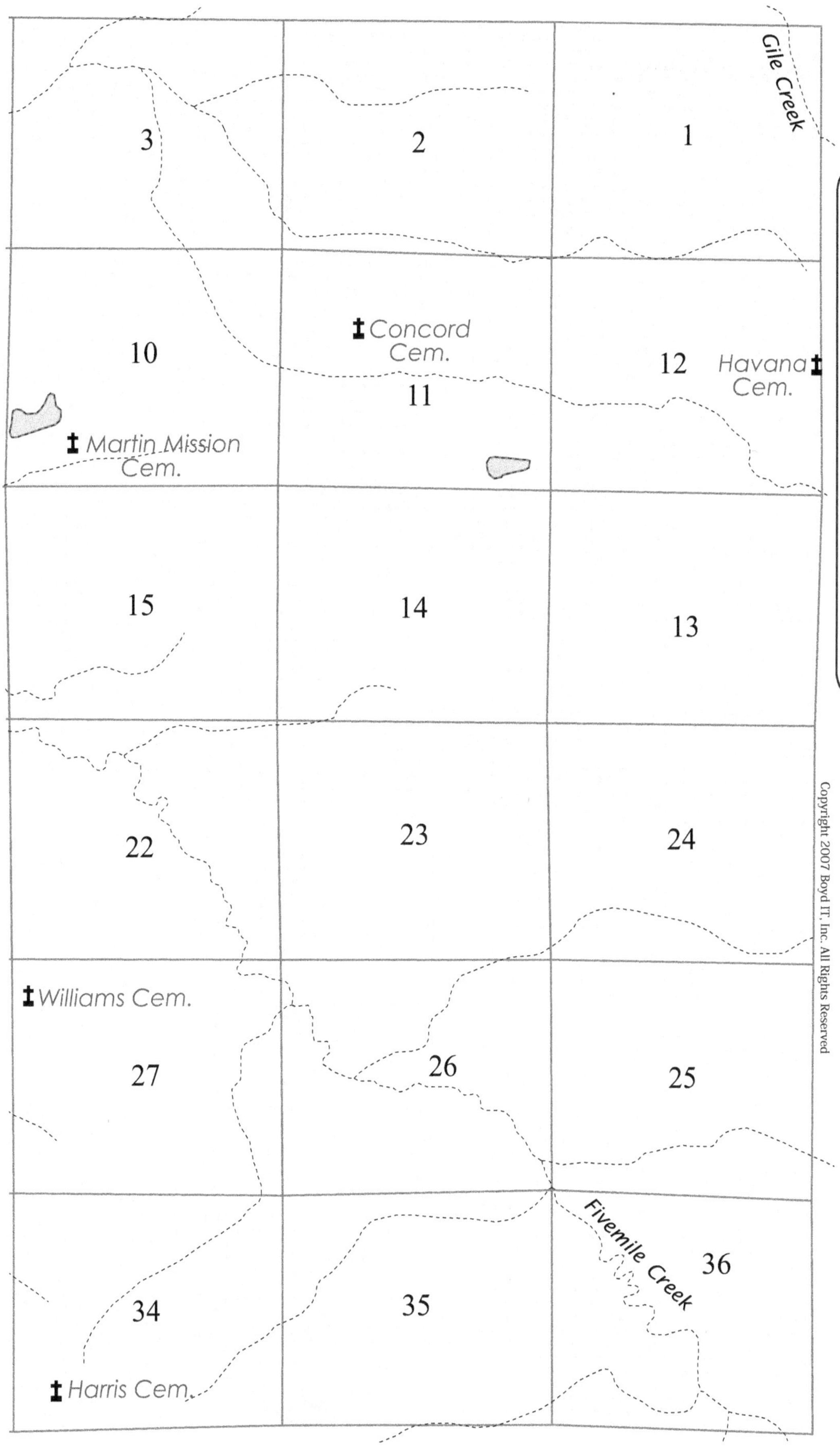
Gile Creek
3
2
1
10
Concord Cem.
11
12
Havana Cem.
Martin Mission Cem.
15
14
13
22
23
24
Williams Cem.
27
26
25
Fivemile Creek
34
35
36
Harris Cem.

Helpful Hints

1. This Map takes a different look at the same Congressional Township displayed in the preceding two maps. It presents features that can help you better envision the historical development of the area: a) Water-bodies (lakes & ponds), b) Water-courses (rivers, streams, etc.), c) Railroads, d) City/town center-points (where they were oftentimes located when first settled), and e) Cemeteries.

2. Using this "Historical" map in tandem with this Township's Patent Map and Road Map, may lead you to some interesting discoveries. You will often find roads, towns, cemeteries, and waterways are named after nearby landowners: sometimes those names will be the ones you are researching. See how many of these research gems you can find here in Hale County.

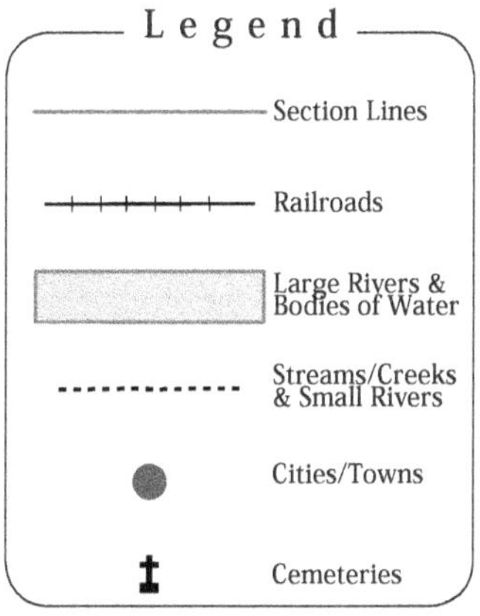
Legend
Section Lines
Railroads
Large Rivers & Bodies of Water
Streams/Creeks & Small Rivers
Cities/Towns
Cemeteries

Scale: Section = 1 mile X 1 mile
(there are some exceptions)

Map Group 7: Index to Land Patents

Township 22-North Range 5-East (St Stephens)

After you locate an individual in this Index, take note of the Section and Section Part then proceed to the Land Patent map on the pages immediately following. You should have no difficulty locating the corresponding parcel of land.

The "For More Info" Column will lead you to more information about the underlying Patents. See the *Legend* at right, and the "How to Use this Book" chapter, for more information.

```
LEGEND
          "For More Info . . . " column
A = Authority (Legislative Act, See Appendix "A")
B = Block or Lot (location in Section unknown)
C = Cancelled Patent
F = Fractional Section
G = Group  (Multi-Patentee Patent, see Appendix "C")
V = Overlaps another Parcel
R = Re-Issued (Parcel patented more than once)
```

(A & G items require you to look in the Appendixes referred to above. All other Letter-designations followed by a number require you to locate line-items in this index that possess the ID number found after the letter).

ID	Individual in Patent	Sec.	Sec. Part	Date Issued	Other Counties	For More Info . . .
1349	ABERNATHY, Coleman H	15	NESE	1858-08-20		A1
1351	" "	15	SESW	1858-08-20		A1
1350	" "	15	SESE	1906-09-25		A1
1529	ADAMS, Owen	34	E½SE	1871-06-13		A1
1530	" "	34	SENE	1871-06-13		A1
1531	" "	35	E½NW	1871-06-13		A1
1532	" "	35	E½SW	1871-06-13		A1
1511	ALLEN, Joseph T	36	SENE	1898-04-18		A1
1453	BARRON, James P	3	NWNW	1837-08-01		A1
1464	BARRON, Jamison	3	NENW	1837-08-01		A1
1544	BARTON, Robert W	23	NWSE	1837-11-02		A1
1540	BOLTON, Robert	31	SWNW	1837-11-02		A1
1541	" "	34	NWSW	1897-02-23		A1
1472	BREWER, Jerry A	10	W½SW	1860-10-01		A1
1386	CALHOUN, Elias	5	NENW	1897-04-10		A1
1387	" "	5	NWNE	1897-04-10		A1
1424	CAMACK, James	22	E½SE	1823-10-01		A1
1427	" "	23	SW	1823-10-01		A1
1426	" "	22	W½SE	1823-12-01		A1
1423	" "	14	E½SW	1824-03-01		A1
1425	" "	22	E½SW	1824-03-01		A1
1352	CAMAK, Daniel	14	W½SE	1837-11-02		A1
1368	CAMAK, David	24	NENW	1837-03-15		A1
1374	" "	27	NWNW	1837-03-15		A1
1361	" "	13	W½SW	1837-08-01		A1
1363	" "	14	E½SE	1837-08-01		A1
1364	" "	15	W½SE	1837-08-01		A1
1367	" "	23	SWNE	1837-08-01		A1
1365	" "	22	W½SW	1837-11-02		A1
1372	" "	26	NENE	1837-11-02		A1
1373	" "	27	NE	1837-11-02		A1
1360	" "	13	NESW	1897-02-17		A1
1362	" "	14	E½NE	1897-02-17		A1
1366	" "	23	E½SE	1897-02-17		A1
1369	" "	24	NWSW	1897-02-17		A1
1370	" "	24	SENW	1897-02-17		A1
1371	" "	24	SWNE	1897-02-17		A1
1429	CAMAK, James	26	NWNE	1835-09-28		A1
1428	" "	23	SWNW	1837-08-01		A1
1430	" "	26	W½NW	1837-11-02		A1
1527	CAMAK, Moses	24	NWNE	1837-03-15		A1
1375	CAMPBELL, David	7	W½NE	1831-12-01		A1
1581	CAMPBELL, William	6	SESE	1858-08-20		A1
1433	CHANDLER, James	30	SENE	1837-11-02		A1
1431	" "	29	SWNW	1839-05-01		A1
1432	" "	30	NESW	1858-08-20		A1

ID	Individual in Patent	Sec.	Sec. Part	Date Issued	Other Counties	For More Info . . .
1549	CHANDLER, Scott	34	S½SW	1837-08-01		A1
1548	" "	29	W½SW	1837-11-02		A1
1607	CHAPMAN, Willis	35	E½SE	1858-08-20		A1 V1466
1608	" "	35	SWSE	1858-08-20		A1
1609	" "	36	NWSW	1858-08-20		A1
1474	CLARY, John	12	E½SE	1837-08-01		A1
1476	" "	13	NENE	1837-08-01		A1
1475	" "	12	SWSE	1837-11-02		A1
1583	CLARY, William	12	NWSE	1837-11-02		A1
1582	" "	12	NE	1858-08-20		A1
1405	COOK, Henry	24	NESE	1858-08-20		A1
1406	" "	24	SENE	1858-08-20		A1
1419	COOK, Jacob M	25	NE	1858-08-20		A1
1584	COOPER, William	5	W½SW	1837-08-01		A1
1585	" "	8	W½NE	1837-08-01		A1
1575	DAVIS, Turner A	30	W½SE	1839-05-01		A1
1573	" "	20	SWSW	1840-11-10		A1
1574	" "	29	NWNW	1840-11-10		A1
1576	" "	31	E½NW	1840-11-10		A1
1577	" "	31	NWNW	1840-11-10		A1
1353	DAY, Daniel	34	SWNW	1858-08-20		A1
1539	DAY, Ransom	33	SESE	1858-08-20		A1
1508	DOWDLE, Joseph P	4	NESW	1837-11-02		A1
1509	" "	4	NWSW	1837-11-02		A1
1480	ELLIOT, John	7	NENE	1837-03-30		A1
1376	ELLIOTT, David R	19	W½SW	1858-08-20		A1
1398	ELLIOTT, George	18	NENW	1837-08-01		A1
1399	" "	23	SENW	1837-08-01		A1
1402	ELLIOTT, George R	8	W½SE	1843-02-01		A1
1400	" "	8	NESW	1858-08-20		A1
1401	" "	8	SESE	1858-08-20		A1
1434	ELLIOTT, James	32	W½NE	1823-10-01		A1
1422	ELLIOTT, James C	29	W½NE	1858-08-20		A1
1481	ELLIOTT, John	7	E½SE	1831-12-01		A1
1482	" "	7	SENE	1835-09-28		A1
1551	ELLIOTT, Thomas	19	E½NW	1823-10-01		A1
1550	" "	18	W½SW	1837-05-15		A1
1554	" "	23	NENW	1837-08-01		A1
1555	" "	23	NWNE	1837-08-01		A1
1552	" "	19	W½NW	1839-05-01		A1
1553	" "	22	E½NE	1858-08-20		A1
1556	" "	23	SWSE	1858-08-20		A1
1557	" "	26	NENW	1858-08-20		A1
1444	FULTOM, James L	14	NWSW	1897-11-05		A2
1558	GEDDIE, Thomas	1	NENE	1853-08-04		A1
1559	" "	1	NWSE	1897-08-16		A1
1560	" "	1	SWNE	1897-08-16		A1
1586	GLOVER, William H	8	NENE	1895-01-31		A2
1542	GREER, Robert	7	W½SE	1831-12-01		A1
1514	GRIFFIN, Killis J	4	SESW	1891-01-15		A2
1438	GUY, James	11	NWSE	1835-09-12		A1
1439	" "	11	SWNE	1835-09-12		A1
1437	" "	11	E½SW	1837-03-15		A1
1435	" "	11	E½NW	1837-11-02		A1
1436	" "	11	E½SE	1837-11-02		A1
1528	GWIN, Moses	28	E½NW	1822-01-01		A1
1587	HARVEY, William	8	W½SW	1822-01-01		A1
1588	HILLHOUSE, William	3	SWNE	1837-11-02		A1
1396	HOGGLE, Fredrick	35	S½NE	1897-01-15		A1
1342	HOLLIS, Calvin D	15	SWSW	1858-08-20		A1
1343	" "	22	W½NW	1858-08-20		A1
1569	HOLLIS, Tire	21	E½NW	1897-02-04		A1
1570	" "	21	E½SW	1897-02-04		A1
1571	" "	21	NENE	1897-02-04		A1
1572	" "	21	W½NE	1897-02-04		A1
1461	HOLSTON, James W	30	SESW	1839-05-01		A1
1458	" "	19	E½SW	1897-01-15		A1
1459	" "	19	SE	1897-01-15		A1
1460	" "	20	NWSW	1897-01-15		A1
1535	HOLSTON, Patrick	30	SWNE	1852-01-01		A1
1533	" "	30	E½NW	1858-08-20		A1
1534	" "	30	NWNE	1858-08-20		A1
1597	HOLSTON, William N	30	W½SW	1895-06-19		A2

ID	Individual in Patent	Sec.	Sec. Part	Date Issued	Other Counties	For More Info . . .
1525	HURLY, Molsy	15	NWSW	1897-01-15		A1
1526	" "	15	SWNW	1897-01-15		A1
1483	HUTT, John	21	W½SW	1897-02-04		A1
1330	INGRAM, Alexander	33	E½NE	1837-05-15		A1 G150
1331	" "	33	SWNE	1837-05-15		A1 G150
1328	" "	27	SWSW	1837-11-02		A1
1329	" "	34	NWNW	1837-11-02		A1
1330	INGRAM, Daniel	33	E½NE	1837-05-15		A1 G150
1331	" "	33	SWNE	1837-05-15		A1 G150
1355	INGRAM, Daniel M	34	NWSE	1858-08-20		A1 R1337
1356	" "	34	SENW	1858-08-20		A1
1357	" "	34	W½NE	1858-08-20		A1
1506	JACKSON, Joseph	9	NESW	1837-11-02		A1
1507	" "	9	NWSE	1837-11-02		A1
1505	" "	34	SWSE	1858-08-20		A1
1599	JANNWAY, William W	20	E½NW	1860-10-01		A1
1473	JOHNSON, Jesse	13	W½SE	1831-12-01		A1
1394	JONES, Frederick W	4	SWNE	1897-01-15		A1
1395	" "	4	SWSW	1897-01-15		A1
1397	JONES, Fredrick	4	E½NE	1897-05-20		A1
1537	JONES, Pinckney	14	SWSW	1850-03-01		A1
1538	" "	23	NWNW	1850-03-01		A1
1388	KNIGHT, Ephraim	22	E½NW	1897-02-17		A1
1389	" "	22	W½NE	1897-02-17		A1
1390	" "	27	E½NW	1897-02-17		A1
1391	" "	27	NESE	1897-02-17		A1
1392	" "	27	SWNW	1897-02-17		A1
1413	LAVENDER, Hugh	21	E½SE	1826-05-15		A1
1412	LAVENDER, Hugh L	4	W½NW	1825-06-06		A1
1493	LAVENDER, John	5	E½NE	1822-01-01		A1
1487	" "	14	NWNW	1835-09-28		A1
1486	" "	14	E½NW	1837-03-30		A1
1489	" "	15	E½NE	1837-08-01		A1
1485	" "	11	SWSW	1837-11-02		A1
1491	" "	15	W½NE	1837-11-02		A1
1492	" "	21	W½SE	1837-11-02		A1
1484	" "	10	S½SE	1897-06-02		A1
1488	" "	14	SWNW	1897-06-02		A1
1490	" "	15	N½NW	1897-06-02		A1
1567	LAVENDER, Thomas	4	NESE	1853-08-01		A1 V1410
1564	" "	10	NWSE	1897-03-02		A1
1565	" "	10	S½NE	1897-03-02		A1
1566	" "	11	NWSW	1897-03-02		A1
1441	LEE, James J	32	E½SE	1837-08-01		A1
1443	" "	33	NWSW	1837-08-01		A1
1442	" "	32	SENE	1840-11-10		A1
1354	LILES, Daniel	36	SE	1858-08-20		A1
1477	LILES, John D	27	NWSW	1897-02-17		A1
1478	" "	27	SESW	1897-02-17		A1
1479	" "	34	NENW	1897-02-17		A1
1593	LILES, William	26	SW	1858-08-20		A1
1592	" "	26	SENW	1861-01-18		A1
1335	LOFTIS, Berryman H	3	S½SW	1837-08-01		A1 V1378
1336	" "	5	E½SW	1837-11-02		A1
1403	LOFTIS, George W	8	NESE	1837-11-02		A1
1404	" "	8	SENE	1837-11-02		A1
1440	LOFTIS, James H	5	SWSE	1837-11-02		A1
1594	LYONS, William	2	W½SW	1897-01-15		A1
1385	MANSKER, Eleanor	18	E½SW	1831-12-01		A1
1448	MARTIN, James	5	W½NW	1823-10-01		A1
1449	" "	6	E½NW	1823-10-01		A1
1450	" "	6	W½SE	1825-06-06		A1
1522	MARTIN, Margaret	6	W½NW	1837-08-01		A1
1598	MARTIN, William S	23	E½NE	1824-03-01		A1
1415	MCCRORY, Hugh	29	SESE	1837-03-20		A1
1414	" "	29	NENW	1837-11-02		A1
1416	" "	33	E½SW	1837-11-02		A1 G191
1417	" "	33	W½SE	1837-11-02		A1 G191
1418	MCCRORY, Isaac I	6	NESE	1858-08-20		A1
1595	MCCRORY, William	20	NE	1897-04-02		A1
1596	" "	21	W½NW	1897-04-02		A1
1578	MCKANE, Whitfield B	29	NWSE	1851-03-01		A1
1579	MCKEAN, Whitfield B	29	NESW	1840-11-10		A1

ID	Individual in Patent	Sec.	Sec. Part	Date Issued	Other Counties	For More Info . . .
1580	MCKEAN, Whitfield B (Cont'd)	29	SENW	1840-11-10		A1
1543	MCKERNIE, Robert	18	W½NW	1823-10-01		A1
1451	MCMASTERS, James	31	E½SW	1826-07-10		A1
1452	NEIGHBOURS, James	36	SESW	1871-06-13		A1
1416	NELSON, Matthew	33	E½SW	1837-11-02		A1 G191
1417	" "	33	W½SE	1837-11-02		A1 G191
1325	OWENS, Alberry	12	SWNW	1837-11-02		A1
1324	" "	12	SENW	1850-03-01		A1
1322	" "	12	NESW	1852-01-01		A1
1323	" "	12	NWSW	1853-08-01		A1
1326	OWENS, Albery	11	E½NE	1897-01-15		A1
1327	" "	12	NWNW	1897-01-15		A1
1462	OWENS, Jameson	12	SESW	1837-11-02		A1
1463	" "	13	NENW	1837-11-02		A1
1547	PATTON, Samuel	35	NWNE	1848-09-01		A1
1393	PECK, F A	31	W½SW	1826-05-12		A1
1561	PERMENTER, Thomas J	5	N½SE	1897-02-17		A1
1562	" "	5	SENW	1897-02-17		A1
1563	" "	8	NENW	1897-02-17		A1
1454	PERRY, James	27	NESW	1858-08-20		A1
1455	" "	27	W½SE	1858-08-20		A1
1512	PERRY, Josiah	33	NESE	1834-08-12		A1
1513	" "	33	NWNE	1834-08-12		A1
1358	PHARES, Daniel	12	SWSW	1837-11-02		A1
1359	" "	13	NWNE	1837-11-02		A1
1568	PILKERTON, Thomas	29	SWSE	1858-08-20		A1
1332	POPE, Alexis D	18	SENW	1839-05-01		A1
1333	" "	8	W½NW	1839-05-01		A1
1495	PRISOC, John	24	NWSE	1848-07-01		A1
1445	REED, James M	20	E½SW	1897-01-15		A1
1446	" "	20	NESE	1897-01-15		A1
1447	" "	20	W½SE	1897-01-15		A1
1504	RICHARDSON, Jonadab	21	SENE	1837-11-02		A1
1456	RYAN, James	14	NWNE	1837-05-15		A1
1496	RYAN, John	24	SWSW	1840-11-10		A1
1494	RYAN, John P	14	SWNE	1837-03-15		A1
1510	RYAN, Joseph	26	SENE	1837-11-02		A1
1334	SEALE, Benton	30	W½NW	1858-08-20		A1
1377	SIMMONS, David	10	NW	1897-01-15		A1
1378	" "	3	SW	1897-01-15		A1 V1335
1338	SIMMS, Burwell G	25	SESW	1897-06-02		A1
1339	" "	36	NW	1897-06-02		A1
1337	SIMS, Burrell G	34	NWSE	1848-09-01		A1 R1355
1341	SIMS, Burwell G	36	W½NE	1860-10-01		A1
1340	" "	36	NESE	1897-01-15		A1
1519	SMITH, Levi	24	SESW	1852-01-01		A1
1518	" "	24	NESW	1858-08-20		A1
1520	" "	24	SWSE	1858-08-20		A1
1467	STEINWINDER, Jefferson	31	SENE	1837-08-01		A1
1380	STEVENS, David	33	SWSW	1835-09-25		A1
1379	" "	33	NWSE	1835-10-01		A1 C
1421	STEVENS, James A	32	NENE	1837-03-30		A1
1344	STICKNEY, Charles L	9	E½SE	1858-08-20		A1
1345	" "	9	NWSW	1858-08-20		A1
1346	" "	9	S½NE	1858-08-20		A1
1347	" "	9	S½SW	1858-08-20		A1
1348	" "	9	SWSE	1858-08-20		A1
1523	SUMMEY, Margaret	15	NESW	1837-11-02		A1
1524	" "	15	SENW	1837-11-02		A1
1536	SUMMEY, Peter H	31	NENE	1835-09-28		A1
1420	SUMMY, Jacob	30	E½SE	1823-10-01		A1
1319	TAYLOR, Absolom	25	SENW	1837-11-02		A1
1320	" "	25	SWNW	1837-11-02		A1
1409	TERRY, Hilliard J	2	SENW	1860-10-01		A1
1407	" "	13	SENW	1870-12-10		A1
1408	" "	13	W½NW	1870-12-10		A1
1457	TERRY, James	24	SESE	1860-10-01		A1
1497	TERRY, John T	12	NENW	1882-10-30		A1
1466	THIGPEN, Jason	35	SESE	1853-08-01		A1 V1607
1465	" "	25	N½NW	1897-04-10		A1
1521	THIGPEN, Lewis	26	SWNE	1860-10-01		A1
1321	TIDMORE, Adam W	9	NWNE	1903-05-19		A2
1381	TIDMORE, David	11	SWSE	1897-01-15		A1

ID	Individual in Patent	Sec.	Sec. Part	Date Issued	Other Counties	For More Info . . .
1410	TIDMORE, Hiram	4	SE	1858-08-20		A1 V1567
1469	TIDMORE, Jeremiah	2	E½E½	1837-08-01		A1
1468	" "	1	SW	1837-11-02		A1
1471	" "	2	W½SE	1837-11-02		A1
1470	" "	2	SWNE	1858-08-20		A1
1498	TIDMORE, John	1	NW	1831-12-01		A1
1499	" "	1	NWNE	1837-08-01		A1
1501	" "	3	NESE	1858-08-20		A1
1500	" "	3	E½NE	1897-01-15		A1
1502	" "	3	NWNE	1897-01-15		A1
1503	WARREN, John	36	SWSW	1839-05-01		A1
1411	WATSON, Hugh A	5	SWNE	1837-11-02		A1
1600	WHEELING, William	4	E½NW	1837-11-02		A1
1601	" "	4	NWNE	1837-11-02		A1
1515	WHITSETT, Lawrence	20	SESE	1837-11-02		A1
1516	" "	29	E½NE	1837-11-02		A1
1517	" "	29	NESE	1837-11-02		A1
1602	WHITSETT, William	24	W½NW	1823-10-01		A1
1384	WILBORN, Edward S	8	SENW	1891-06-29		A2
1545	WILLIAMSON, Robert	17	E½NE	1834-06-12		A1
1546	" "	28	W½NW	1837-11-02		A1
1383	WILSON, Drury	31	SWNE	1837-11-02		A1
1382	" "	31	NWNE	1839-05-01		A1
1589	WILSON, William I	13	S½NE	1858-08-20		A1
1590	WILSON, William J	13	SESW	1837-11-02		A1
1591	" "	24	NENE	1837-11-02		A1
1603	WOOTEN, William	25	SWSW	1871-06-13		A1
1604	" "	26	S½SE	1871-06-13		A1
1605	" "	36	NENE	1871-06-13		A1
1606	WOOTON, William	26	N½SE	1860-10-01		A1

Patent Map

T22-N R5-E
St Stephens Meridian

Map Group 7

Township Statistics

Parcels Mapped	:	291
Number of Patents	:	245
Number of Individuals	:	142
Patentees Identified	:	142
Number of Surnames	:	90
Multi-Patentee Parcels	:	4
Oldest Patent Date	:	1/1/1822
Most Recent Patent	:	9/25/1906
Block/Lot Parcels	:	0
Parcels Re-Issued	:	1
Parcels that Overlap	:	6
Cities and Towns	:	3
Cemeteries	:	6

Section 6
MARTIN Margaret 1837 · MARTIN James 1823 · MARTIN James 1825 · MCCRORY Isaac I 1858 · CAMPBELL William 1858

Section 5
MARTIN James 1823 · CALHOUN Elias 1897 · PERMENTER Thomas J 1897 · COOPER William 1837 · LOFTIS Berryman H 1837

Section 4
CALHOUN Elias 1897 · WATSON Hugh A 1837 · LAVENDER John 1822 · LAVENDER Hugh L 1825 · WHEELING William 1837 · WHEELING William 1837 · JONES Frederick W 1897 · JONES Fredrick 1897 · PERMENTER Thomas J 1897 · LOFTIS James H 1837 · DOWDLE Joseph P 1837 · DOWDLE Joseph P 1837 · TIDMORE Hiram 1858 · LAVENDER Thomas 1853 · JONES Frederick W 1897 · GRIFFIN Killis J 1891

Section 7
CAMPBELL David 1831 · ELLIOT John 1837 · ELLIOTT John 1835 · GREER Robert 1831 · ELLIOTT John 1831

Section 8
POPE Alexis D 1839 · PERMENTER Thomas J 1897 · COOPER William 1837 · WILBORN Edward S 1891 · HARVEY William 1822 · ELLIOTT George R 1858 · ELLIOTT George R 1843

Section 9
GLOVER William H 1895 · LOFTIS George W 1837 · LOFTIS George W 1837 · TIDMORE Adam W 1903 · STICKNEY Charles L 1858 · STICKNEY Charles L 1858 · JACKSON Joseph 1837 · JACKSON Joseph 1837 · ELLIOTT George R 1858 · STICKNEY Charles L 1858 · STICKNEY Charles L 1858 · STICKNEY Charles L 1858

Section 18
MCKERNIE Robert 1823 · ELLIOTT George 1837 · POPE Alexis D 1839 · MANSKER Eleanor 1831 · ELLIOTT Thomas 1837

Section 17
WILLIAMSON Robert 1834

Section 16

Section 19
ELLIOTT Thomas 1839 · ELLIOTT Thomas 1823 · ELLIOTT David R 1858 · HOLSTON James W 1897 · HOLSTON James W 1897

Section 20
JANNWAY William W 1860 · MCCRORY William 1897 · HOLSTON James W 1897 · DAVIS Turner A 1840 · REED James M 1897 · REED James M 1897 · REED James M 1897

Section 21
MCCRORY William 1897 · HOLLIS Tire 1897 · HOLLIS Tire 1897 · HOLLIS Tire 1897 · RICHARDSON Jonadab 1837 · HUTT John 1897 · WHITSETT Lawrence 1837 · HOLLIS Tire 1897 · LAVENDER John 1837 · LAVENDER Hugh 1826

Section 30
SEALE Benton 1858 · HOLSTON Patrick 1858 · HOLSTON Patrick 1858 · HOLSTON Patrick 1852 · CHANDLER James 1837 · CHANDLER James 1858 · HOLSTON William N 1895 · HOLSTON James W 1839 · DAVIS Turner A 1839 · SUMMY Jacob 1823

Section 29
DAVIS Turner A 1840 · MCCRORY Hugh 1837 · ELLIOTT James C 1858 · WHITSETT Lawrence 1837 · CHANDLER James 1839 · MCKEAN Whitfield B 1840 · CHANDLER Scott 1837 · MCKEAN Whitfield B 1840 · MCKANE Whitfield B 1851 · WHITSETT Lawrence 1837 · PILKERTON Thomas 1858 · MCCRORY Hugh 1837

Section 28
WILLIAMSON Robert 1837 · GWIN Moses 1822

Section 31
DAVIS Turner A 1840 · BOLTON Robert 1837 · WILSON Drury 1839 · DAVIS Turner A 1840 · WILSON Drury 1837 · SUMMEY Peter H 1835 · STEINWINDER Jefferson 1837 · PECK F A 1826 · MCMASTERS James 1826

Section 32
ELLIOTT James 1823 · LEE James J 1840 · LEE James J 1837

Section 33
STEVENS James A 1837 · PERRY Josiah 1834 · INGRAM [150] Alexander 1837 · INGRAM [150] Alexander 1837 · LEE James J 1837 · STEVENS David 1835 · MCCRORY [191] Hugh 1837 · MCCRORY [191] Hugh 1837 · STEVENS David 1835 · PERRY Josiah 1834 · DAY Ransom 1858

Map (Section grid)

Section 3
BARRON James P 1837
BARRON Jamison 1837
TIDMORE John 1897
HILLHOUSE William 1837
TIDMORE John 1897
SIMMONS David 1897
TIDMORE John 1858
LOFTIS Berryman H 1837

Section 2
TERRY Hilliard J 1860
TIDMORE Jeremiah 1858
LYONS William 1897
TIDMORE Jeremiah 1837

Section 1
TIDMORE Jeremiah 1837
TIDMORE John 1831
TIDMORE John 1837
GEDDIE Thomas 1853
GEDDIE Thomas 1897
GEDDIE Thomas 1897
TIDMORE Jeremiah 1837

Section 10
SIMMONS David 1897
LAVENDER Thomas 1897
LAVENDER Thomas 1897
LAVENDER John 1897
BREWER Jerry A 1860

Section 11
GUY James 1837
GUY James 1835
GUY James 1835
LAVENDER Thomas 1897
GUY James 1837
LAVENDER John 1837
OWENS Albery 1897
GUY James 1837
TIDMORE David 1897

Section 12
OWENS Albery 1897
TERRY John T 1882
OWENS Alberry 1837
OWENS Alberry 1850
CLARY William 1858
OWENS Alberry 1853
OWENS Alberry 1852
CLARY William 1837
CLARY John 1837
PHARES Daniel 1837
OWENS Jameson 1837
CLARY John 1837

Section 15
LAVENDER John 1897
LAVENDER John 1837
LAVENDER John 1837
HURLY Molsy 1897
SUMMEY Margaret 1837
HURLY Molsy 1897
SUMMEY Margaret 1837
CAMAK David 1837
ABERNATHY Coleman H 1858
HOLLIS Calvin D 1858
ABERNATHY Coleman H 1858
ABERNATHY Coleman H 1906

Section 14
LAVENDER John 1835
LAVENDER John 1837
LAVENDER John 1897
RYAN James 1837
RYAN John P 1837
CAMAK David 1897
FULTOM James L 1897
CAMACK James 1824
CAMAK Daniel 1837
JONES Pinckney 1850
CAMAK David 1837

Section 13
OWENS Jameson 1837
PHARES Daniel 1837
CLARY John 1837
TERRY Hilliard J 1870
TERRY Hilliard J 1870
WILSON William I 1858
CAMAK David 1837
CAMAK David 1897
WILSON William J 1837

Section 22
HOLLIS Calvin D 1858
KNIGHT Ephraim 1897
KNIGHT Ephraim 1897
ELLIOTT Thomas 1858
CAMAK David 1837
CAMACK James 1824
CAMACK James 1823
CAMACK James 1823

Section 23
JONES Pinckney 1850
ELLIOTT Thomas 1837
ELLIOTT Thomas 1837
CAMAK James 1837
ELLIOTT George 1837
CAMAK David 1837
MARTIN William S 1824
CAMACK James 1823
BARTON Robert W 1837
ELLIOTT Thomas 1858
CAMAK David 1897

Section 24
CAMAK David 1837
CAMAK Moses 1837
WILSON William J 1837
WHITSETT William 1823
CAMAK David 1897
CAMAK David 1897
COOK Henry 1858
CAMAK David 1897
SMITH Levi 1858
PRISOC John 1848
COOK Henry 1858
RYAN John 1840
SMITH Levi 1852
SMITH Levi 1858
TERRY James 1860

Section 27
CAMAK David 1837
KNIGHT Ephraim 1897
KNIGHT Ephraim 1897
CAMAK David 1837
LILES John D 1897
PERRY James 1858
PERRY James 1858
KNIGHT Ephraim 1897
INGRAM Alexander 1837
LILES John D 1897

Section 26
CAMAK James 1837
ELLIOTT Thomas 1858
CAMAK James 1835
CAMAK David 1837
LILES William 1861
THIGPEN Lewis 1860
RYAN Joseph 1837
LILES William 1858
WOOTON William 1860
WOOTEN William 1871

Section 25
THIGPEN Jason 1897
TAYLOR Absolom 1837
TAYLOR Absolom 1837
COOK Jacob M 1858
WOOTEN William 1871
SIMMS Burwell G 1897

Section 34
INGRAM Alexander 1837
LILES John D 1897
INGRAM Daniel M 1858
DAY Daniel 1858
INGRAM Daniel M 1858
ADAMS Owen 1871
INGRAM Daniel M 1858
SIMS Burrell G 1848
BOLTON Robert 1897
CHANDLER Scott 1837
JACKSON Joseph 1858
ADAMS Owen 1871

Section 35
ADAMS Owen 1871
PATTON Samuel 1848
HOGGLE Fredrick 1897
ADAMS Owen 1871
CHAPMAN Willis 1858
CHAPMAN Willis 1858

Section 36
SIMMS Burwell G 1897
SIMS Burwell G 1860
WOOTEN William 1871
ALLEN Joseph T 1898
CHAPMAN Willis 1858
SIMS Burwell G 1897
THIGPEN Jason 1853
WARREN John 1839
NEIGHBOURS James 1871
LILES Daniel 1858

Helpful Hints

1. This Map's INDEX can be found on the preceding pages.
2. Refer to Map "C" to see where this Township lies within Hale County, Alabama.
3. Numbers within square brackets [ ] denote a multi-patentee land parcel (multi-owner). Refer to Appendix "C" for a full list of members in this group.
4. Areas that look to be crowded with Patentees usually indicate multiple sales of the same parcel (Re-issues) or Overlapping parcels. See this Township's Index for an explanation of these and other circumstances that might explain "odd" groupings of Patentees on this map.

Legend

— Patent Boundary
— Section Boundary
No Patents Found (or Outside County)
1., 2., 3., ... Lot Numbers (when beside a name)
[ ] Group Number (see Appendix "C")

Scale: Section = 1 mile X 1 mile (generally, with some exceptions)

Road Map

T22-N R5-E
St Stephens Meridian

Map Group 7

Cities & Towns
Harper Hill
Havana
Ingram

Cemeteries
Harris Cemetery
Liberty Cemetery
Macedonia Cemetery
Pruitt Springs Cemetery
Star of Bethlehem Cemetery
Whitsitt-Perry Cemetery

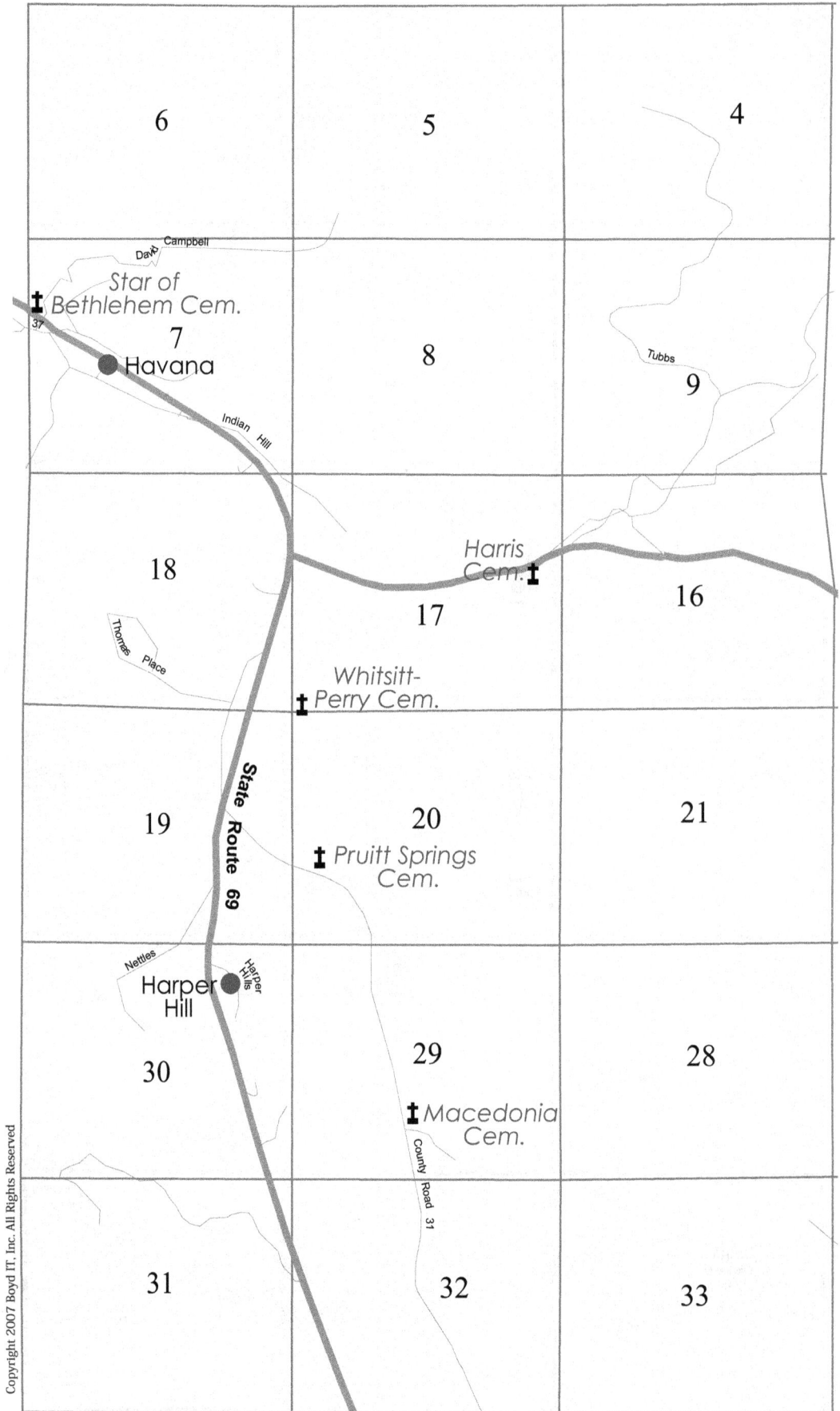

6

5

4

Davis Campbell

Star of Bethlehem Cem.

37

7

● Havana

8

Tubbs

9

Indian Hill

18

Harris Cem.

17

16

Thomas Place

Whitsitt-Perry Cem.

State Route 69

19

20

21

Pruitt Springs Cem.

Nettles

Harper Hills

Harper Hill ●

30

29

28

Macedonia Cem.

County Road 31

31

32

33

3	2	1
10	11	12
15	14	13
22	23	24
27	26	25
34	35	36

Barks

Greenleaf

County Road 29

Liberty Cem.

Ingram

Strawberry

Ramey

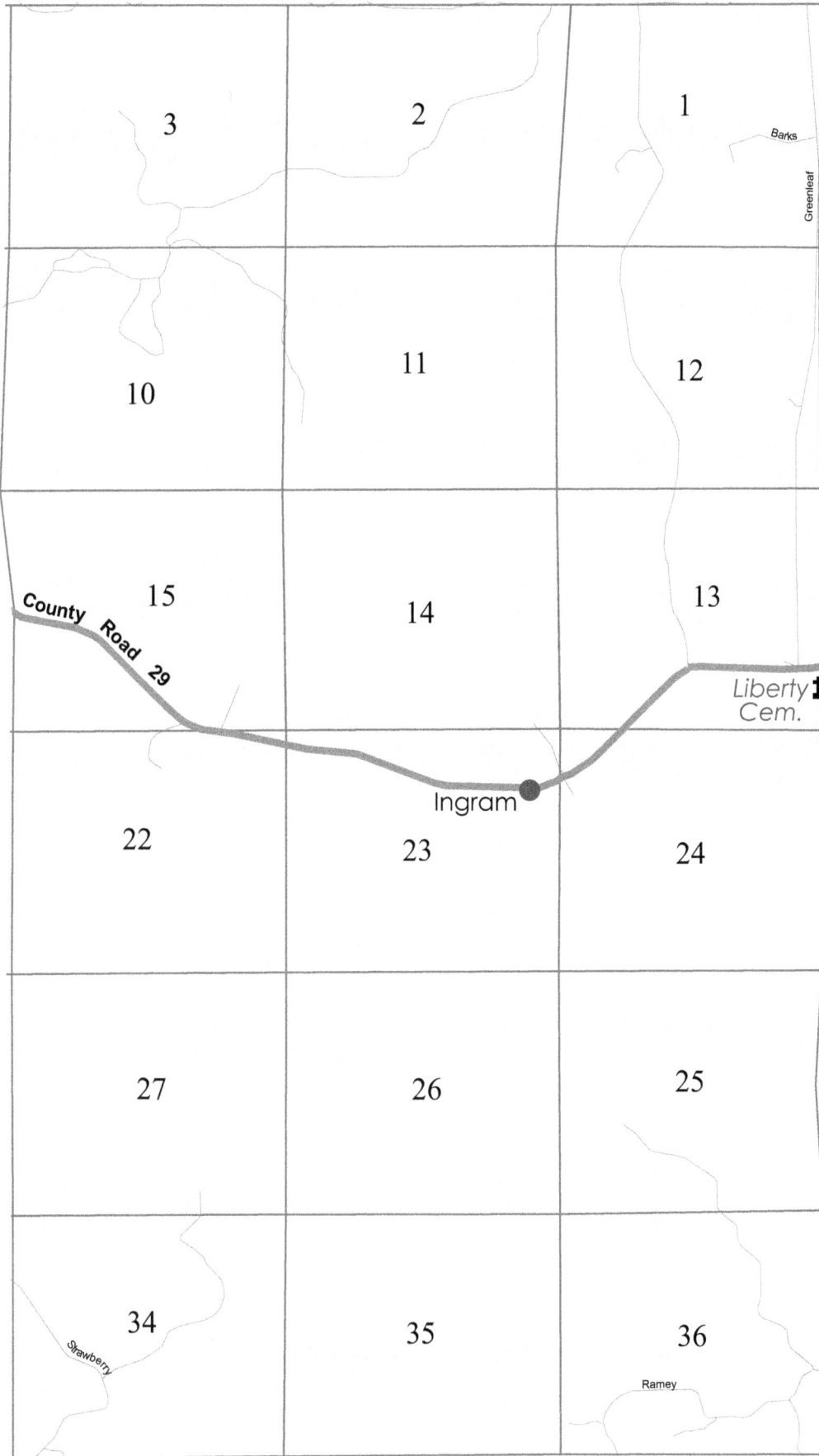

Helpful Hints

1. This road map has a number of uses, but primarily it is to help you: a) find the present location of land owned by your ancestors (at least the general area), b) find cemeteries and city-centers, and c) estimate the route/roads used by Census-takers & tax-assessors.

2. If you plan to travel to Hale County to locate cemeteries or land parcels, please pick up a modern travel map for the area before you do. Mapping old land parcels on modern maps is not as exact a science as you might think. Just the slightest variations in public land survey coordinates, estimates of parcel boundaries, or road-map deviations can greatly alter a map's representation of how a road either does or doesn't cross a particular parcel of land.

Legend

————	Section Lines
════	Interstates
▬▬▬	Highways
————	Other Roads
●	Cities/Towns
⚰	Cemeteries

Scale: Section = 1 mile X 1 mile
(generally, with some exceptions)

Historical Map

T22-N R5-E
St Stephens Meridian

Map Group 7

Cities & Towns
Harper Hill
Havana
Ingram

6

5

4

Gabriel Creek

✝ Star of Bethlehem Cem.

7

● Havana

Gile Creek

8

9

18

Harris Cem. ✝

17

16

✝ Whitsitt-Perry Cem.

19

Pruitt Spring
✝ Pruitt Springs Cem.

20

21

Cemeteries
Harris Cemetery
Liberty Cemetery
Macedonia Cemetery
Pruitt Springs Cemetery
Star of Bethlehem Cemetery
Whitsitt-Perry Cemetery

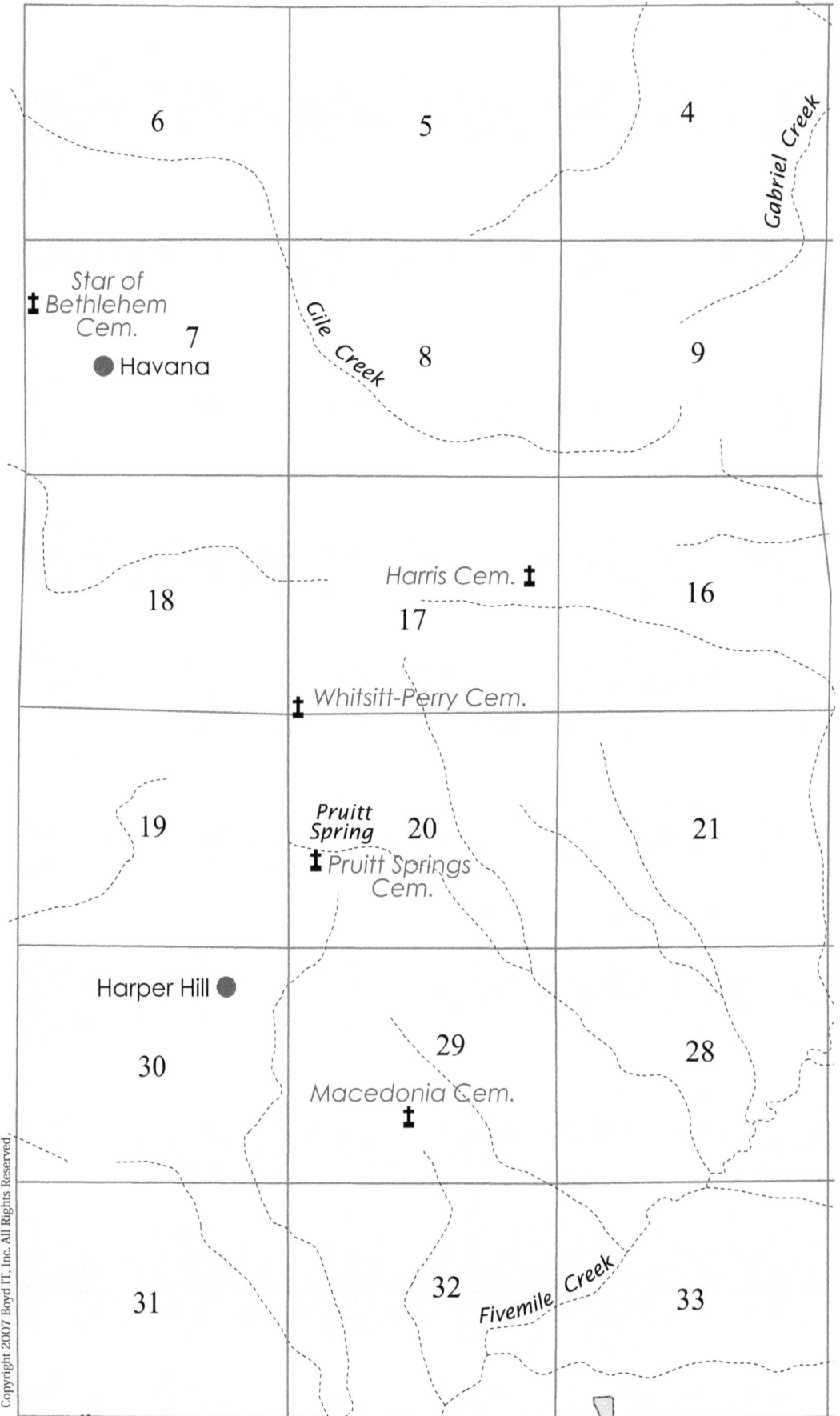

Harper Hill ●

30

29

Macedonia Cem. ✝

28

31

32

Fivemile Creek

33

Copyright 2007 Boyd IT, Inc. All Rights Reserved.

3

2

1

10

11

12

15

14

13

Liberty ✝
Cem.

Ingram ●

Fivemile Creek

22

23

24

27

26

25

34

35

36

Helpful Hints

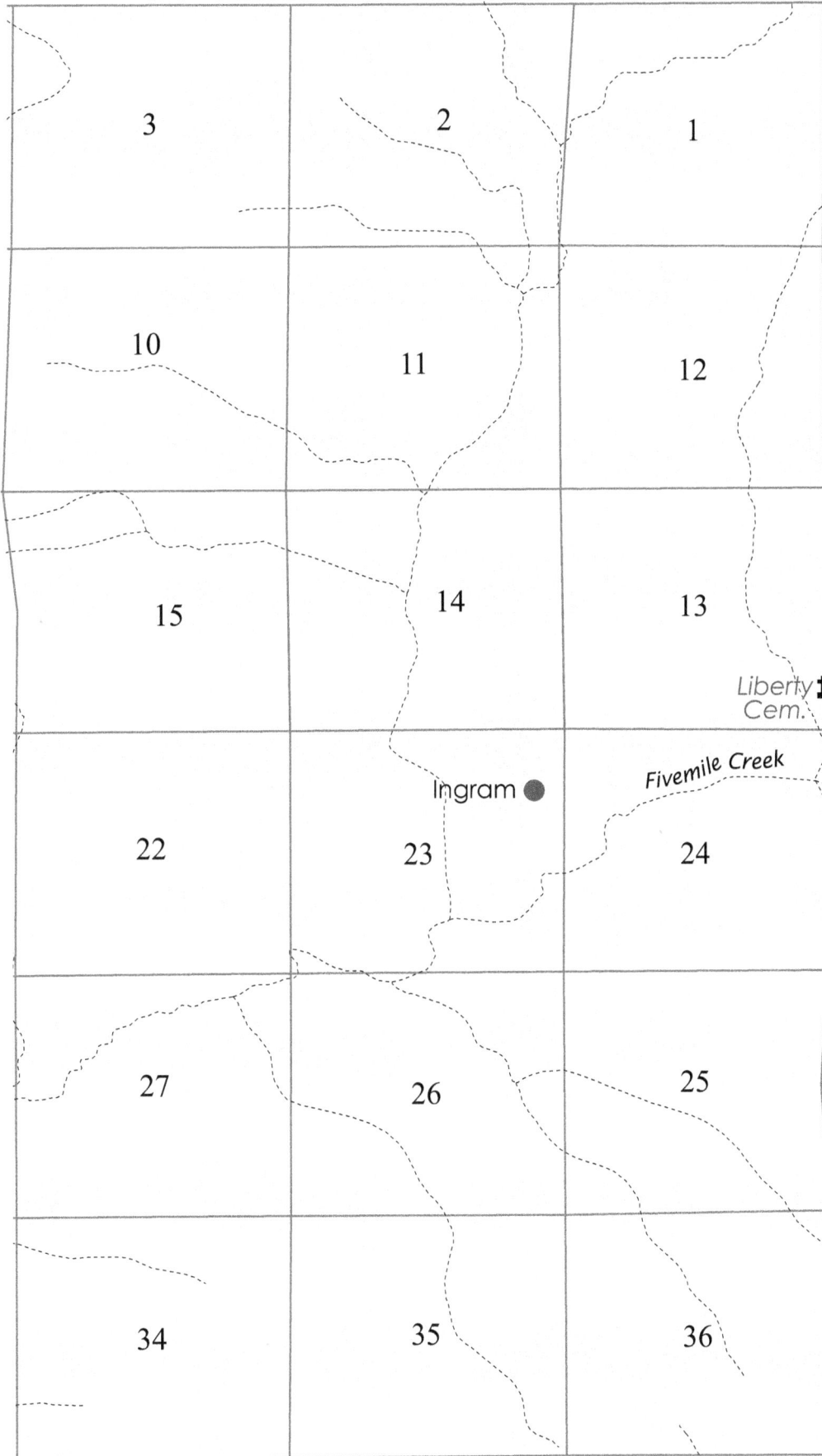

1. This Map takes a different look at the same Congressional Township displayed in the preceding two maps. It presents features that can help you better envision the historical development of the area: a) Water-bodies (lakes & ponds), b) Water-courses (rivers, streams, etc.), c) Railroads, d) City/town center-points (where they were oftentimes located when first settled), and e) Cemeteries.

2. Using this "Historical" map in tandem with this Township's Patent Map and Road Map, may lead you to some interesting discoveries. You will often find roads, towns, cemeteries, and waterways are named after nearby landowners: sometimes those names will be the ones you are researching. See how many of these research gems you can find here in Hale County.

Legend

————————	Section Lines
—+—+—+—+—	Railroads
▭	Large Rivers & Bodies of Water
- - - - - - - -	Streams/Creeks & Small Rivers
●	Cities/Towns
✝	Cemeteries

Scale: Section = 1 mile X 1 mile
(there are some exceptions)

Map Group 8: Index to Land Patents

Township 22-North Range 6-East (St Stephens)

After you locate an individual in this Index, take note of the Section and Section Part then proceed to the Land Patent map on the pages immediately following. You should have no difficulty locating the corresponding parcel of land.

The "For More Info" Column will lead you to more information about the underlying Patents. See the *Legend* at right, and the "How to Use this Book" chapter, for more information.

```
                         LEGEND
              "For More Info . . . " column
A = Authority (Legislative Act, See Appendix "A")
B = Block or Lot (location in Section unknown)
C = Cancelled Patent
F = Fractional Section
G = Group (Multi-Patentee Patent, see Appendix "C")
V = Overlaps another Parcel
R = Re-Issued (Parcel patented more than once)

(A & G items require you to look in the Appendixes referred
to above. All other Letter-designations followed by a number
require you to locate line-items in this index that possess
the ID number found after the letter).
```

ID	Individual in Patent	Sec.	Sec. Part	Date Issued	Other Counties	For More Info . . .
1845	ALLEN, Joseph T	31	W½NW	1852-02-02		A1
1844	" "	31	E½NW	1854-07-15		A1
1843	" "	30	SWSW	1858-11-01		A1
1842	" "	30	SESW	1860-04-02		A1
1910	ALLEN, Thomas	31	SENE	1858-11-01		A1
1911	" "	31	W½NE	1858-11-01		A1
1909	" "	30	SESE	1860-04-02		A1
1657	ARNOLD, Charles W	2	SESE	1898-08-15		A2
1887	ARNOLD, Quincey	2	NENE	1860-04-02		A1
1889	ARNOLD, Quincy	2	NESE	1862-01-01		A1
1890	" "	2	NESW	1862-01-01		A1
1891	" "	2	SENE	1862-01-01		A1
1888	" "	2	E½NW	1895-01-31		A2
1892	" "	2	SWNE	1895-01-31		A2
1976	ARNOLD, Yancy	2	NWSE	1858-11-01		A1
1695	AVERA, Hardy	23	E½SE	1831-06-01		A1
1696	AVERITT, Hardy	23	NWSE	1834-08-12		A1
1697	" "	23	SENE	1834-08-12		A1
1681	BENNETT, George	21	NWSW	1837-08-10		A1
1682	" "	21	SWNE	1837-08-10		A1
1630	BLACKWOOD, Anderson	21	SESE	1840-10-10		A1
1624	BLAND, Allen P	35	NESE	1862-01-01		A1
1625	" "	36	NWSW	1862-01-01		A1
1766	BLAND, James O	33	SENE	1860-04-02		A1
1767	" "	34	NWSW	1860-04-02		A1
1768	" "	34	W½NW	1860-04-02		A1
1645	BOGGS, Benjamin F	36	NW	1860-04-02		A1
1642	" "	25	E½SW	1898-05-02		A1
1643	" "	25	NWSW	1898-05-02		A1
1644	" "	25	SENW	1898-05-02		A1
1954	BOYD, William I	21	E½NE	1898-05-02		A1
1955	" "	21	NESE	1898-05-02		A1
1956	" "	22	NWNW	1898-05-02		A1
1796	BROWN, John	6	SW	1885-12-10		A2
1744	BUSHARD, James	27	SWNE	1860-04-02		A1
1745	BUZZARD, James	8	NWSW	1837-08-12		A1
1936	CALDWELL, Washington J	4	NWSW	1860-04-02		A1
1937	" "	4	SENW	1860-04-02		A1
1780	CARLISLE, Jane	35	SESE	1837-08-02		A1
1779	" "	35	SENE	1837-08-09		A1
1617	CLAREY, Adam	17	NWNW	1837-08-18		A1
1618	CLARY, Adam	30	NENW	1860-04-02		A1
1752	CLARY, James H	22	E½NW	1892-01-18		A2
1680	CLEMENT, Gabriel	25	SWNW	1860-04-02		A1
1855	CLEMENT, Lewellen	28	NWSW	1858-11-01		A1
1856	" "	29	NESE	1858-11-01		A1

ID	Individual in Patent	Sec.	Sec. Part	Date Issued	Other Counties	For More Info . . .
1854	CLEMENT, Lewellen (Cont'd)	28	NESW	1860-04-02		A1
1857	" "	29	SENE	1860-04-02		A1
1694	COLBURN, Giles W	12	SESE	1908-08-03		A1
1972	COLBURN, William W	14	W½NW	1913-03-03		A2
1701	COOK, Henry	19	SWNW	1837-08-02		A1
1702	" "	20	NW	1837-08-02		A1
1698	" "	18	SENE	1837-08-14		A1
1699	" "	19	NESW	1837-08-14		A1
1700	" "	19	NWSW	1837-08-14		A1
1734	COOK, Jacob	36	SWSW	1854-10-02		A1
1787	COOK, John A	20	W½SW	1860-12-01		A1
1868	COOK, Martin	19	SWNE	1835-11-20		A1
1870	" "	19	E½NE	1837-08-02		A1 G66
1871	" "	19	NWNE	1837-08-02		A1 G66
1867	" "	19	NWSE	1838-07-28		A1
1869	" "	28	SWSW	1850-08-10		A1
1865	" "	12	E½NE	1860-04-02		A1
1866	" "	12	NESE	1860-04-02		A1
1710	COUNTS, Henry M	33	E½SW	1843-02-01		A1
1711	" "	33	SWNE	1848-05-03		A1
1737	COUNTS, Jacob W	32	SENE	1852-02-02		A1
1665	DAVIS, Edward W	17	SWSE	1852-02-02		A1
1666	" "	8	SESE	1852-02-02		A1
1748	DAVIS, James	25	E½SE	1858-11-01		A1
1798	DAVIS, John	29	NENW	1849-09-01		A1
1824	DAVIS, John S	8	NESW	1852-02-02		A1
1825	" "	8	W½NW	1858-11-01		A1
1860	DAVIS, Lydia	17	SENW	1837-08-02		A1
1917	DUKE, Thomas J	31	E½SE	1837-08-15		A1
1918	" "	32	W½SW	1837-08-15		A1
1870	DUNKIN, William	19	E½NE	1837-08-02		A1 G66
1871	" "	19	NWNE	1837-08-02		A1 G66
1799	ELLIS, John	35	W½SE	1860-04-02		A1
1800	" "	36	NESW	1860-04-02		A1
1916	EVANS, Thomas H	26	E½NE	1860-04-02		A1
1783	EVRIET, Jesse	24	SENW	1837-08-14		A1
1784	" "	25	NWNW	1837-08-14		A1
1782	" "	24	NENW	1860-04-02		A1
1912	EVRIET, Thomas	13	SWSE	1837-08-14		A1
1913	" "	24	NWNE	1837-08-14		A1
1803	FISHER, John	35	NWNE	1834-06-12		A1
1804	" "	35	SWNE	1837-08-02		A1
1932	FISHER, Thomas W	34	E½NE	1858-11-01		A1
1929	" "	25	SWSW	1860-04-02		A1
1930	" "	26	E½SE	1860-04-02		A1 V1931
1931	" "	26	N½SE	1860-04-02		A1 V1930
1933	" "	35	NENE	1860-04-02		A1
1934	" "	35	SENW	1860-04-02		A1
1938	FISHER, William A	26	SWSE	1837-04-10		A1
1939	" "	35	NENW	1837-08-02		A1
1940	" "	36	SESE	1850-08-10		A1
1941	" "	36	SWSE	1858-11-01		A1
1877	GAREY, Mathias E	21	NW	1831-06-01		A1 G91
1877	GAREY, William	21	NW	1831-06-01		A1 G91
1958	GAY, William L	32	NWNE	1858-11-01		A1
1662	GEDDIE, Dugald	7	S½NW	1837-08-12		A1
1769	GEDDIE, James R	6	NW	1892-03-07		A2
1914	GEDDIE, Thomas	6	SENE	1837-08-18		A1
1915	" "	6	W½NE	1837-08-18		A1
1663	GEDIE, Dugald	7	N½SW	1898-05-02		A1
1664	" "	7	NWSE	1898-05-02		A1
1667	GEORGE, Elias	34	NESE	1860-04-02		A1
1668	" "	34	NESW	1860-04-02		A1
1669	" "	34	SENW	1860-04-02		A1
1670	" "	35	NWSW	1860-04-02		A1
1950	GEORGE, William H	35	SESW	1860-04-02		A1
1735	GLENN, Jacob	24	W½SW	1833-08-02		A1
1812	GOODDIN, John	26	SWSW	1837-08-18		A1
1841	GOODEN, Joseph M	12	N½NW	1905-04-18		A2
1706	GOODWIN, Henry	15	N½NW	1898-05-02		A1
1750	GOODWIN, James	22	NWSE	1835-10-01		A1
1751	" "	22	SWNW	1837-08-10		A1
1948	GOODWIN, William	1	W½NE	1860-04-02		A1

ID	Individual in Patent	Sec.	Sec. Part	Date Issued	Other Counties	For More Info . . .
1949	GOODWIN, William (Cont'd)	1	W½SE	1860-04-02		A1
1947	" "	1	E½NW	1898-05-02		A1
1651	GRIFFIN, Charles	18	NENW	1904-09-28		A2
1960	GUY, William L	32	SWNE	1852-02-02		A1
1961	" "	4	E½SE	1858-11-01		A1
1962	" "	4	NWSE	1858-11-01		A1
1964	" "	9	NENE	1858-11-01		A1
1959	" "	3	SWSW	1860-04-02		A1
1963	" "	4	SWNE	1860-04-02		A1
1951	HILL, William H	28	NENE	1858-11-01		A1
1677	HOGGLE, Frederick	9	SENW	1858-11-01		A1
1678	" "	9	SWNE	1858-11-01		A1
1675	" "	9	NENW	1875-04-20		A1
1676	" "	9	NWNE	1875-04-20		A1
1679	HOGGLE, Fredrick E	29	NESW	1898-06-01		A2
1685	HOGGLE, George	4	NENW	1860-04-02		A1
1686	" "	4	NWNW	1860-04-02		A1
1683	" "	29	SENW	1898-05-02		A1
1684	" "	29	SWSE	1898-05-02		A1
1749	HOGGLE, James F	29	NWSE	1858-11-01		A1
1813	HOGGLE, John	19	SESE	1858-11-01		A1
1814	" "	30	NENE	1858-11-01		A1
1816	" "	30	NWNE	1860-04-02		A1
1817	" "	30	SENE	1860-04-02		A1
1815	" "	30	NESE	1860-12-01		A1
1878	HOGGLE, Mathias	32	NESW	1858-11-01		A1
1879	" "	32	SESW	1858-11-01		A1
1658	HOLMAN, David	28	NWSE	1843-02-01		A1
1632	HORN, Andrew J	26	SWNE	1862-04-10		A1
1707	HORN, Henry	28	NESE	1860-04-02		A1
1708	" "	35	SWNW	1860-04-02		A1
1733	HORNE, Jackson	36	SESW	1837-04-10		A1
1821	JENKINS, John L	17	NWSE	1837-04-10		A1
1822	" "	17	SWNE	1837-04-10		A1
1835	JENKINS, John W	17	NWNE	1837-08-01		A1
1646	JOHNSON, Burrel	9	NESW	1858-11-01		A1
1673	JOHNSON, Francis M	12	S½NW	1875-04-20		A1
1674	" "	12	W½NE	1875-04-20		A1
1687	JOHNSON, George W	6	NENE	1891-05-29		A2
1736	JOHNSON, Jacob	24	SWNW	1835-09-12		A1
1772	JOHNSON, James W	32	NWSE	1858-11-01		A1
1921	JOHNSON, Thomas	17	SESE	1837-08-12		A1
1922	" "	20	SESW	1837-08-12		A1
1647	JOHNSTON, Burrell	20	NESW	1898-05-02		A1
1648	" "	9	SWNW	1898-05-02		A1
1649	" "	9	SWSW	1898-05-02		A1
1872	JOHNSTON, Martin	21	NWNE	1835-09-12		A1 G159
1923	JOHNSTON, Thomas	20	NE	1831-06-01		A1
1924	" "	20	NESE	1837-05-15		A1
1952	JOHNSTON, William H	3	NENW	1860-04-02		A1
1953	" "	3	NWNE	1860-04-02		A1
1709	KINARD, Henry	24	S½SE	1905-04-18		A2
1880	KINARD, Mathias	29	W½NW	1858-11-01		A1
1946	KINARD, William F	19	SWSE	1860-04-02		A1
1746	LANGFORD, James C	27	NESW	1898-05-02		A1
1747	" "	27	W½SE	1898-05-02		A1
1897	LANGFORD, Samuel	23	SENW	1837-08-12		A1
1898	" "	23	SWNE	1837-08-12		A1
1899	" "	26	N½NW	1861-09-10		A1
1942	LANGFORD, William A	28	SENW	1860-04-02		A1
1943	" "	28	SWNE	1860-04-02		A1
1944	" "	28	W½NW	1860-04-02		A1
1945	LATNER, William D	4	E½NE	1883-07-03		A2
1640	LAWLESS, Asahel	7	E½NE	1860-04-02		A1
1641	" "	7	SWNE	1860-04-02		A1
1704	LAWLESS, Henry E	2	W½NW	1888-06-30		A1 G175
1705	" "	2	W½SW	1888-06-30		A1 G175
1703	" "	10	N½NE	1888-09-12		A1 G175
1757	LAWLESS, James M	6	SWSE	1860-04-02		A1
1758	" "	7	NENW	1860-04-02		A1
1759	" "	7	NWNE	1860-04-02		A1
1760	" "	8	SESW	1860-04-02		A1
1761	" "	8	SWSE	1860-04-02		A1

ID	Individual in Patent	Sec.	Sec. Part	Date Issued	Other Counties	For More Info . . .
1762	LAWLESS, James M (Cont'd)	8	SWSW	1860-04-02		A1
1902	LAWSON, Shelton	8	N½SE	1860-04-02		A1
1903	" "	8	SENE	1860-04-02		A1
1904	" "	8	SENW	1860-04-02		A1
1957	LEE, William J	25	S½NE	1898-05-02		A1
1925	MCCONNELL, Thomas	31	SW	1837-04-10		A1
1688	MCFARLAND, George W	27	NWSW	1860-04-02		A1
1689	" "	27	SWNW	1860-04-02		A1
1690	" "	28	SESE	1860-04-02		A1
1755	MCFARLAND, James J	28	SWSE	1860-04-02		A1
1756	" "	33	NENW	1860-04-02		A1
1753	MORGAN, James H	13	SESE	1898-05-02		A1
1754	" "	24	NENE	1898-05-02		A1
1901	MORGAN, Samuel	24	SENE	1860-04-02		A1
1900	" "	24	NESE	1898-05-02		A1
1691	MORRIS, George W	33	NENE	1860-04-02		A1
1692	" "	33	SWSW	1860-04-02		A1
1621	MORRISON, Allen	11	NWNE	1898-05-02		A1
1622	" "	2	SESW	1898-05-02		A1
1623	" "	2	SWSE	1898-05-02		A1
1631	MORRISON, Andrew B	14	S½SW	1896-03-30		A2
1639	MORRISON, Angus	5	NWSW	1898-05-02		A1
1863	MORRISON, Malcom	6	E½SE	1837-08-02		A1
1864	" "	6	NWSE	1837-08-12		A1
1861	" "	12	SESW	1898-05-02		A1
1862	" "	13	E½NW	1898-05-02		A1
1882	MORRISON, Norman	24	NWSE	1860-04-02		A1
1883	" "	24	SESW	1860-04-02		A1
1884	" "	24	SWNE	1860-04-02		A1
1885	" "	25	NENW	1860-04-02		A1
1886	" "	25	NWNE	1860-04-02		A1
1967	MORRISON, William	5	E½NE	1858-11-01		A1
1968	" "	5	NWNE	1858-11-01		A1
1966	" "	4	NWNW	1860-04-02		A1
1715	OSBORN, Isaac H	17	NESE	1852-02-02		A1
1716	" "	17	SENE	1852-02-02		A1
1717	" "	21	NWSE	1852-02-02		A1
1713	" "	10	W½SW	1858-11-01		A1
1714	" "	15	N½SW	1858-11-01		A1
1718	" "	9	NESE	1858-11-01		A1
1720	" "	9	SESE	1858-11-01		A1
1721	" "	9	W½SE	1858-11-01		A1
1712	" "	10	SWNW	1860-04-02		A1
1719	" "	9	SENE	1860-04-02		A1
1774	OWENS, Jamison	3	N½SW	1860-04-02		A1
1775	" "	3	NWSE	1860-04-02		A1
1776	" "	5	NENW	1860-04-02		A1
1777	" "	5	S½SW	1860-04-02		A1
1778	" "	5	W½NW	1860-04-02		A1
1785	OWENS, Jimmerson	5	SENW	1852-02-02		A1
1704	OWENS, Patrick F	2	W½NW	1888-06-30		A1 G175
1705	" "	2	W½SW	1888-06-30		A1 G175
1703	" "	10	N½NE	1888-09-12		A1 G175
1740	PAYNE, Jacob W	13	W½NW	1858-11-01		A1
1741	" "	14	NENE	1858-11-01		A1
1738	" "	11	E½SE	1860-04-02		A1
1739	" "	11	SWSE	1860-04-02		A1
1742	" "	14	NWNE	1860-04-02		A1
1743	" "	23	N½NE	1860-04-02		A1
1763	PAYNE, James M	29	SESE	1860-04-02		A1
1764	" "	32	NENE	1860-04-02		A1
1765	" "	33	NWNW	1860-04-02		A1
1935	PAYNE, Thomas W	12	W½SW	1880-02-20		A2
1724	PHARES, Isaac	4	SESW	1858-11-01		A1
1723	" "	4	NESW	1860-04-02		A1
1725	" "	4	SWSE	1860-04-02		A1
1726	" "	4	SWSW	1860-04-02		A1
1727	" "	9	NWNW	1860-04-02		A1
1652	PHILLIPS, Charles J	10	NESE	1852-12-01		A1
1653	" "	10	SENE	1860-04-02		A1
1654	" "	10	SESE	1860-04-02		A1
1655	" "	11	NWSW	1860-04-02		A1
1656	" "	11	SWNW	1860-04-02		A1

ID	Individual in Patent	Sec.	Sec. Part	Date Issued	Other Counties	For More Info . . .
1722	POOL, Isaac M	27	SESW	1898-05-02		A1
1858	RAGLAND, Loney L	25	NENE	1916-10-20		A1
1660	RICARD, David	17	W½SW	1835-10-01		A1
1661	" "	19	SENW	1837-08-14		A1
1659	" "	17	NENE	1838-07-28		A1
1786	RICHARDSON, Job P	20	W½SE	1858-11-01		A1
1834	RICHARDSON, John T	28	NENW	1922-12-11		A1
1838	RICHARDSON, Jonadab	17	E½SW	1831-07-01		A1
1840	" "	17	SWNW	1837-08-02		A1
1839	" "	17	NENW	1838-07-28		A1
1650	RUSSEL, Caleb	23	NWSW	1835-09-12		A1
1633	RUSSELL, Andrew J	20	SESE	1860-04-02		A1
1634	" "	21	E½SW	1860-04-02		A1
1635	" "	21	SWSW	1860-04-02		A1
1872	RUSSELL, Gibson	21	NWNE	1835-09-12		A1 G159
1811	RUSSELL, John G	8	SWNE	1852-02-02		A1
1805	" "	10	E½NW	1860-04-02		A1
1806	" "	10	E½SW	1860-04-02		A1
1807	" "	10	NWNW	1860-04-02		A1
1808	" "	10	SWNE	1860-04-02		A1
1809	" "	4	SWNW	1860-04-02		A1
1810	" "	5	NESE	1860-04-02		A1
1965	RUSSELL, William M	36	N½SE	1860-04-02		A1
1732	RYAN, Isaac	18	SW	1831-07-01		A1 G220
1728	" "	21	SWSE	1860-04-02		A1
1729	" "	27	NWNW	1860-04-02		A1
1730	" "	28	NWNE	1860-04-02		A1
1731	" "	28	SENE	1860-04-02		A1
1770	RYAN, James	7	SWSE	1837-08-14		A1
1732	RYAN, John	18	SW	1831-07-01		A1 G220
1789	RYAN, John B	18	W½NE	1837-08-12		A1
1791	" "	19	NWNW	1837-08-12		A1
1790	" "	18	W½NW	1837-08-14		A1
1792	" "	22	E½NE	1860-04-02		A1
1794	" "	22	SWNE	1860-04-02		A1
1788	" "	15	S½SE	1898-05-02		A1
1793	" "	22	NWNE	1898-05-02		A1
1795	" "	23	W½NW	1898-05-02		A1
1801	SHAFFER, John F	33	NWNE	1854-07-15		A1
1802	" "	33	SWSE	1854-07-15		A1
1973	SIMS, William W	31	NENE	1837-08-14		A1
1974	" "	32	E½NW	1837-08-14		A1
1975	" "	32	W½NW	1837-08-14		A1
1626	SMELLEY, Allen	24	NESW	1835-04-02		A1
1906	SMELLEY, Stephen	23	SWSW	1835-04-02		A1
1907	" "	27	NENW	1835-04-02		A1
1908	" "	27	NWNE	1837-08-12		A1
1905	SMELLEY, Stephen F	2	NWNE	1917-01-27		A2
1818	SMITH, John J	23	E½SW	1837-08-09		A1
1819	" "	23	SWSE	1837-08-09		A1
1820	" "	26	NWNE	1837-08-09		A1
1850	SMITH, Levi	18	E½SE	1837-04-10		A1
1852	" "	18	W½SE	1837-08-02		A1
1851	" "	18	SENW	1837-08-14		A1
1853	" "	19	NESE	1838-07-28		A1
1859	SMITH, Luke	27	SWSW	1850-08-10		A1
1876	SMITH, Mathew	34	S½SW	1858-11-01		A1
1874	" "	33	E½SE	1860-04-02		A1
1875	" "	33	NWSE	1860-04-02		A1
1926	SMITH, Thomas	32	E½SE	1833-09-16		A1
1928	" "	33	NWSW	1837-08-12		A1
1927	" "	32	SWSE	1854-10-02		A1
1619	SPENCE, Alexander	22	NESE	1834-10-21		A1
1893	STEEDMAN, Ralph	26	NESW	1860-04-02		A1
1894	" "	26	NWSW	1860-04-02		A1
1895	" "	26	SENW	1860-04-02		A1
1896	" "	26	SWNW	1860-04-02		A1
1637	STEPHENS, Andrew W	25	W½SE	1898-05-02		A1
1638	" "	36	NE	1898-05-02		A1
1693	STEPHENS, Gideon	27	SENW	1854-10-02		A1
1827	STEPHENS, John	29	SWNE	1837-08-15		A1
1826	STEPHENS, John S	10	W½SE	1891-09-01		A2
1881	STEPHENS, Myer	12	NESW	1860-04-02		A1

ID	Individual in Patent	Sec.	Sec. Part	Date Issued	Other Counties	For More Info . . .
1823	STEVENS, John M	34	W½NE	1860-04-02		A1
1636	STEWARD, Andrew	12	SWSE	1860-04-02		A1
1828	STEWARD, John	13	NESE	1860-04-02		A1
1829	" "	13	NESW	1860-04-02		A1
1831	" "	13	NWSE	1860-04-02		A1
1832	" "	13	SESW	1860-04-02		A1
1833	" "	13	SWNE	1860-04-02		A1
1830	" "	13	NWNE	1898-05-02		A1
1620	STEWART, Alfred	18	NENE	1838-07-28		A1
1848	TARRANT, Larkin Y	14	NESE	1852-02-02		A1
1849	" "	14	S½NE	1852-02-02		A1
1610	TAYLOR, Absalom	5	SWSE	1860-04-02		A1
1611	" "	8	NENW	1860-04-02		A1
1612	" "	8	NWNE	1860-04-02		A1
1613	TAYLOR, Absolom	5	NWSE	1898-05-02		A1
1614	" "	5	SESE	1898-05-02		A1
1615	" "	5	SWNE	1898-05-02		A1
1616	" "	8	NENE	1898-05-02		A1
1969	TAYLOR, William	27	NESE	1860-04-02		A1
1970	" "	27	SENE	1860-04-02		A1
1771	TERRY, James	19	S½SW	1860-04-02		A1
1627	THIGPEN, Allen	30	SENW	1860-04-02		A1
1628	" "	30	SWNE	1860-04-02		A1
1629	" "	30	W½SE	1860-04-02		A1
1671	THIGPEN, Elizabeth	29	SESW	1896-11-21		A1
1672	" "	29	W½SW	1896-11-21		A1
1781	THIGPEN, Jason	30	N½SW	1858-11-01		A1
1846	THIGPEN, Joseph	31	W½SE	1858-11-01		A1
1847	TINGLE, Josiah	24	NWNW	1837-08-14		A1
1919	TINGLE, Thomas J	26	SESW	1837-08-12		A1
1920	" "	35	NWNW	1837-08-12		A1
1971	TUBB, William	5	NESW	1838-07-28		A1
1836	WEEKS, John	15	SWSW	1898-05-02		A1
1773	WILLIAMS, James	14	W½SE	1848-05-03		A1
1837	WILSON, John	7	SESE	1850-08-10		A1
1873	WILSON, Mary	22	SW	1831-06-01		A1 G245
1873	WILSON, William	22	SW	1831-06-01		A1 G245
1797	WYATT, John C	30	W½NW	1895-02-23		A2

Patent Map

T22-N R6-E
St Stephens Meridian

Map Group 8

Township Statistics

Parcels Mapped	:	367
Number of Patents	:	260
Number of Individuals	:	173
Patentees Identified	:	169
Number of Surnames	:	89
Multi-Patentee Parcels	:	9
Oldest Patent Date	:	6/1/1831
Most Recent Patent	:	12/11/1922
Block/Lot Parcels	:	0
Parcels Re - Issued	:	0
Parcels that Overlap	:	2
Cities and Towns	:	2
Cemeteries	:	8

Section 6
GEDDIE Thomas 1837 · JOHNSON George W 1891 · GEDDIE James R 1892 · GEDDIE Thomas 1837 · MORRISON Malcom 1837 · MORRISON Malcom 1837 · BROWN John 1885 · LAWLESS James M 1860

Section 5
OWENS Jamison 1860 · MORRISON William 1858 · OWENS Jamison 1860 · OWENS Jimmerson 1852 · TAYLOR Absolom 1898 · MORRISON William 1858 · MORRISON Angus 1898 · TUBB William 1838 · TAYLOR Absolom 1898 · RUSSELL John G 1860 · OWENS Jamison 1860 · TAYLOR Absolom 1860 · TAYLOR Absolom 1898

Section 4
MORRISON William 1860 · HOGGLE George 1860 · HOGGLE George 1860 · LATNER William D 1883 · RUSSELL John G 1860 · CALDWELL Washington J 1860 · GUY William L 1860 · CALDWELL Washington J 1860 · PHARES Isaac 1860 · GUY William L 1858 · GUY William L 1858

Section 7
LAWLESS James M 1860 · LAWLESS James M 1860 · LAWLESS Asahel 1860 · GEDDIE Dugald 1837 · LAWLESS Asahel 1860 · GEDIE Dugald 1898 · GEDIE Dugald 1898 · RYAN James 1837 · WILSON John 1850

Section 8
DAVIS John S 1858 · TAYLOR Absalom 1860 · TAYLOR Absalom 1860 · TAYLOR Absolom 1898 · LAWSON Shelton 1860 · RUSSELL John G 1852 · LAWSON Shelton 1860 · BUZZARD James 1837 · DAVIS John S 1852 · LAWSON Shelton 1860 · LAWLESS James M 1860 · LAWLESS James M 1860 · LAWLESS James M 1860 · DAVIS Edward W 1852

Section 9
PHARES Isaac 1860 · PHARES Isaac 1858 · PHARES Isaac 1860 · PHARES Isaac 1860 · HOGGLE Frederick 1875 · HOGGLE Frederick 1875 · GUY William L 1858 · JOHNSTON Burrell 1898 · HOGGLE Frederick 1858 · HOGGLE Frederick 1858 · OSBORN Isaac H 1860 · JOHNSON Burrell 1858 · OSBORN Isaac H 1858 · JOHNSTON Burrell 1898 · OSBORN Isaac H 1858 · OSBORN Isaac H 1858

Section 18
GRIFFIN Charles 1904 · RYAN John B 1837 · STEWART Alfred 1838 · RYAN John B 1837 · SMITH Levi 1837 · COOK Henry 1837 · RYAN [220] Isaac 1831 · SMITH Levi 1837 · SMITH Levi 1837

Section 17
CLAREY Adam 1837 · RICHARDSON Jonadab 1838 · RICHARDSON Jonadab 1837 · DAVIS Lydia 1837 · RICARD David 1835 · RICHARDSON Jonadab 1831

Section 16
JENKINS John W 1837 · RICARD David 1838 · JENKINS John L 1837 · OSBORN Isaac H 1852 · JENKINS John L 1837 · OSBORN Isaac H 1852 · DAVIS Edward W 1852 · JOHNSON Thomas 1837

Section 19
RYAN John B 1837 · COOK [66] Martin 1837 · COOK [66] Martin 1837 · COOK Henry 1837 · RICARD David 1837 · COOK Martin 1835 · COOK Henry 1837 · COOK Henry 1837 · COOK Martin 1838 · SMITH Levi 1838 · TERRY James 1860 · KINARD William F 1860 · HOGGLE John 1858

Section 20
COOK Henry 1837 · JOHNSTON Thomas 1831 · COOK John A 1860 · JOHNSTON Burrell 1898 · RICHARDSON Job P 1858 · JOHNSTON Thomas 1837 · JOHNSON Thomas 1837

Section 21
GAREY [91] Mathias E 1831 · JOHNSTON [159] Martin 1835 · BENNETT George 1837 · BENNETT George 1837 · RUSSELL Andrew J 1860 · RUSSELL Andrew J 1860 · RUSSELL Andrew J 1860 · BOYD William I 1898

Section 28
LANGFORD William A 1860 · RICHARDSON John T 1922 · RYAN Isaac 1860 · HILL William H 1858 · LANGFORD William A 1860 · LANGFORD William A 1860 · RYAN Isaac 1860 · OSBORN Isaac H 1852 · BOYD William I 1898 · RYAN Isaac 1860 · BLACKWOOD Anderson 1840 · CLEMENT Lewellen 1858 · CLEMENT Lewellen 1860 · HOLMAN David 1843 · HORN Henry 1860 · COOK Martin 1850 · MCFARLAND James J 1860 · MCFARLAND George W 1860

Section 29
JOHNSTON Thomas 1831 · KINARD Mathias 1858 · DAVIS John 1849 · HOGGLE George 1898 · STEPHENS John 1837 · CLEMENT Lewellen 1860 · HOGGLE Fredrick E 1898 · HOGGLE James F 1858 · CLEMENT Lewellen 1858 · THIGPEN Elizabeth 1896 · HOGGLE George 1898 · PAYNE James M 1860

Section 30
WYATT John C 1895 · CLARY Adam 1860 · HOGGLE John 1858 · HOGGLE John 1858 · THIGPEN Allen 1860 · HOGGLE John 1860 · THIGPEN Jason 1858 · HOGGLE John 1860 · ALLEN Joseph T 1858 · ALLEN Joseph T 1860 · THIGPEN Allen 1860 · ALLEN Thomas 1860

Section 31
ALLEN Joseph T 1852 · ALLEN Joseph T 1854 · ALLEN Thomas 1858 · MCCONNELL Thomas 1837 · THIGPEN Joseph 1858

Section 32
SIMS William W 1837 · SIMS William W 1837 · ALLEN Thomas 1858 · SIMS William W 1837 · GAY William L 1858 · PAYNE James M 1860 · GUY William L 1852 · COUNTS Jacob W 1852 · HOGGLE Mathias 1858 · JOHNSON James W 1858 · SMITH Thomas 1833 · DUKE Thomas J 1837 · HOGGLE Mathias 1858 · SMITH Thomas 1854

Section 33
PAYNE James M 1860 · MCFARLAND James J 1860 · SHAFFER John F 1854 · MORRIS George W 1860 · COUNTS Henry M 1848 · BLAND James O 1860 · SMITH Thomas 1837 · COUNTS Henry M 1843 · SMITH Mathew 1860 · MORRIS George W 1860 · SHAFFER John F 1854 · SMITH Mathew 1860 · DUKE Thomas J 1837 · SMITH Mathew 1860

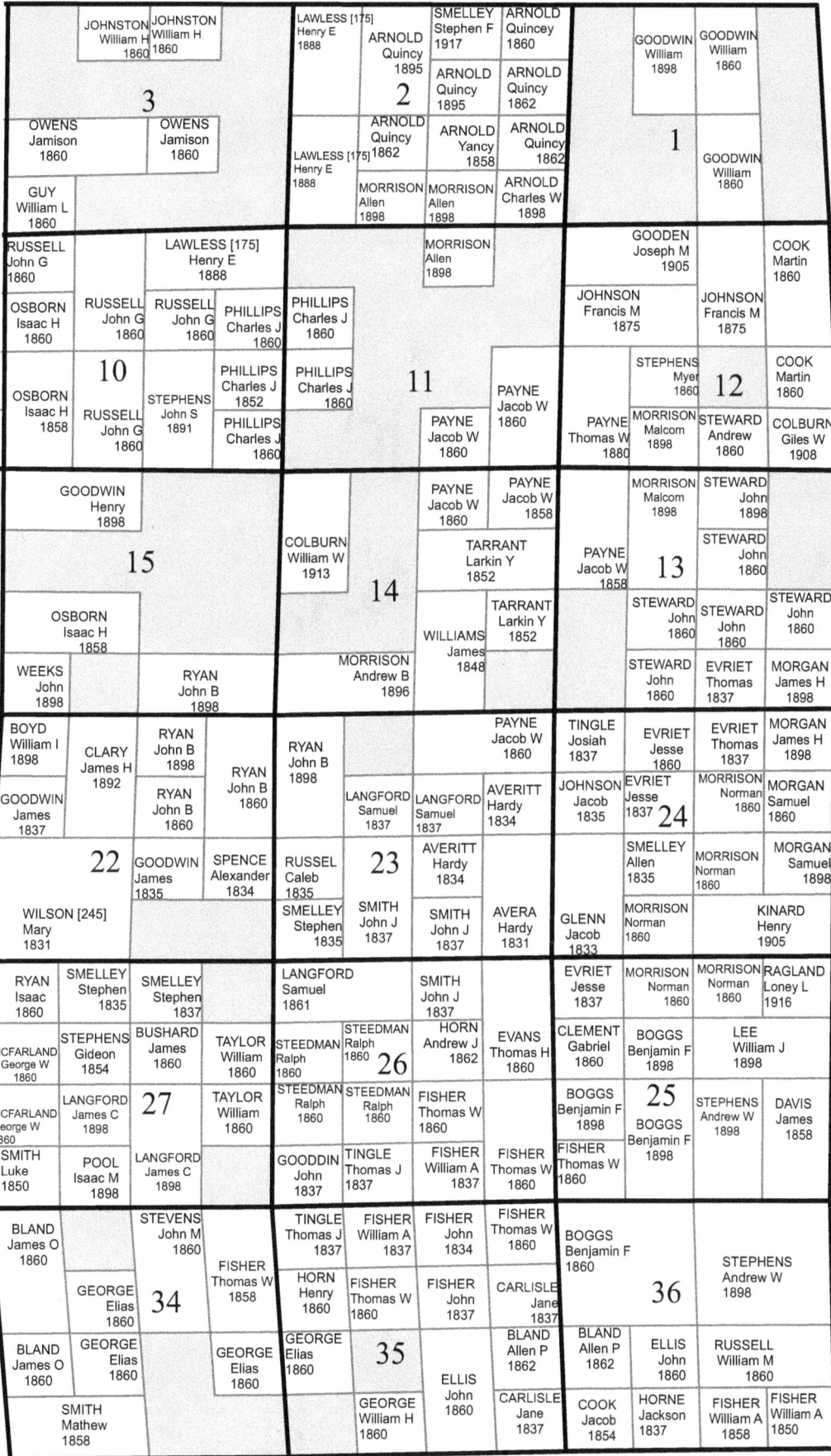

JOHNSTON William H 1860	JOHNSTON William H 1860	LAWLESS [175] Henry E 1888	SMELLEY Stephen F 1917	ARNOLD Quincey 1860	GOODWIN William 1898	GOODWIN William 1860

3

OWENS Jamison 1860 — OWENS Jamison 1860

GUY William L 1860

2
ARNOLD Quincy 1895
ARNOLD Quincy 1895 — ARNOLD Quincy 1862
ARNOLD Quincy 1862 — ARNOLD Yancy 1858 — ARNOLD Quincy 1862
LAWLESS [175] Henry E 1888
MORRISON Allen 1898 — MORRISON Allen 1898 — ARNOLD Charles W 1898

1
GOODWIN William 1860

RUSSELL John G 1860 — LAWLESS [175] Henry E 1888

OSBORN Isaac H 1860 — RUSSELL John G 1860 — RUSSELL John G 1860 — PHILLIPS Charles J 1860 — PHILLIPS Charles J 1860

10
OSBORN Isaac H 1858 — STEPHENS John S 1891 — RUSSELL John G 1860 — PHILLIPS Charles J 1852 — PHILLIPS Charles J 1860 — PHILLIPS Charles J 1860

11
MORRISON Allen 1898
PAYNE Jacob W 1860
PAYNE Jacob W 1860

GOODEN Joseph M 1905 — COOK Martin 1860
JOHNSON Francis M 1875 — JOHNSON Francis M 1875
STEPHENS Myer 1860 — COOK Martin 1860
12
PAYNE Thomas W 1880 — MORRISON Malcom 1898 — STEWARD Andrew 1860 — COLBURN Giles W 1908

GOODWIN Henry 1898

15

OSBORN Isaac H 1858

WEEKS John 1898 — RYAN John B 1898

COLBURN William W 1913

14

PAYNE Jacob W 1860 — PAYNE Jacob W 1858
TARRANT Larkin Y 1852
TARRANT Larkin Y 1852
WILLIAMS James 1848
MORRISON Andrew B 1896

MORRISON Malcom 1898 — STEWARD John 1898
STEWARD John 1860
13
STEWARD John 1860 — STEWARD John 1860 — STEWARD John 1860
STEWARD John 1860 — EVRIET Thomas 1837 — MORGAN James H 1898

BOYD William I 1898 — CLARY James H 1892 — RYAN John B 1898 — RYAN John B 1898
GOODWIN James 1837 — RYAN John B 1860 — RYAN John B 1860
22
GOODWIN James 1835 — SPENCE Alexander 1834
WILSON [245] Mary 1831

RYAN John B 1898
RUSSEL Caleb 1835
SMELLEY Stephen 1835
23
LANGFORD Samuel 1837 — LANGFORD Samuel 1837 — AVERITT Hardy 1834
AVERITT Hardy 1834
SMITH John J 1837 — SMITH John J 1837 — AVERA Hardy 1831

PAYNE Jacob W 1860 — TINGLE Josiah 1837 — EVRIET Jesse 1860 — EVRIET Thomas 1837 — MORGAN James H 1898
JOHNSON Jacob 1835 — EVRIET Jesse 1837 — MORRISON Norman 1860 — MORGAN Samuel 1860
24
SMELLEY Allen 1835 — MORRISON Norman 1860 — MORGAN Samuel 1898
GLENN Jacob 1833 — MORRISON Norman 1860 — KINARD Henry 1905

RYAN Isaac 1860 — SMELLEY Stephen 1835 — SMELLEY Stephen 1837
MCFARLAND George W 1860 — STEPHENS Gideon 1854 — BUSHARD James 1860 — TAYLOR William 1860
MCFARLAND George W 1860 — LANGFORD James C 1898 — **27** — TAYLOR William 1860
SMITH Luke 1850 — POOL Isaac M 1898 — LANGFORD James C 1898

LANGFORD Samuel 1861
STEEDMAN Ralph 1860 — STEEDMAN Ralph 1860 — **26**
STEEDMAN Ralph 1860 — STEEDMAN Ralph 1860 — FISHER Thomas W 1860
GOODDIN John 1837 — TINGLE Thomas J 1837 — FISHER William A 1837

SMITH John J 1837
HORN Andrew J 1862 — EVANS Thomas H 1860
FISHER Thomas W 1860

EVRIET Jesse 1837 — MORRISON Norman 1860 — MORRISON Norman 1860 — RAGLAND Loney L 1916
CLEMENT Gabriel 1860 — BOGGS Benjamin F 1898 — LEE William J 1898
BOGGS Benjamin F 1898 — **25** — STEPHENS Andrew W 1898 — DAVIS James 1858
BOGGS Benjamin F 1898
FISHER Thomas W 1860

BLAND James O 1860 — STEVENS John M 1860
GEORGE Elias 1860 — **34** — FISHER Thomas W 1858
BLAND James O 1860 — GEORGE Elias 1860 — GEORGE Elias 1860

TINGLE Thomas J 1837 — FISHER William A 1837 — FISHER John 1834 — FISHER Thomas W 1860
HORN Henry 1860 — FISHER Thomas W 1860 — FISHER John 1837 — CARLISLE Jane 1837
GEORGE Elias 1860 — **35** — ELLIS John 1860
GEORGE William H 1860

BOGGS Benjamin F 1860
STEPHENS Andrew W 1898
36

BLAND Allen P 1862 — BLAND Allen P 1862 — ELLIS John 1860 — RUSSELL William M 1860
CARLISLE Jane 1837 — COOK Jacob 1854 — HORNE Jackson 1837 — FISHER William A 1858 — FISHER William A 1850

SMITH Mathew 1858

Helpful Hints

1. This Map's INDEX can be found on the preceding pages.

2. Refer to Map "C" to see where this Township lies within Hale County, Alabama.

3. Numbers within square brackets [ ] denote a multi-patentee land parcel (multi-owner). Refer to Appendix "C" for a full list of members in this group.

4. Areas that look to be crowded with Patentees usually indicate multiple sales of the same parcel (Re-issues) or Overlapping parcels. See this Township's Index for an explanation of these and other circumstances that might explain "odd" groupings of Patentees on this map.

Legend

— Patent Boundary

━ Section Boundary

No Patents Found (or Outside County)

1., 2., 3., ... Lot Numbers (when beside a name)

[ ] Group Number (see Appendix "C")

Scale: Section = 1 mile X 1 mile (generally, with some exceptions)

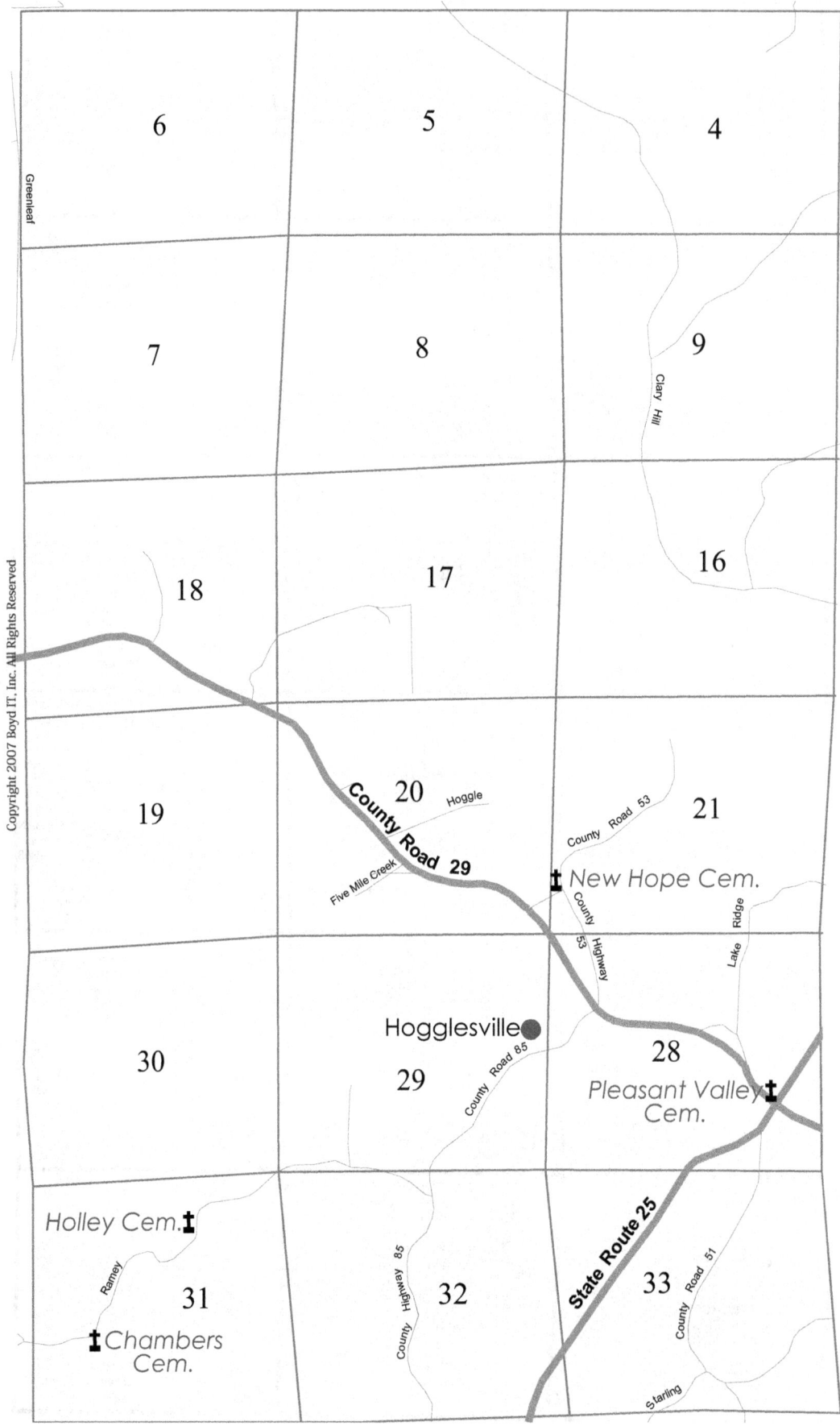

Road Map

T22-N R6-E
St Stephens Meridian

Map Group 8

Cities & Towns
Hogglesville
Wateroak

Cemeteries
Chambers Cemetery
Holley Cemetery
New Hope Cemetery
New Shiloh Cemetery
Old Shiloh Cemetery
Pine Flat Cemetery
Pisgah Cemetery
Pleasant Valley Cemetery

3

Nat'l Forest Road 708

2

Pine Flat

✝ Pine Flat Cem.

1

Forest Road 715

County Road 49

10

11

12

15

County Road 71

14

✝ Pisgah Cem.

National Forest Road 717

13

Clary Hill

22

23

Spring Hill

24

● Wateroak

Bobcat

State Route 25

27

Old Shiloh ✝
Cem.

Nat Forest Rd 716

26

25

✝

New Shiloh
Cem.

34

County Road 29

Calhoun

35

Water Oak

36

Copyright 2007 Boyd IT, Inc. All Rights Reserved

Helpful Hints

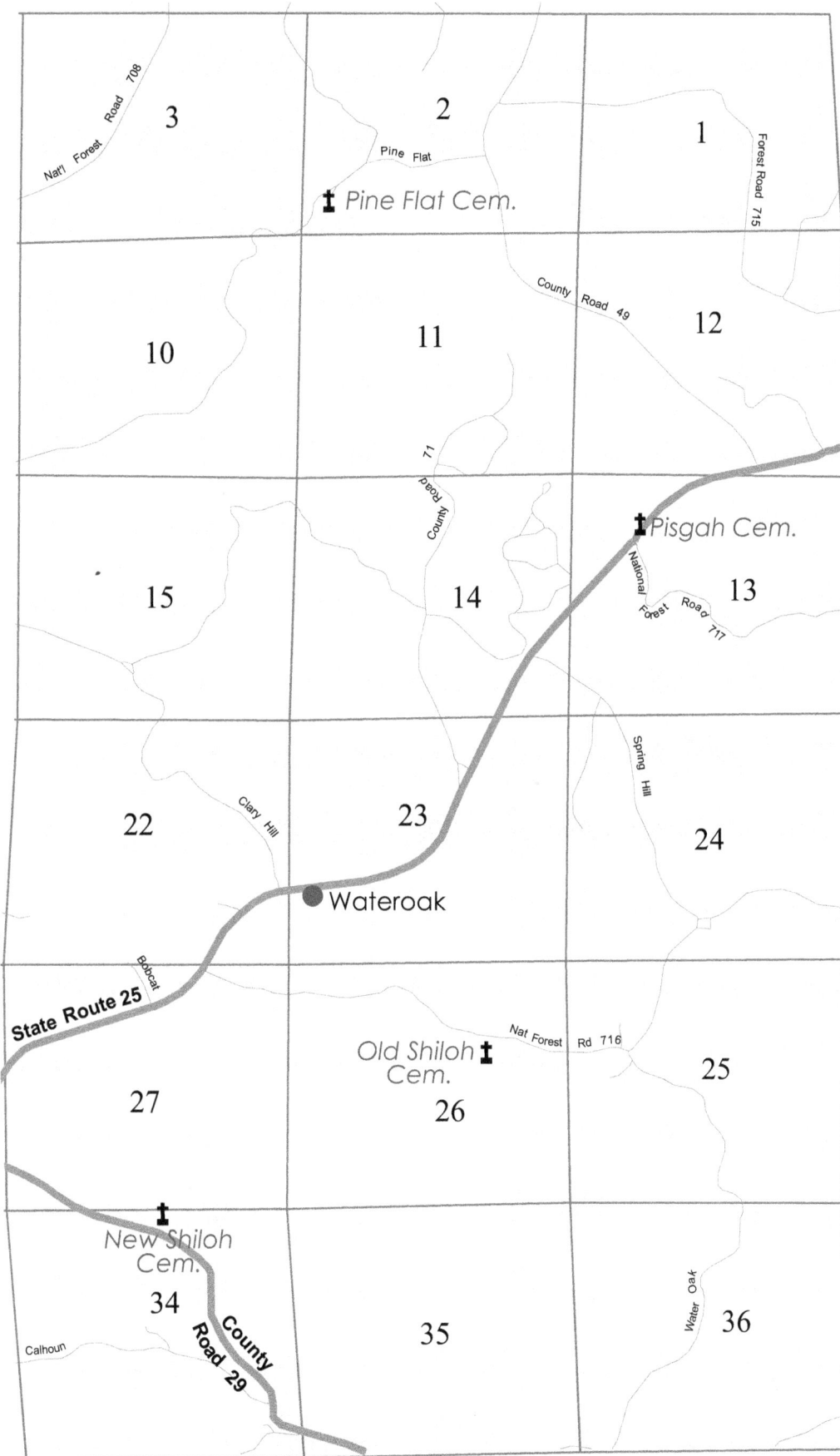

1. This road map has a number of uses, but primarily it is to help you: a) find the present location of land owned by your ancestors (at least the general area), b) find cemeteries and city-centers, and c) estimate the route/roads used by Census-takers & tax-assessors.

2. If you plan to travel to Hale County to locate cemeteries or land parcels, please pick up a modern travel map for the area before you do. Mapping old land parcels on modern maps is not as exact a science as you might think. Just the slightest variations in public land survey coordinates, estimates of parcel boundaries, or road-map deviations can greatly alter a map's representation of how a road either does or doesn't cross a particular parcel of land.

L e g e n d

— Section Lines

≡ Interstates

▬ Highways

— Other Roads

● Cities/Towns

✝ Cemeteries

Scale: Section = 1 mile X 1 mile
(generally, with some exceptions)

133

Historical Map

T22-N R6-E
St Stephens Meridian

Map Group 8

Cities & Towns
Hogglesville
Wateroak

Cemeteries
Chambers Cemetery
Holley Cemetery
New Hope Cemetery
New Shiloh Cemetery
Old Shiloh Cemetery
Pine Flat Cemetery
Pisgah Cemetery
Pleasant Valley Cemetery

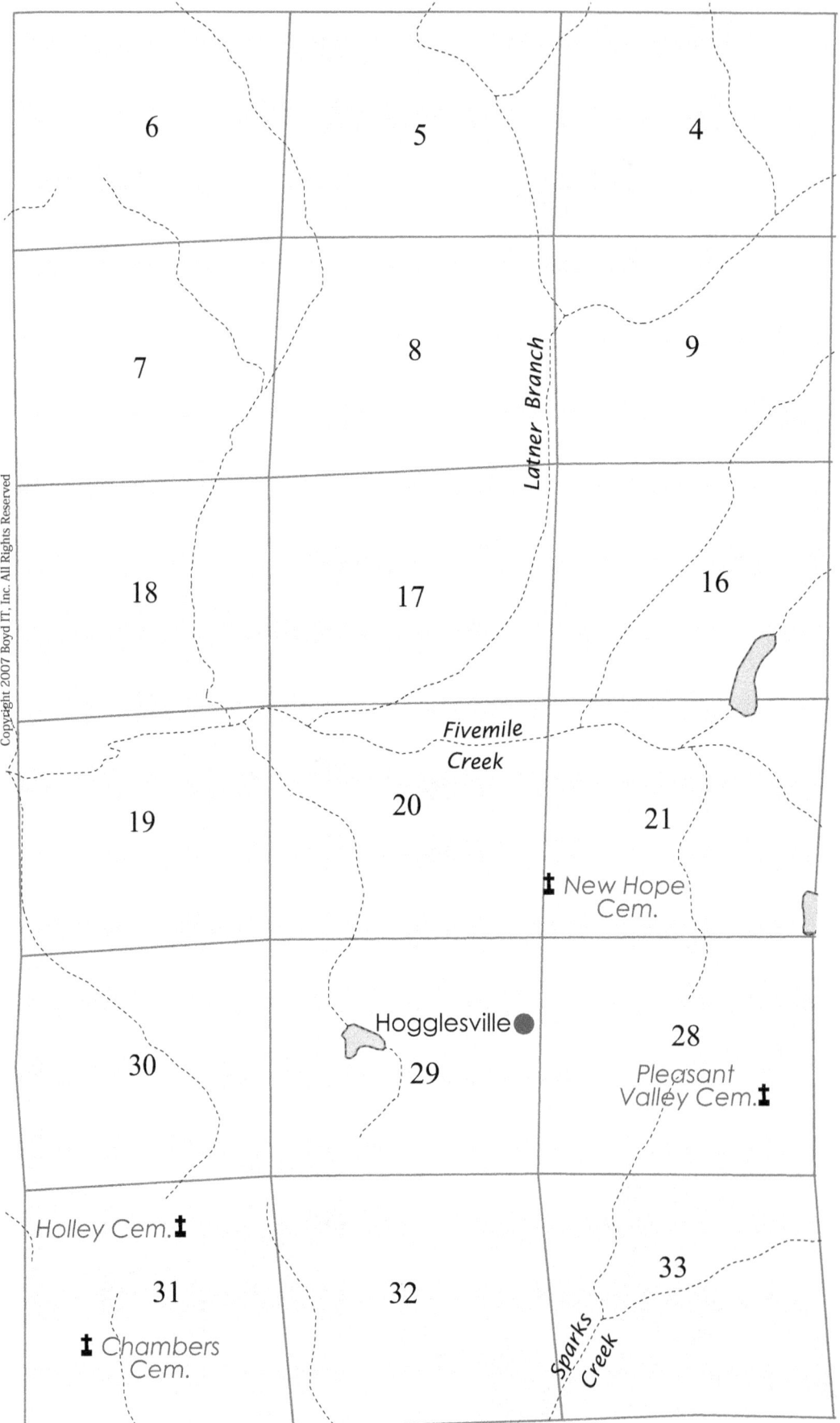

6

5

4

7

8

9

Latner Branch

18

17

16

Fivemile Creek

19

20

21

✝ *New Hope Cem.*

30

Hogglesville ●

29

28

Pleasant Valley Cem. ✝

Holley Cem. ✝

31

32

33

✝ *Chambers Cem.*

Sparks Creek

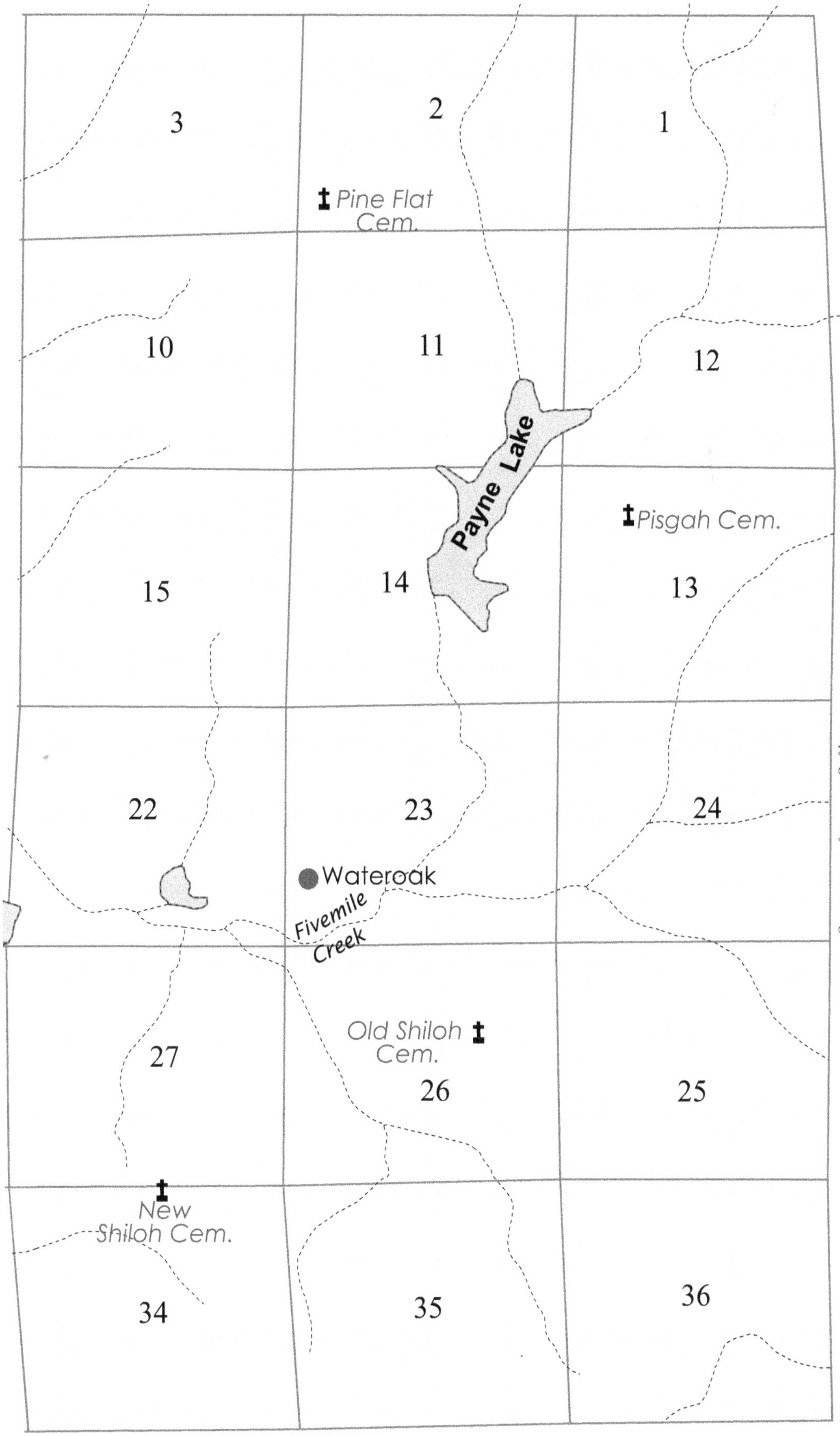
3
2
1
Pine Flat Cem.
10
11
12
Payne Lake
15
14
13
Pisgah Cem.
22
23
24
Wateroak
Fivemile Creek
27
26
25
Old Shiloh Cem.
New Shiloh Cem.
34
35
36

Helpful Hints

1. This Map takes a different look at the same Congressional Township displayed in the preceding two maps. It presents features that can help you better envision the historical development of the area: a) Water-bodies (lakes & ponds), b) Water-courses (rivers, streams, etc.), c) Railroads, d) City/town center-points (where they were oftentimes located when first settled), and e) Cemeteries.
2. Using this "Historical" map in tandem with this Township's Patent Map and Road Map, may lead you to some interesting discoveries. You will often find roads, towns, cemeteries, and waterways are named after nearby landowners: sometimes those names will be the ones you are researching. See how many of these research gems you can find here in Hale County.

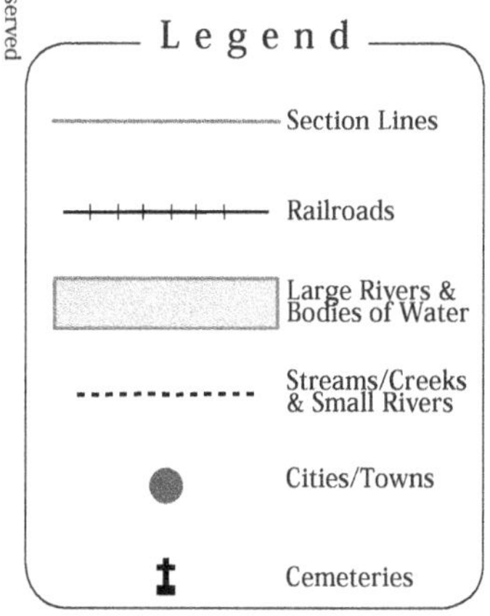
Legend
Section Lines
Railroads
Large Rivers & Bodies of Water
Streams/Creeks & Small Rivers
Cities/Towns
Cemeteries

Scale: Section = 1 mile X 1 mile
(there are some exceptions)

Map Group 9: Index to Land Patents

Township 21-North Range 2-East (St Stephens)

After you locate an individual in this Index, take note of the Section and Section Part then proceed to the Land Patent map on the pages immediately following. You should have no difficulty locating the corresponding parcel of land.

The "For More Info" Column will lead you to more information about the underlying Patents. See the *Legend* at right, and the "How to Use this Book" chapter, for more information.

```
                        LEGEND
              "For More Info . . . " column
  A = Authority (Legislative Act, See Appendix "A")
  B = Block or Lot (location in Section unknown)
  C = Cancelled Patent
  F = Fractional Section
  G = Group  (Multi-Patentee Patent, see Appendix "C")
  V = Overlaps another Parcel
  R = Re-Issued (Parcel patented more than once)

  (A & G items require you to look in the Appendixes referred
  to above. All other Letter-designations followed by a number
  require you to locate line-items in this index that possess
  the ID number found after the letter).
```

ID	Individual in Patent	Sec.	Sec. Part	Date Issued	Other Counties	For More Info . . .
2004	BELL, William	24	NE	1835-09-22	Greene	A1 F
1995	CO, Scott Sims And	26	NW	1826-06-10	Greene	A1 G70 F
1980	COMPANY, Sims Banks And	26	W½	1825-04-25	Greene	A1 G221 F R1984
1984	"	26	W½	1825-04-25	Greene	A1 G229 F R1980
1981	"	27	E½	1825-04-25	Greene	A1 G221 F
1982	"	35	N½	1825-04-25	Greene	A1 G221 F
1983	"	35	NW	1825-04-25	Greene	A1 G221 F
1993	CRESWELL, John T	26	NE	1831-08-25	Greene	A1 F R1985
1994	"	27	NE	1833-05-30	Greene	A1
1992	"	24	SWNW	1837-03-15	Greene	A1
1995	CRISWELL, John T	26	NW	1826-06-10	Greene	A1 G70 F
1986	HAYS, George	35	NE	1831-09-01	Greene	A1 F
1985	"	26	NE	1837-03-30	Greene	A1 F R1993
2002	HOUPT, Sebastian	27	SE	1825-06-20	Greene	A1 F
1987	LEWIS, Henry	26	N½SW	1895-06-19	Greene	A2
1988	"	26	S½NW	1895-06-19	Greene	A2
1999	MASON, Reuben	27	W½NW	1833-05-30	Greene	A1
2000	MASON, Ruben	27	NENW	1835-09-22	Greene	A1
1991	MCDOWELL, John N	35	E½SE	1837-03-15	Greene	A1
1989	MCLAURIN, James	25	SE	1835-09-22	Greene	A1 F R2009
2005	MURPHY, William	24	S½	1835-09-22	Greene	A1 F
2006	"	24	SE	1835-09-22	Greene	A1 F
2007	"	25	NE	1835-09-22	Greene	A1
2008	"	25	NW	1835-09-22	Greene	A1 F
2009	"	25	SE	1835-09-22	Greene	A1 F R1989
2010	"	25	SW	1835-09-22	Greene	A1 F
1977	NORWOOD, Andrew	35	E½SW	1830-12-15	Greene	A1 F
1978	"	35	W½SE	1833-05-30	Greene	A1
1979	"	35	W½SW	1835-10-28	Greene	A1
2003	RIDDLE, Thomas	24	E½NW	1835-09-28	Greene	A1
1990	RODEN, James	24	NWNW	1835-09-22	Greene	A1
1980	SCOTT, David	26	W½	1825-04-25	Greene	A1 G221 F R1984
1981	"	27	E½	1825-04-25	Greene	A1 G221 F
1982	"	35	N½	1825-04-25	Greene	A1 G221 F
1983	"	35	NW	1825-04-25	Greene	A1 G221 F
1984	SIMS, Edward	26	W½	1825-04-25	Greene	A1 G229 F R1980
2001	SIMS, Scott	26	SW	1826-06-10	Greene	A1 F
1996	TALBOT, Mathew	27	W½SW	1837-03-15	Greene	A1
1997	TALBOT, Mathieu	27	E½SW	1837-03-15	Greene	A1
1998	TALBOT, Matthew	27	SENW	1837-03-30	Greene	A1

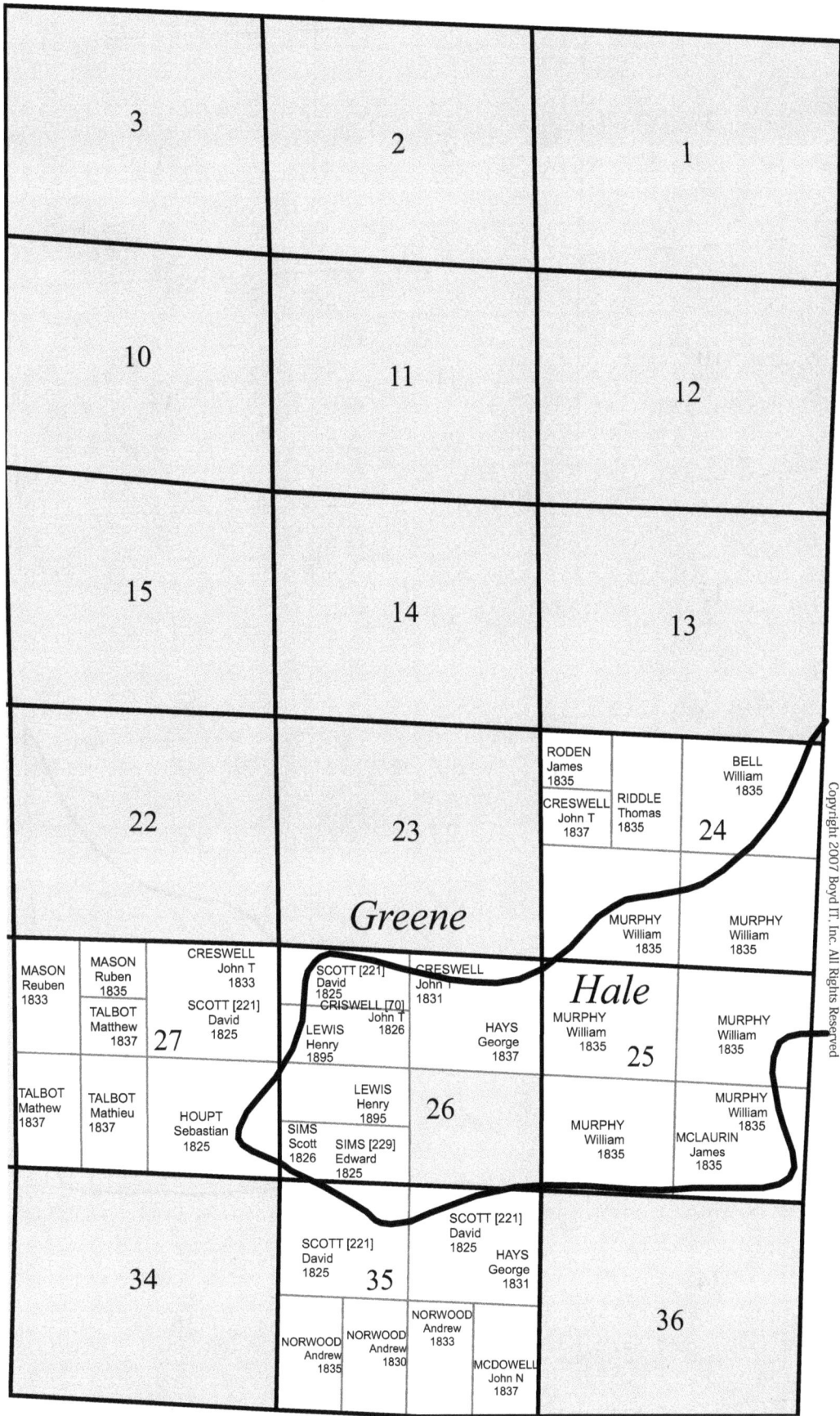

Patent Map

T21-N R2-E
St Stephens Meridian

Map Group 9

Township Statistics

Parcels Mapped	:	34
Number of Patents	:	33
Number of Individuals	:	22
Patentees Identified	:	20
Number of Surnames	:	18
Multi-Patentee Parcels	:	6
Oldest Patent Date	:	4/25/1825
Most Recent Patent	:	6/19/1895
Block/Lot Parcels	:	0
Parcels Re - Issued	:	3
Parcels that Overlap	:	0
Cities and Towns	:	0
Cemeteries	:	0

Note: the area contained in this map amounts to far less than a full Township. Therefore, its contents are completely on this single page (instead of a "normal" 2-page spread).

Legend

———————	Patent Boundary
————————	Section Boundary
░░░░░░	No Patents Found (or Outside County)
1., 2., 3., ...	Lot Numbers (when beside a name)
[ ]	Group Number (see Appendix "C")

Scale: Section = 1 mile X 1 mile (generally, with some exceptions)

Map sections:

Section 3, 2, 1, 10, 11, 12, 15, 14, 13, 22, 23, 34, 35, 36

Greene

Hale

Section 24:
- RODEN James 1835
- CRESWELL John T 1837
- RIDDLE Thomas 1835
- BELL William 1835

Section 25:
- MURPHY William 1835
- MURPHY William 1835
- MURPHY William 1835
- MURPHY William 1835
- MURPHY William 1835
- MURPHY William 1835
- MCLAURIN James 1835

Section 27:
- MASON Reuben 1833
- MASON Ruben 1835
- CRESWELL John T 1833
- SCOTT [221] David 1825
- TALBOT Matthew 1837
- TALBOT Mathew 1837
- TALBOT Mathieu 1837
- HOUPT Sebastian 1825

Section 26:
- SCOTT [221] David 1825
- CRESWELL John T 1831
- CRISWELL [70] John T 1826
- LEWIS Henry 1895
- HAYS George 1837
- LEWIS Henry 1895
- SIMS Scott 1826
- SIMS [229] Edward 1825

Section 35:
- SCOTT [221] David 1825
- SCOTT [221] David 1825
- HAYS George 1831
- NORWOOD Andrew 1833
- NORWOOD Andrew 1835
- NORWOOD Andrew 1830
- MCDOWELL John N 1837

Road Map

T21-N R2-E
St Stephens Meridian

Map Group 9

Note: the area contained in this map amounts to far less than a full Township. Therefore, its contents are completely on this single page (instead of a "normal" 2-page spread).

Cities & Towns
None

Cemeteries
None

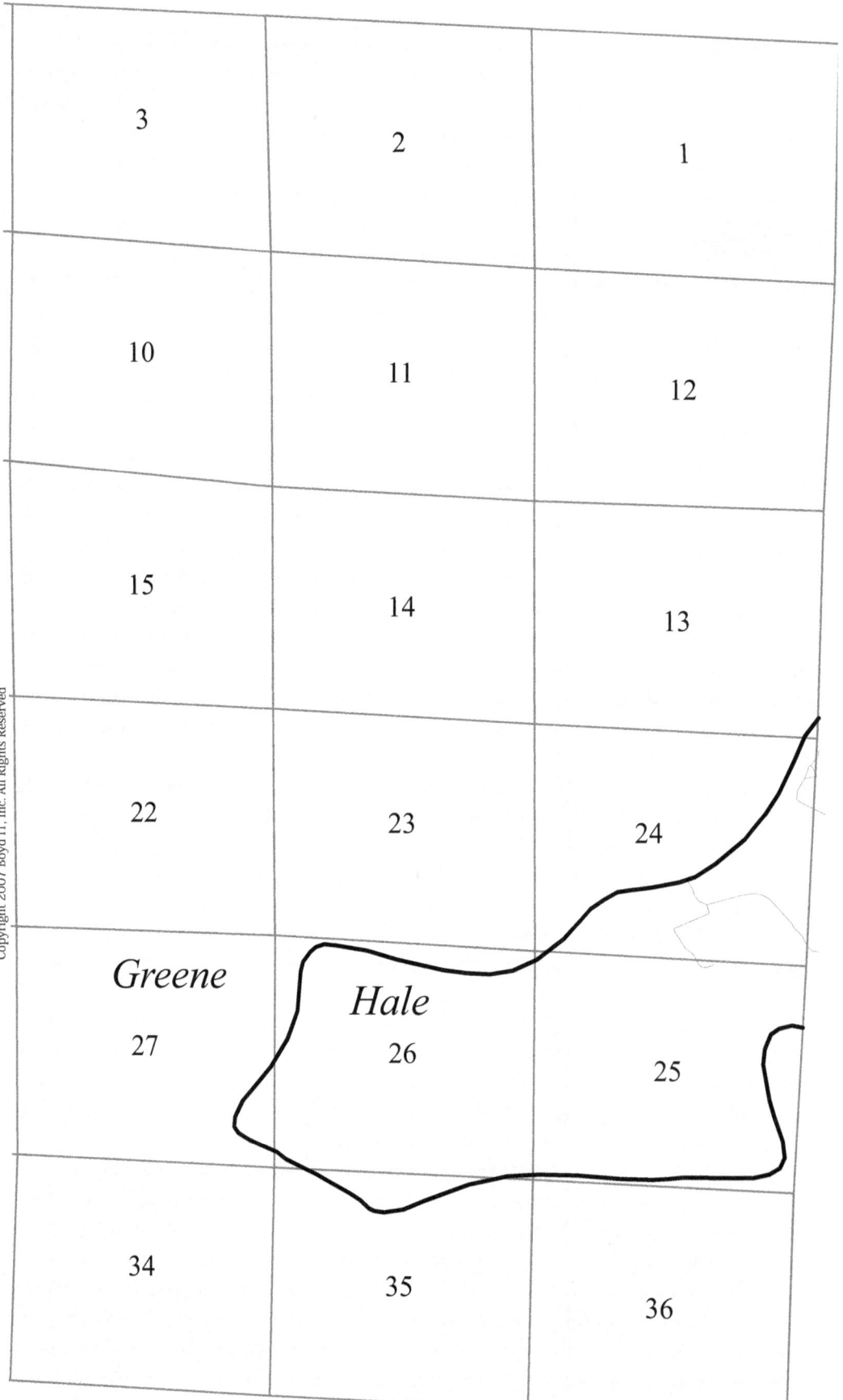

Legend

————————	Section Lines
═══════════	Interstates
━━━━━━━━━	Highways
———————	Other Roads
●	Cities/Towns
✝	Cemeteries

Scale: Section = 1 mile X 1 mile
(generally, with some exceptions)

3	2	1
10	11	12
15	14	13
22	23	24
27	26	25
34	35	36

Greene

Hale

3	2	1
10	11	12
15	14	13
22	23	24
27	26	25
34	35	36

Greene

Hale

Black Warrior River

Historical Map

T21-N R2-E
St Stephens Meridian

Map Group 9

Note: the area contained in this map amounts to far less than a full Township. Therefore, its contents are completely on this single page (instead of a "normal" 2-page spread).

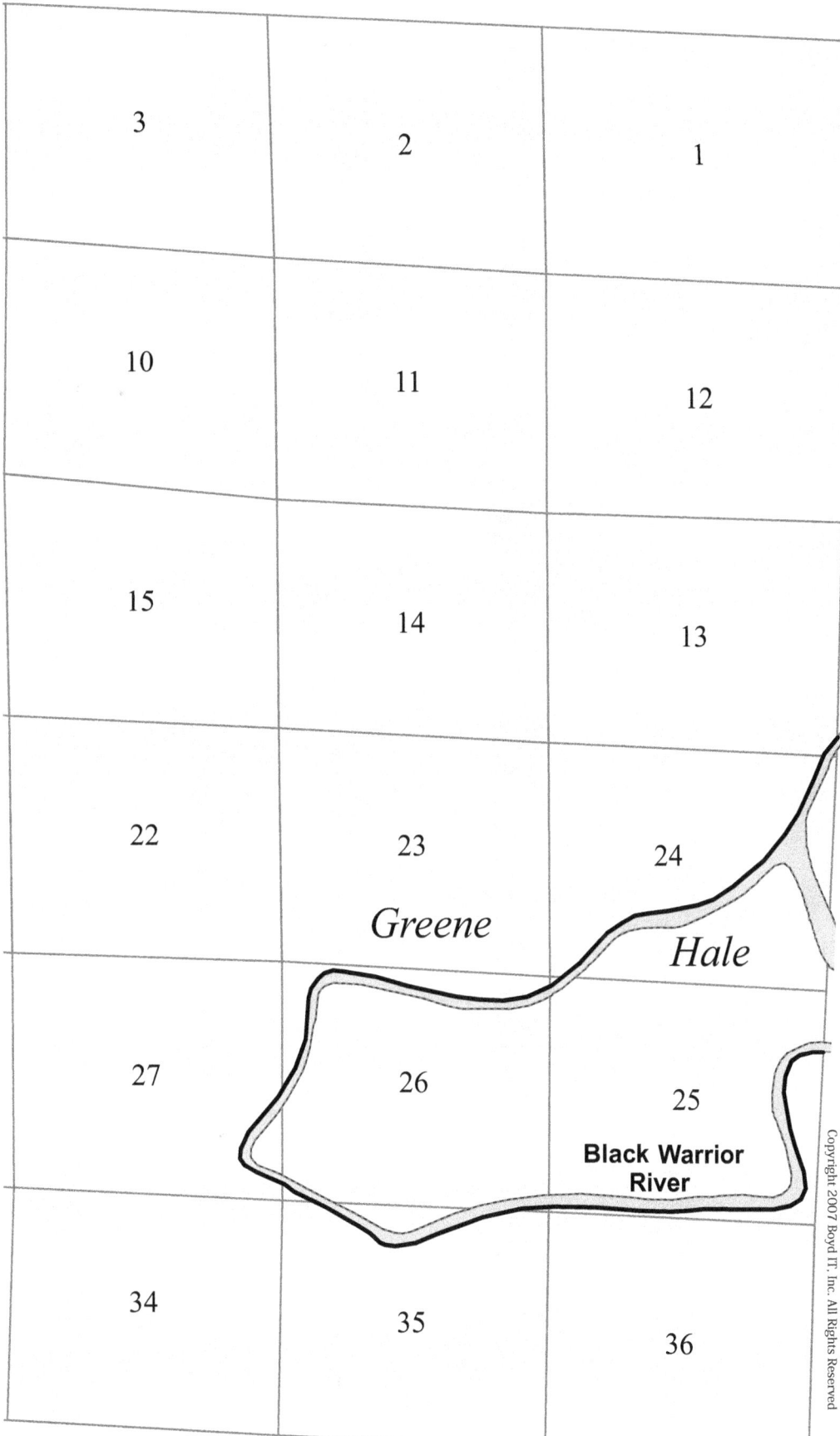

Cities & Towns
None

Cemeteries
None

Legend
— Section Lines
+++++ Railroads
▓ Large Rivers & Bodies of Water
---- Streams/Creeks & Small Rivers
● Cities/Towns
✝ Cemeteries

Scale: Section = 1 mile X 1 mile
(there are some exceptions)

Map Group 10: Index to Land Patents

Township 21-North Range 3-East (St Stephens)

After you locate an individual in this Index, take note of the Section and Section Part then proceed to the Land Patent map on the pages immediately following. You should have no difficulty locating the corresponding parcel of land.

The "For More Info" Column will lead you to more information about the underlying Patents. See the *Legend* at right, and the "How to Use this Book" chapter, for more information.

ID	Individual in Patent	Sec.	Sec. Part	Date Issued	Other Counties	For More Info . . .
2118	ADCOCK, John	22	E½SE	1825-04-20		A1
2119	" "	22	E½SW	1825-05-25		A1
2015	ARRINGTON, Anthony	29	E½NE	1831-08-25		A1
2122	BATES, John M	28	E½SE	1824-10-20		A1
2123	" "	29	W½SE	1824-10-20		A1 F
2186	BERRY, Samuel	13	SWSE	1835-10-20		A1
2187	" "	24	NENE	1835-10-20		A1
2261	BROWN, William P	27	E½NW	1825-05-25		A1
2260	" "	20	SWSW	1835-10-01		A1
2262	" "	29	NWNW	1835-10-01		A1
2173	BUFORD, Phillemon	6	SE	1826-06-10	Greene	A1 F R2055
2022	BURY, Clinton	13	NWSE	1835-09-28		A1
2211	CALDWELL, William	35	E½SE	1824-10-20		A1
2212	CALWELL, William	36	W½SW	1824-10-20		A1 G38
2012	CAMPBELL, Anguish	25	E½SW	1824-10-20		A1
2013	" "	25	W½SW	1824-10-20		A1
2164	CARSON, Mary	15	E½SE	1824-10-20		A1
2165	" "	15	E½SW	1824-10-20		A1
2166	" "	15	W½SE	1824-10-20		A1
2167	" "	15	W½SW	1824-10-20		A1
2168	" "	22	E½NE	1824-10-20		A1
2169	" "	22	W½NE	1824-10-20		A1
2016	CLEMENTS, Benjamin	10	W½NW	1824-10-20		A1 G57
2017	" "	9	E½NE	1824-10-20		A1 G57
2018	" "	9	E½SE	1824-10-20		A1 G57
2036	COMPANY, Sims Banks And	26	W½NW	1824-10-20		A1 G221
2037	" "	27	E½NE	1824-10-20		A1 G221
2047	" "	27	E½SE	1824-10-20		A1 G229
2147	" "	34	E½SW	1824-10-20		A1 G167
2142	CRISWELL, John T	3	W½NE	1825-04-20		A1 V2027, 2058
2182	DAVIDSON, Reuben	36	E½NW	1824-10-20		A1 G71
2181	" "	36	E½SW	1824-10-20		A1 G72
2180	" "	36	W½NW	1824-10-20		A1
2179	" "	26	E½SE	1829-03-06		A1
2077	DERDEN, James	22	W½SE	1825-04-20		A1
2079	" "	25	E½NW	1825-06-20		A1
2076	" "	21	E½SE	1826-02-01		A1
2078	" "	22	W½SW	1826-02-01		A1
2080	" "	26	W½NE	1830-12-01		A1
2081	DONUGH, James	34	E½SE	1824-10-20		A1
2082	" "	34	W½SE	1824-10-20		A1
2083	DORDON, James	26	E½SW	1824-10-20		A1
2085	" "	26	W½SW	1824-10-20		A1
2084	" "	26	W½SE	1825-04-20		A1
2087	DOROUGH, James	34	W½SW	1824-10-20		A1
2086	" "	33	E½SE	1825-05-25		A1

ID	Individual in Patent	Sec.	Sec. Part	Date Issued	Other Counties	For More Info . . .
2120	DUKE, John	27	W½SW	1824-10-20		A1
2137	DUKE, John R	28	E½SW	1824-10-20		A1
2138	" "	28	W½SE	1824-10-20		A1
2195	DUKE, Seaborn	28	W½NW	1829-07-07		A1
2055	FERRIS, Fergus P	6	SE	1837-11-02	Greene	A1 F R2173
2056	" "	7	NE	1837-11-02	Greene	A1 F
2161	FINNEY, Manassah	1	W½NW	1824-10-20		A1 G83
2216	FORSTER, William H	24	E½SE	1826-02-01		A1
2139	FOSTER, John S	23	W½NW	1825-05-25		A1
2188	FOWLER, Samuel	29	SWNW	1837-08-01		A1
2104	GILMORE, James M	24	NWNW	1835-09-25		A1
2215	GILMORE, William	24	W½SE	1825-05-25		A1
2214	" "	23	NENE	1835-10-20		A1
2062	GRANT, Green W	27	W½NE	1829-03-06		A1
2183	GRAVES, Robert	23	E½SE	1825-05-25		A1
2184	" "	24	W½SW	1825-05-25		A1
2121	GRAY, John H	18	D	1839-05-01	Greene	A1
2152	GRAY, Joseph P	18	NW	1837-03-30	Greene	A1 F
2172	GREEN, Peleg	28	E½NW	1835-09-22		A1
2171	" "	21	SWSW	1835-10-01		A1
2051	HENLEY, Elizabeth J	23	E½NW	1824-10-20		A1 G143
2052	" "	23	W½SW	1824-10-20		A1 G143
2053	" "	23	E½SW	1826-08-20		A1 G142
2051	HENLEY, John T	23	E½NW	1824-10-20		A1 G143
2052	" "	23	W½SW	1824-10-20		A1 G143
2053	" "	23	E½SW	1826-08-20		A1 G142
2206	HERNDON, Thomas H	33	W½SE	1825-05-25		A1
2202	" "	2	W½NW	1826-02-01		A1
2203	" "	32	E½W½S½	1831-08-25	Greene	A1 F
2204	" "	32	NW	1831-08-25	Greene	A1 R2140
2205	" "	33	E½SW	1835-10-01		A1
2057	HILL, Gabriel L	3	SENW	1837-03-15		A1
2058	" "	3	SWNE	1837-03-15		A1 V2142
2059	" "	3	W½NW	1837-03-15		A1
2060	" "	4	E½NW	1837-03-15		A1
2061	" "	4	NE	1837-03-15		A1
2217	HINTON, William	21	E½NE	1835-10-20		A1
2218	HINTON, William K	17	N½	1837-03-15		A1
2219	" "	18	NE	1837-03-15	Greene	A1 F
2220	" "	18	SE	1837-03-15	Greene	A1 F
2221	" "	19	N½NE	1837-03-15		A1
2222	" "	21	NW	1837-03-15		A1
2223	" "	21	W½NE	1837-03-15		A1
2224	" "	5	W½SE	1837-03-15		A1
2226	" "	8	NE	1837-03-15		A1
2227	" "	8	NW	1837-03-15		A1 F
2228	" "	9	SW	1837-03-15		A1
2229	" "	9	W½SE	1837-03-15		A1
2225	" "	7	SE	1839-05-01	Greene	A1 R2191
2049	HOPKINS, Elizabeth	15	E½NW	1824-10-20		A1
2050	" "	15	W½NW	1824-10-20		A1
2153	HOPKINS, Lambeth	25	W½NW	1825-05-25		A1
2154	" "	26	E½NE	1825-05-25		A1
2031	JACKSON, David	21	E½SW	1831-08-25		A1
2033	" "	22	W½NW	1835-09-22		A1
2030	" "	20	N½SE	1835-10-01		A1
2032	" "	21	NWSW	1837-03-30		A1
2029	" "	20	N½	1837-08-01		A1
2162	JACKSON, Margaret	20	N½SW	1835-10-01		A1
2185	JEMISON, Robert	15	W½NE	1824-10-20		A1 G156
2190	JENNINGS, Samuel K	5	SW	1837-03-15		A1
2191	" "	7	SE	1837-03-15	Greene	A1 F R2225
2192	" "	8	SE	1837-03-15		A1
2193	" "	8	SW	1837-03-15		A1
2182	JIMISON, William	36	E½NW	1824-10-20		A1 G71
2088	KENNEDY, James	10	E½NW	1824-10-20		A1
2016	" "	10	W½NW	1824-10-20		A1 G57
2090	" "	10	W½SW	1824-10-20		A1
2091	" "	13	E½NE	1824-10-20		A1
2092	" "	14	W½SE	1824-10-20		A1
2103	" "	14	W½SW	1824-10-20		A1 G165
2093	" "	27	W½NW	1824-10-20		A1
2094	" "	28	E½NE	1824-10-20		A1

ID	Individual in Patent	Sec.	Sec. Part	Date Issued	Other Counties	For More Info . . .
2017	KENNEDY, James (Cont'd)	9	E½NE	1824-10-20		A1 G57
2018	" "	9	E½SE	1824-10-20		A1 G57
2089	" "	10	E½SW	1830-12-01		A1
2096	" "	4	SWNW	1835-09-28		A1
2098	" "	5	E½SE	1835-09-28		A1
2097	" "	5	E½NE	1835-10-20		A1
2099	" "	5	NW	1835-10-20		A1
2095	" "	4	E½SW	1837-03-15		A1
2101	" "	9	W½NE	1837-03-15		A1
2100	" "	9	NW	1837-05-15		A1
2102	" "	14	E½SE	1895-06-11		A1 G165
2230	KENNEDY, William	14	E½SW	1825-05-25		A1
2146	LANE, John W	10	E½NE	1824-10-20		A1 G169
2144	" "	11	W½NW	1824-10-20		A1 G168
2145	" "	11	W½SW	1824-10-20		A1 G168
2147	" "	34	E½SW	1824-10-20		A1 G167
2148	" "	36	W½SE	1824-10-20		A1 G174
2212	" "	36	W½SW	1824-10-20		A1 G38
2075	LEE, James B	22	E½NW	1835-09-25		A1
2144	LIPSCOMB, Joel	11	W½NW	1824-10-20		A1 G168
2145	" "	11	W½SW	1824-10-20		A1 G168
2112	" "	11	E½NW	1825-05-25		A1
2114	" "	14	W½NE	1825-05-25		A1
2117	" "	3	E½SE	1830-12-15		A1 V2231
2113	" "	14	SENE	1835-09-28		A1
2116	" "	2	SWSW	1835-10-20		A1
2115	" "	2	NWSW	1837-03-30		A1
2146	LIPSCOMB, John	10	E½NE	1824-10-20		A1 G169
2210	LIPSCOMB, William C	14	E½NW	1824-10-20		A1 G176
2209	" "	14	W½NW	1824-10-20		A1
2025	MAY, Daniel	14	NENE	1835-10-20		A1
2065	MAY, Henry	23	W½NE	1825-04-20		A1
2064	" "	23	SENE	1835-09-22		A1
2063	" "	13	W½SW	1835-09-25		A1
2105	MAY, James	11	W½SE	1824-10-20		A1
2124	MAY, John	10	W½NE	1824-10-20		A1
2126	" "	11	E½NE	1824-10-20		A1
2127	" "	11	E½SE	1824-10-20		A1
2128	" "	11	E½SW	1824-10-20		A1
2129	" "	11	W½NE	1824-10-20		A1
2130	" "	13	W½NE	1824-10-20		A1
2132	" "	23	W½SE	1824-10-20		A1
2125	" "	10	W½SE	1825-04-20		A1
2131	" "	2	W½SE	1825-04-20		A1
2135	" "	3	W½SE	1825-04-20		A1 G187 V2231
2133	" "	4	E½SE	1835-10-20		A1 ·
2134	" "	4	W½SE	1835-10-20		A1
2150	MAY, Jonathan	24	SENE	1835-09-22		A1
2149	" "	24	E½NW	1835-09-25		A1
2163	MAY, Mary A	24	NESW	1835-09-25		A1
2199	MAY, Stephen	12	W½SW	1831-09-01		A1
2200	" "	4	W½SW	1831-09-01		A1
2196	" "	12	SENW	1835-09-28		A1
2197	" "	12	SESW	1835-09-28		A1
2198	" "	12	W½NW	1835-09-28		A1
2231	MAY, William	3	SE	1825-04-20		A1 V2135, 2117
2135	" "	3	W½SE	1825-04-20		A1 G187 V2231
2011	MCGEHEE, Abraham	25	E½SE	1824-10-20		A1
2136	MCLAUREN, John	32	W½SW	1831-09-01	Greene	A1
2021	MEADOR, Clement	30	NE	1831-09-01	Greene	A1 F
2067	MEADOR, Hugh	13	E½SE	1835-10-20		A1
2143	MEADOR, John V	28	W½NE	1831-08-25		A1
2170	MEADOR, Obadiah	30	SE	1831-08-25	Greene	A1 F
2233	MEADOR, William	27	E½SW	1824-10-20		A1
2234	" "	27	W½SE	1824-10-20		A1
2232	" "	25	W½NE	1825-05-25		A1
2014	MELTON, Ann	20	SWSE	1837-08-01		A1
2235	MELTON, William	29	SW	1824-10-20		A1 F
2213	MONETT, William F	24	W½NE	1826-06-10		A1
2151	MOORE, Jordon	30	SEE½	1831-09-01	Greene	A1
2236	MURPHREY, William	34	W½NE	1824-10-20		A1
2240	" "	35	E½NW	1824-10-20		A1 G205
2241	" "	35	E½SW	1824-10-20		A1 G205

ID	Individual in Patent	Sec.	Sec. Part	Date Issued	Other Counties	For More Info . . .
2237	MURPHREY, William (Cont'd)	35	W½NE	1824-10-20		A1
2238	" "	35	W½NW	1824-10-20		A1
2239	" "	35	W½SE	1824-10-20		A1
2242	" "	35	W½SW	1824-10-20		A1 G205
2243	MURPHRY, William	32	SE	1833-05-30	Greene	A1
2244	" "	32	SENE	1835-10-28	Greene	A1
2257	MURPHY, William	34	E½NE	1825-05-25		A1
2247	" "	18	SW	1835-09-22	Greene	A1
2249	" "	19	E½NW	1835-09-22		A1
2250	" "	19	E½SE	1835-09-22		A1
2251	" "	19	E½SW	1835-09-22		A1
2253	" "	19	W½NW	1835-09-22		A1
2255	" "	19	W½SW	1835-09-22		A1
2256	" "	30	NW	1835-09-22	Greene	A1 F
2254	" "	19	W½SE	1837-03-15		A1
2252	" "	19	S½NE	1837-11-02		A1
2245	" "	18	A	1840-11-10	Greene	A1
2246	" "	18	B	1840-11-10	Greene	A1
2248	" "	18	W½NW	1840-11-10	Greene	A1
2072	MUSSINA, Jacob	12	N½NE	1837-11-02		A1
2073	" "	17	S½	1837-11-02		A1
2074	" "	5	W½NE	1837-11-02		A1
2258	NEWTON, William	20	SESE	1837-03-30		A1
2259	" "	20	SESW	1837-03-30		A1
2023	PUCKETT, Dabney	1	W½SW	1835-10-01		A1
2106	RANEY, James	26	E½NW	1826-08-20		A1
2019	RIDGEWAY, Bradley H	7	W½	1837-11-02	Greene	A1
2103	SAMPLE, Daniel B	14	W½SW	1824-10-20		A1 G165
2024	" "	13	E½SW	1835-09-28		A1
2102	" "	14	E½SE	1895-06-11		A1 G165
2034	SCOTT, David	1	E½NE	1824-10-20		A1 G226
2161	" "	1	W½NW	1824-10-20		A1 G83
2210	" "	14	E½NW	1824-10-20		A1 G176
2041	" "	15	E½NE	1824-10-20		A1 G228
2035	" "	2	W½NE	1824-10-20		A1 G225
2036	" "	26	W½NW	1824-10-20		A1 G221
2037	" "	27	E½NE	1824-10-20		A1 G221
2038	" "	36	E½NE	1824-10-20		A1 G227
2181	" "	36	E½SW	1824-10-20		A1 G72
2040	" "	36	W½NE	1824-10-20		A1 G227
2039	" "	36	E½SE	1825-05-25		A1 G227
2140	SCOTT, John	32	NW	1825-05-25	Greene	A1 R2204
2141	SIKES, John	35	E½NE	1824-10-20		A1 V2201
2044	SIMS, Edward	1	W½NE	1824-10-20		A1 G230
2048	" "	10	E½SE	1824-10-20		A1 G235
2047	" "	27	E½SE	1824-10-20		A1 G229
2045	" "	33	E½NE	1824-10-20		A1 G234
2046	" "	34	E½NW	1824-10-20		A1 G234
2240	" "	35	E½NW	1824-10-20		A1 G205
2241	" "	35	E½SW	1824-10-20		A1 G205
2242	" "	35	W½SW	1824-10-20		A1 G205
2042	" "	6	E½	1824-10-20	Greene	A1 F
2043	" "	6	NW	1825-04-25	Greene	A1 F R2189
2068	SNEDECOR, Isaac C	28	SWSW	1837-03-15		A1
2069	" "	32	NENE	1837-03-15	Greene	A1
2070	" "	33	W½NW	1837-03-15		A1
2071	" "	33	W½SW	1837-03-15		A1
2155	TAYLOR, Leah	6	SW	1837-03-30	Greene	A1
2156	" "	7	W½NE	1837-11-02	Greene	A1 F
2194	TAYLOR, Samuel	8	W½	1831-01-01		A1 F
2026	THOMPSON, Daniel	3	E½NE	1829-03-06		A1
2027	" "	3	NWNE	1835-09-25		A1 V2142
2066	THOMPSON, Henry	3	NENW	1835-10-01		A1
2053	TORBERT, Sarah P	23	E½SW	1826-08-20		A1 G142
2051	TORBUT, Elizabeth P	23	E½NW	1824-10-20		A1 G143
2052	" "	23	W½SW	1824-10-20		A1 G143
2035	TRUE, Martin	2	W½NE	1824-10-20		A1 G225
2028	WATSON, Daniel	30	S½SW	1837-08-01	Greene	A1
2107	WEDGEWORTH, James	1	E½NW	1824-10-20		A1
2108	" "	1	E½SE	1824-10-20		A1
2110	" "	2	E½NE	1824-10-20		A1
2109	" "	1	W½SE	1825-05-25		A1
2263	WEDGEWORTH, William	2	E½SE	1825-05-25		A1

ID	Individual in Patent	Sec.	Sec. Part	Date Issued	Other Counties	For More Info . . .
2034	WEDGWORTH, James	1	E½NE	1824-10-20		A1 G226
2044	" "	1	W½NE	1824-10-20		A1 G230
2111	" "	1	E½SW	1837-03-15		A1
2189	WHITWORTH, Samuel J	6	NW	1826-08-20	Greene	A1 F R2043
2201	WILLIAMS, Susan H	35	NENE	1835-09-25		A1 V2141
2038	WILLIAMS, Thomas	36	E½NE	1824-10-20		A1 G227
2040	" "	36	W½NE	1824-10-20		A1 G227
2148	" "	36	W½SE	1824-10-20		A1 G174
2208	" "	25	W½SE	1825-04-20		A1
2039	" "	36	E½SE	1825-05-25		A1 G227
2207	" "	25	SENE	1835-10-28		A1
2270	WILLINGHAM, William	13	W½NE	1824-10-20		A1
2268	" "	12	W½SE	1825-04-20		A1
2269	" "	13	E½NW	1835-09-25		A1
2266	" "	12	SENE	1835-10-20		A1
2267	" "	12	SWNE	1835-10-20		A1
2264	" "	12	NENW	1837-03-15		A1
2265	" "	12	NESW	1837-03-15		A1
2271	WIN, William	2	E½SW	1831-08-25		A1
2020	WINDHAM, Charles	24	SWNW	1835-09-25		A1
2158	WINDHAM, Lewis	12	E½SE	1825-04-20		A1
2159	" "	2	E½NW	1826-02-01		A1
2160	" "	24	SESW	1835-10-20		A1
2157	WRIGHT, Leland	33	E½NW	1831-08-25		A1
2045	WRIGHT, Pleasant	33	E½NE	1824-10-20		A1 G234
2046	" "	34	E½NW	1824-10-20		A1 G234
2178	" "	34	W½NW	1824-10-20		A1
2177	" "	33	W½NE	1825-05-25		A1
2175	" "	29	E½SE	1835-10-20		A1
2174	" "	29	E½NW	1837-03-15		A1
2176	" "	29	W½NE	1837-03-15		A1
2054	WYNNE, Erasmus	28	NWSW	1835-10-28		A1
2048	YARBOROUGH, William	10	E½SE	1824-10-20		A1 G235
2041	" "	15	E½NE	1824-10-20		A1 G228
2185	" "	15	W½NE	1824-10-20		A1 G156
2272	" "	21	W½SE	1824-10-20		A1

Patent Map

T21-N R3-E
St Stephens Meridian

Map Group 10

Township Statistics

Parcels Mapped	:	262
Number of Patents	:	260
Number of Individuals	:	109
Patentees Identified	:	120
Number of Surnames	:	79
Multi-Patentee Parcels	:	36
Oldest Patent Date	:	10/20/1824
Most Recent Patent	:	6/11/1895
Block/Lot Parcels	:	3
Parcels Re - Issued	:	4
Parcels that Overlap	:	8
Cities and Towns	:	2
Cemeteries	:	4

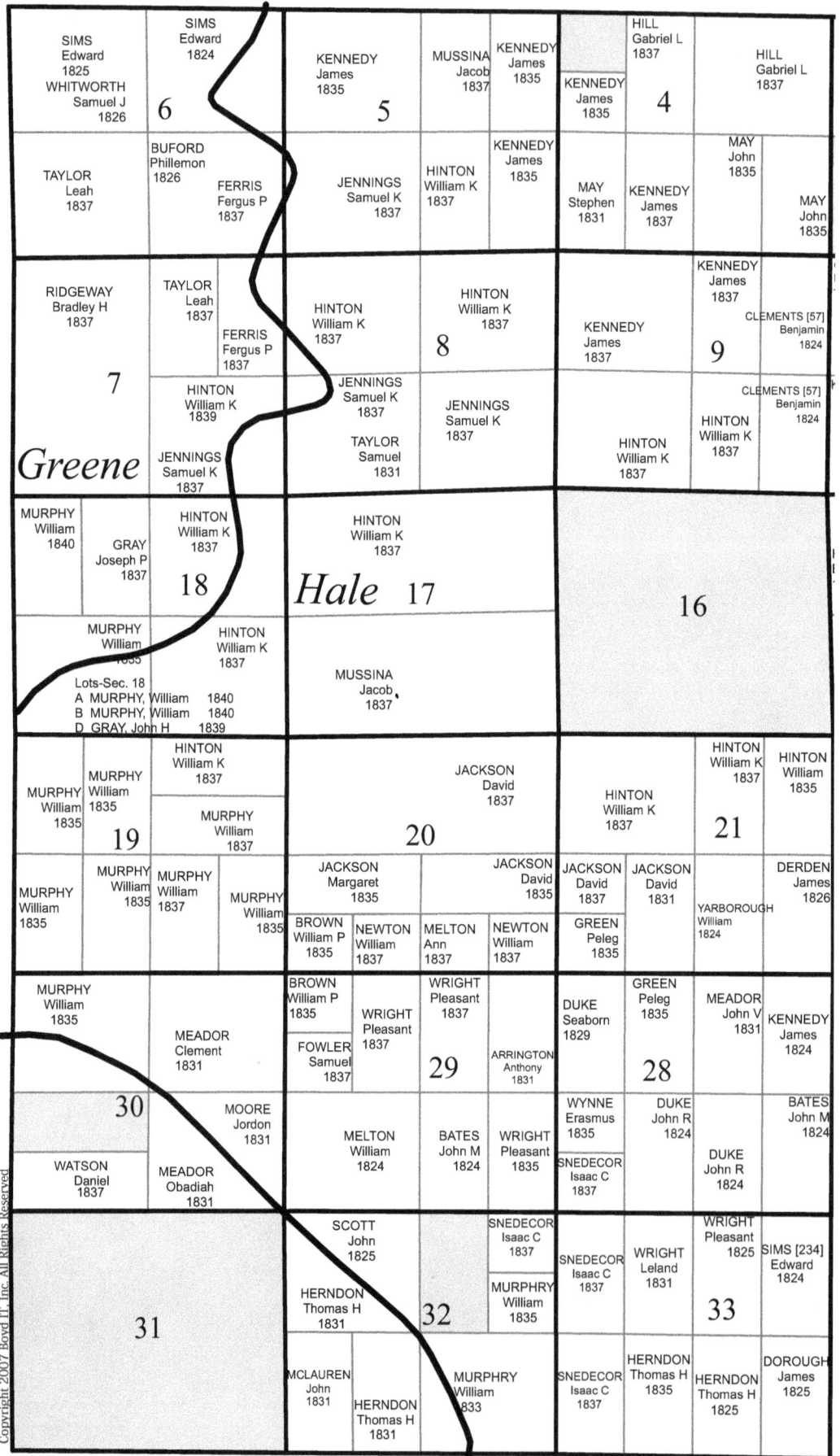

Section 6
SIMS Edward 1825
WHITWORTH Samuel J 1826
SIMS Edward 1824
TAYLOR Leah 1837
BUFORD Phillemon 1826
FERRIS Fergus P 1837

Section 5
KENNEDY James 1835
MUSSINA Jacob 1837
KENNEDY James 1835
JENNINGS Samuel K 1837
HINTON William K 1837
KENNEDY James 1835

Section 4
HILL Gabriel L 1837
KENNEDY James 1835
HILL Gabriel L 1837
MAY John 1835
MAY Stephen 1831
KENNEDY James 1837
MAY John 1835

Section 7 — Greene
RIDGEWAY Bradley H 1837
TAYLOR Leah 1837
FERRIS Fergus P 1837
HINTON William K 1839
JENNINGS Samuel K 1837

Section 8
HINTON William K 1837
HINTON William K 1837
JENNINGS Samuel K 1837
JENNINGS Samuel K 1837
TAYLOR Samuel 1831

Section 9
KENNEDY James 1837
KENNEDY James 1837
CLEMENTS [57] Benjamin 1824
CLEMENTS [57] Benjamin 1824
HINTON William K 1837
HINTON William K 1837

Section 18 — Hale
MURPHY William 1840
GRAY Joseph P 1837
HINTON William K 1837
MURPHY William
HINTON William K 1837

Lots-Sec. 18
A MURPHY, William 1840
B MURPHY, William 1840
D GRAY, John H 1839

Section 17 — Hale
HINTON William K 1837
MUSSINA Jacob 1837

Section 16

Section 19
MURPHY William 1835
MURPHY William 1835
HINTON William K 1837
MURPHY William 1837
MURPHY William 1835
MURPHY William 1835
MURPHY William 1837
MURPHY William 1835

Section 20
JACKSON David 1837
JACKSON Margaret 1835
JACKSON David 1835
BROWN William P 1835
NEWTON William 1837
MELTON Ann 1837
NEWTON William 1837

Section 21
HINTON William K 1837
HINTON William K 1837
HINTON William 1835
JACKSON David 1837
JACKSON David 1831
YARBOROUGH William 1824
DERDEN James 1826
GREEN Peleg 1835

Section 30
MURPHY William 1835
MEADOR Clement 1831
MOORE Jordon 1831
WATSON Daniel 1837
MEADOR Obadiah 1831

Section 29
BROWN William P 1835
FOWLER Samuel 1837
WRIGHT Pleasant 1837
WRIGHT Pleasant 1837
MELTON William 1824
BATES John M 1824
WRIGHT Pleasant 1835
ARRINGTON Anthony 1831

Section 28
DUKE Seaborn 1829
GREEN Peleg 1835
MEADOR John V 1831
KENNEDY James 1824
WYNNE Erasmus 1835
DUKE John R 1824
SNEDECOR Isaac C 1837
DUKE John R 1824
BATES John M 1824

Section 31

Section 32
SCOTT John 1825
HERNDON Thomas H 1831
SNEDECOR Isaac C 1837
MURPHRY William 1835
MCLAUREN John 1831
HERNDON Thomas H 1831
MURPHRY William 1833

Section 33
SNEDECOR Isaac C 1837
WRIGHT Leland 1831
WRIGHT Pleasant 1825
SIMS [234] Edward 1824
SNEDECOR Isaac C 1837
HERNDON Thomas H 1835
HERNDON Thomas H 1825
DOROUGH James 1825

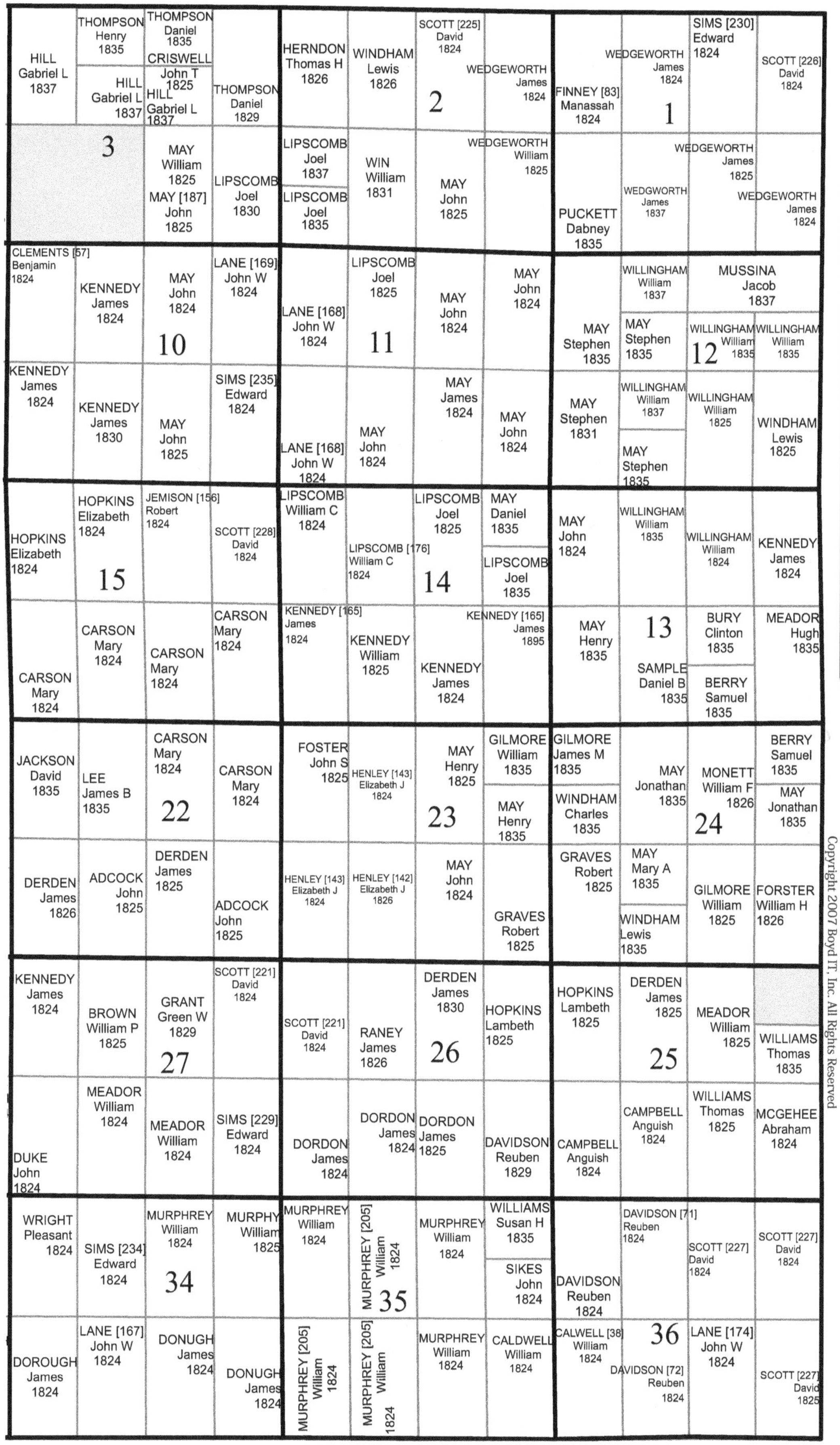

THOMPSON Henry 1835
THOMPSON Daniel 1835
CRISWELL John T 1825
HILL Gabriel L 1837
HILL Gabriel L 1837
HILL Gabriel L 1837
THOMPSON Daniel 1829
3
MAY William 1825
MAY [187] John 1825
LIPSCOMB Joel 1830
HERNDON Thomas H 1826
WINDHAM Lewis 1826
SCOTT [225] David 1824
WEDGEWORTH James 1824
2
LIPSCOMB Joel 1837
LIPSCOMB Joel 1835
WIN William 1831
MAY John 1825
WEDGEWORTH William 1825
FINNEY [83] Manassah 1824
WEDGEWORTH James 1824
SIMS [230] Edward 1824
SCOTT [226] David 1824
1
PUCKETT Dabney 1835
WEDGWORTH James 1837
WEDGEWORTH James 1825
WEDGEWORTH James 1824
CLEMENTS [57] Benjamin 1824
KENNEDY James 1824
MAY John 1824
LANE [169] John W 1824
10
KENNEDY James 1824
KENNEDY James 1830
MAY John 1825
SIMS [235] Edward 1824
LANE [168] John W 1824
LIPSCOMB Joel 1825
MAY John 1824
MAY John 1824
11
LANE [168] John W 1824
MAY John 1824
MAY James 1824
MAY John 1824
MAY Stephen 1835
MAY Stephen 1835
WILLINGHAM William 1837
MUSSINA Jacob 1837
WILLINGHAM William 1835
WILLINGHAM William 1835
12
MAY Stephen 1831
WILLINGHAM William 1837
WILLINGHAM William 1825
WINDHAM Lewis 1825
MAY Stephen 1835
HOPKINS Elizabeth 1824
HOPKINS Elizabeth 1824
JEMISON [156] Robert 1824
SCOTT [228] David 1824
15
CARSON Mary 1824
CARSON Mary 1824
CARSON Mary 1824
CARSON Mary 1824
LIPSCOMB William C 1824
LIPSCOMB [176] William C 1824
LIPSCOMB Joel 1825
MAY Daniel 1835
LIPSCOMB Joel 1835
14
KENNEDY [165] James 1824
KENNEDY William 1825
KENNEDY James 1824
KENNEDY [165] James 1895
MAY John 1824
WILLINGHAM William 1835
WILLINGHAM William 1824
KENNEDY James 1824
MAY Henry 1835
13
BURY Clinton 1835
MEADOR Hugh 1835
SAMPLE Daniel B 1835
BERRY Samuel 1835
JACKSON David 1835
LEE James B 1835
CARSON Mary 1824
CARSON Mary 1824
22
DERDEN James 1826
ADCOCK John 1825
DERDEN James 1825
ADCOCK John 1825
FOSTER John S 1825
HENLEY [143] Elizabeth J 1824
MAY Henry 1825
GILMORE William 1835
23
MAY Henry 1835
HENLEY [143] Elizabeth J 1824
HENLEY [142] Elizabeth J 1826
MAY John 1824
GRAVES Robert 1825
GILMORE James M 1835
MAY Jonathan 1835
MONETT William F 1826
BERRY Samuel 1835
MAY Jonathan 1835
WINDHAM Charles 1835
24
GRAVES Robert 1825
MAY Mary A 1835
WINDHAM Lewis 1835
GILMORE William 1825
FORSTER William H 1826
KENNEDY James 1824
BROWN William P 1825
GRANT Green W 1829
SCOTT [221] David 1824
27
MEADOR William 1824
MEADOR William 1824
SIMS [229] Edward 1824
DUKE John 1824
SCOTT [221] David 1824
RANEY James 1826
DERDEN James 1830
26
HOPKINS Lambeth 1825
DORDON James 1824
DORDON James 1824
DORDON James 1825
DAVIDSON Reuben 1829
HOPKINS Lambeth 1825
DERDEN James 1825
MEADOR William 1825
WILLIAMS Thomas 1835
25
CAMPBELL Anguish 1824
CAMPBELL Anguish 1824
WILLIAMS Thomas 1825
MCGEHEE Abraham 1824
WRIGHT Pleasant 1824
SIMS [234] Edward 1824
MURPHREY William 1824
MURPHY William 1825
34
LANE [167] John W 1824
DOROUGH James 1824
DONUGH James 1824
DONUGH James 1824
MURPHREY William 1824
MURPHREY [205] William 1824
35
MURPHREY William 1824
WILLIAMS Susan H 1835
SIKES John 1824
MURPHREY [205] William 1824
MURPHREY [205] William 1824
MURPHREY William 1824
CALDWELL William 1824
DAVIDSON [71] Reuben 1824
SCOTT [227] David 1824
SCOTT [227] David 1824
DAVIDSON Reuben 1824
CALWELL [38] William 1824
36
DAVIDSON [72] Reuben 1824
LANE [174] John W 1824
SCOTT [227] David 1825

Helpful Hints

1. This Map's INDEX can be found on the preceding pages.
2. Refer to Map "C" to see where this Township lies within Hale County, Alabama.
3. Numbers within square brackets [ ] denote a multi-patentee land parcel (multi-owner). Refer to Appendix "C" for a full list of members in this group.
4. Areas that look to be crowded with Patentees usually indicate multiple sales of the same parcel (Re-issues) or Overlapping parcels. See this Township's Index for an explanation of these and other circumstances that might explain "odd" groupings of Patentees on this map.

Legend

Patent Boundary

Section Boundary

No Patents Found (or Outside County)

1., 2., 3., ... Lot Numbers (when beside a name)

[ ] Group Number (see Appendix "C")

Scale: Section = 1 mile X 1 mile (generally, with some exceptions)

Road Map

T21-N R3-E
St Stephens Meridian

Map Group 10

Cities & Towns
East Port Landing
Wedgeworth

6

5

4

R. O. Cobucks
Landing

Jennings Ferry

State Route 14

7

Anchor

8

9

Clear Creek

Fawn

Greene

Hale

18

17

16

Lock 7

County Road 38

19

20

21

Cemeteries
Bethlehem Cemetery
Bethlehem Cemetery
Jackson Chapel Cemetery
Mays Cemetery

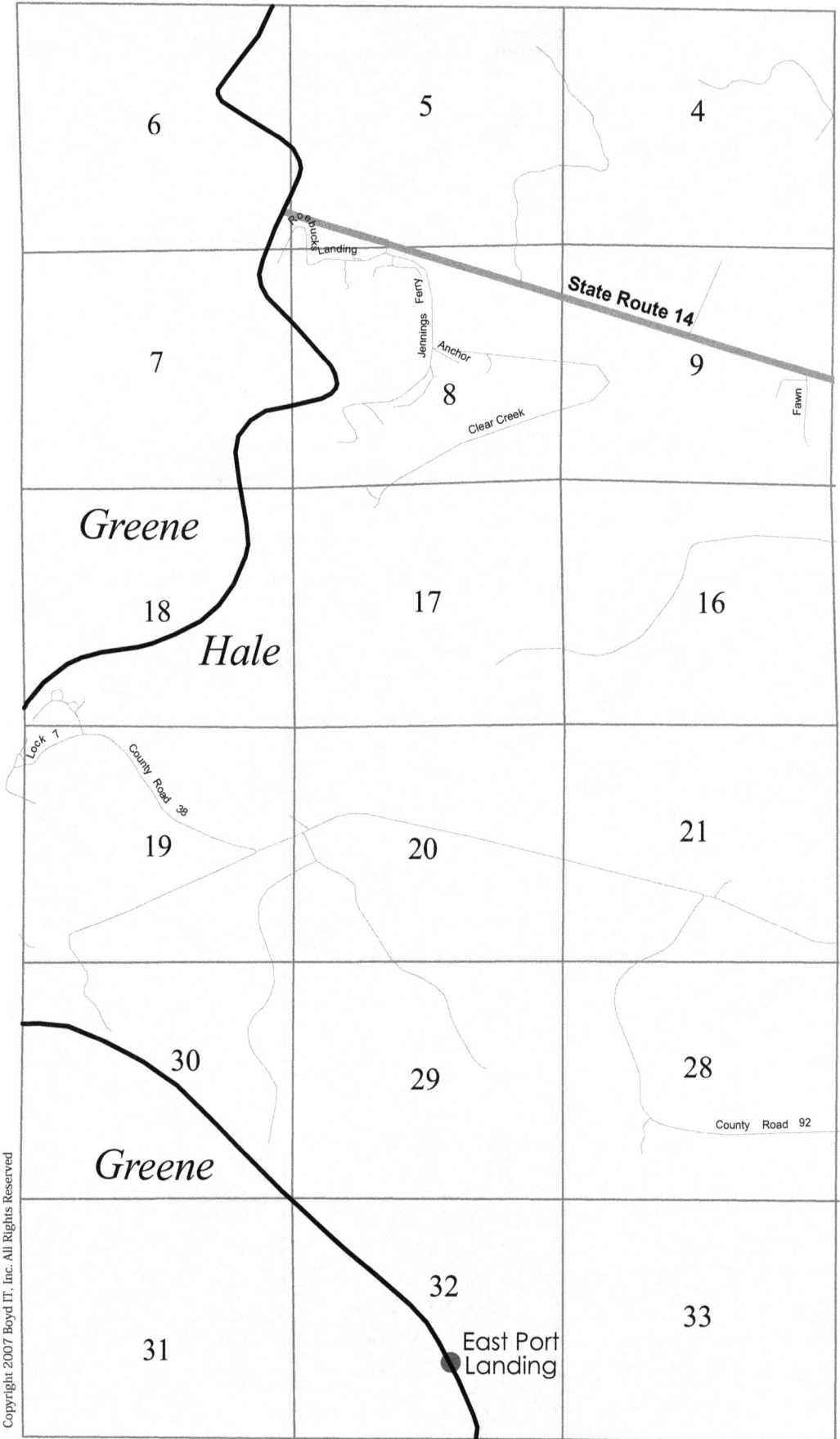

30

29

28

County Road 92

Greene

32

33

31

East Port
Landing

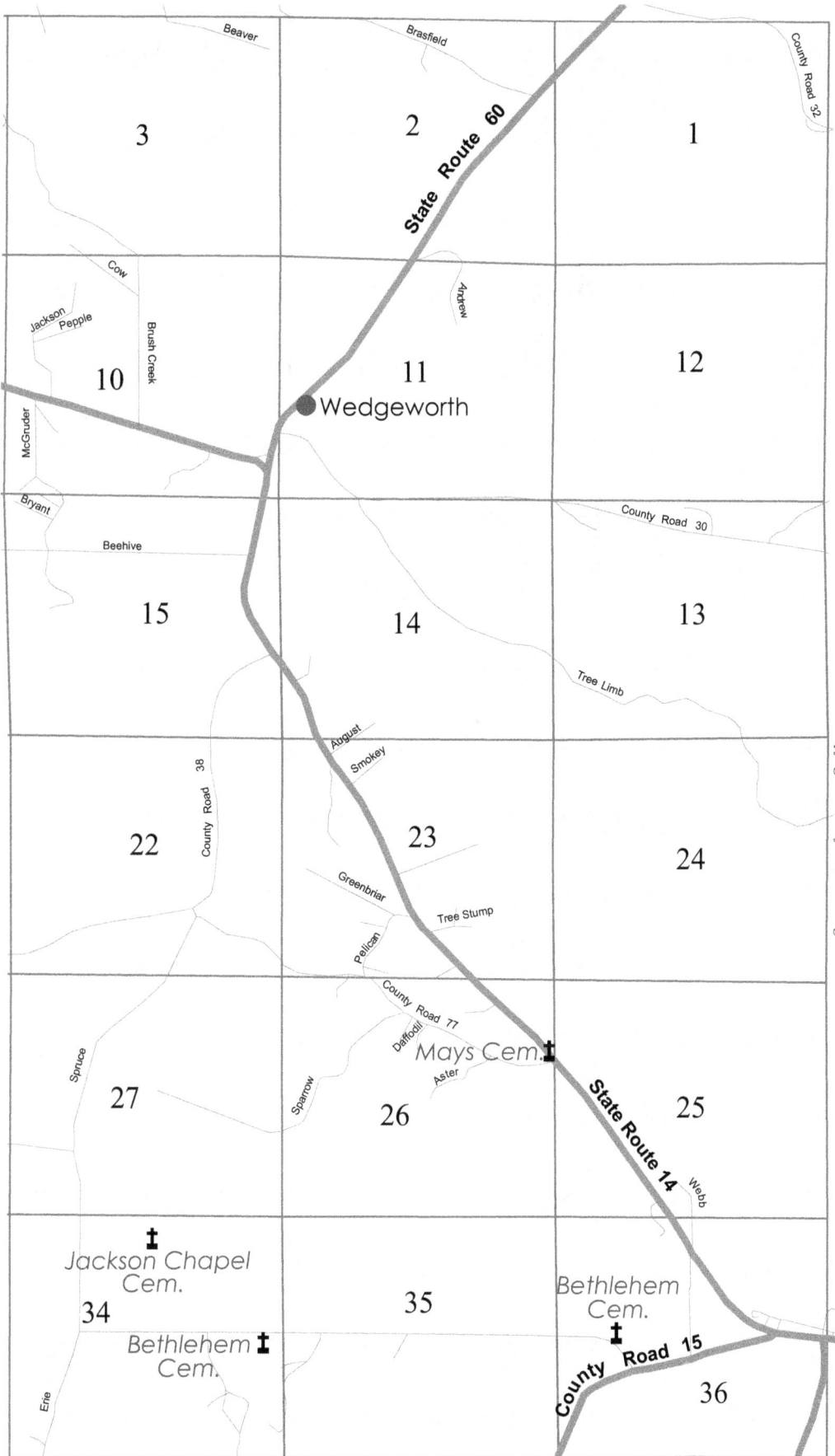

Helpful Hints

1. This road map has a number of uses, but primarily it is to help you: a) find the present location of land owned by your ancestors (at least the general area), b) find cemeteries and city-centers, and c) estimate the route/roads used by Census-takers & tax-assessors.

2. If you plan to travel to Hale County to locate cemeteries or land parcels, please pick up a modern travel map for the area before you do. Mapping old land parcels on modern maps is not as exact a science as you might think. Just the slightest variations in public land survey coordinates, estimates of parcel boundaries, or road-map deviations can greatly alter a map's representation of how a road either does or doesn't cross a particular parcel of land.

Legend

———————	Section Lines
═══════	Interstates
▬▬▬▬▬	Highways
———————	Other Roads
●	Cities/Towns
✝	Cemeteries

Scale: Section = 1 mile X 1 mile (generally, with some exceptions)

Historical Map

T21-N R3-E
St Stephens Meridian

Map Group 10

Cities & Towns
East Port Landing
Wedgeworth

Cemeteries
Bethlehem Cemetery
Bethlehem Cemetery
Jackson Chapel Cemetery
Mays Cemetery

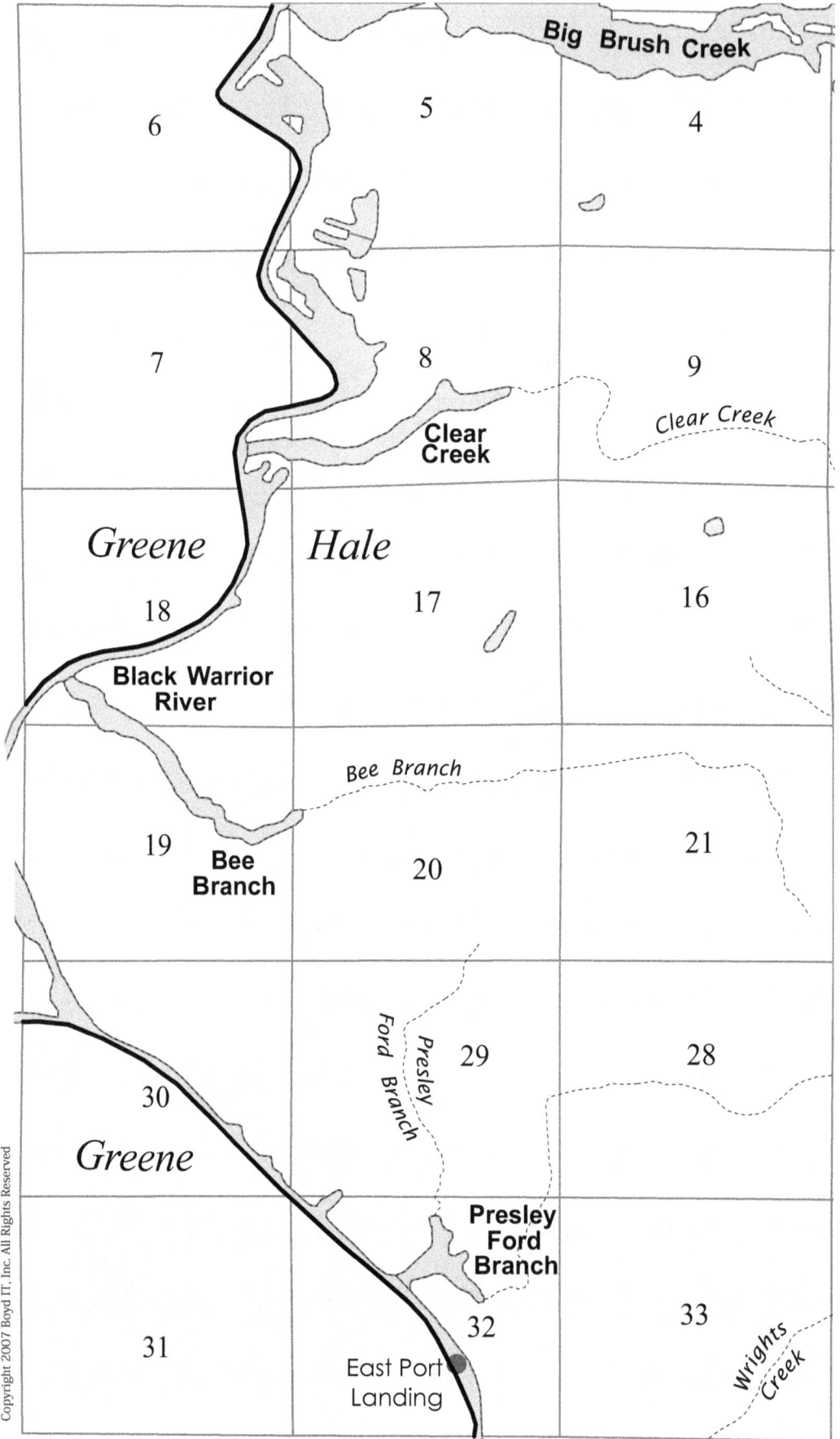

Big Brush Creek

6

5

4

7

8

9

Clear Creek

Clear
Creek

Greene

Hale

18

17

16

Black Warrior
River

Bee Branch

19

20

21

Bee
Branch

Greene

30

29

28

Presley
Ford
Branch

Presley
Ford
Branch

31

32

33

East Port
Landing

Wrights
Creek

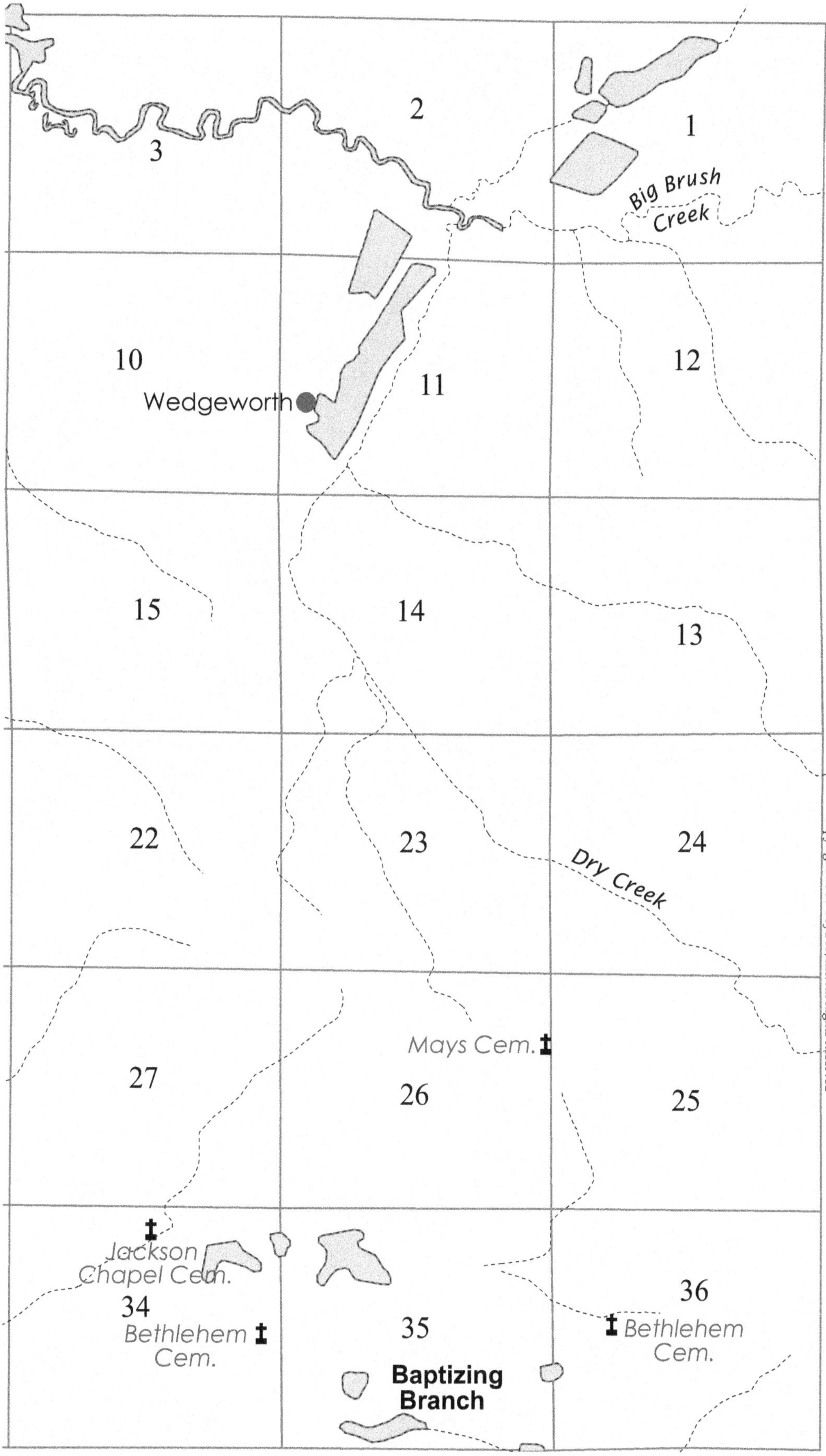
2
1
3
Big Brush Creek
10
12
11
Wedgeworth
15
14
13
22
23
24
Dry Creek
27
Mays Cem.
26
25
Jackson Chapel Cem.
34
Bethlehem Cem.
35
36
Bethlehem Cem.
Baptizing Branch

Helpful Hints

1. This Map takes a different look at the same Congressional Township displayed in the preceding two maps. It presents features that can help you better envision the historical development of the area: a) Water-bodies (lakes & ponds), b) Water-courses (rivers, streams, etc.), c) Railroads, d) City/town center-points (where they were oftentimes located when first settled), and e) Cemeteries.

2. Using this "Historical" map in tandem with this Township's Patent Map and Road Map, may lead you to some interesting discoveries. You will often find roads, towns, cemeteries, and waterways are named after nearby landowners: sometimes those names will be the ones you are researching. See how many of these research gems you can find here in Hale County.

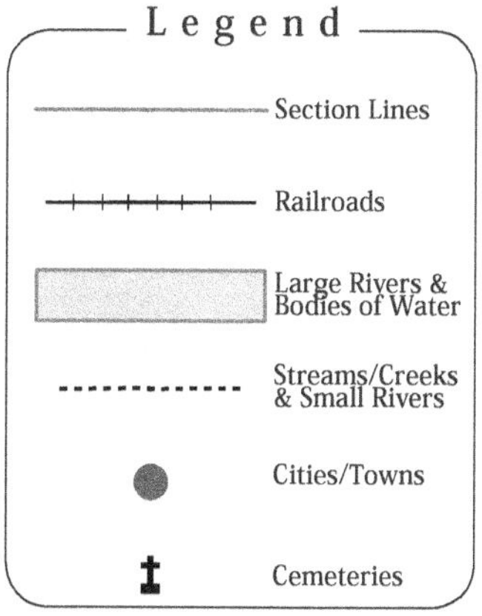
Legend
Section Lines
Railroads
Large Rivers & Bodies of Water
Streams/Creeks & Small Rivers
Cities/Towns
Cemeteries

Scale: Section = 1 mile X 1 mile
(there are some exceptions)

Map Group 11: Index to Land Patents

Township 21-North Range 4-East (St Stephens)

After you locate an individual in this Index, take note of the Section and Section Part then proceed to the Land Patent map on the pages immediately following. You should have no difficulty locating the corresponding parcel of land.

The "For More Info" Column will lead you to more information about the underlying Patents. See the *Legend* at right, and the "How to Use this Book" chapter, for more information.

<table>
<tr><td colspan="2">LEGEND</td></tr>
<tr><td colspan="2">"For More Info . . . " column</td></tr>
<tr><td>A =</td><td>Authority (Legislative Act, See Appendix "A")</td></tr>
<tr><td>B =</td><td>Block or Lot (location in Section unknown)</td></tr>
<tr><td>C =</td><td>Cancelled Patent</td></tr>
<tr><td>F =</td><td>Fractional Section</td></tr>
<tr><td>G =</td><td>Group (Multi-Patentee Patent, see Appendix "C")</td></tr>
<tr><td>V =</td><td>Overlaps another Parcel</td></tr>
<tr><td>R =</td><td>Re-Issued (Parcel patented more than once)</td></tr>
</table>

(A & G items require you to look in the Appendixes referred to above. All other Letter-designations followed by a number require you to locate line-items in this index that possess the ID number found after the letter).

ID	Individual in Patent	Sec.	Sec. Part	Date Issued	Other Counties	For More Info . . .
2542	ALLISON, Thomas	1	E½NE	1824-10-20		A1 G3
2539	" "	1	E½NW	1824-10-20		A1
2541	" "	1	W½NE	1824-10-20		A1
2540	" "	1	E½SE	1837-03-30		A1
2408	ANDERS, James	5	E½NW	1825-04-20		A1
2295	ANDERSON, Benjamin	10	W½SE	1824-10-20		A1 G4
2294	" "	14	E½NW	1824-10-20		A1
2296	" "	14	W½NW	1824-10-20		A1 G4
2297	" "	15	E½NE	1824-10-20		A1 G4
2298	" "	15	W½NE	1824-10-20		A1 G4 R2363
2409	ANDERSON, James	26	W½NW	1825-04-20		A1
2476	ANDERSON, Joshua	14	E½SW	1824-10-20		A1
2478	" "	14	W½SW	1824-10-20		A1
2477	"	14	NE	1825-05-25		A1
2566	ANDERSON, William	23	W½SW	1825-05-25		A1
2568	ANDERSON, William C	23	E½NW	1824-10-20		A1
2569	" "	23	W½NE	1824-10-20		A1
2300	ARNOLD, Bryant	34	SENE	1837-03-20		A1
2447	AVERY, John	35	E½NE	1825-04-20		A1
2457	BATES, John M	32	E½SW	1824-10-20		A1 G15
2410	BAXTER, James	13	W½NW	1837-03-30		A1 G22
2410	BAXTER, Mary	13	W½NW	1837-03-30		A1 G22
2410	BAXTER, Sarah L	13	W½NW	1837-03-30		A1 G22
2410	BAXTER, Thomas	13	W½NW	1837-03-30		A1 G22
2273	BECK, Abner	20	SESW	1835-10-01		A1
2293	BREAZEALE, Barzilla	34	W½NE	1824-10-20		A1 G33
2293	BREAZEALE, Cynthia	34	W½NE	1824-10-20		A1 G33
2293	BREAZEALE, Elijah	34	W½NE	1824-10-20		A1 G33
2293	BREAZEALE, Huldith	34	W½NE	1824-10-20		A1 G33
2299	BREWER, Benjamin B	25	W½NE	1837-11-02		A1
2581	BRITTON, William W	10	E½NE	1835-10-28		A1
2582	" "	10	E½NW	1835-10-28		A1
2584	" "	15	E½NW	1835-10-28		A1
2585	" "	15	SW	1835-10-28		A1
2583	" "	11	SWNW	1837-03-30		A1
2479	BROWN, Kimbrough	21	E½NE	1837-05-15		A1
2411	CARROLL, James	21	SESE	1850-03-01		A1
2567	CARTER, William B	28	SESE	1835-10-20		A1
2501	CHAMBERS, Mordecai	29	NENW	1835-09-25		A1
2503	CHAMBERS, Mordica	29	W½NW	1835-10-20		A1
2507	CLARKE, Patrick C	36	W½NW	1825-05-25		A1
2295	CLEMENTS, Benjamin	10	W½SE	1824-10-20		A1 G4
2296	" "	14	W½NW	1824-10-20		A1 G4
2297	" "	15	E½NE	1824-10-20		A1 G4
2298	" "	15	W½NE	1824-10-20		A1 G4 R2363
2518	COCHRAN, Peyton	24	W½NW	1826-02-01		A1

ID	Individual in Patent	Sec.	Sec. Part	Date Issued	Other Counties	For More Info . . .
2303	COLLINS, Daniel	9	W½NE	1824-10-20		A1 G62
2302	" "	4	W½SE	1826-06-10		A1
2573	COLLINS, William	9	E½NW	1824-10-20		A1
2570	" "	15	E½SE	1825-09-15		A1
2571	" "	17	W½SW	1826-06-10		A1
2572	" "	18	W½SE	1826-08-20		A1 R2524
2316	COMPANY, Sims Banks And	10	E½SE	1824-10-20		A1 G221
2317	" "	11	W½SW	1824-10-20		A1 G221
2318	" "	17	E½NE	1824-10-20		A1 G221
2340	" "	24	E½NW	1824-10-20		A1 G229
2320	" "	26	E½SE	1824-10-20		A1 G221
2341	" "	26	W½NE	1824-10-20		A1 G229
2321	" "	32	W½SE	1824-10-20		A1 G221
2322	" "	32	W½SW	1824-10-20		A1 G221
2324	" "	36	E½SE	1824-10-20		A1 G221
2325	" "	36	E½SW	1824-10-20		A1 G221
2326	" "	36	W½SE	1824-10-20		A1 G221
2342	" "	4	W½SW	1824-10-20		A1 G229
2343	" "	8	E½NE	1824-10-20		A1 G229
2344	" "	8	E½SE	1824-10-20		A1 G229
2345	" "	9	W½NW	1824-10-20		A1 G229
2319	" "	25	W½SW	1825-05-25		A1 G221
2323	" "	36	E½NW	1825-05-25		A1 G221
2449	CUNNINGHAM, John	27	E½SE	1826-02-01		A1
2370	DAVIS, George W	22	W½SW	1852-01-01		A1
2398	DAY, Ingram	33	E½SW	1824-10-20		A1 R2301
2399	" "	33	W½SW	1824-10-20		A1
2412	DERDEN, James	19	E½SW	1826-02-01		A1
2450	DERDEN, John	7	E½NE	1826-02-01		A1
2451	" "	8	W½NW	1826-02-01		A1
2414	DORDON, James	7	W½NW	1825-04-20		A1
2413	" "	7	E½NW	1825-05-25		A1
2522	ELLIS, Robert N	17	SESW	1858-08-20		A1
2535	EVANS, Stephen	32	E½NE	1830-12-01		A1
2575	GAREY, William	13	E½SW	1826-02-01		A1 C R2576
2577	" "	13	W½NE	1826-02-01		A1
2576	" "	13	E½SW	1912-04-27		A1 R2575
2304	GREEN, Daniel	10	W½NW	1824-10-20		A1
2305	" "	9	E½NE	1824-10-20		A1
2306	" "	9	E½SW	1824-10-20		A1
2307	" "	9	W½SE	1824-10-20		A1
2308	GUIN, Daniel	23	E½NE	1837-03-15		A1
2301	HAMLETT, Charles	33	E½SW	1825-06-20		A1 R2398
2480	HANIS, Lacy	36	W½SW	1824-10-20		A1
2361	HARRIS, Ervin R	4	E½NW	1835-10-01		A1
2362	HARRIS, Evin R	4	SESW	1835-10-28		A1
2452	HARRIS, John	8	W½NE	1827-06-20		A1
2530	HARRIS, Sanford	8	NWSE	1837-03-30		A1
2531	HARRIS, Sherrard	11	E½SE	1825-04-20		A1
2532	HARRIS, Simeon	5	E½SE	1826-02-01		A1 F
2559	HARRIS, Tillman P	14	W½SE	1824-10-20		A1
2561	" "	9	W½SW	1825-04-20		A1
2558	" "	13	W½SE	1825-05-25		A1
2560	" "	24	E½NE	1826-02-01		A1 F
2562	HARRIS, Tilmon P	14	E½SE	1824-10-20		A1 G140 R2513
2454	HARRY, John J	13	SENE	1837-03-15		A1
2453	" "	13	NENE	1837-11-02		A1
2544	HARRY, Thomas	1	SWNW	1837-05-15		A1
2545	" "	1	W½SW	1837-11-02		A1
2485	HARVEY, Margaret	1	NWNW	1835-10-20		A1
2403	HENRY, Isham	11	E½NW	1835-10-01		A1
2404	" "	11	NWNE	1837-03-30		A1
2515	HENRY, Perry	2	SWSW	1837-03-15		A1
2513	" "	14	E½SE	1837-03-30		A1 R2562
2514	" "	2	SESW	1837-03-30		A1
2543	HERNDON, Thomas H	7	E½SW	1833-05-30		A1
2274	HESTER, Abraham	17	SWSE	1843-02-01		A1
2490	HOBSON, Matthew	35	E½SW	1835-09-28		A1
2491	" "	35	NWSE	1835-09-28		A1
2415	JOHNSON, James	35	E½SE	1826-02-01		A1
2493	JOHNSON, Miles	23	E½SE	1825-05-25		A1
2494	" "	24	W½SW	1825-05-25		A1
2521	JOHNSTON, Richard	36	E½NE	1825-06-20		A1

ID	Individual in Patent	Sec.	Sec. Part	Date Issued	Other Counties	For More Info . . .
2331	KING, Drury E	21	NESE	1850-03-01		A1
2455	KING, John	17	NESW	1837-05-15		A1
2456	" "	17	NWSE	1837-05-15		A1
2363	LANDRY, Francis	15	W½NE	1830-12-15		A1 R2298
2366	" "	22	W½NE	1831-08-25		A1
2364	" "	22	NENW	1837-03-15		A1
2365	" "	22	SENW	1837-11-02		A1
2469	LANE, John S	11	W½SE	1825-05-25		A1
2471	LANE, John W	31	E½SW	1824-10-20		A1 G172
2470	" "	33	E½SE	1824-10-20		A1 G171
2574	LAWLESS, William G	17	SENW	1858-08-20		A1
2292	LIVINGSTON, Barney B	2	W½NE	1905-03-30		A2
2417	MARTIN, James	22	NWSE	1837-03-15		A1
2416	" "	22	NESW	1837-11-02		A1
2459	MAY, John	27	W½SE	1825-05-25		A1
2460	" "	7	W½NE	1825-05-25		A1
2472	MAY, Jonathan	30	NWNW	1835-09-22		A1 R2536
2508	MAY, Patrick	24	E½SE	1825-04-20		A1
2510	" "	25	E½NE	1825-04-20		A1
2509	" "	24	W½SE	1826-02-01		A1
2282	MCALPIN, Alexander	30	E½SE	1824-10-20		A1
2284	" "	31	W½NE	1824-10-20		A1
2285	" "	31	W½SE	1824-10-20		A1 R2286
2286	" "	31	W½SE	1824-10-20		A1 R2285
2457	" "	32	E½SW	1824-10-20		A1 G15
2288	" "	32	W½NW	1825-05-25		A1
2287	" "	32	E½NW	1826-02-01		A1
2283	" "	31	E½NE	1826-12-20		A1
2289	" "	34	NESE	1835-09-25		A1
2533	MCALPIN, Solomon	34	E½SW	1824-10-20		A1
2534	" "	34	W½SE	1825-05-25		A1
2418	MCCARTER, James	22	E½NE	1825-04-20		A1
2419	" "	23	W½NW	1825-05-25		A1
2420	" "	23	W½SE	1825-05-25		A1
2275	MCGEHEE, Abraham	30	E½SW	1824-10-20		A1
2279	" "	33	E½NE	1824-10-20		A1 G194
2470	" "	33	E½SE	1824-10-20		A1 G171
2280	" "	33	W½NE	1824-10-20		A1 G196
2281	" "	34	W½SW	1824-10-20		A1 G196
2278	" "	35	E½NW	1825-04-20		A1 V2473
2277	" "	33	W½SE	1825-05-25		A1
2276	" "	33	E½NW	1827-07-02		A1
2279	MCLANE, James	33	E½NE	1824-10-20		A1 G194
2461	MCMILLAN, John	26	E½NE	1826-02-01		A1
2462	MEADER, John	30	W½NE	1825-09-15		A1
2396	MEADOR, Holden U	17	NWNE	1837-11-02		A1
2463	MEADOR, John	30	E½NW	1826-02-01		A1
2502	MEADOR, Mordecai J	17	NENW	1837-05-15		A1
2506	MEADOR, Obadiah	19	W½SW	1824-10-20		A1
2505	" "	19	W½NW	1826-02-01		A1
2547	MELTON, Thomas	10	W½NE	1824-10-20		A1
2564	MELTON, West A	10	E½SW	1824-10-20		A1 G199
2565	" "	10	W½SW	1824-10-20		A1 G199
2563	" "	15	W½NW	1826-06-10		A1
2458	MILLEN, John M	23	E½SW	1824-10-20		A1 G200
2309	MON, Daniel	18	E½SE	1824-10-20		A1
2421	MONETT, James	19	E½SE	1825-04-20		A1
2483	MORRISON, Malcolm	5	W½SE	1825-05-25		A1
2484	MORRISSON, Malcolm	35	SWSE	1835-10-20		A1
2389	MUNNERLYN, Henry B	12	E½NE	1837-11-02		A1
2390	" "	12	SENW	1837-11-02		A1
2391	" "	12	SWNE	1837-11-02		A1
2422	MUNNERLYN, James	12	E½SE	1848-07-01		A1
2423	" "	12	SWSE	1848-07-01		A1
2387	NORDIN, Hardy	20	NESW	1835-10-01		A1 R2371
2388	" "	29	SENW	1835-10-20		A1
2511	NORRIS, Patrick	32	E½SE	1824-10-20		A1
2392	PARR, Henry	29	E½SE	1835-10-20		A1
2467	PARR, John	30	NWSE	1835-10-01		A1
2468	" "	30	SWSE	1835-10-20		A1
2339	PECK, E	36	W½NE	1826-02-01		A1 G209
2349	PECK, Edwin	25	W½NW	1825-09-15		A1 G210
2347	" "	25	E½NW	1826-02-01		A1 G210

ID	Individual in Patent	Sec.	Sec. Part	Date Issued	Other Counties	For More Info . . .
2348	PECK, Edwin (Cont'd)	25	E½SW	1826-02-01		A1 G210
2346	" "	25	W½SE	1835-10-20		A1
2339	PECK, F	36	W½NE	1826-02-01		A1 G209
2349	PECK, Frederick	25	W½NW	1825-09-15		A1 G210
2347	" "	25	E½NW	1826-02-01		A1 G210
2348	" "	25	E½SW	1826-02-01		A1 G210
2402	PHARIS, Isaac	30	E½NE	1824-10-20		A1
2400	" "	29	E½SW	1825-04-20		A1
2401	" "	29	W½SW	1825-04-20		A1
2448	PHARIS, John C	32	W½NE	1824-10-20		A1
2471	PICKENS, Samuel	31	E½SW	1824-10-20		A1 G172
2527	" "	31	W½NW	1824-10-20		A1 G212
2526	" "	31	W½SW	1824-10-20		A1
2525	" "	31	E½NW	1825-05-25		A1
2579	POUNDS, William	20	NENW	1837-05-15		A1
2393	PRISOCK, Henry W	2	E½SE	1860-10-01		A1
2580	PURNELL, William	27	NW	1837-05-15		A1
2424	RANEY, James	19	E½NE	1824-10-20		A1
2290	READ, Alexander W	22	SESW	1840-11-10		A1
2351	REDDING, Eli K	21	N½NE	1837-03-30		A1
2519	REDDING, Randolph	21	SENW	1837-03-20		A1
2520	" "	21	SWNW	1837-03-20		A1
2523	REDDING, Robert	21	SWNE	1837-05-15		A1
2372	ROBERTS, George W	20	NWSW	1835-10-20		A1
2371	" "	20	NESW	1837-05-15		A1 R2387
2464	ROBERTSON, John P	17	E½SE	1837-11-02		A1
2465	" "	20	E½NE	1837-11-02		A1
2466	" "	20	NWNE	1837-11-02		A1
2373	RUFF, George W	19	W½NE	1835-09-28		A1
2374	" "	19	W½SE	1835-09-28		A1
2375	" "	20	SWSW	1835-09-28		A1
2316	SCOTT, David	10	E½SE	1824-10-20		A1 G221
2564	" "	10	E½SW	1824-10-20		A1 G199
2565	" "	10	W½SW	1824-10-20		A1 G199
2317	" "	11	W½SW	1824-10-20		A1 G221
2318	" "	17	E½NE	1824-10-20		A1 G221
2320	" "	26	E½SE	1824-10-20		A1 G221
2321	" "	32	W½SE	1824-10-20		A1 G221
2322	" "	32	W½SW	1824-10-20		A1 G221
2324	" "	36	E½SE	1824-10-20		A1 G221
2325	" "	36	E½SW	1824-10-20		A1 G221
2326	" "	36	W½SE	1824-10-20		A1 G221
2312	" "	5	E½SW	1824-10-20		A1 G223
2313	" "	5	W½SW	1824-10-20		A1 G223
2314	" "	6	E½SE	1824-10-20		A1 G223
2315	" "	6	W½SE	1824-10-20		A1 G223
2327	" "	9	E½SE	1824-10-20		A1 G224
2319	" "	25	W½SW	1825-05-25		A1 G221
2323	" "	36	E½NW	1825-05-25		A1 G221
2353	SIMPSON, Enoch	35	W½SW	1824-10-20		A1
2562	SIMS, Edward	14	E½SE	1824-10-20		A1 G140 R2513
2458	" "	23	E½SW	1824-10-20		A1 G200
2340	" "	24	E½NW	1824-10-20		A1 G229
2341	" "	26	W½NE	1824-10-20		A1 G229
2342	" "	4	W½SW	1824-10-20		A1 G229
2343	" "	8	E½NE	1824-10-20		A1 G229
2344	" "	8	E½SE	1824-10-20		A1 G229
2303	" "	9	W½NE	1824-10-20		A1 G62
2345	" "	9	W½NW	1824-10-20		A1 G229
2310	SMALL, Daniel	22	E½SE	1837-03-15		A1
2311	" "	22	SWSE	1837-05-15		A1
2350	SMITH, Eli B	34	NENE	1835-10-28		A1
2428	SPEED, James	4	E½SE	1825-09-15		A1
2425	SPEED, James S	12	NESW	1860-10-01		A1
2426	" "	12	SWSW	1860-10-01		A1
2312	SPEED, Martin	5	E½SW	1824-10-20		A1 G223
2313	" "	5	W½SW	1824-10-20		A1 G223
2314	" "	6	E½SE	1824-10-20		A1 G223
2315	" "	6	W½SE	1824-10-20		A1 G223
2488	" "	5	W½NW	1825-09-15		A1
2489	" "	6	E½NE	1825-09-15		A1
2486	" "	5	E½NE	1826-06-10		A1
2487	" "	5	W½NE	1826-06-10		A1

ID	Individual in Patent	Sec.	Sec. Part	Date Issued	Other Counties	For More Info . . .
2327	SPEED, William	9	E½SE	1824-10-20		A1 G224
2546	SPIVEY, Thomas L	21	W½SW	1835-09-22		A1
2386	STALLINGS, Green B	7	W½SE	1835-10-20		A1
2495	STEPHENSON, Miles	12	NWNE	1837-03-15		A1
2496	"	12	W½NW	1837-03-15		A1
2499	STEPHENSON, Mills	11	E½NE	1826-10-02		A1
2500	"	12	NENW	1835-10-20		A1
2497	"	1	E½SW	1837-03-30		A1
2498	"	1	W½SE	1837-03-30		A1
2473	STICKNEY, Joseph B	35	NW	1837-03-20		A1 V2278
2474	"	35	SWNE	1837-03-20		A1
2357	STRINGFELLON, Enock	2	N½SW	1837-08-01		A1
2352	STRINGFELLOW, Elizabeth	2	S½NW	1837-11-02		A1
2356	STRINGFELLOW, Enoch	34	E½NW	1835-09-22		A1
2355	"	27	W½SW	1837-03-20		A1
2354	"	2	E½NE	1860-10-01		A1
2358	STRINGFELLOW, Enock	28	NESE	1837-03-30		A1 V2552
2359	"	28	W½SE	1837-03-30		A1 V2552
2360	STRINGFELLOW, Erasmus	2	W½SE	1858-08-20		A1
2492	STRINGFELLOW, Mcdonald	27	E½SW	1837-03-20		A1
2524	STRINGFELLOW, Robert	18	W½SE	1825-04-20		A1 R2572
2578	STRINGFELLOW, William M	2	N½NW	1858-08-20		A1
2542	SUMMEY, Jacob	1	E½NE	1824-10-20		A1 G3
2406	SUMMY, Jacob	13	W½SW	1824-10-20		A1
2291	THOMAS, Anne	20	W½NW	1825-05-25		A1
2504	THOMASON, Nicholson	13	NENW	1840-11-10		A1
2368	TOLAND, Francis	20	SWNE	1835-09-22		A1
2369	"	20	W½SE	1835-09-22		A1
2367	"	20	NESE	1837-08-01		A1
2429	TOLAND, James	29	NE	1835-10-28		A1 G238
2430	"	29	W½SE	1835-10-28		A1 G238
2475	TOLAND, Joseph	20	SESE	1835-09-25		A1
2429	"	29	NE	1835-10-28		A1 G238
2430	"	29	W½SE	1835-10-28		A1 G238
2328	TOWNSEND, David	11	E½SW	1825-05-25		A1
2329	"	4	W½NW	1825-05-25		A1
2481	TURNER, Lemargues D	7	W½SW	1829-03-06		A1
2394	WATSON, Henry	25	E½SE	1837-11-02		A1
2397	WATSON, Hugh	27	W½NE	1825-05-25		A1
2431	WEDGEWORTH, James	6	E½NW	1824-10-20		A1
2432	"	6	E½SW	1824-10-20		A1
2433	"	6	W½NE	1824-10-20		A1
2434	"	6	W½NW	1824-10-20		A1
2435	"	6	W½SW	1824-10-20		A1
2332	WHITE, Durrett	26	E½NW	1825-09-15		A1
2333	"	26	E½SW	1825-09-15		A1
2334	"	26	W½SE	1826-02-01		A1
2335	"	26	W½SW	1826-02-01		A1
2336	"	27	E½NE	1826-06-10		A1
2337	"	34	SESE	1835-09-22		A1
2338	"	35	NWNE	1835-09-22		A1
2330	WILLIAMS, David	18	E½SW	1835-10-20		A1
2436	WILLIAMS, James	24	E½SW	1825-05-25		A1
2512	WILLIAMS, Paul	22	W½NW	1840-11-10		A1
2517	WILLIAMS, Peter	8	SWSE	1835-09-22		A1
2516	"	17	SWNE	1837-03-30		A1
2528	WILLIAMS, Samuel	21	NWNE	1835-10-20		A1
2529	"	3	NENE	1837-08-01		A1
2536	WILLIAMS, Susan H	30	NWNW	1837-03-15		A1 R2472
2527	WILLIAMS, Thomas	31	W½NW	1824-10-20		A1 G212
2280	"	33	W½NE	1824-10-20		A1 G196
2281	"	34	W½SW	1824-10-20		A1 G196
2556	"	30	W½SW	1825-09-15		A1
2548	"	21	E½SW	1835-09-25		A1
2549	"	21	W½SE	1835-09-25		A1
2550	"	28	E½NW	1835-09-25		A1
2551	"	28	E½SW	1835-09-25		A1
2552	"	28	N½SE	1835-09-25		A1 V2358, 2359
2553	"	28	NE	1835-09-25		A1
2554	"	28	W½NW	1835-09-25		A1
2557	"	33	W½NW	1835-09-25		A1
2555	"	30	SWNW	1835-10-28		A1
2586	WILLINGHAM, William	18	E½NW	1837-03-15		A1

ID	Individual in Patent	Sec.	Sec. Part	Date Issued	Other Counties	For More Info . . .
2395	WILSON, Henry	13	E½SE	1825-09-15		A1
2405	WILSON, Jackonias	12	NWSE	1858-08-20		A1
2407	WILSON, Jaconiah	12	SESW	1851-03-01		A1
2427	WILSON, James S	11	NWNW	1843-02-01		A1
2437	WILSON, Jane	3	NENW	1835-09-22		A1
2438	WILSON, Jechonias	13	SENW	1837-03-30		A1
2443	WILSON, John A	3	W½NW	1824-10-20		A1
2444	" "	4	E½NE	1824-10-20		A1
2445	" "	4	NESW	1835-10-01		A1
2446	" "	4	W½NE	1835-10-01		A1
2440	" "	3	SENW	1837-03-30		A1
2441	" "	3	SW	1837-03-30		A1
2442	" "	3	SWSE	1837-03-30		A1
2439	" "	3	NWSE	1840-11-10		A1
2537	WILSON, Thomas A	11	SWNE	1837-03-15		A1
2538	" "	12	NWSW	1837-03-30		A1
2482	WINDHAM, Lewis	18	W½NW	1825-04-20		A1
2377	YARBOROUGH, George	18	E½NE	1824-10-20		A1
2382	" "	8	E½NW	1824-10-20		A1
2380	" "	19	E½NW	1835-09-22		A1
2384	" "	8	NWSW	1835-09-25		A1
2378	" "	18	NWNE	1835-10-28		A1
2381	" "	7	E½SE	1835-10-28		A1
2383	" "	8	E½SW	1837-03-15		A1
2385	" "	8	SWSW	1837-03-15		A1
2379	" "	18	SWNE	1837-03-20		A1
2376	" "	17	W½NW	1837-08-01		A1

Patent Map

T21-N R4-E
St Stephens Meridian

Map Group 11

Township Statistics

Parcels Mapped	:	314
Number of Patents	:	307
Number of Individuals	:	170
Patentees Identified	:	168
Number of Surnames	:	104
Multi-Patentee Parcels	:	47
Oldest Patent Date	:	10/20/1824
Most Recent Patent	:	4/27/1912
Block/Lot Parcels	:	0
Parcels Re - Issued	:	8
Parcels that Overlap	:	5
Cities and Towns	:	1
Cemeteries	:	5

Section 3
WILSON John A 1824 · WILSON Jane 1835 · WILSON John A 1837 · WILLIAMS Samuel 1837 · 3 · WILSON John A 1840 · WILSON John A 1837 · WILSON John A 1837

Section 2
STRINGFELLOW William M 1858 · LIVINGSTON Barney B 1905 · STRINGFELLOW Enoch 1860 · STRINGFELLOW Elizabeth 1837 · STRINGFELLON Enock 1837 · STRINGFELLOW Erasmus 1858 · HENRY Perry 1837 · HENRY Perry 1837 · PRISOCK Henry W 1860

Section 1
HARVEY Margaret 1835 · ALLISON Thomas 1824 · ALLISON Thomas 1824 · ALLISON [3] Thomas 1824 · HARRY Thomas 1837 · 1 · STEPHENSON Mills 1837 · STEPHENSON Mills 1837 · HARRY Thomas 1837 · ALLISON Thomas 1837

Section 10
GREEN Daniel 1824 · BRITTON William W 1835 · MELTON Thomas 1824 · BRITTON William W 1835 · 10 · MELTON [199] West A 1824 · MELTON [199] West A 1824 · SCOTT [221] David 1824 · ANDERSON [4] Benjamin 1824

Section 11
WILSON James S 1843 · HENRY Isham 1837 · HENRY Isham 1835 · HENRY Isham 1835 · WILSON Thomas A 1837 · STEPHENSON Mills 1826 · BRITTON William W 1837 · 11 · SCOTT [221] David 1824 · TOWNSEND David 1825 · LANE John S 1825 · HARRIS Sherrard 1825

Section 12
STEPHENSON Mills 1835 · STEPHENSON Miles 1837 · MUNNERLYN Henry B 1837 · STEPHENSON Miles 1837 · MUNNERLYN Henry B 1837 · MUNNERLYN Henry B 1837 · 12 · WILSON Thomas A 1837 · SPEED James S 1860 · WILSON Jackonias 1858 · MUNNERLYN James 1848 · SPEED James S 1860 · WILSON Jaconiah 1851 · MUNNERLYN James 1848

Section 15
MELTON West A 1826 · BRITTON William W 1835 · ANDERSON [4] Benjamin 1824 · ANDERSON [4] Benjamin 1824 · LANDRY Francis 1830 · 15 · BRITTON William W 1835 · COLLINS William 1825

Section 14
ANDERSON [4] Benjamin 1824 · ANDERSON Benjamin 1824 · ANDERSON Joshua 1825 · 14 · ANDERSON Joshua 1824 · ANDERSON Joshua 1824 · HARRIS Tillman P 1824

Section 13
BAXTER [22] James 1837 · THOMASON Nicholson 1840 · GAREY William 1826 · HARRY John J 1837 · WILSON Jechonias 1837 · HARRY John J 1837 · 13 · HARRIS [140] Tilmon P 1824 · HENRY Perry 1837 · SUMMY Jacob 1824 · GAREY William 1912 · GAREY William 1826 · HARRIS Tillman P 1825 · WILSON Henry 1825

Section 22
WILLIAMS Paul 1840 · LANDRY Francis 1837 · LANDRY Francis 1831 · MCCARTER James 1825 · LANDRY Francis 1837 · 22 · MARTIN James 1837 · MARTIN James 1837 · SMALL Daniel 1837 · DAVIS George W 1852 · READ Alexander W 1840 · SMALL Daniel 1837

Section 23
MCCARTER James 1825 · ANDERSON William C 1824 · ANDERSON William C 1824 · GUIN Daniel 1837 · 23 · ANDERSON William 1825 · MILLEN [200] John M 1824 · MCCARTER James 1825 · JOHNSON Miles 1825

Section 24
SIMS [229] Edward 1824 · COCHRAN Peyton 1826 · HARRIS Tillman P 1826 · 24 · JOHNSON Miles 1825 · WILLIAMS James 1825 · MAY Patrick 1826 · MAY Patrick 1825

Section 27
WILLIAMS Paul 1840 · WATSON Hugh 1825 · WHITE Durrett 1826 · PURNELL William 1837 · 27 · STRINGFELLOW Enoch 1837 · MAY John 1825 · STRINGFELLOW Mcdonald 1837 · CUNNINGHAM John 1826

Section 26
ANDERSON James 1825 · WHITE Durrett 1825 · SIMS [229] Edward 1824 · MCMILLAN John 1826 · WHITE Durrett 1825 · 26 · SCOTT [221] David 1824 · WHITE Durrett 1826 · WHITE Durrett 1826

Section 25
PECK [210] Edwin 1825 · PECK [210] Edwin 1826 · BREWER Benjamin B 1837 · MAY Patrick 1825 · 25 · SCOTT [221] David 1825 · PECK [210] Edwin 1826 · PECK Edwin 1835 · WATSON Henry 1837

Section 34
STRINGFELLOW Enoch 1835 · SMITH Eli B 1835 · BREAZEALE [33] Barzilla 1824 · ARNOLD Bryant 1837 · 34 · MCGEHEE [196] Abraham 1824 · MCALPIN Solomon 1824 · MCALPIN Solomon 1825

Section 35
MCGEHEE Abraham 1825 · WHITE Durrett 1835 · AVERY John 1825 · STICKNEY Joseph B 1837 · STICKNEY Joseph B 1837 · 35 · MCALPIN Alexander 1835 · WHITE Durrett 1835 · SIMPSON Enoch 1824 · HOBSON Matthew 1835 · HOBSON Matthew 1835 · JOHNSON James 1826 · MORRISSON Malcolm 1835

Section 36
CLARKE Patrick C 1825 · PECK [209] E 1826 · JOHNSTON Richard 1825 · SCOTT [221] David 1825 · 36 · HANIS Lacy 1824 · SCOTT [221] David 1824 · SCOTT [221] David 1824 · SCOTT [221] David 1824

Helpful Hints

1. This Map's INDEX can be found on the preceding pages.

2. Refer to Map "C" to see where this Township lies within Hale County, Alabama.

3. Numbers within square brackets [ ] denote a multi-patentee land parcel (multi-owner). Refer to Appendix "C" for a full list of members in this group.

4. Areas that look to be crowded with Patentees usually indicate multiple sales of the same parcel (Re-issues) or Overlapping parcels. See this Township's Index for an explanation of these and other circumstances that might explain "odd" groupings of Patentees on this map.

Legend

- ——— Patent Boundary
- ▬▬▬ Section Boundary
- No Patents Found (or Outside County)
- 1., 2., 3., ... Lot Numbers (when beside a name)
- [ ] Group Number (see Appendix "C")

Scale: Section = 1 mile X 1 mile (generally, with some exceptions)

Road Map

T21-N R4-E
St Stephens Meridian

Map Group 11

Cities & Towns
Sawyerville

Cemeteries
Langham Cemetery
Martian Cemetery
Rhone Cemetery
Robertson Cemetery
Wilson Cemetery

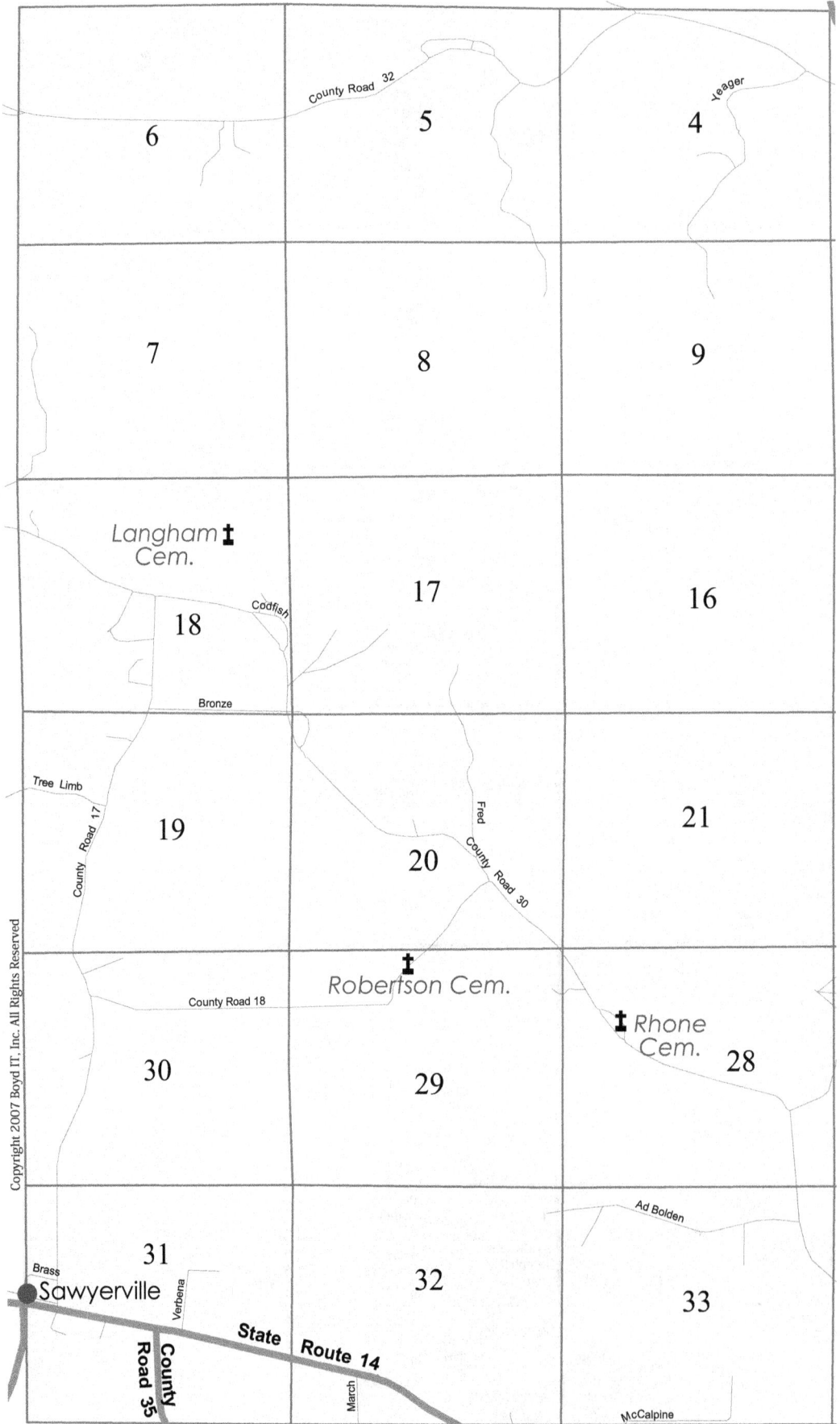

County Road 32

Yeager

6

5

4

7

8

9

Langham Cem.

Codfish

18

17

16

Bronze

Tree Limb

County Road 17

19

20

Fred

County Road 30

21

County Road 18

Robertson Cem.

Rhone Cem.

30

29

28

Ad Bolden

Brass

31

Sawyerville

Verbena

County Road 35

State Route 14

March

32

McCalpine

33

Wilson Cem.

County Highway 32

3

2

1

Hubbard

Raspberry

Dunson

10

11

12

County Road 32

15

14

13

County Road 21

22

23

24

Tree Top

27

26

25

Big Brush

Saffron

34

35

36

County Road 30 Osprey

Martian Cem.

Brown

Sage

Helpful Hints

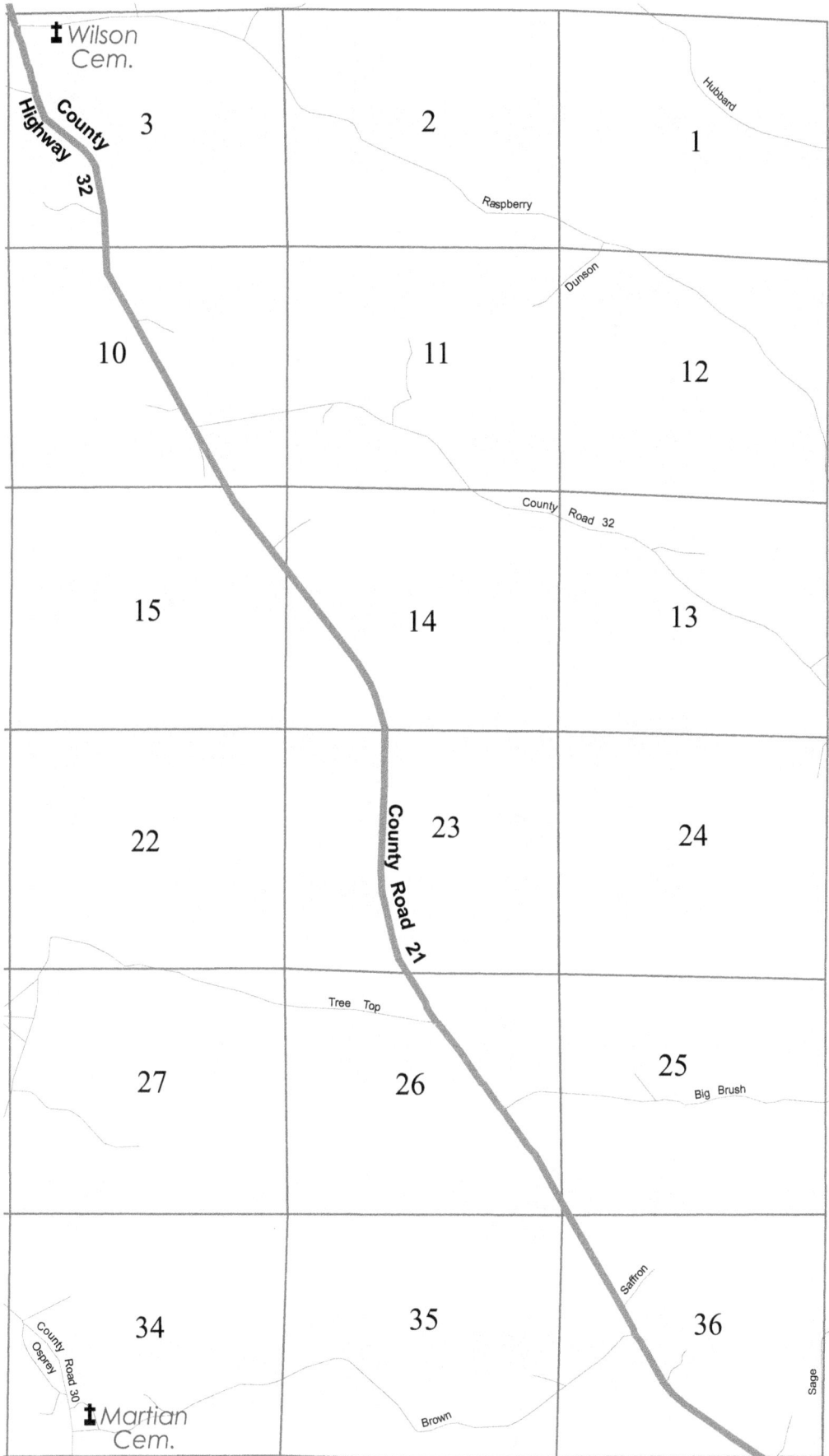

1. This road map has a number of uses, but primarily it is to help you: a) find the present location of land owned by your ancestors (at least the general area), b) find cemeteries and city-centers, and c) estimate the route/roads used by Census-takers & tax-assessors.

2. If you plan to travel to Hale County to locate cemeteries or land parcels, please pick up a modern travel map for the area before you do. Mapping old land parcels on modern maps is not as exact a science as you might think. Just the slightest variations in public land survey coordinates, estimates of parcel boundaries, or road-map deviations can greatly alter a map's representation of how a road either does or doesn't cross a particular parcel of land.

Legend

——————— Section Lines

═══════ Interstates

━━━━━━━ Highways

——————— Other Roads

● Cities/Towns

✝ Cemeteries

Scale: Section = 1 mile X 1 mile
(generally, with some exceptions)

Historical Map

T21-N R4-E
St Stephens Meridian

Map Group 11

Cities & Towns
Sawyerville

Cemeteries
Langham Cemetery
Martian Cemetery
Rhone Cemetery
Robertson Cemetery
Wilson Cemetery

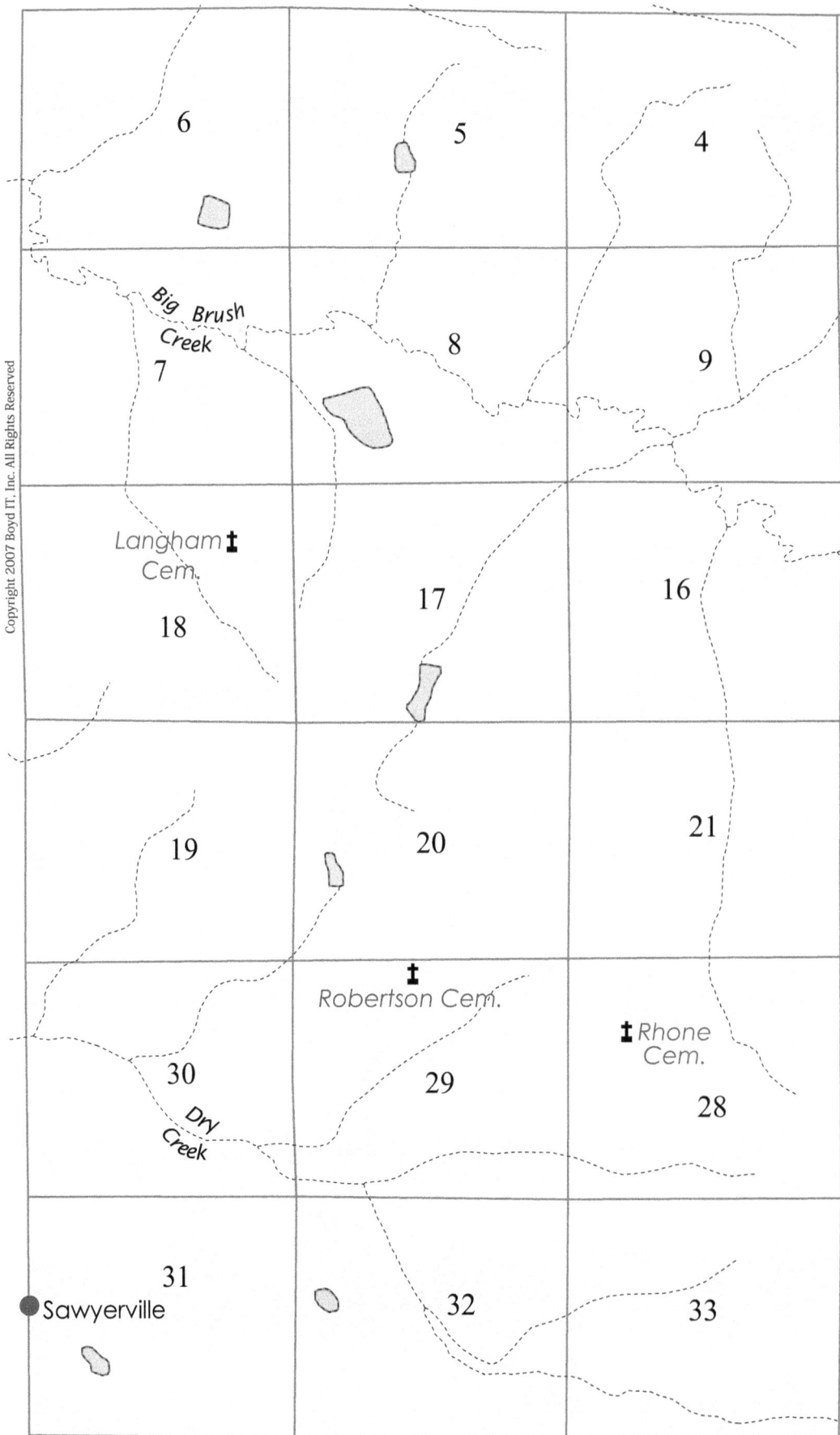

6

5

4

Big Brush
Creek
7

8

9

Langham ✝
Cem.

18

17

16

19

20

21

✝
Robertson Cem.

✝ Rhone
Cem.

30

Dry
Creek

29

28

31

● Sawyerville

32

33

‡ Wilson
Cem.

3

2

1

Fivemile Creek

Helpful Hints

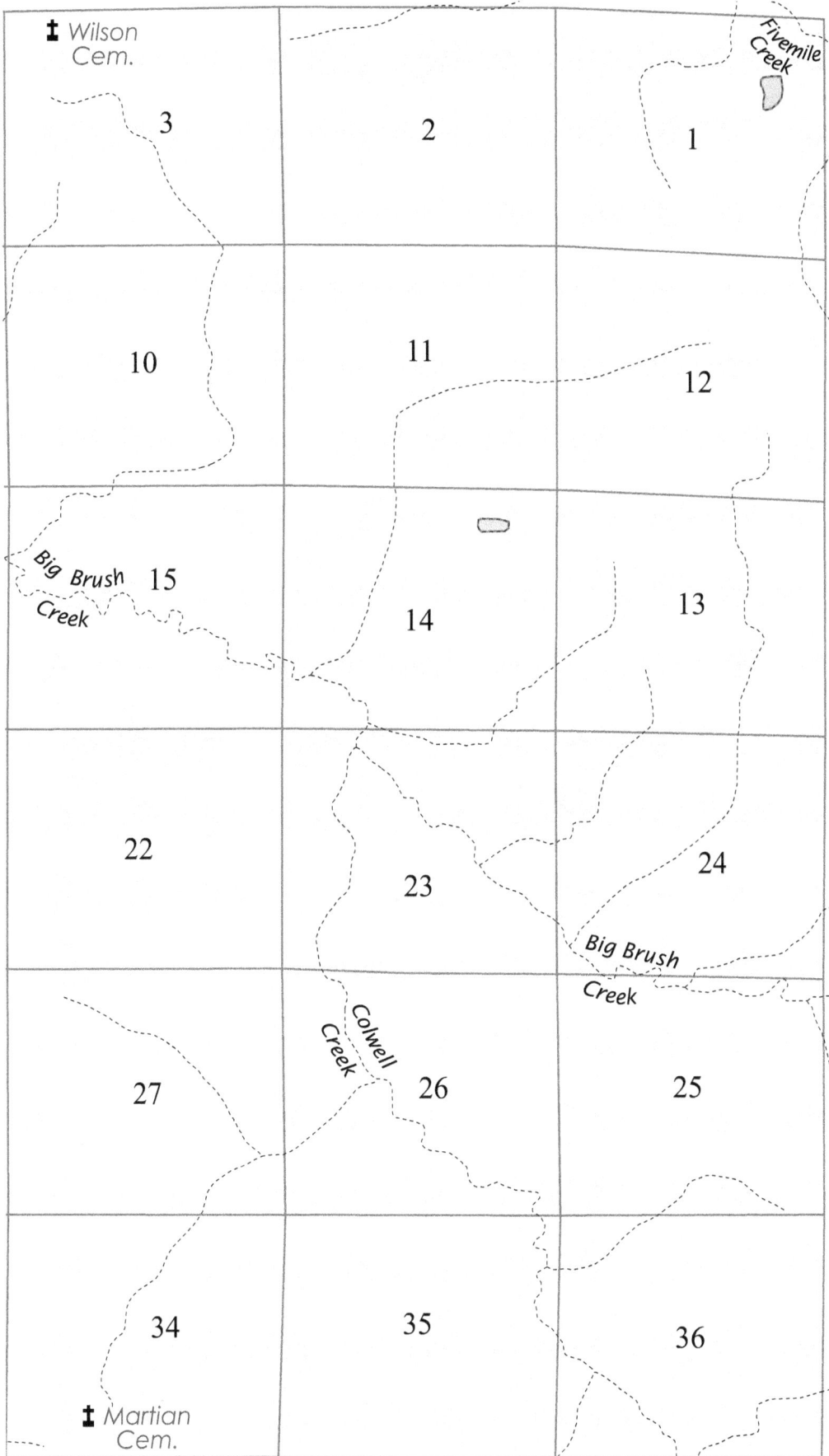

1. This Map takes a different look at the same Congressional Township displayed in the preceding two maps. It presents features that can help you better envision the historical development of the area: a) Water-bodies (lakes & ponds), b) Water-courses (rivers, streams, etc.), c) Railroads, d) City/town center-points (where they were oftentimes located when first settled), and e) Cemeteries.

2. Using this "Historical" map in tandem with this Township's Patent Map and Road Map, may lead you to some interesting discoveries. You will often find roads, towns, cemeteries, and waterways are named after nearby landowners: sometimes those names will be the ones you are researching. See how many of these research gems you can find here in Hale County.

10

11

12

Big Brush Creek

15

14

13

22

23

24

Big Brush Creek

Colwell Creek

27

26

25

34

35

36

‡ Martian Cem.

Legend

— Section Lines

+‑+‑+‑+‑+ Railroads

Large Rivers & Bodies of Water

----------- Streams/Creeks & Small Rivers

● Cities/Towns

‡ Cemeteries

Scale: Section = 1 mile X 1 mile
(there are some exceptions)

Map Group 12: Index to Land Patents

Township 21-North Range 5-East (St Stephens)

After you locate an individual in this Index, take note of the Section and Section Part then proceed to the Land Patent map on the pages immediately following. You should have no difficulty locating the corresponding parcel of land.

The "For More Info" Column will lead you to more information about the underlying Patents. See the *Legend* at right, and the "How to Use this Book" chapter, for more information.

ID	Individual in Patent	Sec.	Sec. Part	Date Issued	Other Counties	For More Info . . .
2783	ADAM, Sally	31	W½SW	1828-04-02		A1
2789	ALLISON, Thomas	6	W½SE	1825-06-06		A1
2791	" "	7	NWNW	1837-03-30		A1
2788	" "	6	NESE	1840-11-10		A1
2790	" "	7	E½NW	1840-11-10		A1
2681	ALSOBROOKE, Jessee	19	NWSW	1837-03-30		A1
2655	ANDERSON, James	11	NWNW	1834-08-20		A1
2657	" "	3	SESE	1834-08-20		A1
2656	" "	11	SWNW	1837-05-15		A1
2683	ANDERSON, John	11	SWSE	1837-05-15		A1
2684	" "	12	SWSE	1837-11-02		A1
2691	BATES, John M	29	NWSW	1837-03-15		A1
2690	" "	17	W½SW	1837-08-01		A1
2692	" "	30	E½SE	1837-11-02		A1
2608	BLOUNT, Archibald	4	W½SW	1825-04-16		A1
2794	BRANTLEY, Thomas	33	E½SW	1837-05-15		A1
2618	BRILEY, Charlton	32	W½NW	1823-10-01		A1
2588	CARR, Abram A	2	SWSE	1837-05-15		A1
2678	CHANDLER, Jeremiah	12	NWNW	1837-05-15		A1
2679	" "	3	E½NW	1837-05-15		A1 G42
2679	CHANDLER, Scott	3	E½NW	1837-05-15		A1 G42
2831	CHAPMAN, Willis	2	NENE	1852-01-01		A1
2832	" "	2	NWNE	1898-11-11		A1
2833	" "	2	SENE	1898-11-11		A1
2602	COOK, Andrew	9	SWNW	1850-03-01		A1
2626	COOK, Elizabeth	9	SW	1837-03-30		A1 G64
2682	COOK, John A	8	SWNE	1837-11-02		A1
2626	COOK, Martin	9	SW	1837-03-30		A1 G64
2703	COUSINS, John R	32	SWSW	1835-09-25		A1
2702	" "	31	SESE	1835-09-28		A1
2785	COUSINS, Samuel W	31	NESE	1837-03-20		A1
2786	" "	32	NWSW	1837-03-20		A1
2628	CRAWFORD, George M	23	NWNW	1835-09-28		A1
2756	DAILEY, Owen	1	NENW	1848-07-01		A1
2757	" "	1	NWNE	1848-07-01		A1
2687	DALE, John	7	SESE	1837-03-30		A1
2686	" "	7	NESE	1837-11-02		A1
2795	DANCE, Thomas	33	W½SE	1837-05-15		A1
2640	DAVIDSON, Holley	33	SWSW	1835-09-28		A1
2587	DAVIS, Abraham	18	W½SE	1821-11-07		A1
2750	DAVIS, Oren	4	SE	1823-10-01		A1
2753	DAVIS, Orren	3	NWSW	1835-10-01		A1
2751	" "	10	NWNW	1837-03-30		A1
2752	" "	3	E½SW	1837-11-02		A1
2810	DAVITT, William	8	N½NW	1837-08-01		A1
2769	DAY, Ransom	13	W½NE	1837-05-15		A1

ID	Individual in Patent	Sec.	Sec. Part	Date Issued	Other Counties	For More Info . . .
2711	DILLARD, John W	31	E½NW	1837-08-01		A1
2620	EDDINS, Daniel	17	E½SE	1837-03-15		A1
2754	EDDINS, Oswell	14	W½SE	1837-03-30		A1
2755	"	23	NWNE	1837-05-15		A1
2611	FAIRCLOTH, Bright	17	NENE	1837-08-01		A1
2742	FIELDS, Michael	8	NESE	1837-05-15		A1
2613	FINLEY, Caswell W	19	NESW	1835-09-12		A1
2660	FOSTER, James H	32	E½NW	1827-07-26		A1
2733	FOSTER, Mary	21	NE	1825-04-20		A1
2735	" "	22	W½NW	1831-12-01		A1
2734	"	22	E½SW	1834-08-20		A1
2779	FREEMAN, Robert	22	W½SW	1829-07-07		A1
2780	" "	27	W½NW	1830-11-16		A1
2808	FREEMAN, Wiley	22	E½NW	1837-11-02		A1
2619	GEWIN, Christopher	7	SENE	1848-09-01		A1 G92
2737	GRANTHAM, Matthew	2	W½NW	1826-07-10		A1
2612	GULLEY, Calvin J	31	E½NE	1837-05-15		A1
2811	HALL, William	33	E½NW	1827-12-10		A1
2796	HARDIN, Thomas	3	W½NW	1823-10-01		A1
2614	HARRISON, Catharine	20	E½NE	1833-06-04		A1
2615	" "	20	W½NE	1833-06-04		A1
2616	" "	21	E½SW	1834-08-20		A1
2771	HARRISON, Richard	4	E½NW	1825-04-16		A1 G141
2641	HARRISS, Hudson	18	W½NW	1832-09-10		A1
2619	HARRY, John J	7	SENE	1848-09-01		A1 G92
2743	HENDERSON, Michael P	18	SENE	1837-03-15		A1
2766	HENDERSON, Pleasant	8	SWSE	1835-09-28		A1 R2590
2767	" "	8	SWSW	1835-09-28		A1
2765	" "	18	NENE	1837-11-02		A1
2607	HUTCHINS, Anthony T	34	SW	1823-10-01		A1
2664	HUTCHINS, James L	27	W½NE	1837-03-30		A1
2665	" "	27	W½SE	1837-03-30		A1
2643	IDOM, Jackson	31	SWSE	1835-09-28		A1
2787	IDOM, Sarah	31	E½SW	1837-03-15		A1
2596	INGREM, Alexander	10	W½SW	1825-04-02		A1
2712	JENKINS, John W	12	N½NE	1839-05-01		A1
2713	" "	12	SESW	1848-07-01		A1
2777	JOHNSON, Richard	32	SWSE	1835-09-12		A1
2776	" "	32	SESW	1835-09-22		A1
2772	" "	29	E½SW	1837-03-15		A1 V2645
2773	" "	31	NWSE	1837-03-30		A1
2774	" "	31	W½NE	1837-03-30		A1
2775	" "	32	NWNE	1837-11-02		A1
2688	KINARD, John	18	E½SE	1837-08-01		A1
2689	" "	7	NESW	1839-05-01		A1
2677	KIRKSEY, Jehu	30	W½SE	1826-07-10		A1
2658	LEE, James B	4	E½SW	1837-03-30		A1
2661	LEE, James J	5	SESE	1837-08-01		A1
2662	" "	8	NENE	1837-08-01		A1
2621	LILES, Daniel	7	SWSE	1837-11-02		A1
2589	LINGALEY, Adam	8	E½SW	1837-08-01		A1
2590	" "	8	SWSE	1837-08-01		A1 R2766
2710	LIVINGSTON, John T	7	NWSE	1858-08-20		A1
2650	MADISON, James A	14	NENW	1837-05-15		A1
2651	" "	15	NESE	1837-05-15		A1
2648	" "	10	W½NE	1858-08-20		A1
2649	" "	10	W½SE	1858-08-20		A1
2758	MADISON, Paton	14	NESW	1835-09-12		A1
2759	" "	14	SWNW	1835-09-12		A1
2760	MADISON, Peyton	14	NWNW	1837-05-15		A1
2761	" "	14	SENE	1837-05-15		A1
2764	" "	15	E½NE	1837-05-15		A1
2763	" "	14	W½SW	1837-08-01		A1
2762	" "	14	SENW	1858-08-20		A1
2744	MCCARTER, Moses	31	SWNW	1837-03-30		A1
2617	MCCOY, Charlotte	8	NWSW	1850-03-01		A1
2812	MCDONALD, William J	11	SENE	1858-08-20		A1
2813	" "	12	NWSW	1858-08-20		A1
2814	" "	12	SWNW	1858-08-20		A1
2599	MCKANE, Alexander	7	NENE	1837-11-02		A1
2600	" "	7	NWNE	1837-11-02		A1
2598	" "	6	SESE	1840-11-10		A1
2603	MCMASTER, Ann	17	W½SE	1834-08-20		A1

ID	Individual in Patent	Sec.	Sec. Part	Date Issued	Other Counties	For More Info . . .
2694	MCMASTER, John	20	SW	1821-11-07		A1
2695	" "	20	W½NW	1821-11-07		A1
2696	" "	28	NW	1821-12-03		A1
2693	" "	20	E½NW	1823-10-01		A1
2667	MCMASTERS, James	18	SW	1823-10-01		A1
2666	" "	18	E½NW	1826-05-01		A1
2778	MEEKS, Riley S	9	NENW	1858-08-20		A1
2770	MITCHELL, Ransom	22	W½NE	1837-05-15		A1
2663	MUNNERLYN, James J	7	SWSW	1848-07-01		A1
2668	NEIGHBOURS, James	1	E½NE	1871-06-13		A1
2669	" "	1	N½SW	1871-06-13		A1
2670	" "	1	S½NW	1871-06-13		A1
2671	" "	1	SWNE	1871-06-13		A1
2782	OLIVER, Robert P	29	W½SE	1837-03-15		A1
2781	" "	29	NESE	1837-03-30		A1
2672	PARKER, James	5	E½SW	1823-10-01		A1
2784	PATTON, Samuel	36	E½SE	1825-04-04		A1
2725	PERRY, Josiah	5	E½NE	1833-09-16		A1
2726	" "	9	E½NE	1837-05-15		A1
2721	" "	10	E½NW	1837-11-02		A1
2722	" "	10	SWNW	1837-11-02		A1
2723	" "	15	NW	1837-11-02		A1
2724	" "	3	SWSW	1837-11-02		A1
2699	PETERSON, John	13	E½NE	1829-05-02		A1
2697	" "	12	E½SE	1837-11-02		A1
2698	" "	12	NWSE	1839-05-01		A1
2736	PETERSON, Mary	1	E½SE	1827-05-15		A1
2818	PETERSON, William	12	S½NE	1837-05-15		A1
2817	" "	1	W½SE	1839-05-01		A1
2819	POOL, William	22	SE	1821-09-27		A1
2738	POWERS, Meredith W	2	E½NW	1858-08-20		A1
2739	" "	2	NESW	1858-08-20		A1
2741	" "	2	SWNE	1858-08-20		A1
2740	" "	2	NWSW	1897-01-15		A1
2728	PRATHER, King	13	W½NW	1837-03-20		A1
2727	" "	13	E½NW	1837-08-01		A1
2592	PRISOC, Adam	17	NESW	1834-08-20		A1
2591	" "	17	E½NW	1837-03-30		A1
2595	" "	17	SWNW	1837-08-01		A1
2593	" "	17	NWNW	1837-11-02		A1
2594	" "	17	SESW	1837-11-02		A1
2700	PRISOC, John	17	SENE	1837-11-02		A1
2701	" "	17	W½NE	1837-11-02		A1
2627	PRISOCK, Epha M	8	SENE	1891-02-16		A2
2633	PRISOCK, Henry W	8	S½NW	1858-08-20		A1
2720	PRISOCK, Joseph	8	NWNE	1897-02-17		A1
2624	PURSELL, Edmund	9	E½SE	1826-05-08		A1
2629	PURTEL, George	2	E½SE	1837-08-01		A1
2644	PURTTE, Jacob	1	SWSW	1837-11-02		A1
2797	PURTTE, Thomas J	2	NWSE	1837-11-02		A1
2706	RAY, John	18	W½NE	1825-04-22		A1
2747	RHODES, Moses	27	SW	1826-05-05		A1
2746	" "	27	SENW	1837-03-30		A1
2745	" "	27	NENW	1837-08-01		A1
2800	RHODES, Thomas	15	SESE	1834-08-05		A1
2801	" "	15	SWSE	1835-09-22		A1
2803	" "	23	E½NW	1837-03-30		A1
2805	" "	23	SWNW	1837-03-30		A1
2804	" "	23	NESW	1837-05-15		A1
2799	" "	15	NWSE	1837-08-01		A1
2802	" "	15	W½NE	1837-08-01		A1
2798	" "	14	SESW	1852-01-01		A1
2707	RYAN, John	26	E½SW	1831-12-01		A1
2708	" "	26	W½SW	1831-12-01		A1
2834	RYAN, Zachariah	27	E½SE	1826-05-15		A1
2601	SEALE, Alexander	3	E½NE	1837-03-30		A1
2605	SEALE, Anthony	11	SENW	1835-09-12		A1
2606	" "	11	SWNE	1835-09-12		A1
2604	" "	11	N½SE	1837-05-15		A1
2609	SEALE, Benton	11	SESE	1837-03-30		A1
2610	" "	3	W½NE	1837-03-30		A1
2637	SEALE, Hezekiah	11	NESW	1858-08-20		A1 V2709
2638	" "	2	SESW	1858-08-20		A1

ID	Individual in Patent	Sec.	Sec. Part	Date Issued	Other Counties	For More Info . . .
2639	SEALE, Hezekiah (Cont'd)	3	NESE	1858-08-20		A1
2673	SEALE, James	10	E½NE	1837-05-15		A1
2674	" "	2	SWSW	1837-05-15		A1
2675	SEALE, Jarvis	10	E½SE	1837-08-01		A1
2676	" "	12	SWSW	1837-08-01		A1
2680	SEALE, Jeremiah	3	NWSE	1896-12-07		A1
2823	SEALE, William R	12	NESW	1837-03-30		A1
2824	" "	12	SENW	1837-03-30		A1
2820	" "	1	SESW	1858-08-20		A1
2821	" "	11	N½NE	1858-08-20		A1
2822	" "	12	NENW	1858-08-20		A1
2653	STEPHENS, James A	9	SENW	1848-09-01		A1
2652	" "	10	SESW	1851-03-01		A1
2623	STEVENS, David	4	W½NW	1826-05-12		A1
2654	STEVENS, James A	10	NESW	1896-12-07		A1
2815	STEVENS, William O	9	NWNW	1897-02-04		A1
2732	STEWART, Larkin	23	E½NE	1835-09-22		A1
2729	" "	13	E½SE	1835-09-25		A1 R2715
2730	" "	13	W½SW	1837-03-30		A1
2731	" "	14	E½SE	1837-03-30		A1
2825	STEWART, William	14	NWNE	1837-05-15		A1
2816	STEWART, William P	14	SWNE	1837-03-30		A1
2792	STONE, Thomas B	32	N½SE	1837-03-15		A1
2793	" "	32	NESW	1837-03-20		A1
2646	SUMMEY, Jacob	5	W½SW	1823-10-01		A1
2647	" "	9	W½SE	1823-10-01		A1
2645	" "	29	SESW	1835-09-28		A1 V2772
2771	SUMMY, Jacob	4	E½NW	1825-04-16		A1 G141
2632	TAYLOE, Henry A	29	SWSW	1837-11-02		A1
2826	THOMAS, William	8	SESE	1837-11-02		A1
2597	WALKER, Alexander M	5	NESE	1837-03-20		A1
2630	WALKER, Goolsby C	29	SESE	1835-09-25		A1
2631	" "	32	SWNE	1835-09-28		A1
2659	WALKER, James D	33	W½NW	1825-04-20		A1
2685	WALKER, John D	33	E½SE	1825-04-20		A1
2709	WALLACE, John S	11	SW	1823-12-01		A1 V2637
2715	WARREN, John	13	E½SE	1823-10-01		A1 R2729
2716	" "	13	W½SE	1827-01-01		A1
2714	" "	1	NWNW	1839-05-01		A1
2634	WATSON, Henry	19	S½SW	1837-11-02		A1
2635	" "	30	SW	1837-11-02		A1
2625	WEBB, Eliza	24	NW	1825-04-04		A1
2636	WEBB, Henry Y	22	E½NE	1823-10-01		A1
2806	WEBB, Thomas	36	E½SW	1826-07-10		A1
2807	" "	36	W½SE	1826-07-10		A1
2749	WEEKS, Newman	9	SWNE	1837-08-01		A1
2748	" "	9	NWNE	1837-11-02		A1
2809	WHITE, William A	14	NENE	1834-08-20		A1
2827	WILLIAMS, William	23	SESW	1835-09-12		A1
2829	" "	23	W½SW	1837-03-30		A1
2828	" "	23	SWNE	1837-08-01		A1
2830	" "	27	E½NE	1837-08-01		A1
2642	WILSON, Jackonias	7	NWSW	1858-08-20		A1
2719	WINGATE, Jonathan	7	SESW	1837-08-01		A1
2622	WITHERSPOON, Daniel M	34	W½SE	1835-09-25		A1
2705	WITHERSPOON, John R	36	W½SW	1828-04-02		A1
2704	" "	36	W½NW	1837-03-30		A1
2718	WOODALL, John	33	NWSW	1835-09-22		A1
2717	" "	32	SESE	1835-09-28		A1
2768	WOODALL, Presley	32	E½NE	1826-05-15		A1

Patent Map

T21-N R5-E
St Stephens Meridian

Map Group 12

Township Statistics

Parcels Mapped	:	248
Number of Patents	:	231
Number of Individuals	:	141
Patentees Identified	:	138
Number of Surnames	:	96
Multi-Patentee Parcels	:	4
Oldest Patent Date	:	9/27/1821
Most Recent Patent	:	11/11/1898
Block/Lot Parcels	:	0
Parcels Re - Issued	:	2
Parcels that Overlap	:	4
Cities and Towns	:	1
Cemeteries	:	9

Section 6
ALLISON Thomas 1825
ALLISON Thomas 1840
MCKANE Alexander 1840

Section 5
SUMMEY Jacob 1823
PARKER James 1823
PERRY Josiah 1833
STEVENS David 1826
WALKER Alexander M 1837
LEE James J 1837

Section 4
HARRISON [141] Richard 1825
BLOUNT Archibald 1825
LEE James B 1837
DAVIS Oren 1823

Section 7
ALLISON Thomas 1837
ALLISON Thomas 1840
MCKANE Alexander 1837
MCKANE Alexander 1837
GEWIN [92] Christopher 1848
WILSON Jackonias 1858
KINARD John 1839
LIVINGSTON John T 1858
DALE John 1837
MUNNERLYN James J 1848
WINGATE Jonathan 1837
LILES Daniel 1837
DALE John 1837

Section 8
DAVITT William 1837
PRISOCK Joseph 1897
LEE James J 1837
PRISOCK Henry W 1858
COOK John A 1837
PRISOCK Epha M 1891
MCCOY Charlotte 1850
LINGALEY Adam 1837
FIELDS Michael 1837
HENDERSON Pleasant 1835
HENDERSON Pleasant 1835
LINGALEY Adam 1837
THOMAS William 1837

Section 9
STEVENS William O 1897
MEEKS Riley S 1858
WEEKS Newman 1837
PERRY Josiah 1837
COOK Andrew 1850
STEPHENS James A 1848
WEEKS Newman 1837
COOK [64] Elizabeth 1837
SUMMEY Jacob 1823
PURSELL Edmund 1826

Section 18
HARRISS Hudson 1832
MCMASTERS James 1826
RAY John 1825
HENDERSON Pleasant 1837
HENDERSON Michael P 1837
MCMASTERS James 1823
DAVIS Abraham 1821
KINARD John 1837

Section 17
PRISOC Adam 1837
PRISOC Adam 1837
PRISOC Adam 1837
PRISOC John 1837
FAIRCLOTH Bright 1837
PRISOC John 1837
BATES John M 1837
PRISOC Adam 1834
PRISOC Adam 1837
MCMASTER Ann 1834
EDDINS Daniel 1837

Section 16

Section 19

ALSOBROOKE Jessee 1837
FINLEY Caswell W 1835
WATSON Henry 1837

Section 20
MCMASTER John 1821
MCMASTER John 1823
HARRISON Catharine 1833
MCMASTER John 1821
HARRISON Catharine 1833

Section 21
FOSTER Mary 1825
HARRISON Catharine 1834

Section 30
WATSON Henry 1837
KIRKSEY Jehu 1826
BATES John M 1837

Section 29
BATES John M 1837
JOHNSON Richard 1837
OLIVER Robert P 1837
TAYLOE Henry A 1837
SUMMEY Jacob 1835
OLIVER Robert P 1837
WALKER Goolsby C 1835

Section 28
MCMASTER John 1821

Section 31
DILLARD John W 1837
JOHNSON Richard 1837
GULLEY Calvin J 1837
MCCARTER Moses 1837
ADAM Sally 1828
IDOM Sarah 1837
JOHNSON Richard 1837
COUSINS Samuel W 1837
IDOM Jackson 1835
COUSINS John R 1835

Section 32
BRILEY Charlton 1823
FOSTER James H 1827
JOHNSON Richard 1837
WALKER Goolsby C 1835
WOODALL Presley 1826
COUSINS Samuel W 1837
STONE Thomas B 1837
STONE Thomas B 1837
COUSINS John R 1835
JOHNSON Richard 1835
JOHNSON Richard 1835
WOODALL John 1835

Section 33
WALKER James D 1825
HALL William 1827
WOODALL John 1835
DAVIDSON Holley 1835
BRANTLEY Thomas 1837
DANCE Thomas 1837
WALKER John D 1825

Section 3
HARDIN Thomas 1823
CHANDLER [42] Jeremiah 1837
SEALE Benton 1837
SEALE Alexander 1837
DAVIS Orren 1835
DAVIS Orren 1837
SEALE Jeremiah 1896
SEALE Hezekiah 1858
PERRY Josiah 1837
ANDERSON James 1834

Section 2
GRANTHAM Matthew 1826
POWERS Meredith W 1858
CHAPMAN Willis 1898
CHAPMAN Willis 1852
POWERS Meredith W 1858
CHAPMAN Willis 1898
POWERS Meredith W 1897
POWERS Meredith W 1858
PURTTE Thomas J 1837
PURTEL George 1837
SEALE James 1837
SEALE Hezekiah 1858
CARR Abram A 1837

Section 1
WARREN John 1839
DAILEY Owen 1848
DAILEY Owen 1848
NEIGHBOURS James 1871
NEIGHBOURS James 1871
NEIGHBOURS James 1871
NEIGHBOURS James 1871
PETERSON William 1839
PETERSON Mary 1827
PURTTE Jacob 1837
SEALE William R 1858

Section 10
DAVIS Orren 1837
MADISON James A 1858
SEALE James 1837
PERRY Josiah 1837
PERRY Josiah 1837
INGREM Alexander 1825
STEVENS James A 1896
STEPHENS James A 1851
MADISON James A 1858
SEALE Jarvis 1837

Section 11
ANDERSON James 1834
SEALE William R 1858
ANDERSON James 1837
SEALE Anthony 1835
SEALE Anthony 1835
MCDONALD William J 1858
SEALE Hezekiah 1858
WALLACE John S 1823
SEALE Anthony 1837
ANDERSON John 1837
SEALE Benton 1837

Section 12
CHANDLER Jeremiah 1837
SEALE William R 1858
JENKINS John W 1839
MCDONALD William J 1858
SEALE William R 1837
PETERSON William 1837
MCDONALD William J 1858
SEALE William R 1837
PETERSON John 1839
PETERSON John 1837
SEALE Jarvis 1837
JENKINS John W 1848
ANDERSON John 1837

Section 15
PERRY Josiah 1837
RHODES Thomas 1837
MADISON Peyton 1837
15
RHODES Thomas 1837
MADISON James A 1837
RHODES Thomas 1835
RHODES Thomas 1834

Section 14
MADISON Peyton 1837
MADISON James A 1837
STEWART William 1837
WHITE William A 1834
MADISON Paton 1835
MADISON Peyton 1858
STEWART William P 1837
MADISON Peyton 1837
MADISON Paton 1835
14
STEWART Larkin 1837
RHODES Thomas 1852
EDDINS Oswell 1837

Section 13
PRATHER King 1837
PRATHER King 1837
DAY Ransom 1837
PETERSON John 1829
13
STEWART Larkin 1837
WARREN John 1827
STEWART Larkin 1835
WARREN John 1823
PETERSON John 1837

Section 22
FOSTER Mary 1831
FREEMAN Wiley 1837
MITCHELL Ransom 1837
WEBB Henry Y 1823
22
FREEMAN Robert 1829
FOSTER Mary 1834
POOL William 1821

Section 23
CRAWFORD George M 1835
RHODES Thomas 1837
EDDINS Oswell 1837
STEWART Larkin 1835
RHODES Thomas 1837
WILLIAMS William 1837
23
RHODES Thomas 1837
WILLIAMS William 1837
WILLIAMS William 1835

Section 24
WEBB Eliza 1825
24

Section 27
RHODES Moses 1837
HUTCHINS James L 1837
FREEMAN Robert 1830
RHODES Moses 1837
WILLIAMS William 1837
27
RYAN Zachariah 1826
RHODES Moses 1826
HUTCHINS James L 1837

Section 26
26
RYAN John 1831
RYAN John 1831

Section 25
25

Section 34
34
WITHERSPOON Daniel M 1835
HUTCHINS Anthony T 1823

Section 35
35

Section 36
WITHERSPOON John R 1837
36
WITHERSPOON John R 1828
WEBB Thomas 1826
WEBB Thomas 1826
PATTON Samuel 1825

Helpful Hints

1. This Map's INDEX can be found on the preceding pages.

2. Refer to Map "C" to see where this Township lies within Hale County, Alabama.

3. Numbers within square brackets [ ] denote a multi-patentee land parcel (multi-owner). Refer to Appendix "C" for a full list of members in this group.

4. Areas that look to be crowded with Patentees usually indicate multiple sales of the same parcel (Re-issues) or Overlapping parcels. See this Township's Index for an explanation of these and other circumstances that might explain "odd" groupings of Patentees on this map.

Legend

——————— Patent Boundary

━━━━━━━ Section Boundary

No Patents Found (or Outside County)

1., 2., 3., ... Lot Numbers (when beside a name)

[ ] Group Number (see Appendix "C")

Scale: Section = 1 mile X 1 mile (generally, with some exceptions)

Road Map

T21-N R5-E
St Stephens Meridian

Map Group 12

Cities & Towns

Dominick

Cemeteries

Antioch Cemetery
Burrough Cemetery
Burroughs Cemetery
Morning Star Cemetery
New Haven Cemetery
Ramey Chapel Cemetery
Rhodes Chapel Cemetery
Saint Johns Cemetery
Shelton Cemetery

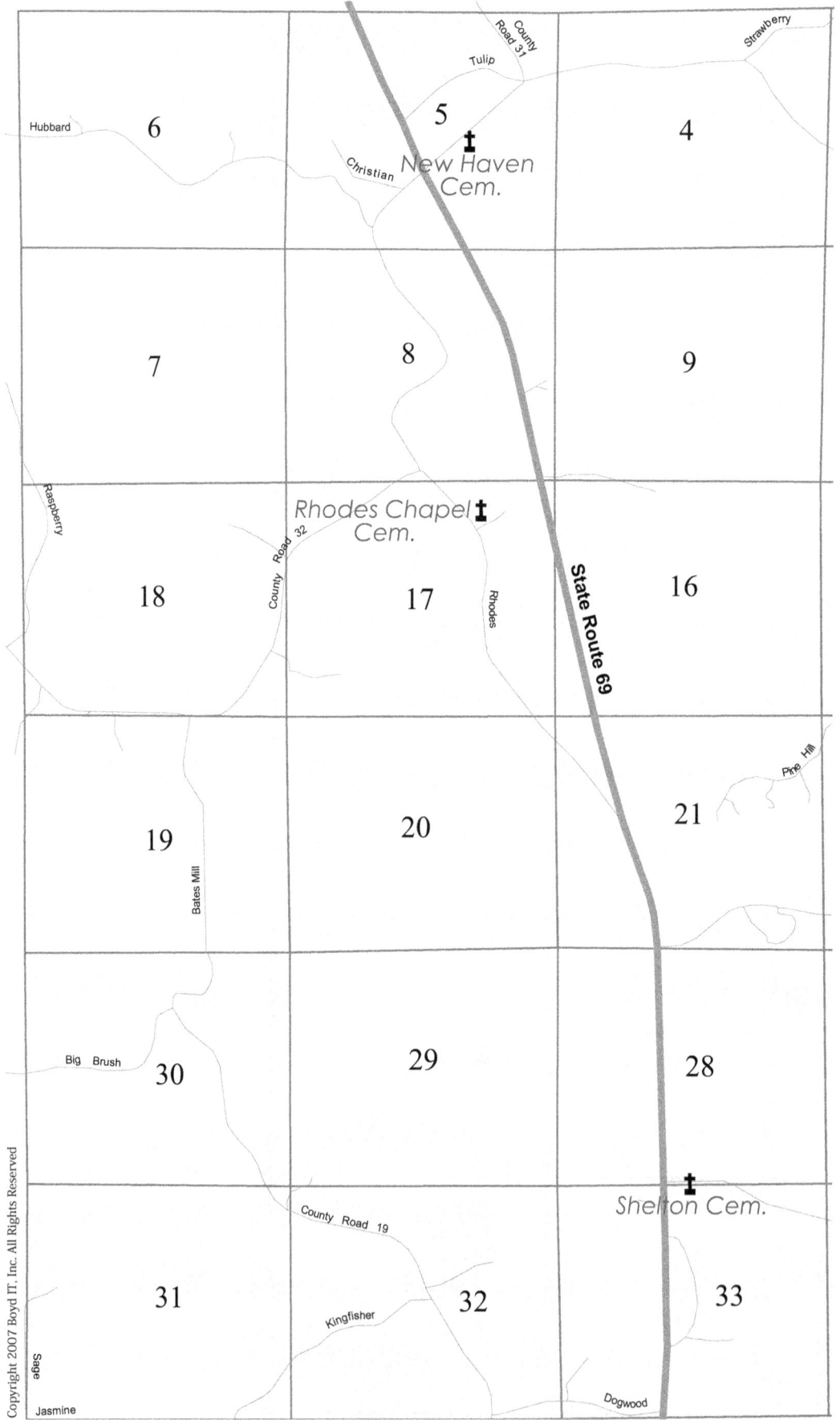

6

Hubbard

5

Tulip

County Road 31

Christian

New Haven Cem.

4

Strawberry

7

8

9

State Route 69

18

Raspberry

County Road 32

Rhodes Chapel Cem.

17

Rhodes

16

19

Bates Mill

20

21

Pine Hill

30

Big Brush

29

28

31

County Road 19

Kingfisher

32

Shelton Cem.

33

Sage

Jasmine

Dogwood

Morning Star
Cem.

3

2

1

Burrough Cem.

Ramey Chapel
Cem.

County Road 32

10

11

Burrough

12

Stalk

Burroughs Cem.

Redwood

15

14

Dominick

13

Antioch Cem.

Red   Wood

22

23

County Road 3

24

Saint Johns
Cem.

Baldwin

County Road   4

State Route 25

Lilac

27

26

Crawford

25

Copyright 2007 Boyd IT, Inc. All Rights Reserved

34

35

County Road 51

36

Shelton

County
Road 7

Helpful Hints

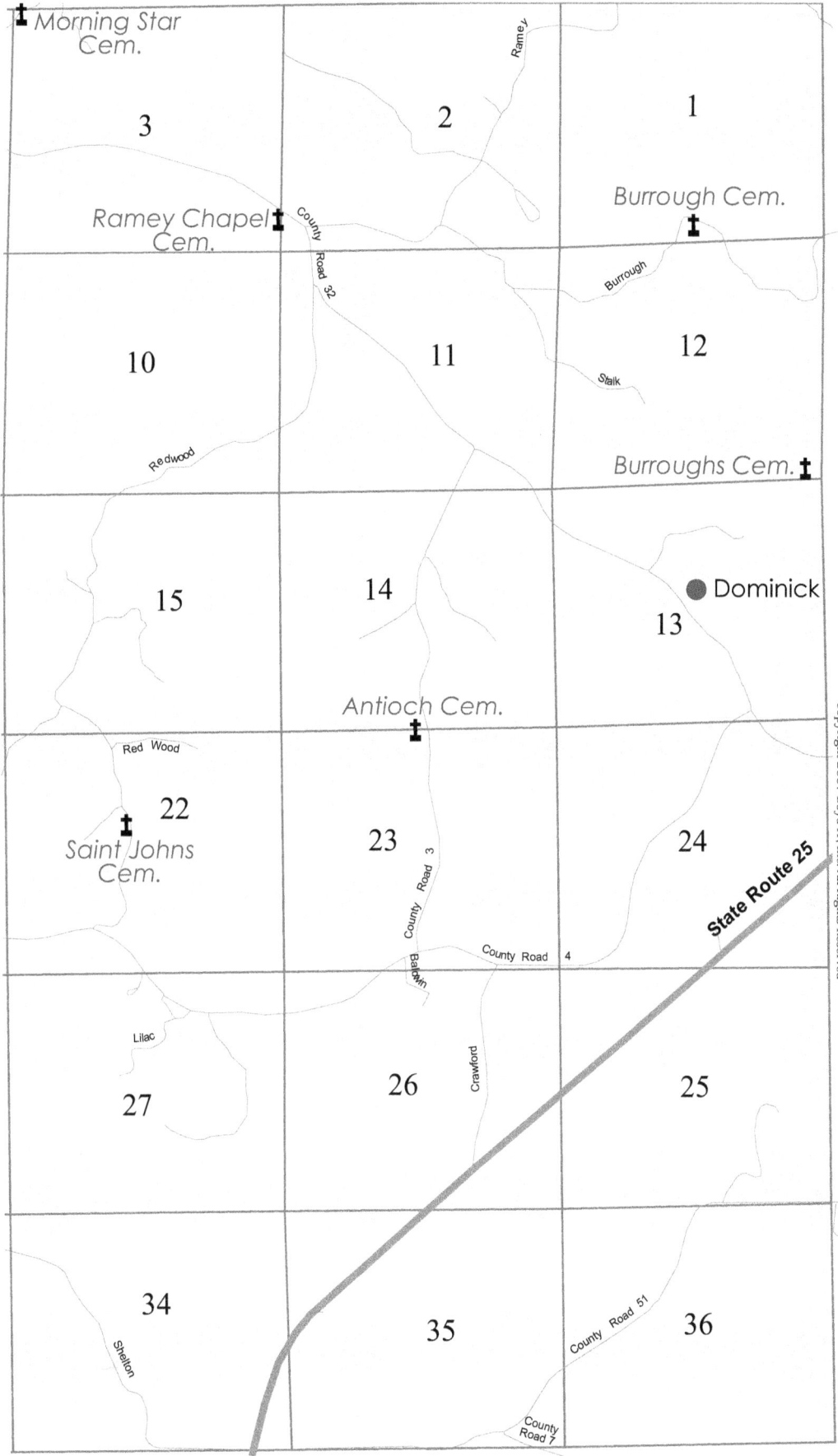

1. This road map has a number of uses, but primarily it is to help you: a) find the present location of land owned by your ancestors (at least the general area), b) find cemeteries and city-centers, and c) estimate the route/roads used by Census-takers & tax-assessors.

2. If you plan to travel to Hale County to locate cemeteries or land parcels, please pick up a modern travel map for the area before you do. Mapping old land parcels on modern maps is not as exact a science as you might think. Just the slightest variations in public land survey coordinates, estimates of parcel boundaries, or road-map deviations can greatly alter a map's representation of how a road either does or doesn't cross a particular parcel of land.

L e g e n d

———— Section Lines

═══ Interstates

——— Highways

——— Other Roads

● Cities/Towns

✝ Cemeteries

Scale: Section = 1 mile X 1 mile
(generally, with some exceptions)

Historical Map

T21-N R5-E
St Stephens Meridian

Map Group 12

Cities & Towns
Dominick

Cemeteries
Antioch Cemetery
Burrough Cemetery
Burroughs Cemetery
Morning Star Cemetery
New Haven Cemetery
Ramey Chapel Cemetery
Rhodes Chapel Cemetery
Saint Johns Cemetery
Shelton Cemetery

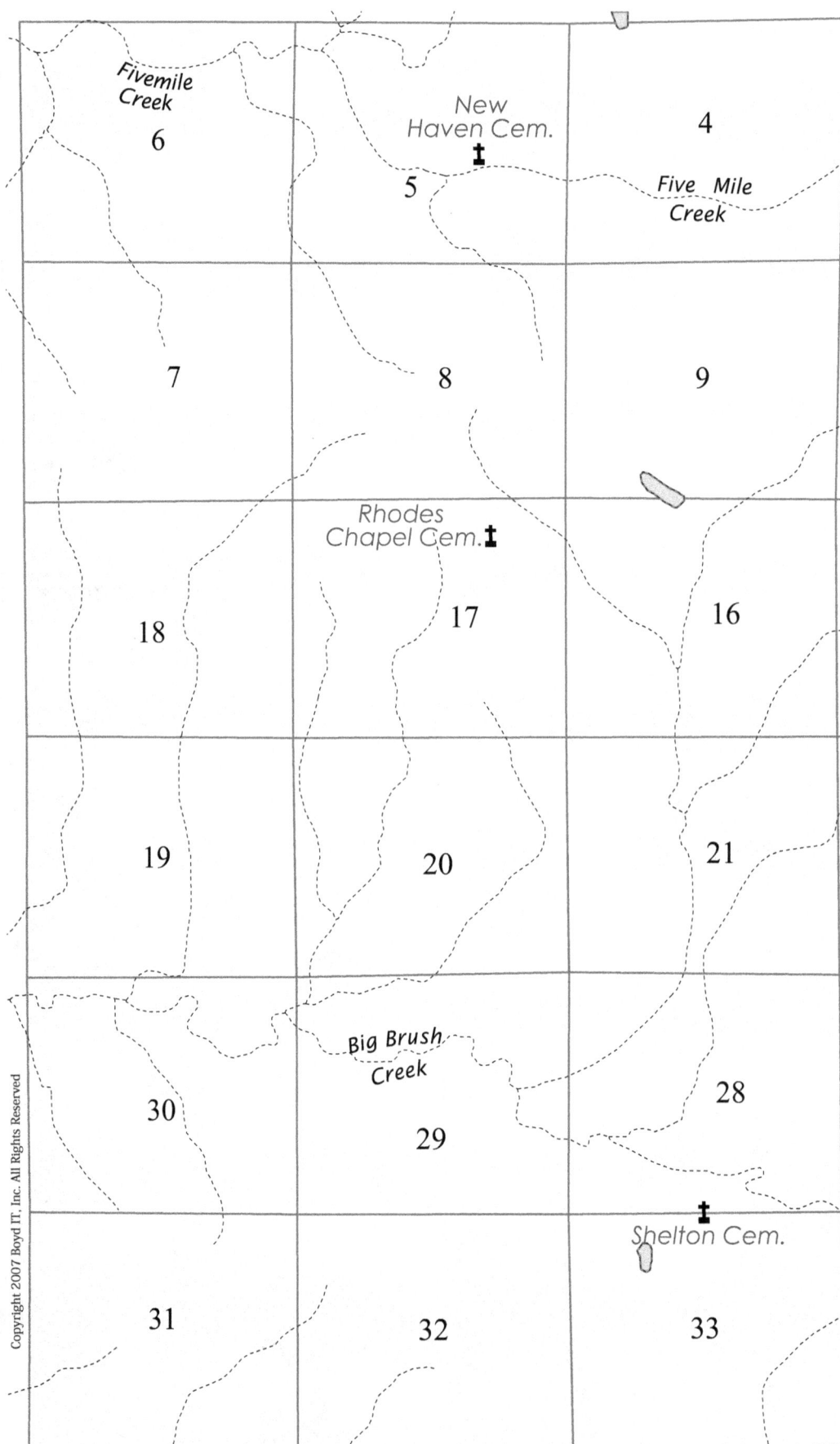

Fivemile Creek

6

New Haven Cem.

5

4

Five Mile Creek

7

8

9

Rhodes Chapel Cem.

18

17

16

19

20

21

Big Brush Creek

30

29

28

Shelton Cem.

31

32

33

Morning Star
Cem.

3

2

1

Ramey
Chapel Cem.

Burrough Cem.

10

11

12

Burroughs
Cem.

15

14

Dominick 13

Saint
Johns Cem.

Antioch Cem.

23

24

22

27

26

25

Sparks
Creek

34

Big Brush
Creek

36

Polecat
Creek

35

Helpful Hints

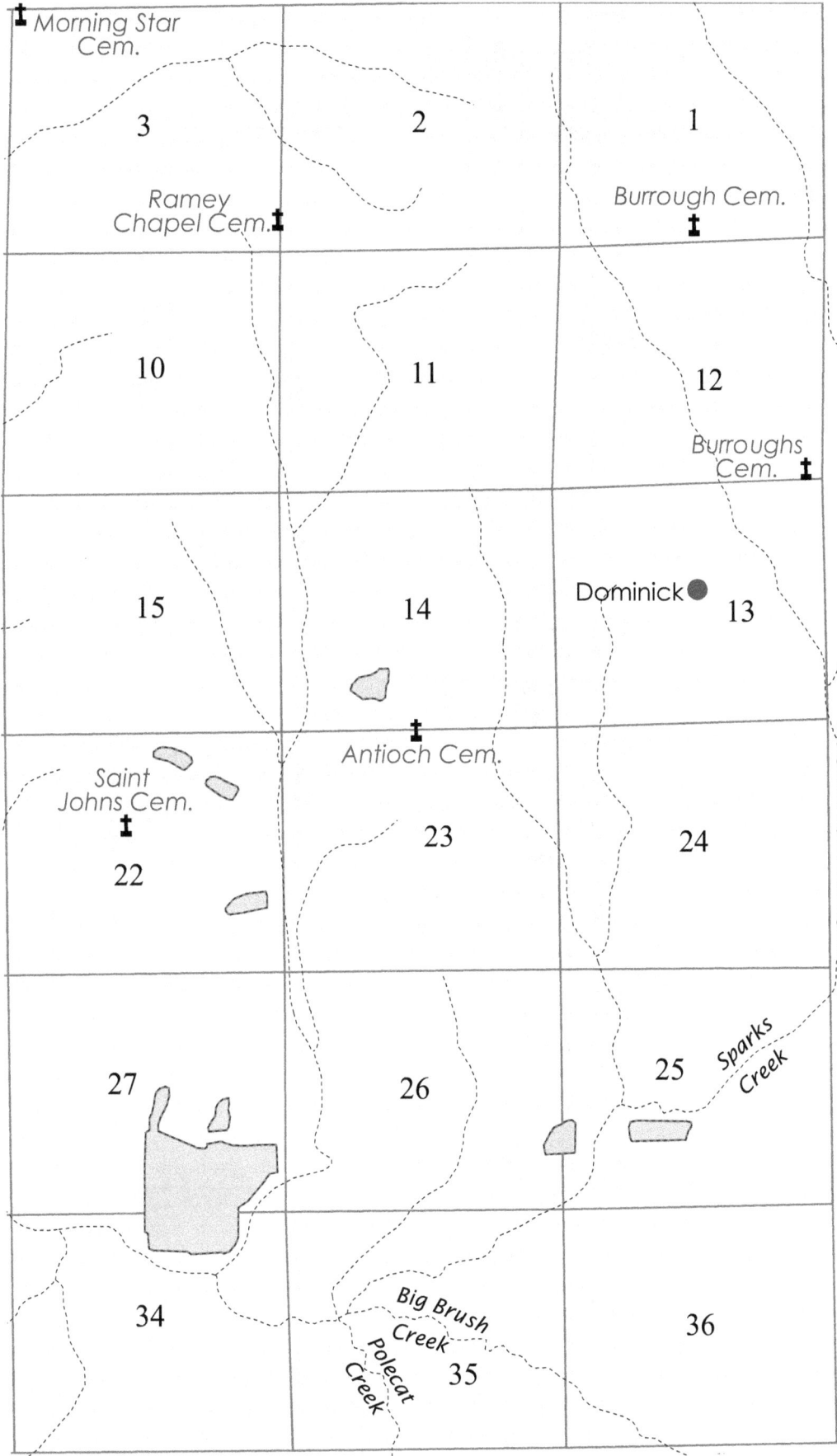

1. This Map takes a different look at the same Congressional Township displayed in the preceding two maps. It presents features that can help you better envision the historical development of the area: a) Water-bodies (lakes & ponds), b) Water-courses (rivers, streams, etc.), c) Railroads, d) City/town center-points (where they were oftentimes located when first settled), and e) Cemeteries.

2. Using this "Historical" map in tandem with this Township's Patent Map and Road Map, may lead you to some interesting discoveries. You will often find roads, towns, cemeteries, and waterways are named after nearby landowners: sometimes those names will be the ones you are researching. See how many of these research gems you can find here in Hale County.

Legend

Section Lines

Railroads

Large Rivers & Bodies of Water

Streams/Creeks & Small Rivers

Cities/Towns

Cemeteries

Scale: Section = 1 mile X 1 mile
(there are some exceptions)

Map Group 13: Index to Land Patents

Township 21-North Range 6-East (St Stephens)

After you locate an individual in this Index, take note of the Section and Section Part then proceed to the Land Patent map on the pages immediately following. You should have no difficulty locating the corresponding parcel of land.

The "For More Info" Column will lead you to more information about the underlying Patents. See the *Legend* at right, and the "How to Use this Book" chapter, for more information.

```
                    LEGEND
         "For More Info . . . " column
A = Authority (Legislative Act, See Appendix "A")
B = Block or Lot (location in Section unknown)
C = Cancelled Patent
F = Fractional Section
G = Group  (Multi-Patentee Patent, see Appendix "C")
V = Overlaps another Parcel
R = Re-Issued (Parcel patented more than once)

(A & G items require you to look in the Appendixes referred
to above. All other Letter-designations followed by a number
require you to locate line-items in this index that possess
the ID number found after the letter).
```

ID	Individual in Patent	Sec.	Sec. Part	Date Issued	Other Counties	For More Info . . .
2942	ABBOTT, Willis	20	NE	1831-12-01		A1 G1
2923	ASH, Thomas	33	E½NE	1822-01-01		A1
2839	AVERY, Bryant	33	W½NW	1831-12-01		A1
2942	BOUNDS, Henry	20	NE	1831-12-01		A1 G1
2912	BRADFORD, Randall	5	NESW	1835-04-02		A1
2913	BRADFORD, Randol	5	SENW	1837-08-12		A1
2914	BRADFORD, Randolph	5	W½NE	1837-05-15		A1
2943	CHANDLER, Wilson N	28	NESE	1837-08-02		A1
2934	CLEMENT, William	9	NE	1837-08-09		A1
2935	" "	9	NWSW	1837-08-09		A1
2936	" "	9	SENW	1837-08-09		A1
2843	COLEMAN, Charles	9	W½SE	1837-08-15		A1
2871	CRAWFORD, James	18	E½NW	1821-12-03		A1
2872	" "	18	E½SW	1821-12-03		A1
2920	DUKE, Robert	9	E½SE	1823-10-01		A1
2925	DUKE, Thomas I	6	SESW	1838-07-28		A1
2899	ELLIOTT, Martin	5	NENW	1854-07-15		A1
2847	FORD, Dorrel	18	SWNW	1835-04-15		A1
2924	GOODWIN, Thomas	28	NWSE	1837-08-02		A1
2901	GRANTHAM, Mathew	5	W½NW	1837-08-14		A1
2902	" "	7	W½NE	1837-08-14		A1
2903	" "	8	W½NW	1837-08-14		A1
2904	GRANTHAM, Matthew	5	NWSW	1834-09-04		A1
2909	" "	7	SENW	1834-09-04		A1
2905	" "	5	SWSW	1837-05-15		A1
2906	" "	6	E½NE	1837-05-15		A1
2907	" "	6	W½SE	1837-05-15		A1
2908	" "	7	NENW	1837-05-15		A1
2910	GRONTHAM, Matthew	6	E½SE	1826-05-05		A1
2849	HOWARD, Edmund	17	SESE	1837-05-15		A1
2850	" "	21	W½NW	1837-05-15		A1
2848	" "	17	NESE	1837-08-14		A1
2889	JENKINS, John W	6	NENW	1837-05-15		A1
2890	" "	6	W½NE	1837-05-15		A1
2886	" "	17	NENW	1837-08-12		A1
2888	" "	17	W½SE	1837-08-12		A1
2885	" "	17	NENE	1837-08-14		A1
2887	" "	17	W½NE	1837-08-14		A1
2891	" "	7	W½NW	1838-07-28		A1
2855	JOHNSON, Frederic	4	NWSE	1847-05-01		A1
2856	" "	4	SESE	1847-05-01		A1
2857	JOHNSON, Frederick	4	SESW	1841-05-20		A1
2858	" "	4	SWSE	1841-05-20		A1
2876	JOHNSON, James W	8	NENE	1837-05-20		A1
2877	" "	9	NWNW	1837-05-20		A1
2851	JONES, Elijah	20	SENW	1837-05-15		A1

ID	Individual in Patent	Sec.	Sec. Part	Date Issued	Other Counties	For More Info . . .
2867	JONES, Humphrey	9	SWSW	1845-07-01		A1
2866	" "	9	NESW	1850-05-01		A1
2926	MCCONNELL, Thomas	6	W½NW	1837-04-10		A1
2873	MEEK, James	17	W½NW	1827-05-30		A1
2880	MEIGS, John	5	SESW	1837-08-09		A1
2921	MURFF, Samuel	31	W½SW	1831-12-01		A1
2838	NEWNUM, Berry	9	SESW	1850-04-01		A1
2922	PATTON, Samuel	18	NWNW	1837-08-09		A1
2881	PETERSON, John	7	W½SW	1829-05-02		A1
2900	PETERSON, Mary	6	W½SW	1827-05-30		A1
2844	PHILLIPS, Charles J	4	NESW	1854-10-02		A1
2882	POOL, John	29	NE	1821-09-27		A1
2868	RHODES, Ingraham	6	NESW	1860-04-02		A1
2869	" "	6	SENW	1860-04-02		A1
2837	RUSSELL, Andrew	4	W½SW	1823-10-01		A1
2842	RUSSELL, Caleb	33	W½NE	1821-12-03		A1
2915	SHACKELFORD, Richard D	20	E½SE	1835-04-02		A1
2874	SHACKLEFORD, James	21	SE	1823-10-01		A1
2875	" "	28	E½SW	1823-10-01		A1
2892	SHACKLEFORD, John W	21	W½SW	1828-04-10		A1
2919	SHACKLEFORD, Richard D	29	E½NW	1821-09-27		A1
2918	" "	28	W½SW	1821-12-03		A1
2916	" "	20	E½SW	1823-12-01		A1
2917	" "	20	W½SE	1823-12-01		A1
2879	SHAFFER, John F	33	E½NW	1832-08-08		A1
2840	SIMS, Burrel G	9	NENW	1837-05-20		A1
2841	" "	9	SWNW	1837-05-20		A1
2937	SIMS, William W	8	SENE	1837-05-15		A1
2852	SLAUGHTER, Ezekiel	5	W½SE	1821-12-03		A1
2854	" "	8	W½NE	1821-12-03		A1
2853	" "	8	E½NW	1823-10-01		A1
2896	SMITH, Mark	4	NE	1823-10-01		A1
2897	" "	5	E½SE	1835-04-08		A1
2895	" "	4	E½NW	1837-08-14		A1
2911	SMITH, Matthew	4	NESE	1845-07-01		A1
2928	SMITH, Thomas	5	NENE	1835-10-01		A1
2929	" "	5	SENE	1837-05-15		A1
2927	" "	4	W½NW	1850-08-10		A1
2845	SPARKS, Christane	20	NENW	1835-10-01		A1
2846	SPARKS, Christenea	17	SENW	1837-05-20		A1
2893	SPARKS, Joseph K	17	SW	1821-10-01		A1
2894	" "	20	W½NW	1821-10-01		A1
2878	STOKES, Jeremiah	28	S½SE	1837-08-08		A1
2870	SUMMEY, Jacob	8	SE	1823-10-01		A1
2884	THOMAS, John	21	SENE	1835-10-01		A1
2883	" "	21	NWNE	1837-05-20		A1
2898	TIDMORE, Mark	21	SESW	1837-05-15		A1
2862	WEBB, Henry Y	7	E½NE	1823-10-01		A1
2863	" "	7	E½SW	1823-10-01		A1
2864	" "	7	SE	1823-10-01		A1
2865	" "	8	SW	1823-10-01		A1
2930	WEBB, Thomas	29	W½NW	1821-12-03		A1
2931	" "	30	E½NE	1821-12-03		A1
2932	" "	31	NESW	1835-10-08		A1
2933	" "	31	SESW	1837-08-02		A1
2859	WILLIAMS, George B	19	E½SE	1823-10-01		A1
2860	" "	20	W½SW	1823-10-01		A1
2861	WILLIAMS, George P	19	SW	1821-09-27		A1
2938	WILSON, William	21	E½NW	1837-08-12		A1
2939	" "	21	NENE	1837-08-12		A1
2940	" "	21	NESW	1837-08-12		A1
2941	" "	21	SWNE	1837-08-12		A1
2835	WINN, Abner	18	W½SW	1823-10-01		A1
2836	" "	19	W½SE	1823-10-01		A1

Patent Map

T21-N R6-E
St Stephens Meridian

Map Group 13

Township Statistics

Parcels Mapped	:	109
Number of Patents	:	101
Number of Individuals	:	63
Patentees Identified	:	62
Number of Surnames	:	45
Multi-Patentee Parcels	:	1
Oldest Patent Date	:	9/27/1821
Most Recent Patent	:	4/2/1860
Block/Lot Parcels	:	0
Parcels Re - Issued	:	0
Parcels that Overlap	:	0
Cities and Towns	:	0
Cemeteries	:	1

Note: the area contained in this map amounts to far less than a full Township. Therefore, its contents are completely on this single page (instead of a "normal" 2-page spread).

Legend

— Patent Boundary

— Section Boundary

No Patents Found (or Outside County)

1., 2., 3., ... Lot Numbers (when beside a name)

[ ] Group Number (see Appendix "C")

Scale: Section = 1 mile X 1 mile (generally, with some exceptions)

Map Grid

Section 6:
- MCCONNELL Thomas 1837
- JENKINS John W 1837
- JENKINS John W 1837
- RHODES Ingraham 1860
- GRANTHAM Matthew 1837
- PETERSON Mary 1827
- RHODES Ingraham 1860
- DUKE Thomas I 1838
- GRANTHAM Matthew 1837
- GRONTHAM Matthew 1826

Section 5:
- GRANTHAM Mathew 1837
- ELLIOTT Martin 1854
- BRADFORD Randol 1837
- BRADFORD Randolph 1837
- SMITH Thomas 1835
- SMITH Thomas 1837
- GRANTHAM Matthew 1834
- BRADFORD Randall 1835
- GRANTHAM Matthew 1837
- MEIGS John 1837
- SLAUGHTER Ezekiel 1821
- SMITH Mark 1835

Section 4:
- SMITH Thomas 1850
- SMITH Mark 1837
- SMITH Mark 1823
- RUSSELL Andrew 1823
- PHILLIPS Charles J 1854
- JOHNSON Frederic 1847
- SMITH Matthew 1845
- JOHNSON Frederick 1841
- JOHNSON Frederick 1841
- JOHNSON Frederic 1847

Section 7:
- JENKINS John W 1838
- GRANTHAM Matthew 1837
- GRANTHAM Matthew 1834
- GRANTHAM Matthew 1837
- WEBB Henry Y 1823
- PETERSON John 1829
- WEBB Henry Y 1823
- WEBB Henry Y 1823

Section 8:
- SLAUGHTER Ezekiel 1823
- GRANTHAM Mathew 1837
- SLAUGHTER Ezekiel 1821
- SIMS William W 1837
- WEBB Henry Y 1823
- SUMMEY Jacob 1823

Section 9:
- JOHNSON James W 1837
- JOHNSON James W 1837
- SIMS Burrel G 1837
- SIMS Burrel G 1837
- CLEMENT William 1837
- CLEMENT William 1837
- CLEMENT William 1837
- JONES Humphrey 1850
- COLEMAN Charles 1837
- JONES Humphrey 1845
- NEWNUM Berry 1850
- DUKE Robert 1823

Section 18:
- PATTON Samuel 1837
- FORD Dorrel 1835
- CRAWFORD James 1821
- WINN Abner 1823
- CRAWFORD James 1821

Section 17:
- MEEK James 1827
- JENKINS John W 1837
- SPARKS Christenea 1837
- JENKINS John W 1837
- JENKINS John W 1837
- SPARKS Joseph K 1821
- JENKINS John W 1837

Section 16:
- (No Patents Found)

Section 19:
- (No Patents Found)

Section 20:
- SPARKS Joseph K 1821
- SPARKS Christane 1835
- JONES Elijah 1837
- ABBOTT [1] Willis 1831
- WILLIAMS George B 1823
- SHACKLEFORD Richard D 1823
- SHACKLEFORD Richard D 1823
- SHACKLEFORD Richard D 1835

Section 21:
- HOWARD Edmund 1837
- WILSON William 1837
- THOMAS John 1837
- WILSON William 1837
- WILSON William 1837
- THOMAS John 1835
- SHACKLEFORD John W 1828
- WILSON William 1837
- TIDMORE Mark 1837
- SHACKLEFORD James 1823

Section 16 area (HOWARD Edmund 1837)

Section 30:
- WILLIAMS George P 1821
- WINN Abner 1823
- WILLIAMS George B 1823
- WEBB Thomas 1821

Section 29:
- WEBB Thomas 1821
- SHACKLEFORD Richard D 1821
- POOL John 1821

Section 28:
- SHACKLEFORD Richard D 1821
- GOODWIN Thomas 1837
- CHANDLER Wilson N 1837
- SHACKLEFORD James 1823
- STOKES Jeremiah 1837

Section 31:
- MURFF Samuel 1831
- WEBB Thomas 1835
- WEBB Thomas 1837

Section 32:
- (No Patents Found)

Section 33:
- AVERY Bryant 1831
- SHAFFER John F 1832
- RUSSELL Caleb 1821
- ASH Thomas 1822

Marmalade

6

Starling

5

County Road 51

4

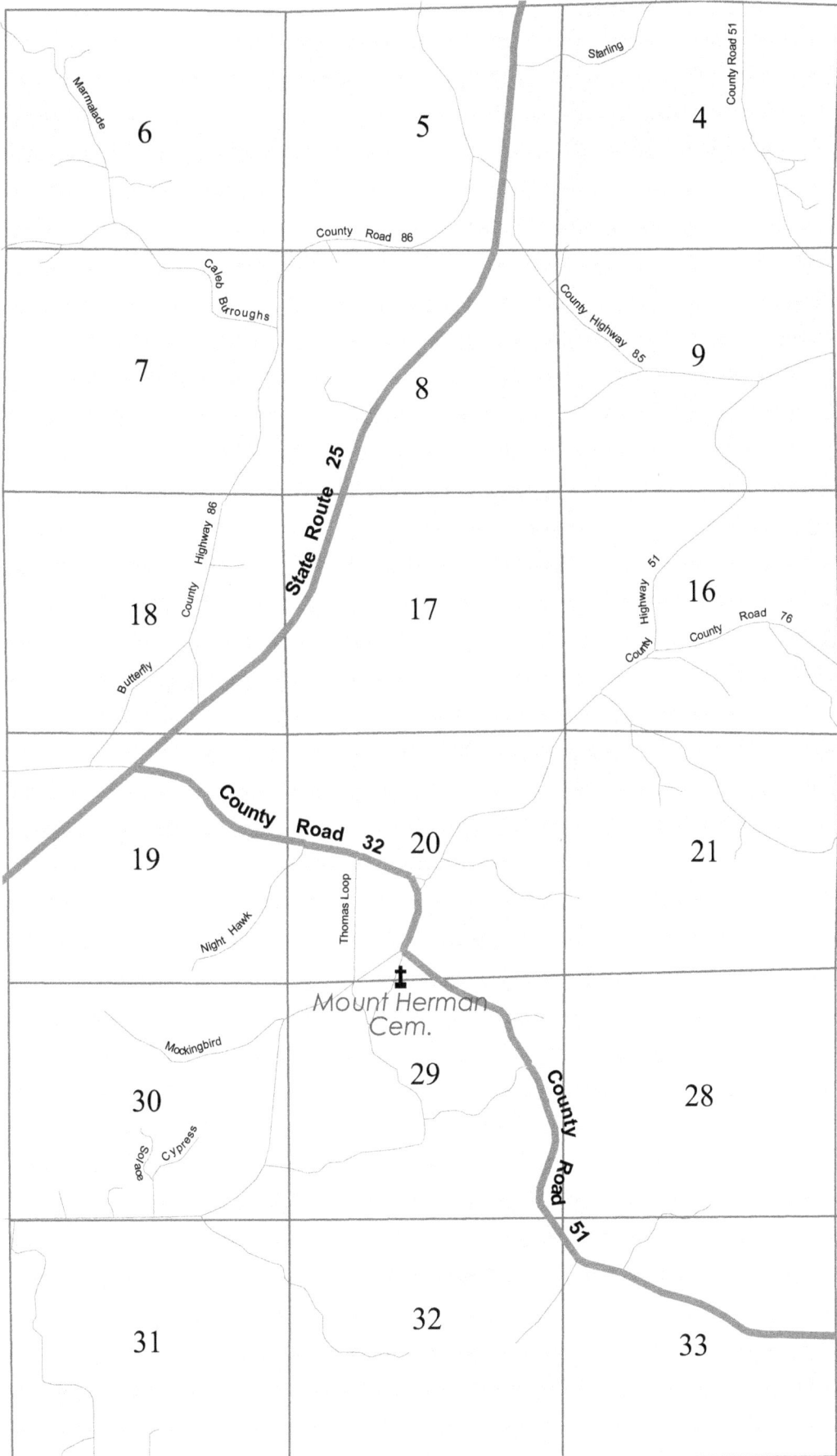

County Road 86

Caleb Burroughs

Note: the area contained in this map amounts to far less than a full Township. Therefore, its contents are completely on this single page (instead of a "normal" 2-page spread).

7

8

County Highway 85

9

State Route 25

County Highway 86

Cities & Towns
None

18

17

County Highway 51

16

County Road 76

Butterfly

Cemeteries
Mount Herman Cemetery

County Road 32

20

19

21

Night Hawk

Thomas Loop

Mount Herman Cem.

Mockingbird

29

28

County Road 51

30

Solace

Cypress

Legend

——— Section Lines

===== Interstates

—— Highways

—— Other Roads

● Cities/Towns

✝ Cemeteries

31

32

33

Scale: Section = 1 mile X 1 mile
(generally, with some exceptions)

Historical Map

T21-N R6-E
St Stephens Meridian

Map Group 13

Note: the area contained in this map amounts to far less than a full Township. Therefore, its contents are completely on this single page (instead of a "normal" 2-page spread).

Cities & Towns
None

Cemeteries
Mount Herman Cemetery

Legend

———— Section Lines

+++++++ Railroads

Large Rivers & Bodies of Water

---------- Streams/Creeks & Small Rivers

● Cities/Towns

✝ Cemeteries

Scale: Section = 1 mile X 1 mile
(there are some exceptions)

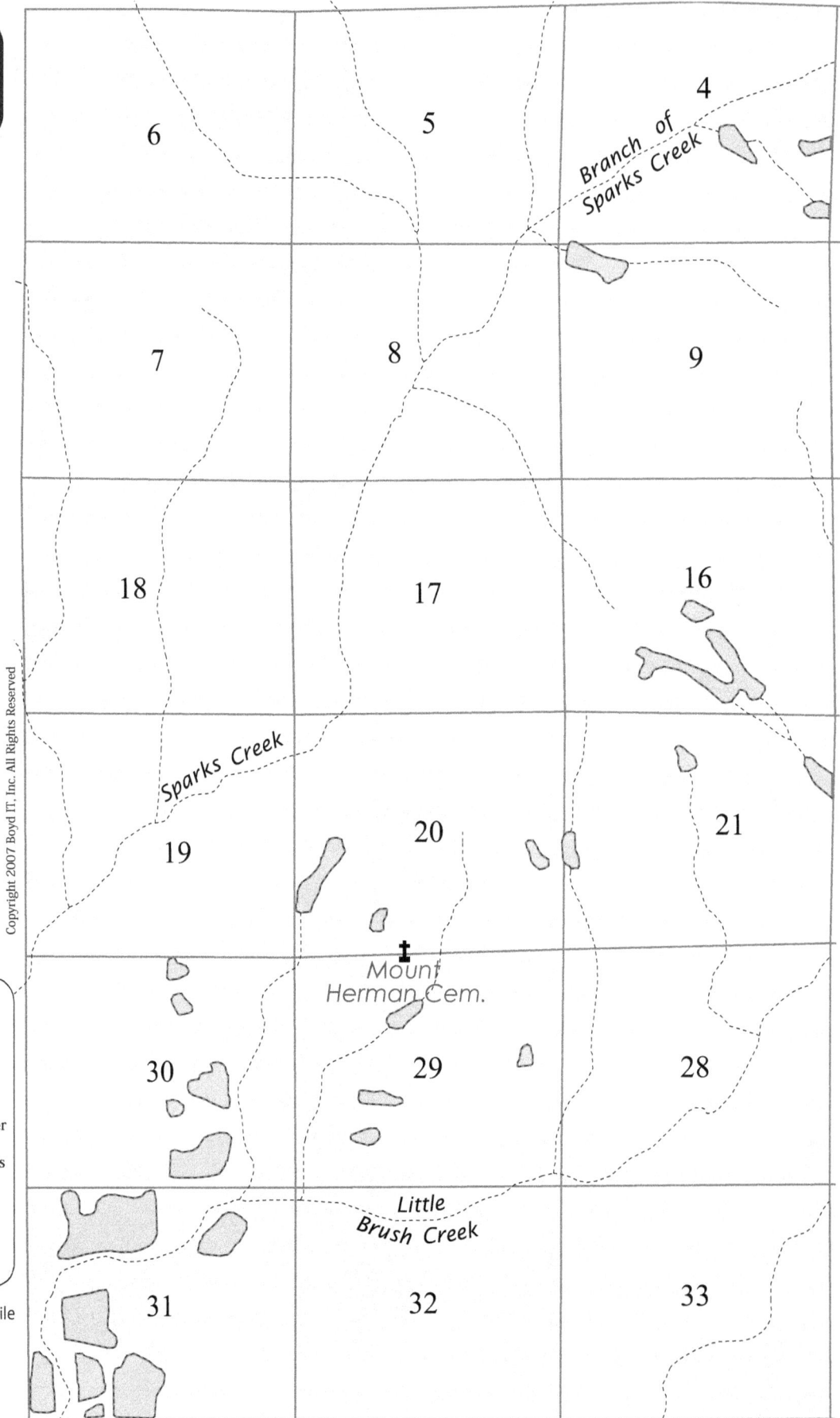

6

5

4

Branch of Sparks Creek

7

8

9

18

17

16

Sparks Creek

19

20

21

✝
Mount Herman Cem.

30

29

28

Little Brush Creek

31

32

33

Map Group 14: Index to Land Patents

Township 20-North Range 2-East (St Stephens)

After you locate an individual in this Index, take note of the Section and Section Part then proceed to the Land Patent map on the pages immediately following. You should have no difficulty locating the corresponding parcel of land.

The "For More Info" Column will lead you to more information about the underlying Patents. See the *Legend* at right, and the "How to Use this Book" chapter, for more information.

```
                    LEGEND
          "For More Info . . . " column
A = Authority (Legislative Act, See Appendix "A")
B = Block or Lot (location in Section unknown)
C = Cancelled Patent
F = Fractional Section
G = Group (Multi-Patentee Patent, see Appendix "C")
V = Overlaps another Parcel
R = Re-Issued (Parcel patented more than once)

(A & G items require you to look in the Appendixes referred
to above. All other Letter-designations followed by a number
require you to locate line-items in this index that possess
the ID number found after the letter).
```

ID	Individual in Patent	Sec.	Sec. Part	Date Issued	Other Counties	For More Info . . .
2953	CHAMBERS, Uriel B	12	S½NE	1839-05-01	Greene	A1 G41
2952	MCALPIN, Solomon	12	SE	1837-03-15	Greene	A1
2960	MCALPIN, William	13	W½SW	1835-10-01	Greene	A1
2954	" "	13	E½SW	1837-03-15	Greene	A1
2956	" "	13	NE	1837-03-15	Greene	A1 F
2957	" "	13	SENW	1837-03-15	Greene	A1
2958	" "	13	SWNW	1837-03-15	Greene	A1
2959	" "	13	W½SE	1837-03-15	Greene	A1
2955	" "	13	N½NW	1837-03-30	Greene	A1
2944	PRITCHARD, Benjamin H	13	E½SE	1839-05-01	Greene	A1
2947	ROBINSON, Franklin	12	SW	1837-03-15	Greene	A1
2945	SIMS, Edward	12	E½	1825-04-25	Greene	A1 F
2946	" "	13	E½	1825-04-25	Greene	A1 F
2950	SNEDECOR, Isaac C	12	NWNE	1837-08-01	Greene	A1
2949	" "	12	A	1839-05-01	Greene	A1
2953	" "	12	S½NE	1839-05-01	Greene	A1 G41
2948	WATSON, George H	12	W½NW	1837-03-15	Greene	A1
2951	WATSON, James A	12	E½NW	1858-08-20	Greene	A1

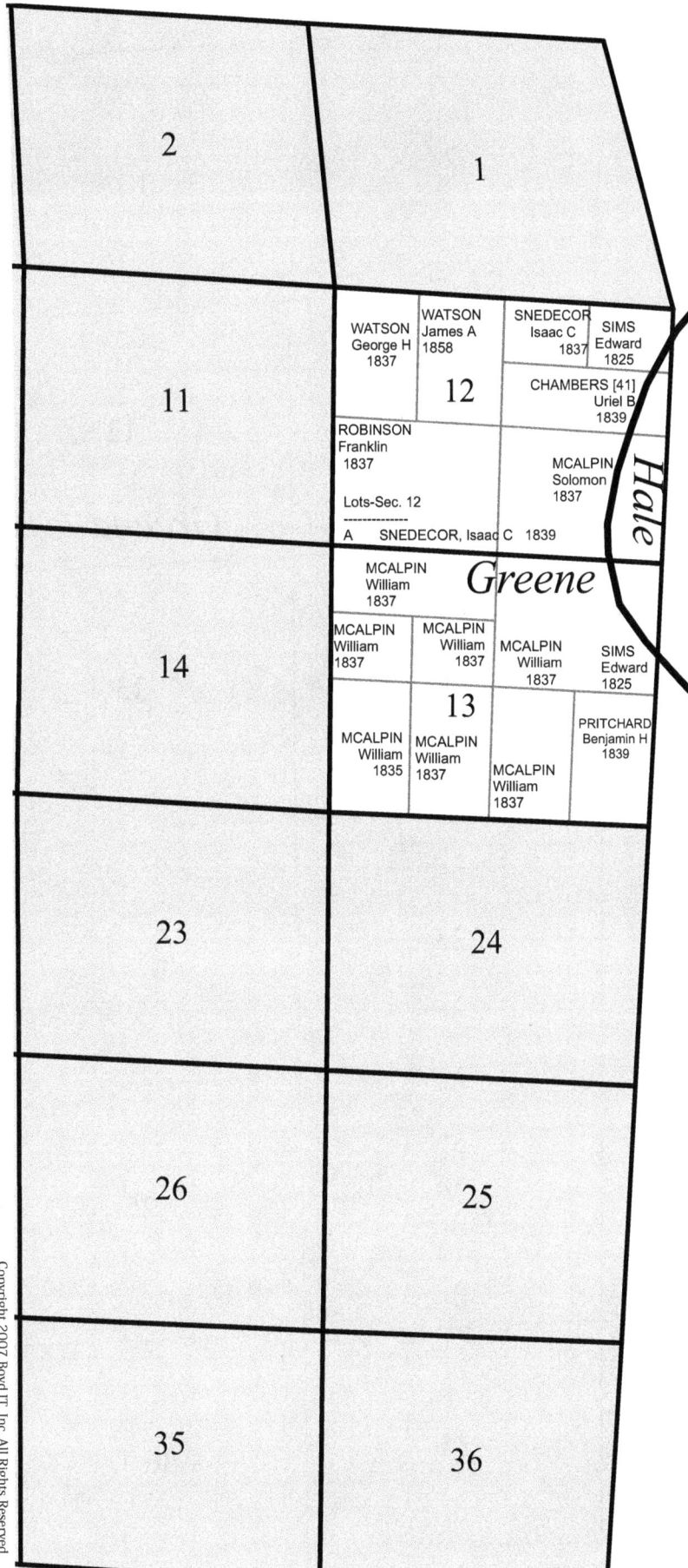

WATSON
George H
1837

WATSON
James A
1858

SNEDECOR
Isaac C
1837

SIMS
Edward
1825

12

CHAMBERS [41]
Uriel B
1839

ROBINSON
Franklin
1837

MCALPIN
Solomon
1837

Lots-Sec. 12

A   SNEDECOR, Isaac C 1839

MCALPIN
William
1837

Greene

MCALPIN
William
1837

MCALPIN
William
1837

MCALPIN
William
1837

SIMS
Edward
1825

13

MCALPIN
William
1835

MCALPIN
William
1837

MCALPIN
William
1837

PRITCHARD
Benjamin H
1839

Hale

Township Statistics

Parcels Mapped	:	17
Number of Patents	:	17
Number of Individuals	:	9
Patentees Identified	:	9
Number of Surnames	:	7
Multi-Patentee Parcels	:	1
Oldest Patent Date	:	4/25/1825
Most Recent Patent	:	8/20/1858
Block/Lot Parcels	:	1
Parcels Re - Issued	:	0
Parcels that Overlap	:	0
Cities and Towns	:	0
Cemeteries	:	0

Note: the area contained in this map amounts to far less than a full Township. Therefore, its contents are completely on this single page (instead of a "normal" 2-page spread).

Legend

———— Patent Boundary

━━━━ Section Boundary

No Patents Found
(or Outside County)

1., 2., 3., ... Lot Numbers
(when beside a name)

[ ] Group Number
(see Appendix "C")

Scale: Section = 1 mile X 1 mile
(generally, with some exceptions)

Road Map

T20-N R2-E
St Stephens Meridian

Map Group 14

Note: the area contained in this map amounts to far less than a full Township. Therefore, its contents are completely on this single page (instead of a "normal" 2-page spread).

Cities & Towns
None

Cemeteries
None

Legend

—————— Section Lines

══════ Interstates

━━━━━━ Highways

—————— Other Roads

● Cities/Towns

✝ Cemeteries

Scale: Section = 1 mile X 1 mile
(generally, with some exceptions)

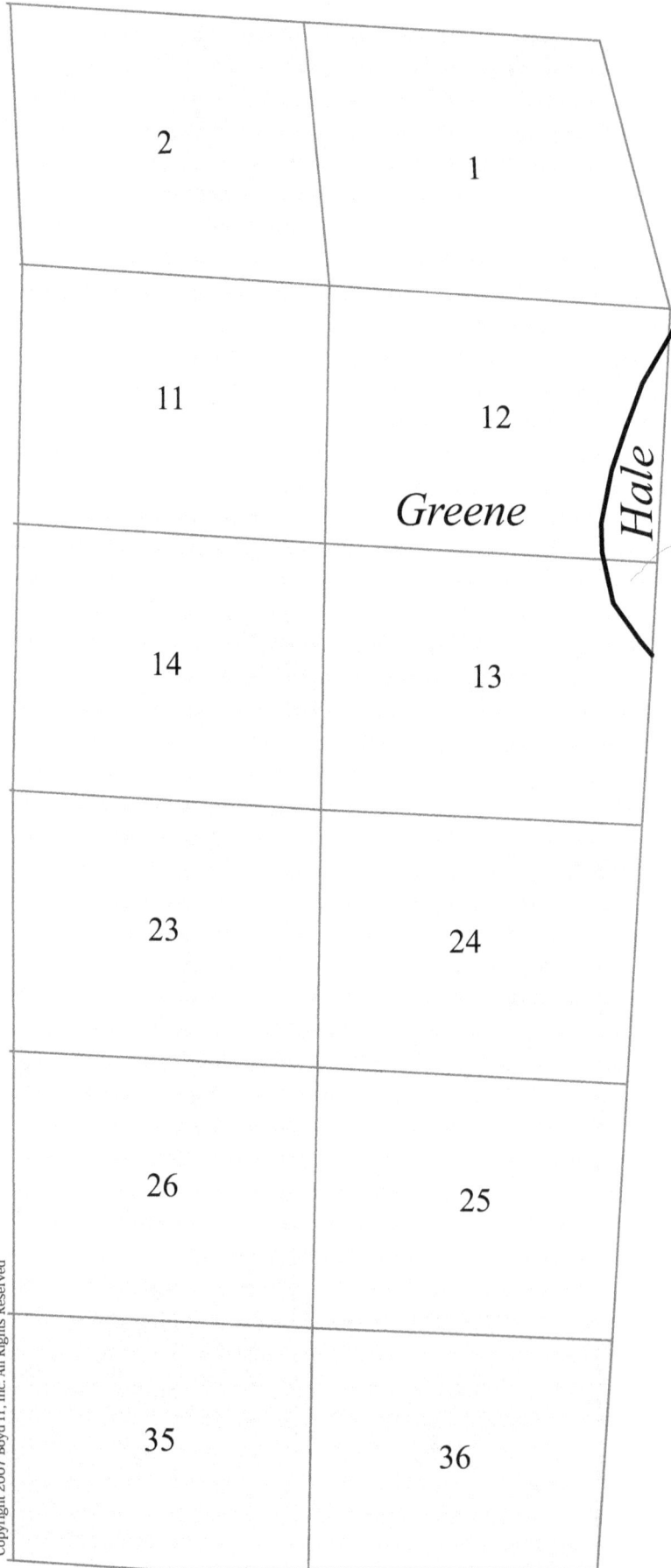

2	1
11	12
14	13
23	24
26	25
35	36

Greene

Hale

2

1

11

12

Greene

Hale

**Black
Warrior River**

14

13

23

24

26

25

35

36

Historical Map

T20-N R2-E
St Stephens Meridian

Map Group 14

Note: the area contained in this map amounts to far less than a full Township. Therefore, its contents are completely on this single page (instead of a "normal" 2-page spread).

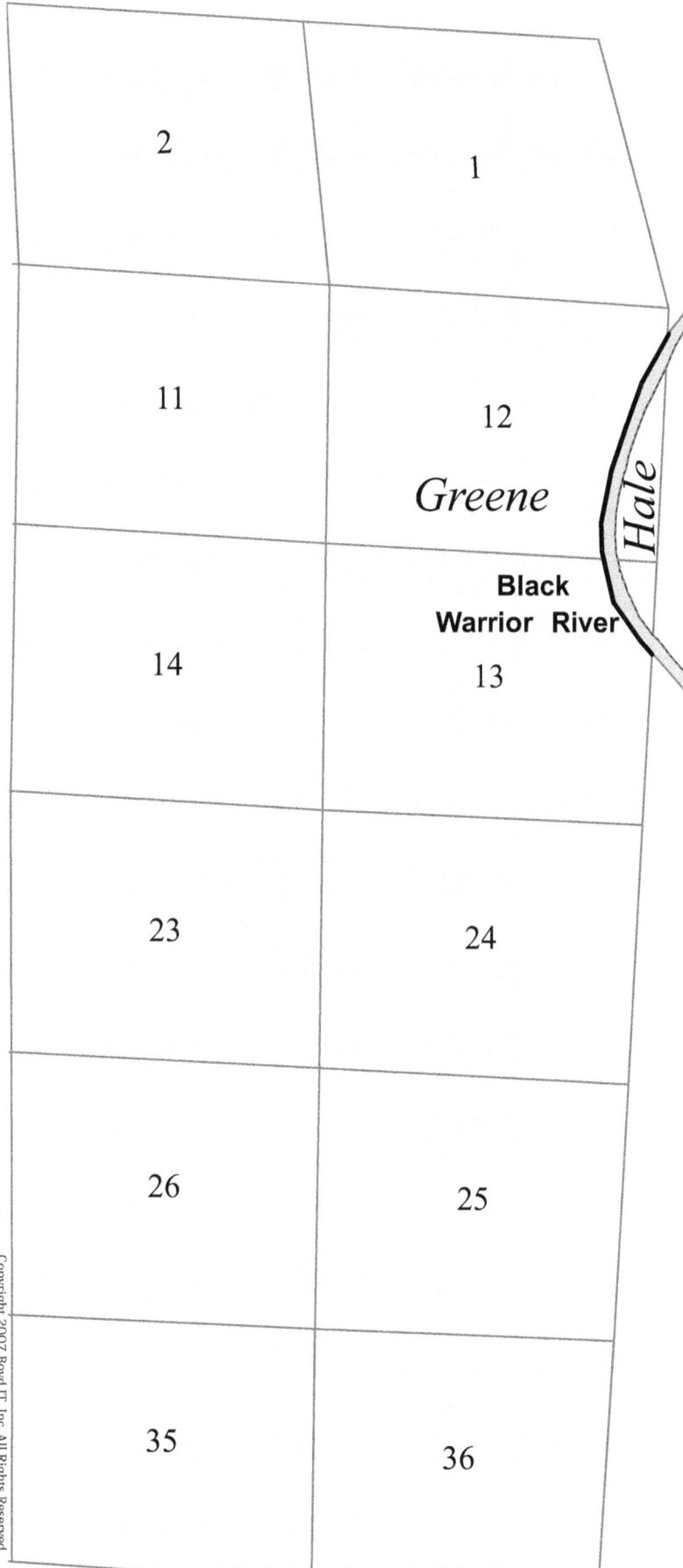

Cities & Towns
None

Cemeteries
None

Legend

——————— Section Lines

+++++++ Railroads

Large Rivers &
Bodies of Water

- - - - - - - Streams/Creeks
& Small Rivers

● Cities/Towns

✝ Cemeteries

Scale: Section = 1 mile X 1 mile
(there are some exceptions)

Map Group 15: Index to Land Patents

Township 20-North Range 3-East (St Stephens)

After you locate an individual in this Index, take note of the Section and Section Part then proceed to the Land Patent map on the pages immediately following. You should have no difficulty locating the corresponding parcel of land.

The "For More Info" Column will lead you to more information about the underlying Patents. See the *Legend* at right, and the "How to Use this Book" chapter, for more information.

```
                        LEGEND
            "For More Info . . . " column
A = Authority (Legislative Act, See Appendix "A")
B = Block or Lot (location in Section unknown)
C = Cancelled Patent
F = Fractional Section
G = Group  (Multi-Patentee Patent, see Appendix "C")
V = Overlaps another Parcel
R = Re-Issued (Parcel patented more than once)

(A & G items require you to look in the Appendixes referred
to above. All other Letter-designations followed by a number
require you to locate line-items in this index that possess
the ID number found after the letter).
```

ID	Individual in Patent	Sec.	Sec. Part	Date Issued	Other Counties	For More Info . . .
3004	DAVIS, Miles	28	E½	1823-10-20	Greene	A1 F
2999	FOWLER, James	6	E½NW	1837-05-15	Greene	A1
3000	" "	6	W½NE	1837-05-15	Greene	A1
3001	" "	6	W½NW	1837-05-15	Greene	A1
2998	" "	27	SE	1837-08-01		A1
3031	FOWLER, Samuel	26	W½NW	1837-08-01		A1
3032	" "	26	W½SE	1837-08-01		A1
3033	" "	26	W½SW	1837-08-01		A1
2981	GRANT, Green W	15	E½SW	1833-05-30		A1
3038	HERNDON, Thomas H	4	NW	1831-09-01		A1
3035	" "	10	W½SW	1833-05-30		A1
3036	" "	15	E½NW	1833-05-30		A1
3037	" "	15	W½NW	1833-05-30		A1
3039	" "	5	ANE	1833-05-30	Greene	A1 F
3040	" "	5	B	1835-09-25	Greene	A1
2976	HINES, Bryan	35	NWNW	1835-09-22	Greene	A1
2961	" "	21	NE	1835-09-25	Greene	A1 F
2964	" "	24	NESE	1835-09-25		A1
2965	" "	25	W½NE	1835-09-25		A1
2972	" "	33	E½NW	1835-09-25	Greene	A1 F
2973	" "	33	SE	1835-09-25	Greene	A1 F
2974	" "	33	W½NE	1835-09-25	Greene	A1
2975	" "	34	W½NW	1835-09-25		A1
2966	" "	26	E½NE	1835-10-01		A1
2967	" "	27	E½NE	1835-10-01		A1
2970	" "	27	W½SW	1835-10-01		A1
2971	" "	33	E½NE	1835-10-01	Greene	A1
2968	" "	27	E½SW	1837-03-15		A1
2969	" "	27	W½NE	1837-03-15		A1
2962	" "	22	SWSE	1837-08-01		A1
2963	" "	23	SW	1837-08-01		A1
2977	HINES, Bryant	25	E½NW	1833-05-30		A1
2978	" "	25	W½NW	1833-05-30		A1
3034	HOUPT, Sebastian	8	W½SE	1825-04-20	Greene	A1
2983	KENNON, Howell D	21	B	1835-10-28	Greene	A1 F
2979	LAWSON, Charles M	17	NW	1823-10-20	Greene	A1 F
3003	LIVINGSTON, Joseph	26	E½SE	1823-10-20		A1
3042	LOW, William B	12	W½NE	1835-10-28		A1
3043	MADISON, William	15	W½SE	1826-10-02		A1
3044	MCALPIN, William	6	SE	1833-05-30	Greene	A1 F
2980	MCLAUREN, Duncan	22	W½NW	1833-05-30		A1
3045	MURPHY, William	5	D	1833-05-30	Greene	A1 F
3046	" "	5	E	1833-05-30	Greene	A1 F
3047	" "	6	E½NE	1833-05-30	Greene	A1
2996	SHEPHERD, Isaac	28	D	1837-03-15	Greene	A1 F
2984	SNEDECOR, Isaac C	15	W½SW	1833-05-30		A1

ID	Individual in Patent	Sec.	Sec. Part	Date Issued	Other Counties	For More Info . . .
2985	SNEDECOR, Isaac C (Cont'd)	22	E½NW	1833-05-30		A1
2986	" "	22	E½SE	1835-09-25		A1
2987	" "	22	NESW	1835-09-25		A1
2988	" "	22	NWSE	1835-09-25		A1
2989	" "	22	NWSW	1835-10-01		A1
2994	" "	6	SW	1837-03-15	Greene	A1
2995	" "	7	NW	1837-03-15	Greene	A1 F
2990	" "	28	E	1837-03-20	Greene	A1
2991	" "	28	NWSW	1837-03-20	Greene	A1
2992	" "	28	SW	1837-03-30	Greene	A1 F
2993	" "	28	W½NW	1837-03-30	Greene	A1
2997	TORBERT, James A	15	E½SE	1825-05-25		A1
2982	TOWNSEND, Henry P	25	E½NE	1823-10-20		A1
3002	WALTON, James M	35	S½	1826-06-10	Greene	A1 F
3041	WILLIAMS, Thomas	1	W½NE	1831-09-01		A1
3014	WITHERS, Robert W	24	W½SE	1833-05-30		A1
3023	" "	35	SE	1833-05-30	Greene	A1 F
3025	" "	36	E½NE	1833-05-30		A1
3029	" "	36	W½NE	1833-05-30		A1
3013	" "	24	SESE	1835-09-22		A1
3026	" "	36	E½SW	1835-09-28		A1
3027	" "	36	NWNW	1835-09-28		A1
3028	" "	36	SWNW	1837-03-15		A1
3030	" "	36	W½SW	1837-03-15		A1
3024	" "	35	SW	1837-03-20	Greene	A1 F
3021	" "	34	SE	1837-03-30		A1
3016	" "	26	E½SW	1837-05-15		A1
3019	" "	34	E½NW	1837-05-15		A1
3020	" "	34	NE	1837-05-15		A1
3022	" "	34	SW	1837-05-15		A1
3015	" "	26	E½NW	1837-08-01		A1
3017	" "	26	W½NE	1837-08-01		A1
3018	" "	33	E½SE	1837-08-01	Greene	A1
3012	WRIGHT, Pleasant	8	SE	1825-05-25	Greene	A1 F
3005	WYNNE, Osman A	21	NESE	1837-03-30	Greene	A1
3006	" "	22	SESW	1837-03-30		A1
3007	" "	27	NW	1837-03-30		A1
3008	WYNNE, Osmond A	21	W½SE	1833-05-30	Greene	A1 F
3010	WYNNE, Osmun A	21	SESE	1835-10-01	Greene	A1
3011	" "	22	SWSW	1835-10-01		A1
3009	" "	21	D	1837-03-30	Greene	A1

Patent Map

T20-N R3-E
St Stephens Meridian

Map Group 15

Township Statistics

Parcels Mapped	:	87
Number of Patents	:	83
Number of Individuals	:	27
Patentees Identified	:	27
Number of Surnames	:	23
Multi-Patentee Parcels	:	0
Oldest Patent Date	:	10/20/1823
Most Recent Patent	:	8/1/1837
Block/Lot Parcels	:	7
Parcels Re - Issued	:	0
Parcels that Overlap	:	0
Cities and Towns	:	1
Cemeteries	:	3

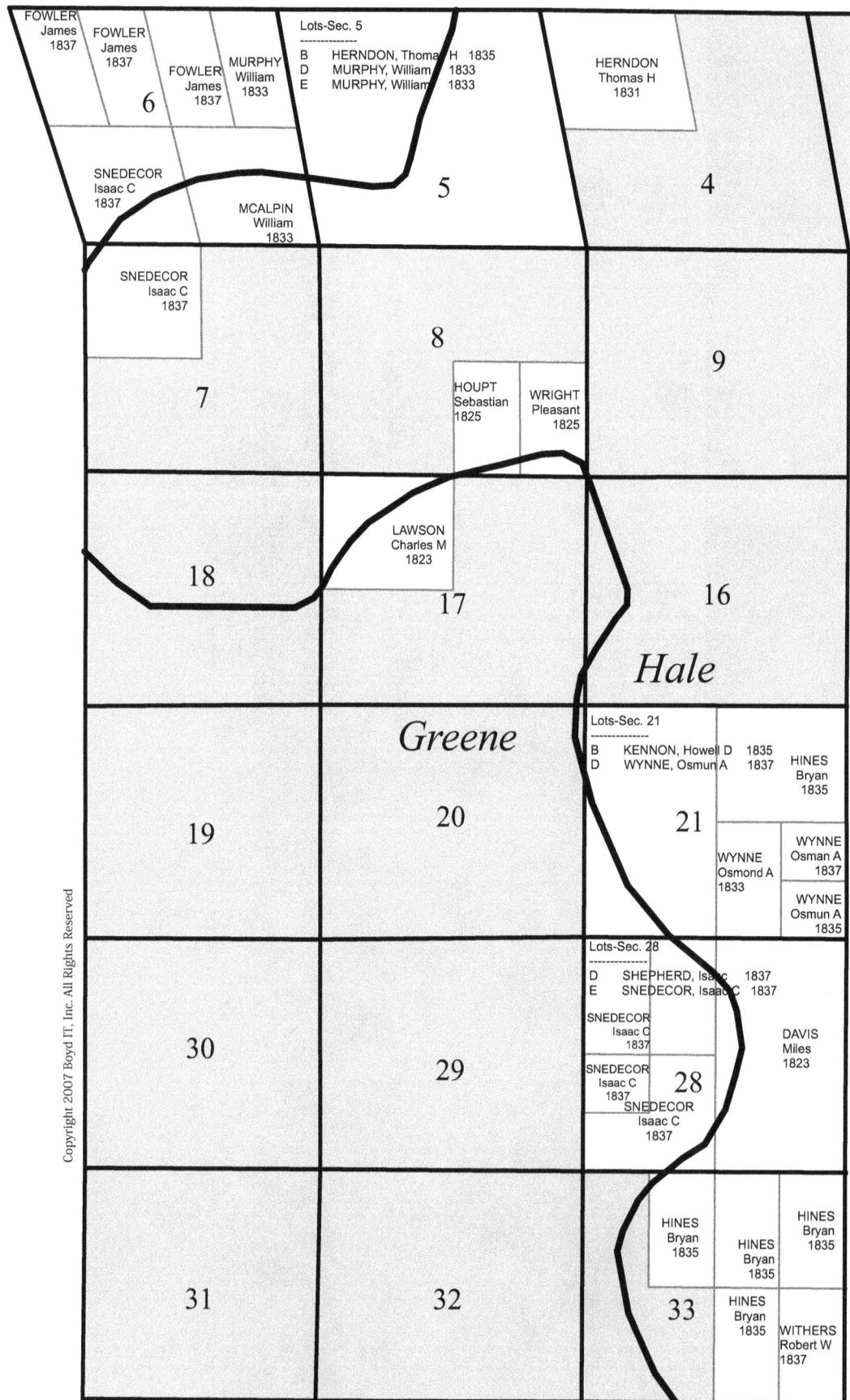

FOWLER
James
1837

FOWLER
James
1837

FOWLER
James
1837

MURPHY
William
1833

6

Lots-Sec. 5

B   HERNDON, Thomas H 1835
D   MURPHY, William   1833
E   MURPHY, William   1833

HERNDON
Thomas H
1831

SNEDECOR
Isaac C
1837

MCALPIN
William
1833

5

4

SNEDECOR
Isaac C
1837

7

8

9

HOUPT
Sebastian
1825

WRIGHT
Pleasant
1825

18

LAWSON
Charles M
1823

17

16

Hale

Greene

19

20

Lots-Sec. 21

B   KENNON, Howell D   1835
D   WYNNE, Osmun A   1837

21

HINES
Bryan
1835

WYNNE
Osmond A
1833

WYNNE
Osman A
1837

WYNNE
Osmun A
1835

30

29

Lots-Sec. 28

D   SHEPHERD, Isaac   1837
E   SNEDECOR, Isaac C 1837

SNEDECOR
Isaac C
1837

SNEDECOR
Isaac C
1837

SNEDECOR
Isaac C
1837

28

DAVIS
Miles
1823

31

32

HINES
Bryan
1835

HINES
Bryan
1835

33

HINES
Bryan
1835

HINES
Bryan
1835

WITHERS
Robert W
1837

		WILLIAMS Thomas 1831
3	2	1

10	11	LOW William B 1835	
HERNDON Thomas H 1833			12

HERNDON Thomas H 1833

HERNDON Thomas H 1833

15

14

13

SNEDECOR Isaac C 1833 | GRANT Green W 1833 | MADISON William 1826 | TORBERT James A 1825

MCLAUREN Duncan 1833 | SNEDECOR Isaac C 1833

22

23

24

SNEDECOR Isaac C 1835 | SNEDECOR Isaac C 1835 | SNEDECOR Isaac C 1835 | SNEDECOR Isaac C 1835 | HINES Bryan 1837

WYNNE Osmun A 1835 | WYNNE Osman A 1837 | HINES Bryan 1837

WITHERS Robert W 1833 | HINES Bryan 1835

WITHERS Robert W 1835

WYNNE Osman A 1837

HINES Bryan 1837 | HINES Bryan 1835 | FOWLER Samuel 1837 | WITHERS Robert W 1837 | WITHERS Robert W 1837 | HINES Bryan 1835 | HINES Bryant 1833 | HINES Bryant 1833 | HINES Bryan 1835 | TOWNSEND Henry P 1823

27

26

HINES Bryan 1835 | HINES Bryan 1837 | FOWLER James 1837

FOWLER Samuel 1837 | WITHERS Robert W 1837 | FOWLER Samuel 1837 | LIVINGSTON Joseph 1823

25

HINES Bryan 1835 | WITHERS Robert W 1837 | WITHERS Robert W 1837 | HINES Bryan 1835 | WITHERS Robert W 1835 | WITHERS Robert W 1833 | WITHERS Robert W 1833

35

WITHERS Robert W 1837

36

WITHERS Robert W 1835

34

WITHERS Robert W 1837

WALTON James M 1826 | WITHERS Robert W 1833 | WITHERS Robert W 1835

WITHERS Robert W 1837

WITHERS Robert W 1837

WITHERS Robert W 1837

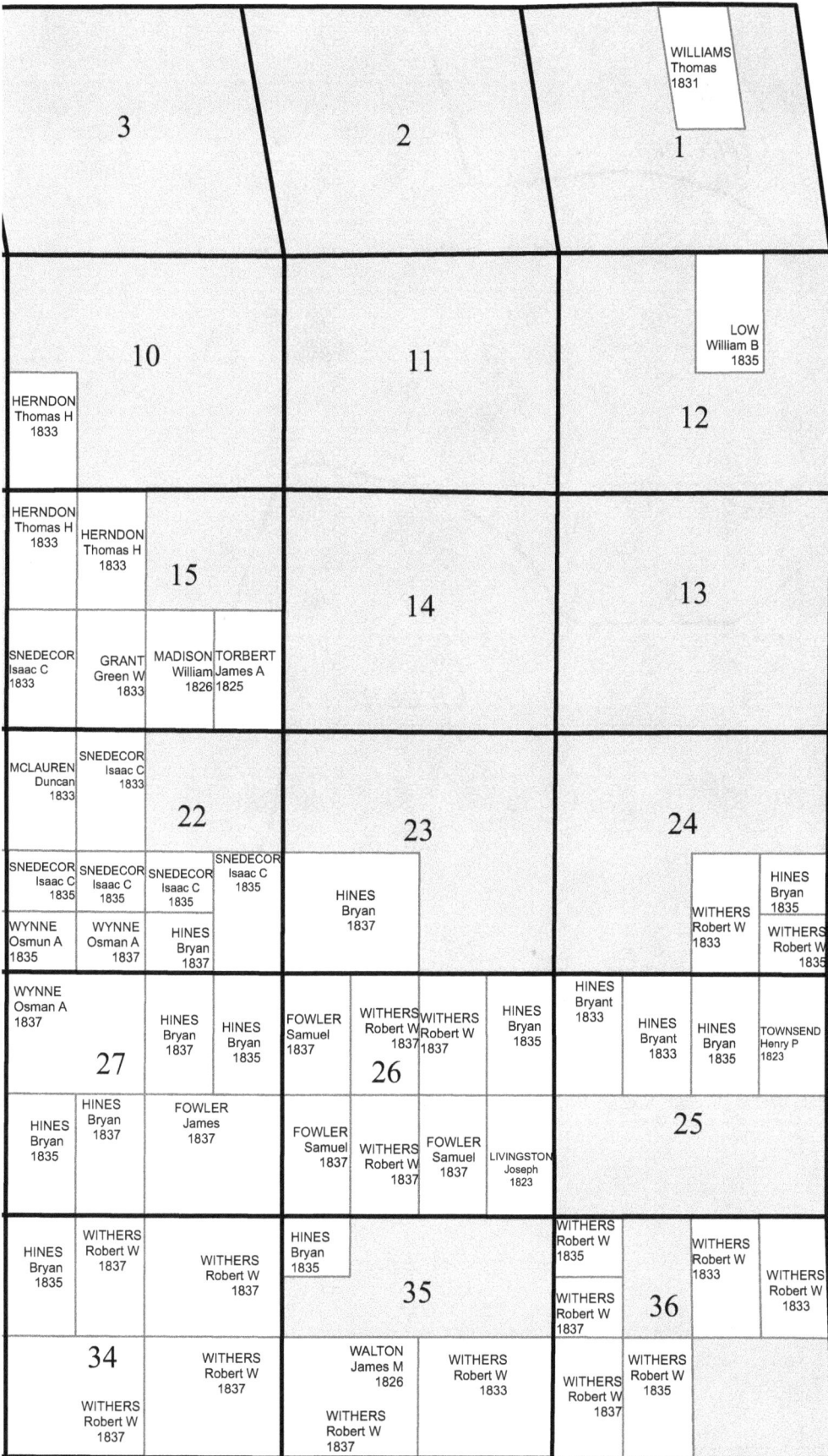

Helpful Hints

1. This Map's INDEX can be found on the preceding pages.

2. Refer to Map "C" to see where this Township lies within Hale County, Alabama.

3. Numbers within square brackets [ ] denote a multi-patentee land parcel (multi-owner). Refer to Appendix "C" for a full list of members in this group.

4. Areas that look to be crowded with Patentees usually indicate multiple sales of the same parcel (Re-issues) or Overlapping parcels. See this Township's Index for an explanation of these and other circumstances that might explain "odd" groupings of Patentees on this map.

Legend

———————— Patent Boundary

━━━━━━━━ Section Boundary

No Patents Found (or Outside County)

1., 2., 3., ... Lot Numbers (when beside a name)

[ ] Group Number (see Appendix "C")

Scale: Section = 1 mile X 1 mile (generally, with some exceptions)

Road Map

T20-N R3-E
St Stephens Meridian

Map Group 15

Cities & Towns
Millwood

Cemeteries
Erie Cemetery
Evans Cemetery
Limestone Cemetery

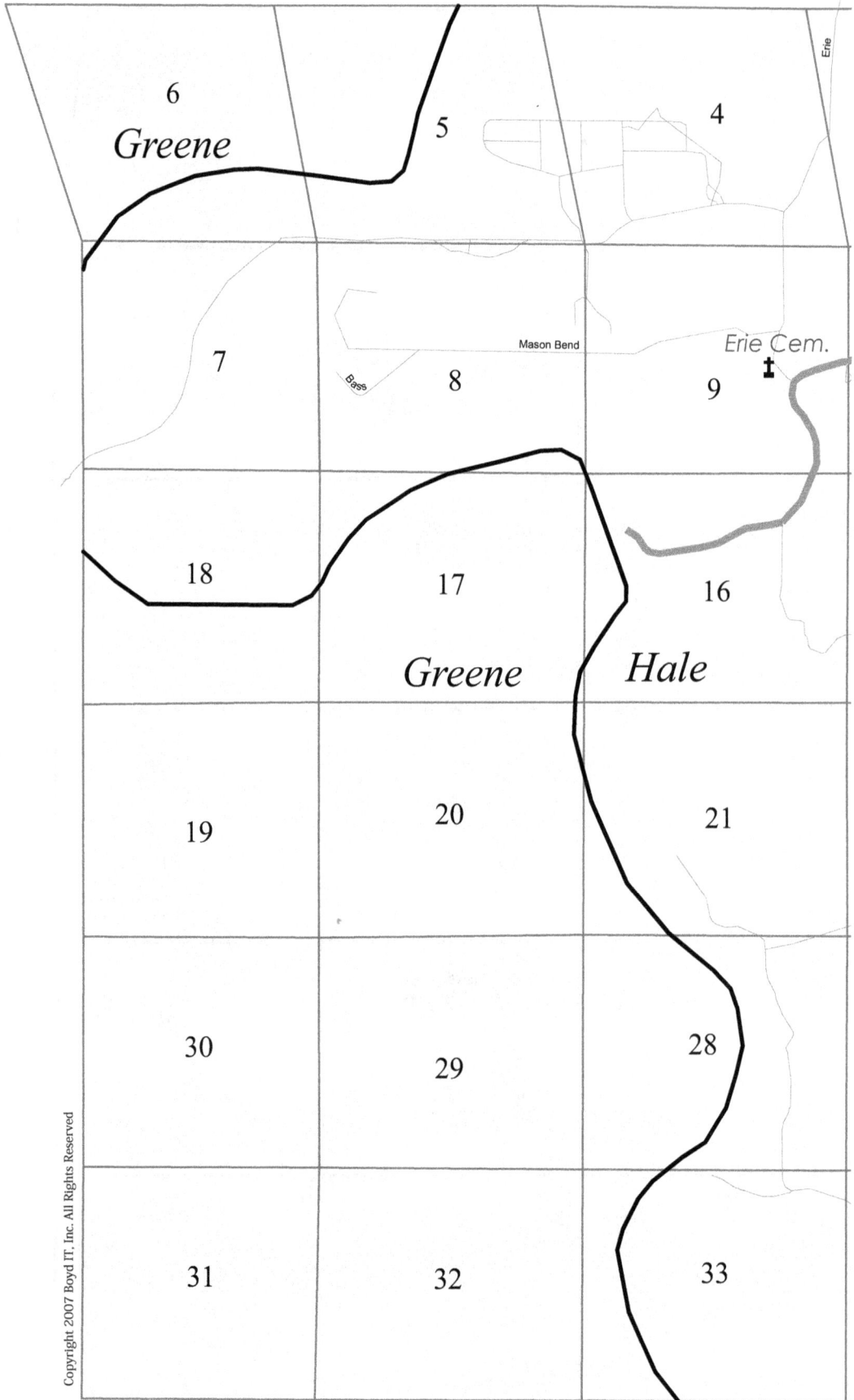

6

Greene

5

4

Erie

7

Mason Bend

Bass

8

Erie Cem.

9

18

17

16

Greene

Hale

19

20

21

30

29

28

31

32

33

3

2

1

Hibiscus

Guiena

Red Mud

Gator

Thrasher

County Road 15

10

11

12

Eloise George

Hines

Quail

Carnation

Pine

County Road 17

15

14

13

Evans Cem.

Carter

Flamingo

22

23

24

New Hope

Limestone Cem.

27

26

25

Millwood

34

35

36

County Road 24

Millwood

Copyright 2007 Boyd IT, Inc. All Rights Reserved

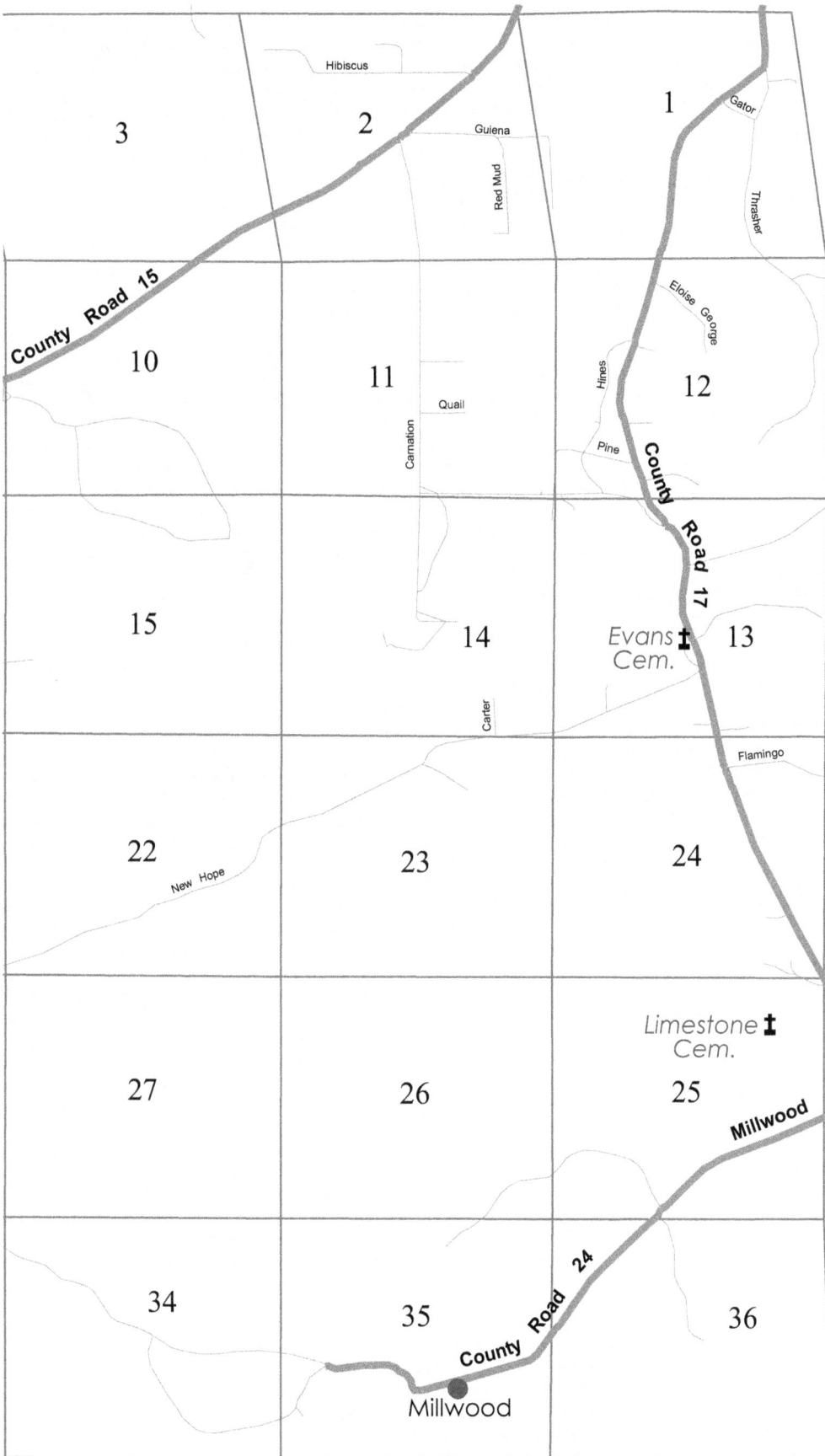

Helpful Hints

1. This road map has a number of uses, but primarily it is to help you: a) find the present location of land owned by your ancestors (at least the general area), b) find cemeteries and city-centers, and c) estimate the route/roads used by Census-takers & tax-assessors.

2. If you plan to travel to Hale County to locate cemeteries or land parcels, please pick up a modern travel map for the area before you do. Mapping old land parcels on modern maps is not as exact a science as you might think. Just the slightest variations in public land survey coordinates, estimates of parcel boundaries, or road-map deviations can greatly alter a map's representation of how a road either does or doesn't cross a particular parcel of land.

L e g e n d

_____ Section Lines

═══════════ Interstates

▬▬▬▬▬▬▬ Highways

_____ Other Roads

● Cities/Towns

✝ Cemeteries

Scale: Section = 1 mile X 1 mile
(generally, with some exceptions)

Historical Map

T20-N R3-E
St Stephens Meridian

Map Group 15

Cities & Towns
Millwood

Greene
Hale

6

5

4

Wrights Creek

Graveyard Branch

7

8

9

Erie Cem.

18

17

Black Warrior River

16

19

20

Hines Creek

21

Cemeteries
Erie Cemetery
Evans Cemetery
Limestone Cemetery

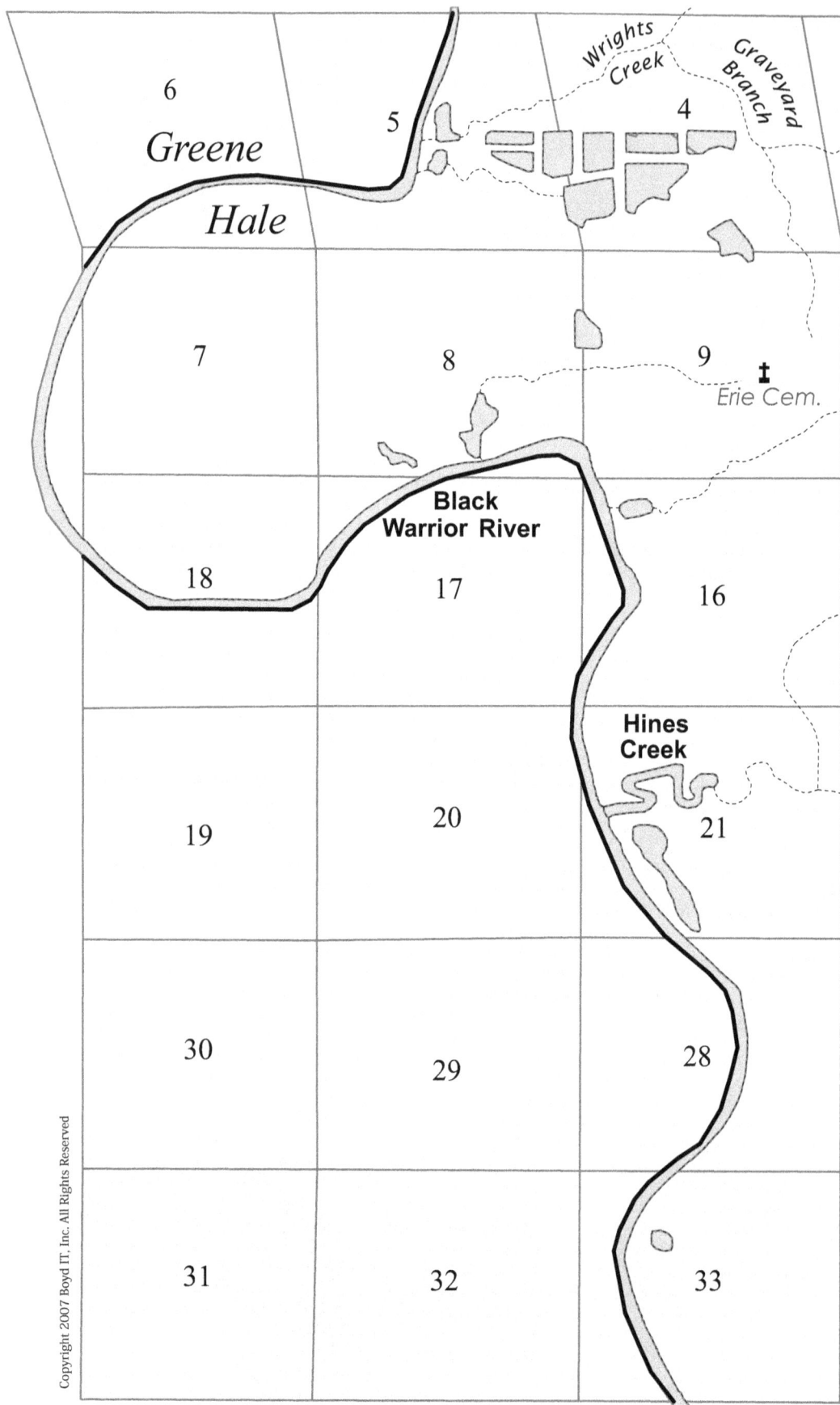

30

29

28

31

32

33

3

2

1

10

11

12

15

14

Hines Creek

13

Evans ✝
Cem.

22

23

24

Limestone Cem ✝

27

26

25

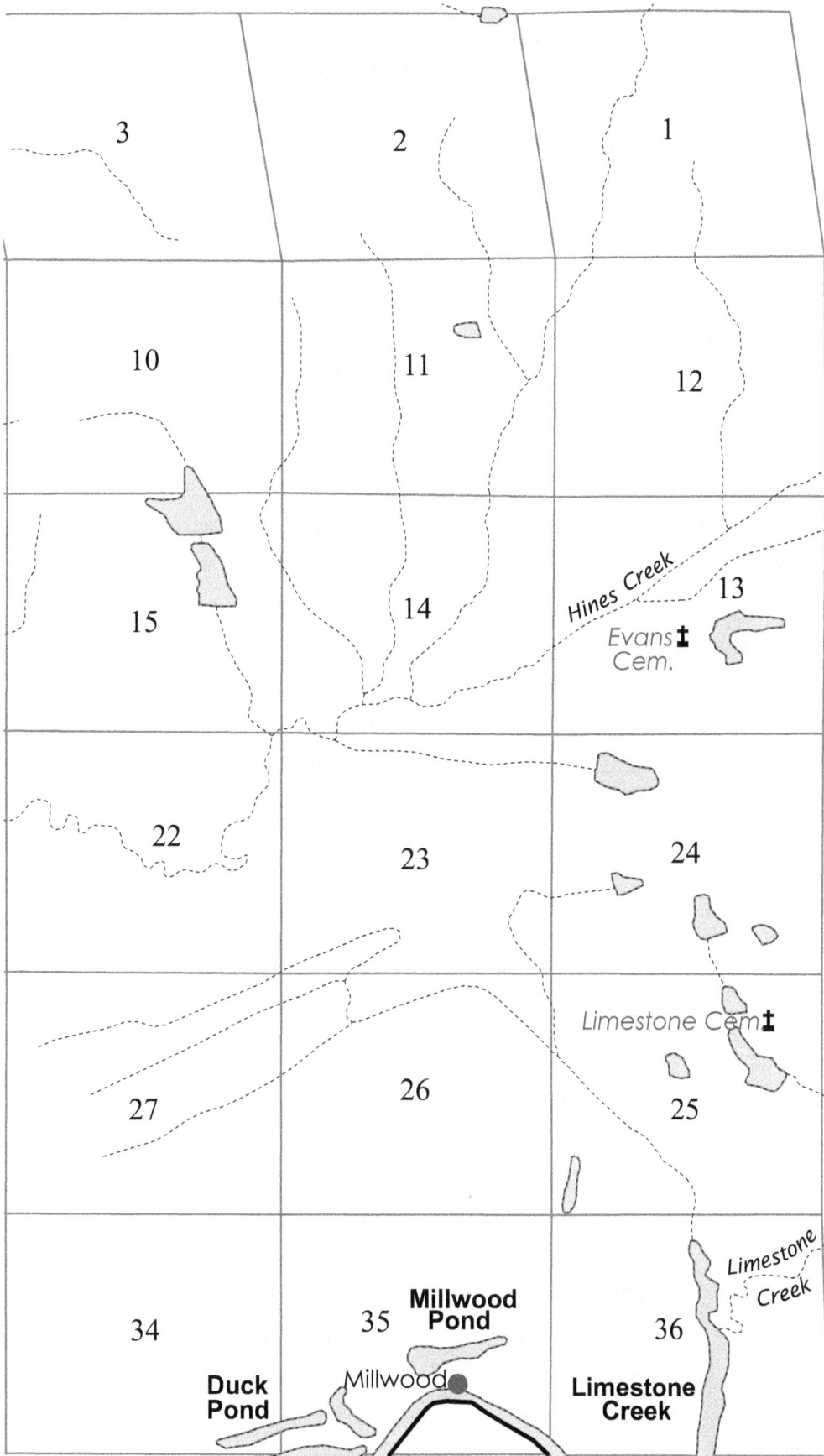

34

35

Millwood Pond

Millwood

36

Duck Pond

Limestone Creek

Limestone Creek

Legend

————————	Section Lines
—+—+—+—+—	Railroads
▭	Large Rivers & Bodies of Water
- - - - - - - -	Streams/Creeks & Small Rivers
●	Cities/Towns
✝	Cemeteries

Scale: Section = 1 mile X 1 mile
(there are some exceptions)

Map Group 16: Index to Land Patents

Township 20-North Range 4-East (St Stephens)

After you locate an individual in this Index, take note of the Section and Section Part then proceed to the Land Patent map on the pages immediately following. You should have no difficulty locating the corresponding parcel of land.

The "For More Info" Column will lead you to more information about the underlying Patents. See the *Legend* at right, and the "How to Use this Book" chapter, for more information.

```
                        LEGEND
                "For More Info . . . " column
A = Authority (Legislative Act, See Appendix "A")
B = Block or Lot (location in Section unknown)
C = Cancelled Patent
F = Fractional Section
G = Group  (Multi-Patentee Patent, see Appendix "C")
V = Overlaps another Parcel
R = Re-Issued (Parcel patented more than once)

(A & G items require you to look in the Appendixes referred
to above. All other Letter-designations followed by a number
require you to locate line-items in this index that possess
the ID number found after the letter).
```

ID	Individual in Patent	Sec.	Sec. Part	Date Issued	Other Counties	For More Info . . .
3070	ANDREWS, Thompson P	33	W½SE	1848-07-01		A1
3061	BORDEN, Joseph	31	E½E½SE	1837-03-30		A1 G29
3052	CHANDRON, Felix	29	E½NW	1837-03-30		A1 G47
3053	"	29	W½SW	1837-03-30		A1 G47
3051	"	30	E½E½SE	1837-03-30		A1 G45
3054	"	30	E½SW	1837-03-30		A1 G47
3055	"	30	SWSW	1837-03-30		A1 G48
3050	COOK, Elizabeth	28	W½SE	1837-03-30		A1 G65
3048	FOURNIER, Alexander	8	E½E½SE	1835-10-01		A1
3049	GLOVER, Allen	33	E½SE	1837-03-30		A1 G103
3064	GREENE, Lodowick	29	W½NE	1837-03-30		A1 G129
3051	GRIFFIN, James	30	E½E½SE	1837-03-30		A1 G45
3066	HALL, Rebecca E	5	SE	1837-03-30		A1
3071	HANCOCK, William B	29	E½NE	1837-03-30		A1 G133
3052	HENLEY, John W	29	E½NW	1837-03-30		A1 G47
3053	"	29	W½SW	1837-03-30		A1 G47
3051	"	30	E½E½SE	1837-03-30		A1 G45
3054	"	30	E½SW	1837-03-30		A1 G47
3055	"	30	SWSW	1837-03-30		A1 G48
3049	LANDRUM, Samuel	33	E½SE	1837-03-30		A1 G103
3061	LANE, Levin B	31	E½E½SE	1837-03-30		A1 G29
3062	MARTINIERE, Julius	21	E½E½SE	1835-09-28		A1
3063	"	29	W½NW	1837-03-30		A1 G186
3056	MCFARLAND, George	34	SE	1837-03-30		A1
3072	MONTGOMERY, William	20	E½E½SE	1839-05-01		A1 G201
3060	MOORE, John E	31	NWSW	1848-07-01		A1
3050	PURNELL, Hortensius	28	W½SE	1837-03-30		A1 G65
3071	"	29	E½NE	1837-03-30		A1 G133
3057	"	29	E½SW	1837-03-30		A1 G216
3064	"	29	W½NE	1837-03-30		A1 G129
3058	PURNELL, Hortentius	28	E½SE	1839-05-01		A1 G217
3072	ROUDET, Peter C	20	E½E½SE	1839-05-01		A1 G201
3059	SCOTT, James B	13	SE	1835-09-28		A1
3055	SEALE, Benton	30	SWSW	1837-03-30		A1 G48
3065	STRICKLAND, Obijah	31	W½NW	1837-03-30		A1 G237
3061	TUCKER, William H	31	E½E½SE	1837-03-30		A1 G29
3063	WALLER, Archibald	29	W½NW	1837-03-30		A1 G186
3057	WHITE, Hiram	29	E½SW	1837-03-30		A1 G216
3058	WHITE, Josiah	28	E½SE	1839-05-01		A1 G217
3065	WITHERS, Robert W	31	W½NW	1837-03-30		A1 G237
3067	"	18	E½E½SE	1841-02-08		A1
3068	"	30	NWSW	1841-02-08		A1
3069	"	30	W½NW	1841-02-08		A1

Patent Map

T20-N R4-E
St Stephens Meridian

Map Group 16

Township Statistics

Parcels Mapped	:	25
Number of Patents	:	23
Number of Individuals	:	28
Patentees Identified	:	21
Number of Surnames	:	26
Multi-Patentee Parcels	:	15
Oldest Patent Date	:	9/28/1835
Most Recent Patent	:	7/1/1848
Block/Lot Parcels	:	0
Parcels Re-Issued	:	0
Parcels that Overlap	:	0
Cities and Towns	:	1
Cemeteries	:	11

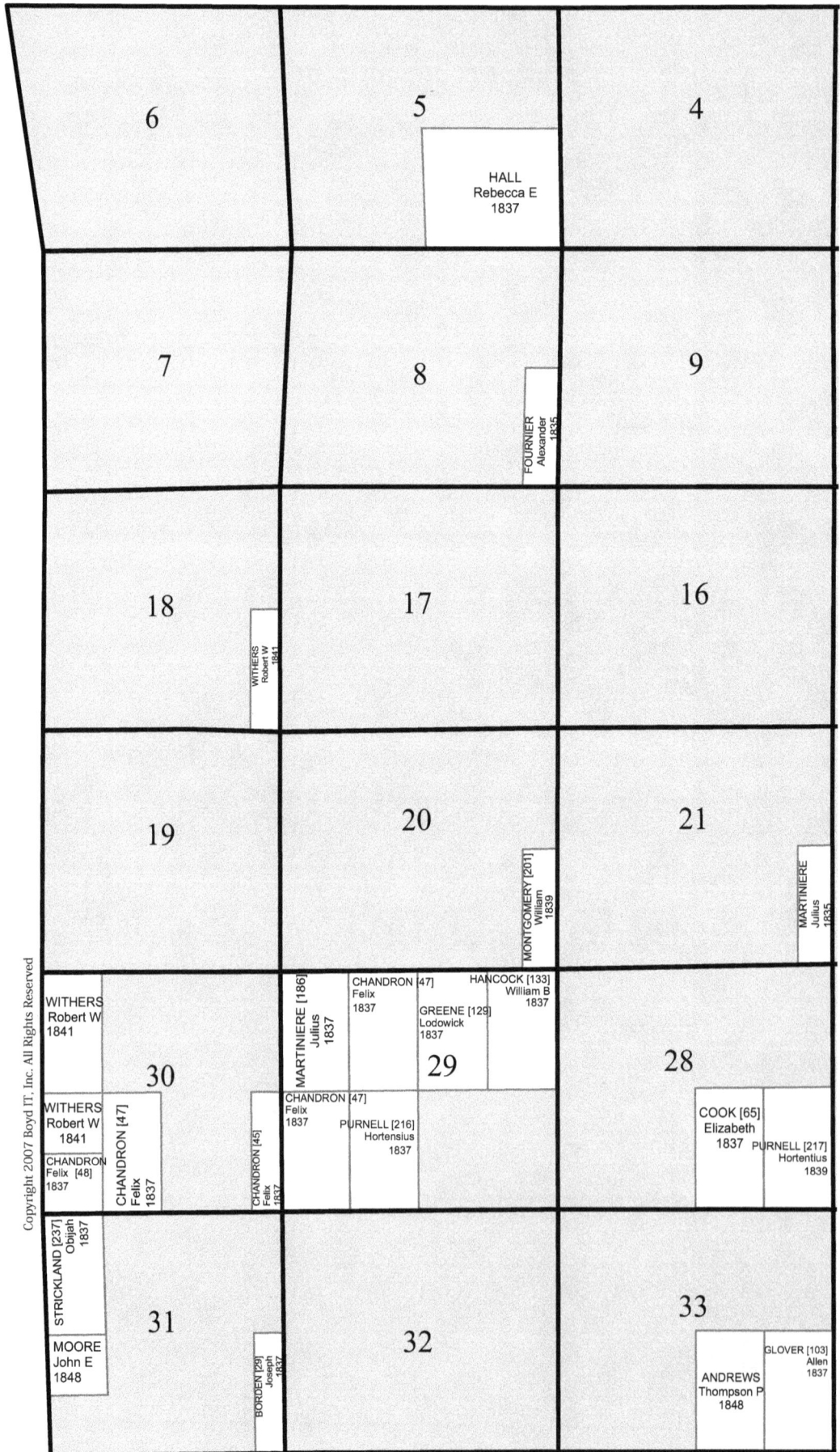

3	2	1
10	11	12
15	14	13 / SCOTT James B 1835
22	23	24
27	26	25
34 / MCFARLAND George 1837	35	36

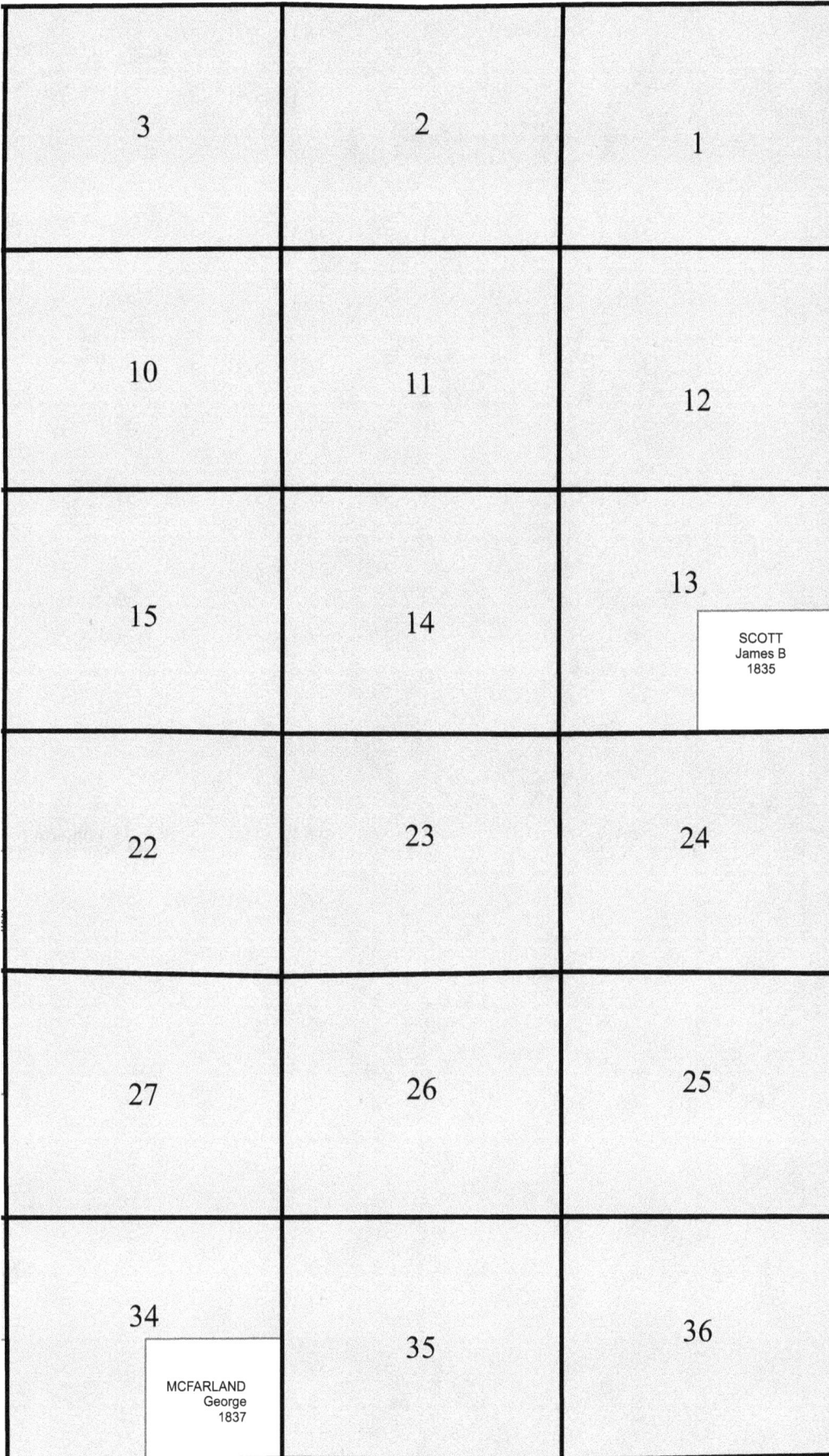

Helpful Hints

1. This Map's INDEX can be found on the preceding pages.

2. Refer to Map "C" to see where this Township lies within Hale County, Alabama.

3. Numbers within square brackets [ ] denote a multi-patentee land parcel (multi-owner). Refer to Appendix "C" for a full list of members in this group.

4. Areas that look to be crowded with Patentees usually indicate multiple sales of the same parcel (Re-issues) or Overlapping parcels. See this Township's Index for an explanation of these and other circumstances that might explain "odd" groupings of Patentees on this map.

Legend

———————— Patent Boundary

━━━━━━━━ Section Boundary

No Patents Found (or Outside County)

1., 2., 3., ...   Lot Numbers (when beside a name)

[ ]   Group Number (see Appendix "C")

Scale: Section = 1 mile X 1 mile (generally, with some exceptions)

Road Map

T20-N R4-E
St Stephens Meridian

Map Group 16

Cities & Towns
Melton

Cemeteries
Boston Cemetery
Burk Cemetery
Crooks Cemetery
Curry Cemetery
Hatche Cemetery
Long Cemetery
Mount Moriah Cemetery
Mount Zion Cemetery
Pickens Cemetery
Ramey Cemetery
Taylor Cemetery

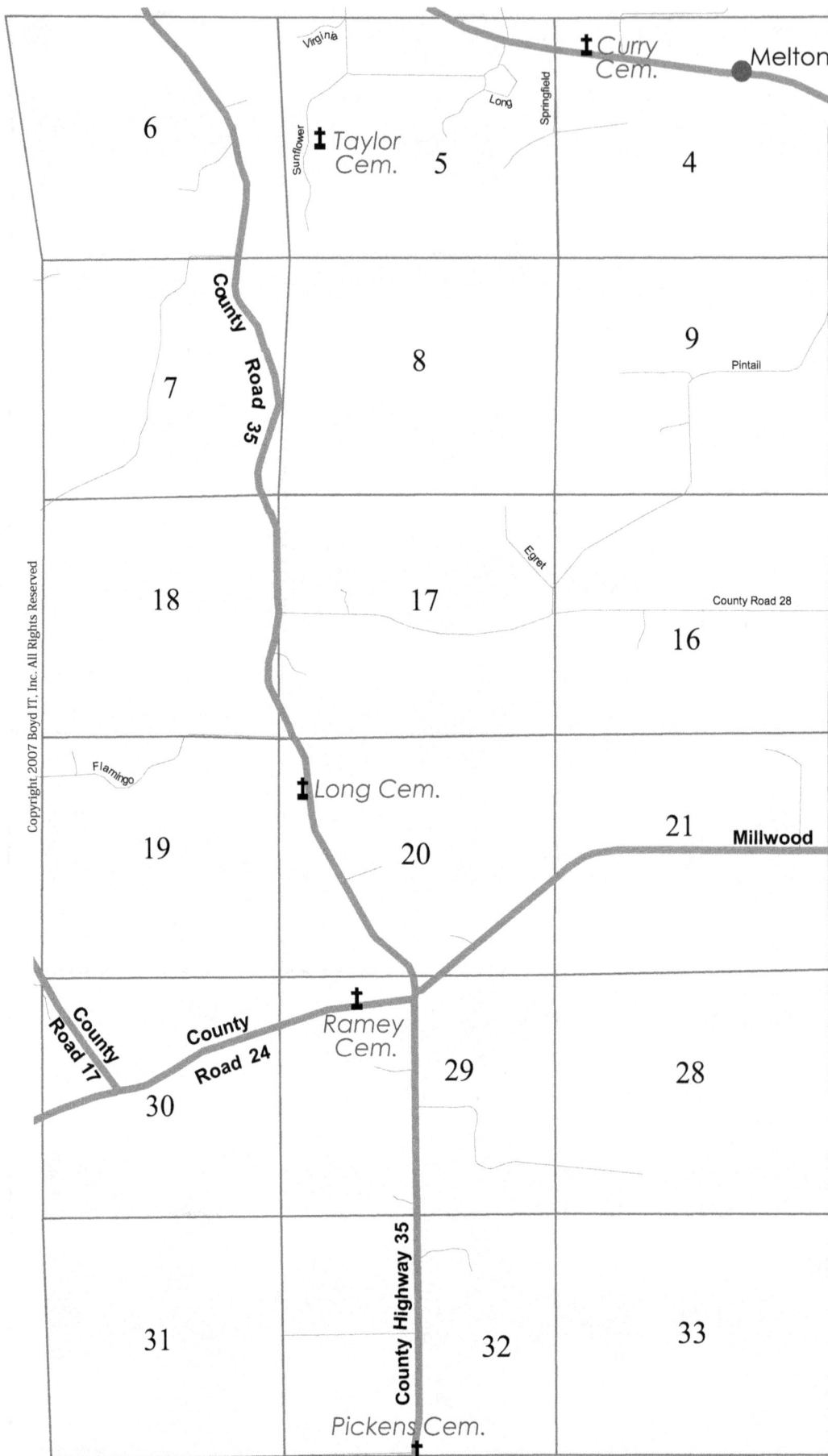

Copyright 2007 Boyd IT. Inc. All Rights Reserved

Virginia

✝ Curry Cem.

● Melton

6

Sunflower

✝ Taylor Cem.

5

Long

Springfield

4

County Road 35

7

8

9

Pintail

18

Egret

17

16

County Road 28

Flamingo

✝ Long Cem.

19

20

21

Millwood

County Road 17

County Road 24

✝ Ramey Cem.

29

28

30

31

County Highway 35

32

33

Pickens Cem.
✝

County Road 30

3

Calico

State Route 14

Hatche Cem.

2

Boston Cem.

1

Burk Cem.

County Road 21

10

Johnson

11

12

Loon

Dillard

Owens

Circle

Holbrook Place

15

July

14

Clements

13

County Road 28

Mount Zion Cem.

Mount Moriah Cem.

Crooks Cem.

Lakewood

22

Airport Loop

23

Kings Hill

24

27

26

25

34

35

36

State Route 69

Copyright 2007 Boyd IT, Inc. All Rights Reserved

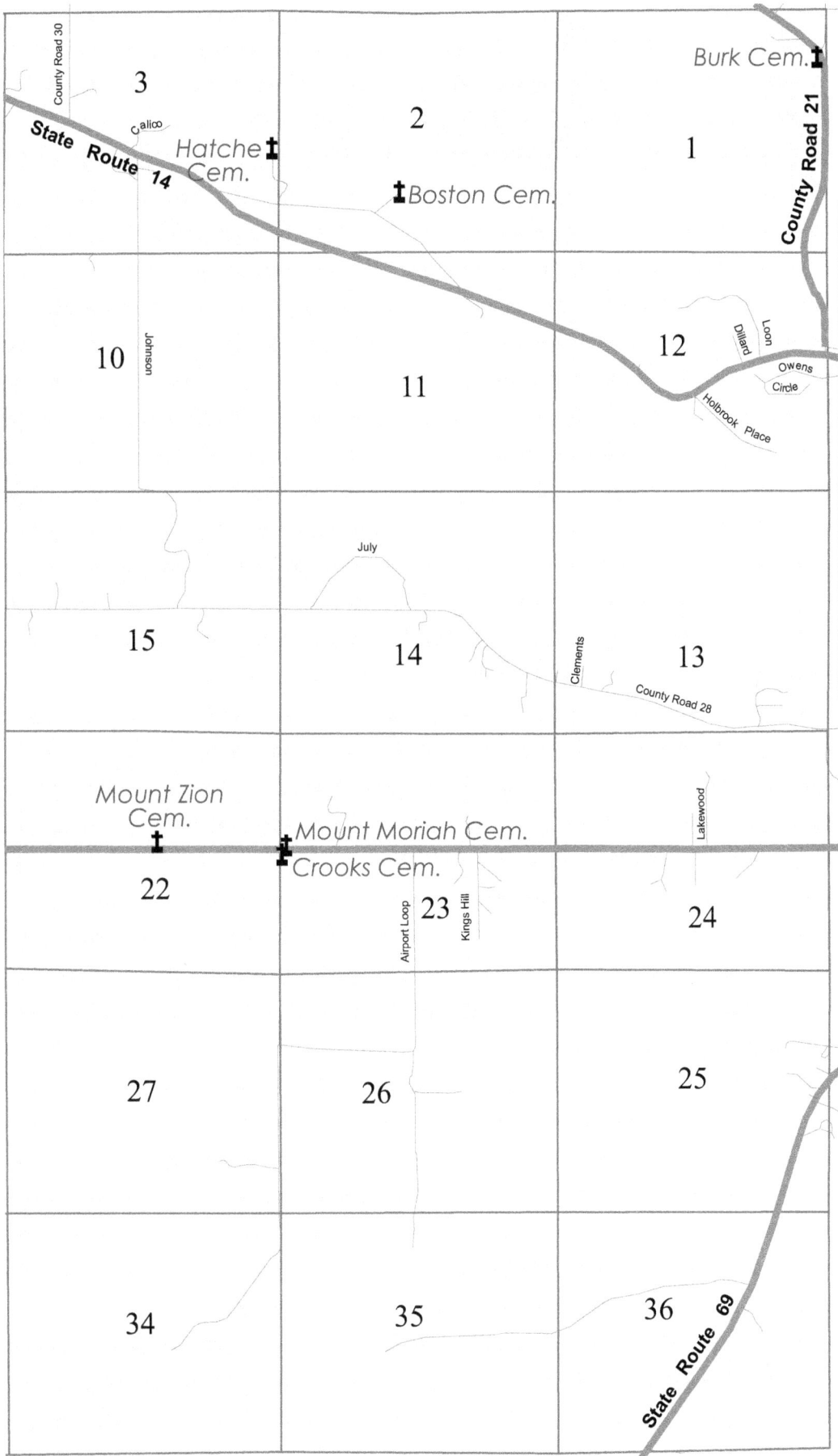

Legend

Section Lines

Interstates

Highways

Other Roads

Cities/Towns

Cemeteries

Scale: Section = 1 mile X 1 mile
(generally, with some exceptions)

Historical Map

T20-N R4-E
St Stephens Meridian

Map Group 16

Cities & Towns
Melton

Cemeteries
Boston Cemetery
Burk Cemetery
Crooks Cemetery
Curry Cemetery
Hatche Cemetery
Long Cemetery
Mount Moriah Cemetery
Mount Zion Cemetery
Pickens Cemetery
Ramey Cemetery
Taylor Cemetery

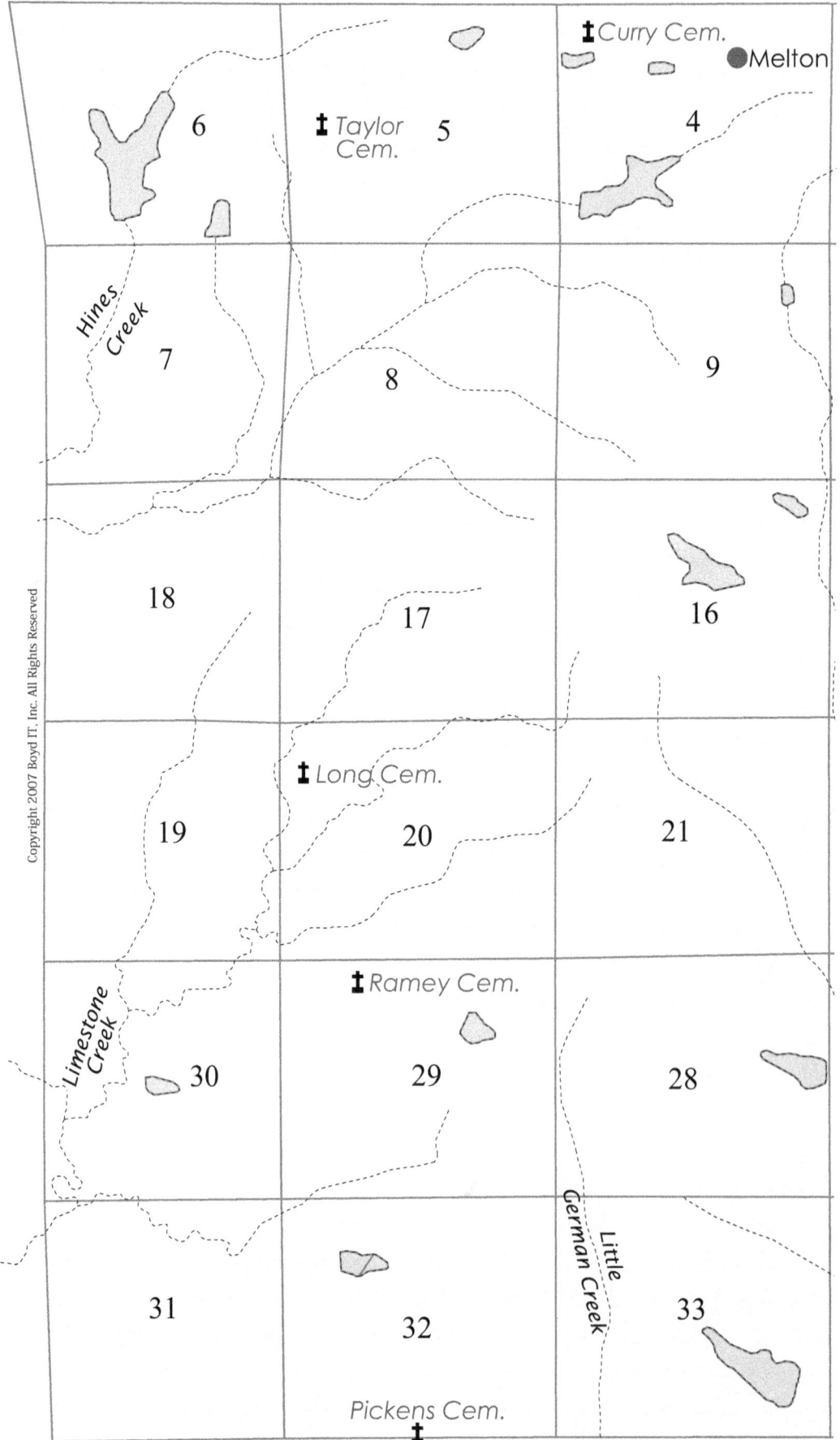

‡ Curry Cem.
● Melton

6

‡ Taylor Cem.   5

4

Hines Creek

7

8

9

18

17

16

Copyright 2007 Boyd IT, Inc. All Rights Reserved

‡ Long Cem.

19

20

21

Limestone Creek

‡ Ramey Cem.

30

29

28

Little German Creek

31

32

33

Pickens Cem.
‡

3

Hatche **✝**
Cem.

Burk Cem. **✝**

Colwell Creek

2

Boston Cem. **✝**

1

10

11

12

15

14

13

Mount
Zion Cem. **✝**
22

✝ Mount Moriah Cem.
Crooks Cem.
23

24

27

Big Little
German Creek
26

25

34

35

36

Helpful Hints

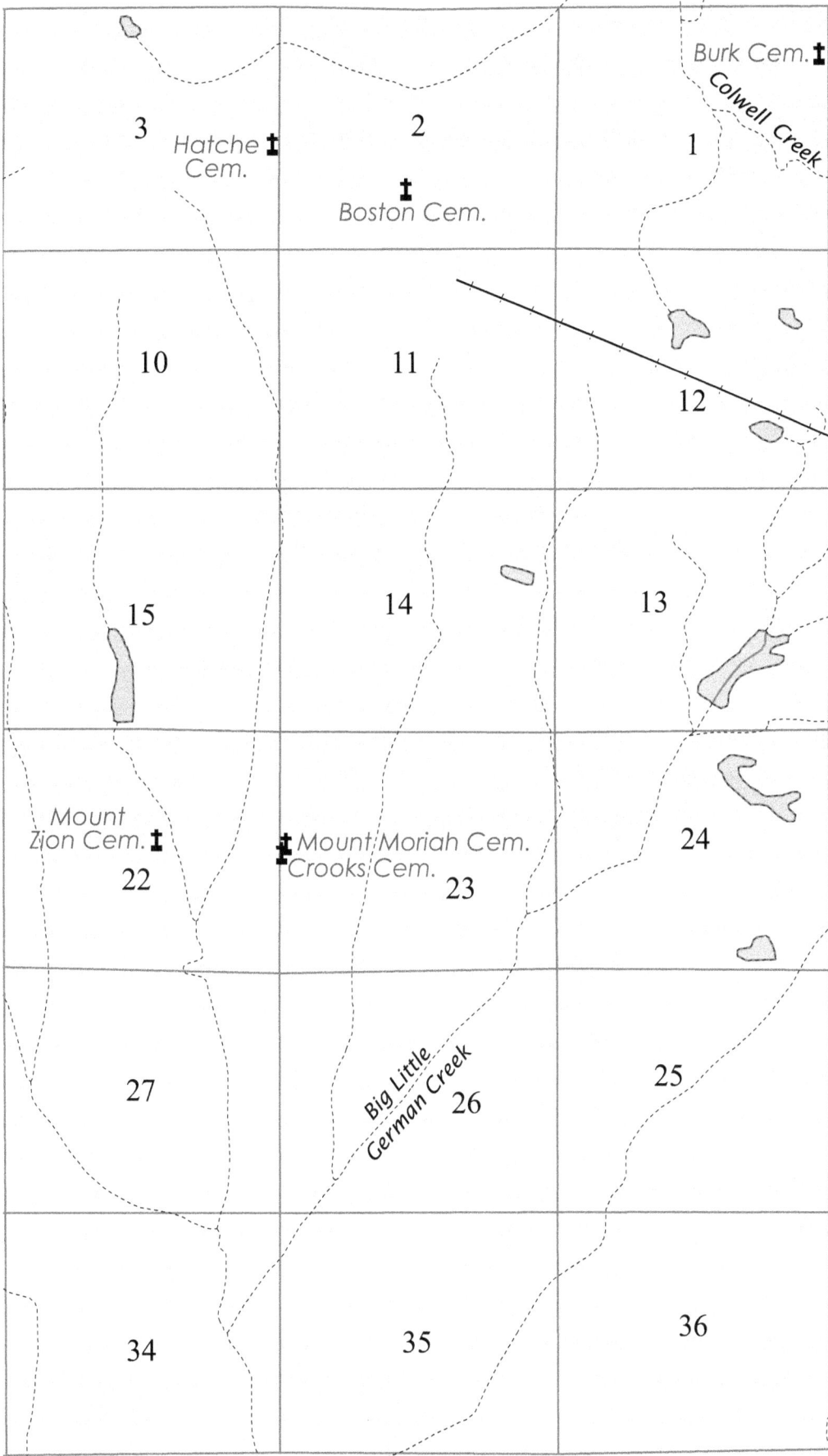

1. This Map takes a different look at the same Congressional Township displayed in the preceding two maps. It presents features that can help you better envision the historical development of the area: a) Water-bodies (lakes & ponds), b) Water-courses (rivers, streams, etc.), c) Railroads, d) City/town center-points (where they were oftentimes located when first settled), and e) Cemeteries.

2. Using this "Historical" map in tandem with this Township's Patent Map and Road Map, may lead you to some interesting discoveries. You will often find roads, towns, cemeteries, and waterways are named after nearby landowners: sometimes those names will be the ones you are researching. See how many of these research gems you can find here in Hale County.

Legend

————	Section Lines
⊢⊢⊢⊢⊢	Railroads
▭	Large Rivers & Bodies of Water
- - - - - -	Streams/Creeks & Small Rivers
●	Cities/Towns
✝	Cemeteries

Scale: Section = 1 mile X 1 mile
(there are some exceptions)

199

Map Group 17: Index to Land Patents

Township 20-North Range 5-East (St Stephens)

After you locate an individual in this Index, take note of the Section and Section Part then proceed to the Land Patent map on the pages immediately following. You should have no difficulty locating the corresponding parcel of land.

The "For More Info" Column will lead you to more information about the underlying Patents. See the *Legend* at right, and the "How to Use this Book" chapter, for more information.

ID	Individual in Patent	Sec.	Sec. Part	Date Issued	Other Counties	For More Info ...
3163	BELL, Will	2	NE	1823-10-01		A1
3164	BELL, William	34	E½NW	1831-12-01		A1
3165	" "	34	E½SW	1831-12-01		A1
3154	BENNETT, Stephen	8	E½NE	1823-10-01		A1
3155	" "	9	W½NW	1823-10-01		A1
3103	BRANTLEY, James	4	SENW	1834-08-12		A1
3104	" "	4	SWNE	1834-08-12		A1
3102	" "	4	N½NE	1837-03-30		A1
3105	BRANTLY, James	4	NENW	1835-09-28		A1
3126	CARTER, John	5	SENW	1835-09-22		A1
3127	" "	5	SWNE	1835-09-22		A1
3095	CHAMBERS, Elizabeth	3	E½NW	1835-09-28		A1
3096	" "	3	NWNW	1835-09-28		A1
3158	CHILDS, Thomas	35	E½SE	1825-04-04		A1 G52
3159	" "	35	W½SE	1825-04-04		A1 G52
3149	DICKENS, Robert	11	W½NE	1837-03-30		A1
3150	" "	13	E½NW	1837-03-30		A1 R3140
3151	" "	13	E½SW	1837-03-30		A1
3152	" "	13	W½NE	1837-03-30		A1
3089	EDDINS, Daniel	3	W½SW	1831-12-01		A1
3088	" "	3	E½SW	1835-09-28		A1
3137	GRIGGS, John W	12	SE	1823-10-01		A1
3138	" "	13	E½NE	1823-10-01		A1
3074	HUTCHINS, Anthony T	10	W½NE	1823-10-01		A1
3075	" "	11	E½NE	1823-10-01		A1
3076	" "	11	E½SW	1823-10-01		A1
3077	" "	11	SE	1823-10-01		A1
3078	" "	11	W½SW	1823-10-01		A1
3079	" "	12	NE	1823-10-01		A1
3080	" "	12	SW	1823-10-01		A1
3081	" "	12	W½NW	1823-10-01		A1
3083	" "	31	SW	1823-10-01		A1
3084	" "	9	E½NW	1823-10-01		A1
3085	" "	9	W½NE	1823-10-01		A1
3082	" "	2	NW	1825-04-16		A1
3106	HUTCHINS, James L	10	E½SW	1823-10-01		A1
3107	" "	10	SE	1823-10-01		A1
3108	" "	14	W½NW	1823-10-01		A1
3112	" "	3	W½SE	1823-10-01		A1
3113	" "	4	SE	1823-10-01		A1
3114	" "	9	E½NE	1823-10-01		A1
3110	" "	3	E½SE	1835-09-25		A1
3111	" "	3	SWNE	1835-09-25		A1
3109	" "	2	W½SW	1837-03-30		A1
3162	HUTCHINS, Washington P	2	E½SW	1832-09-10		A1
3145	JOHNSON, Miles	8	E½NW	1825-04-02		A1

ID	Individual in Patent	Sec.	Sec. Part	Date Issued	Other Counties	For More Info . . .
3146	JOHNSON, Miles (Cont'd)	8	W½NW	1825-04-02		A1
3141	LAKE, Justus	25	E½NW	1825-04-04		A1
3128	MARRAST, John	20	E½SW	1825-04-04		A1
3166	MARTIN, William	6	E½NE	1823-10-01		A1
3167	" "	6	W½NE	1826-05-01		A1
3129	MAY, John	30	E½SE	1823-10-01		A1
3130	" "	30	W½SE	1823-10-01		A1
3160	MAYFIELD, Thomas	10	W½SW	1823-10-01		A1
3116	MCCARTER, James	6	E½SW	1821-12-03		A1
3115	" "	6	E½NW	1823-10-01		A1
3117	" "	6	W½NW	1823-10-01		A1
3118	" "	6	W½SW	1823-10-01		A1
3142	MURFF, Levi	1	W½NE	1828-04-10		A1
3153	MURFF, Samuel	1	E½NE	1826-05-05		A1
3140	NICHOLSON, Joseph W	13	E½NE	1860-07-02		A1 R3150
3098	PECK, Frederick	5	E½NE	1835-09-22		A1
3100	PICKENS, Israel	32	E½NE	1825-04-04		A1
3101	" "	32	W½NE	1825-04-04		A1
3099	PURDOM, Henry	14	W½NE	1825-06-06		A1
3073	RACKLEY, Anthony	2	SE	1823-10-01		A1
3124	RACKLEY, Jesse	14	E½NW	1823-10-01		A1
3147	RANDOLPH, Robert C	10	E½NE	1835-09-25		A1
3148	" "	11	NW	1835-09-25		A1
3087	RHODES, Bryan	3	NWNE	1835-09-22		A1
3120	SANDERS, Jeremiah	36	W½SW	1821-09-27		A1
3119	" "	36	E½SW	1821-11-07		A1
3158	" "	35	E½SE	1825-04-04		A1 G52
3159	" "	35	W½SE	1825-04-04		A1 G52
3121	SAUNDERS, Jeremiah	14	E½NE	1823-10-01		A1
3122	" "	25	W½NW	1825-04-04		A1
3123	" "	26	E½NE	1831-12-01		A1
3086	SEALE, Bluford	28	W½SE	1831-12-01		A1
3125	SHIVERS, Jesse	18	W½SE	1831-12-01		A1
3093	SIMS, Edward	27	E½NW	1825-04-04		A1
3094	" "	27	W½NW	1825-04-04		A1
3168	SIMS, William	1	W½NW	1821-12-03		A1
3097	SPEED, Elizabeth	4	W½NW	1825-04-16		A1
3143	STEPHENS, Lewis	33	E½SE	1829-07-06		A1
3144	" "	33	W½SE	1832-08-08		A1
3169	STEPHENS, William	13	W½SW	1832-08-08		A1
3134	STOKES, John	8	SE	1821-09-27		A1
3135	" "	8	W½NE	1823-10-01		A1
3132	" "	3	SWNW	1835-09-22		A1
3133	" "	4	SENE	1835-09-22		A1
3156	STONE, Thomas B	5	NENW	1835-09-25		A1
3157	" "	5	NWNE	1835-09-25		A1
3161	THURMOND, Thomas	13	SE	1834-09-04		A1
3136	TIDMORE, John	34	W½SW	1831-12-01		A1
3092	TURNER, David	4	W½SW	1825-04-22		A1
3091	" "	4	SESW	1835-09-12		A1
3090	" "	4	NESW	1835-09-22		A1
3139	WISDOM, John	12	E½NW	1821-12-03		A1
3131	WITHERSPOON, John R	1	E½NW	1835-09-25		A1

Patent Map

T20-N R5-E
St Stephens Meridian

Map Group 17

Township Statistics

Parcels Mapped	:	97
Number of Patents	:	97
Number of Individuals	:	47
Patentees Identified	:	47
Number of Surnames	:	40
Multi-Patentee Parcels	:	2
Oldest Patent Date	:	9/27/1821
Most Recent Patent	:	7/2/1860
Block/Lot Parcels	:	0
Parcels Re-Issued	:	1
Parcels that Overlap	:	0
Cities and Towns	:	1
Cemeteries	:	16

6

MCCARTER James 1823
MCCARTER James 1823
MARTIN William 1826
MARTIN William 1823
MCCARTER James 1823
MCCARTER James 1821

5

STONE Thomas B 1835
STONE Thomas B 1835
PECK Frederick 1835
CARTER John 1835
CARTER John 1835

4

SPEED Elizabeth 1825
BRANTLY James 1835
BRANTLEY James 1837
BRANTLEY James 1834
BRANTLEY James 1834
STOKES John 1835
TURNER David 1825
TURNER David 1835
TURNER David 1835
HUTCHINS James L 1823

7

8

JOHNSON Miles 1825
JOHNSON Miles 1825
STOKES John 1823
BENNETT Stephen 1823
STOKES John 1821

9

BENNETT Stephen 1823
HUTCHINS Anthony T 1823
HUTCHINS Anthony T 1823
HUTCHINS James L 1823

18 SHIVERS Jesse 1831

17

16

19

20 MARRAST John 1825

21

30 MAY John 1823 / MAY John 1823

29

28 SEALE Bluford 1831

31 HUTCHINS Anthony T 1823

32 PICKENS Israel 1825 / PICKENS Israel 1825

33 STEPHENS Lewis 1832 / STEPHENS Lewis 1829

CHAMBERS Elizabeth 1835	CHAMBERS Elizabeth 1835	RHODES Bryan 1835		HUTCHINS Anthony T 1825	BELL Will 1823	SIMS William 1821	WITHERSPOON John R 1835	MURFF Levi 1828	MURFF Samuel 1826

3

2

STOKES John 1835

HUTCHINS James L 1835

EDDINS Daniel 1831

EDDINS Daniel 1835

HUTCHINS James L 1823

HUTCHINS James L 1835

HUTCHINS James L 1837

HUTCHINS Washington P 1832

RACKLEY Anthony 1823

1

HUTCHINS Anthony T 1823

RANDOLPH Robert C 1835

10

RANDOLPH Robert C 1835

DICKENS Robert 1837

HUTCHINS Anthony T 1823

HUTCHINS Anthony T 1823

WISDOM John 1821

HUTCHINS Anthony T 1823

11

12

MAYFIELD Thomas 1823

HUTCHINS James L 1823

HUTCHINS James L 1823

HUTCHINS Anthony T 1823

HUTCHINS Anthony T 1823

HUTCHINS Anthony T 1823

HUTCHINS Anthony T 1823

GRIGGS John W 1823

15

HUTCHINS James L 1823

RACKLEY Jesse 1823

PURDOM Henry 1825

SAUNDERS Jeremiah 1823

NICHOLSON Joseph W 1860

DICKENS Robert 1837

GRIGGS John W 1823

14

DICKENS Robert 1837

13

STEPHENS William 1832

DICKENS Robert 1837

THURMOND Thomas 1834

22

23

24

SIMS Edward 1825

27

SIMS Edward 1825

SAUNDERS Jeremiah 1831

SAUNDERS Jeremiah 1825

LAKE Justus 1825

26

25

BELL William 1831

34

35

36

TIDMORE John 1831

BELL William 1831

CHILDS [52] Thomas 1825

CHILDS [52] Thomas 1825

SANDERS Jeremiah 1821

SANDERS Jeremiah 1821

Helpful Hints

1. This Map's INDEX can be found on the preceding pages.

2. Refer to Map "C" to see where this Township lies within Hale County, Alabama.

3. Numbers within square brackets [ ] denote a multi-patentee land parcel (multi-owner). Refer to Appendix "C" for a full list of members in this group.

4. Areas that look to be crowded with Patentees usually indicate multiple sales of the same parcel (Re-issues) or Overlapping parcels. See this Township's Index for an explanation of these and other circumstances that might explain "odd" groupings of Patentees on this map.

Legend

——— Patent Boundary

━━━ Section Boundary

No Patents Found (or Outside County)

1., 2., 3., ... Lot Numbers (when beside a name)

[ ] Group Number (see Appendix "C")

Scale: Section = 1 mile X 1 mile (generally, with some exceptions)

Road Map

T20-N R5-E
St Stephens Meridian

Map Group 17

Cities & Towns
Greensboro

Cemeteries
Burton Cemetery
Greenleaf Cemetery
Greensboro Cemetery
Hill Place Cemetery
Jenkins Place Cemetery
Jerusalem Cemetery
May Cemetery
McCoy Cemetery
Oakwood Cemetery
Pine Grove Cemetery
Pleasant Grove Cemetery
Redick Cemetery
Saint Marys Cemetery
Stokes Cemetery
Union Grove Cemetery
Weaver Cemetery

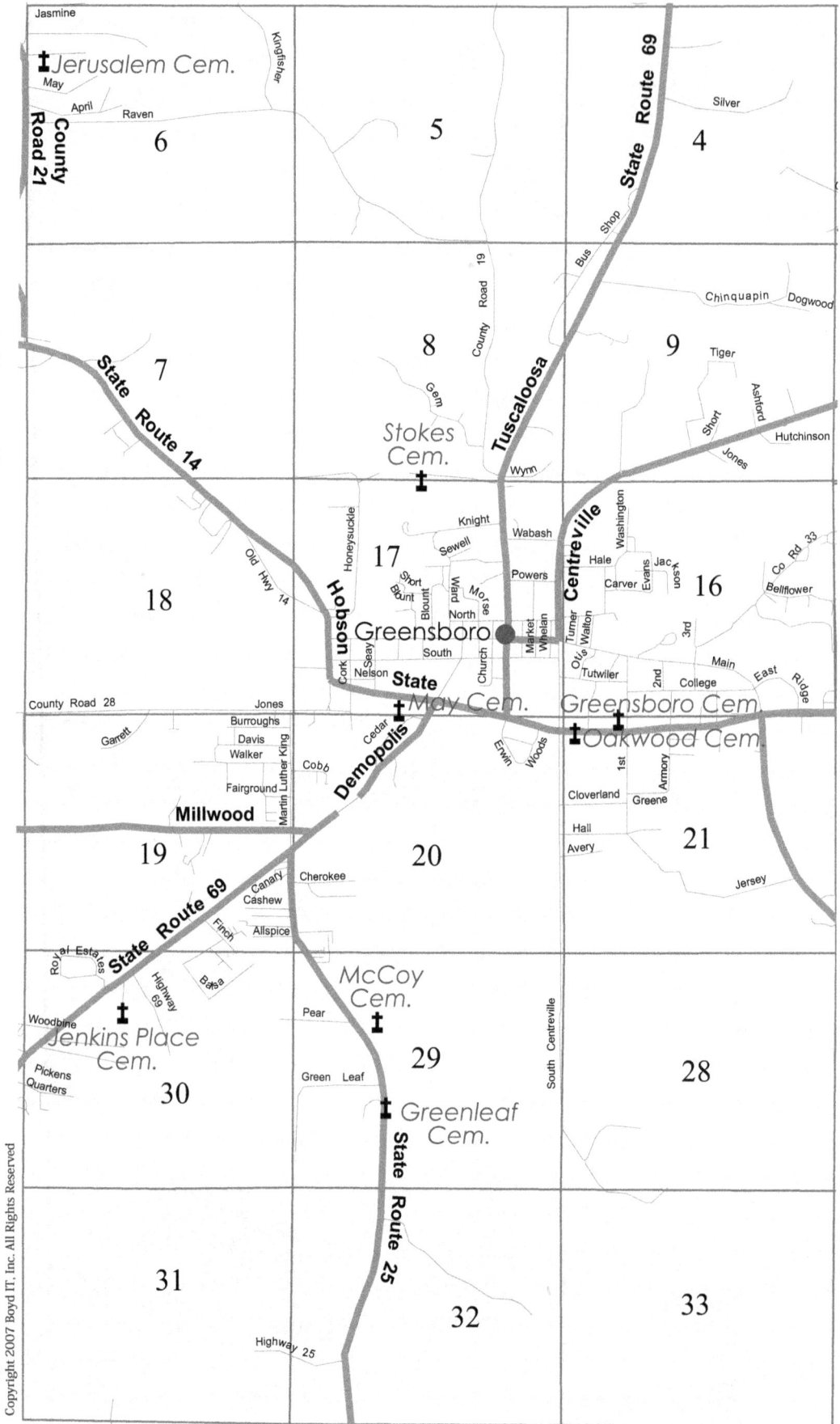

Jasmine

Jerusalem Cem.

May
April
Raven
Kingfisher

County Road 21

6

5

State Route 69
Silver

Chinquapin Dogwood

State Route 14

7

County Road 19

8

Tuscaloosa

9

Tiger
Ashford
Short
Jones
Hutchinson

Gem

Stokes Cem.

Wynn

Honeysuckle

Knight
Wabash

Centreville
Washington
Hale
Jackson
Evans
Carver

17
Sewell
Short
Blount
Ward
Morse
North
Powers

16
Co Rd 33
Bellflower

Old Hwy 14

18

Hobson

Greensboro

South
Church
Seay
Nelson

Market
Whelan
Otis Walton
Turner
Tutwiler

3rd
2nd
Main
College
East Ridge

State

May Cem.

Greensboro Cem

County Road 28
Jones
Burroughs

Demopolis
Cedar
Cobb
Erwin
Woods

Oakwood Cem.

Garrett
Davis
Walker
Martin Luther King
Fairground

Cloverland
Greene
Hall
Avery

1st
Armory

Millwood

19

State Route 69

Cherokee

20

21
Jersey

Canary
Cashew
Finch
Allspice

Royal Estates
Highway 69
Balsa

McCoy Cem.
Pear

South Centreville

Woodbine

Jenkins Place Cem.

Pickens Quarters

30

Green Leaf

29

Greenleaf Cem.

State Route 25

28

31

Highway 25

32

33

204

Shelton

County Road 51

County Road 7

Redick Cem. ✝ Oakwood

Lynns

Shiloh

3

2

1

Lakewood Farm

Marchant

Castlewood

Shady

State Route 25

10

11

12

Burton Cem. ✝

Union Grove

Swift

Union Grove Cem. ✝

County Road 7

15

14

13

Orchid

Robert Burroughs

Beverly

State Route 14

Pleasant Grove Cem. ✝

22

23

24

Stringfellow

Persimmon

Highway 7

Apple

25

State Route 61

Daisy

27

Willow

County

26

✝ Pine Grove Cem.

Hill Place Cem.

Bobwhite

Saint Marys Cem. ✝

Weaver ✝ Cem.

36

Rosemary

34

Horseshoe Bend

35

Marion

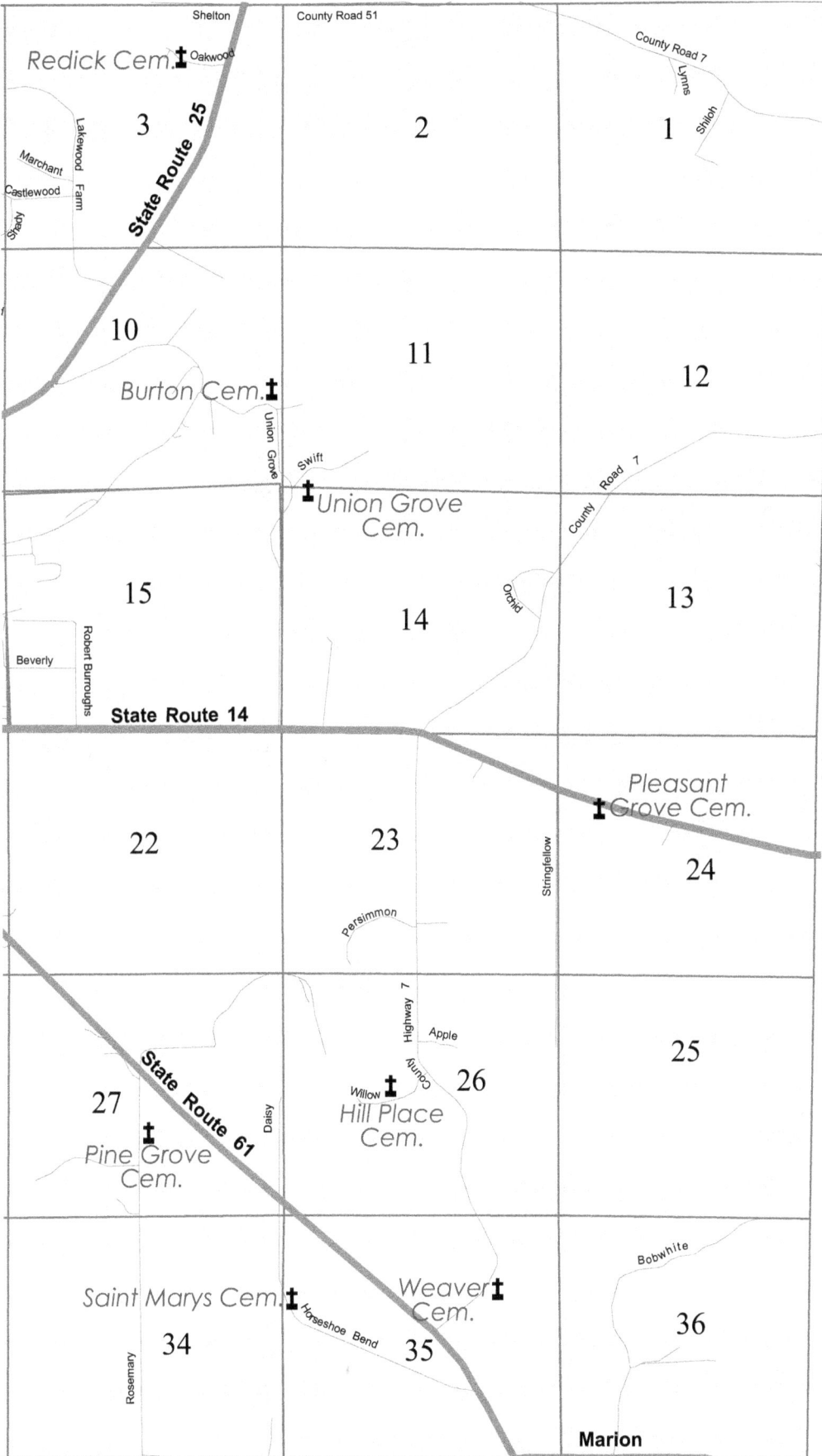

Helpful Hints

1. This road map has a number of uses, but primarily it is to help you: a) find the present location of land owned by your ancestors (at least the general area), b) find cemeteries and city-centers, and c) estimate the route/roads used by Census-takers & tax-assessors.

2. If you plan to travel to Hale County to locate cemeteries or land parcels, please pick up a modern travel map for the area before you do. Mapping old land parcels on modern maps is not as exact a science as you might think. Just the slightest variations in public land survey coordinates, estimates of parcel boundaries, or road-map deviations can greatly alter a map's representation of how a road either does or doesn't cross a particular parcel of land.

Legend

— Section Lines

≡ Interstates

— Highways

— Other Roads

● Cities/Towns

✝ Cemeteries

Scale: Section = 1 mile X 1 mile
(generally, with some exceptions)

Historical Map

T20-N R5-E
St Stephens Meridian

Map Group 17

Cities & Towns
Greensboro

Cemeteries
Burton Cemetery
Greenleaf Cemetery
Greensboro Cemetery
Hill Place Cemetery
Jenkins Place Cemetery
Jerusalem Cemetery
May Cemetery
McCoy Cemetery
Oakwood Cemetery
Pine Grove Cemetery
Pleasant Grove Cemetery
Redick Cemetery
Saint Marys Cemetery
Stokes Cemetery
Union Grove Cemetery
Weaver Cemetery

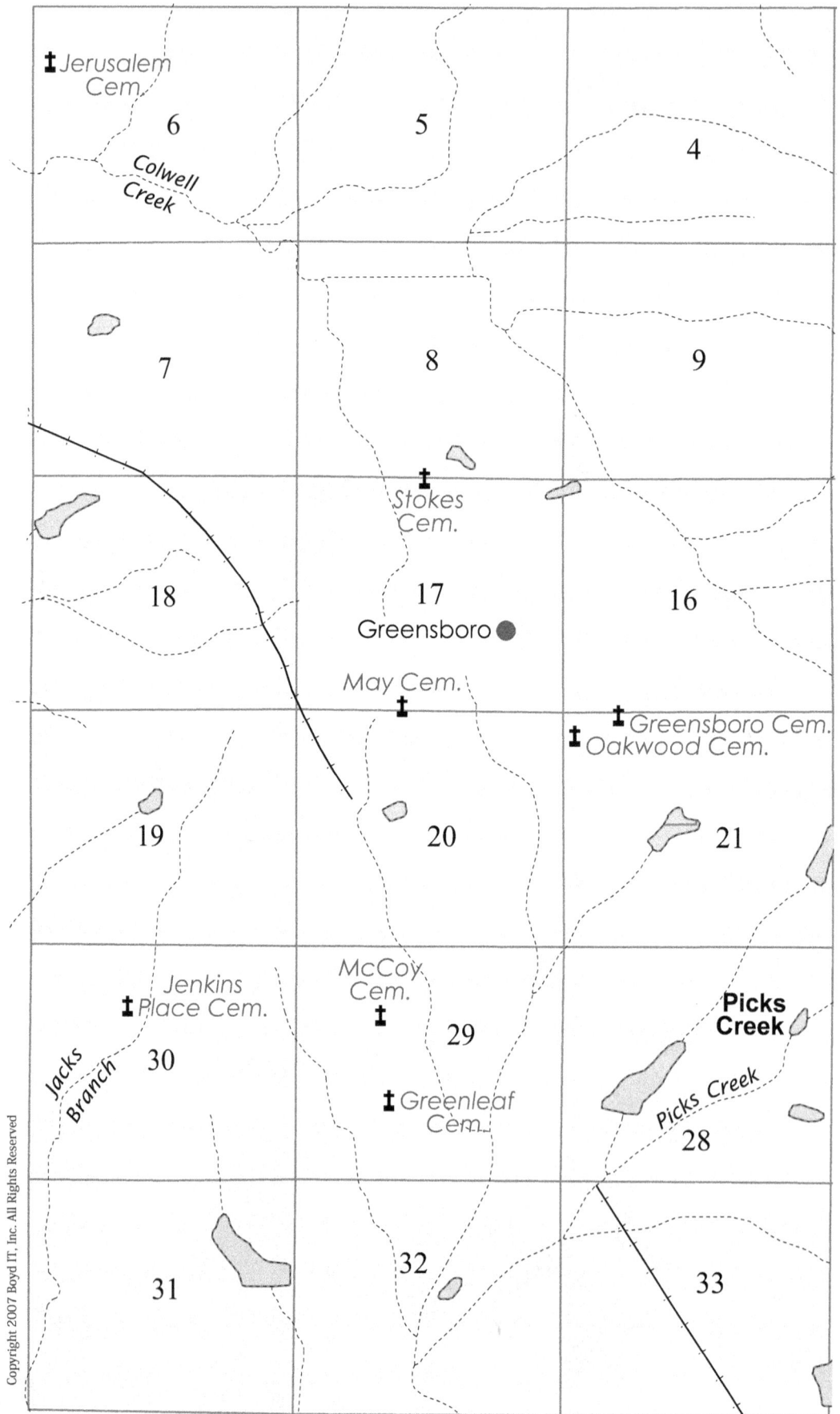

‡ Jerusalem Cem.

Colwell Creek

6

5

4

7

8

9

‡ Stokes Cem.

18

17

Greensboro ●

16

May Cem.
‡

‡ Greensboro Cem.
‡ Oakwood Cem.

19

20

21

Jenkins Place Cem. ‡

McCoy Cem.
‡

Picks Creek

30

29

28

Jacks Branch

‡ Greenleaf Cem.

Picks Creek

31

32

33

✝
Redick
Cem.

3

2

Big Brush
Creek

1

Polecat
Creek

10

Burton ✝
Cem.

11

12

✝
Union Grove
Cem.

15

14

13

22

23

Pleasant
✝ *Grove Cem.*

Whitsitt
Creek   24

27

Hill
Place Cem.
✝
26

25

✝
Pine Grove
Cem.

Weaver
Cem.

✝ *Saint Marys*
Cem.

✝

35

34

Whitsitt
Creek

36

Helpful Hints

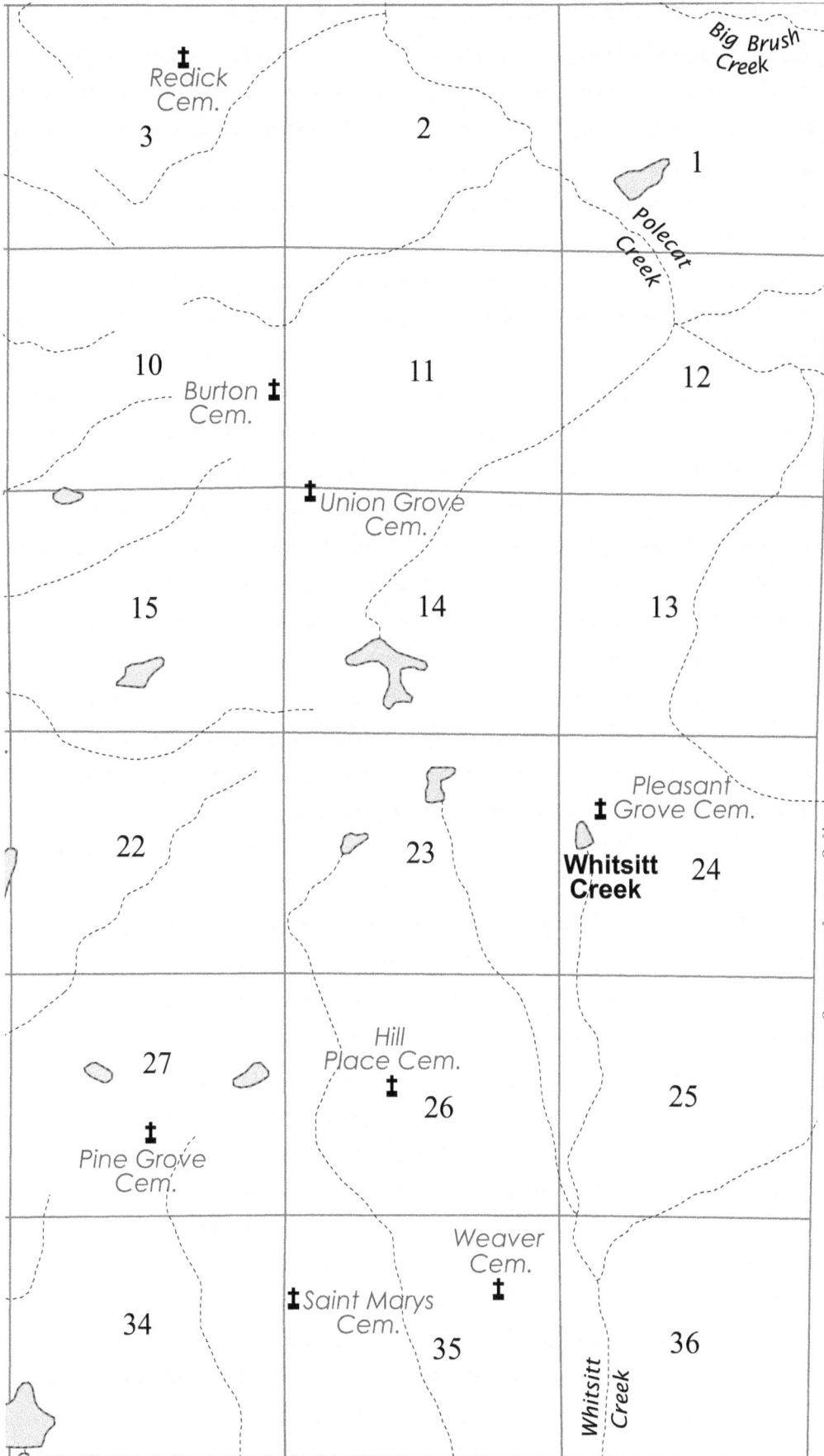

1. This Map takes a different look at the same Congressional Township displayed in the preceding two maps. It presents features that can help you better envision the historical development of the area: a) Water-bodies (lakes & ponds), b) Water-courses (rivers, streams, etc.), c) Railroads, d) City/town center-points (where they were oftentimes located when first settled), and e) Cemeteries.

2. Using this "Historical" map in tandem with this Township's Patent Map and Road Map, may lead you to some interesting discoveries. You will often find roads, towns, cemeteries, and waterways are named after nearby landowners: sometimes those names will be the ones you are researching. See how many of these research gems you can find here in Hale County.

Legend

———————— Section Lines

+–+–+–+–+ Railroads

Large Rivers &
Bodies of Water

------------- Streams/Creeks
& Small Rivers

● Cities/Towns

✝ Cemeteries

Scale: Section = 1 mile X 1 mile
(there are some exceptions)

207

Map Group 18: Index to Land Patents

Township 20-North Range 6-East (St Stephens)

After you locate an individual in this Index, take note of the Section and Section Part then proceed to the Land Patent map on the pages immediately following. You should have no difficulty locating the corresponding parcel of land.

The "For More Info" Column will lead you to more information about the underlying Patents. See the *Legend* at right, and the "How to Use this Book" chapter, for more information.

```
                        LEGEND
              "For More Info . . . " column
A = Authority (Legislative Act, See Appendix "A")
B = Block or Lot (location in Section unknown)
C = Cancelled Patent
F = Fractional Section
G = Group  (Multi-Patentee Patent, see Appendix "C")
V = Overlaps another Parcel
R = Re-Issued (Parcel patented more than once)

(A & G items require you to look in the Appendixes referred
to above. All other Letter-designations followed by a number
require you to locate line-items in this index that possess
the ID number found after the letter).
```

ID	Individual in Patent	Sec.	Sec. Part	Date Issued	Other Counties	For More Info . . .
3257	ALLEN, Samuel	6	SESW	1835-09-12		A1 G2
3256	" "	6	SWSE	1835-10-01		A1
3255	" "	6	NWSE	1849-09-01		A1
3261	ALLEN, Thomas	8	NENE	1837-04-15		A1
3262	ASH, Thomas	4	NE	1822-01-01		A1 V3177
3174	AVERY, Allen	5	N½NE	1837-08-12		A1
3177	AVERY, Bryan	4	S½NE	1835-04-02		A1 V3262
3178	" "	5	N½SW	1845-07-01		A1
3179	" "	6	SESE	1845-07-01		A1
3180	" "	8	NWNW	1845-07-01		A1
3189	AVERY, David	9	NENE	1847-05-01		A1
3188	" "	4	NESE	1849-09-01		A1
3268	BELL, William	6	W½SW	1823-10-01		A1
3269	" "	7	NW	1823-10-01		A1
3221	BLACKBURN, James L	4	E½NW	1837-08-08		A1
3276	BOHANNAN, Young	31	W½NE	1827-04-09		A1
3259	BRILEY, Shadrach	18	E½NW	1826-05-01		A1
3190	CADE, Drury B	32	W½SW	1825-04-04		A1
3219	CHAMBERS, James B	32	E½NW	1825-04-04		A1 G40
3220	" "	32	W½NW	1825-04-04		A1 G40
3206	CHATHAM, George K	8	SWSE	1835-10-01		A1
3243	CHRISTOPHER, R G	32	E½SW	1825-04-04		A1 G53
3244	" "	32	E½SE	1825-04-08		A1 G54
3250	COPELAND, Robert	21	E½NW	1831-08-01		A1
3200	COUSINS, Edward G	17	E½NE	1823-10-01		A1
3251	CRAIG, Robert G	28	E½SE	1831-12-01		A1
3253	" "	33	E½NE	1831-12-01		A1
3252	" "	28	E½SW	1835-09-19		A1
3212	CURRY, Jabez	28	E½NW	1831-08-01		A1
3209	" "	17	S½	1835-10-08		A1
3210	" "	20	E½NW	1835-10-08		A1
3211	" "	20	NE	1835-10-08		A1
3249	DAVIS, Richard	18	E½SE	1831-05-17		A1
3175	FOLLEY, Asa	17	W½NE	1826-05-08		A1
3215	FRAZIER, Jacob	8	SENW	1835-04-08		A1
3214	" "	5	NESE	1837-04-10		A1
3213	" "	4	NWSW	1838-07-28		A1
3226	FRAZIER, John	9	NENW	1837-04-10		A1
3227	" "	9	SENE	1840-10-10		A1
3239	GAGE, Mathew	28	W½NW	1825-04-04		A1 G89
3240	GAGE, Matthew	18	E½SW	1825-06-06		A1
3241	" "	18	W½SE	1827-12-10		A1
3242	" "	18	W½SW	1827-12-10		A1
3184	GRIFFIN, Claiborne	31	E½NE	1825-04-04		A1
3270	GRIFFIN, William	9	NWNE	1848-05-03		A1
3201	HARPER, Edward	33	E½NW	1823-10-01		A1

ID	Individual in Patent	Sec.	Sec. Part	Date Issued	Other Counties	For More Info . . .
3204	HARPER, Edward (Cont'd)	33	SW	1825-04-04		A1
3202	" "	33	E½SE	1834-10-21		A1
3205	" "	33	SWNW	1835-10-08		A1
3203	" "	33	NWNW	1837-05-15		A1
3264	HARPER, Wilkens	9	SENW	1837-08-01		A1
3265	" "	9	SWNE	1837-08-01		A1
3266	HARPER, Wilkins	9	SWSW	1834-10-21		A1
3267	" "	9	W½SE	1837-08-01		A1 F
3170	HOLLINGSWORTH, Abraham	5	SESE	1837-08-10		A1
3192	HOPSON, Edmund	20	E½SE	1825-04-04		A1
3196	" "	21	W½SW	1825-04-04		A1
3194	" "	20	W½SE	1826-05-01		A1
3195	" "	21	W½NW	1831-08-01		A1
3193	" "	20	W½NW	1834-01-21		A1
3239	JAMISON, Robert	28	W½NW	1825-04-04		A1 G89
3230	JOHNSON, Joseph	28	NWSW	1835-10-08		A1
3231	" "	28	SWSW	1835-11-20		A1
3208	KEITH, Gilbert R	4	SESW	1837-08-15		A1
3207	KENNARD, George W	8	W½SW	1826-05-05		A1
3260	LOW, Sherwood	17	E½NW	1826-05-05		A1
3228	MARRAST, John	21	W½NE	1827-01-01		A1
3222	MARS, James	9	E½SW	1826-05-12		A1
3263	MAYFIELD, Thomas	21	E½SW	1826-05-01		A1
3272	MCKEE, William	5	NWSE	1838-07-28		A1
3171	MOODY, Alex	7	W½SW	1823-10-01		A1 G202
3173	MOODY, Alexander	18	W½NW	1826-05-01		A1 G203
3172	" "	17	W½NW	1826-05-05		A1 G203
3171	MOODY, Martin	7	W½SW	1823-10-01		A1 G202
3173	" "	18	W½NW	1826-05-01		A1 G203
3172	" "	17	W½NW	1826-05-05		A1 G203
3237	" "	18	W½NE	1835-10-14		A1
3238	" "	8	E½SE	1835-10-16		A1
3181	MURFF, Charles	5	SWSE	1837-08-08		A1
3182	" "	8	NENW	1837-08-08		A1
3183	" "	9	NWNW	1837-08-08		A1
3185	MURFF, Daniel	7	E½SE	1831-12-01		A1
3187	" "	7	W½SE	1831-12-01		A1
3186	" "	7	S½NE	1835-04-08		A1
3216	MURFF, Jacob	8	SWNW	1837-04-10		A1
3225	MURFF, Jeremiah	8	NWNE	1837-08-01		A1
3224	" "	4	SWSW	1837-08-12		A1
3273	NERTZ, William	8	E½SW	1835-04-08		A1
3229	PAGE, John	18	E½NE	1833-06-04		A1
3191	PECK, E	21	E½NE	1826-05-05		A1 G209
3191	PECK, F	21	E½NE	1826-05-05		A1 G209
3197	POWERS, Edmund	8	NWSE	1835-10-01		A1
3199	" "	8	SWNE	1837-04-10		A1
3198	" "	8	SENE	1837-08-01		A1
3223	REED, James	9	NESE	1837-08-15		A1
3235	REED, Lewis W	28	E½NE	1832-09-10		A1
3236	" "	9	SESE	1837-08-01		A1
3176	REYNOLDS, Benjamin	4	W½NW	1823-10-01		A1
3271	RHODES, William K	6	NESE	1847-05-01		A1
3219	SANDERS, Jeremiah	32	E½NW	1825-04-04		A1 G40
3220	" "	32	W½NW	1825-04-04		A1 G40
3247	SHACKLEFORD, Richard D	6	E½NE	1821-12-03		A1
3248	" "	6	W½NE	1823-10-01		A1
3243	SIMS, Edward	32	E½SW	1825-04-04		A1 G53
3254	SPEED, Robert	7	E½SW	1830-11-16		A1
3274	STOKES, William W	4	NESW	1837-08-12		A1
3275	" "	4	NWSE	1837-08-12		A1
3258	STRADWICK, Samuel	5	NW	1822-01-01		A1
3217	SUMMEY, Jacob	6	E½NW	1823-10-01		A1
3218	SUMMY, Jacob	6	W½NW	1823-10-01		A1
3232	THIGPEN, Joseph	5	S½SW	1834-08-12		A1
3257	THIGPEN, Joshua	6	SESW	1835-09-12		A1 G2
3233	" "	6	NESW	1835-10-01		A1
3234	" "	7	N½NE	1835-10-01		A1
3244	WALTHALL, R B	32	E½SE	1825-04-08		A1 G54
3245	WALTHALL, Richard B	9	NWSW	1837-08-09		A1
3246	" "	9	SWNW	1837-08-09		A1

Patent Map

T20-N R6-E
St Stephens Meridian

Map Group 18

Township Statistics

Parcels Mapped	:	107
Number of Patents	:	104
Number of Individuals	:	68
Patentees Identified	:	65
Number of Surnames	:	51
Multi-Patentee Parcels	:	10
Oldest Patent Date	:	12/3/1821
Most Recent Patent	:	9/1/1849
Block/Lot Parcels	:	0
Parcels Re - Issued	:	0
Parcels that Overlap	:	2
Cities and Towns	:	0
Cemeteries	:	0

Note: the area contained in this map amounts to far less than a full Township. Therefore, its contents are completely on this single page (instead of a "normal" 2-page spread).

Legend

Patent Boundary

Section Boundary

No Patents Found
(or Outside County)

1., 2., 3., ... Lot Numbers
(when beside a name)

[ ] Group Number
(see Appendix "C")

Scale: Section = 1 mile X 1 mile
(generally, with some exceptions)

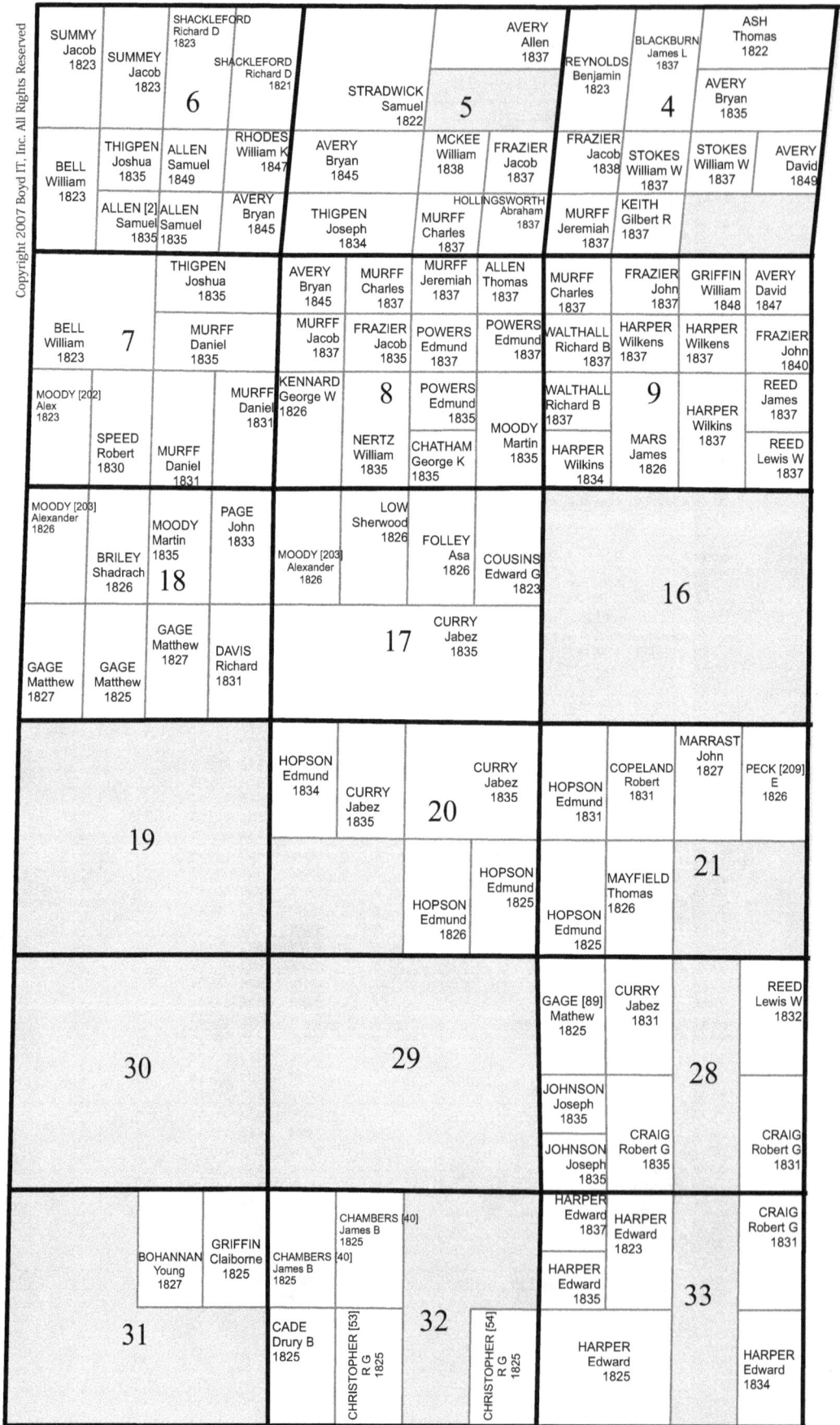

Section 6
SUMMY Jacob 1823
SUMMEY Jacob 1823
SHACKLEFORD Richard D 1823
SHACKLEFORD Richard D 1821
BELL William 1823
THIGPEN Joshua 1835
ALLEN Samuel 1849
RHODES William K 1847
ALLEN [2] Samuel 1835
ALLEN Samuel 1835
AVERY Bryan 1845

Section 5
STRADWICK Samuel 1822
AVERY Allen 1837
AVERY Bryan 1845
MCKEE William 1838
FRAZIER Jacob 1837
THIGPEN Joseph 1834
MURFF Charles 1837
HOLLINGSWORTH Abraham 1837

Section 4
REYNOLDS Benjamin 1823
BLACKBURN James L 1837
ASH Thomas 1822
AVERY Bryan 1835
FRAZIER Jacob 1838
STOKES William W 1837
STOKES William W 1837
AVERY David 1849
MURFF Jeremiah 1837
KEITH Gilbert R 1837

Section 7
BELL William 1823
THIGPEN Joshua 1835
MURFF Daniel 1835
MOODY [202] Alex 1823
SPEED Robert 1830
MURFF Daniel 1831
MURFF Daniel 1831

Section 8
AVERY Bryan 1845
MURFF Charles 1837
MURFF Jeremiah 1837
ALLEN Thomas 1837
MURFF Jacob 1837
FRAZIER Jacob 1835
POWERS Edmund 1837
POWERS Edmund 1837
KENNARD George W 1826
POWERS Edmund 1835
NERTZ William 1835
CHATHAM George K 1835
MOODY Martin 1835

Section 9
MURFF Charles 1837
FRAZIER John 1837
GRIFFIN William 1848
AVERY David 1847
WALTHALL Richard B 1837
HARPER Wilkens 1837
HARPER Wilkens 1837
FRAZIER John 1840
WALTHALL Richard B 1837
HARPER Wilkins 1837
REED James 1837
HARPER Wilkins 1834
MARS James 1826
REED Lewis W 1837

Section 18
MOODY [203] Alexander 1826
BRILEY Shadrach 1826
MOODY Martin 1835
PAGE John 1833
GAGE Matthew 1827
GAGE Matthew 1825
GAGE Matthew 1827
DAVIS Richard 1831

Section 17
MOODY [203] Alexander 1826
LOW Sherwood 1826
FOLLEY Asa 1826
COUSINS Edward G 1823
CURRY Jabez 1835

Section 16

Section 19

Section 20
HOPSON Edmund 1834
CURRY Jabez 1835
CURRY Jabez 1835
HOPSON Edmund 1826
HOPSON Edmund 1825

Section 21
HOPSON Edmund 1831
COPELAND Robert 1831
MARRAST John 1827
PECK [209] E 1826
MAYFIELD Thomas 1826
HOPSON Edmund 1825

Section 30

Section 29
GAGE [89] Mathew 1825
CURRY Jabez 1831
JOHNSON Joseph 1835
JOHNSON Joseph 1835
CRAIG Robert G 1835

Section 28
REED Lewis W 1832
CRAIG Robert G 1831

Section 31
BOHANNAN Young 1827
GRIFFIN Claiborne 1825

Section 32
CHAMBERS [40] James B 1825
CHAMBERS [40] James B 1825
CADE Drury B 1825
CHRISTOPHER [53] R G 1825
CHRISTOPHER [54] R G 1825

Section 33
HARPER Edward 1837
HARPER Edward 1823
HARPER Edward 1835
HARPER Edward 1825
CRAIG Robert G 1831
HARPER Edward 1834

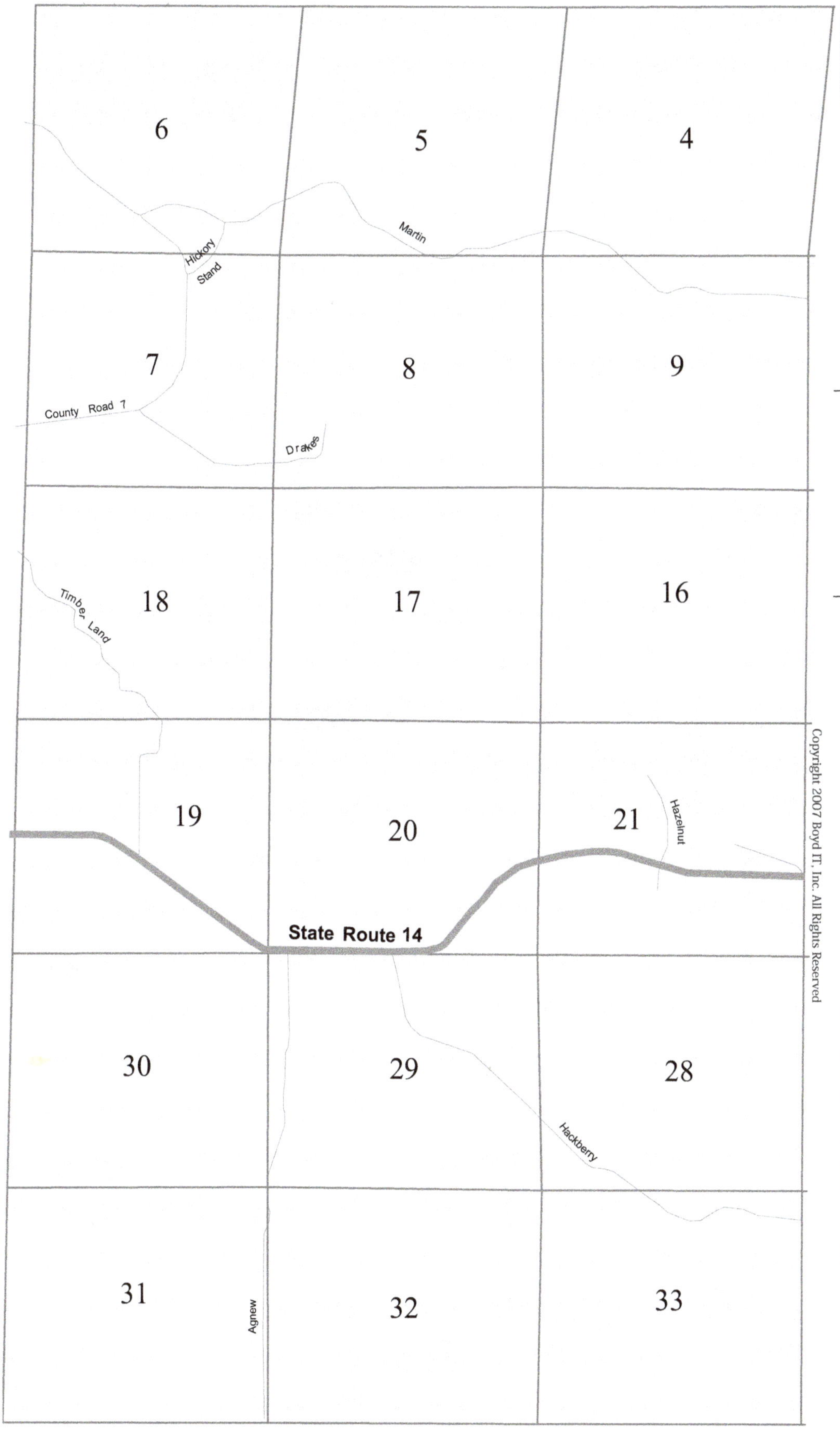
6
5
4
Hickory Stand
Martin
7
8
9
County Road 7
Drakes
18
17
16
Timber Land
19
20
21
Hazelnut
State Route 14
30
29
28
Hackberry
31
32
33
Agnew
Copyright 2007 Boyd IT, Inc. All Rights Reserved

Road Map

T20-N R6-E
St Stephens Meridian

Map Group 18

Note: the area contained in this map amounts to far less than a full Township. Therefore, its contents are completely on this single page (instead of a "normal" 2-page spread).

Cities & Towns

None

Cemeteries

None

Legend

- Section Lines
- Interstates
- Highways
- Other Roads
- Cities/Towns
- Cemeteries

Scale: Section = 1 mile X 1 mile
(generally, with some exceptions)

Historical Map

T20-N R6-E
St Stephens Meridian

Map Group 18

Note: the area contained in this map amounts to far less than a full Township. Therefore, its contents are completely on this single page (instead of a "normal" 2-page spread).

Cities & Towns
None

Cemeteries
None

Big Brush Creek

Brush Creek

6

5

4

7

8

9

18

17

Polecat Creek

16

19

20

21

30

29

28

31

32

33

Legend

————	Section Lines
+++++	Railroads
▬▬▬	Large Rivers & Bodies of Water
- - - - -	Streams/Creeks & Small Rivers
●	Cities/Towns
✝	Cemeteries

Scale: Section = 1 mile X 1 mile
(there are some exceptions)

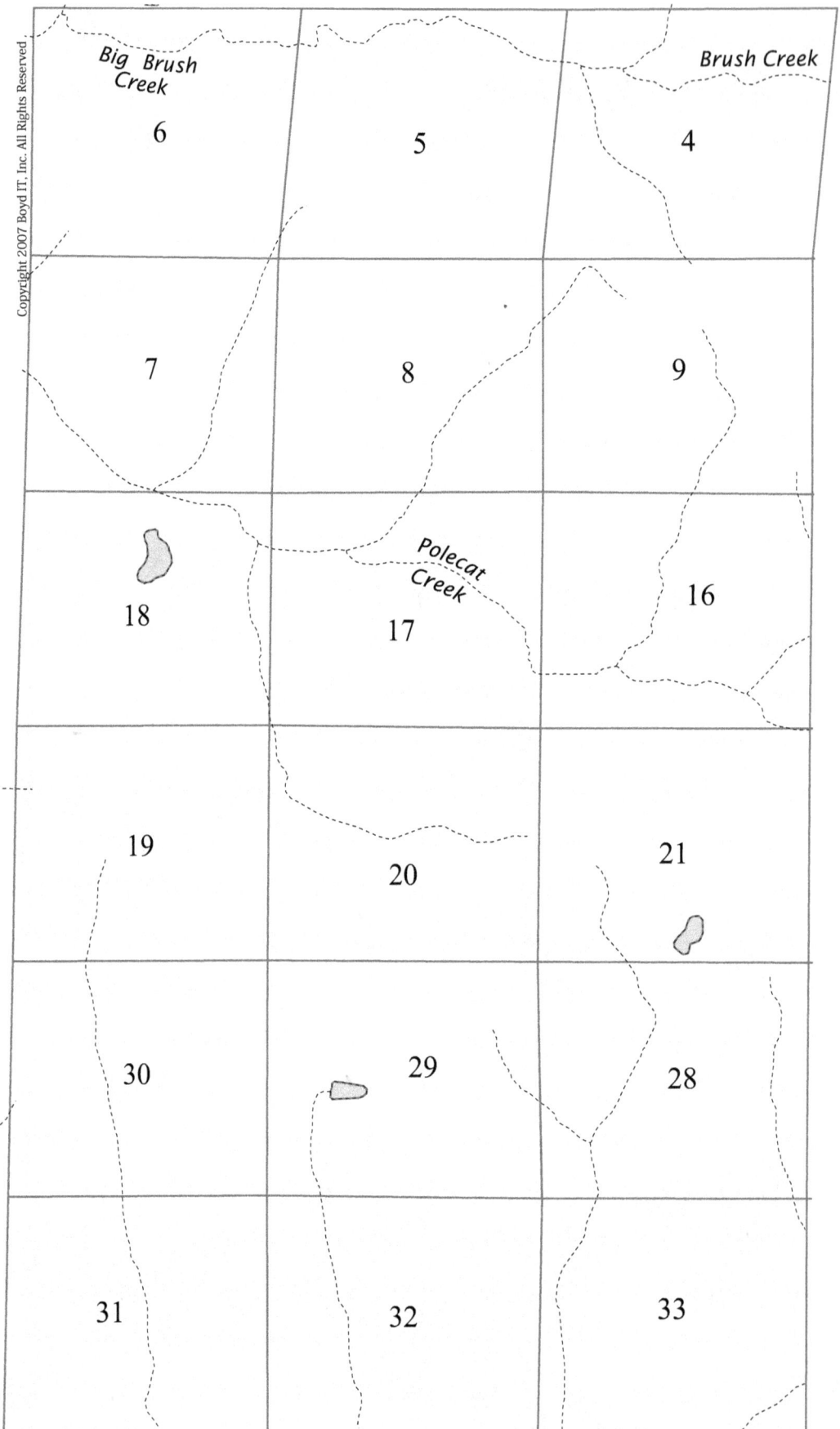

Map Group 19: Index to Land Patents

Township 19-North Range 3-East (St Stephens)

After you locate an individual in this Index, take note of the Section and Section Part then proceed to the Land Patent map on the pages immediately following. You should have no difficulty locating the corresponding parcel of land.

The "For More Info" Column will lead you to more information about the underlying Patents. See the *Legend* at right, and the "How to Use this Book" chapter, for more information.

```
                    LEGEND
           "For More Info . . . " column
A = Authority (Legislative Act, See Appendix "A")
B = Block or Lot (location in Section unknown)
C = Cancelled Patent
F = Fractional Section
G = Group  (Multi-Patentee Patent, see Appendix "C")
V = Overlaps another Parcel
R = Re-Issued (Parcel patented more than once)

(A & G items require you to look in the Appendixes referred
to above. All other Letter-designations followed by a number
require you to locate line-items in this index that possess
the ID number found after the letter).
```

ID	Individual in Patent	Sec.	Sec. Part	Date Issued	Other Counties	For More Info . . .
3284	ARRINGTON, Anthony S	20	NWNW	1837-03-20	Greene	A1
3295	ARRINGTON, Elizabeth W	20	NENW	1837-03-15	Greene	A1
3366	ARRINGTON, Nicholas	20	E½SE	1835-09-25	Greene	A1
3368	"	20	SWNW	1835-09-25	Greene	A1
3367	"	20	NWSE	1837-03-15	Greene	A1
3369	"	20	W½SW	1837-03-15	Greene	A1
3370	"	27	N½SW	1837-03-15	Greene	A1 V3333
3337	DABNEY, John M	14	SE	1837-11-02	Greene	A1 F
3338	"	15	E½SE	1837-11-02		A1
3334	DONELSON, John	20	NE	1835-10-01	Greene	A1 F R3298
3335	"	21	N½	1835-10-01	Greene	A1 F
3292	DRUMMOND, Charles H	23	B	1837-03-15	Greene	A1 G77
3387	EARBEE, William	10	NE	1837-03-15	Greene	A1 F
3389	"	2	W½SW	1837-03-15	Greene	A1
3390	"	3	B	1837-03-15	Greene	A1
3388	"	2	E½SW	1837-03-20	Greene	A1
3293	FILES, David	4	A	1917-11-24	Greene	A1 G82
3294	"	4	W½NW	1917-11-24	Greene	A1 G82
3377	FITZ, Robert	26	SE	1835-09-28	Greene	A1 F
3279	GLOVER, Allen	8	N½	1833-05-30	Greene	A1 F
3311	GRIFFIN, Goodman G	28	SWSW	1837-03-30	Greene	A1 G130
3286	HINES, Bryan	2	NWNW	1835-09-25	Greene	A1 F
3287	"	3	N½	1837-03-15	Greene	A1 F
3288	"	4	NE	1837-03-15	Greene	A1 F
3324	LITTLE, Holland	10	SESE	1837-11-02	Greene	A1
3378	LOWRY, Solomon	33	W½NW	1837-03-30	Greene	A1
3296	MARTIN, Francis	20	E½SW	1837-03-15	Greene	A1
3345	MARTIN, Maims	28	W½NW	1837-03-20	Greene	A1
3365	MARTIN, Marius	20	SWSE	1837-03-15	Greene	A1 G180
3352	"	23	E½SW	1837-03-15	Greene	A1
3357	"	27	W½SE	1837-03-15	Greene	A1
3358	"	28	E½NW	1837-03-15	Greene	A1
3355	"	24	SW	1837-03-20	Greene	A1 F
3356	"	27	E½SE	1837-03-20	Greene	A1
3359	"	28	W½NE	1837-03-20	Greene	A1
3347	"	22	NW	1837-03-30	Greene	A1
3346	"	20	SENW	1837-05-15	Greene	A1
3360	"	10	B	1837-08-01	Greene	A1 G181 F
3361	"	10	E½SW	1837-08-01	Greene	A1 G181
3362	"	10	SWSW	1837-08-01	Greene	A1 G181
3363	"	15	NW	1837-08-01		A1 G181
3364	"	15	SW	1837-08-01		A1 G181
3350	"	23	D	1838-12-10	Greene	A1
3348	"	23	A	1839-05-01	Greene	A1
3349	"	23	C	1839-05-01	Greene	A1
3351	"	23	E	1839-05-01	Greene	A1

ID	Individual in Patent	Sec.	Sec. Part	Date Issued	Other Counties	For More Info . . .
3353	MARTIN, Marius (Cont'd)	23	F	1839-05-01	Greene	A1
3354	" "	23	NENW	1839-09-02	Greene	A1
3381	MARTIN, Virginius	23	W½SW	1837-03-15	Greene	A1
3382	" "	27	E½NE	1837-03-30	Greene	A1
3379	" "	10	A	1837-08-01	Greene	A1 F
3383	" "	15	W½SE	1837-08-01		A1 G183
3384	" "	9	SW	1837-08-01	Greene	A1 G183 F
3380	" "	17	NESE	1837-11-02	Greene	A1
3385	MARTIN, Virginus	17	E	1839-05-01	Greene	A1
3386	" "	17	F	1839-05-01	Greene	A1
3344	MASON, Littleberry	28	NWSW	1897-03-02	Greene	A1
3331	MAY, James	25	NW	1831-09-01	Greene	A1 F
3330	" "	25	E½NE	1837-03-20	Greene	A1
3372	MAY, Pleasant	36	W½NE	1831-01-01		A1
3371	" "	25	SE	1833-05-30	Greene	A1 F
3373	" "	36	W½NW	1837-03-20		A1
3332	MCCOY, James	33	SW	1835-09-22	Greene	A1 F
3392	MCDANIEL, William	8	SW	1833-05-30	Greene	A1 F
3293	MCINTIRE, Thomas L	4	A	1917-11-24	Greene	A1 G82
3294	" "	4	W½NW	1917-11-24	Greene	A1 G82
3374	MEADE, Richard E	12	NE	1835-10-01		A1
3375	" "	12	SE	1837-03-15		A1
3376	" "	2	C	1837-03-30	Greene	A1 G198
3328	MUSSINA, Jacob	17	E½NE	1837-11-02	Greene	A1
3329	" "	8	SE	1837-11-02	Greene	A1
3282	MYERS, Amanda	10	N½SE	1837-03-20	Greene	A1 G206
3280	" "	10	C	1839-05-01	Greene	A1 G206
3281	" "	10	D	1839-05-01	Greene	A1 G206
3282	MYERS, Ann	10	N½SE	1837-03-20	Greene	A1 G206
3280	" "	10	C	1839-05-01	Greene	A1 G206
3281	" "	10	D	1839-05-01	Greene	A1 G206
3283	MYERS, Ann L	11	NE	1835-10-20	Greene	A1 F
3282	MYERS, Pleasant	10	N½SE	1837-03-20	Greene	A1 G206
3280	" "	10	C	1839-05-01	Greene	A1 G206
3281	" "	10	D	1839-05-01	Greene	A1 G206
3282	MYERS, William	10	N½SE	1837-03-20	Greene	A1 G206
3280	" "	10	C	1839-05-01	Greene	A1 G206
3281	" "	10	D	1839-05-01	Greene	A1 G206
3311	OSBORN, Esaias H	28	SWSW	1837-03-30	Greene	A1 G130
3333	PHARES, John C	27	SW	1837-03-15	Greene	A1 R3299 V3370
3297	RAVESIES, Frederic	17	SW	1835-10-20	Greene	A1 F
3298	"	20	NE	1835-10-20	Greene	A1 F R3334
3305	RAVESIES, Frederick	34	SW	1831-09-01	Greene	A1 F
3299	" "	27	SW	1833-05-30	Greene	A1 F R3333
3300	" "	28	SE	1833-05-30	Greene	A1 F R3301
3301	" "	28	SE	1833-05-30	Greene	A1 F R3300
3302	" "	33	N½E½	1833-05-30	Greene	A1 F
3303	" "	33	SE	1833-05-30	Greene	A1 F R3310
3304	" "	34	NW	1833-05-30	Greene	A1 F
3306	RAVISIES, Frederick	28	E½SW	1837-03-15	Greene	A1
3365	RAY, John	20	SWSE	1837-03-15	Greene	A1 G180
3313	ROBERTSON, Henry C	11	E	1837-03-30	Greene	A1
3376	" "	2	C	1837-03-30	Greene	A1 G198
3316	" "	2	N½SE	1837-03-30	Greene	A1 F
3317	" "	23	SWSE	1837-03-30	Greene	A1
3318	" "	27	NW	1837-03-30	Greene	A1
3319	" "	27	W½NE	1837-03-30	Greene	A1
3312	" "	11	D	1839-01-08	Greene	A1
3315	" "	11	NENW	1839-01-08	Greene	A1
3314	" "	11	G	1843-02-01	Greene	A1
3393	SHAFFER, William	36	E½NW	1835-10-20		A1
3307	SIMS, Garry	10	NWSW	1837-05-15	Greene	A1
3308	" "	9	SE	1837-05-15	Greene	A1
3339	SIMS, John	10	SWSE	1837-08-01	Greene	A1
3341	SIMS, Julius H	3	CSW	1835-10-28	Greene	A1 F
3342	" "	4	B	1835-10-28	Greene	A1 F
3343	" "	9	A	1837-03-30	Greene	A1 F
3327	SNEDECOR, Isaac	4	E½SW	1835-10-01	Greene	A1
3326	SNEDECOR, Isaac C	4	W½SW	1835-09-25	Greene	A1
3325	" "	4	W½SE	1835-10-01	Greene	A1
3360	" "	10	B	1837-08-01	Greene	A1 G181 F
3361	" "	10	E½SW	1837-08-01	Greene	A1 G181
3362	" "	10	SWSW	1837-08-01	Greene	A1 G181

ID	Individual in Patent	Sec.	Sec. Part	Date Issued	Other Counties	For More Info . . .
3363	SNEDECOR, Isaac C (Cont'd)	15	NW	1837-08-01		A1 G181
3364	" "	15	SW	1837-08-01		A1 G181
3336	STEPHENS, John J	22	SESW	1899-12-07	Greene	A2
3309	STEWART, George N	33	ANE	1831-09-01	Greene	A1
3310	" "	33	SE	1831-09-01	Greene	A1 F R3303
3320	STICKNEY, Henry	14	N½	1837-03-30	Greene	A1 G236
3321	" "	14	SW	1837-03-30	Greene	A1 G236 F
3322	" "	15	W½NE	1837-03-30		A1 G236
3340	STICKNEY, Joseph B	15	E½NE	1837-03-20		A1
3320	" "	14	N½	1837-03-30	Greene	A1 G236
3321	" "	14	SW	1837-03-30	Greene	A1 G236 F
3322	" "	15	W½NE	1837-03-30		A1 G236
3292	TALIAFERRO, Benjamin	23	B	1837-03-15	Greene	A1 G77
3383	WALLER, Archibald	15	W½SE	1837-08-01		A1 G183
3285	" "	9	B	1837-08-01	Greene	A1 F
3384	" "	9	SW	1837-08-01	Greene	A1 G183 F
3323	WARD, Hiram	28	E½NE	1858-08-20	Greene	A1
3289	WATKINS, Bryan	17	D	1835-10-01	Greene	A1
3290	" "	8	A	1835-10-01	Greene	A1
3291	" "	8	B	1835-10-01	Greene	A1
3391	WHITSITT, William H	11	BSE	1835-09-25	Greene	A1
3277	WRIGHT, Alexander	36	NENE	1835-09-25		A1
3278	" "	36	SENE	1837-03-30		A1

Patent Map

T19-N R3-E
St Stephens Meridian

Map Group 19

Township Statistics

Parcels Mapped	:	117
Number of Patents	:	112
Number of Individuals	:	55
Patentees Identified	:	52
Number of Surnames	:	39
Multi-Patentee Parcels	:	19
Oldest Patent Date	:	1/1/1831
Most Recent Patent	:	11/24/1917
Block/Lot Parcels	:	24
Parcels Re - Issued	:	4
Parcels that Overlap	:	2
Cities and Towns	:	4
Cemeteries	:	2

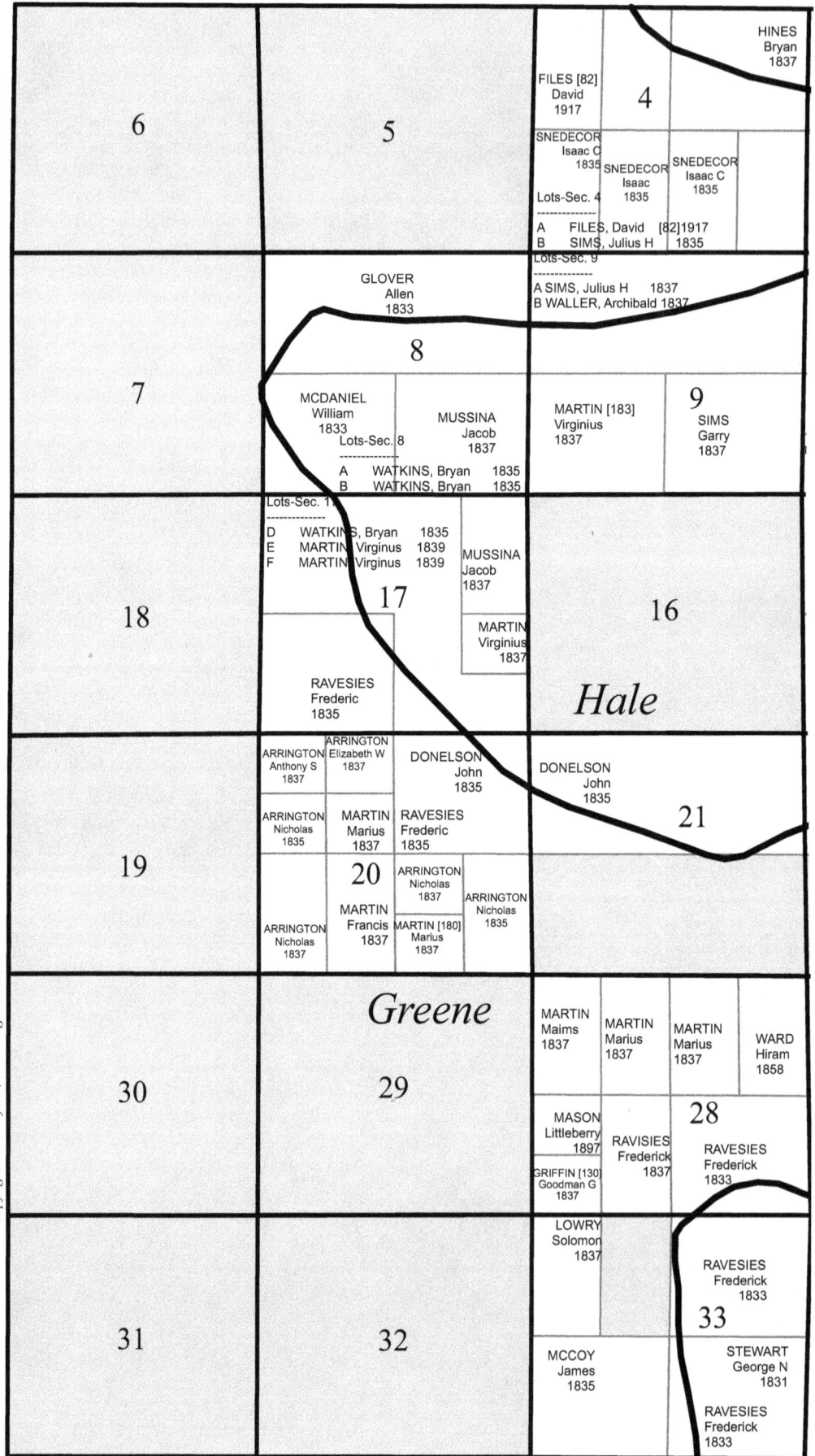

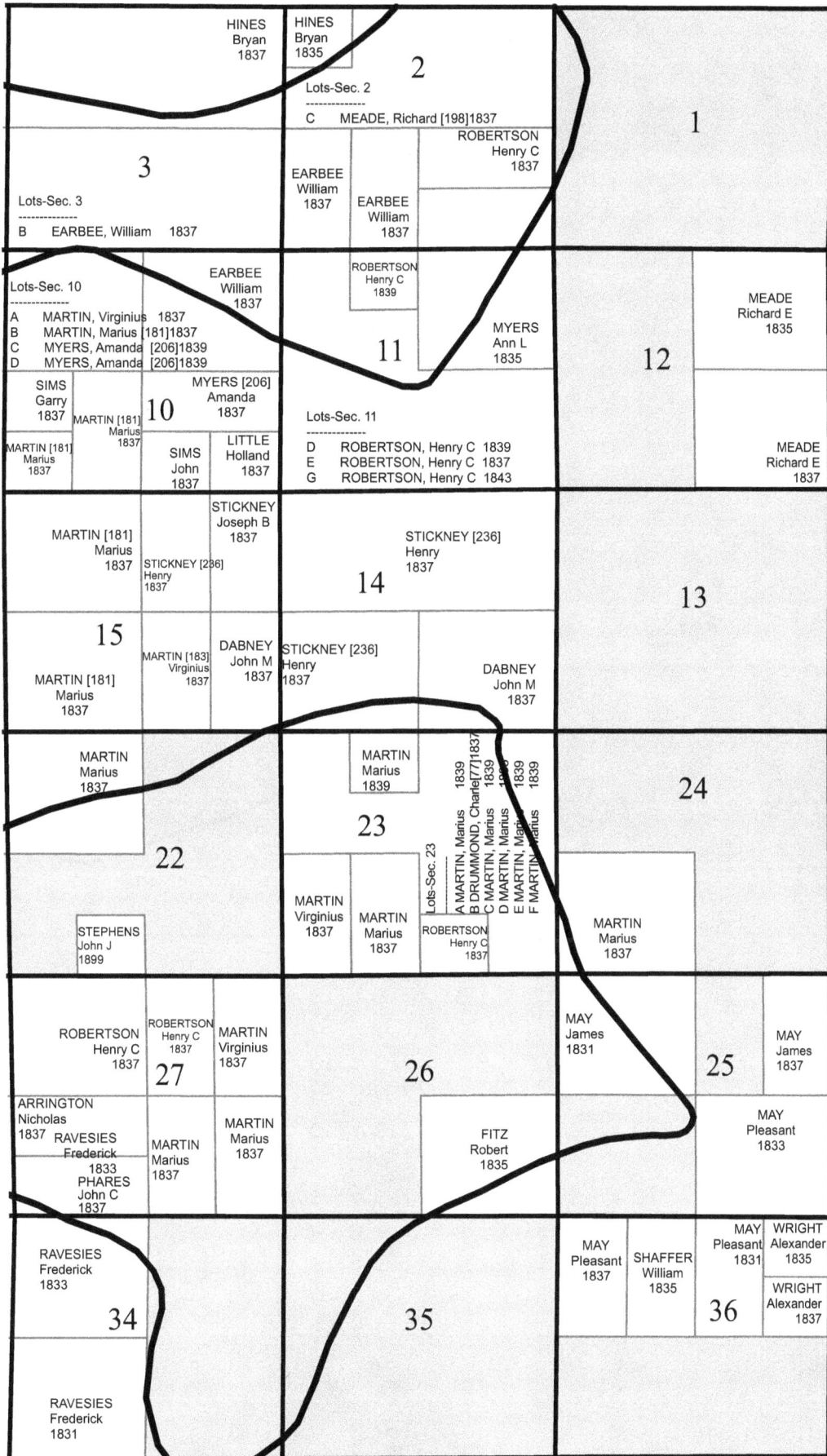

Helpful Hints

1. This Map's INDEX can be found on the preceding pages.

2. Refer to Map "C" to see where this Township lies within Hale County, Alabama.

3. Numbers within square brackets [ ] denote a multi-patentee land parcel (multi-owner). Refer to Appendix "C" for a full list of members in this group.

4. Areas that look to be crowded with Patentees usually indicate multiple sales of the same parcel (Re-issues) or Overlapping parcels. See this Township's Index for an explanation of these and other circumstances that might explain "odd" groupings of Patentees on this map.

Legend

———	Patent Boundary
▬▬▬	Section Boundary
(shaded)	No Patents Found (or Outside County)
1., 2., 3., ...	Lot Numbers (when beside a name)
[ ]	Group Number (see Appendix "C")

Scale: Section = 1 mile X 1 mile (generally, with some exceptions)

219

Road Map

T19-N R3-E
St Stephens Meridian

Map Group 19

Cities & Towns
Gilmore Quarters
Lake Bend Landing
Lock Five
Port Royal

Cemeteries
Pickens Cemetery
Washington Cemetery

6	5	4
7	●Lake Bend Landing 8	9 Jimmy Phillips●
18	17	16
19	20	21
30	29	28
31	32	33

Hale

3

2

1

Port Royal

11

Gilmore
Quarters
Gilmore Quarters

10

Owl

12

15

14

Owl

13

Pickens Cem. †

Owl

Jimmie
Phillips

Hale

Greene

22

23

24

27

26

25

Jackson
Branch
Grouse

Candys
Landing

County Road 16

Sandpiper

Lock Five

Savanna

Hale

34

Blue Heron
Meadowlark
Prairie Creek
Ramsey

35

Bailey

Butternut

36

Bailey

Washington Cem. †

Copyright 2007 Boyd IT, Inc. All Rights Reserved

Helpful Hints

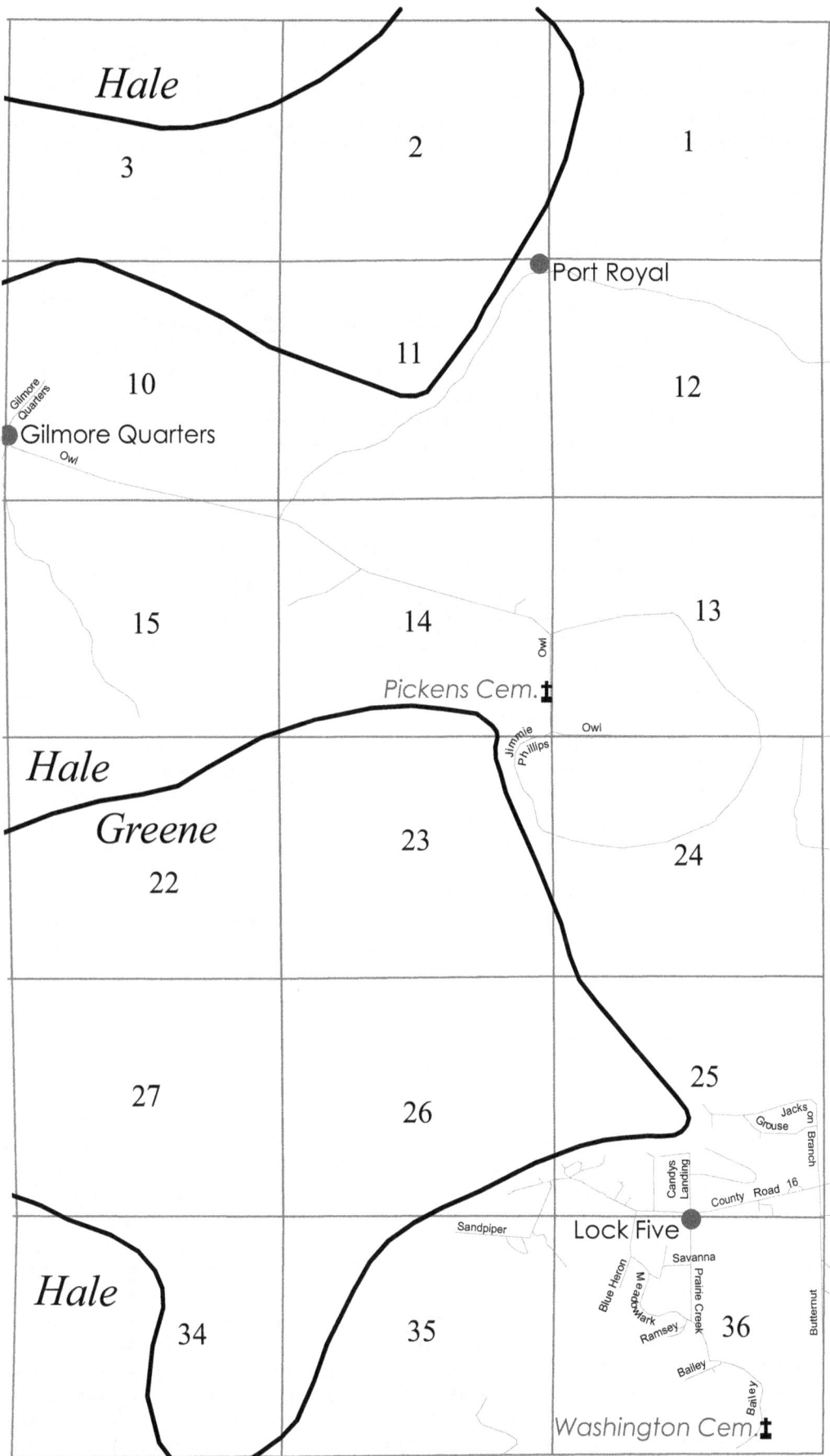

1. This road map has a number of uses, but primarily it is to help you: a) find the present location of land owned by your ancestors (at least the general area), b) find cemeteries and city-centers, and c) estimate the route/roads used by Census-takers & tax-assessors.

2. If you plan to travel to Hale County to locate cemeteries or land parcels, please pick up a modern travel map for the area before you do. Mapping old land parcels on modern maps is not as exact a science as you might think. Just the slightest variations in public land survey coordinates, estimates of parcel boundaries, or road-map deviations can greatly alter a map's representation of how a road either does or doesn't cross a particular parcel of land.

Legend

————	Section Lines
══════	Interstates
————	Highways
————	Other Roads
●	Cities/Towns
†	Cemeteries

Scale: Section = 1 mile X 1 mile
(generally, with some exceptions)

Historical Map

T19-N R3-E
St Stephens Meridian

Map Group 19

Cities & Towns
Gilmore Quarters
Lake Bend Landing
Lock Five
Port Royal

Cemeteries
Pickens Cemetery
Washington Cemetery

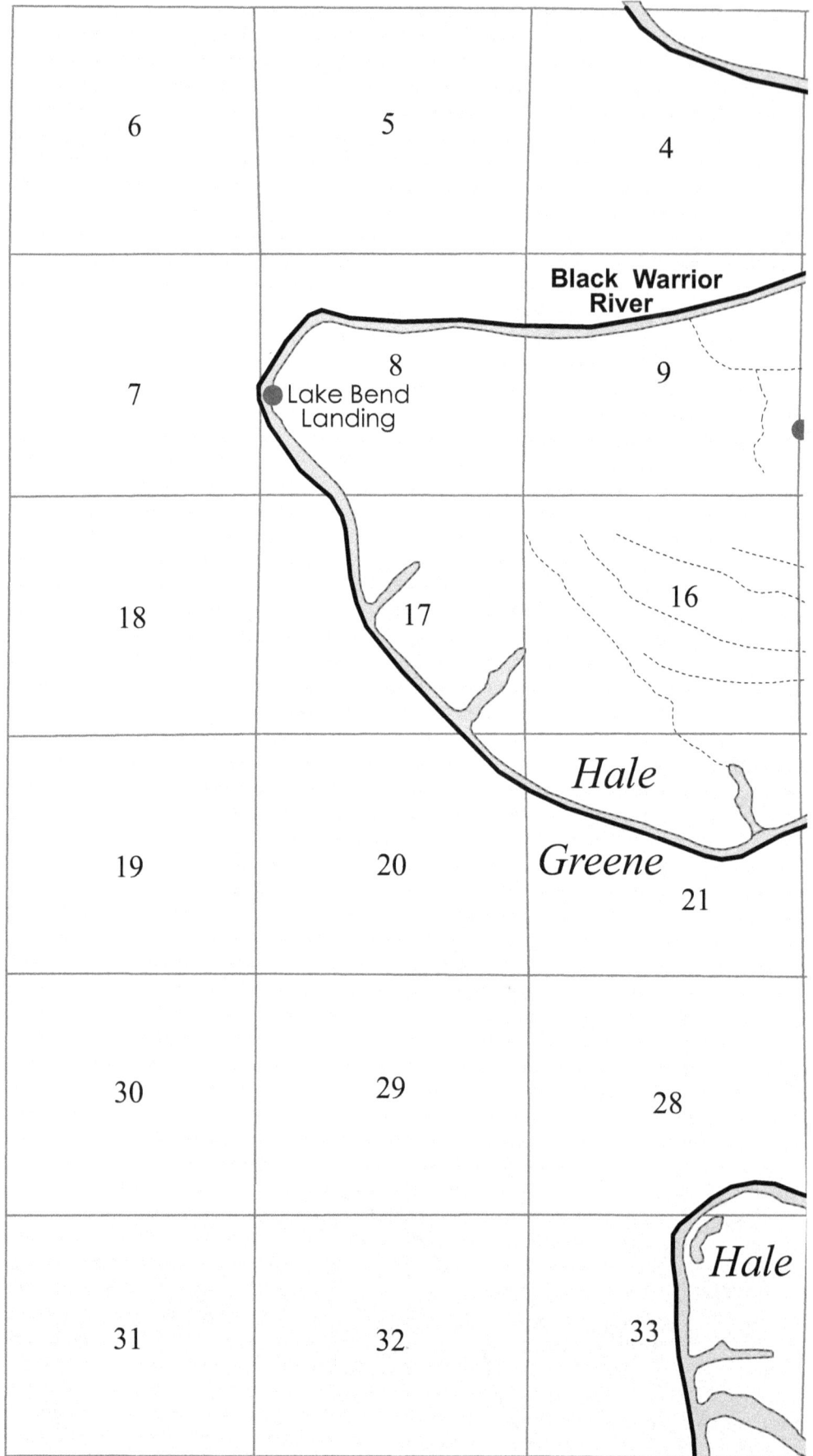

6	5	4
7	8 — Lake Bend Landing	9
18	17	16
19	20	Hale / Greene 21
30	29	28
31	32	33 Hale

Black Warrior River

Hale

Greene

Hale

3

2

1

Limestone Creek

● Port Royal

11

10

● Gilmore Quarters

12

15

14

13

✝ *Pickens Cem.*

Lake Demopolis 24

22

23

27

26

25

Demopolis Lake

34

Big Prairie Creek

35

● Lock Five

Demopolis Lake

36

Washington Cem.

✝

Helpful Hints

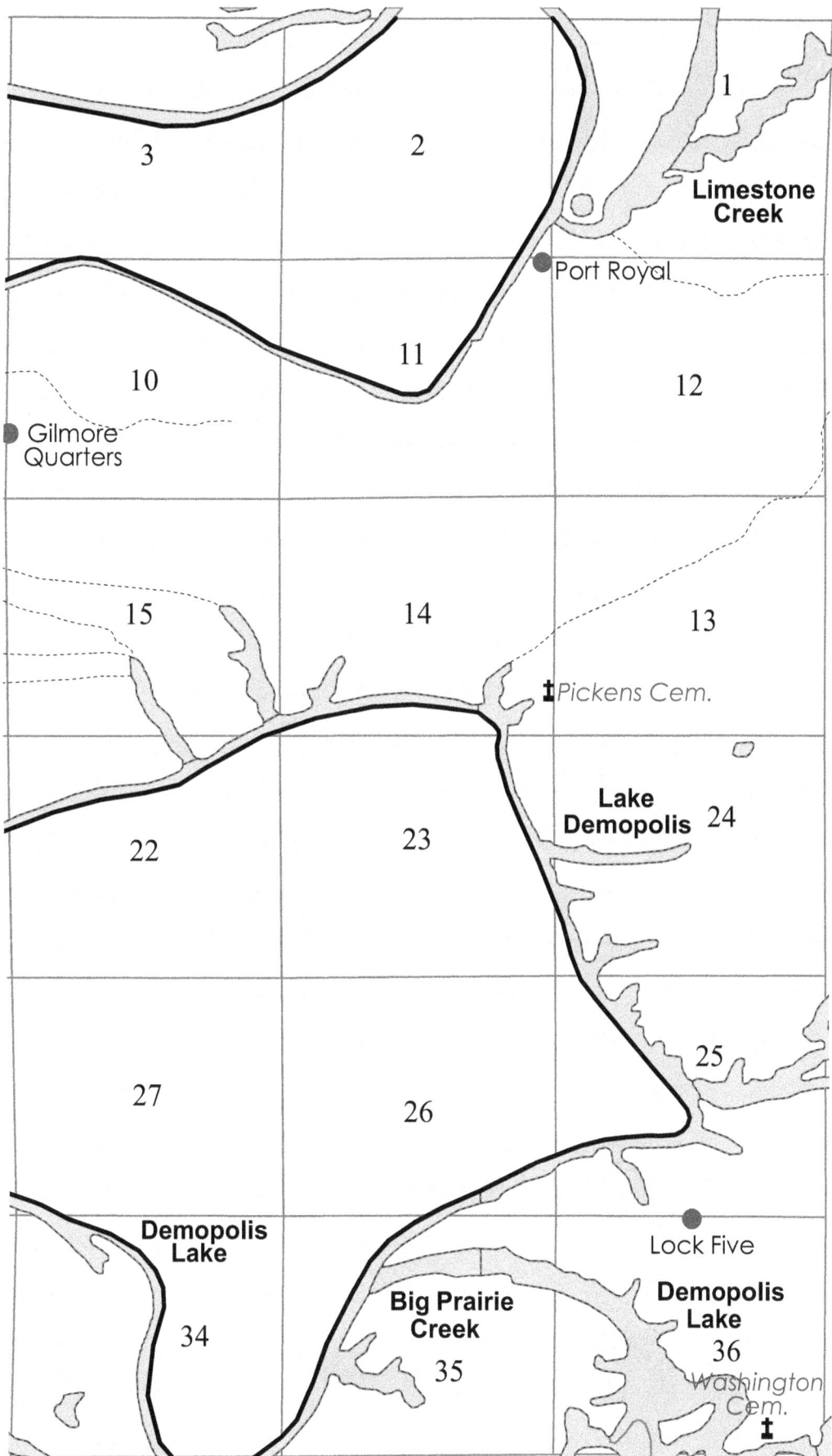

1. This Map takes a different look at the same Congressional Township displayed in the preceding two maps. It presents features that can help you better envision the historical development of the area: a) Water-bodies (lakes & ponds), b) Water-courses (rivers, streams, etc.), c) Railroads, d) City/town center-points (where they were oftentimes located when first settled), and e) Cemeteries.

2. Using this "Historical" map in tandem with this Township's Patent Map and Road Map, may lead you to some interesting discoveries. You will often find roads, towns, cemeteries, and waterways are named after nearby landowners: sometimes those names will be the ones you are researching. See how many of these research gems you can find here in Hale County.

Legend

——————	Section Lines
┼┼┼┼┼┼┼	Railroads
▭	Large Rivers & Bodies of Water
- - - - - - -	Streams/Creeks & Small Rivers
●	Cities/Towns
✝	Cemeteries

Scale: Section = 1 mile X 1 mile
(there are some exceptions)

Map Group 20: Index to Land Patents

Township 19-North Range 4-East (St Stephens)

After you locate an individual in this Index, take note of the Section and Section Part then proceed to the Land Patent map on the pages immediately following. You should have no difficulty locating the corresponding parcel of land.

The "For More Info" Column will lead you to more information about the underlying Patents. See the *Legend* at right, and the "How to Use this Book" chapter, for more information.

ID	Individual in Patent	Sec.	Sec. Part	Date Issued	Other Counties	For More Info ...
3435	BARNES, Pittkin	9	E½NE	1837-03-30		A1 G10
3437	" "	9	E½NW	1837-03-30		A1 G12
3434	" "	9	E½SE	1837-03-30		A1 G9
3436	" "	9	W½NE	1837-03-30		A1 G11
3438	" "	9	W½SE	1837-03-30		A1 G8
3450	BEARD, Willis	21	NWSW	1848-09-01		A1
3451	" "	21	W½NW	1848-09-01		A1
3429	BUCHANNAN, May	30	W½SE	1848-07-01		A1
3445	BUCHANNAN, Samuel	17	E½SE	1837-05-15		A1 G35
3444	" "	17	W½SE	1837-05-15		A1 G34
3432	CARTER, Pannel C	12	W½SW	1840-11-10		A1 G39
3420	CHANDLER, Jeremiah	32	E½SE	1837-05-15		A1 G43
3446	CHANDLER, Scott	33	W½SW	1837-05-15		A1 G44
3414	CHANDRON, Felix	32	E½NE	1837-03-30		A1 G46
3413	" "	33	E½SE	1837-03-30		A1 G49
3412	" "	33	W½NW	1837-03-30		A1 G50
3418	COPELAND, James	33	NE	1843-09-23		A1
3444	COWAN, Jehu	17	W½SE	1837-05-15		A1 G34
3445	COWAN, Robert	17	E½SE	1837-05-15		A1 G35
3409	CUMMINGS, Edith L	16	S½S½NENE	1945-11-19		A1
3410	" "	16	SENE	1945-11-19		A1
3419	DIXON, James	12	SE	1837-03-30		A1
3404	DRUMMOND, Charles H	29	E½SE	1837-03-30		A1 G77
3405	" "	29	W½SE	1837-03-30		A1 G77
3406	" "	31	E½SE	1837-03-30		A1 G77
3407	" "	31	W½SE	1837-03-30		A1 G77
3422	EDWARDS, John B	32	NW	1843-10-04		A1
3421	GARRETT, Jesse H	20	SE	1911-04-13		A1
3401	GLOVER, Allen	22	E½SE	1837-03-30		A1 G108
3398	" "	22	W½SE	1837-03-30		A1 G96
3397	" "	24	E½SW	1837-03-30		A1 G105
3396	" "	24	W½NW	1837-03-30		A1 G111
3395	" "	24	W½SW	1837-03-30		A1 G112
3399	" "	27	E½SE	1837-03-30		A1 G107
3400	" "	12	E½NE	1843-02-01		A1 G113
3432	GOOLE, Daniel	12	W½SW	1840-11-10		A1 G39
3417	HALBERT, Henry	12	NW	1840-11-10		A1 G132
3398	HARRELL, Gordon	22	W½SE	1837-03-30		A1 G96
3415	HARRIS, Hattie R	16	SENW	1949-08-08		A1
3414	HARRISON, Nathaniel	32	E½NE	1837-03-30		A1 G46
3414	HENLEY, John W	32	E½NE	1837-03-30		A1 G46
3413	" "	33	E½SE	1837-03-30		A1 G49
3412	" "	33	W½NW	1837-03-30		A1 G50
3394	INGRAM, Alexander	29	E½SW	1837-05-15		A1 G151
3408	INGRAM, Daniel	29	W½SW	1837-05-15		A1
3443	LEWIS, Samuel A	32	SW	1847-11-05		A1

ID	Individual in Patent	Sec.	Sec. Part	Date Issued	Other Counties	For More Info . . .
3426	LOWREY, Leonard M	16	E½SW	1951-06-21		A2
3397	MANESS, Enoch	24	E½SW	1837-03-30		A1 G105
3427	MARTIN, Marius	30	E½SE	1837-03-30		A1 G182
3394	"	29	E½SW	1837-05-15		A1 G151
3420	"	32	E½SE	1837-05-15		A1 G43
3446	"	33	W½SW	1837-05-15		A1 G44
3433	MAY, Patrick	4	E½SE	1837-03-30		A1 G188
3438	MCCLURE, William	9	W½SE	1837-03-30		A1 G8
3399	MCGAW, John P	27	E½SE	1837-03-30		A1 G107
3401	MCGAW, William	22	E½SE	1837-03-30		A1 G108
3449	MCNALLY, Thomas	4	W½SE	1848-09-01		A1
3434	MILLER, Frederick	9	E½SE	1837-03-30		A1 G9
3433	OVERTON, Jesse B	4	E½SE	1837-03-30		A1 G188
3396	PEACOCK, Elizabeth	24	W½NW	1837-03-30		A1 G111
3417	PEARSON, Joseph J	12	NW	1840-11-10		A1 G132
3395	PERRITT, Charlotte	24	W½SW	1837-03-30		A1 G112
3400	PHILLIPS, Thomas	12	E½NE	1843-02-01		A1 G113
3425	RABORN, Joseph	33	E½NW	1837-11-02		A1
3402	RACKLEY, Anthony	33	E½SW	1848-09-01		A1
3403	"	33	W½SE	1848-09-01		A1
3411	REID, Edwin D	23	E½E½SE	1848-07-01		A1
3416	ROBERTSON, Henry C	29	NW	1839-05-01		A1 G219
3416	ROYALL, John D	29	NW	1839-05-01		A1 G219
3447	SEXTON, Seaborn	32	W½NE	1837-11-02		A1
3430	SKINNER, Nathan	12	E½SW	1841-09-08		A1
3439	STEWART, Quinn Lewis	16	N½N½NWSW	1949-09-01		A1
3440	"	16	SWNW	1949-09-01		A1
3404	TALIAFERRO, Benjamin	29	E½SE	1837-03-30		A1 G77
3405	"	29	W½SE	1837-03-30		A1 G77
3406	"	31	E½SE	1837-03-30		A1 G77
3407	"	31	W½SE	1837-03-30		A1 G77
3413	THORNTON, Mitchell	33	E½SE	1837-03-30		A1 G49
3431	THRASH, Nathan	12	W½NE	1843-02-01		A1
3441	TUCKER, Richard	10	W½SW	1837-05-15		A1
3423	VEST, John P	29	NE	1843-02-01		A1 C R3424
3424	"	29	NE	1847-11-05		A1 R3423
3427	WALLER, Catherine	30	E½SE	1837-03-30		A1 G182
3448	WARD, Stephen	32	W½SE	1847-11-05		A1
3435	WHITE, Griffin	9	E½NE	1837-03-30		A1 G10
3442	WHITE, Robert	10	E½E½SE	1837-03-30		A1 G243
3442	WHITWORTH, Jeremiah	10	E½E½SE	1837-03-30		A1 G243
3428	WILSON, Martha Johnston	16	NWNW	1949-08-19		A1 G244
3428	WILSON, Preston Oliver	16	NWNW	1949-08-19		A1 G244
3412	WOODARD, Charles E	33	W½NW	1837-03-30		A1 G50
3436	WOODARD, Moses	9	W½NE	1837-03-30		A1 G11
3437	WOODWARD, Sarah	9	E½NW	1837-03-30		A1 G12

Patent Map

T19-N R4-E
St Stephens Meridian

Map Group 20

Township Statistics

Parcels Mapped	:	58
Number of Patents	:	54
Number of Individuals	:	63
Patentees Identified	:	50
Number of Surnames	:	55
Multi-Patentee Parcels	:	31
Oldest Patent Date	:	3/30/1837
Most Recent Patent	:	6/21/1951
Block/Lot Parcels	:	0
Parcels Re - Issued	:	1
Parcels that Overlap	:	0
Cities and Towns	:	2
Cemeteries	:	5

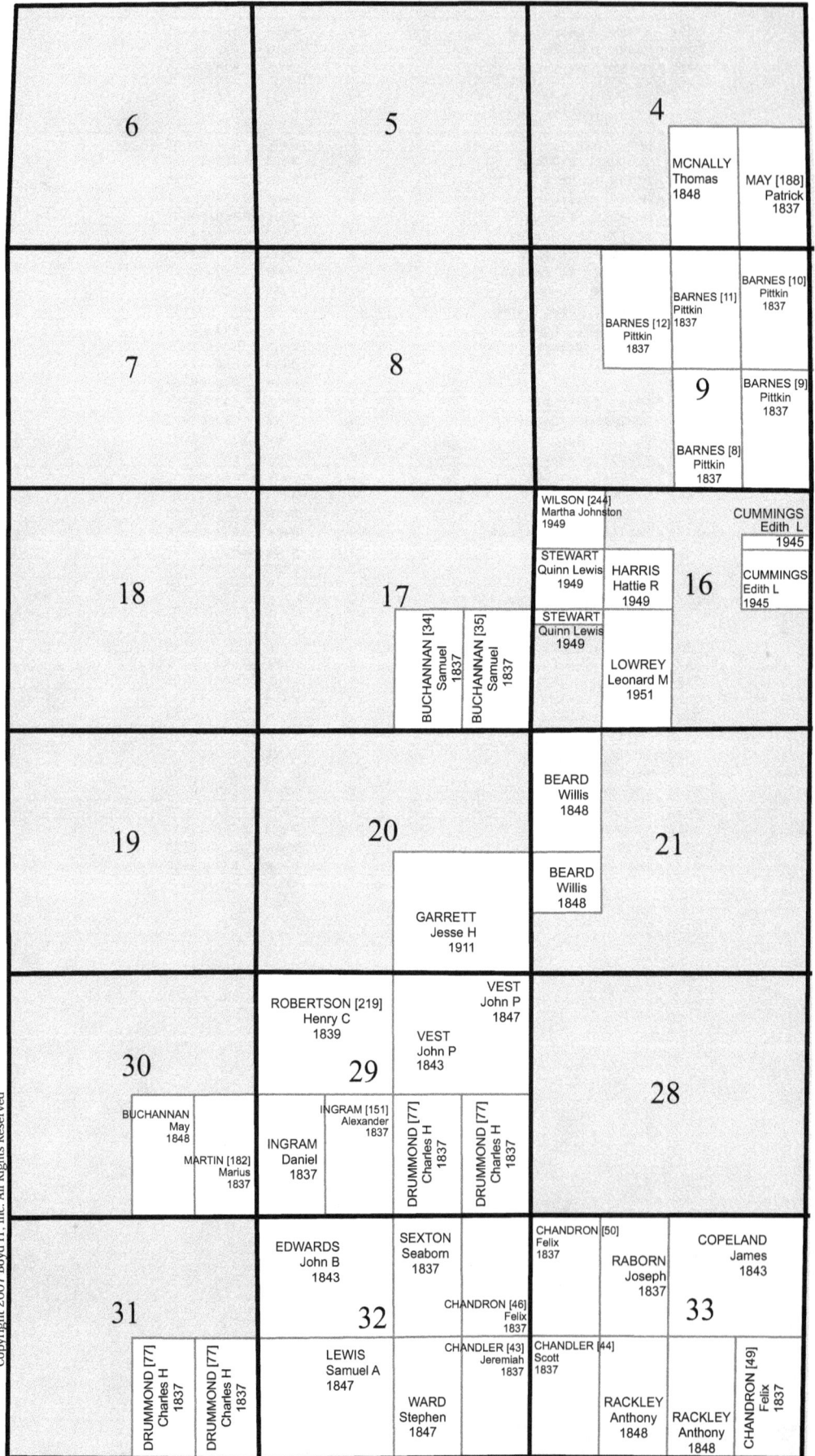

6

5

4

MCNALLY
Thomas
1848

MAY [188]
Patrick
1837

7

8

BARNES [12]
Pittkin
1837

BARNES [11]
Pittkin
1837

BARNES [10]
Pittkin
1837

9

BARNES [9]
Pittkin
1837

BARNES [8]
Pittkin
1837

18

17

BUCHANNAN [34]
Samuel
1837

BUCHANNAN [35]
Samuel
1837

WILSON [244]
Martha Johnston
1949

STEWART
Quinn Lewis
1949

HARRIS
Hattie R
1949

STEWART
Quinn Lewis
1949

LOWREY
Leonard M
1951

16

CUMMINGS
Edith L
1945

CUMMINGS
Edith L
1945

19

20

GARRETT
Jesse H
1911

BEARD
Willis
1848

BEARD
Willis
1848

21

30

BUCHANNAN
May
1848

MARTIN [182]
Marius
1837

29

ROBERTSON [219]
Henry C
1839

INGRAM [151]
Alexander
1837

INGRAM
Daniel
1837

VEST
John P
1847

VEST
John P
1843

DRUMMOND [77]
Charles H
1837

DRUMMOND [77]
Charles H
1837

28

31

DRUMMOND [77]
Charles H
1837

DRUMMOND [77]
Charles H
1837

32

EDWARDS
John B
1843

LEWIS
Samuel A
1847

SEXTON
Seaborn
1837

CHANDRON [46]
Felix
1837

CHANDLER [43]
Jeremiah
1837

WARD
Stephen
1847

CHANDRON [50]
Felix
1837

CHANDLER [44]
Scott
1837

RABORN
Joseph
1837

33

COPELAND
James
1843

RACKLEY
Anthony
1848

RACKLEY
Anthony
1848

CHANDRON [49]
Felix
1837

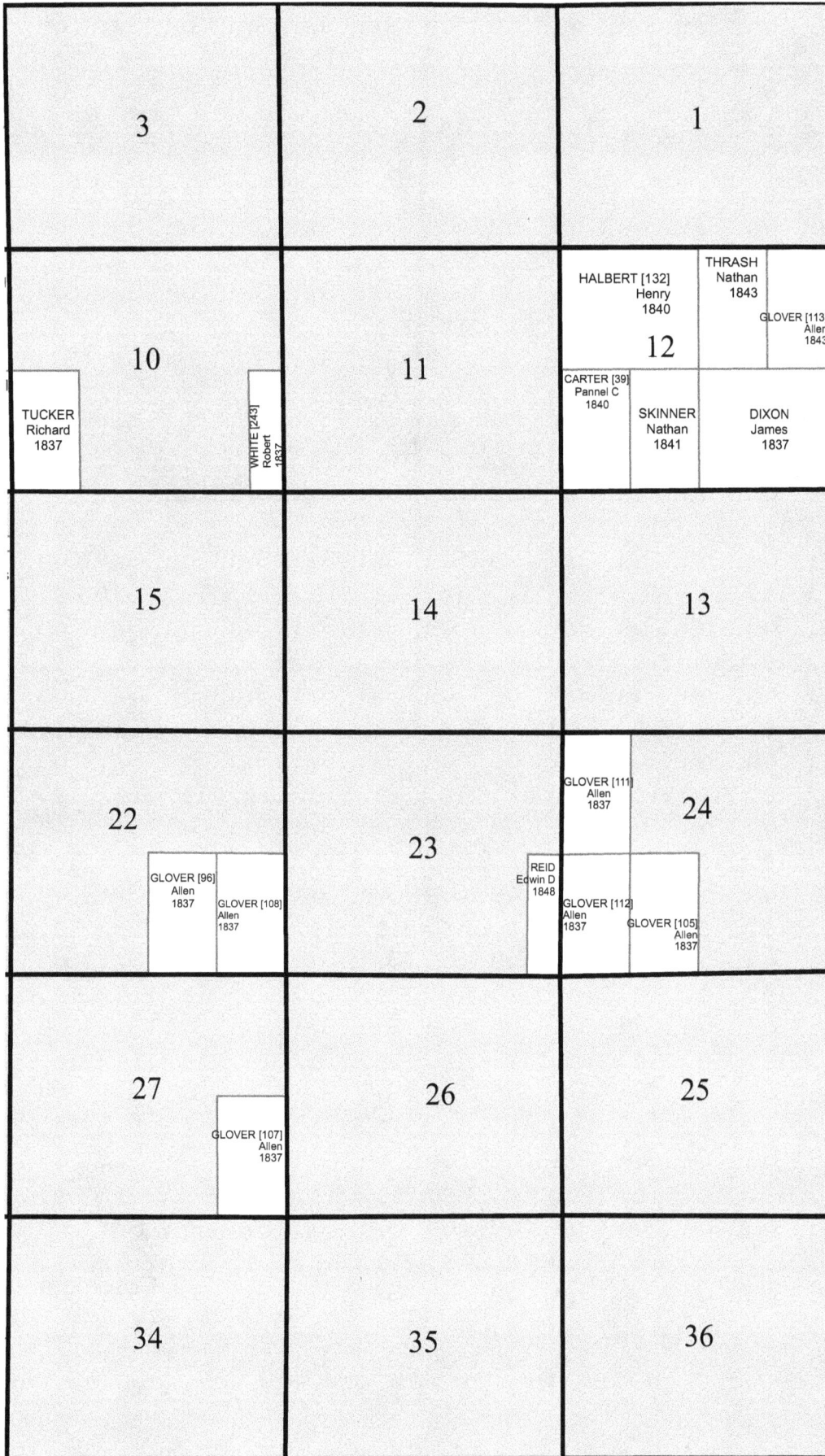

| 3 | 2 | 1 |

| 10 | 11 | 12 |

HALBERT [132]
Henry
1840

THRASH
Nathan
1843

GLOVER [113]
Allen
1843

CARTER [39]
Pannel C
1840

SKINNER
Nathan
1841

DIXON
James
1837

TUCKER
Richard
1837

WHITE [243]
Robert
1837

| 15 | 14 | 13 |

| 22 | 23 | 24 |

GLOVER [96]
Allen
1837

GLOVER [108]
Allen
1837

GLOVER [111]
Allen
1837

REID
Edwin D
1848

GLOVER [112]
Allen
1837

GLOVER [105]
Allen
1837

| 27 | 26 | 25 |

GLOVER [107]
Allen
1837

| 34 | 35 | 36 |

Helpful Hints

1. This Map's INDEX can be found on the preceding pages.

2. Refer to Map "C" to see where this Township lies within Hale County, Alabama.

3. Numbers within square brackets [ ] denote a multi-patentee land parcel (multi-owner). Refer to Appendix "C" for a full list of members in this group.

4. Areas that look to be crowded with Patentees usually indicate multiple sales of the same parcel (Re-issues) or Overlapping parcels. See this Township's Index for an explanation of these and other circumstances that might explain "odd" groupings of Patentees on this map.

Legend

———— Patent Boundary

━━━━ Section Boundary

No Patents Found
(or Outside County)

1., 2., 3., ... Lot Numbers
(when beside a name)

[ ] Group Number
(see Appendix "C")

Scale: Section = 1 mile X 1 mile
(generally, with some exceptions)

Road Map

T19-N R4-E
St Stephens Meridian

Map Group 20

Cities & Towns
Casemore
Cedarville

Cemeteries
Casemore Cemetery
Eaton Cemetery
Micken Cemetery
Pine Grove Cemetery
Saint Pauls Cemetery

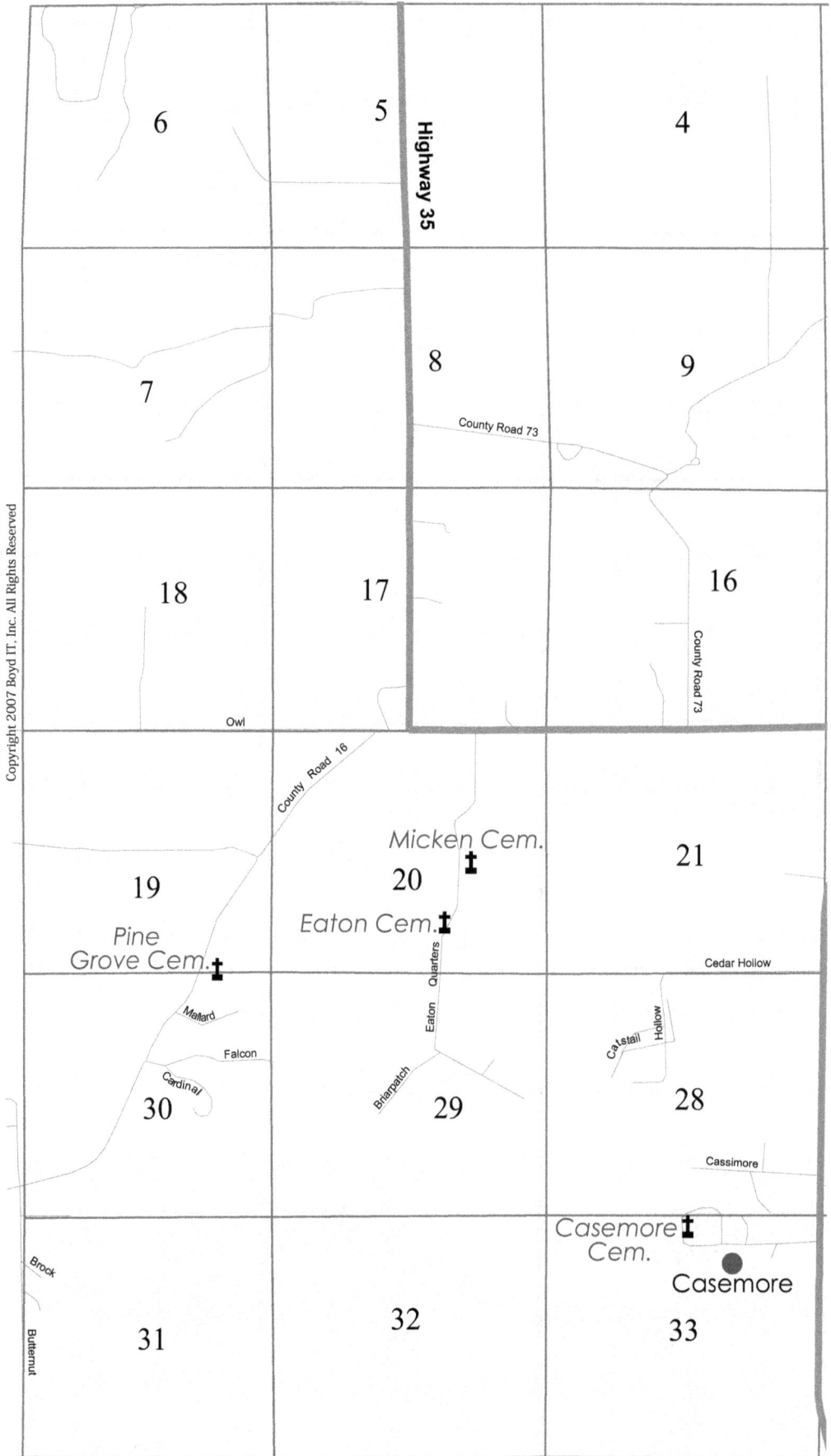

6

5

Highway 35

4

7

8

9

County Road 73

18

17

16

County Road 73

Owl

County Road 16

Micken Cem.

19

20

21

Eaton Cem.

Pine
Grove Cem.

Cedar Hollow

Mallard

Eaton Quarters

Catstail Hollow

Falcon

Cardinal

Briarpatch

30

29

28

Cassimore

Brock

Casemore
Cem.

Casemore

Butternut

31

32

33

3

2

County Road 54

1

Saint Pauls
Cem. †

State Route 69

10

11

12

15

14

13

Cedarville

County Road 16

22

23

County Road 9

24

27

26

25

34

35

36

Copyright 2007 Boyd IT, Inc. All Rights Reserved

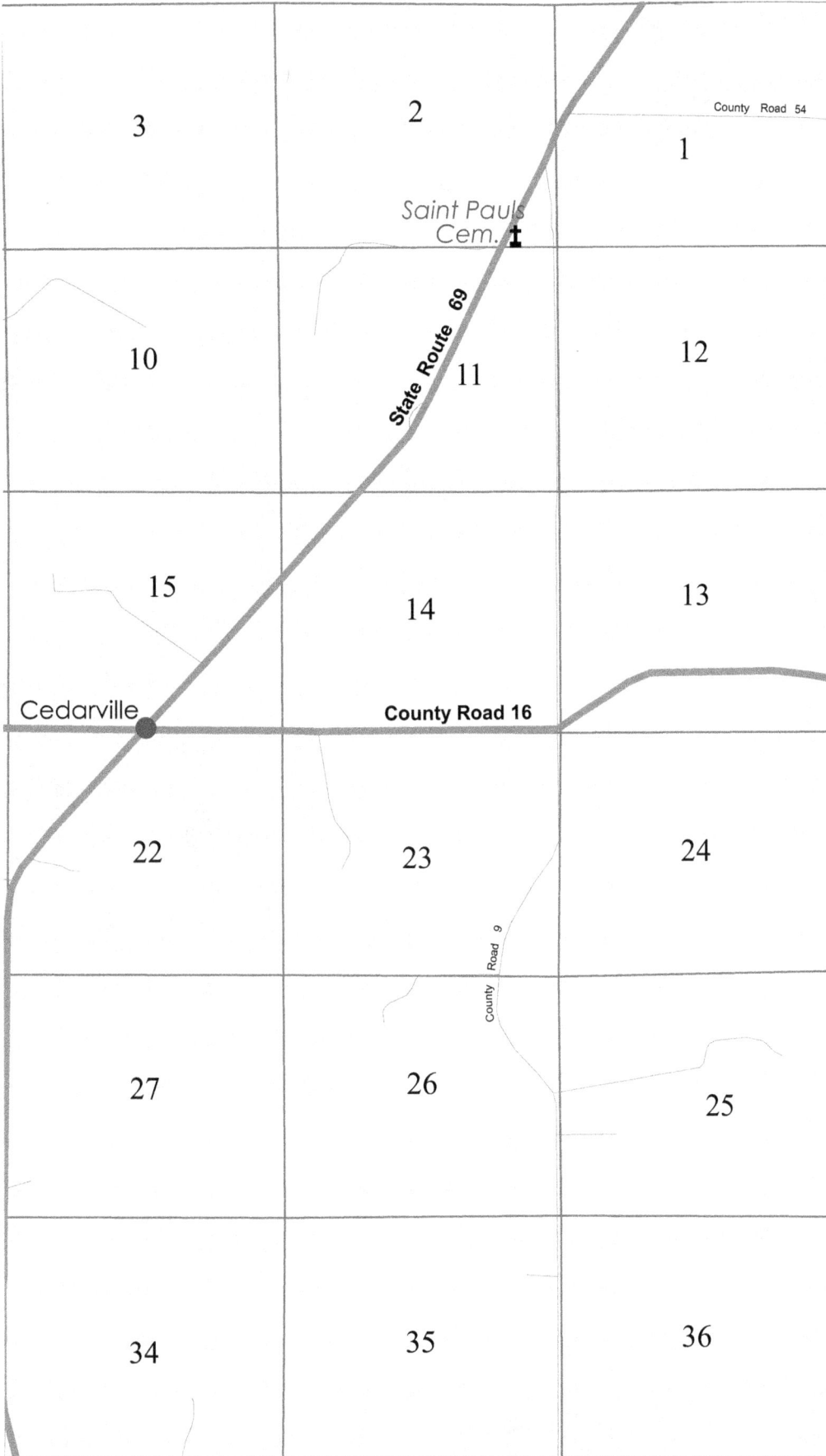

Legend

——— Section Lines

═══ Interstates

▬▬▬ Highways

——— Other Roads

● Cities/Towns

† Cemeteries

Scale: Section = 1 mile X 1 mile
(generally, with some exceptions)

229

Historical Map

T19-N R4-E
St Stephens Meridian

Map Group 20

Cities & Towns
Casemore
Cedarville

Cemeteries
Casemore Cemetery
Eaton Cemetery
Micken Cemetery
Pine Grove Cemetery
Saint Pauls Cemetery

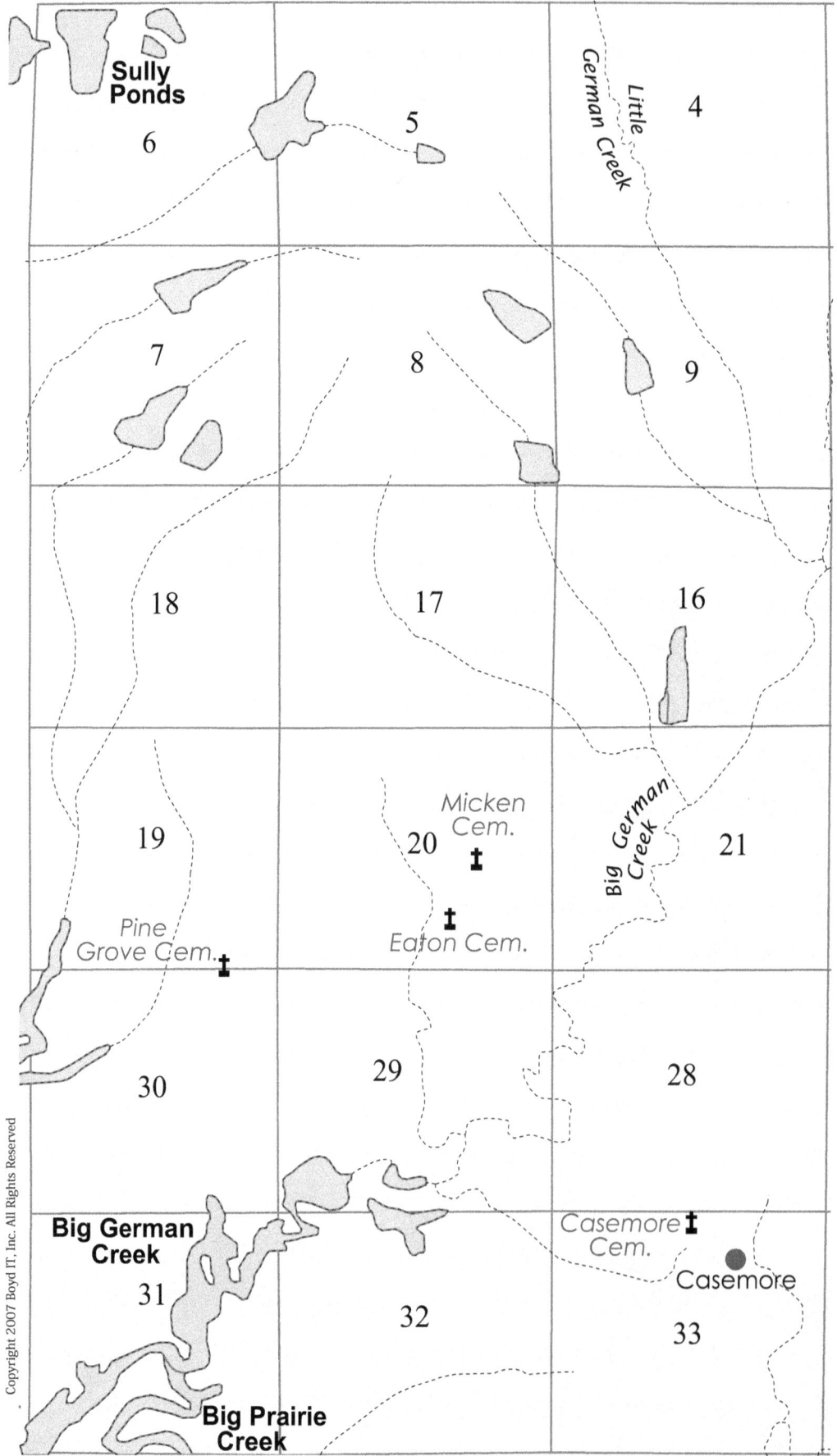

Sully Ponds

6

5

Little German Creek

4

7

8

9

18

17

16

19

Micken Cem.

20

✝

Big German Creek

21

Pine Grove Cem.

✝

Eaton Cem.

✝

30

29

28

Big German Creek

31

32

Casemore Cem. ✝

● **Casemore**

33

Big Prairie Creek

Copyright 2007 Boyd IT, Inc. All Rights Reserved

3

2

1

Saint Pauls Cem. †

Big Little German Creek

10

11

Jacks Branch

12

15

14

13

● Cedarville

22

23

24

Picks Creek

27

26

25

34

35

36

Little Prarie Creek

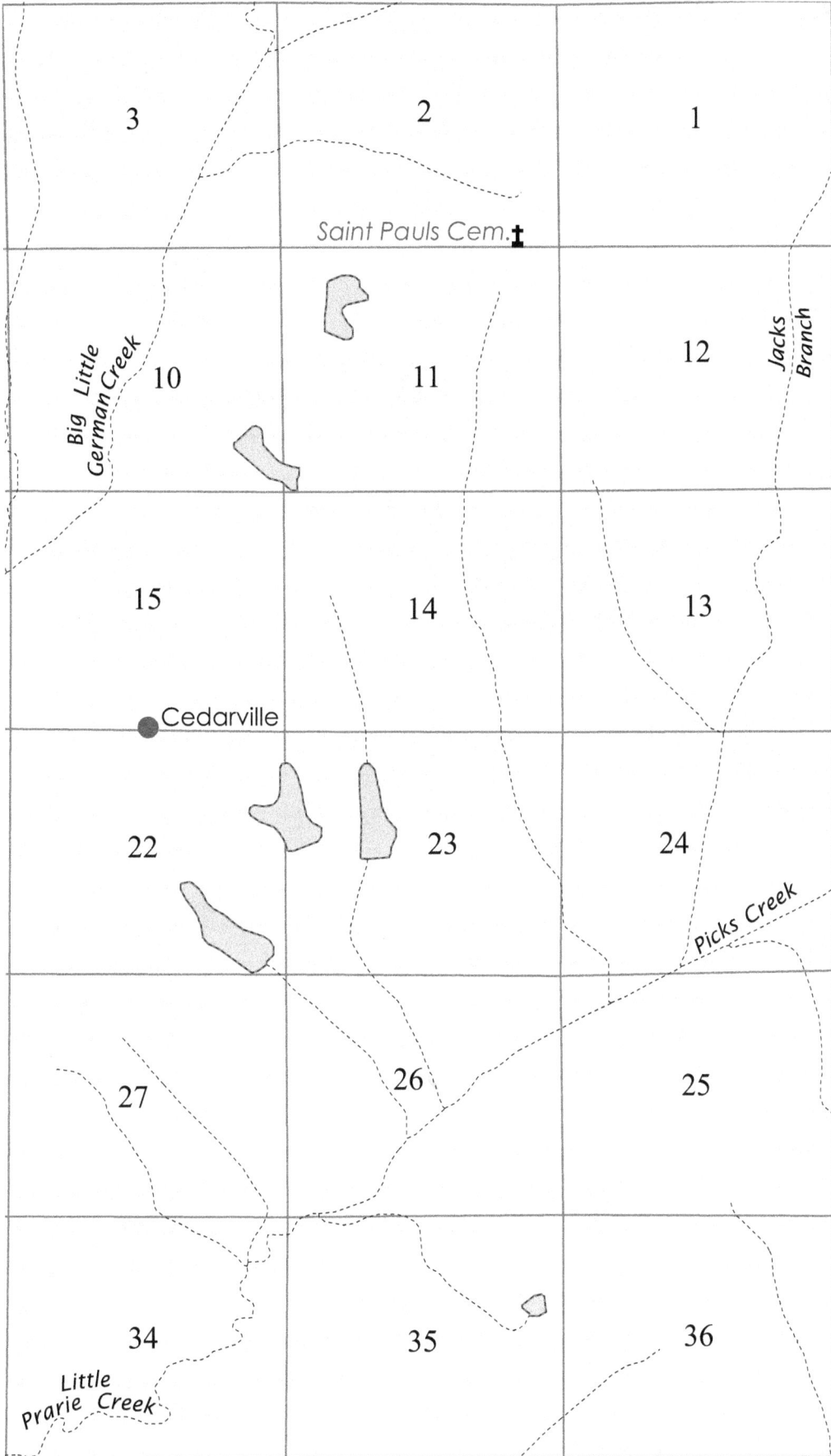

Helpful Hints

1. This Map takes a different look at the same Congressional Township displayed in the preceding two maps. It presents features that can help you better envision the historical development of the area: a) Water-bodies (lakes & ponds), b) Water-courses (rivers, streams, etc.), c) Railroads, d) City/town center-points (where they were oftentimes located when first settled), and e) Cemeteries.

2. Using this "Historical" map in tandem with this Township's Patent Map and Road Map, may lead you to some interesting discoveries. You will often find roads, towns, cemeteries, and waterways are named after nearby landowners: sometimes those names will be the ones you are researching. See how many of these research gems you can find here in Hale County.

Legend

Section Lines

Railroads

Large Rivers & Bodies of Water

Streams/Creeks & Small Rivers

● Cities/Towns

† Cemeteries

Scale: Section = 1 mile X 1 mile
(there are some exceptions)

Map Group 21: Index to Land Patents

Township 19-North Range 5-East (St Stephens)

After you locate an individual in this Index, take note of the Section and Section Part then proceed to the Land Patent map on the pages immediately following. You should have no difficulty locating the corresponding parcel of land.

The "For More Info" Column will lead you to more information about the underlying Patents. See the *Legend* at right, and the "How to Use this Book" chapter, for more information.

```
LEGEND
        "For More Info . . . " column
A = Authority (Legislative Act, See Appendix "A")
B = Block or Lot (location in Section unknown)
C = Cancelled Patent
F = Fractional Section
G = Group  (Multi-Patentee Patent, see Appendix "C")
V = Overlaps another Parcel
R = Re-Issued (Parcel patented more than once)

(A & G items require you to look in the Appendixes referred
to above. All other Letter-designations followed by a number
require you to locate line-items in this index that possess
the ID number found after the letter).
```

ID	Individual in Patent	Sec.	Sec. Part	Date Issued	Other Counties	For More Info . . .
3604	ABBOTT, Willis	28	W½NW	1831-12-01		A1
3564	ARINGTON, Nicholas	18	W½NW	1832-08-08		A1
3588	BELL, William	4	E½NE	1832-08-08		A1 G26
3589	"	4	W½NE	1832-08-08		A1 G26
3520	BLACKBURN, John	25	NE	1821-12-03		A1
3544	BORDEN, Joseph	26	E½NW	1835-09-22		A1
3545	" "	26	W½SW	1835-09-22		A1
3546	" "	27	E½NE	1835-09-22		A1
3547	" "	35	E½SE	1835-09-22		A1
3550	" "	35	NW	1835-09-22		A1 G27
3548	" "	36	NW	1835-09-22		A1
3549	" "	36	W½NE	1835-09-22		A1
3580	BORDEN, Thomas R	36	E½SW	1833-08-02		A1
3581	" "	36	NWSW	1834-08-20		A1
3550	" "	35	NW	1835-09-22		A1 G27
3579	" "	36	E½NE	1835-09-22		A1
3575	" "	25	W½SW	1835-09-25		A1
3574	" "	25	E½SW	1835-09-28		A1
3578	" "	35	SW	1835-09-28		A1
3576	" "	31	W½NW	1835-10-16		A1
3577	" "	35	NWSE	1837-03-15		A1
3492	BOUNDS, Henry	3	E½SW	1831-07-27		A1 R3541
3522	BOYD, John	13	W½NE	1821-12-03		A1
3523	" "	1	W½NE	1825-04-04		A1 G31
3521	" "	13	E½NW	1831-12-01		A1
3457	BUCKHALTER, Allen	19	E½SE	1831-12-01		A1
3477	CADE, Drury B	24	W½SE	1827-01-01		A1
3519	CALLOWAY, Job	6	NE	1823-10-01		A1
3562	CARTER, Meshach	19	E½NW	1831-12-01		A1
3572	CHILDS, Thomas	1	E½NE	1825-04-04		A1 G51
3582	CHILDS, Walter	26	W½SE	1823-10-01		A1
3567	CHRISTOPHER, R G	25	E½NW	1827-01-01		A1
3526	COATES, John	34	W½NW	1827-02-16		A1
3524	" "	27	W½NW	1830-11-16		A1
3525	" "	34	E½SW	1833-11-14		A1
3527	COATS, John	15	W½NE	1830-11-16		A1
3528	" "	34	W½NE	1833-11-14		A1
3600	COATS, William W	29	E½NW	1830-11-16		A1
3601	" "	33	E½SE	1831-08-01		A1
3516	CRAWFORD, Jesse	14	SW	1821-12-03		A1 R3517
3518	" "	23	E½NW	1823-10-01		A1
3517	" "	14	SW	1936-10-16		A1 R3516
3459	CRENSHAW, Anderson	3	E½SE	1831-12-01		A1
3460	" "	3	W½NE	1831-12-01		A1
3584	CROOM, Wiley J	23	SWNW	1835-10-01		A1
3572	CURRY, Jabez	1	E½NE	1825-04-04		A1 G51

ID	Individual in Patent	Sec.	Sec. Part	Date Issued	Other Counties	For More Info . . .
3473	DAVIS, Darling W	8	W½NE	1831-12-01		A1
3502	DEW, James	27	W½SE	1837-03-30		A1 G75 R3467
3472	EASLEY, Daniel W	24	E½NW	1827-01-01		A1
3474	ELLIOTT, David	10	E½NW	1831-08-01		A1
3485	FARISH, George W	11	SW	1831-08-01		A1
3569	FIELD, Stephen G	14	W½SE	1833-11-14		A1
3529	GARRETT, John M	19	W½NE	1831-12-01		A1
3502	GLOVER, Allen	27	W½SE	1837-03-30		A1 G75 R3467
3551	HALBERT, Joshua	6	SE	1821-10-01		A1
3471	HAMER, Daniel	24	W½NW	1821-12-03		A1
3503	HANNA, James	11	E½SE	1831-12-01		A1
3504	" "	11	W½SE	1831-12-01		A1
3505	" "	3	W½SW	1832-08-08		A1
3506	" "	4	E½SW	1834-09-04		A1
3557	HARBIN, Mark	26	E½SE	1823-10-01		A1
3558	" "	35	W½NE	1823-10-01		A1
3452	HARDIN, Absalom	25	W½NW	1827-04-09		A1
3453	HARDIN, Absolom C	26	W½NE	1835-09-22		A1
3560	HARDIN, Mark	35	E½NE	1825-04-02		A1
3559	" "	26	E½SW	1834-08-20		A1
3507	HEAD, James	1	E½SW	1831-12-01		A1
3597	HENDON, William T	34	E½SE	1835-10-01		A1
3598	" "	34	W½SE	1835-10-01		A1
3566	HODGES, Philemon	18	E½SE	1831-12-01		A1 G146
3484	HOPPER, George	13	W½NW	1831-12-01		A1
3455	HORTON, Albert C	8	E½SE	1831-07-01		A1
3456	" "	8	E½SW	1831-12-01		A1
3570	HORTON, Stephen	15	W½SW	1832-08-08		A1
3586	HOUSE, Wiley J	24	E½SE	1830-11-16		A1
3587	" "	24	E½SW	1830-11-16		A1
3585	" "	24	E½NE	1833-11-14		A1
3490	HUCKABEE, Green	27	E½SE	1835-09-22		A1
3593	JENKINS, William	19	SW	1831-12-01		A1
3594	" "	19	W½NW	1832-08-08		A1
3483	KING, George C	23	NWNW	1835-09-12		A1
3538	LIPSCOMB, John P	22	E½NE	1835-09-22		A1
3539	" "	22	NESE	1835-09-22		A1
3540	" "	22	SESE	1835-09-22		A1
3561	LITCHFIELD, Melzer	35	SWSE	1834-06-12		A1
3454	LUDLOW, Adam	30	E½NE	1831-12-01		A1
3556	LUDLOW, Lewis	30	W½NE	1831-12-01		A1
3511	MABRY, James T	2	W½SW	1823-10-01		A1
3583	MABRY, Walter	2	E½SW	1821-12-03		A1
3458	MCDONALD, Allen	33	W½SE	1829-05-06		A1
3509	MCDONALD, James	18	E½NE	1831-12-01		A1 G192
3566	" "	18	E½SE	1831-12-01		A1 G146
3510	" "	18	W½SE	1831-12-01		A1 G192
3508	" "	19	E½NE	1831-12-01		A1
3465	MIDDLEBROOKS, Baxter	29	W½NW	1830-11-16		A1
3466	" "	9	E½NW	1832-08-08		A1
3498	MIDDLEBROOKS, Ibzan	11	W½NW	1826-07-10		A1
3497	" "	11	E½NW	1830-11-16		A1
3495	" "	10	E½NW	1831-12-01		A1
3496	" "	10	W½NW	1831-12-01		A1
3500	" "	3	W½SE	1831-12-01		A1
3499	" "	17	W½NE	1833-06-04		A1
3530	MILES, John	19	W½SE	1831-12-01		A1
3533	NELSON, John	22	W½SW	1829-05-06		A1
3532	" "	21	E½NE	1830-11-16		A1
3509	" "	18	E½NE	1831-12-01		A1 G192
3531	" "	18	E½NW	1831-12-01		A1
3566	" "	18	E½SE	1831-12-01		A1 G146
3510	" "	18	W½SE	1831-12-01		A1 G192
3536	" "	7	E½SW	1834-01-21		A1
3537	" "	7	W½SW	1835-09-12		A1
3534	" "	6	SESW	1837-03-15		A1
3535	" "	7	E½NW	1837-03-15		A1
3491	PERKINS, Hardin	9	SE	1926-04-24		A1
3501	PETEET, J	7	W½NW	1823-10-01		A1 G211
3541	PETETE, John	3	E½SW	1831-12-01		A1 R3492
3470	PHILLIPS, Charles	13	W½SE	1829-05-02		A1
3568	PICKENS, Samuel	30	NW	1829-05-04		A1
3464	PRESTWOOD, Austin	13	E½SE	1830-11-16		A1

Family Maps of Hale County, Alabama

ID	Individual in Patent	Sec.	Sec. Part	Date Issued	Other Counties	For More Info . . .
3488	RICE, George W	8	E½NW	1831-12-01		A1
3487	" "	7	W½SE	1834-01-21		A1
3486	" "	6	NESW	1835-09-12		A1
3501	ROAN, W J	7	W½NW	1823-10-01		A1 G211
3606	ROAN, Willis J	8	W½SE	1825-06-06		A1
3605	" "	18	E½SW	1831-08-01		A1
3607	ROANE, Willis J	18	W½SW	1832-08-08		A1
3469	SEABROOK, Bowen	36	SWSW	1835-09-22		A1
3461	SEAL, Anthony	22	W½SE	1823-10-01		A1
3462	" "	29	E½NE	1829-04-10		A1
3468	SEAL, Beaufort	24	W½SW	1823-10-01		A1
3463	SEALE, Anthony	22	E½SW	1830-11-16		A1
3467	SEALE, Beauford	27	W½SE	1833-11-14		A1 R3502
3478	SEALE, Eli	15	E½SW	1828-04-09		A1
3479	" "	34	W½SW	1833-11-14		A1
3514	SEALE, Jarvis	27	E½SW	1833-11-14		A1
3515	" "	34	E½NE	1833-11-14		A1
3595	SEALE, William	10	W½NE	1831-08-01		A1
3608	SEALE, Wright	9	E½NE	1831-12-01		A1
3609	" "	9	W½NE	1831-12-01		A1
3480	SEALES, Eli	34	E½NW	1830-11-16		A1
3542	STANFILL, John	8	E½NE	1831-12-01		A1
3596	STANFILL, William	9	W½NW	1831-12-01		A1
3573	STARKE, Thomas L	29	SW	1909-11-22		A1
3475	STEPHENS, David T	15	E½SW	1831-12-01		A1
3476	" "	15	W½SE	1832-08-08		A1
3523	THOMAS, Francis	1	W½NE	1825-04-04		A1 G31
3599	THOMAS, William	13	E½NE	1821-12-03		A1
3543	TIDMORE, John	22	W½NW	1831-12-01		A1
3554	WALKER, Lawrence W	27	E½NW	1827-02-16		A1
3555	" "	27	W½NE	1827-04-09		A1
3552	" "	24	W½NE	1830-11-16		A1
3553	" "	25	SE	1837-03-15		A1
3482	WALTERS, Frederic S	10	W½SE	1830-11-16		A1
3489	WALTON, George	33	W½SW	1831-07-27		A1
3602	WALTON, William W	28	E½NW	1831-12-01		A1
3563	WARREN, Moses	27	W½SW	1830-11-16		A1
3590	WARREN, William H	10	E½SW	1831-12-01		A1
3591	" "	10	W½SW	1831-12-01		A1
3588	" "	4	E½NE	1832-08-08		A1 G26
3589	" "	4	W½NE	1832-08-08		A1 G26
3493	WESTBROOK, Hudson	21	W½NE	1829-05-06		A1
3494	" "	14	NW	1936-10-16		A1 G242
3571	WESTBROOK, Thomas B	10	E½SE	1827-07-26		A1
3494	WESTBROOK, William	14	NW	1936-10-16		A1 G242
3512	WHITSETT, James	23	E½SE	1823-10-01		A1
3513	" "	23	W½SE	1825-04-04		A1
3592	WHITSETT, William H	23	W½SW	1827-02-16		A1
3603	WILLIAMS, William	15	E½SE	1830-11-16		A1
3481	WOOD, Elisha B	29	W½NE	1830-11-16		A1
3565	WOOD, Obadiah M	17	E½NE	1832-08-08		A1

Patent Map

T19-N R5-E
St Stephens Meridian

Map Group 21

Township Statistics

Parcels Mapped	:	158
Number of Patents	:	158
Number of Individuals	:	100
Patentees Identified	:	99
Number of Surnames	:	75
Multi-Patentee Parcels	:	11
Oldest Patent Date	:	10/1/1821
Most Recent Patent	:	10/16/1936
Block/Lot Parcels	:	0
Parcels Re - Issued	:	3
Parcels that Overlap	:	0
Cities and Towns	:	3
Cemeteries	:	4

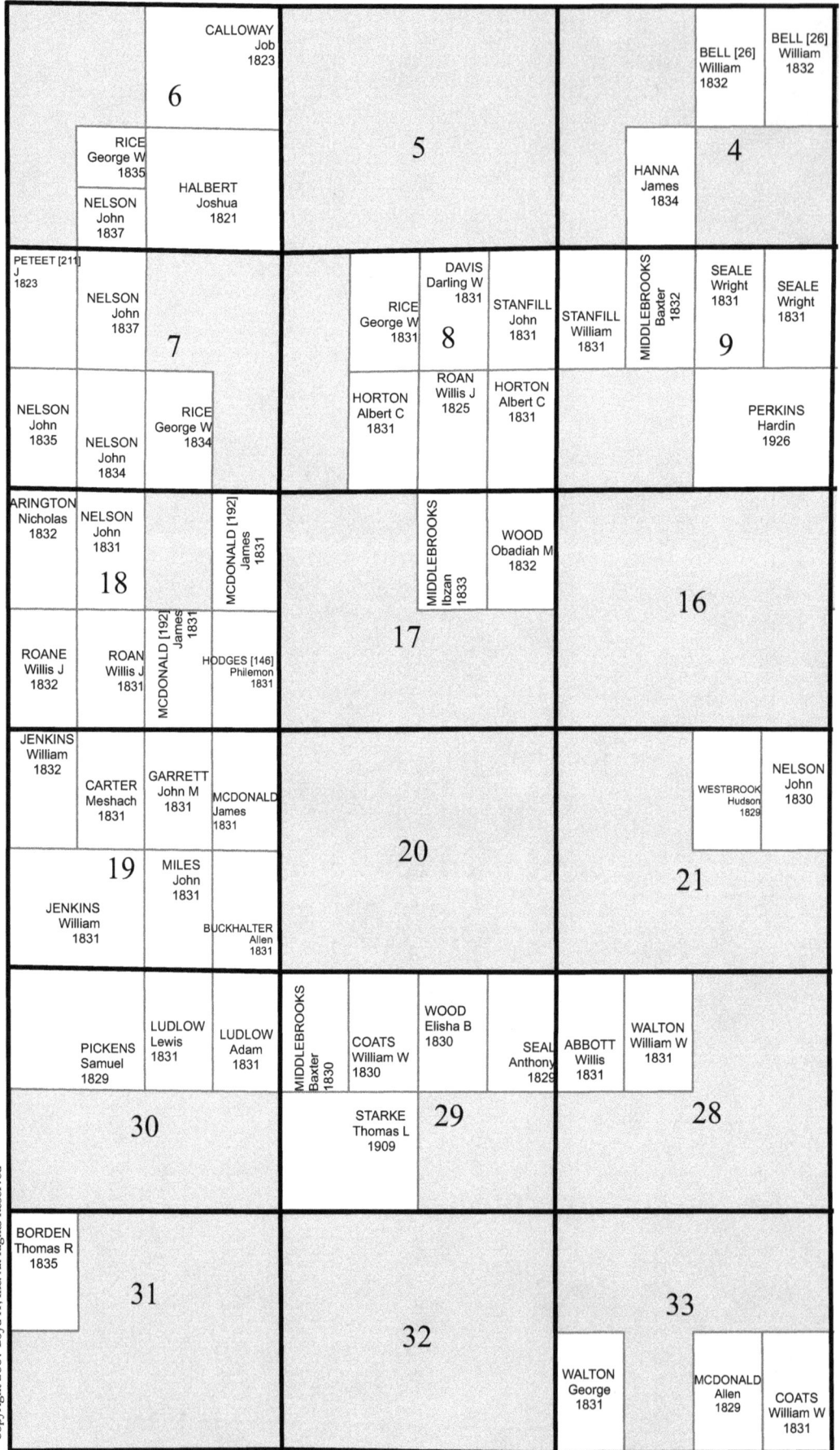

6

CALLOWAY
Job
1823

RICE
George W
1835

NELSON
John
1837

HALBERT
Joshua
1821

5

BELL [26]
William
1832

BELL [26]
William
1832

HANNA
James
1834

4

PETEET [211]
J
1823

NELSON
John
1837

7

NELSON
John
1835

NELSON
John
1834

RICE
George W
1834

RICE
George W
1831

DAVIS
Darling W
1831

STANFILL
John
1831

8

HORTON
Albert C
1831

ROAN
Willis J
1825

HORTON
Albert C
1831

STANFILL
William
1831

MIDDLEBROOKS
Baxter
1832

SEALE
Wright
1831

SEALE
Wright
1831

9

PERKINS
Hardin
1926

ARINGTON
Nicholas
1832

NELSON
John
1831

18

MCDONALD [192]
James
1831

ROANE
Willis J
1832

ROAN
Willis J
1831

MCDONALD [192]
James
1831

HODGES [146]
Philemon
1831

MIDDLEBROOKS
Ibzan
1833

WOOD
Obadiah M
1832

17

16

JENKINS
William
1832

CARTER
Meshach
1831

GARRETT
John M
1831

MCDONALD
James
1831

19

MILES
John
1831

JENKINS
William
1831

BUCKHALTER
Allen
1831

20

WESTBROOK
Hudson
1829

NELSON
John
1830

21

PICKENS
Samuel
1829

LUDLOW
Lewis
1831

LUDLOW
Adam
1831

30

MIDDLEBROOKS
Baxter
1830

COATS
William W
1830

WOOD
Elisha B
1830

STARKE
Thomas L
1909

29

SEAL
Anthony
1829

ABBOTT
Willis
1831

WALTON
William W
1831

28

BORDEN
Thomas R
1835

31

32

WALTON
George
1831

33

MCDONALD
Allen
1829

COATS
William W
1831

Section 3
CRENSHAW Anderson 1831

3

HANNA James 1832 | PETETE John 1831 / BOUNDS Henry 1831 | MIDDLEBROOKS Ibzan 1831 | CRENSHAW Anderson 1831

Section 2
2

MABRY James T 1823 | MABRY Walter 1821

Section 1
BOYD [31] John 1825 | CHILDS [51] Thomas 1825

1

HEAD James 1831

Section 10
MIDDLEBROOKS Ibzan 1831 | MIDDLEBROOKS Ibzan 1831 | SEALE William 1831 | ELLIOTT David 1831

10

WARREN William H 1831 | WARREN William H 1831 | WALTERS Frederic S 1830 | WESTBROOK Thomas B 1827

Section 11
MIDDLEBROOKS Ibzan 1826 | MIDDLEBROOKS Ibzan 1830

11

FARISH George W 1831 | HANNA James 1831 | HANNA James 1831

Section 12
12

Section 15
15

COATS John 1830 | SEALE Eli 1828

HORTON Stephen 1832 | STEPHENS David T 1831 | STEPHENS David T 1832 | WILLIAMS William 1830

Section 14
14

WESTBROOK [242] Hudson 1936

CRAWFORD Jesse 1821 / CRAWFORD Jesse 1936 | FIELD Stephen G 1833

Section 13
HOPPER George 1831 | BOYD John 1821 | THOMAS William 1821

BOYD John 1831 **13**

PHILLIPS Charles 1829

PRESTWOOD Austin 1830

Section 22
TIDMORE John 1831 | LIPSCOMB John P 1835

22

NELSON John 1829 | SEALE Anthony 1830 / SEAL Anthony 1823 | LIPSCOMB John P 1835 / LIPSCOMB John P 1835

Section 23
KING George C 1835 / CROOM Wiley J 1835 | CRAWFORD Jesse 1823

23

WHITSETT William H 1827 | WHITSETT James 1825 | WHITSETT James 1823

Section 24
HAMER Daniel 1821 | EASLEY Daniel W 1827 | WALKER Lawrence W 1830 | HOUSE Wiley J 1833

24

SEAL Beaufort 1823 | HOUSE Wiley J 1830 | CADE Drury B 1827 | HOUSE Wiley J 1830

Section 27
COATES John 1830 | WALKER Lawrence W 1827 | WALKER Lawrence W 1827 | BORDEN Joseph 1835

27

SEALE Jarvis 1833 | SEALE Beauford 1833 / DEW [75] James 1837 | HUCKABEE Green 1835

WARREN Moses 1830

Section 26
BORDEN Joseph 1835

26

HARDIN Absolom C 1835

BORDEN Joseph 1835 | HARDIN Mark 1834 | CHILDS Walter 1823

Section 25
CHRISTOPHER R G 1827

HARDIN Absolom 1827 | BLACKBURN John 1821

25

BORDEN Thomas R 1835 | BORDEN Thomas R 1835 | WALKER Lawrence W 1837

HARBIN Mark 1823

Section 34
COATES John 1827 | COATS John 1833 | SEALE Jarvis 1833

SEALES Eli 1830 **34**

COATES John 1833 | SEALE Eli 1833 | HENDON William T 1835 | HENDON William T 1835

Section 35
BORDEN [27] Joseph 1835 | HARBIN Mark 1823 | HARDIN Mark 1825

35

BORDEN Thomas R 1835 | BORDEN Thomas R 1837 / LITCHFIELD Melzer 1834 | BORDEN Joseph 1835

Section 36
BORDEN Joseph 1835 | BORDEN Joseph 1835 | BORDEN Thomas R 1835

36

BORDEN Thomas R 1834 | BORDEN Thomas R 1834 | BORDEN Thomas R 1833

SEABROOK Bowen 1835

Helpful Hints

1. This Map's INDEX can be found on the preceding pages.

2. Refer to Map "C" to see where this Township lies within Hale County, Alabama.

3. Numbers within square brackets [ ] denote a multi-patentee land parcel (multi-owner). Refer to Appendix "C" for a full list of members in this group.

4. Areas that look to be crowded with Patentees usually indicate multiple sales of the same parcel (Re-issues) or Overlapping parcels. See this Township's Index for an explanation of these and other circumstances that might explain "odd" groupings of Patentees on this map.

Legend

———— Patent Boundary

▬▬▬▬ Section Boundary

No Patents Found (or Outside County)

1., 2., 3., ... Lot Numbers (when beside a name)

[   ] Group Number (see Appendix "C")

Scale: Section = 1 mile X 1 mile (generally, with some exceptions)

Road Map

T19-N R5-E
St Stephens Meridian

Map Group 21

Cities & Towns
Newbern
Rosemary
Whitsitt

Cemeteries
McCreary Cemetery
Newbern Cemetery
Terrell Cemetery
Washington Cemetery

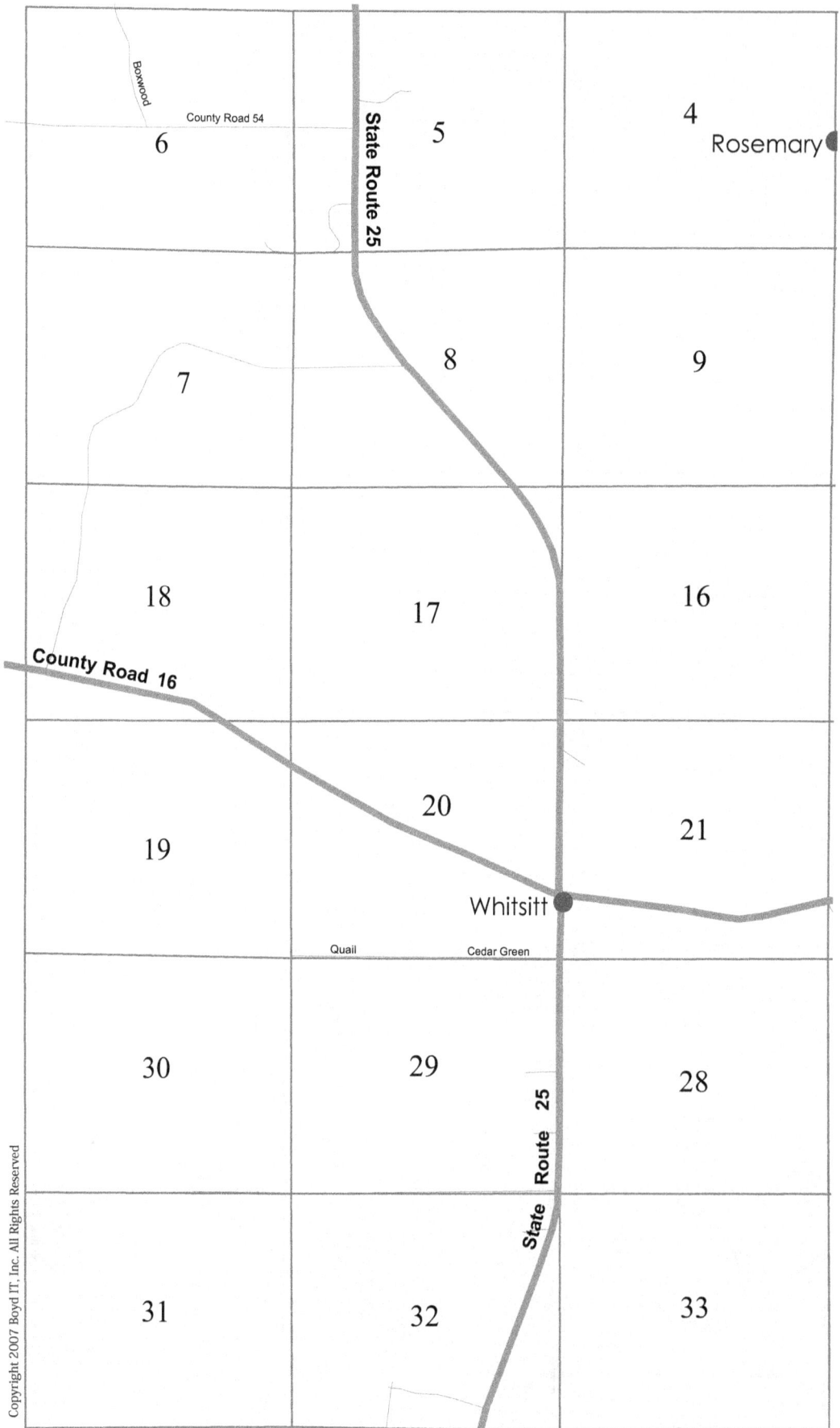

Boxwood

County Road 54

State Route 25

6

5

4

Rosemary

7

8

9

18

17

16

County Road 16

20

19

21

Whitsitt

Quail

Cedar Green

30

29

28

State Route 25

31

32

33

3

2

Terrell Cem.

Washington Cem.

Marion

1

Allen Acres

State Route 61

10

Rosemary

11

12

Pheasant

15

14

13

County Road 48

Pheasant

22

Canvas Back

Whitsitt

24

Lewis

Honey Dew

23

Killdeer

School

Beach

Newbern Cem.

Baby

Newbern

25

Bear

Bryant

Bryant Spur

27

26

Woods

Live Oak

Woods

Loop

County Road 20

Mt Valley

Bayler

34

35

36

McCreary Cem.

Helpful Hints

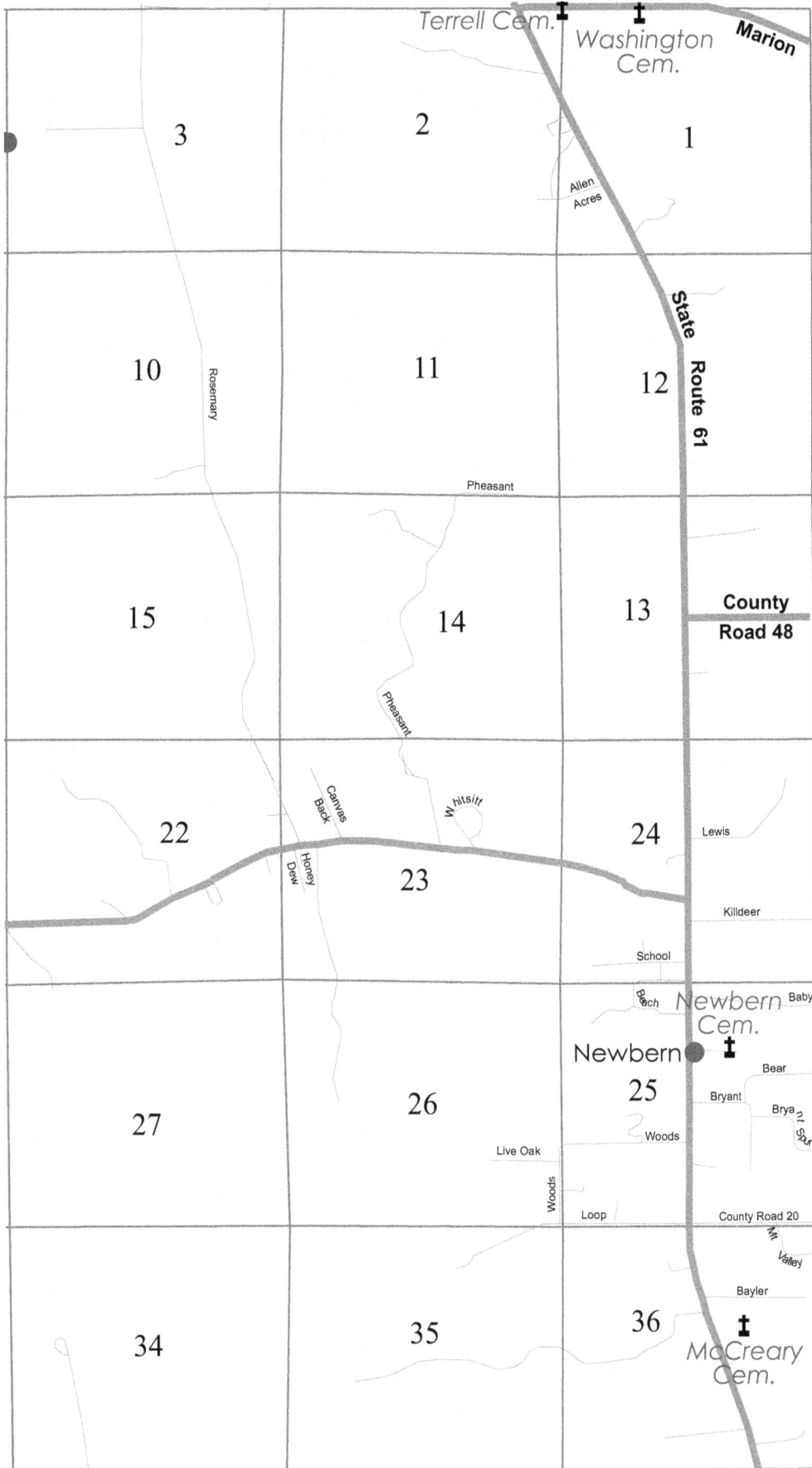

1. This road map has a number of uses, but primarily it is to help you: a) find the present location of land owned by your ancestors (at least the general area), b) find cemeteries and city-centers, and c) estimate the route/roads used by Census-takers & tax-assessors.

2. If you plan to travel to Hale County to locate cemeteries or land parcels, please pick up a modern travel map for the area before you do. Mapping old land parcels on modern maps is not as exact a science as you might think. Just the slightest variations in public land survey coordinates, estimates of parcel boundaries, or road-map deviations can greatly alter a map's representation of how a road either does or doesn't cross a particular parcel of land.

Legend

Section Lines
Interstates
Highways
Other Roads
Cities/Towns
Cemeteries

Scale: Section = 1 mile X 1 mile
(generally, with some exceptions)

Historical Map

T19-N R5-E
St Stephens Meridian

Map Group 21

Cities & Towns
Newbern
Rosemary
Whitsitt

Cemeteries
McCreary Cemetery
Newbern Cemetery
Terrell Cemetery
Washington Cemetery

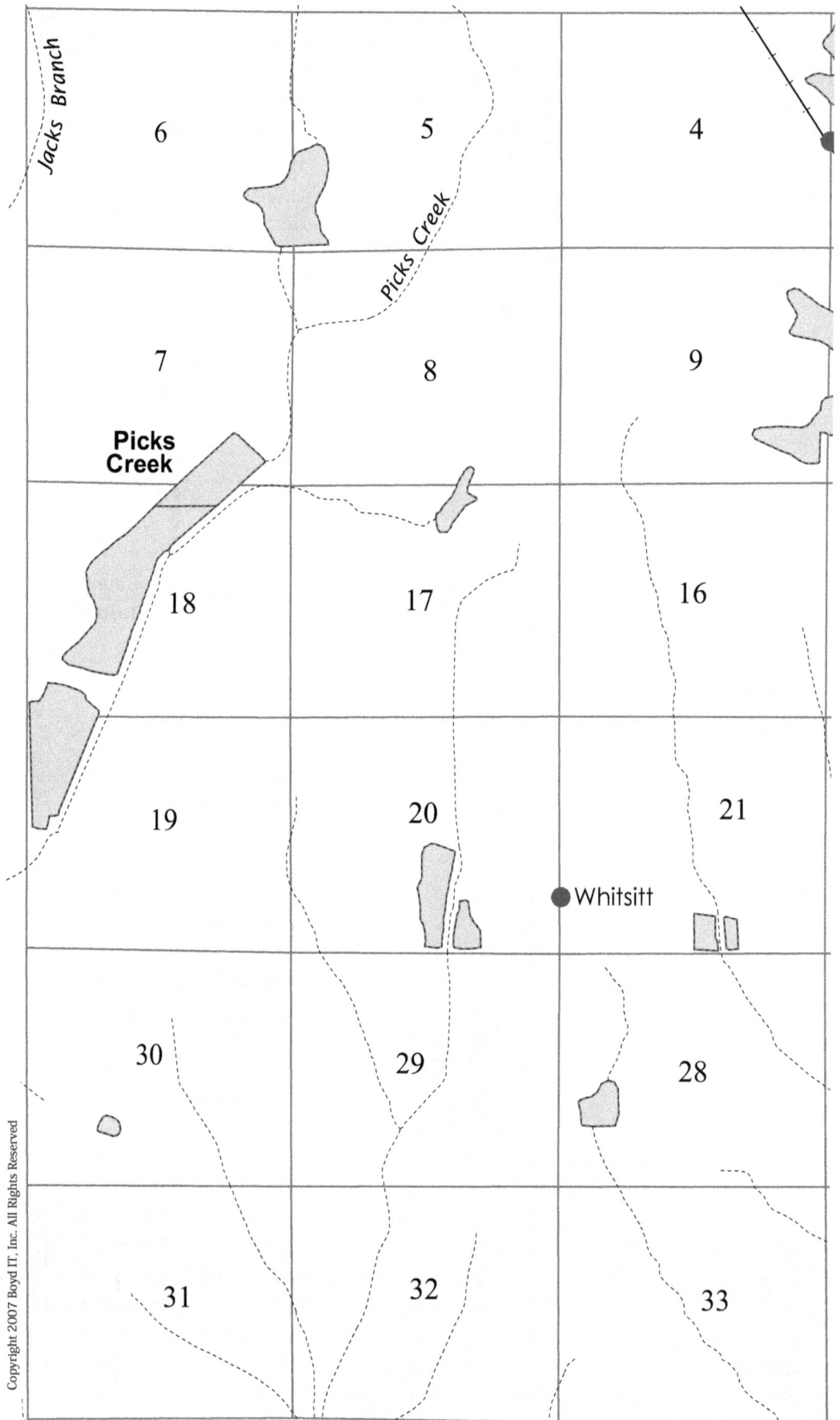

Jacks Branch

6

5

4

Picks Creek

7

8

9

**Picks
Creek**

18

17

16

19

20

21

● Whitsitt

30

29

28

31

32

33

Terrell Cem.

Washington Cem.

3

Rosemary

2

1

10

11

12

Whitsitt Creek

15

14

13

22

23

24

Newbern Cem.

Newbern

26

25

27

McCreary Cem.

34

35

36

Big Prairie Creek

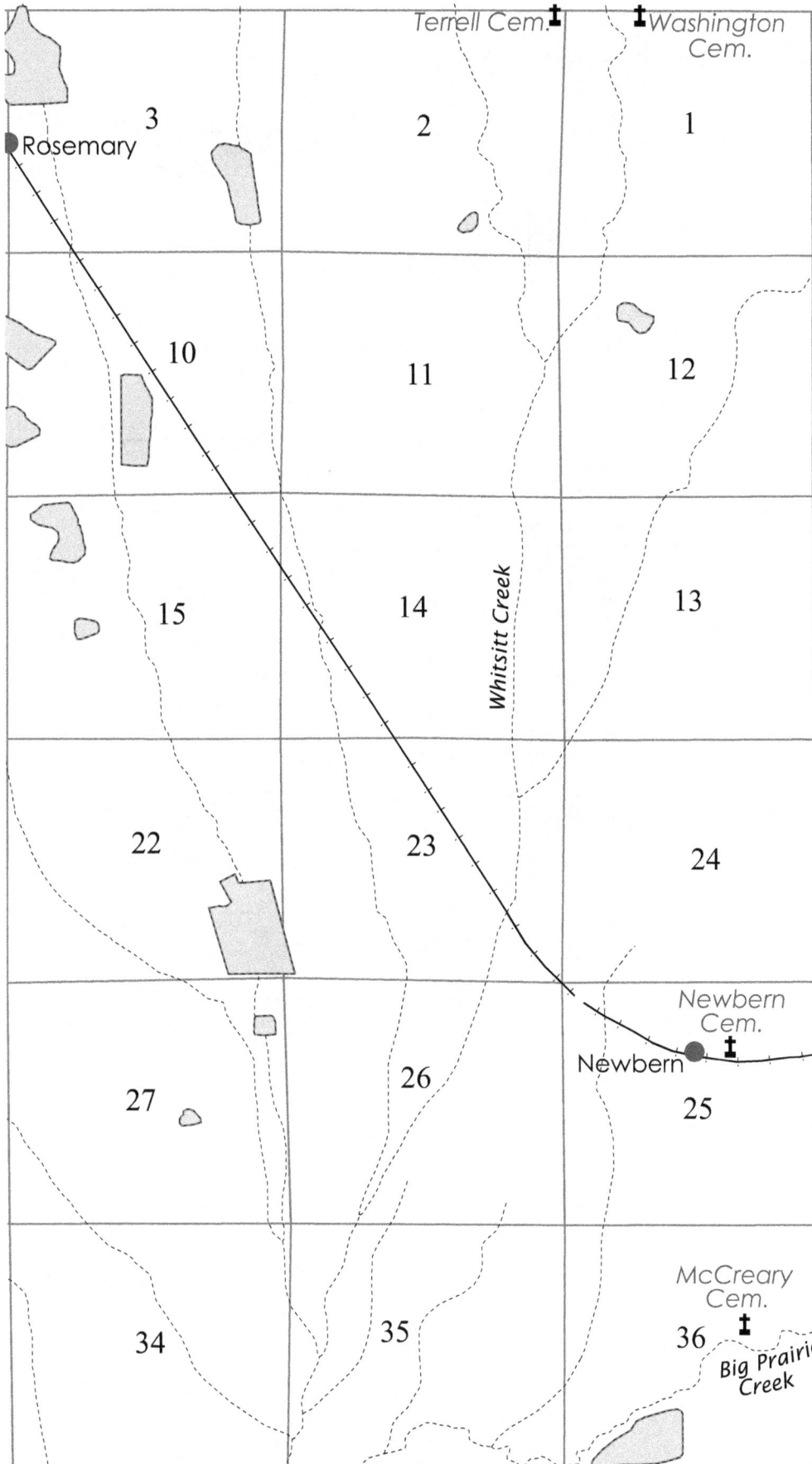

Helpful Hints

1. This Map takes a different look at the same Congressional Township displayed in the preceding two maps. It presents features that can help you better envision the historical development of the area: a) Water-bodies (lakes & ponds), b) Water-courses (rivers, streams, etc.), c) Railroads, d) City/town center-points (where they were oftentimes located when first settled), and e) Cemeteries.

2. Using this "Historical" map in tandem with this Township's Patent Map and Road Map, may lead you to some interesting discoveries. You will often find roads, towns, cemeteries, and waterways are named after nearby landowners: sometimes those names will be the ones you are researching. See how many of these research gems you can find here in Hale County.

L e g e n d

————————	Section Lines
+++++++++	Railroads
▭	Large Rivers & Bodies of Water
- - - - - - - -	Streams/Creeks & Small Rivers
●	Cities/Towns
✝	Cemeteries

Scale: Section = 1 mile X 1 mile
(there are some exceptions)

Map Group 22: Index to Land Patents

Township 18-North Range 3-East (St Stephens)

After you locate an individual in this Index, take note of the Section and Section Part then proceed to the Land Patent map on the pages immediately following. You should have no difficulty locating the corresponding parcel of land.

The "For More Info" Column will lead you to more information about the underlying Patents. See the *Legend* at right, and the "How to Use this Book" chapter, for more information.

```
LEGEND
            "For More Info . . . " column
A = Authority (Legislative Act, See Appendix "A")
B = Block or Lot (location in Section unknown)
C = Cancelled Patent
F = Fractional Section
G = Group  (Multi-Patentee Patent, see Appendix "C")
V = Overlaps another Parcel
R = Re-Issued (Parcel patented more than once)

(A & G items require you to look in the Appendixes referred
to above. All other Letter-designations followed by a number
require you to locate line-items in this index that possess
the ID number found after the letter).
```

ID	Individual in Patent	Sec.	Sec. Part	Date Issued	Other Counties	For More Info . . .
3627	BREADY, John	5	N½NE	1837-03-30	Greene	A1 G32
3619	CONNER, Charles D	14	NE	1835-09-28		A1
3621	CONNOR, Ephraim D	4	L	1847-12-16	Greene	A1
3622	"	4	M	1847-12-16	Greene	A1
3623	"	4	SWSW	1847-12-16	Greene	A1
3624	CONNOR, Eveline D	5	E½	1858-08-20	Greene	A1 F
3610	FORNIER, Alexander	5	W½SE	1837-03-30	Greene	A1 G85 F
3613	GLOVER, Allen	14	E½NW	1837-03-30		A1 G117
3616	"	4	B	1837-03-30	Greene	A1 G104
3614	"	5	E½SW	1837-03-30	Greene	A1 G116
3627	"	5	N½NE	1837-03-30	Greene	A1 G32
3617	"	5	W½SW	1837-03-30	Greene	A1 G118
3611	"	4	A	1837-11-02	Greene	A1 G109
3612	"	4	E½SE	1839-05-01	Greene	A1 G98
3615	"	4	W½SE	1839-05-01	Greene	A1 G100
3612	HOLTAM, Elijah S	4	E½SE	1839-05-01	Greene	A1 G98
3620	JAMES, Edmund B	4	C	1837-11-02	Greene	A1 F
3615	JAMES, Thomas	4	W½SE	1839-05-01	Greene	A1 G100
3625	KAMBER, Francis	16	SE	1835-09-28		A1
3616	LANDRUM, Zachariah	4	B	1837-03-30	Greene	A1 G104
3611	MCLEAN, Alfred	4	A	1837-11-02	Greene	A1 G109
3628	OSBORN, John H	8	SE	1858-08-20	Greene	A1 F
3629	PHILLIPS, William H	5	A	1837-11-02	Greene	A1
3626	RAVESIES, Frederick	2	SE	1835-09-28		A1
3610	SCISM, Joseph	5	W½SE	1837-03-30	Greene	A1 G85 F
3618	WALLER, Archibald	5	NW	1837-03-30	Greene	A1 G241
3618	WALLER, Catherine	5	NW	1837-03-30	Greene	A1 G241
3614	WHITE, James	5	E½SW	1837-03-30	Greene	A1 G116
3613	WHITE, James J	14	E½NW	1837-03-30		A1 G117
3617	WHITE, Zedekiah	5	W½SW	1837-03-30	Greene	A1 G118

Patent Map

T18-N R3-E
St Stephens Meridian

Map Group 22

Township Statistics

Parcels Mapped	:	20
Number of Patents	:	18
Number of Individuals	:	21
Patentees Identified	:	18
Number of Surnames	:	16
Multi-Patentee Parcels	:	10
Oldest Patent Date	:	9/28/1835
Most Recent Patent	:	8/20/1858
Block/Lot Parcels	:	6
Parcels Re - Issued	:	0
Parcels that Overlap	:	0
Cities and Towns	:	1
Cemeteries	:	2

Note: the area contained in this map amounts to far less than a full Township. Therefore, its contents are completely on this single page (instead of a "normal" 2-page spread).

Legend

— Patent Boundary

━━ Section Boundary

No Patents Found
(or Outside County)

1., 2., 3., ... Lot Numbers
(when beside a name)

[ ] Group Number
(see Appendix "C")

Scale: Section = 1 mile X 1 mile
(generally, with some exceptions)

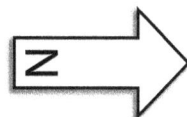

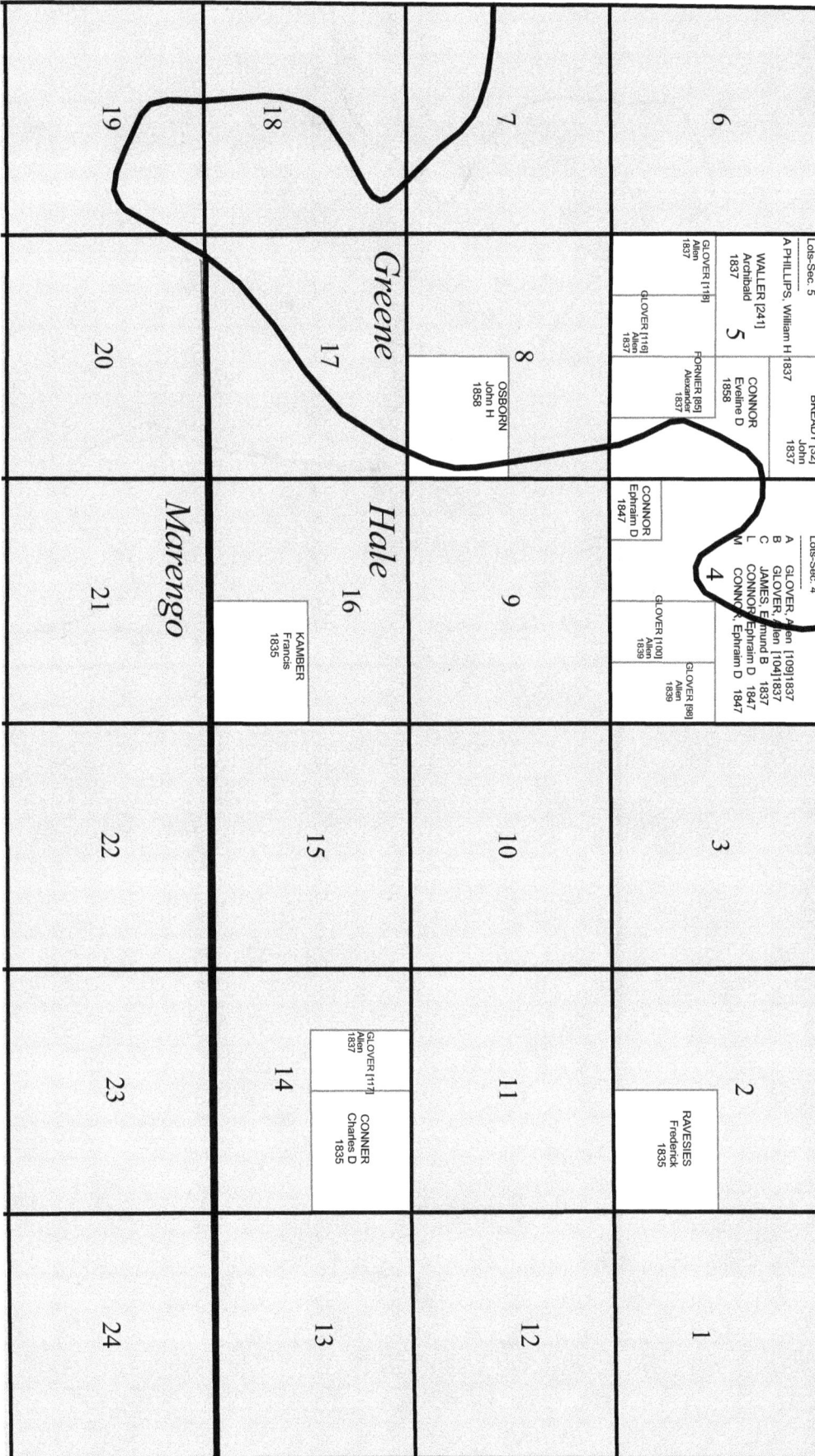

Map grid (sections and patents):

- 19
- 18
- 7
- 6
- 20
- 17 *Greene*
- 8
- OSBORN John H 1858
- CONNOR Eveline D 1858
- FORNIER [85] Alexander 1837
- GLOVER [116] Allen 1837
- GLOVER [118] Allen 1837
- WALLER [241] Archibald 1837
- A PHILLIPS, William H 1837
- Lots-Sec. 5
- 5
- BREADY [32] John 1837
- 21 *Marengo*
- 16 *Hale*
- KAMBER Francis 1835
- 9
- CONNOR Ephraim D 1847
- GLOVER [100] Allen 1839
- GLOVER [98] Allen 1839
- Lots-Sec. 4
- A GLOVER, Allen [109]1837
- B GLOVER, Allen [104]1837
- C JAMES, Edmund B 1837
- L CONNOR, Ephraim D 1847
- M CONNOR, Ephraim D 1847
- 4
- 22
- 15
- 10
- 3
- 23
- 14
- GLOVER [117] Allen 1837
- CONNER Charles D 1835
- 11
- 2
- RAVESIES Frederick 1835
- 24
- 13
- 12
- 1

N

Road Map

T18-N R3-E
St Stephens Meridian

Map Group 22

Note: the area contained in this map amounts to far less than a full Township. Therefore, its contents are completely on this single page (instead of a "normal" 2-page spread).

Cities & Towns
Arcola

Cemeteries
Evening Star Cemetery
Jerusalem Cemetery

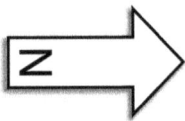

N

Legend

Section Lines

Interstates

Highways

Other Roads

● Cities/Towns

✝ Cemeteries

Scale: Section = 1 mile X 1 mile
(generally, with some exceptions)

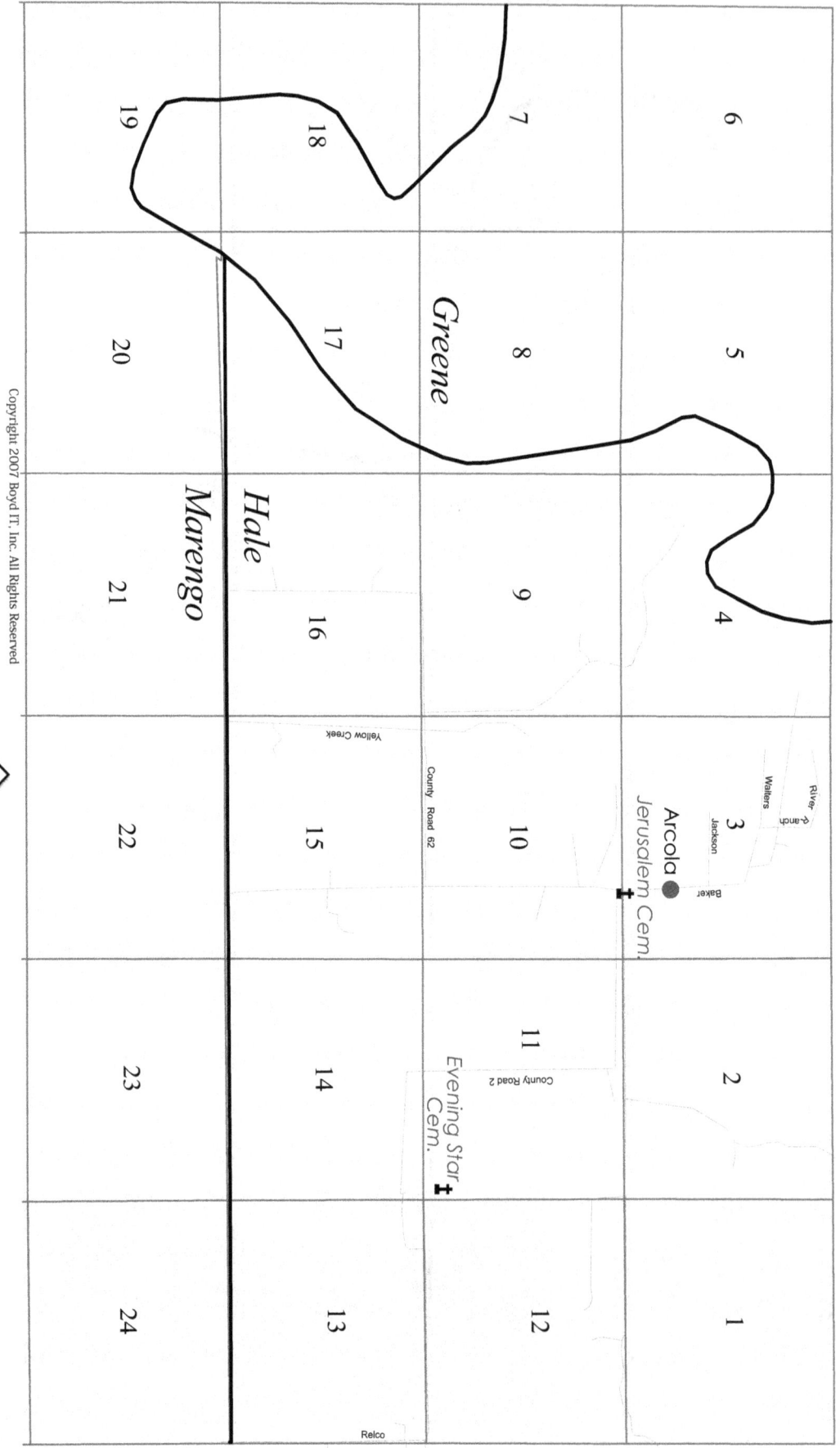

19	18	7		6	
20	17	*Greene*	8	5	
21	*Marengo* *Hale*	16	9	4	
22	15	10		2	
23	14	11			
24	13	12		1	

Greene

Marengo Hale

Yellow Creek

County Road 62

Arcola

Jerusalem Cem.

Walters

River Ranch

Jackson 3

Baker

Evening Star Cem.

County Road 2

Relco

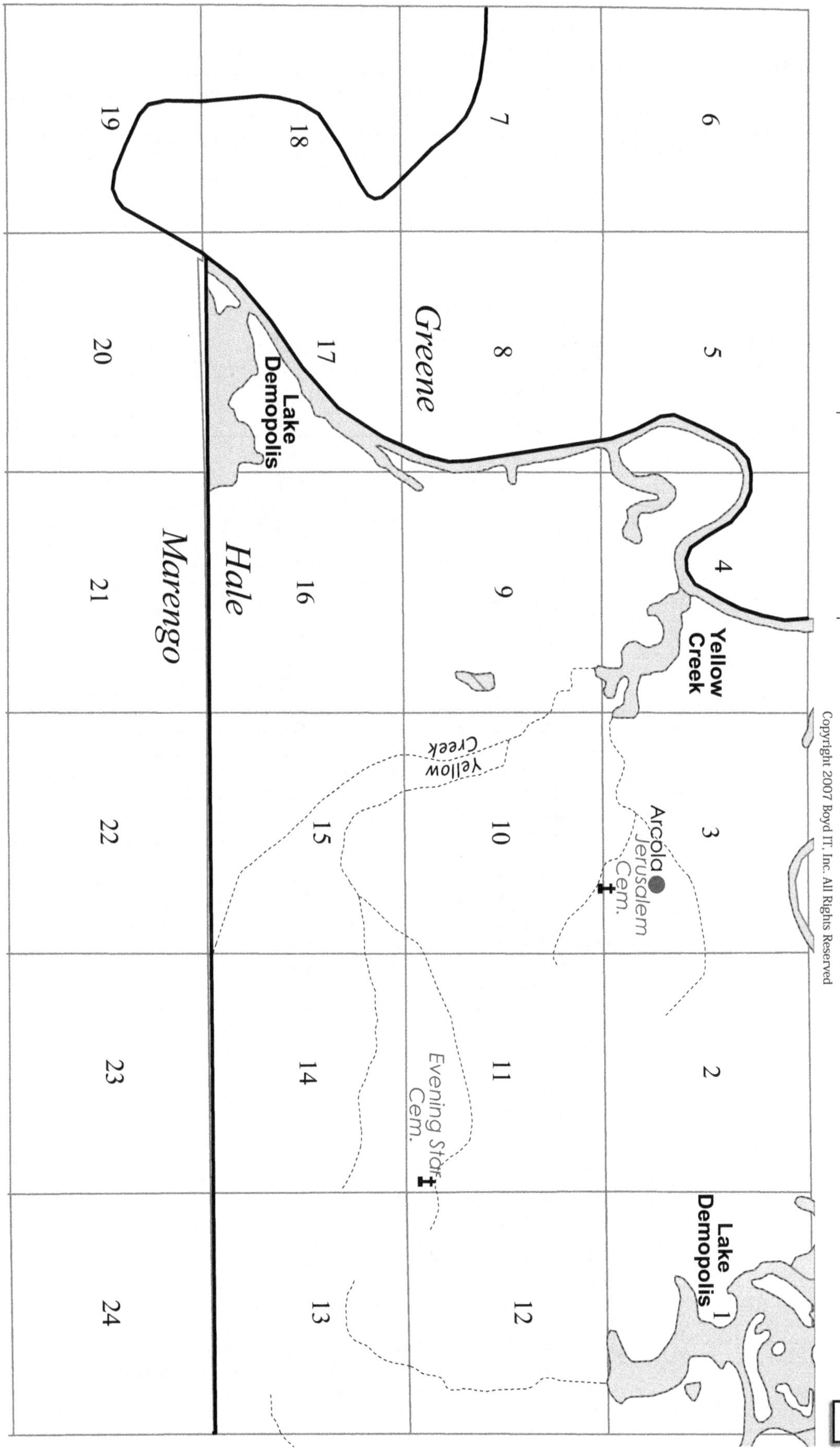

Historical Map

T18-N R3-E
St Stephens Meridian

Map Group 22

Note: the area contained in this map amounts to far less than a full Township. Therefore, its contents are completely on this single page (instead of a "normal" 2-page spread).

Cities & Towns

Arcola

Cemeteries

Evening Star Cemetery
Jerusalem Cemetery

Legend

- Section Lines
- Railroads
- Large Rivers & Bodies of Water
- Streams/Creeks & Small Rivers
- Cities/Towns
- Cemeteries

Scale: Section = 1 mile X 1 mile
(there are some exceptions)

N

Map Group 23: Index to Land Patents

Township 18-North Range 4-East (St Stephens)

After you locate an individual in this Index, take note of the Section and Section Part then proceed to the Land Patent map on the pages immediately following. You should have no difficulty locating the corresponding parcel of land.

The "For More Info" Column will lead you to more information about the underlying Patents. See the *Legend* at right, and the "How to Use this Book" chapter, for more information.

```
              LEGEND
        "For More Info . . . " column
A = Authority (Legislative Act, See Appendix "A")
B = Block or Lot (location in Section unknown)
C = Cancelled Patent
F = Fractional Section
G = Group (Multi-Patentee Patent, see Appendix "C")
V = Overlaps another Parcel
R = Re-Issued (Parcel patented more than once)

(A & G items require you to look in the Appendixes referred
to above. All other Letter-designations followed by a number
require you to locate line-items in this index that possess
the ID number found after the letter).
```

ID	Individual in Patent	Sec.	Sec. Part	Date Issued	Other Counties	For More Info . . .
3668	BARRETT, Starling	6	E½E½SE	1837-03-30		A1 G13
3653	BAUMGARTHER, John E	19	NE	1835-09-28		A1
3659	BRANCH, Julius C	29	W½NW	1848-07-01		A1
3652	BROWN, John	24	NENE	1892-06-10		A2
3651	BRYAN, James R	31	SW	1835-10-01		A1
3663	COCKE, Richard	29	SW	1839-05-01		A1
3671	CRAIG, William J	35	W½E½SE	1835-10-01		A1
3672	" "	35	W½SE	1835-10-01		A1
3647	GAGE, James B	3	NE	1835-10-01		A1 G88
3669	GAINSLEY, William	6	E½NW	1837-03-30		A1 G90
3641	GLOVER, Allen	13	E½SE	1837-03-30		A1 G95
3634	" "	13	W½SE	1837-03-30		A1 G94
3635	" "	15	E½SE	1837-03-30		A1 G99
3638	" "	15	W½SE	1837-03-30		A1 G110
3636	" "	16	E½E½SE	1837-03-30		A1 G101
3639	" "	31	W½NW	1837-03-30		A1 G97
3640	" "	34	E½SW	1837-03-30		A1 G102
3631	" "	34	SWSW	1837-03-30		A1
3637	" "	5	E½SE	1837-03-30		A1 G115
3633	" "	5	W½SE	1837-03-30		A1 G106
3668	" "	6	E½E½SE	1837-03-30		A1 G13
3669	" "	6	E½NW	1837-03-30		A1 G90
3632	" "	8	N½SE	1837-03-30		A1 C R3648
3642	" "	8	N½SW	1837-03-30		A1 G114
3649	GRAY, James	34	SE	1835-10-01		A1
3670	GREER, William	9	NW	1837-03-30		A1
3665	HAMMONDS, Samuel	9	SW	1835-09-28		A1
3634	HARDY, Henry	13	W½SE	1837-03-30		A1 G94
3641	HARDY, William	13	E½SE	1837-03-30		A1 G95
3644	HILL, Gabriel L	33	SE	1835-09-28		A1
3639	HILL, Sterling	31	W½NW	1837-03-30		A1 G97
3635	HOWELL, Ira	15	E½SE	1837-03-30		A1 G99
3645	HUDSON, Isaac	24	SE	1835-10-01		A1
3636	JOHNSON, James	16	E½E½SE	1837-03-30		A1 G101
3640	JOHNSON, Thomas W	34	E½SW	1837-03-30		A1 G102
3658	LOMAX, John T	3	E½NW	1839-05-01		A1 G178
3657	" "	3	W½NW	1839-05-01		A1 G177
3648	LYON, James B	8	N½SE	1840-11-10		A1 R3632
3647	MALONE, John	3	NE	1835-10-01		A1 G88
3633	MANESS, Ezekiel	5	W½SE	1837-03-30		A1 G106
3658	MANNING, Amos R	3	E½NW	1839-05-01		A1 G178
3657	" "	3	W½NW	1839-05-01		A1 G177
3630	MARTIN, Albert	26	W½NW	1837-03-30		A1 G179
3630	MARTIN, Esther	26	W½NW	1837-03-30		A1 G179
3630	MARTIN, Francis	26	W½NW	1837-03-30		A1 G179
3630	MARTIN, Laura	26	W½NW	1837-03-30		A1 G179

ID	Individual in Patent	Sec.	Sec. Part	Date Issued	Other Counties	For More Info . . .
3630	MARTIN, Peter	26	W½NW	1837-03-30		A1 G179
3630	MARTIN, Sarah	26	W½NW	1837-03-30		A1 G179
3630	MARTIN, Wesley	26	W½NW	1837-03-30		A1 G179
3660	MARTINIER, Julius	6	W½NE	1837-03-30		A1 G184
3661	MARTINIERE, Julius	6	E½NE	1837-03-30		A1 G185
3643	MCRAE, Christopher	9	NE	1837-03-30		A1
3654	MCRAE, John	19	SW	1835-09-28		A1
3660	MOORE, James	6	W½NE	1837-03-30		A1 G184
3638	MORGAN, Silas	15	W½SE	1837-03-30		A1 G110
3656	MOSS, John S	24	E½SW	1825-06-20		A1
3661	RIDGILL, Joel	6	E½NE	1837-03-30		A1 G185
3655	ROBERTSON, John R	32	SE	1835-09-28		A1
3667	ROGERS, Simon G	26	SW	1835-10-01		A1
3650	RUFFIN, James H	7	E½E½SE	1837-03-30		A1
3662	SANDERSON, Lemuel G	21	SE	1835-09-28		A1
3673	SHULTZ, William N	28	E½E½SE	1835-09-28		A1
3642	SURGINER, William	8	N½SW	1837-03-30		A1 G114
3646	SWANN, Isaac	19	NW	1835-09-28		A1
3661	TALIAFERRO, Benjamin	6	E½NE	1837-03-30		A1 G185
3660	TALLIAFERRO, Benjamin	6	W½NE	1837-03-30		A1 G184
3658	TUCKER, Richard H	3	E½NW	1839-05-01		A1 G178
3637	WADE, Joshua A	5	E½SE	1837-03-30		A1 G115
3666	WILSON, Samuel	3	SW	1835-10-01		A1
3664	WITHERSPOON, Robert F	2	SE	1835-09-28		A1

Patent Map

T18-N R4-E
St Stephens Meridian

Map Group 23

Township Statistics

Parcels Mapped	:	44
Number of Patents	:	43
Number of Individuals	:	54
Patentees Identified	:	42
Number of Surnames	:	44
Multi-Patentee Parcels	:	18
Oldest Patent Date	:	6/20/1825
Most Recent Patent	:	6/10/1892
Block/Lot Parcels	:	0
Parcels Re - Issued	:	1
Parcels that Overlap	:	0
Cities and Towns	:	4
Cemeteries	:	5

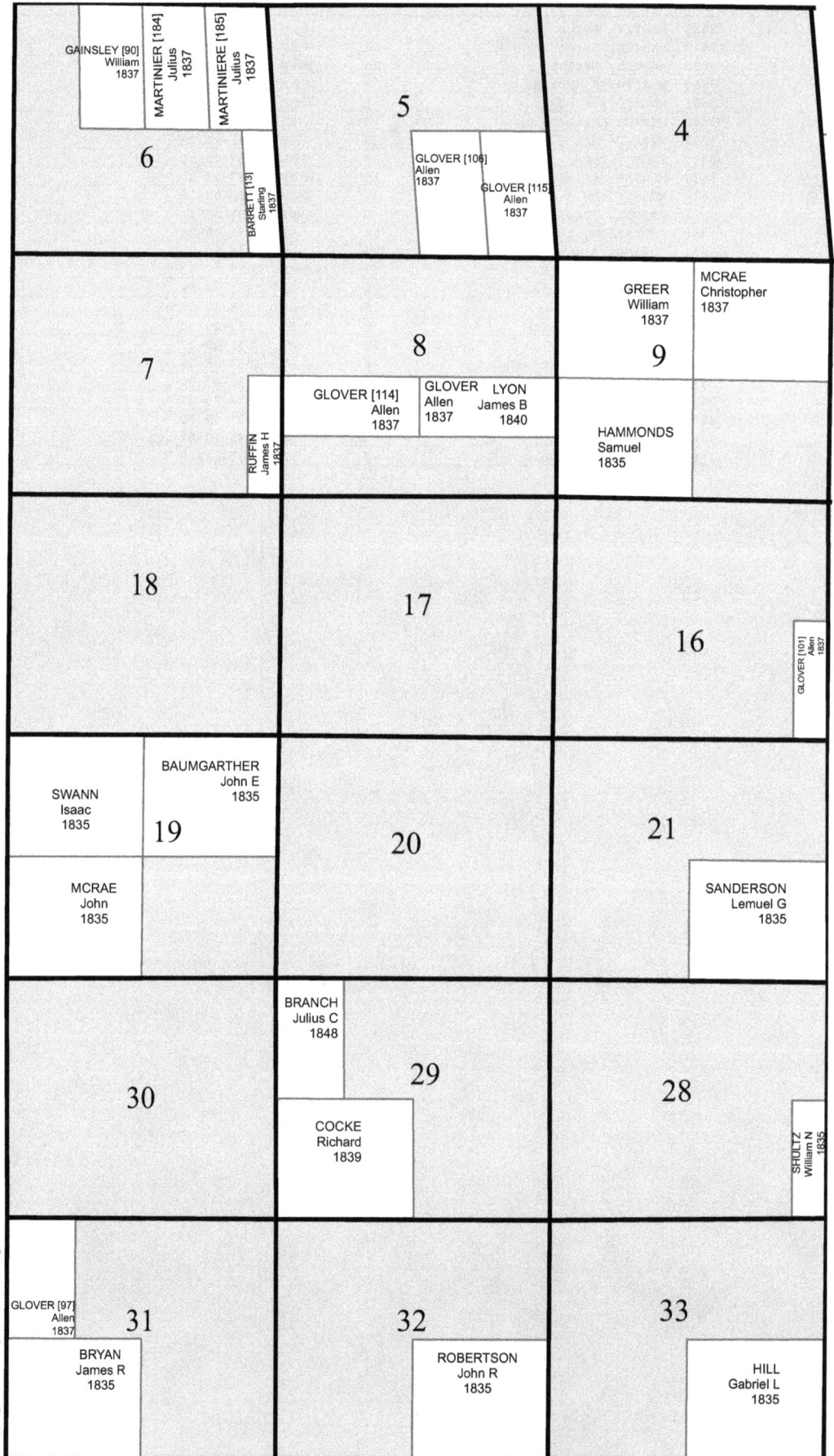

GAINSLEY [90]
William
1837

MARTINIER [184]
Julius
1837

MARTINIERE [185]
Julius
1837

6

5

4

BARRETT [13]
Starling
1837

GLOVER [106]
Allen
1837

GLOVER [115]
Allen
1837

7

8

GREER
William
1837

MCRAE
Christopher
1837

9

RUFFIN
James H
1837

GLOVER [114]
Allen
1837

GLOVER
Allen
1837

LYON
James B
1840

HAMMONDS
Samuel
1835

18

17

16

GLOVER [101]
Allen
1837

SWANN
Isaac
1835

BAUMGARTHER
John E
1835

19

MCRAE
John
1835

20

21

SANDERSON
Lemuel G
1835

30

BRANCH
Julius C
1848

29

COCKE
Richard
1839

28

SHULTZ
William N
1835

GLOVER [97]
Allen
1837

31

BRYAN
James R
1835

32

ROBERTSON
John R
1835

33

HILL
Gabriel L
1835

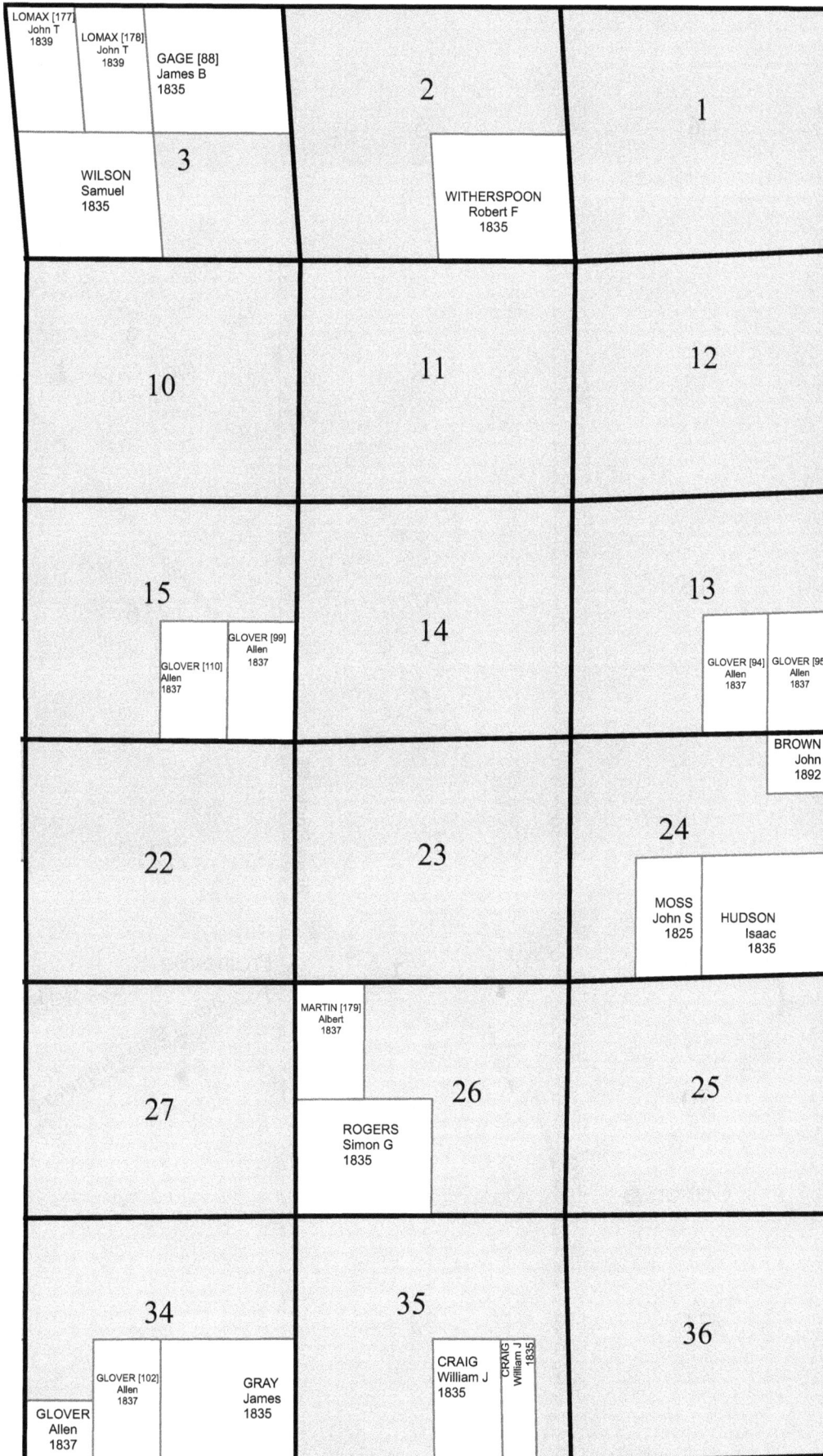

LOMAX [177]
John T
1839

LOMAX [178]
John T
1839

GAGE [88]
James B
1835

WILSON
Samuel
1835

3

2

1

WITHERSPOON
Robert F
1835

10

11

12

15

GLOVER [110]
Allen
1837

GLOVER [99]
Allen
1837

14

13

GLOVER [94]
Allen
1837

GLOVER [95]
Allen
1837

BROWN
John
1892

22

23

24

MOSS
John S
1825

HUDSON
Isaac
1835

27

MARTIN [179]
Albert
1837

ROGERS
Simon G
1835

26

25

34

GLOVER [102]
Allen
1837

GLOVER
Allen
1837

GRAY
James
1835

35

CRAIG
William J
1835

CRAIG
William J
1835

36

Helpful Hints

1. This Map's INDEX can be found on the preceding pages.

2. Refer to Map "C" to see where this Township lies within Hale County, Alabama.

3. Numbers within square brackets [ ] denote a multi-patentee land parcel (multi-owner). Refer to Appendix "C" for a full list of members in this group.

4. Areas that look to be crowded with Patentees usually indicate multiple sales of the same parcel (Re-issues) or Overlapping parcels. See this Township's Index for an explanation of these and other circumstances that might explain "odd" groupings of Patentees on this map.

Legend

_____ Patent Boundary

━━━━━━━━━━ Section Boundary

No Patents Found
(or Outside County)

1., 2., 3., ... Lot Numbers
(when beside a name)

[ ] Group Number
(see Appendix "C")

Scale: Section = 1 mile X 1 mile
(generally, with some exceptions)

Road Map

T18-N R4-E
St Stephens Meridian

Map Group 23

Cities & Towns
Allenville
Gallion
Oak Grove
Prairieville

Cemeteries
Allenville Cemetery
Mount Olive Cemetery
Oak Grove Cemetery
Saint Andrews Cemetery
Willis-Scott Cemetery

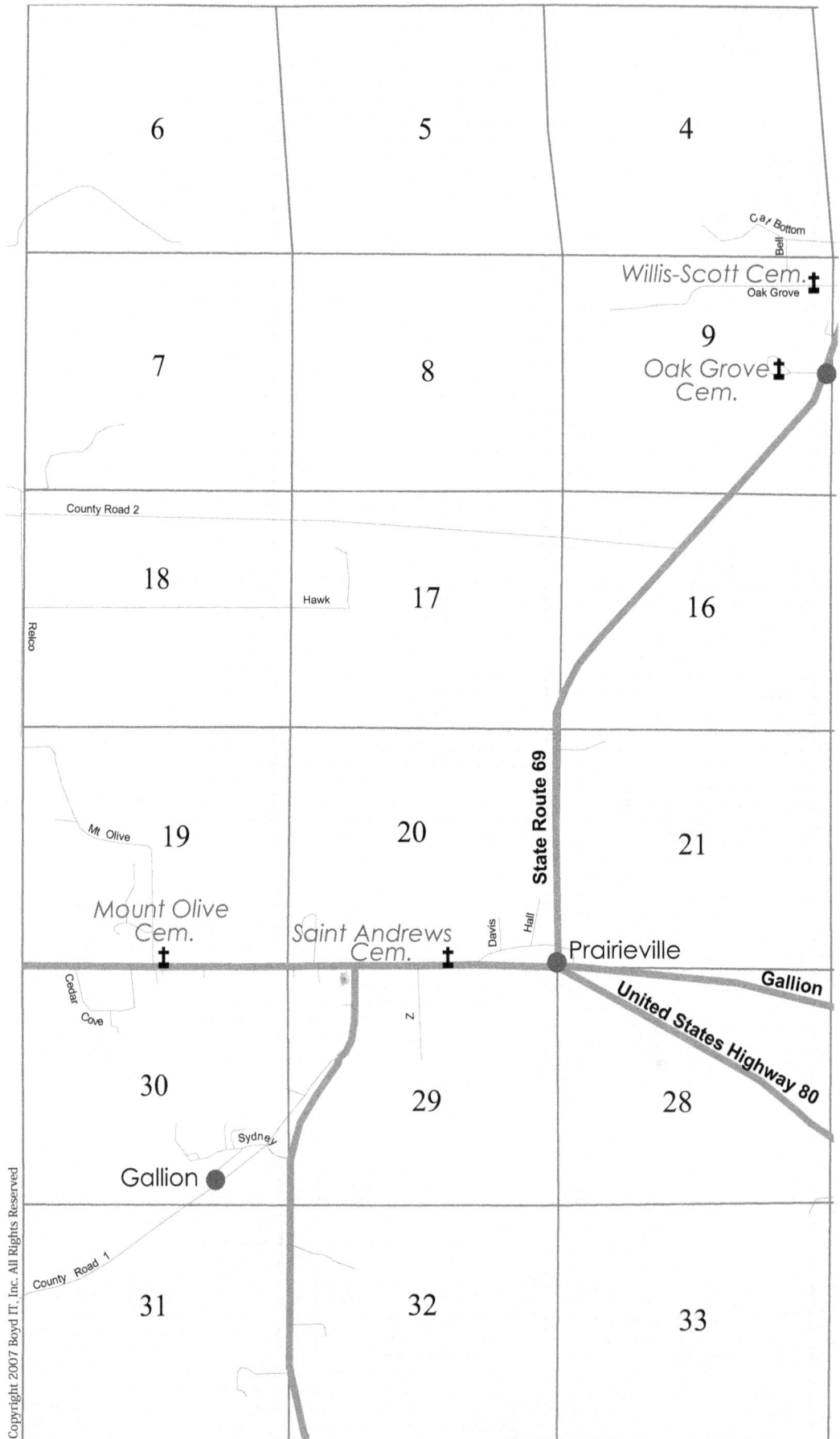

6

5

4

Ca/ Bottom

Bell

Willis-Scott Cem. †
Oak Grove

7

8

9

Oak Grove †
Cem.

County Road 2

18

Hawk

17

16

Relco

State Route 69

19

Mt Olive

20

21

Mount Olive
Cem. †

Saint Andrews
Cem. †

Davis

Hall

Prairieville

Gallion

United States Highway 80

Cedar
Cove

30

29

28

Z

Sydney

Gallion

31

County Road 1

32

33

3

2

1

County Road 9

County Road 10

Pecan

Oak Grove
10

11

Garris

12

15

14

13

22

23

24

County Road 12

Robin

David

Gallion

27

26

25

✝ *Allenville Cem.*

Ash

Allenville

Apricot

Allenville

34

35

36

Allenville

Helpful Hints

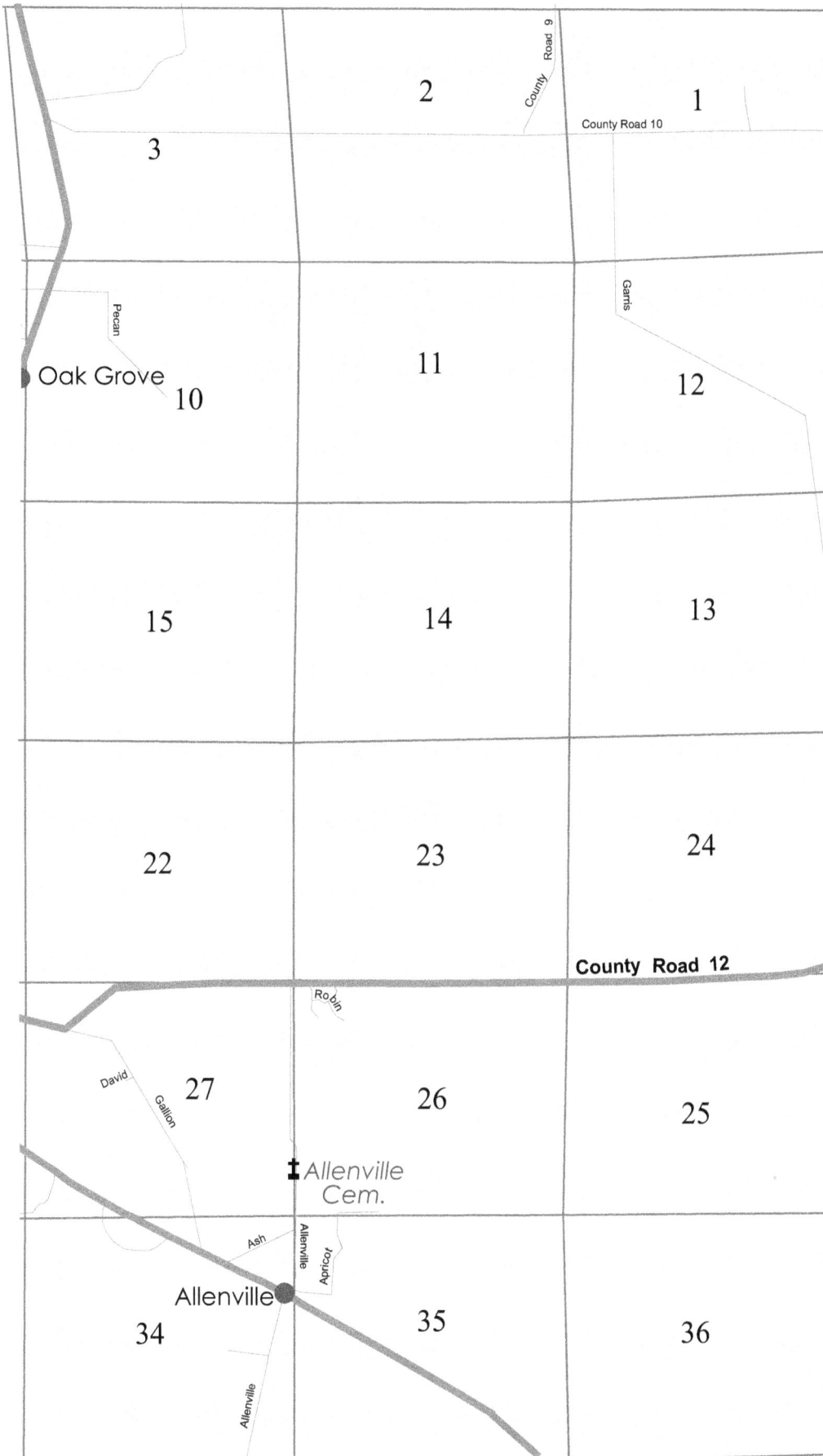

1. This road map has a number of uses, but primarily it is to help you: a) find the present location of land owned by your ancestors (at least the general area), b) find cemeteries and city-centers, and c) estimate the route/roads used by Census-takers & tax-assessors.

2. If you plan to travel to Hale County to locate cemeteries or land parcels, please pick up a modern travel map for the area before you do. Mapping old land parcels on modern maps is not as exact a science as you might think. Just the slightest variations in public land survey coordinates, estimates of parcel boundaries, or road-map deviations can greatly alter a map's representation of how a road either does or doesn't cross a particular parcel of land.

L e g e n d

——————— Section Lines

═══════ Interstates

▬▬▬▬▬ Highways

——————— Other Roads

● Cities/Towns

✝ Cemeteries

Scale: Section = 1 mile X 1 mile
(generally, with some exceptions)

Historical Map

T18-N R4-E
St Stephens Meridian

Map Group 23

Cities & Towns
Allenville
Gallion
Oak Grove
Prairieville

Cemeteries
Allenville Cemetery
Mount Olive Cemetery
Oak Grove Cemetery
Saint Andrews Cemetery
Willis-Scott Cemetery

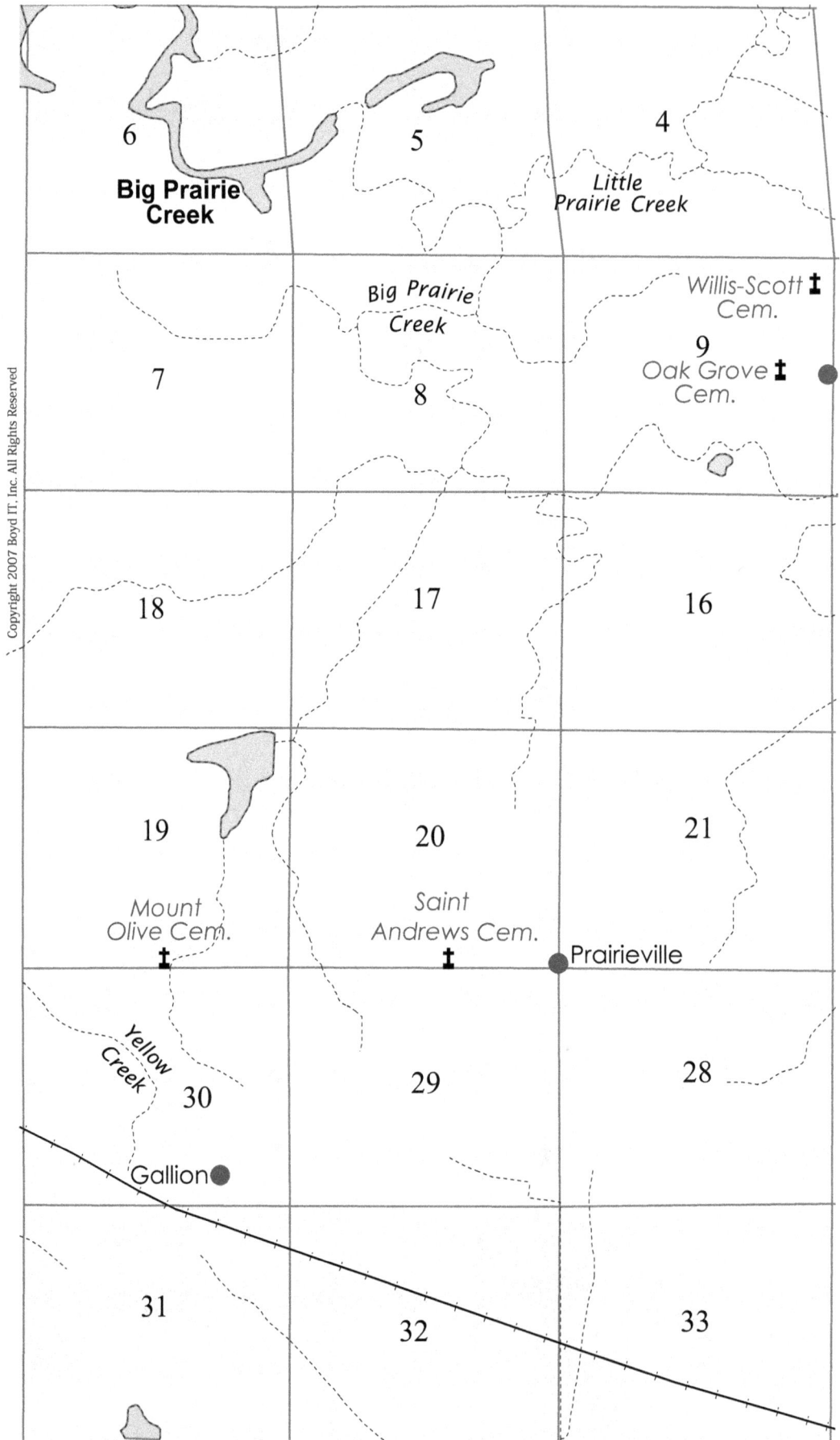

6

5

4

Big Prairie
Creek

Little
Prairie Creek

7

Big Prairie
Creek

8

Willis-Scott
Cem.

9

Oak Grove
Cem.

18

17

16

19

20

21

Mount
Olive Cem.

Saint
Andrews Cem.

Prairieville

30

Yellow
Creek

29

28

Gallion

31

32

33

3

2

1

Helpful Hints

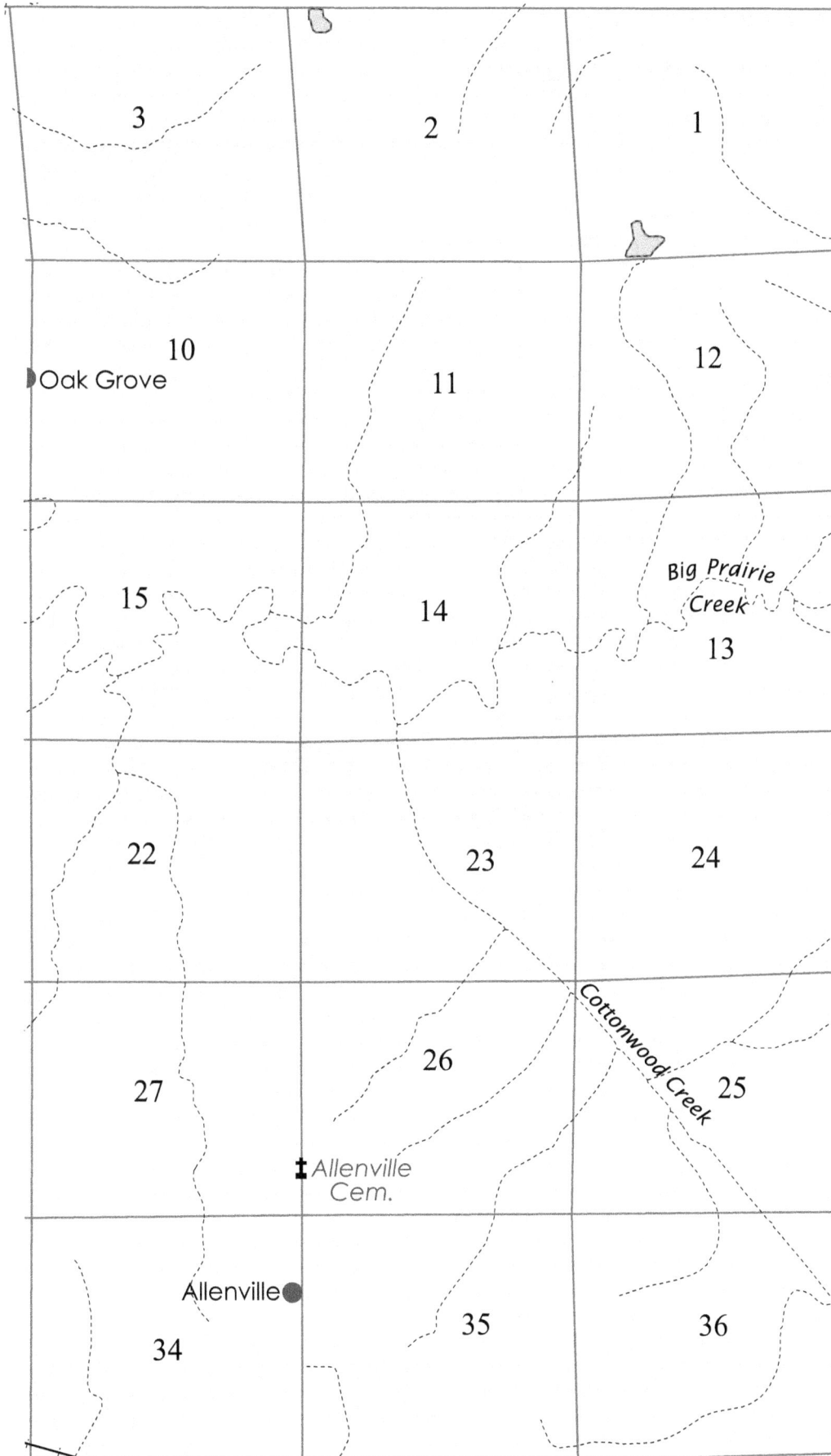

1. This Map takes a different look at the same Congressional Township displayed in the preceding two maps. It presents features that can help you better envision the historical development of the area: a) Water-bodies (lakes & ponds), b) Water-courses (rivers, streams, etc.), c) Railroads, d) City/town center-points (where they were oftentimes located when first settled), and e) Cemeteries.

2. Using this "Historical" map in tandem with this Township's Patent Map and Road Map, may lead you to some interesting discoveries. You will often find roads, towns, cemeteries, and waterways are named after nearby landowners: sometimes those names will be the ones you are researching. See how many of these research gems you can find here in Hale County.

10

Oak Grove

11

12

15

14

Big Prairie Creek

13

22

23

24

Cottonwood Creek

26

25

27

‡ Allenville Cem.

Allenville

34

35

36

Legend

————————	Section Lines
+++++++++	Railroads
▭	Large Rivers & Bodies of Water
- - - - - - -	Streams/Creeks & Small Rivers
●	Cities/Towns
‡	Cemeteries

Scale: Section = 1 mile X 1 mile
(there are some exceptions)

Map Group 24: Index to Land Patents

Township 18-North Range 5-East (St Stephens)

After you locate an individual in this Index, take note of the Section and Section Part then proceed to the Land Patent map on the pages immediately following. You should have no difficulty locating the corresponding parcel of land.

The "For More Info" Column will lead you to more information about the underlying Patents. See the *Legend* at right, and the "How to Use this Book" chapter, for more information.

```
┌──────────────────────────────────────────────────────┐
│                      LEGEND                            │
│           "For More Info . . . " column                │
│ ──────────────────────────────────────────────────    │
│ A = Authority (Legislative Act, See Appendix "A")      │
│ B = Block or Lot (location in Section unknown)         │
│ C = Cancelled Patent                                   │
│ F = Fractional Section                                 │
│ G = Group  (Multi-Patentee Patent, see Appendix "C")   │
│ V = Overlaps another Parcel                            │
│ R = Re-Issued (Parcel patented more than once)         │
│                                                        │
│ (A & G items require you to look in the Appendixes     │
│ referred to above. All other Letter-designations       │
│ followed by a number require you to locate line-items  │
│ in this index that possess the ID number found after   │
│ the letter).                                           │
└──────────────────────────────────────────────────────┘
```

ID	Individual in Patent	Sec.	Sec. Part	Date Issued	Other Counties	For More Info . . .
3710	ADAMS, David W	18	SENW	1837-03-30		A1
3870	ALSTON, Nathaniel	35	E½NE	1831-07-01		A1
3871	" "	35	E½SE	1831-07-01		A1
3782	AVERA, John	20	W½NW	1831-06-01		A1
3783	" "	20	W½SW	1831-06-01		A1
3784	" "	21	W½SW	1831-08-01		A1
3894	BAGGETT, Silas	24	W½SW	1831-05-17		A1
3741	BANNON, James	4	SWSW	1835-09-28		A1
3890	BANNON, Robert O	4	SWSE	1835-09-22		A1
3785	BARRON, John	10	E½NE	1834-01-21		A1
3877	BELL, Robert	22	W½NE	1831-06-01		A1
3930	BENNETT, William	5	E½NW	1831-06-01		A1
3931	" "	7	N½NE	1831-06-01		A1
3836	BORDEN, Joseph	22	W½SW	1833-09-16		A1
3835	" "	22	E½SW	1833-11-14		A1
3830	" "	11	E½SW	1835-09-22		A1
3841	" "	11	SE	1835-09-22		A1 G28
3831	" "	11	W½NE	1835-09-22		A1
3832	" "	12	E½NW	1835-09-22		A1
3842	" "	12	E½SW	1835-09-22		A1 G28
3843	" "	12	SE	1835-09-22		A1 G28
3833	" "	12	W½NE	1835-09-22		A1
3834	" "	12	W½SW	1835-09-22		A1
3837	" "	27	NW	1835-09-22		A1
3838	" "	27	NWNE	1835-09-22		A1
3839	" "	28	NENE	1835-09-22		A1
3840	" "	9	E½SE	1835-09-28		A1
3917	BORDEN, Thomas R	1	E½NE	1831-08-01		A1
3919	" "	21	E½SW	1833-08-02		A1
3918	" "	12	NENE	1834-08-20		A1
3841	" "	11	SE	1835-09-22		A1 G28
3842	" "	12	E½SW	1835-09-22		A1 G28
3843	" "	12	SE	1835-09-22		A1 G28
3920	" "	10	SE	1837-03-15		A1 G30
3921	" "	11	NW	1837-03-15		A1 G30
3922	" "	11	W½SW	1837-03-15		A1 G30
3933	BROWN, William	36	SWNE	1834-09-04		A1
3932	" "	36	NWNE	1835-09-25		A1
3739	BURKE, Hannah C	18	NWNE	1835-10-01		A1
3786	BURKE, John	17	W½NE	1831-06-01		A1
3793	" "	19	W½SE	1831-06-01		A1
3792	" "	19	W½NE	1831-07-01		A1
3788	" "	18	E½SE	1833-06-04		A1
3787	" "	17	W½SW	1834-08-12		A1
3789	" "	18	E½SW	1834-08-12		A1
3791	" "	18	W½SE	1834-08-12		A1

ID	Individual in Patent	Sec.	Sec. Part	Date Issued	Other Counties	For More Info . . .
3790	BURKE, John (Cont'd)	18	S½NE	1835-09-25		A1
3718	CABANISS, Elijah	33	W½NE	1831-05-17		A1
3740	CHAMBERS, James B	15	SESE	1834-08-20		A1
3844	CHAMBERS, Joseph	13	S½NW	1834-08-20		A1
3827	CHAMBERS, Joseph B	23	E½NE	1831-06-01		A1
3829	" "	24	W½NW	1831-06-01		A1
3824	" "	14	E½SW	1831-07-01		A1
3828	" "	23	W½SE	1831-07-01		A1
3825	" "	14	S½NE	1835-09-12		A1
3826	" "	14	W½SW	1835-09-12		A1
3797	COATS, John	19	E½SW	1831-07-01		A1 G61
3798	" "	19	W½SW	1831-07-01		A1 G61
3796	" "	30	E½NW	1831-07-01		A1
3799	" "	30	W½NW	1831-07-01		A1 G61
3794	" "	19	E½NE	1831-08-01		A1
3795	" "	19	NW	1831-08-01		A1
3797	COLE, David	19	E½SW	1831-07-01		A1 G61
3798	" "	19	W½SW	1831-07-01		A1 G61
3799	" "	30	W½NW	1831-07-01		A1 G61
3863	CRENSHAW, Micajah	25	S½SW	1834-08-20		A1
3778	CROOM, Jesse H	30	W½NE	1835-09-12		A1
3775	" "	18	W½SW	1835-09-22		A1
3776	" "	28	SW	1835-09-22		A1
3777	" "	28	W½SE	1835-09-22		A1
3923	CROOM, Wiley	28	W½NW	1835-09-19		A1
3924	" "	29	E½SE	1835-09-19		A1
3925	CROOM, Wiley J	32	E½NE	1834-05-12		A1
3927	" "	32	SW	1834-05-12		A1
3928	" "	32	W½NE	1834-05-12		A1
3929	" "	32	W½NW	1834-05-12		A1
3926	" "	32	SE	1834-09-04		A1
3878	DICKENS, Robert	33	NWNW	1837-03-15		A1
3879	" "	33	SESW	1837-05-15		A1
3880	DICKINS, Robert	17	NWNW	1835-10-01		A1
3881	" "	18	NENE	1835-10-01		A1
3882	" "	27	N½SW	1835-10-01		A1
3883	" "	28	E½NW	1835-10-01		A1
3884	" "	28	SENE	1835-10-01		A1
3885	" "	28	W½NE	1835-10-01		A1
3887	" "	9	E½SW	1835-10-01		A1
3888	" "	9	W½SE	1835-10-01		A1
3886	" "	7	S½SE	1837-03-15		A1 V3702
3686	ELLIOTT, Andrew	22	E½NE	1831-06-01		A1
3687	" "	23	W½NW	1831-06-01		A1
3855	FINNEY, Manasseh	34	E½SE	1831-06-01		A1
3856	" "	35	W½SW	1831-06-01		A1
3889	FREEMAN, Robert	34	W½SE	1833-06-04		A1
3820	FRIERSON, John W	6	E½NE	1831-07-01		A1
3821	" "	7	E½NW	1831-07-01		A1
3717	GABEL, Elias	21	NE	1831-06-01		A1
3859	GAREY, Mathias E	22	E½SE	1831-06-01		A1
3934	GAREY, William	20	E½NW	1831-06-01		A1
3899	GARRETSON, Thomas	17	SWNW	1834-08-20		A1
3869	GILL, Nathan J	12	SENE	1835-09-22		A1
3822	GILMORE, John W	35	W½NE	1831-07-01		A1
3823	" "	36	W½SW	1831-07-01		A1
3677	GRANTHAM, Adam	23	E½SE	1831-05-17		A1
3900	GREEN, Thomas	28	E½SE	1831-08-01		A1
3688	GREER, Anthony W	29	W½SW	1833-06-04		A1
3849	GREER, Joseph	34	NE	1831-06-01		A1
3847	" "	29	W½NE	1831-07-01		A1
3845	" "	29	E½NE	1831-08-01		A1
3846	" "	29	E½SW	1831-08-01		A1
3850	" "	35	W½NW	1831-08-01		A1
3848	" "	32	E½NW	1833-06-04		A1
3892	GREER, Samuel	20	E½SE	1831-07-01		A1
3893	" "	21	E½SE	1831-08-01		A1
3902	GREER, Thomas	33	E½NE	1831-05-17		A1
3904	" "	34	W½NW	1831-05-17		A1
3903	" "	34	E½NW	1831-07-01		A1
3901	" "	27	S½SW	1835-09-12		A1
3725	GRIFFIN, Goodman G	34	SW	1835-09-22		A1
3697	HANNAN, Burrel	2	W½SW	1831-07-01		A1

ID	Individual in Patent	Sec.	Sec. Part	Date Issued	Other Counties	For More Info . . .
3706	HARDING, Daniel	33	NESW	1834-08-12		A1
3707	" "	33	SWNW	1834-08-12		A1
3708	HARDING, David	6	E½NW	1831-07-01		A1
3709	" "	6	W½NE	1831-07-01		A1
3698	HARMAN, Burrel	3	E½SE	1831-08-01		A1
3743	HARPER, James	36	E½SW	1831-08-01		A1
3742	" "	35	W½SE	1834-09-04		A1
3744	" "	36	NWSE	1834-09-04		A1
3711	HAYES, Dempsey	6	SE	1831-06-01		A1
3943	HEMPHILL, William	18	NENW	1835-10-01		A1
3700	HOOKS, Charles W	7	NWSE	1834-09-04		A1
3699	" "	7	NESE	1835-09-25		A1 V3702
3728	HUCKABEE, Gray	3	NENW	1835-09-28		A1
3730	" "	3	SWNW	1835-09-28		A1
3726	" "	10	NWNW	1835-10-01		A1
3727	" "	3	E½SW	1835-10-01		A1
3731	" "	3	W½SW	1835-10-01		A1
3732	" "	4	E½SE	1835-10-01		A1
3733	" "	8	NE	1835-10-01		A1
3734	" "	8	SE	1835-10-01		A1
3735	" "	9	E½NW	1835-10-01		A1
3736	" "	9	S½NE	1835-10-01		A1
3737	" "	9	W½NW	1835-10-01		A1
3738	" "	9	W½SW	1835-10-01		A1
3729	" "	3	SWNE	1837-03-20		A1
3701	HUDSON, Christopher	36	E½NE	1831-06-01		A1
3944	INGREM, William	24	W½SE	1831-05-17		A1
3810	JEMISON, John M	12	W½NW	1833-07-18		A1 G153
3935	JEMISON, William H	13	E½SE	1833-11-14		A1
3810	JEMISON, William W	12	W½NW	1833-07-18		A1 G153
3702	JOHNSON, Clabourn	7	E½SE	1835-09-22		A1 V3699, 3886
3703	JOHNSON, Claiborne	22	E½NW	1831-07-01		A1
3704	" "	22	W½NW	1831-07-01		A1
3705	" "	22	W½SE	1831-07-01		A1
3809	KNOX, John	21	W½SE	1831-07-01		A1
3936	LAWRENCE, William H	30	E½SW	1834-09-04		A1
3938	" "	31	E½NW	1834-09-04		A1
3937	" "	30	W½SW	1835-09-12		A1
3939	" "	31	W½NW	1835-09-12		A1
3867	LAWSON, Mumford	24	E½NE	1831-07-01		A1
3868	" "	24	E½SE	1831-07-01		A1
3691	LINCOLN, Barney B	11	E½NE	1834-03-12		A1
3945	LITCHFIELD, William	7	W½SW	1831-06-01		A1
3694	LOFTES, Berryman H	20	W½NE	1831-06-01		A1
3695	" "	20	W½SE	1831-06-01		A1
3676	LUMPKIN, Achilles	29	W½SE	1835-09-12		A1
3745	MARTIN, James	23	SW	1831-05-17		A1
3751	" "	36	E½NW	1831-07-01		A1 R3772
3746	" "	26	E½SW	1835-09-19		A1
3747	" "	26	W½SW	1835-09-19		A1
3748	" "	27	E½SE	1835-09-19		A1
3750	" "	27	W½SE	1835-09-19		A1
3749	" "	27	SWNE	1835-09-25		A1
3906	MCCONNEL, Thomas	15	NESW	1835-09-28		A1
3908	MCCONNELL, Thomas	15	W½SW	1831-08-01		A1
3907	" "	15	SESW	1834-08-20		A1
3679	MCDONALD, Allen	4	E½NW	1831-06-01		A1
3682	" "	4	W½NE	1831-06-01		A1
3678	" "	4	E½NE	1835-09-22		A1
3680	" "	4	NESW	1835-09-22		A1
3681	" "	4	NWSE	1835-09-22		A1
3865	MCGEE, Micajah	31	W½SW	1831-07-01		A1
3866	" "	30	E½NE	1831-12-01		A1 G193
3864	" "	31	E½SW	1831-12-01		A1
3866	MCGEE, Thomas	30	E½NE	1831-12-01		A1 G193
3909	" "	31	E½SE	1831-12-01		A1
3910	" "	31	W½SE	1834-05-12		A1
3693	MIDDLEBROOKS, Baxter	24	E½SW	1831-05-17		A1
3692	" "	2	S½NE	1831-06-01		A1
3860	MOORE, Matthew	21	E½NW	1831-08-01		A1
3862	" "	29	E½NW	1831-08-01		A1
3861	" "	27	E½NE	1834-08-20		A1
3812	MORRISSETT, John	13	SW	1831-07-01		A1

ID	Individual in Patent	Sec.	Sec. Part	Date Issued	Other Counties	For More Info . . .
3814	MORRISSETT, John (Cont'd)	13	W½SE	1831-07-01		A1
3816	" "	14	SE	1831-07-01		A1
3813	" "	13	W½NE	1834-05-12		A1
3811	" "	13	N½NW	1834-09-04		A1
3815	" "	14	N½NE	1834-09-04		A1
3803	NASH, John H	33	E½NW	1834-08-12		A1
3804	" "	33	W½SW	1834-08-12		A1
3674	NELSON, Abisha	1	E½NW	1831-05-17		A1 G207
3675	" "	23	E½NW	1831-05-17		A1 G207
3674	NELSON, Asa	1	E½NW	1831-05-17		A1 G207
3675	" "	23	E½NW	1831-05-17		A1 G207
3689	" "	2	E½NW	1831-07-01		A1 G208
3690	" "	2	W½NW	1831-07-01		A1 G208
3724	NELSON, Francis J	1	SW	1833-06-04		A1
3851	NELSON, Joseph	1	W½NW	1831-05-17		A1
3852	" "	24	E½NW	1831-05-17		A1
3914	NELSON, Thomas	23	W½NE	1831-05-17		A1
3913	" "	2	N½NE	1831-06-01		A1
3911	" "	10	W½NE	1833-09-16		A1
3912	" "	10	W½SW	1833-09-16		A1
3905	NELSON, Thomas J	1	SE	1832-09-10		A1
3891	OBANNON, Robert	4	SESW	1837-03-15		A1
3916	OBANNON, Thomas	9	NWNE	1835-09-22		A1
3915	" "	9	NENE	1835-10-01		A1
3805	ORMOND, John J	14	NW	1834-09-04		A1
3806	" "	15	N½	1834-09-04		A1
3807	" "	15	N½SE	1834-09-04		A1
3808	" "	15	SWSE	1835-09-25		A1
3854	PERRY, Lawrence W	3	NWNE	1834-08-20		A1
3762	PICKENS, James	5	NE	1831-06-01		A1
3756	" "	17	W½SE	1831-07-01		A1
3759	" "	4	W½NW	1831-07-01		A1
3761	" "	5	E½SW	1831-07-01		A1
3763	" "	5	W½NW	1831-07-01		A1
3764	" "	5	W½SE	1831-07-01		A1
3757	" "	21	W½NW	1831-08-01		A1
3760	" "	5	E½SE	1832-08-08		A1
3752	" "	17	E½NW	1833-06-04		A1
3755	" "	17	SENE	1834-08-12		A1
3758	" "	4	NWSW	1834-08-12		A1
3765	" "	5	W½SW	1834-08-12		A1
3753	" "	17	E½SW	1834-08-20		A1
3766	" "	8	E½NW	1835-10-01		A1
3767	" "	8	E½SW	1835-10-01		A1
3754	" "	17	NENE	1837-03-30		A1
3721	PRUITT, Ezekiel	29	W½NW	1831-07-01		A1 G215
3722	" "	35	E½SW	1831-07-01		A1 G215
3723	" "	36	E½SE	1831-07-01		A1 G215
3774	REEVES, Jeremiah	20	E½SW	1831-08-01		A1
3895	RHODES, Solomon	1	W½NE	1831-07-01		A1
3779	ROAN, Jesse J	6	SW	1831-05-17		A1
3857	ROAN, Mary	20	E½NE	1831-06-01		A1
3858	" "	7	S½NE	1831-06-01		A1
3719	ROGERS, Enos	3	E½NE	1837-03-20		A1
3720	" "	3	W½SE	1837-03-20		A1
3780	RYAN, Jesse	17	E½SE	1831-06-01		A1
3781	" "	19	E½SE	1831-06-01		A1
3898	SHAFFER, Susan	13	E½NE	1834-09-04		A1
3841	SHELDON, George	11	SE	1835-09-22		A1 G28
3842	" "	12	E½SW	1835-09-22		A1 G28
3843	" "	12	SE	1835-09-22		A1 G28
3920	SHELDON, Israel	10	SE	1837-03-15		A1 G30
3921	" "	11	NW	1837-03-15		A1 G30
3922	" "	11	W½SW	1837-03-15		A1 G30
3684	SMITH, Allen	30	W½SE	1834-09-04		A1
3683	" "	30	E½SE	1835-09-12		A1
3685	" "	31	NE	1835-09-12		A1
3896	SORRELL, Starling	3	NWNW	1834-08-05		A1
3897	" "	3	SENW	1835-09-22		A1
3817	SWIFT, John	25	W½NW	1831-08-01		A1
3818	" "	26	NE	1831-08-01		A1
3819	" "	26	W½NW	1831-08-01		A1
3696	TEW, Blackman	36	SWSE	1834-09-04		A1

ID	Individual in Patent	Sec.	Sec. Part	Date Issued	Other Counties	For More Info . . .
3713	TRAVIS, Doctor W	6	W½NW	1831-07-01		A1
3714	" "	7	W½NW	1831-07-01		A1
3712	" "	18	W½NW	1832-09-10		A1
3875	VARNELL, Ransom P	35	E½NW	1833-09-16		A1
3715	VAUGHAN, Edward B	8	W½NW	1835-10-01		A1
3716	" "	8	W½SW	1835-10-01		A1
3771	WALLACE, James	2	W½SE	1831-08-01		A1
3768	" "	2	E½SE	1833-08-02		A1
3769	" "	2	NESW	1835-09-22		A1
3770	" "	2	SESW	1835-09-25		A1
3800	WALLACE, John E	10	E½NW	1833-08-02		A1
3801	" "	10	E½SW	1833-09-16		A1
3802	" "	10	SWNW	1835-09-22		A1
3773	WATSON, Jason	24	W½NE	1831-05-17		A1
3721	WEAVER, Philip J	29	W½NW	1831-07-01		A1 G215
3722	" "	35	E½SW	1831-07-01		A1 G215
3723	" "	36	E½SE	1831-07-01		A1 G215
3872	" "	25	E½SE	1831-08-01		A1
3873	" "	26	SE	1831-08-01		A1
3874	" "	33	SE	1831-08-01		A1
3876	WEDGEWORTH, Reuben	25	W½NE	1834-06-12		A1
3946	WEDGEWORTH, William	25	E½NE	1833-09-16		A1
3940	WEDGEWORTH, William H	25	E½NW	1834-06-12		A1
3941	" "	25	N½SW	1834-08-20		A1
3942	" "	25	W½SE	1834-08-20		A1
3689	WELLS, James H	2	E½NW	1831-07-01		A1 G208
3690	" "	2	W½NW	1831-07-01		A1 G208
3772	WILLIAMS, James	36	E½NW	1834-03-12		A1 R3751
3853	WILLIAMS, Joseph	36	W½NW	1833-11-14		A1

Patent Map

T18-N R5-E
St Stephens Meridian

Map Group 24

Township Statistics

Parcels Mapped	:	273
Number of Patents	:	273
Number of Individuals	:	114
Patentees Identified	:	113
Number of Surnames	:	86
Multi-Patentee Parcels	:	18
Oldest Patent Date	:	5/17/1831
Most Recent Patent	:	5/15/1837
Block/Lot Parcels	:	0
Parcels Re - Issued	:	1
Parcels that Overlap	:	3
Cities and Towns	:	2
Cemeteries	:	8

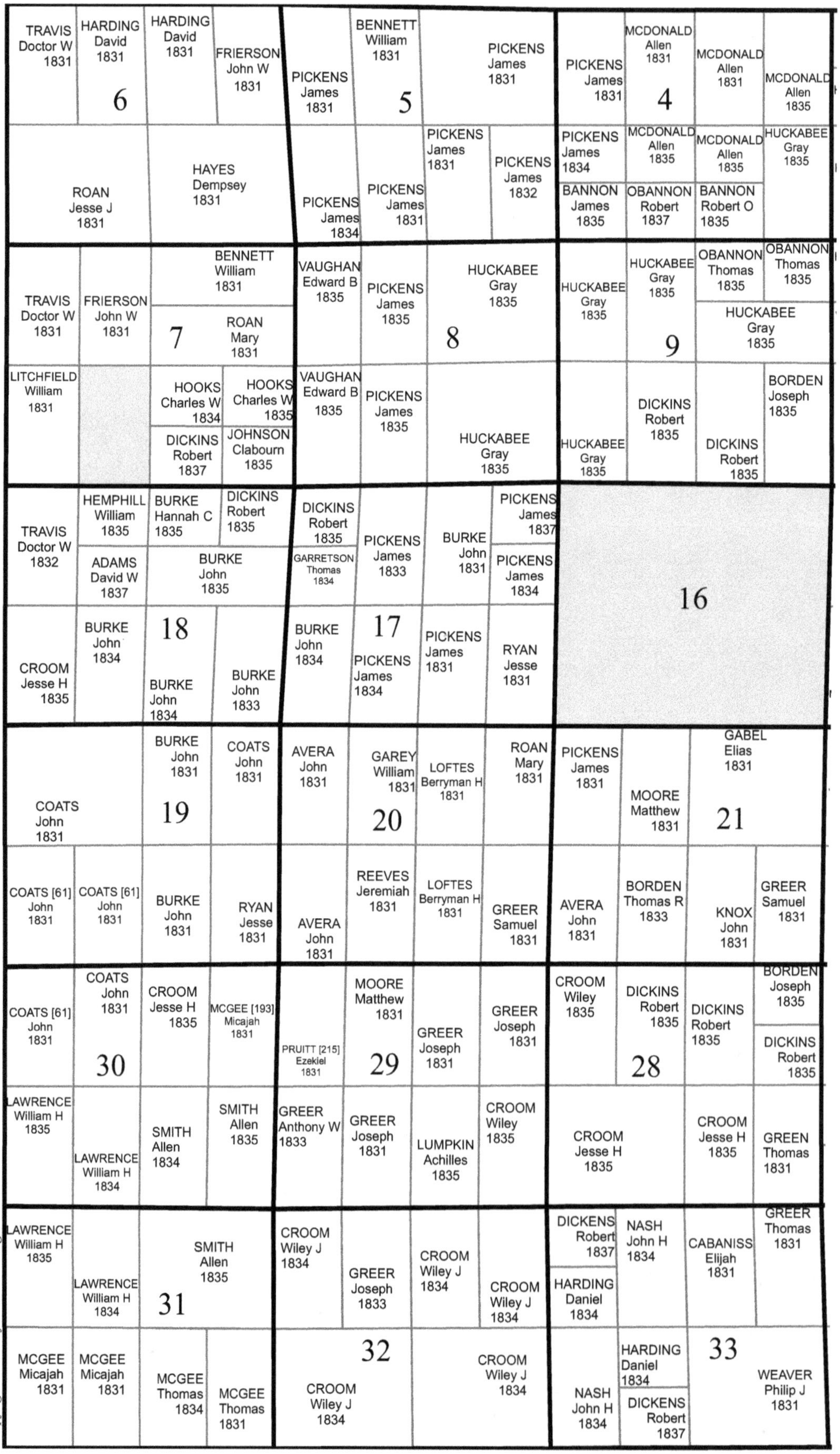

SORRELL Starling 1834	HUCKABEE Gray 1835	PERRY Lawrence W 1834	ROGERS Enos 1837	NELSON [208] Asa 1831	NELSON Thomas 1831	NELSON Joseph 1831	NELSON [207] Abisha 1831	RHODES Solomon 1831	BORDEN Thomas R 1831
HUCKABEE Gray 1835	SORRELL Starling 1835	HUCKABEE Gray 1837		NELSON [208] Asa 1831 **2**	MIDDLEBROOKS Baxter 1831			**1**	
HUCKABEE Gray 1835 **3**	ROGERS Enos 1837	HARMAN Burrel 1831	HANNAN Burrel 1831	WALLACE James 1835	WALLACE James 1831	WALLACE James 1833	NELSON Francis J 1833		
HUCKABEE Gray 1835	HUCKABEE Gray 1835			WALLACE James 1835				NELSON Thomas J 1832	

HUCKABEE Gray 1835	WALLACE John E 1833	NELSON Thomas 1833	BARRON John 1834	BORDEN [30] Thomas R 1837	BORDEN Joseph 1835	LINCOLN Barney B 1834	JEMISON [153] John M 1833	BORDEN Joseph 1835	BORDEN Thomas R 1834
WALLACE John E 1835				**11**			BORDEN Joseph 1835		GILL Nathan J 1835
NELSON Thomas 1833	WALLACE John E 1833 **10**	BORDEN [30] Thomas R 1837	BORDEN [30] Thomas R 1837	BORDEN Joseph 1835	BORDEN [28] Joseph 1835	BORDEN Joseph 1835	BORDEN [28] Joseph 1835 **12**	BORDEN [28] Joseph 1835	

ORMOND John J 1834 **15**		ORMOND John J 1834 **14**	MORRISSETT John 1834	MORRISSETT John 1834	MORRISSETT John 1834		
			CHAMBERS Joseph B 1835	CHAMBERS Joseph 1834	SHAFFER Susan 1834		
MCCONNEL Thomas 1835	ORMOND John J 1834	CHAMBERS Joseph B 1835	CHAMBERS Joseph B 1831	MORRISSETT John 1831	**13**		
MCCONNELL Thomas 1834	ORMOND John J 1835	CHAMBERS James B 1834		MORRISSETT John 1831	MORRISSETT John 1831	JEMISON William H 1833	
MCCONNELL Thomas 1831							

JOHNSON Claiborne 1831	JOHNSON Claiborne 1831	BELL Robert 1831 **22**	ELLIOTT Andrew 1831	ELLIOTT Andrew 1831	NELSON [207] Abisha 1831	NELSON Thomas 1831 **23**	1831	CHAMBERS Joseph B	WATSON Jason 1831 **24**	LAWSON Mumford 1831
BORDEN Joseph 1833	BORDEN Joseph 1833	JOHNSON Claiborne 1831	GAREY Mathias E 1831	MARTIN James 1831	CHAMBERS Joseph B 1831	GRANTHAM Adam 1831	BAGGETT Silas 1831	MIDDLEBROOKS Baxter 1831	INGREM William 1831	LAWSON Mumford 1831

BORDEN Joseph 1835 **27**	BORDEN Joseph 1835	MOORE Matthew 1834	SWIFT John 1831 **26**	SWIFT John 1831	SWIFT John 1831	WEDGEWORTH William H 1834	WEDGEWORTH William 1833
	MARTIN James 1835					WEDGEWORTH Reuben 1834	**25**
DICKINS Robert 1835	GREER Thomas 1835	MARTIN James 1835	MARTIN James 1835	MARTIN James 1835	WEAVER Philip J 1831	WEDGEWORTH William H 1834	WEDGEWORTH William H 1834
	MARTIN James 1835		MARTIN James 1835			CRENSHAW Micajah 1834	WEAVER Philip J 1831

GREER Thomas 1831	GREER Thomas 1831	GREER Joseph 1831 **34**	GREER Joseph 1831	VARNELL Ransom P 1833	ALSTON Nathaniel 1831	WILLIAMS Joseph 1833	MARTIN James 1831	BROWN William 1835	HUDSON Christopher 1831
				GILMORE John W 1831		WILLIAMS James 1834	BROWN William 1834		
GRIFFIN Goodman G 1835	FREEMAN Robert 1833	FINNEY Manasseh 1831	FINNEY Manasseh 1831	PRUITT [215] Ezekiel 1831	**35**	ALSTON Nathaniel 1831	**36**	HARPER James 1834	PRUITT [215] Ezekiel 1831
				HARPER James 1834		GILMORE John W 1831	HARPER James 1831	TEW Blackman 1834	

Helpful Hints

1. This Map's INDEX can be found on the preceding pages.

2. Refer to Map "C" to see where this Township lies within Hale County, Alabama.

3. Numbers within square brackets [ ] denote a multi-patentee land parcel (multi-owner). Refer to Appendix "C" for a full list of members in this group.

4. Areas that look to be crowded with Patentees usually indicate multiple sales of the same parcel (Re-issues) or Overlapping parcels. See this Township's Index for an explanation of these and other circumstances that might explain "odd" groupings of Patentees on this map.

Legend

———— Patent Boundary

▬▬▬▬ Section Boundary

No Patents Found (or Outside County)

1., 2., 3., ... Lot Numbers (when beside a name)

[ ] Group Number (see Appendix "C")

Scale: Section = 1 mile X 1 mile (generally, with some exceptions)

Road Map

T18-N R5-E
St Stephens Meridian

Map Group 24

Cities & Towns

Laneville
Sunshine

Cemeteries

Alexander Cemetery
Cottrell Cemetery
Curry Grove Cemetery
Fowler Cemetery
Greer Cemetery
Hunter Chapel Cemetery
Jones Cemetery
Tunstall Cemetery

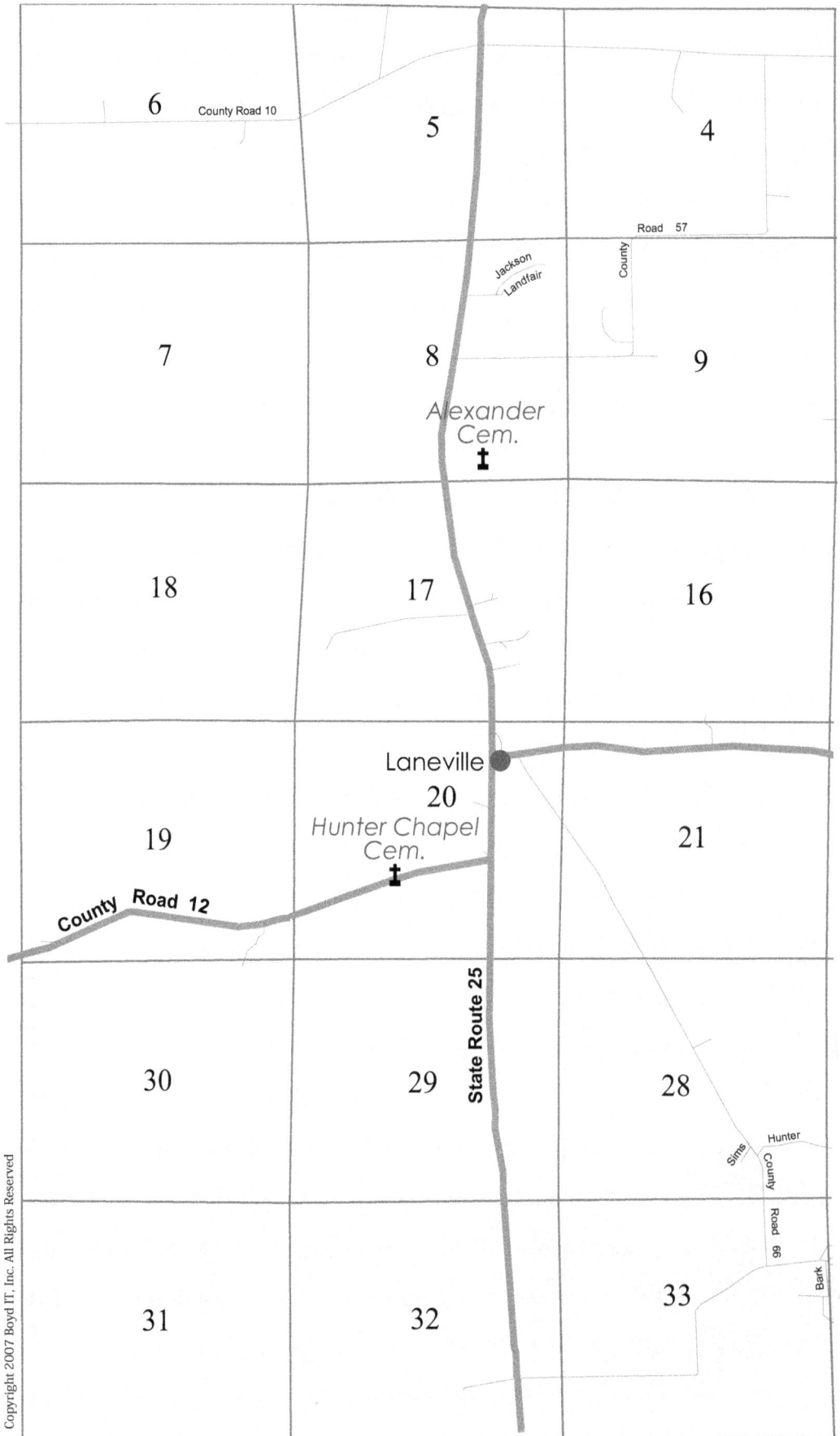

6

County Road 10

5

4

Road 57

Jackson
Landfair

County

7

8

9

Alexander Cem.

18

17

16

Laneville

20

21

Hunter Chapel Cem.

19

County Road 12

State Route 25

30

29

28

Sims
Hunter
County
Road 66
Bark

31

32

33

County Road 10

Dodge City

3

Blossom

2

● Sunshine

1

✝
Curry Grove
Cem.

McKinley

County Road 39

10

11

12

County Road 58

Lily

Dry Creek

15

14

13

Red Bamberg

County Road 12

24

✝ Tunstall
Cem.

22

23

✝
Fowler Cem.

Cottrell ✝
Cem.

State Route 61

27

26

25

Gasline

Foot
Wash

✝ Greer
Cem.

Greer Creek

34

35

✝ Jones Cem.

36

Birch

County
Road
26

Helpful Hints

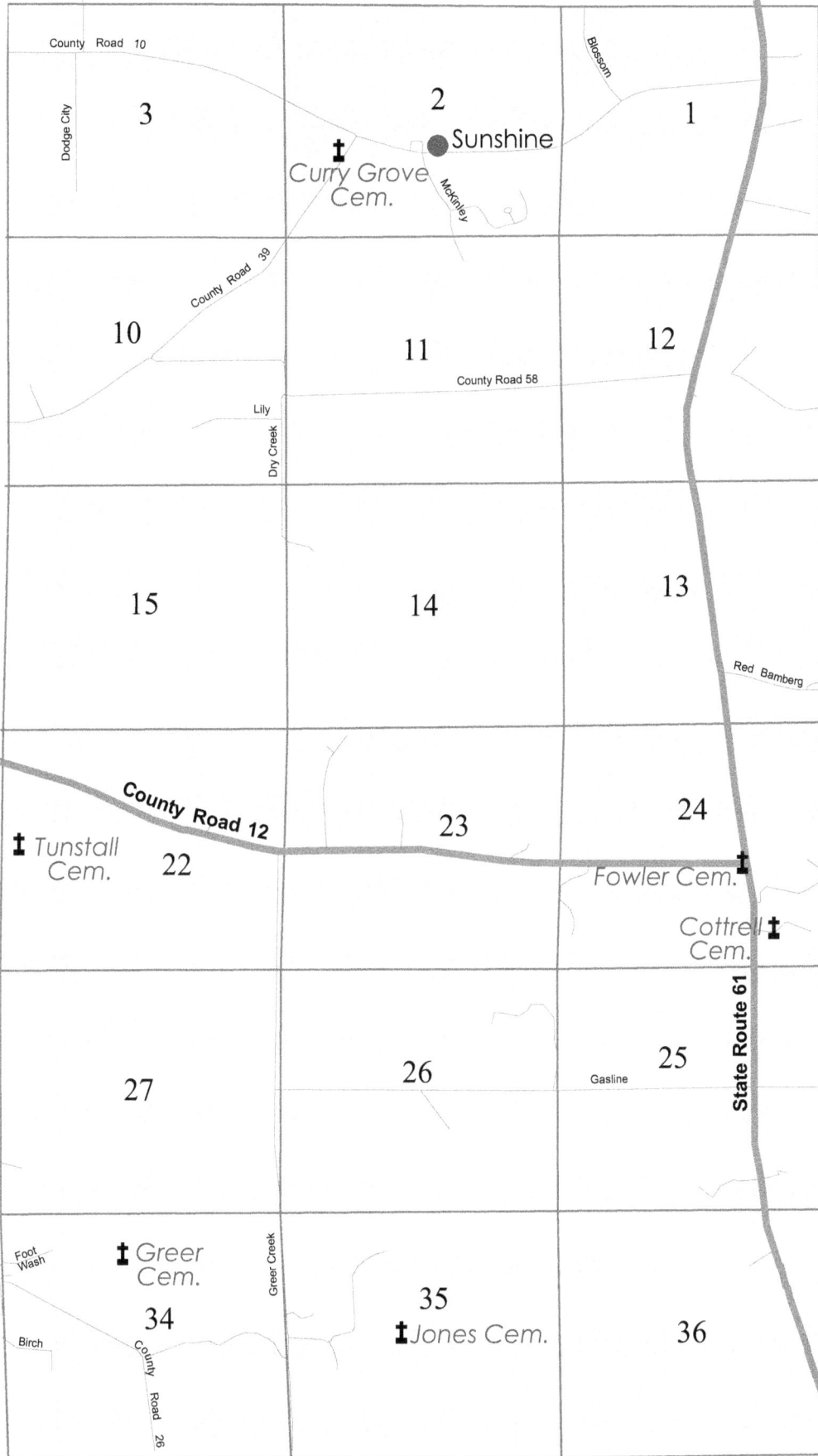

1. This road map has a number of uses, but primarily it is to help you: a) find the present location of land owned by your ancestors (at least the general area), b) find cemeteries and city-centers, and c) estimate the route/roads used by Census-takers & tax-assessors.

2. If you plan to travel to Hale County to locate cemeteries or land parcels, please pick up a modern travel map for the area before you do. Mapping old land parcels on modern maps is not as exact a science as you might think. Just the slightest variations in public land survey coordinates, estimates of parcel boundaries, or road-map deviations can greatly alter a map's representation of how a road either does or doesn't cross a particular parcel of land.

Legend

——————	Section Lines
═══════	Interstates
━━━━━━	Highways
——————	Other Roads
●	Cities/Towns
✝	Cemeteries

Scale: Section = 1 mile X 1 mile
(generally, with some exceptions)

Historical Map

T18-N R5-E
St Stephens Meridian

Map Group 24

Cities & Towns
Laneville
Sunshine

Cemeteries
Alexander Cemetery
Cottrell Cemetery
Curry Grove Cemetery
Fowler Cemetery
Greer Cemetery
Hunter Chapel Cemetery
Jones Cemetery
Tunstall Cemetery

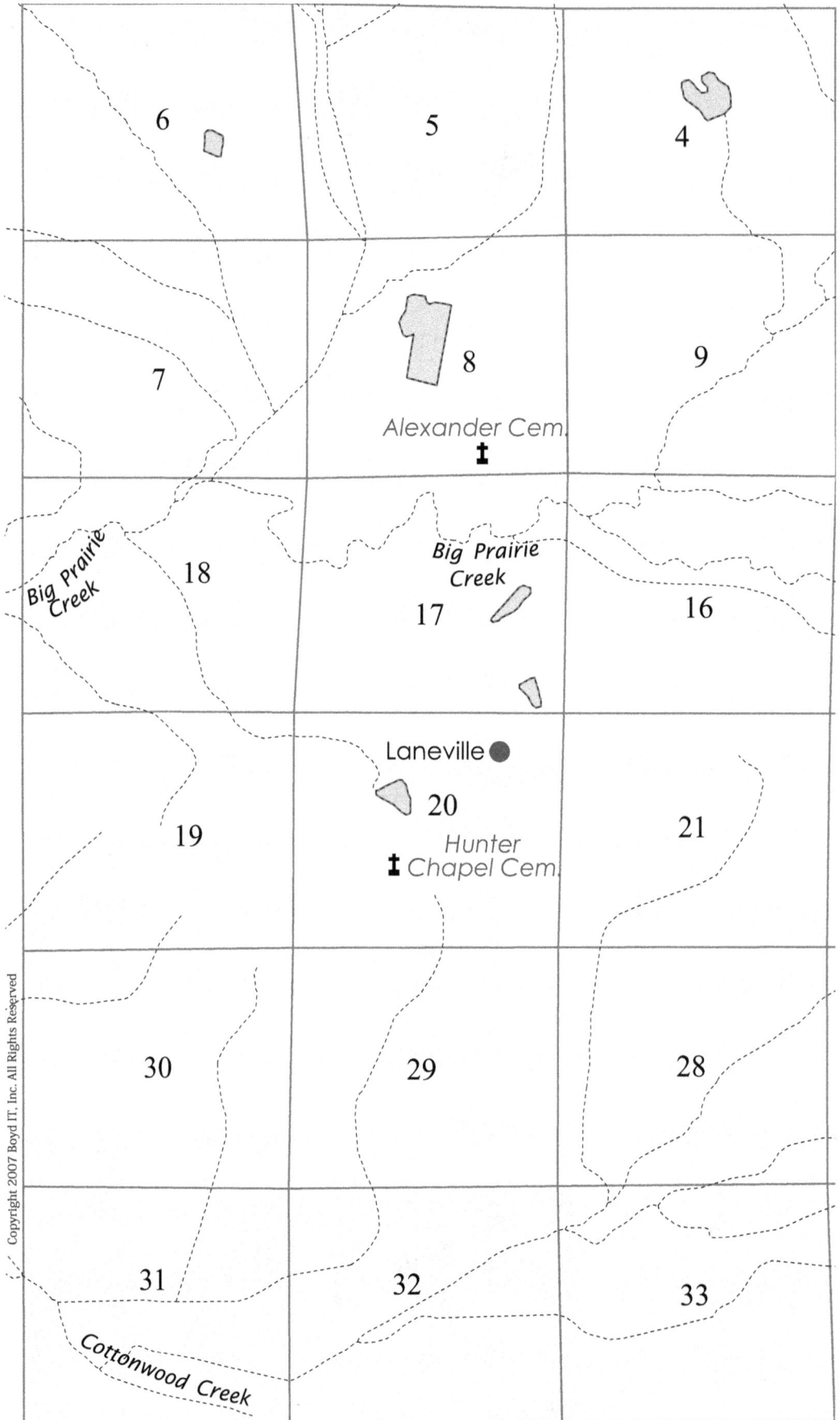

6 5 4

7 8 9

Alexander Cem.

Big Prairie Creek

18 17 16

Big Prairie Creek

Laneville

19 20 21

Hunter Chapel Cem.

30 29 28

31 32 33

Cottonwood Creek

3	2 ●Sunshine	1

✝ Curry Grove Cem.

Big Prairie Creek

10	11	12

Dry Creek 15	14	13

24 *Fowler Cem.* ✝

✝*Tunstall Cem.*
22

23

Cottrell ✝ *Cem.*

27	26	25

Greer Creek

✝ *Greer Cem.*

34	35 ✝*Jones Cem.*	36

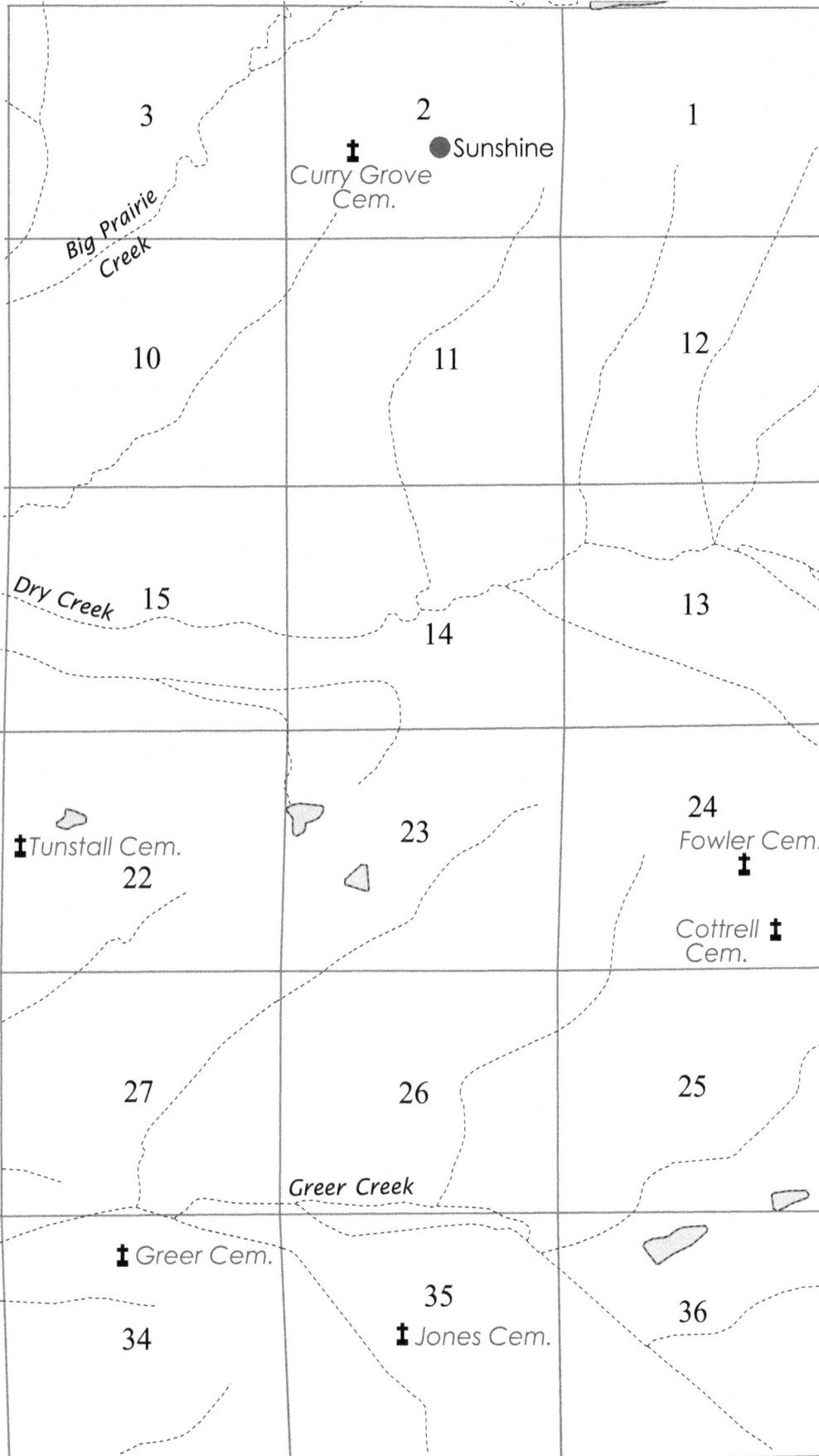

Helpful Hints

1. This Map takes a different look at the same Congressional Township displayed in the preceding two maps. It presents features that can help you better envision the historical development of the area: a) Water-bodies (lakes & ponds), b) Water-courses (rivers, streams, etc.), c) Railroads, d) City/town center-points (where they were oftentimes located when first settled), and e) Cemeteries.

2. Using this "Historical" map in tandem with this Township's Patent Map and Road Map, may lead you to some interesting discoveries. You will often find roads, towns, cemeteries, and waterways are named after nearby landowners: sometimes those names will be the ones you are researching. See how many of these research gems you can find here in Hale County.

Legend

— Section Lines
+++++ Railroads
▭ Large Rivers & Bodies of Water
····· Streams/Creeks & Small Rivers
● Cities/Towns
✝ Cemeteries

Scale: Section = 1 mile X 1 mile
(there are some exceptions)

Appendices

Appendix A - Acts of Congress Authorizing the Patents Contained in this Book

The following Acts of Congress are referred to throughout the Indexes in this book. The text of the Federal Statutes referred to below can usually be found on the web. For more information on such laws, check out the publishers's web-site at *www.arphax.com*, go to the "Research" page, and click on the "Land-Law" link.

Ref. No.	Date and Act of Congress	Number of Parcels of Land
1	April 24, 1820: Sale-Cash Entry (3 Stat. 566)	3822
2	May 20, 1862: Homestead EntryOriginal (12 Stat. 392)	124

Appendix B - Section Parts (Aliquot Parts)

The following represent the various abbreviations we have found thus far in describing the parts of a Public Land Section. Some of these are very obscure and rarely used, but we wanted to list them for just that reason. A full section is 1 square mile or 640 acres.

Section Part	Description	Acres
<none>	Full Acre (if no Section Part is listed, presumed a full Section)	640
<1-??>	A number represents a Lot Number and can be of various sizes	?
E½	East Half-Section	320
E½E½	East Half of East Half-Section	160
E½E½SE	East Half of East Half of Southeast Quarter-Section	40
E½N½	East Half of North Half-Section	160
E½NE	East Half of Northeast Quarter-Section	80
E½NENE	East Half of Northeast Quarter of Northeast Quarter-Section	20
E½NENW	East Half of Northeast Quarter of Northwest Quarter-Section	20
E½NESE	East Half of Northeast Quarter of Southeast Quarter-Section	20
E½NESW	East Half of Northeast Quarter of Southwest Quarter-Section	20
E½NW	East Half of Northwest Quarter-Section	80
E½NWNE	East Half of Northwest Quarter of Northeast Quarter-Section	20
E½NWNW	East Half of Northwest Quarter of Northwest Quarter-Section	20
E½NWSE	East Half of Northwest Quarter of Southeast Quarter-Section	20
E½NWSW	East Half of Northwest Quarter of Southwest Quarter-Section	20
E½S½	East Half of South Half-Section	160
E½SE	East Half of Southeast Quarter-Section	80
E½SENE	East Half of Southeast Quarter of Northeast Quarter-Section	20
E½SENW	East Half of Southeast Quarter of Northwest Quarter-Section	20
E½SESE	East Half of Southeast Quarter of Southeast Quarter-Section	20
E½SESW	East Half of Southeast Quarter of Southwest Quarter-Section	20
E½SW	East Half of Southwest Quarter-Section	80
E½SWNE	East Half of Southwest Quarter of Northeast Quarter-Section	20
E½SWNW	East Half of Southwest Quarter of Northwest Quarter-Section	20
E½SWSE	East Half of Southwest Quarter of Southeast Quarter-Section	20
E½SWSW	East Half of Southwest Quarter of Southwest Quarter-Section	20
E½W½	East Half of West Half-Section	160
N½	North Half-Section	320
N½E½NE	North Half of East Half of Northeast Quarter-Section	40
N½E½NW	North Half of East Half of Northwest Quarter-Section	40
N½E½SE	North Half of East Half of Southeast Quarter-Section	40
N½E½SW	North Half of East Half of Southwest Quarter-Section	40
N½N½	North Half of North Half-Section	160
N½NE	North Half of Northeast Quarter-Section	80
N½NENE	North Half of Northeast Quarter of Northeast Quarter-Section	20
N½NENW	North Half of Northeast Quarter of Northwest Quarter-Section	20
N½NESE	North Half of Northeast Quarter of Southeast Quarter-Section	20
N½NESW	North Half of Northeast Quarter of Southwest Quarter-Section	20
N½NW	North Half of Northwest Quarter-Section	80
N½NWNE	North Half of Northwest Quarter of Northeast Quarter-Section	20
N½NWNW	North Half of Northwest Quarter of Northwest Quarter-Section	20
N½NWSE	North Half of Northwest Quarter of Southeast Quarter-Section	20
N½NWSW	North Half of Northwest Quarter of Southwest Quarter-Section	20
N½S½	North Half of South Half-Section	160
N½SE	North Half of Southeast Quarter-Section	80
N½SENE	North Half of Southeast Quarter of Northeast Quarter-Section	20
N½SENW	North Half of Southeast Quarter of Northwest Quarter-Section	20
N½SESE	North Half of Southeast Quarter of Southeast Quarter-Section	20

Section Part	Description	Acres
N½SESW	North Half of Southeast Quarter of Southwest Quarter-Section	20
N½SESW	North Half of Southeast Quarter of Southwest Quarter-Section	20
N½SW	North Half of Southwest Quarter-Section	80
N½SWNE	North Half of Southwest Quarter of Northeast Quarter-Section	20
N½SWNW	North Half of Southwest Quarter of Northwest Quarter-Section	20
N½SWSE	North Half of Southwest Quarter of Southeast Quarter-Section	20
N½SWSE	North Half of Southwest Quarter of Southeast Quarter-Section	20
N½SWSW	North Half of Southwest Quarter of Southwest Quarter-Section	20
N½W½NW	North Half of West Half of Northwest Quarter-Section	40
N½W½SE	North Half of West Half of Southeast Quarter-Section	40
N½W½SW	North Half of West Half of Southwest Quarter-Section	40
NE	Northeast Quarter-Section	160
NEN½	Northeast Quarter of North Half-Section	80
NENE	Northeast Quarter of Northeast Quarter-Section	40
NENENE	Northeast Quarter of Northeast Quarter of Northeast Quarter	10
NENENW	Northeast Quarter of Northeast Quarter of Northwest Quarter	10
NENESE	Northeast Quarter of Northeast Quarter of Southeast Quarter	10
NENESW	Northeast Quarter of Northeast Quarter of Southwest Quarter	10
NENW	Northeast Quarter of Northwest Quarter-Section	40
NENWNE	Northeast Quarter of Northwest Quarter of Northeast Quarter	10
NENWNW	Northeast Quarter of Northwest Quarter of Northwest Quarter	10
NENWSE	Northeast Quarter of Northwest Quarter of Southeast Quarter	10
NENWSW	Northeast Quarter of Northwest Quarter of Southwest Quarter	10
NESE	Northeast Quarter of Southeast Quarter-Section	40
NESENE	Northeast Quarter of Southeast Quarter of Northeast Quarter	10
NESENW	Northeast Quarter of Southeast Quarter of Northwest Quarter	10
NESESE	Northeast Quarter of Southeast Quarter of Southeast Quarter	10
NESESW	Northeast Quarter of Southeast Quarter of Southwest Quarter	10
NESW	Northeast Quarter of Southwest Quarter-Section	40
NESWNE	Northeast Quarter of Southwest Quarter of Northeast Quarter	10
NESWNW	Northeast Quarter of Southwest Quarter of Northwest Quarter	10
NESWSE	Northeast Quarter of Southwest Quarter of Southeast Quarter	10
NESWSW	Northeast Quarter of Southwest Quarter of Southwest Quarter	10
NW	Northwest Quarter-Section	160
NWE½	Northwest Quarter of Eastern Half-Section	80
NWN½	Northwest Quarter of North Half-Section	80
NWNE	Northwest Quarter of Northeast Quarter-Section	40
NWNENE	Northwest Quarter of Northeast Quarter of Northeast Quarter	10
NWNENW	Northwest Quarter of Northeast Quarter of Northwest Quarter	10
NWNESE	Northwest Quarter of Northeast Quarter of Southeast Quarter	10
NWNESW	Northwest Quarter of Northeast Quarter of Southwest Quarter	10
NWNW	Northwest Quarter of Northwest Quarter-Section	40
NWNWNE	Northwest Quarter of Northwest Quarter of Northeast Quarter	10
NWNWNW	Northwest Quarter of Northwest Quarter of Northwest Quarter	10
NWNWSE	Northwest Quarter of Northwest Quarter of Southeast Quarter	10
NWNWSW	Northwest Quarter of Northwest Quarter of Southwest Quarter	10
NWSE	Northwest Quarter of Southeast Quarter-Section	40
NWSENE	Northwest Quarter of Southeast Quarter of Northeast Quarter	10
NWSENW	Northwest Quarter of Southeast Quarter of Northwest Quarter	10
NWSESE	Northwest Quarter of Southeast Quarter of Southeast Quarter	10
NWSESW	Northwest Quarter of Southeast Quarter of Southwest Quarter	10
NWSW	Northwest Quarter of Southwest Quarter-Section	40
NWSWNE	Northwest Quarter of Southwest Quarter of Northeast Quarter	10
NWSWNW	Northwest Quarter of Southwest Quarter of Northwest Quarter	10
NWSWSE	Northwest Quarter of Southwest Quarter of Southeast Quarter	10
NWSWSW	Northwest Quarter of Southwest Quarter of Southwest Quarter	10
S½	South Half-Section	320
S½E½NE	South Half of East Half of Northeast Quarter-Section	40
S½E½NW	South Half of East Half of Northwest Quarter-Section	40
S½E½SE	South Half of East Half of Southeast Quarter-Section	40

Section Part	Description	Acres
S½E½SW	South Half of East Half of Southwest Quarter-Section	40
S½N½	South Half of North Half-Section	160
S½NE	South Half of Northeast Quarter-Section	80
S½NENE	South Half of Northeast Quarter of Northeast Quarter-Section	20
S½NENW	South Half of Northeast Quarter of Northwest Quarter-Section	20
S½NESE	South Half of Northeast Quarter of Southeast Quarter-Section	20
S½NESW	South Half of Northeast Quarter of Southwest Quarter-Section	20
S½NW	South Half of Northwest Quarter-Section	80
S½NWNE	South Half of Northwest Quarter of Northeast Quarter-Section	20
S½NWNW	South Half of Northwest Quarter of Northwest Quarter-Section	20
S½NWSE	South Half of Northwest Quarter of Southeast Quarter-Section	20
S½NWSW	South Half of Northwest Quarter of Southwest Quarter-Section	20
S½S½	South Half of South Half-Section	160
S½SE	South Half of Southeast Quarter-Section	80
S½SENE	South Half of Southeast Quarter of Northeast Quarter-Section	20
S½SENW	South Half of Southeast Quarter of Northwest Quarter-Section	20
S½SESE	South Half of Southeast Quarter of Southeast Quarter-Section	20
S½SESW	South Half of Southeast Quarter of Southwest Quarter-Section	20
S½SESW	South Half of Southeast Quarter of Southwest Quarter-Section	20
S½SW	South Half of Southwest Quarter-Section	80
S½SWNE	South Half of Southwest Quarter of Northeast Quarter-Section	20
S½SWNW	South Half of Southwest Quarter of Northwest Quarter-Section	20
S½SWSE	South Half of Southwest Quarter of Southeast Quarter-Section	20
S½SWSE	South Half of Southwest Quarter of Southeast Quarter-Section	20
S½SWSW	South Half of Southwest Quarter of Southwest Quarter-Section	20
S½W½NE	South Half of West Half of Northeast Quarter-Section	40
S½W½NW	South Half of West Half of Northwest Quarter-Section	40
S½W½SE	South Half of West Half of Southeast Quarter-Section	40
S½W½SW	South Half of West Half of Southwest Quarter-Section	40
SE	Southeast Quarter Section	160
SEN½	Southeast Quarter of North Half-Section	80
SENE	Southeast Quarter of Northeast Quarter-Section	40
SENENE	Southeast Quarter of Northeast Quarter of Northeast Quarter	10
SENENW	Southeast Quarter of Northeast Quarter of Northwest Quarter	10
SENESE	Southeast Quarter of Northeast Quarter of Southeast Quarter	10
SENESW	Southeast Quarter of Northeast Quarter of Southwest Quarter	10
SENW	Southeast Quarter of Northwest Quarter-Section	40
SENWNE	Southeast Quarter of Northwest Quarter of Northeast Quarter	10
SENWNW	Southeast Quarter of Northwest Quarter of Northwest Quarter	10
SENWSE	Souteast Quarter of Northwest Quarter of Southeast Quarter	10
SENWSW	Southeast Quarter of Northwest Quarter of Southwest Quarter	10
SESE	Southeast Quarter of Southeast Quarter-Section	40
SESENE	SoutheastQuarter of Southeast Quarter of Northeast Quarter	10
SESENW	Southeast Quarter of Southeast Quarter of Northwest Quarter	10
SESESE	Southeast Quarter of Southeast Quarter of Southeast Quarter	10
SESESW	Southeast Quarter of Southeast Quarter of Southwest Quarter	10
SESW	Southeast Quarter of Southwest Quarter-Section	40
SESWNE	Southeast Quarter of Southwest Quarter of Northeast Quarter	10
SESWNW	Southeast Quarter of Southwest Quarter of Northwest Quarter	10
SESWSE	Southeast Quarter of Southwest Quarter of Southeast Quarter	10
SESWSW	Southeast Quarter of Southwest Quarter of Southwest Quarter	10
SW	Southwest Quarter-Section	160
SWNE	Southwest Quarter of Northeast Quarter-Section	40
SWNENE	Southwest Quarter of Northeast Quarter of Northeast Quarter	10
SWNENW	Southwest Quarter of Northeast Quarter of Northwest Quarter	10
SWNESE	Southwest Quarter of Northeast Quarter of Southeast Quarter	10
SWNESW	Southwest Quarter of Northeast Quarter of Southwest Quarter	10
SWNW	Southwest Quarter of Northwest Quarter-Section	40
SWNWNE	Southwest Quarter of Northwest Quarter of Northeast Quarter	10
SWNWNW	Southwest Quarter of Northwest Quarter of Northwest Quarter	10

Section Part	Description	Acres
SWNWSE	Southwest Quarter of Northwest Quarter of Southeast Quarter	10
SWNWSW	Southwest Quarter of Northwest Quarter of Southwest Quarter	10
SWSE	Southwest Quarter of Southeast Quarter-Section	40
SWSENE	Southwest Quarter of Southeast Quarter of Northeast Quarter	10
SWSENW	Southwest Quarter of Southeast Quarter of Northwest Quarter	10
SWSESE	Southwest Quarter of Southeast Quarter of Southeast Quarter	10
SWSESW	Southwest Quarter of Southeast Quarter of Southwest Quarter	10
SWSW	Southwest Quarter of Southwest Quarter-Section	40
SWSWNE	Southwest Quarter of Southwest Quarter of Northeast Quarter	10
SWSWNW	Southwest Quarter of Southwest Quarter of Northwest Quarter	10
SWSWSE	Southwest Quarter of Southwest Quarter of Southeast Quarter	10
SWSWSW	Southwest Quarter of Southwest Quarter of Southwest Quarter	10
W½	West Half-Section	320
W½E½	West Half of East Half-Section	160
W½N½	West Half of North Half-Section (same as NW)	160
W½NE	West Half of Northeast Quarter	80
W½NENE	West Half of Northeast Quarter of Northeast Quarter-Section	20
W½NENW	West Half of Northeast Quarter of Northwest Quarter-Section	20
W½NESE	West Half of Northeast Quarter of Southeast Quarter-Section	20
W½NESW	West Half of Northeast Quarter of Southwest Quarter-Section	20
W½NW	West Half of Northwest Quarter-Section	80
W½NWNE	West Half of Northwest Quarter of Northeast Quarter-Section	20
W½NWNW	West Half of Northwest Quarter of Northwest Quarter-Section	20
W½NWSE	West Half of Northwest Quarter of Southeast Quarter-Section	20
W½NWSW	West Half of Northwest Quarter of Southwest Quarter-Section	20
W½S½	West Half of South Half-Section	160
W½SE	West Half of Southeast Quarter-Section	80
W½SENE	West Half of Southeast Quarter of Northeast Quarter-Section	20
W½SENW	West Half of Southeast Quarter of Northwest Quarter-Section	20
W½SESE	West Half of Southeast Quarter of Southeast Quarter-Section	20
W½SESW	West Half of Southeast Quarter of Southwest Quarter-Section	20
W½SW	West Half of Southwest Quarter-Section	80
W½SWNE	West Half of Southwest Quarter of Northeast Quarter-Section	20
W½SWNW	West Half of Southwest Quarter of Northwest Quarter-Section	20
W½SWSE	West Half of Southwest Quarter of Southeast Quarter-Section	20
W½SWSW	West Half of Southwest Quarter of Southwest Quarter-Section	20
W½W½	West Half of West Half-Section	160

Appendix C - Multi-Patentee Groups

The following index presents groups of people who jointly received patents in Hale County, Alabama. The Group Numbers are used in the Patent Maps and their Indexes so that you may then turn to this Appendix in order to identify all the members of the each buying group.

Group Number 1
ABBOTT, Willis; BOUNDS, Henry

Group Number 2
ALLEN, Samuel; THIGPEN, Joshua

Group Number 3
ALLISON, Thomas; SUMMEY, Jacob

Group Number 4
ANDERSON, Benjamin; CLEMENTS, Benjamin

Group Number 5
ANDERSON, Thomas J; CLEMENTS, Benjamin

Group Number 6
ANDERSON, Thomas J; DIAL, David M

Group Number 7
ANDERSON, Thomas J; SCOTT, David

Group Number 8
BARNES, Pittkin; MCCLURE, William

Group Number 9
BARNES, Pittkin; MILLER, Frederick

Group Number 10
BARNES, Pittkin; WHITE, Griffin

Group Number 11
BARNES, Pittkin; WOODARD, Moses

Group Number 12
BARNES, Pittkin; WOODWARD, Sarah

Group Number 13
BARRETT, Starling; GLOVER, Allen

Group Number 14
BATES, John M; DIAL, David M

Group Number 15
BATES, John M; MCALPIN, Alexander

Group Number 16
BATTLE, Alfred; FOSTER, James

Group Number 17
BATTLE, Alfred; GREENE, Daniel

Group Number 18
BATTLE, Alfred; GUNN, Peter; MEARS, John; RAMIE, Robert; SMITH, Moss

Group Number 19
BATTLE, Alfred; JEMISON, Robert

Group Number 20
BATTLE, Alfred; MARR, William M

Group Number 21
BATTLE, Alfred; PARKER, James

Group Number 22
BAXTER, James; BAXTER, Mary; BAXTER, Sarah L; BAXTER, Thomas

Group Number 23
BEALE, John S; BLOUNT, James G; BURROUGHS, Benjamin

Group Number 24
BEALE, John S; BLOUNT, James G; RICHARDS, John D

Group Number 25
BEALE, John; RICHARDS, John D

Group Number 26
BELL, William; WARREN, William H

Group Number 27
BORDEN, Joseph; BORDEN, Thomas R

Group Number 28
BORDEN, Joseph; BORDEN, Thomas R; SHELDON, George

Group Number 29
BORDEN, Joseph; LANE, Levin B; TUCKER, William H

Group Number 30
BORDEN, Thomas R; SHELDON, Israel

Group Number 31
BOYD, John; THOMAS, Francis

Group Number 32
BREADY, John; GLOVER, Allen

Group Number 33
BREAZEALE, Barzilla; BREAZEALE, Cynthia;
BREAZEALE, Elijah; BREAZEALE, Huldith

Group Number 34
BUCHANNAN, Samuel; COWAN, Jehu

Group Number 35
BUCHANNAN, Samuel; COWAN, Robert

Group Number 36
BUFORD, Goodlow; LANE, John W

Group Number 37
BURROUGHS, Benjamin; JEMISON, Robert

Group Number 38
CALWELL, William; LANE, John W

Group Number 39
CARTER, Pannel C; GOOLE, Daniel

Group Number 40
CHAMBERS, James B; SANDERS, Jeremiah

Group Number 41
CHAMBERS, Uriel B; SNEDECOR, Isaac C

Group Number 42
CHANDLER, Jeremiah; CHANDLER, Scott

Group Number 43
CHANDLER, Jeremiah; MARTIN, Marius

Group Number 44
CHANDLER, Scott; MARTIN, Marius

Group Number 45
CHANDRON, Felix; GRIFFIN, James; HENLEY, John W

Group Number 46
CHANDRON, Felix; HARRISON, Nathaniel; HENLEY,
John W

Group Number 47
CHANDRON, Felix; HENLEY, John W

Group Number 48
CHANDRON, Felix; HENLEY, John W; SEALE, Benton

Group Number 49
CHANDRON, Felix; HENLEY, John W; THORNTON,
Mitchell

Group Number 50
CHANDRON, Felix; HENLEY, John W; WOODARD,
Charles E

Group Number 51
CHILDS, Thomas; CURRY, Jabez

Group Number 52
CHILDS, Thomas; SANDERS, Jeremiah

Group Number 53
CHRISTOPHER, R G; SIMS, Edward

Group Number 54
CHRISTOPHER, R G; WALTHALL, R B

Group Number 55
CLEMENTS, Benjamin; DIAL, David M

Group Number 56
CLEMENTS, Benjamin; HANIS, Evin

Group Number 57
CLEMENTS, Benjamin; KENNEDY, James

Group Number 58
CLEMENTS, Benjamin; WILLIAMS, Charles

Group Number 59
CLEMENTS, Jesse B; HATTER, Richard

Group Number 60
CLEMENTS, Jesse B; LONG, Lunerford

Group Number 61
COATS, John; COLE, David

Group Number 62
COLLINS, Daniel; SIMS, Edward

Group Number 63
COLLINS, James W; SCOTT, David

Group Number 64
COOK, Elizabeth; COOK, Martin

Group Number 65
COOK, Elizabeth; PURNELL, Hortensius

Group Number 66
COOK, Martin; DUNKIN, William

Group Number 67
COOPE, George; SIMS, Edward

Group Number 68
COOPER, George; SCOTT, David

Group Number 69
COOPER, George; SIMS, Edward

Group Number 70
CRISWELL, John T; CO, Scott Sims And

Group Number 71
DAVIDSON, Reuben; JIMISON, William

Group Number 72
DAVIDSON, Reuben; SCOTT, David

Group Number 73
DAVIS, George; DEVANE, Irelon C

Group Number 74
DAVIS, George; GUNN, Radford

Group Number 75
DEW, James; GLOVER, Allen

Group Number 76
DIAL, David M; JIMISON, William

Group Number 77
DRUMMOND, Charles H; TALIAFERRO, Benjamin

Group Number 78
DUNLAP, William; MAY, William

Group Number 79
ELLIOTT, David; SEALE, William

Group Number 80
ELLIS, Stephen; SCOTT, David

Group Number 81
ELLIS, Stephen; SIMS, Edward

Group Number 82
FILES, David; MCINTIRE, Thomas L

Group Number 83
FINNEY, Manassah; SCOTT, David

Group Number 84
FLEMING, Plinny R; LANE, John W

Group Number 85
FORNIER, Alexander; SCISM, Joseph

Group Number 86
FRIEDMAN, Bernard; JEMISON, Robert; LOVEMAN, Emanuel

Group Number 87
FULTON, Paul; LANE, John W

Group Number 88
GAGE, James B; MALONE, John

Group Number 89
GAGE, Mathew; JAMISON, Robert

Group Number 90
GAINSLEY, William; GLOVER, Allen

Group Number 91
GAREY, Mathias E; GAREY, William

Group Number 92
GEWIN, Christopher; HARRY, John J

Group Number 93
GLENN, Simeon; SIMS, Edward

Group Number 94
GLOVER, Allen; HARDY, Henry

Group Number 95
GLOVER, Allen; HARDY, William

Group Number 96
GLOVER, Allen; HARRELL, Gordon

Group Number 97
GLOVER, Allen; HILL, Sterling

Group Number 98
GLOVER, Allen; HOLTAM, Elijah S

Group Number 99
GLOVER, Allen; HOWELL, Ira

Group Number 100
GLOVER, Allen; JAMES, Thomas

Group Number 101
GLOVER, Allen; JOHNSON, James

Group Number 102
GLOVER, Allen; JOHNSON, Thomas W

Group Number 103
GLOVER, Allen; LANDRUM, Samuel

Group Number 104
GLOVER, Allen; LANDRUM, Zachariah

Group Number 105
GLOVER, Allen; MANESS, Enoch

Group Number 106
GLOVER, Allen; MANESS, Ezekiel

Group Number 107
GLOVER, Allen; MCGAW, John P

Group Number 108
GLOVER, Allen; MCGAW, William

Group Number 109
GLOVER, Allen; MCLEAN, Alfred

Group Number 110
GLOVER, Allen; MORGAN, Silas

Group Number 111
GLOVER, Allen; PEACOCK, Elizabeth

Group Number 112
GLOVER, Allen; PERRITT, Charlotte

Group Number 113
GLOVER, Allen; PHILLIPS, Thomas

Group Number 114
GLOVER, Allen; SURGINER, William

Group Number 115
GLOVER, Allen; WADE, Joshua A

Group Number 116
GLOVER, Allen; WHITE, James

Group Number 117
GLOVER, Allen; WHITE, James J

Group Number 118
GLOVER, Allen; WHITE, Zedekiah

Group Number 119
GRAY, Hezekiah; GRAY, William; HADEN, Anselm L

Group Number 120
GRAY, James; KENNON, William

Group Number 121
GRAY, James; KORNEGAY, Thomas W

Group Number 122
GRAY, John; SIMS, Edward

Group Number 123
GRAY, Thomas; SIMS, Edward

Group Number 124
GREEN, Daniel; HILL, Green

Group Number 125
GREEN, Daniel; TRAVIS, Doctor W

Group Number 126
GREENE, Daniel; KENNON, William

Group Number 127
GREENE, Daniel; MCMILLAN, Alexander

Group Number 128
GREENE, Daniel; SIMS, Edward

Group Number 129
GREENE, Lodowick; PURNELL, Hortensius

Group Number 130
GRIFFIN, Goodman G; OSBORN, Esaias H

Group Number 131
GUNN, Radford; MORRIS, John

Group Number 132
HALBERT, Henry; PEARSON, Joseph J

Group Number 133
HANCOCK, William B; PURNELL, Hortensius

Group Number 134
HANIS, John; SIMS, Edward

Group Number 135
HANNA, Andrew M; HANNA, Robert C

Group Number 136
HANNA, Robert C; LANE, John W

Group Number 137
HARDWICK, Garland; JEMISON, Robert

Group Number 138
HARPER, John; WEBB, James

Group Number 139
HARRIS, John; LANE, John W

Group Number 140
HARRIS, Tilmon P; SIMS, Edward

Group Number 141
HARRISON, Richard; SUMMY, Jacob

Group Number 142
HENLEY, Elizabeth J; HENLEY, John T; TORBERT, Sarah P

Group Number 143
HENLEY, Elizabeth J; HENLEY, John T; TORBUT, Elizabeth P

Group Number 144
HENNON, William; JONES, William; MCGEHEE, Abraham

Group Number 145
HOBSON, Baker; SIMS, Edward

Group Number 146
HODGES, Philemon; MCDONALD, James; NELSON, John

Group Number 147
HOLBROOK, Burrel; SIMS, Edward

Group Number 148
HOLBROOK, Jacob; SCOTT, David

Group Number 149
HUBBARD, Samuel; LEWIS, Rufus G; TAPPAN, John

Group Number 150
INGRAM, Alexander; INGRAM, Daniel

Group Number 151
INGRAM, Alexander; MARTIN, Marius

Group Number 152
JACKSON, Joseph; ROE, Churchwell

Group Number 153
JEMISON, John M; JEMISON, William W

Group Number 154
JEMISON, Robert; SIMS, Edward

Group Number 155
JEMISON, Robert; TOOSING, Joseph

Group Number 156
JEMISON, Robert; YARBOROUGH, William

Group Number 157
JIMISON, William; COMPANY, Sims Banks And

Group Number 158
JOHNSON, Daniel J; JOHNSON, Shelottie

Group Number 159
JOHNSTON, Martin; RUSSELL, Gibson

Group Number 160
JONES, James; JONES, John; JONES, Thomas; JONES, William

Group Number 161
JONES, William; POPE, Willis

Group Number 162
JONES, William; TRAVIS, Amos

Group Number 163
KEATON, John; RICHARDS, John D

Group Number 164
KELLY, Mamie L; TUBBS, Mamie L

Group Number 165
KENNEDY, James; SAMPLE, Daniel B

Group Number 166
KENNON, William; LANE, John W

Group Number 167
LANE, John W; COMPANY, Sims Banks And

Group Number 168
LANE, John W; LIPSCOMB, Joel

Group Number 169
LANE, John W; LIPSCOMB, John

Group Number 170
LANE, John W; MCCOWN, Sampson; MCRAE, Malcolm

Group Number 171
LANE, John W; MCGEHEE, Abraham

Group Number 172
LANE, John W; PICKENS, Samuel

Group Number 173
LANE, John W; WILLIAMS, Samuel

Group Number 174
LANE, John W; WILLIAMS, Thomas

Group Number 175
LAWLESS, Henry E; OWENS, Patrick F

Group Number 176
LIPSCOMB, William C; SCOTT, David

Group Number 177
LOMAX, John T; MANNING, Amos R

Group Number 178
LOMAX, John T; MANNING, Amos R; TUCKER, Richard H

Group Number 179
MARTIN, Albert; MARTIN, Esther; MARTIN, Francis; MARTIN, Laura; MARTIN, Peter; MARTIN, Sarah; MARTIN, Wesley

Group Number 180
MARTIN, Marius; RAY, John

Group Number 181
MARTIN, Marius; SNEDECOR, Isaac C

Group Number 182
MARTIN, Marius; WALLER, Catherine

Group Number 183
MARTIN, Virginius; WALLER, Archibald

Group Number 184
MARTINIER, Julius; MOORE, James; TALLIAFERRO, Benjamin

Group Number 185
MARTINIERE, Julius; RIDGILL, Joel; TALIAFERRO, Benjamin

Group Number 186
MARTINIERE, Julius; WALLER, Archibald

Group Number 187
MAY, John; MAY, William

Group Number 188
MAY, Patrick; OVERTON, Jesse B

Group Number 189
MCCOWN, Sampson; MCRAE, Malcom

Group Number 190
MCCRAE, Daniel; MCMILLEN, James

Group Number 191
MCCRORY, Hugh; NELSON, Matthew

Group Number 192
MCDONALD, James; NELSON, John

Group Number 193
MCGEE, Micajah; MCGEE, Thomas

Group Number 194
MCGEHEE, Abraham; MCLANE, James

Group Number 195
MCGEHEE, Abraham; SIMS, Edward

Group Number 196
MCGEHEE, Abraham; WILLIAMS, Thomas

Group Number 197
MCGIFFORD, James; PAUL, James

Group Number 198
MEADE, Richard E; ROBERTSON, Henry C

Group Number 199
MELTON, West A; SCOTT, David

Group Number 200
MILLEN, John M; SIMS, Edward

Group Number 201
MONTGOMERY, William; ROUDET, Peter C

Group Number 202
MOODY, Alex; MOODY, Martin

Group Number 203
MOODY, Alexander; MOODY, Martin

Group Number 204
MOSS, Johnson; RICHARDS, John D

Group Number 205
MURPHREY, William; SIMS, Edward

Group Number 206
MYERS, Amanda; MYERS, Ann; MYERS, Pleasant;
MYERS, William

Group Number 207
NELSON, Abisha; NELSON, Asa

Group Number 208
NELSON, Asa; WELLS, James H

Group Number 209
PECK, E; PECK, F

Group Number 210
PECK, Edwin; PECK, Frederick

Group Number 211
PETEET, J; ROAN, W J

Group Number 212
PICKENS, Samuel; WILLIAMS, Thomas

Group Number 213
PRICKET, Dabney; SCOTT, David

Group Number 214
PRICKETT, Dabney; SCOTT, David

Group Number 215
PRUITT, Ezekiel; WEAVER, Philip J

Group Number 216
PURNELL, Hortensius; WHITE, Hiram

Group Number 217
PURNELL, Hortentius; WHITE, Josiah

Group Number 218
RICHARDS, John D; SIMS, Edward

Group Number 219
ROBERTSON, Henry C; ROYALL, John D

Group Number 220
RYAN, Isaac; RYAN, John

Group Number 221
SCOTT, David; COMPANY, Sims Banks And

Group Number 222
SCOTT, David; SIMS, Edward

Group Number 223
SCOTT, David; SPEED, Martin

Group Number 224
SCOTT, David; SPEED, William

Group Number 225
SCOTT, David; TRUE, Martin

Group Number 226
SCOTT, David; WEDGWORTH, James

Group Number 227
SCOTT, David; WILLIAMS, Thomas

Group Number 228
SCOTT, David; YARBOROUGH, William

Group Number 229
SIMS, Edward; COMPANY, Sims Banks And

Group Number 230
SIMS, Edward; WEDGWORTH, James

Group Number 231
SIMS, Edward; WILLIAMS, David

Group Number 232
SIMS, Edward; WILLIAMS, Henry

Group Number 233
SIMS, Edward; WILLIAMS, Samuel

Group Number 234
SIMS, Edward; WRIGHT, Pleasant

Group Number 235
SIMS, Edward; YARBOROUGH, William

Group Number 236
STICKNEY, Henry; STICKNEY, Joseph B

Group Number 237
STRICKLAND, Obijah; WITHERS, Robert W

Group Number 238
TOLAND, James; TOLAND, Joseph

Group Number 239
TRAVIS, Doctor W; TRAVIS, Jesse

Group Number 240
WADKINS, G W; WADKINS, John; WADKINS, Lacy;
WADKINS, Lucy; WADKINS, Mary; WADKINS, Tabitha

Group Number 241
WALLER, Archibald; WALLER, Catherine

Group Number 242
WESTBROOK, Hudson; WESTBROOK, William

Group Number 243
WHITE, Robert; WHITWORTH, Jeremiah

Group Number 244
WILSON, Martha Johnston; WILSON, Preston Oliver

Group Number 245
WILSON, Mary; WILSON, William

Extra! Extra! (about our Indexes)

We purposefully do not have an all-name index in the back of this volume so that our readers do not miss one of the best uses of this book: finding misspelled names among more specialized indexes.

Without repeating the text of our "How-to" chapter, we have nonetheless tried to assist our more anxious researchers by delivering a short-cut to the two county-wide Surname Indexes, the second of which will lead you to all-name indexes for each Congressional Township mapped in this volume :

For your convenience, the "How To Use this Book" Chart on page 2 is repeated on the reverse of this page.

We should be releasing new titles every week for the foreseeable future. We urge you to write, fax, call, or email us any time for a current list of titles. Of course, our web-page will always have the most current information about current and upcoming books.

Arphax Publishing Co.
2210 Research Park Blvd.
Norman, Oklahoma 73069
(800) 681-5298 toll-free
(405) 366-6181 local
(405) 366-8184 fax
info@arphax.com

www.arphax.com

How to Use This Book - A Graphical Summary

Part I
"The Big Picture"

Map A ▸ *Counties in the State*

Map B ▸ *Surrounding Counties*

Map C ▸ *Congressional Townships (Map Groups) in the County*

Map D ▸ *Cities & Towns in the County*

Map E ▸ *Cemeteries in the County*

Surnames in the County ▸ *Number of Land-Parcels for Each Surname*

Surname/Township Index ▸ Directs you to Township Map Groups in Part II

The Surname/Township Index can direct you to any number of **Township Map Groups**

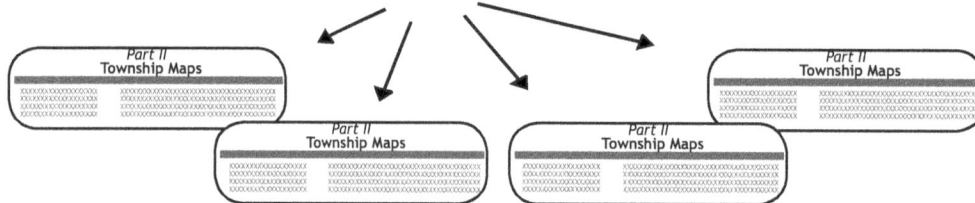

Part II
Township Maps

Part II
Township Maps

Part II
Township Maps

Part II
Township Maps

Part II
Township Maps

Part II
Township Map Groups
(1 for each Township in the County)

Each Township Map Group contains all four of of the following tools . . .

Land Patent Index ▸ *Every-name Index of Patents Mapped in this Township*

Land Patent Map ▸ *Map of Patents as listed in above Index*

Road Map ▸ *Map of Roads, City-centers, and Cemeteries in the Township*

Historical Map ▸ *Map of Railroads, Lakes, Rivers, Creeks, City-Centers, and Cemeteries*

Appendices

Appendix A ▸ *Congressional Authority enabling Patents within our Maps*

Appendix B ▸ *Section-Parts / Aliquot Parts (a comprehensive list)*

Appendix C ▸ *Multi-patentee Groups (Individuals within Buying Groups)*

www.ingramcontent.com/pod-product-compliance
Lightning Source LLC
Chambersburg PA
CBHW080232270326

41926CB00020B/4211